DARK MATTERS

Dark Matters

PESSIMISM AND THE PROBLEM OF SUFFERING

Mara van der Lugt

PRINCETON UNIVERSITY PRESS
PRINCETON & OXFORD

Published by Princeton University Press
41 William Street, Princeton, New Jersey 08540
99 Banbury Road, Oxford OX2 6JX

press.princeton.edu

First paperback printing, 2023
Paper ISBN 9780691226149
Cloth ISBN 9780691206622
ISBN (e-book) 9780691226156

British Library Cataloging-in-Publication Data is available

Editorial: Ben Tate and Josh Drake
Production Editorial: Debbie Tegarden and Natalie Baan
Jacket/Cover Design: Karl Spurzem
Production: Danielle Amitucci
Publicity: Alyssa Sanford and Amy Stewart
Copyeditor: Geoffrey D. Palmer

This book has been composed in Miller

In memory of my father

Bart van der Lugt

(1942–2006)

who will hiere the gleoman when the tales he tells is blaec
who locs at the heofon if it brings him regn
who locs in the mere when there seems no end to its deopness

PAUL KINGSNORTH, *THE WAKE*

Éléments, animaux, humains, tout est en guerre.
Il le faut avouer, le mal est sur la terre . . .

VOLTAIRE

. . . die Philosophie hebt, wie die Ouvertüre zum Don Juan, mit einem Mollakkord an.

ARTHUR SCHOPENHAUER

Je vois le mal sur la terre.

JEAN-JACQUES ROUSSEAU

CONTENTS

DARK MATTERS

INTRODUCTION

Philosophy in a Minor Chord

But after [all philosophical systems] have completed their demonstrations and sung their song of the best world, then at last comes, in the back of the system, as a late avenger of the illusory, like a ghost out of the grave, like the stone guest to Don Juan, the question of the origin of evil, of monstrous, nameless evil, of the terrible, heart-breaking misery in the world:—and they fall silent, or have nothing but words, empty, resounding words, in order to close such a heavy account.

ARTHUR SCHOPENHAUER[1]

IT BEGINS WITH an observation.

Say that you were walking the earth for the first time, and your eyes were wide with wonder.

Around you, you perceive the beauty of creation, the trees and plants and flowers, 'the wild world of beauty and complexity and dark magic', 'this strange little garden leafing and blooming in the frozen, fiery tempest of cosmic reality', and all things singing with 'the soft music of the world'.[2] Around you, too, the strange splendours of the animal world, where the lion and the antelope run wild and free, where 'the birds of the sky nest by the waters; they sing among the branches'; 'the sea, vast and spacious, teeming with creatures beyond number'.[3] Above you, 'the heavens declare the glory of God; the skies proclaim the work of his hands'; while science lets you 'read about this speck of glittering planet in gravitational thrall

1. Schopenhauer, *Über den Willen in der Natur* (*Hauptwerke*, III.423). Adapted from Cartwright's translation ('Schopenhauer on Suffering', 60).

2. Kingsnorth, *Confessions*, 160; Robinson, *The Givenness of Things*, 86; Monk of Enlli, cited in Macfarlane, *The Wild Places*, 29.

3. Psalm 104:12; and Psalm 104:24–5 (New International Version).

to a star at the fringe of a whorl of galaxy in a roaring surging universe'.[4] Within you, you perceive 'the moral law', as wondrous perhaps as the 'starry heavens' above you; the 'gorgeous blossoming of consciousness' we call *thought*.[5] By the time you have observed it all, you are already deep in love.

But something happens. The serpent enters the garden. You see the lion eat the antelope. You see the natural world devastated by floods and earthquakes. You see things brushed off from the game of life like so many flecks of dust. You see drought in the thirstiest of regions, while the rains pour endlessly into the sea. You see everywhere reminders that 'nature does not love us or want us to be happy: Lyme disease, birth defects, and the everyday theatre of wild suffering'.[6] You scan the news for trials and tribulations on every scale imaginable, from personal to national to global; you have traced the spread of a strange new virus across the earth. You read about the 'crimes and misfortunes' of history; you have travelled the world and taken home with you the sight of beggars in the street.[7] Or you are struck down yourself, by illness or addiction or bereavement, with 'Darkness and Dimness and a bewildering Shame, and Pain that is utterly Lord over us',[8] and sit sorrowful among the ashes like a latter-day Job.[9] Until you cannot help but say, with Jean-Jacques Rousseau, that single sentence: 'I see evil on earth.'[10]

What happens then? Do we speak, or do we fall silent? If we speak, what do we say; how do we say it?

This book is about the question what happens next, once evil has been perceived. It is also about the kinds of questions that arise in the wake of this perception, if it is a philosopher asking them. Is life worth living? Do the goods of human existence outweigh the evils? Could it ever be said, for any being, that it would be better for it never to have been? How could God have created a truly miserable creature? Indeed, if life is as bad as it seems to be, how could God have created us at all; how dare anyone ever create another person?

Such questions form part and parcel of what has been known, for centuries, as *the problem of evil*, and the various ways in which they have been

4. Psalm 19:1; Robinson, *Givenness*, 82.

5. Kant, *KpV* 5:161 (the famous passage was also inscribed on Kant's tombstone in Kaliningrad); Robinson, *Givenness*, 143.

6. Purdy, *After Nature*, 10.

7. Bayle, *Manicheans*[1].*D.*

8. Samuel Taylor Coleridge, cited in Macfarlane, *The Wild Places*, 210.

9. Job 2:8.

10. Rousseau, *Emile*, IV, 278: 'Je vois le mal sur la terre.'

answered have created the competing philosophical traditions known as *optimism* and *pessimism*. These are terms that have lent themselves to many misunderstandings, especially on the side of pessimism, which has become so pejorative a term that, these days, to call someone a pessimist is often enough to undermine their position.[11] This tendency to take pessimism less than seriously is both understandable, since pessimism intrudes so darkly into our existence as to lead us to ask whether life is in fact worth living at all, and deeply mistaken, since this tendency withholds from inquiry one of the deepest parts of our being: our capacity to suffer. A large part of the aim of this book is to clear up some of these confusions, and try to do justice to both sides of the debate, to optimists as well as pessimists, by uncovering what I call the *moral background* of their arguments: the way their ideas are crucially rooted not in abstract metaphysics, but in a deep and widely shared concern over how to speak truthfully, meaningfully, and compassionately about human (and sometimes even animal) suffering.

But what exactly is pessimism; what is the problem of evil?

The Problem of Evil

The 'problem of evil' designates a specific kind of question posed by philosophers, theologians, and the curious of mind, a question that can be broadly described as a conflict between God's presumed attributes and the fact that bad things happen in the world. Possibly the shortest and nicest formulation ever written comes from Marilynne Robinson: 'If God is God, why does he permit evil and suffering and death?'[12]

If God is God—but who is God, or what is God? That is, what are the attributes that are hard to square with 'evil and suffering and death'? Traditionally, there are three: omniscience, omnipotence, and omnibenevolence. In the classic formulation of the dilemma or 'trilemma' of evil attributed to Epicurus (ca. 300 BCE), the problem then becomes as follows:

> Is [God] willing to prevent evil, but not able? then is he impotent.
> Is he able, but not willing? then is he malevolent.
> Is he both able and willing? Whence then is evil?[13]

11. Dienstag, *Pessimism*, 'Preface' and chapter 1.

12. Robinson, *Givenness*, 268.

13. This formulation cited from Hume, *Dialogues concerning Natural Religion*, 74. Originally attributed by Lactantius to Epicurus in his *De ira dei* and cited by Bayle in *Paulicians*[1].*E*.

For evil to exist, God must be either unaware of it (so not all-knowing), or unable to prevent it (so not all-powerful), or unwilling to prevent it (so not perfectly good). A wonderful set-up for one of philosophy's favourite puzzles, Epicurus's formulation is most striking in that the parameters have scarcely altered since then: these are still the main terms of the debate as it is carried out today.[14] But some things have changed, and tracking these shifts and changes will form a large part of this book—especially in the seventeenth and eighteenth centuries, when the problem of evil is like a house stripped down and partially rebuilt, its inner and outer workings reinvented almost entirely.

For one thing, there have been shifts throughout the ages in which of God's attributes receives priority, and we can group certain 'theodicies' accordingly (*theodicy* being the label used, after Leibniz, to denote any systematic response to the problem of evil).[15] Thus Steven Nadler has grouped the seventeenth-century philosophers Malebranche and Leibniz together by virtue of their prioritisation of God's wisdom and understanding (i.e. his omniscience), in opposition to Arnauld, who instead prioritises God's power and sovereignty (i.e. his omnipotence).[16] To these, a third line could be added in the form of philosophers such as Bayle, whose name will be a red thread throughout this book, and who ardently gave the greatest weight to God's goodness above all other characteristics, as Rousseau would in his wake.[17] Kant in turn supplies an alternative trichotomy of divine attributes—holiness, goodness, and justice—which he relates to three distinct kinds of conflict, three kinds of problem of evil.

This ties in with another kind of shift we can trace throughout thinkers grappling with theodicy, having to do with the question of what really

14. Though there are changes in the *kinds of evil* that are considered most problematic, and the debate has become increasingly formalised, with, for example, distinctions between 'logical' and 'evidential' problems of evil; for an overview, see Adams and Adams, 'Introduction', Michael Tooley's entry 'The Problem of Evil' in the SEP, and Newlands, 'Hume on Evil'.

15. While I appreciate Paul Rateau's reservations with regard to the widespread use of 'theodicy' outside Leibniz's very particular philosophical project, I follow contemporary usage of the term as designating any systematic attempt to answer the problem of evil (see Rateau, 'The Theoretical Foundations', 93).

16. Nadler, 'Choosing a Theodicy', and his *Best of Possible Worlds*, chapter 6. In fact, the Jansenist Arnauld thinks it is mistaken to even distinguish God's wisdom from his will (Nadler, *Best of Possible Worlds*, 161–2).

17. In fact, many authors in the centuries that follow consider goodness the most relevant attribute—such as Hume and also Schopenhauer, who defines the problem of evil as 'the contradiction between the goodness of God and the misery of the world' (*WWR*.I.407n.).

constitutes a *problem* of evil: Wherein lies the *problematic* bit? Kant, again, thinks there are three kinds of problems having to do with three kinds of 'counterpurposiveness' (*Zweckwidrigkeit*): three kinds of observations about the world that we interpret as bad, evil, or unjust. First, there are *moral evils*, which we nowadays think about when we call something or someone 'evil': bad actions, bad people. How could God in his holiness have created humans as bad as they are, or as capable of badness? Second, there are 'the countless ills and pains of the rational beings of the world', which philosophers generally classify under *natural or physical evils*: things like death, illness, earthquakes, and misfortune. How could God in his goodness allow such bad things to happen to his creatures? Third, there is the observation of *misalignment* between the two: the fact that wicked people often go unpunished or even prosper, and what this seems to suggest about the deeper injustice of things. How could God in his justice permit that 'the depraved [should] go unpunished in the world'?[18]

This third category is especially interesting, since it did not tend to feature in earlier 'taxonomies' of evils—which is not to say that it was not in question throughout the history of theodicy. In fact, the observation of misalignment is a crucial dimension to the deep moral investment shared by many of these thinkers, on all sides of the debate (optimists and pessimists, theodicy and anti-theodicy),[19] from Bayle to Schopenhauer and beyond. Most of the time, however, this misalignment extends further than it does in Kant's version: the problem is not just that the wicked prosper but, equally, that *the righteous suffer*.[20] Misalignment generally addresses two opposed yet connected moral outrages: a Rufinus—the fourth-century Roman consul whose prosperity and depravity caused the poet Claudian to doubt providence; and a Job—a bad person prospering, and a good person suffering.[21] The idea is that our sense of cosmic indignation or existential doubt arises at its strongest when we witness the suffering of the good or the prosperity of the wicked, what Schopenhauer calls *poetic injustice*:

18. Kant, 'Essay' (8:256–62).

19. 'Anti-theodicy' was originally defined by Zachary Braiterman as 'any religious response to the problem of evil whose proponents refuse to justify, explain, or accept as somehow meaningful the relationship between God and suffering' (Braiterman, *(God) After Auschwitz*, 31). I follow N.N. Trakakis ['Anti-theodicy' (1) and (2)] in allowing for non-religious interpretations of the project of anti-theodicy, which I will define, even more loosely, as any rejection of theodicy on moral grounds.

20. Kant does, in fact, see this as a problem, but of a different kind; see chapter 7.

21. Bayle discusses Flavius Rufinus in his dictionary article *Rufinus*; see my *Bayle, Jurieu*, 180.

> [Such a view] sees the wicked man, after misdeeds and cruelties of every kind, live a life of pleasure, and quit the world undisturbed. It sees the oppressed person drag out to the end a life full of suffering without the appearance of an avenger or vindicator.[22]

While some scholars see misalignment as 'the intractable question' of theodicy,[23] I disagree: far from being the major or fundamental problem of theodicy, misalignment represents only one of its more striking instances. As I hope to show throughout this book, the deepest and darkest thinkers on the problem of evil will question not only why the wicked flourish, but why the wicked *suffer*, and more than this: *why the wicked are wicked at all.* Can we help the way we have been created? Is it not one of the greatest misfortunes in life to have been born with such a constitution as to make our happiness depend on the suffering of others? How can God be responsible for *any* of our evils, whether moral or physical, aligned or misaligned; or how can we save him from this responsibility? Under what conditions do we believe creation, of any kind, to be justified—and were those conditions met by God? Are they met, for that matter, by those of us choosing to create (that is, *pro*create) in modern times?

Such arguments have a striking force far beyond the debates in which they were first formulated, interrogating the very value of existence as well as the ethics of creation, and it is precisely in such questions (I will argue) that pessimism proves its point, its meaning, its urgency, and its continued relevance for us today. Throughout this book, in tracing the various shifting ways in which the problem of evil is formulated and conceived, I am also interrogating the background sense of why and how such questions matter, if they matter at all.

A third shift has to with the kinds of things that qualify as evils, and which of these are considered most problematic. After all, how do we decide what constitutes an evil or an ill? The categories of *moral* and *physical* (or *natural*) evil are often considered to be more or less static, as though our understanding of them were the same now as it was in the early modern age. In fact, the similarity of the names conceals a thick mass of work and argument that is going on behind the scenes, by which the categories we know now are constantly invested with new meanings. The very relationship between moral and physical evil is a deeply fraught one.

22. Schopenhauer, *WWR*.I.353; see also *WWR*.I.253–4 on poetic injustice.

23. E.g. Neiman, 'Metaphysics, Philosophy', 158: 'The fact that moral and physical evils have no intelligible connection—that it is, very often, wicked people who thrive while righteous people suffer—is the intractable question.'

Originally closely linked by the Augustinian narrative that interpreted all physical evils (suffering) as punishment for moral evils (sin), the two categories came to be disentangled in the course of the seventeenth century, with dire consequences for the older Genesis-inspired narrative and the very concept of original sin. One result of this disentangling was that physical evil or suffering in general begins to play an increasingly important part in the story I am trying to tell. For while physical evil, for most of the history of theodicy, used to be the lesser problematic kind of evil, it ends up being the *more* problematic kind, and is still seen as such today.[24]

This rise in prominence of the concept of suffering is closely related to the story of pessimism, and is itself marked by a series of theoretical revolutions. For one thing, Bayle reinvents the concept of physical evil by defining it as whatever is experienced as such, resisting any tendency to explain away such evils by arguing they could have been prevented or are otherwise justified as a form of punishment. The result is a highly modern conception that not only gives full weight to the experience of the individual sufferer, but also extends suffering to a much-neglected category in the theodicean debate: that of animals. Aside from this, the category of physical evil is itself deepened and unfolded into the two subcategories of pain and sorrow, of physical and psychological suffering, and in another modern moment, the latter gradually come to include our very dispositions. We can now be said to suffer not only the things that happen to us, but also the feelings we experience internally, and the very temperament that disposes us to feel that way.

The crucial ingredients, then, of the traditional problem of evil are the identity of God with his attributes, on the one hand, and the overall 'fact' of evils, on the other—but within this overall framework, the central questions are often drastically different. For this reason (as I will argue in chapter 1), it is perhaps somewhat deceptive to speak of *the problem of evil* at all, when in fact there are almost as many different *problems* of evil as there are thinkers formulating them. For the sake of brevity, convenience, and the like, I have chosen to continue to use the common label, but I do so on strongly Wittgensteinian assumptions: my 'problem of evil' works more like a 'family resemblance' class, gathering overlapping categories,

24. This is the overwhelming tendency in contemporary philosophy of religion and has been the trend throughout the twentieth century; see, e.g., C.S. Lewis, *The Problem of Pain*, and the contributions to Adams and Adams's collection *The Problem of Evil*, but also the recent volume edited by N.N. Trakakis, *The Problem of Evil: Eight Views in Dialogue*, where 'the problem of evil' is sometimes equated with 'the problem of suffering' (as in Stump, 'The Problem of Suffering'; see also her *Wandering in Darkness*).

than as a single category that can be clearly defined (it cannot). Part of the challenge, throughout this book, will be to tease out these different underlying questions and problems and concerns, and to do so in a way that clarifies more than it confuses. As such, I will be treating the problem of evil mainly as a problem of suffering, sometimes as a problem of creation, sometimes as a problem of suicide, and sometimes not as a problem at all.

The connecting factor or common thread throughout these debates is perhaps not so much the formal framework (how can a good God, etc.), but the sense that all of this *matters* in some deeply significant way. For some reason, philosophers have continued to dust off the old creaking question of evil throughout the ages; to pick it up, tweak its bits, and do something new with it, in an ongoing attempt to either make sense of the evils of existence or to unmake the sense made of them by others. As Susan Neiman writes, and here I agree:

> Two kinds of standpoint can be traced from the early Enlightenment to the present day, regardless of what sort of evil is in question, and each is guided more by ethical than by epistemological concerns. The one, from Rousseau to Arendt, insists that morality demands that we make evil intelligible. The other, from Voltaire to Jean Améry, insists that morality demands that we don't.[25]

Throughout, this sense of ethical concern (which I interpret somewhat differently) is paramount: a concern that is partly directed towards the creator, but partly, and increasingly, also towards *the creature*; and the latter category begins to include more beings as the debate progresses. Thus, while animals had traditionally been excluded from the 'problem' posed by evil and suffering, by the time Charles Darwin muses on the question, the balance is overturned entirely:

> That there is much suffering in the world no one disputes. Some have attempted to explain this in reference to man by imagining that it serves for his moral improvement. But the number of men in the world is as nothing compared with that of all other sentient beings, and these often suffer greatly without any moral improvement. A being so powerful and so full of knowledge as a God who could create the universe, is to our finite minds omnipotent and omniscient, and it revolts our understanding to suppose that this benevolence is not unbounded, for

25. Neiman, *Evil*, 8. Her sympathies lie with the former option; mine (as will become clear) rather with the latter.

> what advantage can there be in the suffering of millions of the lower animals throughout almost endless time?[26]

If there is one thing that connects the authors loosely classified as 'pessimists' in this book, it is this concern to give due weight to the suffering of others, and to let evils, moral and physical, stand as a kind of cosmic residue, 'the remainder, or the insoluble precipitate',[27] which sticks to our hands just when we have washed them of all other problems. If there is one thing that connects the authors of the opposing tradition categorised just as loosely under 'optimism', it is the sense that this very effort gets something fundamentally wrong, not just about our conception of God and the cosmos, but about what it is to be human, and what it is that a human being needs to live fruitfully and undespairingly within this fractured world.

Pessimism and Optimism

But what exactly is pessimism, or optimism for that matter? These are terms that we have all used and encountered in daily life, and their meanings may seem nothing other than straightforward. Like so many other terms, they mean something different in philosophy than they do in everyday life, and in fact they often mean different things in philosophy itself. So much the worse for philosophy, we might say. But this would be too quick a judgement for, as I will argue, the most common use of optimism and pessimism is also the least interesting one, turning them into somewhat empty concepts, easy labels to stick on one's opponent's coat without another thought. 'Optimism' (in its common sense of thinking things are going to get better) is often used as shorthand for a kind of naïvety or wishful thinking, in which case the converse concept of pessimism is one of heroic realism and maturity, of being brave enough to live without illusions: 'Despair is my *virtue*, and my health.'[28] At the same time, 'pessimism' (in its common sense of thinking things are going to get worse)

26. Darwin, *Autobiography*, 90. See also Darwin's letter to Asa Gray (22 May 1860): 'There seems to me too much misery in the world. I cannot persuade myself that a beneficent and omnipotent God would have designedly created the Ichneumonidæ with the express intention of their feeding within the living bodies of caterpillars, or that a cat should play with mice' (*Darwin Correspondence Project*, Letter no. 2814). See Nagasawa, 'The Problem of Evil for Atheists', 152–3.

27. Schopenhauer, *PP*.I.64.

28. 'Le désespoir est ma *vertu* à moi, et ma santé.' André Comte-Sponville, *Traité du désespoir et de la béatitude*, 20 (my translation).

tends to be used as shorthand for despair, fatalism, giving up, giving in to doom. The converse concept of optimism is, then, one of heroic persistence, of *not* giving up, of maintaining courage even against all odds: 'optimism over despair'![29]

There is also an underdoggish tendency of both sides to suggest that fashion favours the opponent. The critics of pessimism do not tire of reminding us that pessimism is 'always fashionable', though it is much rarer for them to give concrete examples of these strident fashionable pessimists.[30] It is with more justification that the defenders of pessimism, such as Joshua Foa Dienstag, criticise the critics in turn for associating pessimism with fatalism or passivity, almost without argument, when in fact pessimism is a philosophical tradition in its own right, one that stands out for its ability to spur political activism.[31]

It seems, then, that both concepts, optimism and pessimism, lend themselves to the kind of exaggeration that is at the same time a deflation, one that flattens these terms until they become almost trivial, denoting little more than a mental attitude, an outlook on day-to-day life. The result of such lazy theorising is a tendency not to take the other side seriously, and to let what could be a meaningful inquiry come to a halt in a silly caricature. And what an inquiry this could be! For both concepts can also be taken to mean something much more profound and interesting, and it is this profundity that has tended to motivate their advocates, not just now but ever since their original conception in the eighteenth century. Pessimism, at its best, is more than a shrug of despair; optimism, at its best, more than a gesture of confidence. Throughout this book, I will try to recover some of those original meanings, setting aside the traditional oppositions, the trivial (*naïveté/fatalism*) and the psychological (*cheerful/glum*), to come to a deeper grasp of the two competing philosophical concepts of optimism and pessimism. But as I mentioned, even philosophers do not agree on how to take these terms. Two overall conceptions can be discerned in modern discussions of the topic, which I will call *future-* and *value-oriented* (I unpack these terms in more detail in chapter 2).

Of these two conceptions, the *future-oriented* version stands closer to the everyday understanding of optimism and pessimism as having

29. This is the title of a recent book collecting interviews with Noam Chomsky.

30. Robinson, *Givenness*, 29: 'Cultural pessimism is always fashionable, and, since we are human, there are always grounds for it. It has the negative consequence of depressing the level of aspiration, the sense of the possible.'

31. Dienstag, *Pessimism*.

something to do with our expectations about the future. But it should be noted here that the two terms, under this conception, are not necessarily symmetrical. Whereas optimism implies a systematic expectation of progress and improvement, and a level of confidence in human perfectibility (that things will get better if we make them so), this does not mean that *pessimism* entails the converse belief: a systematic expectation that *things will get worse*. As Dienstag argues in his book exploring the political–philosophical tradition of pessimism, pessimists define themselves precisely by their resistance to such expectations: '*The pessimist expects nothing*'.[32] Pessimism, in this view, implies a lack of any systematic belief about the future, or at most the contrary belief that we cannot know or expect anything from the future, considering our human limitations. At most, pessimists express a deep awareness that we are locked in time, and that the quality of being thus locked is a central part of the human predicament. As Schopenhauer argues, belief in decline is as unwarranted as belief in progress: 'In this world of the phenomenon, true loss is as little possible as is true gain.'[33]

A greater symmetry exists in the other conception of optimism and pessimism, which I call *value-oriented*, and which applies itself to questions such as whether life is worth living, whether the goods or evils weigh out in life, and how to weigh them adequately. On this conception, 'pessimism is a judgement of value regarding life or reality as a whole, which results from the conflict between man's *supreme* value and the supposed facts of life' (the same would go for optimism).[34] While Dienstag, in the only modern book-length study of philosophical pessimism to date, focuses purely on future-oriented pessimism, I will engage mostly with value-oriented pessimism (and optimism), which I will argue is the more fundamental kind, and is also how these terms were originally conceived.

As the title of this book suggests, I will be saying more about pessimism than optimism, a focus I believe to be justified by my sense that pessimism is by far the more misunderstood of the two: in all the history of philosophy, it is perhaps the intellectual tradition most prone to confusion, exaggeration, and misrepresentation. Of the two traditions, pessimism is also the less studied, to such an extent that it might be called a

32. Ibid., 40; his emphasis.

33. Schopenhauer, *WWR*.I.184.

34. Krusé, 'The Inadequacy of the Hedonistic Interpretation', 395.

shadow tradition, one that has been considered mostly negatively as the counterpart of optimism, in the shadow of which it has always seemed to stand. My focus on pessimism is further necessitated by the fact that I will be studying these questions in tandem with the problem of evil, from which they often spring, and while the problem of evil has as much to do with the goods of life as with the evils, the goods are not where the *problem* resides.

But the two traditions go hand in hand, and in discussing the philosophical interest in pessimism throughout the centuries, I will necessarily also be discussing the philosophical interest in optimism, a tradition that has also lent itself to much exaggeration and dulling down by its critics and opponents. The risk, in trying to achieve a more meaningful view of pessimism, is that our sympathies simply shift from one side to the other, so that optimism is flattened in the same proportion as pessimism is deepened. This, I fear, is what happens in some parts of Dienstag's book, which, in the course of complicating our conceptions of pessimism, ends up painting a too simple (and sometimes caricatural) picture of optimism.[35] This is a tendency and temptation against which I will be constantly on guard, and that I will counter by trying to do justice to the deep moral intuitions and investments that stand behind the projects of such arch-optimists as Leibniz and King. My aim is to excavate a deeper understanding of pessimism, but my hope is that in the course of making pessimism more interesting, this will make optimism more interesting too.

The outcome of this attempt, to lift the curtain just a little, is that I will end up conceiving of optimism and pessimism in sets of shared concerns rather than in purely theoretical commitments: concerns having to do with the status of creaturely experience against the cosmic perspective, but also with the question of how to speak sensitively and meaningfully of human (and sometimes animal) suffering, over and against the question of how to explain suffering in a way that can justify existence. A large part of my argument will be that there is a profound intellectual *but also ethical* drive in both positions, giving us a reason to take both sides deeply seriously. Interestingly, while both traditions are marked by a number of distinct concerns, they are also bound together by a twofold moral focus that powers the majority of their confrontations, having to do with *hope*, *compassion*, and *consolation*. These, I argue, are the axes or orientations

35. As in this passage: 'Optimism is to time what metaphysics is to space. It projects perfection elsewhere, or, more properly, elsewhen. It teaches one to despise the here and now, which ultimately means to despise oneself' (Dienstag, *Pessimism*, 41).

that form a common moral horizon shared by both optimism and pessimism, but do so unbeknownst to either side: a long history of mutual misunderstandings begins here.

Discovering such moral impetus in optimism may be less surprising to us than finding it in pessimism, which so often is seen as a kind of hardened arrogance or intellectual self-indulgence. And sometimes, it must be admitted, it is just that. But for most of these philosophers, their pessimism is marked by a sense of urgency, of deep personal investment. Reading them, we gain the sense that all of this *matters*, and matters deeply; that far from being a facile or fatuous provocation, there is something very pivotal and personal about their pessimism: it doesn't just matter, it matters to *them*. It is this element of existential questioning, this personal dimension, that sets pessimism aside from most other philosophical topics; it does the same for the problem of evil. There are times when, reading into these dark matters, we will come across a deepening, a widening of sorts, something as hard to define as it is to miss, something having to do with the *point of pessimism*, which, when present, is what makes pessimism worthwhile, and, when absent, marks the moment when pessimism (like optimism) slips into its own unfeeling parody. This is why, throughout this book, I will be unthreading the moral concerns that appear and disappear and reappear throughout these debates—concerns that, perhaps more than the theoretical foundations, give a continuity and focus to both traditions, from the seventeenth century to today. By unearthing these ethical commitments, I hope to afford an entirely new perspective on pessimism as a tradition that has not only its own epistemological and methodological concerns and presuppositions but, crucially, its own sets of virtues and moral aims.

Plato famously lets Socrates say that 'wonder is the feeling of a philosopher, and philosophy begins in wonder'.[36] To which Schopenhauer added that this wonder or 'astonishment' in turn begins with an awareness of evil, of suffering, of the darker side of life: 'philosophical astonishment is at bottom one that is dismayed and distressed; philosophy, like the overture to *Don Juan*, starts with a minor chord'.[37] Pessimism, for Schopenhauer as for other pessimists, not only leads us to recognise this dark side of existence: it leads us to philosophy itself.

36. Plato, *Theaetetus*, 155d; see also Aristotle, *Metaphysics*, 982b.
37. Schopenhauer, *WWR*.II.171.

Maps and Methods

It is traditional at this point to discuss some historiography, to supply a helpful (if tedious) overview of the state of scholarship to date. I don't intend to be so helpful, in part because such overviews have been adequately supplied by other authors before me, and in part because it will be more fruitful and enjoyable for everyone if I engage with the literature as we go along, in the specific contexts where it will be most relevant.[38]

Having said that, I will here briefly draw attention to two authors whose names will be recurrent guests throughout this book, and whose own books each supply a kind of map into the dual debates of pessimism and the problem of evil: Joshua Foa Dienstag's *Pessimism: Philosophy, Ethic, Spirit* (on pessimism) and Susan Neiman's *Evil in Modern Thought: An Alternative History of Philosophy* (on the problem of evil). Both will feature a lot in the pages and especially the footnotes to follow, where I will cite them mostly to offer my own adjustments to their central historical and philosophical arguments. This may give the impression that I am primarily critical of these works, which is assuredly *not* the case. Both are works of the kind we call seminal; they have been enormously helpful in shaping my own thoughts on these matters, and the current book is intended as a complement to rather than a replacement of either study. If disagreements nevertheless ensue, these are themselves based on deeper agreements and affinities, especially in the background understanding that these questions matter in ways we are only beginning to understand.

With that disclaimer, here are my problems. To begin with Neiman's work on the problem of evil: this is an approach that, like my own, combines historical and philosophical perspectives, and indicates a major shift in the development of the problem of evil, which she links to Voltaire and Kant in particular. My deepest concern with this narrative is that the historical argument does not work: Neiman, like many others before her, places far too much weight on Voltaire and the Lisbon earthquake, when in fact, as I will argue, by the mid-eighteenth century most of the major innovations in the debate on evil had already been set in motion or even carried to their furthest conclusions. Far from being theological dead wood in the seventeenth century, the problem of evil was reinvented and re-explored by some of that age's best philosophers, such as Malebranche,

38. See especially chapter 1 (for sources on the problem of evil in the history of philosophy) and chapter 2 (for sources on pessimism); and see later chapters for sources on these issues in specific authors.

who put physical evil firmly back on the agenda, and Bayle, who drew from this a pessimism that would haunt thinkers for decades, maybe centuries, to come. To her credit, Neiman does devote some pages to Bayle, but does so without recognition of precisely those innovations that were so troubling to optimists such as Leibniz and King: the case for pessimism made in the heated pages of Bayle's article *Xenophanes*.[39]

More generally, her approach misses some of the key developments in the longer debate on evil, especially its reorientation to *physical evil* and its widening of that category by the inclusion of psychological and (sometimes) animal suffering. Neiman is right to stress the sharpening of the distinction between moral and physical evils throughout the eighteenth century, but this distinction hinges crucially on a number of conceptual and methodological innovations, for which Bayle supplied the groundwork in basing his discussion of physical evil not a priori on the concept of sin, but a posteriori on the observation of experience. These deeper, subtler developments within the debate on physical evil (which is also a debate on pessimism) precede the Lisbon earthquake by half a century and serve to explain not only how Lisbon could have the impact that it did, but also why philosophers today still tend to think of physical evils as the more problematic part of the problem of evil, the most robust 'remainder' or 'precipitate' (Schopenhauer) that remains once all other problems (or evils) have been dealt with. Hence, throughout this book, I will offer several critical adjustments to Neiman's theory (to which I am nevertheless sympathetic) that 'the problem of evil is the root from which modern philosophy springs'.[40]

Moving on to Dienstag's work on pessimism, I cannot stress enough the importance of this study, especially since there is hardly any literature on the philosophical tradition of pessimism, and I share several of Dienstag's starting points. The main distinction between our approaches (aside from my combining this topic with the problem of evil) has to do with the conception of pessimism that is at the basis of our studies. While Dienstag sees the pessimist tradition as driven mainly by a *future-oriented* pessimism, I believe it is *value-oriented* pessimism that is better placed

39. Bayle remains a philosopher rarely studied in sufficient depth, which may be due to the simple fact that there's so much of him, and yet so little available in modern translations. Popkin's *Selections*, which seem to be Neiman's only primary source for Bayle, do not include articles such as *Xenophanes*, though Jenkinson's selection of *Political Writings* does.

40. Neiman, *Evil*, 13. Neiman is excellent on moral evil (see also her *Moral Clarity*), and so another way of framing the contrast is to see my book, which focuses on *physical* evil, as a complement to Neiman's work on *moral* evil.

to make this claim. As such, I take issue with Dienstag's suggestion that value-oriented pessimism is at most a subcategory or more trivial extension of the main future-oriented variety, and that to understand pessimism as saying something about the value of existence or the weighing of goods and evils is mistaken.[41] Against this, I will argue that we can also trace, with equal or even *greater* justification, a sophisticated modern pessimist tradition in terms of the evaluation of existence as a whole, in which the weighing of goods and evils has its proper place. Far from being a superficial pursuit, furthermore, this evaluative exercise is something to which these thinkers are deeply committed. Fundamental to this tradition, again, is the sense that much is at stake in answering these questions; that they *matter*, and matter deeply.

This may seem to be a minor point, but it feeds into a wider problem that shadows Dienstag's project as a whole, which is ultimately a problem of circularity. Having chosen a specific conception of pessimism (as future-oriented), Dienstag uses this to reconstruct a coherent pessimist tradition, but the very choice of this conception of pessimism is itself based on a specific and necessarily selective reading of not only the tradition (in which Bayle, Hume, and Voltaire are absent) but of the very philosophers he makes central to his argument (especially Schopenhauer). As such, his argument becomes a kind of self-fulfilling prophecy. It is what makes his approach so very appealing and coherent, but it is also what limits it.[42] By reason of this starting point, Dienstag's project excludes entrenched philosophical pessimists on either side of the tradition (from Bayle to Benatar), while it places a figure as ambiguous as Rousseau at the heart of the modern pessimist tradition. (On my interpretation, as will become clear, it is rather Bayle who should have this place, while Rousseau is more rightly featured among the optimists.) The result of this disagreement about our starting points is that I will be critiquing Dienstag, too, throughout this

41. See, e.g., Dienstag, *Pessimism*, 6n.: on the 'misconception' of conceiving pessimism as 'merely positing an excess of pain over pleasure in life'. This is itself an exaggeration: value-oriented pessimism does more than posit an excess of pain; it tries to *weigh* (not calculate) goods and evils in a more meaningful (though ever problematic) way.

42. It could be argued, of course, that I'm open to the same critique, choosing to start with value-oriented pessimism and then reading it into the sources in order to form something like a 'tradition'. While I'm aware of this risk, which is intrinsic to the exercise of intellectual history, I nevertheless believe my approach to be warranted by those very sources: if we take into account what self-proclaimed philosophical pessimists consider to be pessimism, and with which other authors they align themselves, then it turns out that value-oriented pessimism is the dominant form in the history of philosophy, with future-oriented pessimism as a kind of offshoot, secondary and derivative.

book, not in an attempt to discredit his work as a whole, but to complement and continue his argument into the wider tradition of value-oriented pessimism, which is itself so closely linked to that other debate: the problem of evil.

This leads me to a third criticism, which is directed equally (and I hope not too unfairly) at both Neiman and Dienstag. It is curious, considering the closeness of their topics, that their books hardly overlap. This, again, has to do with their specific orientations: Neiman focuses primarily on the problem of *moral* evil, Dienstag on the tradition of *future-oriented* pessimism. These approaches, again, are highly valuable in their own right, but they miss something vital about their subject matter, something that emerges only once the two topics are studied in connection with each other. Once the focus is placed instead on *physical* evil (the problem of suffering) and *value-oriented* pessimism (the question of whether life is worth living), we find that these two issues are crucially interconnected, to such an extent that it makes little sense to study one without the other: it is only by an appreciation of this connectedness that either tradition can properly be understood. It is from this intersection between pessimism and the problem of evil that this book takes its cue.

HISTORY, PHILOSOPHY, SYMPATHY

This brings me to a word on method. The originality of this study, again, lies first and foremost in its consideration of both topics at the same time and in connection with each other, both historically and philosophically. This dual orientation of my work, which has one foot in the discipline of history and another in that of philosophy, places it in the twilight fields known as intellectual history, the history of ideas, and the history of philosophy, labels that are all to some extent appropriate but to which I prefer not to commit myself (some chapters will have me move more in the direction of intellectual history, others in that of philosophy and its history). My method, for this reason, is a fluid one, consisting mainly of in-depth analysis of specific sources in connection with each other, by which I seek to trace the inner mechanics of these debates as they develop over time. Contextually, I have maintained a rather light touch (maybe too light for some readers), choosing to focus primarily on the ideas of the philosophers in question, and on the intuitions and preconceptions that are active in the background—sometimes boldly stated, sometimes only subtly implied. Methodologically, then, this book would seem to fit most comfortably in the history of philosophy, where the emphasis lies on *philosophy*.

This has other consequences too. It may be clear by now that the point of this study is partly historical, partly philosophical, but also partly ethical or evaluative. It is marked throughout by an attempt to *detrivialise* certain questions, to place them in a new perspective, on the assumption that at least some of them are up for re-evaluation. To some extent, reading my way into these debates was like learning a new language, a new way of thinking, and my primary concern throughout the writing of this book has been to open up these debates and 'translate' these modes of thought in such a way that they may still speak to us today. This is a far from straightforward exercise: after all, the results of the dual debates of pessimism and the problem of evil are not necessarily of the kind any of us might find convincing. In the words of Paul Ricoeur: 'One might say that the problem of evil offers at the same time the most considerable challenge to think and the most deceptive invitation to talk nonsense, as if evil were an always premature problem where the ends of reason always exceed its means.'[43] The same could equally be said of pessimism and optimism, with the result that, throughout this book, we will be going back and forth rather a lot between the nonsensical and the profound.

For this reason, I have attempted to maintain what might be called a *hermeneutics of sympathy*, by which I mean simply the effort to give these authors the benefit of the doubt as much as possible, even when they seem just silly or ridiculous or outrageous (at times even *immoral*): to try to do them justice nonetheless.[44] This is something I believe to be all the more required because the topic in question is such an *unsympathetic* one, especially in the case of pessimism, which continues to raise eyebrows and suspicions of poor taste. ('Why not *optimism*?' some people ask me, sometimes with concern, when I tell them what I've been working on.) But the many misunderstandings of philosophical pessimism have done just as much damage to the reputation of philosophical *optimism*, which is all too easily dismissed as just silly and deluded (we still tend to read Leibniz through Voltaire, who probably didn't really read Leibniz in any depth at all).[45]

43. Ricoeur, *Symbolism*, 165.

44. This can be taken as a more morally invested version of the 'principle of charity'; I am inspired here by Ricoeur's intuition that any hermeneutics of suspicion must be offset by a hermeneutics of intention or sympathy: 'Hermeneutics seems to me to be animated by this double motivation: willingness to suspect, willingness to listen; vow of rigor, vow of obedience.' Ricoeur, *Freud and Philosophy*, 27.

45. At least, not before attacking 'optimism' in *Candide*: see chapter 3.

This is a dance that has characterised the cultural clash between optimism and pessimism from the beginning, both sides failing miserably to take the other seriously and, in particular, to recognise in the other the presence of a deep ethical impulse, a moral drive. It is in an attempt to recover something from their encounter that was lost by virtue of this misunderstanding that I employ a hermeneutics of sympathy—towards the pessimists but *also* towards the optimists (which is sometimes the more challenging part). These thinkers are seldom lazy or uncaring: they tend to have good reasons for thinking and writing as they do, even if these reasons seem almost incomprehensible to us now. For this reason, I ask the reader to adopt some of the same 'sympathetic' attitude as we explore these many voices, even when they try to drown each other out.

However, trying to be generous in our interpretations does not mean that our sympathies need to be equally distributed, if such a thing were even possible. Again, in the words of Paul Ricoeur,

> nobody asks questions from nowhere. One must be in a position to hear and to understand. It is a great illusion to think that one could make himself a pure spectator, without weight, without memory, without perspective, and regard everything with equal sympathy. Such indifference, in the strict sense of the word, destroys the possibility of appropriation.[46]

Appropriation may be too strong a word, or perhaps not: part of the aim of this book is indeed to draw something out of these debates and traditions that may still serve us today. As such, there is also a *dialogic* aspect to this exercise, and in several ways. For instance, Pierre Bayle may not have been able to respond to Rousseau's critique of pessimism, but we can nevertheless reconstruct a hypothetical response and, true to Bayle's own practices, continue this conversation across the centuries.[47] As such, there is a dialogic aspect to my method, not just in my own interrogations of these authors, but in my attempt to bring in voices from the past (and sometimes the future) to cross-examine later thinkers; the reader should not be surprised to hear Bayle's voice asking questions in a chapter on Schopenhauer. If this exercise is historically suspect (and I think it is not, since all of these authors are elaborating on common themes), it is also philosophically valuable.

46. Ricoeur, *Symbolism*, 306.

47. See my *Bayle, Jurieu*, chapter 1, on Bayle's own dialogic method.

But this book is also dialogic in the deeper sense of drawing out these ideas into modern times, picking them up, and turning them around to see if they are still able to speak to us. This may at times incur me the charge of overinterpreting, to which I respond with the words of someone who used to teach me philosophy:

> Let it be said from the start that such an interpretation is violent, to which I should immediately add, that *any* interpretation is violent. In the conversation with history the latter always appears as the history *of* and *for us*.[48]

And maybe, at heart, this is really all this book intends to do: simply to continue a conversation.

The Question

More specifically, this is a book about a question, or a set of questions, having to do with the dark side of existence, 'the terrible side of life'.[49] Are there more evils than goods in our lives? Is life worth living for all of us, for any of us? Why do some people choose death despite their blessings; why do some people choose life despite their sufferings? Do animals suffer as we do? Are we responsible for our own happiness? *Is it better never to have been?* The various ways in which these questions have been answered throughout the centuries have created the competing philosophical traditions known as optimism and pessimism. This book traces the intersection of the debate on the problem of evil with the debate on pessimism from the late seventeenth century onwards, seeking throughout to evaluate pessimism on its own terms. My main thesis is twofold.

First, I argue that the age-old philosophical debate on the problem of evil was reinvented and imbued with a new sense of urgency in the second half of the seventeenth century. This itself is not a very original point: many scholars have argued for some kind of 'theodicean turn' in the eighteenth century, beginning at least with Leibniz and ending (or *seeming* to end) abruptly in the death sentence delivered on this topic by Immanuel Kant; and others before me have pushed this development further back into the seventeenth century. My interest lies in tracing the fate of *physical evil* in particular, and in showing how the intensification and

48. Prins, *Uit Verveling*, 45, taking here a Gadamerian stance (my translation; emphasis in original).

49. Schopenhauer (*WWR*.I.252; *WWR*.II.433, 435; *PP*.I.421).

reorientation of the debate on evil created an entirely new philosophical tradition: one eventually known as *pessimism*. When the debate on theodicy burns out in the eighteenth century, pessimism continues to push some of its central questions, such as the ethics of creation and the justification of existence, which return in Schopenhauer's philosophy as well as in the contemporary anti-natalist philosopher David Benatar.[50]

Second, I argue that, even from its earliest beginnings, pessimism is driven by a crucial moral orientation, which in many cases it shares with the competing tradition of optimism, and revolves around the key concepts of *hope*, *compassion*, and *consolation*. Throughout these debates, pessimists show themselves concerned to speak of suffering in such a way that does justice to the human experience and yet is able to offer something in the way of consolation, compassion, or even hope: *pessimism*, I argue throughout, *does not want to be a philosophy of despair*. This moral orientation is shared with the optimists, who are in turn concerned that pessimists place such emphasis on suffering as to make suffering worse, thus leaving no room for either hope or consolation. These concepts turn out to be crucial for understanding the inner mechanics of pessimism, and I argue that it is precisely this ethical drive that gives focus and force to the pessimist tradition, which is why pessimism may be reinterpreted as a moral source.

The central figure in all of these questions, and the main character of the cast of philosophers featured in this book, is Pierre Bayle, the French philosopher who fled to the Dutch Republic at the end of the seventeenth century and remained a household name in the canon of philosophy for a long time before he was, temporarily, displaced within the folds of history. In the past few decades, Bayle scholarship has taken flight again, but in the dearth of solid modern editions of, in particular, the *Dictionnaire*, he remains a shadowy passenger through the pages of most books. It may therefore come as some surprise that I will be placing Bayle at the heart and origins of a pessimist tradition (which I conceive as value-oriented, so with different priorities than Dienstag's future-oriented tradition), replacing Dienstag's Rousseau as the 'patriarch of pessimism'.[51] I believe this placement is nevertheless warranted, both in terms of influence and orientation: not only is Bayle responsible for putting pessimism firmly on the eighteenth century's philosophical agenda, but his arguments and

50. There are many parallels between Benatar's argument against procreation and Bayle's attack on (rational) theodicy; while I do not discuss Benatar centrally, he is a recurrent visitor in the footnotes of this book.

51. This phrase of Walter Starkie's is cited by Dienstag, *Pessimism*, 49.

preoccupations bear close affinities to those of later pessimists such as Schopenhauer and David Benatar.

To trace this tradition, and ground Bayle's role in it, I will be circling around a set of recurrent questions, which stand at the intersection of these two debates: *pessimism and the problem of evil.* Such questions include the status of animal suffering, the meaning and justification of suicide, the level of control we have over our own happiness (and, correspondingly, our sufferings), the virtues of Stoicism, and a central methodological concern: How can we find out whether life's evils outweigh the goods? By revisiting these themes in a variety of contexts, we will travel ever more deeply into the core concerns of the pessimist (as well as the optimist) tradition. In doing so, I hope to reveal the inherent ambiguities and ambivalence in the position of pessimism and optimism alike, and to show how both traditions crucially depend on each other and develop in opposition to each other. I hope to show, furthermore, that far from presenting a series of trivial and purely descriptive points, these philosophers are engaged in serious and significant attempts to tackle cogent philosophical questions, having to do with the value of existence, with philosophy's relation to hope and consolation, and with the ethics of creation.

As a result of my 'bifocal' approach, some of the chapters in this book will be oriented more towards the problem of evil, others more towards pessimism, but it should be recalled that, throughout, both issues are at stake. I open with two chapters that reconstruct the first major confrontation between optimism and pessimism through the works of Bayle and Malebranche (chapter 1) and Leibniz and King (chapter 2). In these chapters, I also offer a more intricate introduction into the problem of evil (chapter 1) and pessimism (chapter 2). This 'first encounter' between optimism and pessimism sets the terms of the debate for a long time to come and is decisive for the future questions and concerns of thinkers in both traditions alike. The following chapters trace the continuation of these arguments in Voltaire and the deists (chapter 3), La Mettrie and Maupertuis (chapter 4), while connecting them to wider cultural attitudes towards the meaning and value of existence (chapter 3) and the eighteenth-century debate on happiness and Stoicism (chapter 4).

I then show how Bayle's arguments on pessimism *and* the problem of evil are taken up and developed by David Hume, who formulates a 'dispositional problem of evil' while radicalising Bayle's case against the consolations of philosophy (chapter 5). An entirely different response to Baylean pessimism (as elaborated by Voltaire and Maupertuis) is examined in the figure of Rousseau, whose writings are marked by an ongoing attempt to formulate an 'art of suffering' (chapter 6). I go on to trace the culmination of the 'theodicean turn' in Kant's seminal essay on the failure of rational theodicy, which articulates the problem of evil in a defining way even while claiming to close it once and for all (chapter 7). Finally, I turn to Schopenhauer's emancipation of pessimism as a philosophy in its own right and on strictly a priori terms, while arguing that his philosophy nevertheless carries a strong debt of inheritance to the theodicean debate, and is haunted by its own concerns with justification (chapter 8).

While my approach is, again, both historical and philosophical in orientation, I insist on the historical part of my argument only for the first part of the book, where a historical awareness of the vagaries of theodicy is essential for understanding the internal mechanics of the debate on evil as well as the development of the pessimist tradition. This is also why my focus throughout is especially on the new concept of *physical evil* as suffering in general, which in its Baylean reformulation begins to push moral evil from the centre of the debate, finally replacing it as the pivotal problem of evil even to this day. But aside from this historical point, I also want to make a deeper philosophical one, having to do with the merit or credit of pessimism, as a philosophy but also as a moral source. In chapter 9, therefore, I will shed some of my caution and attempt to make the case for a valuable pessimism, out of an intuition that something very meaningful is being articulated by these authors over time, something that we lose or forfeit at our peril, something having to do not only with hope and consolation, but with a deep sense of the fragility of life.

A Note of Caution

Finally, a note of caution. These questions are of the kind that are not just philosophically but also personally interesting, by which I mean that they may be relevant to individual human beings reflecting upon the value of their lives. This bestows a sense of responsibility on the author, especially when discussing the question of suicide. As historian Róisín Healy writes,

> If it is proven that an intellectual culture that defends suicide as a right and a society that views it as an understandable response to despair have contributed to the rise in suicides, great responsibility rests on the shoulders of all who discuss suicide, including historians.[52]

52. Healy, 'Suicide in Early Modern and Modern Europe', 919. To which I would add that this responsibility exists even if such a link were never proven.

This sense of responsibility is present in many of the authors in this book, in optimists as well as pessimists, though in some more than others. The debate on pessimism is itself shadowed by the spectre of Hegesias, the Cyrenaic philosopher who supposedly painted so bleak a picture of life that it drove its readers to kill themselves, as Descartes writes: 'the false philosophy of Hegesias, whose book was prohibited by Ptolemy and was the cause that many killed themselves after having read it, as it tried to argue that this life is evil'.[53] 'Maybe [Ptolemy] was right,' Pierre de Maupertuis adds a century onwards: 'a work that painted our evils too vividly would be pernicious, if it did not at the same time present us with ways by which they become bearable, and if it did not indicate their remedies'.[54]

Such concerns become especially poignant in the matter of suicide, where written thoughts may have dramatic consequences. Here it should be noted, not for the only time in this book, that the idea that pessimists tend to promote or advocate suicide is just another common misconception clinging to this tradition with tenacity: often, it is precisely the pessimists who write most sensitively and concernedly about suicide, whereas the optimists repeatedly slide into a more callous and dismissive stance. Since part of my approach consists in an ongoing ethical interrogation of my sources, I will not hold back on evaluating their authors accordingly: where there is this horizon of concern, I will take this to be to the thinker's credit; where it is lacking, I will consider it something for which they can and should be held accountable. On the part of the reader, furthermore, a level of awareness needs to exist that while these issues are sometimes discussed as mere items of curiosity, for some people they are questions of burning urgency, questions with which they struggle every day. For this reason, this book might not be for everyone: some bleak pages will certainly follow.

But also some brighter ones. For one thing, the pessimists tend to be rather wonderful to read. This has to do not only with their style but also with their sense of audacity, of courage perhaps, and sometimes of outright outrageousness. Schopenhauer is particularly dazzling on this score:

> The two main requirements for philosophising are: firstly, to have the courage not to keep any question back; and secondly, to attain a clear

53. Descartes to Elisabeth of Bohemia, 6 October 1645, *Correspondence*, 121.
54. Maupertuis, *EPM*, xvii.

consciousness of anything that *goes without saying* so as to comprehend it as a problem.[55]

I mention this striking quote because it applies equally to many of the philosophers who will be speaking in these pages, especially where they are at their most controversial, and perhaps least amenable to our intuitive grasp of life. Many of these thinkers go against the grain of truths universally acknowledged, whether in their own time or in all times, rethinking things that are supposed to be commonsensical or self-evident, things that are believed to *go without saying*. For instance, that life is necessarily worth living, or that creation is by definition a good thing, whether this means creation by God (in the case of earlier debates) or by humans (in the case of later ones).

'Write, as though you were alone in the Universe', Julien Offray de La Mettrie advises his fellow philosophers.[56] And again Schopenhauer:

> the world wants to hear that it is praiseworthy and excellent, and philosophers want to please the world. With me it is different: I have seen what pleases the world and will, in order to please it, not deviate a single step from the path of truth.[57]

What sets many of these philosophers apart is that, as in Schopenhauer's quote, they keep no question back, and they problematise that which is supposed to go without saying: they do, more often than not, write as though they were alone in the universe. Whether or not we agree with them, this seems to me an effort worth our attention and consideration. The pessimists may not always be right in their answers, but even where they are wrong, they may still be right in the kinds of questions they ask: questions we would be mistaken to dismiss or disregard too easily. As Schopenhauer himself closes the preface to his *magnum opus*: 'life is short, and truth works far and lives long: let us speak the truth'.[58]

I end, perhaps controversially, on a personal note. As optimists have kept telling pessimists for centuries, and as today's 'wellness' mentality keeps reminding us: focusing our minds too much on suffering will only make us all the more miserable; we should try to focus instead on the

55. Schopenhauer, 'On Philosophy and its Method', here in Hollingdale's translation (*Essays and Aphorisms*, 117; Schopenhauer's emphasis); see *PP*.II.8.

56. La Mettrie, 'Discours préliminaire', 247: 'Écrivez, comme si vous étiez seul dans l'Univers . . .'.

57. Schopenhauer, *Hauptwerke*, III.423 (my translation).

58. Schopenhauer, *WWR*.I.xvii.

good, the bright, the sunny side of life. So why this topic? Why would anyone choose to spend years of her life studying pessimism, evil, and suffering? Why, for that matter, would readers want to spend their time gazing into these dark matters? Part of the goal of this book is to give an answer to this question (which is at the same time a criticism); I hope I have gone some way towards answering it already. But to offer a glimpse of what is to come: there is more here than 'mere' intellectual curiosity: I see these as matters of a greater and deeper value than that confined to the pages of history, and in this perception there is something of a personal motivation too. *Personal*, which is not the same as *autobiographical*: let us resist throughout the all-too-common tendency to reduce pessimism to a matter of temperament or character or biography, as though the only reason to be interested in these topics is because one is personally miserable or damaged or unhappy with one's life. A *reductio ad biographiam*: surely we can do better than that.

I am reminded of what philosopher Alex Douglas writes about philosophy and hope, itself a recurrent theme throughout this book. There is a widespread assumption among contemporary philosophers that philosophy should not concern itself at all with matters such as hope or consolation; we shouldn't be exercising philosophy in order to find comfort. But what, he asks, is so wrong with hope or comfort? After all:

> The blighted bagatelle of ordinary life contains more than enough to make us hard-headed and cautious in our hopes. There is no need for philosophy to join the party, and I choose to spend my time with the philosophers who don't.[59]

I more than agree with this sentiment: indeed, I applaud it. But it again raises that question: Why, then, do *I* want to spend my time with philosophers who focus on the dark side of life, on its pains and sorrows and, sometimes, its hopelessness?

Strangely, for a similar reason. Because I find in these philosophers something that is missing or understated in many others, something having to do with a due appreciation of the fragility of life: with a sense that sometimes we may try to the best of our abilities *and yet we may fail* to achieve happiness or even just to avoid great suffering. This is something the pessimists knew very deeply, and it is a truth that is beginning to slip away from us in current times. But is this hopelessness? Not necessarily.

59. Douglas, 'Philosophy and Hope', 28.

Rather, it is a sense of the profound and insurmountable fragility of existence, and of hope itself. At its best and deepest, what this kind of dark thinking, which is also a *fragile thinking*,[60] achieves, is neither desperate nor passive nor fatalist: it is to open up new horizons of compassion and consolation. This, briefly, is part of my reason for delving into these dark matters. Let us begin.

60. I draw this term (in the original Dutch: *broos denken*) from Prins, 'Het wordt niet beter, het kan niet beter.'

CHAPTER ONE

The Complaint

BAYLE AND MALEBRANCHE ON PHYSICAL EVIL

Bayle knows more than anyone, and so I'll seek him out:
But, balances in hand, Bayle teaches but to doubt . . .

VOLTAIRE[1]

It is the only problem. The problem of suffering is the only problem. It all boils down to that.

MURIEL SPARK[2]

ONE OF THE MOST DEFINING problems of the history of philosophy is the problem of evil: the question of how an all-good, all-knowing, and all-powerful God could permit the existence of evil in the world. Although this question goes back to the dawn of Christianity and further still, throughout the ages there have been striking shifts in how it has been conceived, formulated, and answered. In past decades, there have been several attempts to inscribe the problem of evil into the history of philosophy, either tracing the problem throughout the ages or in a specific period—sometimes leading to bold yet thought-provoking claims, such as Susan Neiman's suggestion that 'the problem of evil was the most important question driving modern philosophy'.[3] The risk in such approaches—

1. Voltaire, 'Poem on the Lisbon Disaster' (my translation).

2. Spark, *The Only Problem*, 20.

3. Neiman, 'What Happened to Evil?', 358; see Neiman, *Evil in Modern Thought*, 13. Neiman's is the most influential recent historical–philosophical work on the problem of evil; other works include Latzer and Kremer (eds.), *The Problem of Evil in Early Modern Philosophy*; Nadler, *The Best of All Possible Worlds*; Hernandez, *Early Modern Women and*

even those that focus on the early modern period alone—is their tendency to treat the problem of evil as a static thing: a problem that has more or less stayed the same throughout the centuries. The idea in the background seems to be that, although the answers and solutions to the problem have differed, it's the same *kind* of problem all the way through.[4]

To some extent, this is a valid assumption. We can indeed describe the problem of evil in roughly the same terms throughout the centuries: as a conflict between God's divine attributes (omnipotence, omniscience, omnibenevolence) and the existence of evils in his creation. However, even if the same schema loosely fits, this does not mean that the problem of evil is the same kind of problem in all cases. Even among authors writing in a shared context, the 'problem of evil' they discuss often corresponds to very distinct concerns, which often but not always overlap. In fact, until sometime in the nineteenth century, the matter is not even framed as *the problem of evil*, but as a discussion of, for instance, the *origins of evil*, or simply, *evil*. Furthermore, in many authors the subject is not seen as a real *problem* at all, but as a necessary, or even a standard, part of the theological corpus: a part of existence that must (and *can*) be explained in order for any theology to be complete.

Instead of asking how the problem of evil was treated or answered in this or that age, it is perhaps more productive to begin by asking *what kind of problem* evil presented in each discussion; what kinds of concerns drove these debates. Was it primarily a problem of sin or of suffering (human or also animal)? A problem of pain or sadness; of monsters or disorders? A problem of suicide or a problem of creation? And: To what extent was it even conceived as a real problem? If we look at the debates on evil with these questions in mind, we find different authors with fundamentally different concerns, some of which overlap while others do not. This results in different problems of evil, which does lead to different answers, but I believe it is in the reframing of the problem itself that the most interesting

---

the Problem of Evil; Hickson, 'A Brief History of Problems of Evil'; Newlands, 'The Problem of Evil'; Fonnesu, 'The Problem of Theodicy'; the Blackwell and Cambridge Companions and Routledge Handbook to the problem of evil; Chignell (ed.), *Evil: A History* (on the concept of evil); Safranski, *Das Böse*, and Dews, *The Idea of Evil* (both on moral evil).

4. For notable recent exceptions, see Hickson, 'A Brief History of Problems of Evil'; Oppy, 'Problems of Evil'; Newlands, 'Hume on Evil' and his other articles, suggesting already a growing refinement in treatments of *problems* of evil. John Bishop disagrees with this diversification: 'we can and should identify a certain problem as *the* problem, or, at least, *the foundational* problem of evil' (Bishop, 'On Identifying the Problem of Evil', 42).

shifts occur, and in the ongoing inclusion of new aspects of existence that had not been considered quite so problematic before.[5]

A full archeology of problems of evil would require a book in itself, and so I will offer but a brief introduction by way of two key elements: the categories into which evils were variously divided, and the strategies for answering the problems they posed. I will then trace some of the shifts and reorientations in the debates on evil in the early modern period, especially in the late seventeenth and early eighteenth century, focusing on two seminal philosophers: the Oratorian priest Nicolas Malebranche and the Calvinist *dictionnairiste* Pierre Bayle. By examining the works of these thinkers in the wider context of this debate, and by tracing the changing role of *physical evil*, I will argue that this period sees an important shift in thinking about evil: that the problem of evil, as it is usually conceived, is reinvented as an entirely different kind of *problem*, incorporating different kinds of *evil*.[6]

Categories

But what is, in fact, an evil? Let's take a look at some 'taxonomies of evil': that is, the various categories into which evil (*malum*) was traditionally, or not so traditionally, divided.[7] The crucial point of reference for Christian authors was Augustine, who divided evil exclusively into these two categories: sin (*peccatum*) and punishment for sin (*poena peccati*).[8] This was at the basis of what was to become the standard vocabulary of the scholastics: *malum culpae* (evil of fault) and *malum poenae* (evil of penalty or punishment); sin on the one hand, and punishment for sin on the other. Human suffering falls into in the latter category, as punishment for, if not actual individual sin, then certainly original sin. However, the question rose among some authors whether these two categories covered every kind of evil. For instance, what about earthquakes and birth defects—cases where there seems to be an evil, which is not necessarily the result of actual sin: How to categorise those? Some scholastics, such as Francisco

5. See Kilby, 'Evil and the Limits of Theology', 22: 'It is clear that the problem of evil as presented by philosophers of religion is not an ahistorical, timeless question, a universal human conundrum, but that in different societies and in different parts of the Christian tradition people have, in the face of various evils, asked very different kinds of questions.'

6. Note that I do not mean to criticise authors on 'the problem of evil' for their use of this term, which I shall continue to use myself, but merely to argue that such use needs to be accompanied by a critical awareness of its shifts in meaning.

7. I borrow the term 'taxonomies of evil' from Antognazza, 'Metaphysical Evil Revisited', 115.

8. Augustine, *De Genesi*, 1.3.

Suárez, placed the categories of *malum culpae* and *malum poenae* under the header of *moral evil*, while adding a new category of *natural evil* for, very roughly speaking, evils that are not connected with moral responsibility. For instance, earthquakes are bad for living beings; pain is bad for animals; a sixth finger is bad for a human.[9]

These new categories (moral and natural evil, with moral evil comprising Augustine's categories of sin and punishment) remain more or less stable—until some point in the second half of the seventeenth century, when they start shifting again, and some intriguing conceptual reinventions take place. For instance, neither Bayle nor Malebranche uses the scholastic category of natural evil; in fact, they seem to be sidestepping the scholastic tradition altogether. Instead, Malebranche goes back to Augustine's two categories, though using a different terminology, substituting *moral evil* for *malum culpae* or evil of sin and *physical evil* for *malum poenae* or evil of punishment.[10] These terms, which Malebranche uses very rarely, correspond to his concept of 'the moral' and 'the physical'; that is, the moral and physical order of things. These have to do with moral actions on the one hand, chosen by man, and the physical results of these actions on the other: things that are not directly done or chosen but happen as a consequence of choice. Thus everything falls ultimately into the moral order, and Malebranche's philosophy remains firmly within an Augustinian framework where sin accounts for suffering (on which, more later). As Steven Nadler describes Malebranche's cosmology: 'This is a world in which justice predominates as much as it can, given the simplest laws, and as many people as possible receive their proper deserts—where rewards and punishments ("the physical") are closely related to deeds ("the moral").'[11]

In Bayle, the matter of mapping categories is more complicated. At times, he also seems to go back to Augustine's categories, equating moral evil with *mal de coulpe* and physical evil with *mal de peine*.[12] But these

9. Suárez, Disputation XI 'On Evil', section II (*Metaphysics*, 181–6). See Antognazza, 'Metaphysical Evil Revisited', 115–17 (also on the distinction between *malum in se* and *malum alteri*); Freddoso, 'Suarez', 10–11.

10. This is not to say that Malebranche coined the term *physical evil*, which comes up in a few seventeenth-century Latin texts, though nowhere nearly as much as *natural evil*. I have not come across the term in French before Malebranche.

11. Nadler, *Best of Worlds*, 118.

12. As far as I can tell, only at one point in the *Dictionnaire* (namely in the discussion of moral pessimism in *Xenophanes¹.E*), does Bayle himself use the more theologically burdened categories *mal de coulpe/mal de peine*; for the rest, he speaks only of *mal moral/mal physique*. In *Manicheans¹.D*, it's the Christian character Melissus equating 'mal physique' with 'la punition du mal moral'.

instances are rare and, on closer reading, not resonant with Bayle's wider discussion of what evil is and how it should be conceived. Bayle does use the categories of moral and physical evil, and does so much more frequently and consistently than Malebranche, but on closer examination, it appears that they are only tangentially related to Augustine's concepts of *malum culpae* and *malum poenae*. For Bayle, moral evil does constitute sin or crime (*doing* evil), but physical evil is just suffering (*experiencing* evil), whether or not that suffering was deserved: it is no longer evil of punishment.[13]

As will be discussed in more detail below, Baylean physical evil consists of either pain or sadness, physical or psychological suffering, such as, on the one hand, the inconveniences of illness and old age, and, on the other, melancholy and personal unhappiness (for instance, by being trapped in a bad marriage).[14] The crucial element here is *experience*: physical evil is evil suffered. There can be no physical evil that is not experienced as an evil; conversely, if something is experienced as an evil, then it *is* an evil. This is also why the scholastic category of natural evil, which included non-experienced evils, makes no sense for Bayle: it cannot be called an evil that a tree has no leaves or a stone has no weight, since these evils are not experienced by them. According to the scholastics, lacking flight is an evil in a bird but not in man; having six fingers or lacking a leg is an evil in man. To which Bayle might say: if a man is miserable because he cannot fly, then the lack of flight is indeed an evil for him; conversely, if he lacks a leg, but does not miss it, this is not an evil. Only what we experience as good or evil is actually good or evil (*RQP*.II.75/*OD*.III.653).

This new conception of physical evil in particular raised some questions among Bayle's critics. Following his works, Leibniz took up these categories of moral and physical evil (sin and suffering), while again adding a third category of *metaphysical evil* to account for 'simple imperfection': such as deformity, earthquakes, and other natural defects (*EdT*, 21.136, *G*.VI.115). As Maria Rosa Antognazza argues, Leibniz's metaphysical evil is designed to perform the same role and capture the same kinds of evils as the scholastic category of natural evil.[15] At roughly the same time, Wil-

13. See also Leibniz, *EdT*, 241.276/*G*.VI.261: '*physical evil*, that is, sorrows, sufferings, miseries' (*les douleurs, les souffrances, les misères*).

14. See Bayle, *Xenophanes*[2].*H*.

15. Antognazza, 'Metaphysical Evil Revisited', 123. In essence, then, this introduction of a third category is not so much an innovation as a strange sort of compromise: an attempt to reinstitute the scholastic 'natural evil' *while at the same time* adhering to the new experience-based conception of Baylean 'physical evil'.

liam King went back to the original categories of moral and *natural* evil, while adding a third category of 'evil of imperfection'.[16] To my mind, this is a mirroring of Leibniz's move to preserve the scholastic category of natural evil (here, evil of imperfection) while maintaining Bayle's categories of moral and physical evil for sin and suffering *tout court*.[17] It is out of a discomfort with Bayle's reduction of evil to mere sin and suffering that Leibniz and King, while taking up his categories of moral and physical evil, feel called upon to reintroduce some third category for the metaphysical residue of evils that are not experienced as such, or at all. (Bayle would dismiss any such alternative category as incoherent: only evils experienced as such by sentient beings can duly be called evils; *RQP*.II.75/*OD*.III.653.)

It is not possible to delve too deeply into this conflict of concepts here, though I will return to some of these elements below. For now, let me just point out that the main contentions of these taxonomies do not reside in moral evil, but in the non-moral kind: evils that appear to be somehow disconnected from human responsibility. In what follows, I will be speaking mostly about these kinds of evils.

Strategies

Bearing these taxonomies in mind, let me sketch out the most common traditional strategies for answering the problem of evil. These can be grouped under two main categories, which were most often combined.[18]

NEGATIVE STRATEGIES

The first group of strategies, which we can regard as 'negative', are not so much attempts to answer or solve the problem of evil as attempts to deny that there is such a problem in the first place. For instance, one influential

16. According to Antognazza ('Metaphysical Evil Revisited', 115), Leibniz and King formulated their triple distinctions more or less simultaneously but probably separately from each other. As Samuel Newlands notes ('Hume on Evil', 627), Samuel Clarke takes up King's categories in his *Demonstration of the Being and Attributes of God* (1705): 'All that we call evil is either an evil of imperfection, as the want of certain faculties and excellencies which other creatures have, or natural evil, as pain, death, and the like, or moral evil, as all kinds of vice' (Clarke, *Demonstration*, 78–9, cited in Newlands, ibid.).

17. In Antognazza's view, King places *malum culpae* and *malum poenae* under moral evil; I believe, rather, that he is echoing Bayle's categories of sin and suffering, and King's natural evil plays the role of Bayle's physical evil.

18. But see Samuel Newlands, 'Hume on Evil', 624–9, for an alternative taxonomy of problems of evil through the four axes of 'force, scope, kinds, and perspective'.

strategy, which goes back to Augustine, is to argue that evil should be characterised strictly as non-being: that evil is not a positive entity, but *privatio boni*, the privation of a good.[19] This *privation approach* is a central strategy throughout the scholastic tradition, although there are debates about whether all kinds of evils are strictly negative, and will remain a crucial element in the theodicies of Leibniz and King.[20]

A second traditional strategy, which I will call *the aesthetic or holistic approach*, warns against focusing too much on appearances: things may *seem* evil to us, but this illusion disappears when we change our view, taking into account the whole of creation. That which seems bad or ugly in its parts becomes good and beautiful when we survey the whole. Thus Augustine had compared the universe to a great mosaic, the beauty of which only appears when one sees the entire picture:

> If a person were to look at an intricate pavement so narrowly as to see only the single tesserae, he would say the artist, lacking a sense of composition, had set the little pieces at haphazard, since he could not take in at once the whole pattern, inlaid to form a single image of beauty.[21]

Thus apparent evils generally serve some greater good, and therefore are not real evils: it is a fault of perspective that creates the appearance of evils in the world.

A third, less common and more controversial, strategy could be called *quantitative optimism*: the view that the evils of life are vastly outweighed (and therefore justified[22]) by the goods. It is found in, for instance, Maimonides's *Guide of the Perplexed*, where he argues that the evils of human existence are amply outnumbered by the goods. For instance, speaking of evils that rise from man's nature as a physical being, Maimonides notes that

> the evils of this kind that befall men are very few and occur only seldom. For you will find cities, existing for thousands of years, that have

19. Augustine, *Enchiridion*, 3.11.

20. On the wider shifts in the early modern reception of 'privation theory', and its eventual eclipse in the philosophy of religion, see Newlands, 'Evils, Privations, and the Early Moderns', and his 'Leibniz on Privations'.

21. Augustine, *De ordine*, 1.1.2; translation cited from Wills, *Saint Augustine*, 3. Another common metaphor in the aesthetic strategy is that of dissonances in music; thus Leibniz combines the examples of both painting and music in his *De rerum origination radicali* of 1697 (G.VII.306–7).

22. This leap from description to justification is nearly always implied, but seldom recognised for the *non sequitur* that it is.

> never been flooded or burned. Also thousands of people are born in perfect health whereas the birth of an infirm human being is an anomaly, or at least . . . such an individual is very rare; for they do not form a hundredth or even a thousandth part of those born in good health.[23]

As for evils that humans inflict upon each other, he grants that these are more numerous, but notes that crimes such as murder or theft are nevertheless rarities: they are exceptions to the rule. Generally, there is less war in the world than peace.[24] Hence, though there are evils in the world, these do not pose a problem for divine justice, since they are either outnumbered by the goods or, as is most often the case, are self-inflicted.[25]

POSITIVE STRATEGIES

Aside from these negative strategies, there is also a second group of *positive* strategies, which do concede that the existence of evils in God's creation seems irreconcilable with the goodness of the creator, and seek to resolve this tension by offering a genealogy of evil—that is, by tracing evil back to its origins: Are these human, or divine? Common to all of these is what may be called the *reduction approach*, which, very roughly sketched, reduces most evils, or even *all* evils, to moral evil: to sin. Thus Augustine quite firmly defined all suffering as punishment for sin, arguing that 'under a just God no one can be miserable, unless they deserve to be'.[26] This is reflected in the two categories of *malum poenae* and *malum culpae,* discussed above; it means that all evil flows from the moral order, either as action or as the result of action. And even where there has been no particular sin, then suffering can be accounted for by original sin, in which all humans participate. This leads to some questionable consequences, which would be hotly debated in the seventeenth century, with its Augustinian revival: for instance, that animals cannot suffer, and that small children are already deserving of punishment, even before they have had a chance to sin.

It also leads to a very concrete problem: If all evils of human existence can be traced back to original sin, whence came sin itself? Surely God

23. Maimonides, *The Guide of the Perplexed*, II.444.

24. Maimonides, *Guide*, II.444; Bayle will argue the opposite in *Xenophanes*[2]*.K.*

25. Ibid., II.445. This is only one aspect of Maimonides's philosophy of good and evil, which is rooted in Neoplatonic as well as Aristotelian sources and has strong aesthetic tendencies: see Lobel, 'Being and the Good'.

26. Augustine, *Contra secundam iuliani responsionem imperfectum opus*, book 1, 39: 'Neque enim sub Deo iusto miser esse quisquam, nisi mereatur, potest.'

could have prevented sin from entering the world; why, then, didn't he? In other words: How to isolate God from any involvement with the origins of evil; that is, the origins of sin? The answer to such questions, which would be rehearsed relentlessly by Bayle (why did God create Adam and Eve as creatures capable of sin; why did he place them in a situation where they would be tempted?), usually accorded an important role to the human faculty of free will, itself a battleground among competing theological factions in the seventeenth century—and Bayle, again, would place an eager finger on each and every one of the sore spots that this lack of Christian consensus had left behind.[27]

The result of these strategies, positive and negative, combined is that the emphasis in discussing evil came to lie overwhelmingly on sin or *malum culpae*, as the ugly residue that remains when all other evils have been explained. And thus, for most Christian authors writing about evil in the seventeenth century, the problem of evil was, first and foremost, a problem of sin.

Malebranche's Monsters

Enter Nicolas Malebranche, one of the most piercing minds of the seventeenth century, whose enormous philosophical project included a systematic attempt to explain why there are so many blatant defects or disorders in God's creation. For instance: that rain falls in the sea, where it is useless; that the plague does not distinguish between the good and the wicked; that one who goes to rescue another is buried in ruins; that one who seeks vengeance finds nothing in his way (*Réponse au livre*, *OCM*.VI.40). And, perhaps most importantly: the birth of a so-called monster or deformed creature, whether viable or non-viable.[28]

For Malebranche, who was himself born with a severe deformation of the spine,[29] 'monsters' are the paradigmatic case of 'defective works' (*OCM*.III.88/*SAT*, 588): of disorders, defects, or imperfections in nature.

27. E.g. Bayle, *Paulicians*^{1}.*F*.

28. In some examples, Malebranche's discusses viable (e.g. *Traité de la nature et de la grâce*, *OCM*.V.32); in others, non-viable monsters (e.g. *Réponse aux réflexions*, *OCM*.VIII.770): see the editorial footnote by Rodis-Lewis in Malebranche, *Œuvres*, 1992, II.1155. Sometimes he focuses specifically on non-human monsters; for example, in animals and plants (*OCM*.III.87/*SAT*, 588). I am especially interested in the case of viable sentient 'monsters' (I will use Malebranche's term throughout).

29. See La Vopa, *Labor of the Mind*, 69. This important biographical fact, which is not often mentioned in the literature, seems to drive at least part of Malebranche's interest in the human 'machine' (ibid., 70–2).

A great part of his philosophy of evil, as well as his theory of reproduction, is aimed at explaining why disorders such as monsters exist.[30] According to Malebranche, there are some aspects of nature for which it is hard to judge if they make the world more perfect or not. But in the case of monsters it is very clear: they make the world *less* perfect: 'There are monsters whose deformity leaps to the eye. . . . A world made up of creatures who lack nothing that they ought to have is more perfect than a world full of monsters' (*Réponse aux réflexions*, *OCM*.VIII.770).[31] The question, then, is how to harmonise the existence of such imperfections with God's perfect attributes: for surely God *could* have made the world more perfect than it is. Thus the problem of evil, for Malebranche, is a problem of visible disorders or defects, a problem of imperfection, and even: a problem of monsters. He sets out to solve this problem, and does so while resisting two traditional strategies of the negative strain, both of which are associated with Augustine, the thinker who, together with Descartes, influenced Malebranche most.[32]

WORSE THAN NOTHING

The first strategy countered by Malebranche is the Augustinian privation approach: to see evil strictly as non-being, as the lack of a good. Going against a long tradition that runs from Augustine well into scholasticism, Malebranche rethinks evil, including physical evil, as something positive.[33] Ontologically speaking, physical evils are not nothing: they can even be *worse* than nothing, *pire que le néant*.[34] This, according to Malebranche, is a blunt fact of experience.

As Denis Moreau has argued, Malebranche's argument on the 'reality of the negative' takes place on several levels: aside from worldly disorder

30. On Malebranche's focusing 'almost obsessively' on the case of monsters in his theodicean project, see Jolley, 'Is Leibniz's Theodicy', 60; Moreau, 'Malebranche on Disorder', 87–90. There are important connections here with Malebranche's influential theory of reproduction, *emboîtement*, on which, see Schrecker, 'Malebranche et le préformisme biologique'.

31. English translation cited from Moreau, 'Malebranche on Disorder', 88.

32. On Malebranche's Cartesian–Augustinian inheritance, see, e.g., La Vopa, *Labor*, chapter 3; Gouhier, *Cartésianisme et Augustinisme*.

33. Moreau, 'Malebranche on Disorder', 88.

34. On this recurrent expression in Malebranche (e.g. *OCM*.III.99, XII.103, XIII.389), see Moreau, *Deux Cartésiens*, 93–4, 119–20; Boudot, 'L'être et le néant'; Guéroult, *Malebranche*, vol. 2, 122–3 and vol. 3, 235–40, 365–7; Litwin, 'Amour de soi et pensée du néant'. Malebranche repeatedly uses this expression to designate the state of the sinner (and especially damnation); I follow Moreau in extending it to physical evils (*Deux Cartésiens*, 94n.).

and sin, it also holds true for concepts such as pain and unhappiness.[35] For instance, Malebranche argues that pain is more than just the privation of pleasure:

> Now it should be pointed out here that pain is a real and true evil [*un mal réel et véritable*], and that it is no more the privation of pleasure than pleasure is the privation of pain, for there is a difference between not feeling pleasure or being deprived of the sensation of pleasure and actually suffering pain. (*Recherche de la vérité*, *OCM*.II.142–4/*SAT*, 348)

Similarly, unhappiness is not the mere lack of happiness, but something *on the other side* of nothingness. Thus a miserable man can desire to re-enter a state of nothingness, for nothingness is not as terrible as the desolate state of living without grace: nothingness is a state *in between* happiness and unhappiness. Unhappiness, therefore, is just as positive a reality as happiness:

> A man without grace can take his own life; he can desire to go back into nothingness [*le néant*]. Yet nothing is not as terrible as that desolate condition of living without that which we love. Nothingness is a condition [*un milieu*] between happiness and misery. Thus, when we are unhappy and desperate in our misery, we can wish not to be [*souhaiter de n'être point*]. (*Traité de morale*, *OCM*.XI.82/*TE*, 91)

The same holds true for evil and defects in general:

> I do not believe evil is just a matter of appearances. I believe that there is evil, that God permits it, and draws good from it. I also believe that there are not only *apparent* defects in the world, but also true defects [*de véritables défauts*]. (*Avis touchant l'entretien*, *OCM*.XV.53; his emphasis)

The novelty of this argument cannot be stressed too much.[36] Centuries of philosophical and theological argumentation had striven precisely to remove evil from positive creation, so that God could not directly be blamed or thought responsible for its lesser or less perfect parts. But if evil is part of positive reality as much as (or even more so) than good, then

35. Moreau, *Deux Cartésiens*, 120.

36. I am indebted to Moreau's work for providing the building blocks for my argument here. Moreau ('Malebranche on Disorder', 93) suggests that Malebranche is 'perhaps the only Cartesian who gives a full ontological value to the sensation of pain'. To which I would add, Bayle too—in so far as he can be called Cartesian, that is (as argued by Todd Ryan, *Pierre Bayle's Cartesian Metaphysics*).

it occupies a central place in God's creation. This is to up the ante to an extreme degree: all now stands or falls with the question of whether or not creation as a whole can yet be justified.

Another intriguing aspect of this argument is that it sidesteps the classic distinction, central to scholastic debates, between negation and privation.[37] According to scholastics such as Suárez, evil is always privative, in that it is based on the absence of some good that the thing *ought to have* according to its nature. Thus the absence of wings is not an evil in a man, but it is an evil in a bird, whose wings are not trivially absent, but meaningfully privative: the bird is deprived whereas man is not. Furthermore, some kinds of evils can be positive in a specific way: the category of *evil for another* was meant to explain, for instance, claws in dangerous animals, which are a good for the animal but can be an evil for us. Such evils are positive not in so far as they are evils, but in so far as they are also goods in themselves: thus for Suárez and other scholastics, privation can in some cases be grounded in something positive.[38]

Malebranche has little patience for these scholastic views, which do not match up to our experience of suffering. Pain and evil must be considered more or worse than mere privation: they need to be positive concepts in themselves, thought out on their own terms.[39] Our experience dictates that evil is an equally positive entity as good; likewise for pain and unhappiness. According to Malebranche (and Bayle after him), pain is bad not because it's privative, but because it's an evil on its own account, just as the good is in itself a good. Hence, Malebranche's willingness to think the reality and positivity of evil on its own terms, and not as relative to or derivative from the good, goes directly against the first negative strategy and thereby flies in the face of centuries of Augustinian and scholastic traditions.

THE GOOD, THE BAD, AND THE UGLY

Malebranche also objects to the second negative strategy mentioned above: the holistic or aesthetic approach. The Jansenist philosopher Antoine Arnauld, in one of his many critiques of Malebranche, had

37. On which, see again Antognazza, 'Metaphysical Evil Revisited', 113–4; Newlands, 'Malebranche', section 3, as well as his 'Leibniz on Privations' and 'Evils, Privations'.

38. Suárez, 'On Evil', section I (*Metaphysics*, 162–80).

39. For more on Malebranche's response to scholastic privation theory, see Newlands, 'Malebranche', who notes that Malebranche accepts privation theory with regard to *moral* evils (section 2; see also section 3).

referred back to Augustine's comparison of the universe to a beautiful mosaic, and added an analogy with music:

> Nothing is more contrary to music than dissonances. . . . And yet, a dissonance, mixed in among many consonances, is what makes for the most excellent harmony. . . . A monstrous animal [*Un animal monstrueux*] is, if you will, a dissonance in the harmony of the universe; but it does not fail to make a contribution to this harmony.[40]

In response, Malebranche strongly resists the aesthetic analogy with either shadows in a painting or dissonances in music offered by philosophers such as Arnauld:

> Shadows are necessary in a painting, and dissonances in Music. Therefore it is necessary that women miscarry [*avortent*], and create an infinity of monsters. What a consequence! I would reply boldly to the Philosophers. . . . I mean that, in the end, none of that makes God's work more perfect. On the contrary, it disfigures it [*le défigure*], and renders it disagreeable to all those who love order. . . . in truth it renders the Universe less perfect. (*Réponse aux réflexions*, *OCM*.VIII.765; see *OCM*.XII.212)

In fact, according to Malebranche, the entire premise of the analogy is misguided, since it focuses exclusively on the end result of the work, without taking into account the ways by which it has been created:

> In order to judge the beauty of a work [*ouvrage*], and by that the wisdom of the worker [*ouvrier*], one should not merely consider the work in itself, one should compare it with the ways [*les voies*] by which it has been formed. . . . To judge the worker by the work, one should therefore not consider the work as much as the way of acting [*la manière d'agir*] of the worker. (*Méditations chrétiennes*, *OCM*.X.70)

An excellent artist or craftsman ought to proportion his action to his work: he does not do something by very complicated ways if he can also do it by simpler ways; he does not act without purpose, and never performs useless efforts (*Traité de la nature et de la grâce*, *OCM*.V.28).

This, in a nutshell, is Malebranche's answer to the problem of evil as he formulated it: as a problem of imperfect creation. Very briefly, according

40. Arnauld, *Réflexions philosophiques*, in *Œuvres*, vol. 39, 205; English translation cited from Nadler, *Best of Worlds*, 153, a work which explores the fascinating triangular intellectual relationship between Malebranche, Arnauld, and Leibniz.

to Malebranche, God's creation is a compound of *work* and *ways*. The world is not as perfect as it could be, absolutely speaking: God could have made it more perfect. But the world is the most perfect *combination* of work and ways. God must choose the ways that most honour his wisdom: and he does this by minimising his particular volitions, which would be needed to prevent cases of monsters. Thus God accepts a lesser perfection of the work if it means a greater perfection of the ways, leading to an optimal total perfection. The world as we have it is a kind of compromise, the optimal combination of various perfections, of work and ways, which Malebranche at some point even expresses in quantitative terms.[41]

In his double defiance of these two strategies, Malebranche goes directly against the traditional Augustinian philosophy of evil, especially in his insistence on the positive reality of evil and pain. However, he also stays true to the positive strategy introduced by Augustine, which links suffering inextricably to sin. For instance, in one of his responses to Arnauld, Malebranche calls pain a true physical evil, *physiquement un vrai mal*, but he also equates this *mal physique* with punishment for sin (that is, *malum poenae*) or moral evil:

> Thus the Sage of the Stoics lied, when he said he was happy in his torments, for pain is not a false evil, but it's physically a true evil [*physiquement un vrai mal*], not a true efficacious evil, but a true formal evil, not a moral evil that corrupts the soul, but a physical evil [*mal physique*], punishment of sin or of moral evil. (Malebranche, *Réponse . . . à la troisième lettre, OCM*.IX.981)

In this sense, there is something subtly deceptive about Malebranche's obsessive insistence on the problematic case of monsters.[42] Monsters are not problematic because they suffer. This suffering is perfectly explicable, according to Malebranche, by the human condition of sin. His philosophy is crucially entrenched in the Augustinian discourse of sin and punishment.[43] The defective creature may suffer without having sinned in this

41. See Malebranche, *Abrégé du traité de la nature et de la grâce* (1704), *OCM*.IX.1085; where he compares two hypothetical creations by the sum [*Perfection of the work*] + [*Perfection of the ways*] = [*Total perfection*]; a lesser creation gives *8* (*work*) + *2* (*ways*) = *10* (*total perfection*), where God's creation would give *6* (*work*) + *6* (*ways*) = *12* (*total perfection*), hence yielding a greater overall perfection, since the ways are more perfect, even though the work is less so. See Moreau's helpful representation of these quantitative relations, which he warns against overinterpreting ('Malebranche on Disorder', 83).

42. See Jolley, 'Is Leibniz's Theodicy', 60, for a similar point.

43. See Newlands, 'Malebranche on the Metaphysics and Ethics of Evil', section 2. Thus sin ultimately remains a greater problem for Malebranche than pain or even monsters:

life, yet it has no legitimate complaint against its creator, since it is ultimately guilty for having participated in original sin. Malebranche, who himself suffered wretchedly throughout his life, does reserve a place for human suffering as part of the positive reality of evil—but this is not where the *problem* of evil resides.

Why, then, are monsters problematic at all? Again, it is not because the monster suffers. It is not from the perspective of the *monster* that there's a problem: rather, monsters are problematic from the perspective of the *universe*, which is disfigured on their account. Malebranche's category of disorder or defect is not so much about suffering as it is about disfigurement, something *visibly* defective—something, we could almost say, that seems ugly rather than evil: or rather, evil on account of its ugliness. It's an almost aesthetic category. Thus, when Malebranche writes that it would be better that there were no monsters ('il serait mieux qu'il n'y en eût point'), he doesn't mean it would be better for the *monster*, but that it would be better *for the universe as a whole* (*OCM*.V.36).

Hence, in Malebranche's philosophy of evil, the traditional justificatory line that connects suffering with sin remains intact. What changes is the positive *reality* of evil. Considering this, he requires a different kind of theodicy: his explanation of the existence of evil must take into account more than the end product, which is *obviously*, *visibly* defective—hence the inclusion of God's ways aside from his works.[44] Thus Malebranche's treatment of evil does a lot of things that are very new and very striking—but what it does *not* do is provide a discourse of evil that allows for the legitimate complaint of the creature against its creator.

Bayle's Balances

Enter Pierre Bayle (1647–1706), one of Malebranche's most avid readers, who started out as a devotee and, though he changed his mind on some of Malebranche's doctrines, did pick up certain key elements of his philosophy of evil. Born into a Calvinist community in the south of Catholic France under Louis XIV, Bayle's life was always going to be a conflicted one, and he did not make things easier for himself by converting, twice,

---

Moreau, *Deux Cartésiens*, 94n.; Guéroult, *Malebranche*, III.235–40; Boudot, 'L'être et le néant', 293.

44. See Moreau, 'Malebranche on Disorder', 93–4: 'According to Malebranche, one can go from the affirmation "this seems evil to me" to the affirmation "it is evil." So, this unusual theodicy appears to be almost a phenomenological one.' As we will see, the same can be said of Bayle's *anti*-theodicy.

in his early twenties: first to Catholicism, then back again. This reconversion turned him into a relapsed heretic and marked the beginning of several itinerant years, as Bayle fled to Geneva, Sedan, and ultimately the Dutch Republic, where he spent the rest of his life and wrote most of his philosophical works in the city of Rotterdam.[45] Among these was the *Dictionnaire historique et critique* (1696).[46] This strangest of books, spanning six million words and four folio volumes by the time Bayle died 'pen in hand', is the main reason why Bayle became one of the household names of the Enlightenment, read avidly by Hume, Voltaire, and the *philosophes*, who all plucked many ideas from its pages (as was surely Bayle's intention). It is also why Bayle found himself at the centre of one of the most divided hermeneutical debates in the history of philosophy, a debate that is still ongoing.

I too have spent years poring over the *Dictionnaire*'s pages, searching for answers to a question that (I finally concluded) was itself unanswerable, at least on Bayle's own terms.[47] This position, if it deserves the name, is itself controversial and has brought upon me the criticism of not answering my own questions. In any other case, that criticism would be warranted: in Bayle's case, I think it is not. My reason for believing this has everything to do with getting to know Bayle as a writer, and understanding what he is *doing* with words even when he isn't saying things outright. To my mind, Bayle is one of the most intelligent, creative, deliberate writers you will ever come across. If he wants to say something, he doesn't mince his words. But he does like to lead his readers in different directions, leaving banana peels for you to slip on in the very passages that seem most straightforward, putting up signposts that may be the clue to what you're looking for, but may also lead you further astray, and scattering breadcrumbs that tempt you onwards until you find yourself tangled

45. On Bayle's life, see Bost, *Pierre Bayle*, Labrousse, *Pierre Bayle*, vol. I. Earlier works of Bayle include the *Pensées diverses* (1682), which argued (among other things) that a society of virtuous atheists was possible, and the *Commentaire philosophique* (1686), one of the most far-reaching pleas for religious toleration of the period. Later works include the *Réponse aux questions d'un provincial* (1704–1707), *Entretiens de Maxime et de Thémiste* (1707), and *Continuation des pensées diverses* (1704).

46. Bayle prepared three editions of the *Dictionnaire* (hereafter *DHC*), in 1696, 1702, and 1720 (published posthumously): each edition contained a vast amount of new material. Following the approach in my earlier work on Bayle, I will cite the fourth edition (now standard) of 1740, while indicating the origin of any passage: e.g. *Xenophanes¹.E* (article *Xenophanes*, Remark E, passage present in the first edition). On the structure of the *DHC*, see my *Bayle, Jurieu*, chapter 1.

47. See the introduction and conclusion to my *Bayle, Jurieu*.

in a dark wood of footnotes and cross-references, where you may have the most exciting, confusing, and exhausting time of your reading life. It's not a real dictionary at all, you see: it's more like a labyrinth of words.

Bayle got in trouble over the *Dictionnaire* as soon as it was published, and one of his problems had everything to do with that of evil.[48] In a nutshell, the 'Bayle enigma' that has baffled scholars to this day consists of these three elements:[49]

i. In the *Dictionnaire*, Bayle goes to great lengths to argue that the problem of evil cannot be solved by reason.
ii. Bayle repeatedly suggests that the only way out of the problem of evil is by 'captivating the understanding under the obedience of faith': a position generally known as *fideism*.[50]
iii. But Bayle doesn't seem to like fideism or any element of irrationalism in religion, and in his other works manifests deeply rationalist tendencies.

So was Bayle 'really' a Calvinist fideist, or was he instead a cunning freethinker, dissembling his deeper irreligion behind a superficial façade of high-hearted faith?[51] The incongruity lies not only in Bayle's statements, but also in the fact that Bayle *did not relent*. There is a sort of double gesture inherent in the *Dictionnaire*, as Bayle appeals to faithful silence with one hand, while with the other he continues to hammer down his objections to 'theodicy' (a term not yet invented), even in subsequent editions of the *Dictionnaire*, and in his later works.[52] On and on the dizzying dance continues, until one would like to exclaim to Bayle, as Elizabeth

48. The *DHC* was examined and censured by the Walloon Consistory of Rotterdam in 1697; the Manichean articles were among those receiving special scrutiny. For details see Bost and McKenna (eds.), *L'Affaire Bayle*.

49. The term 'the Bayle Enigma' comes from Thomas Lennon (*Reading Bayle*, 14).

50. *captivare intellectum in obsequium fidei*; see my *Bayle, Jurieu*, 172.

51. These opposing positions, here bluntly stated, represent the main avenues of interpretation in Bayle scholarship, exemplified in their strongest forms by Elisabeth Labrousse and Walter Rex on the 'fideist' side, and Gianluca Mori and Antony McKenna on the 'irreligious' side; see the introduction to my *Bayle, Jurieu*.

52. See my *Bayle, Jurieu*, chapter 5. Leibniz coined the term 'theodicy' with his *Essais de Théodicée* of 1710 (on which, see chapter 2), composing it out of the Greek terms *theos* (god) and *dikē* (justice); but Paul Rateau notes that Leibniz used the term in a letter to Etienne Chauvin as early as 1696 ('Theoretical Foundations', 92). I prefer the adjective 'theodicean' to the awkward 'theodical' (common in analytic philosophers), to preserve continuity with the terms *théodicée*/*theodicy*/*theodicist*.

Bennett does to her Mr Darcy: 'I do not get on at all. I hear such different accounts of you as puzzle me exceedingly.'[53]

But what if *puzzled* is precisely what we are meant to be? What if the point of the entire exercise is not so much to deliver a single fixed opinion, but to explore varieties of philosophical pathways, and to invite readers to do the same? What if the duality of the dictionary is integral to what it means to think, and write, like Bayle? To borrow a football metaphor from John Robertson: perhaps we should see Bayle as a philosophical 'midfielder', passing the ball in various directions, though by the time 'the reader receives what they take to be the final pass (the "assist", as it's now called), it's no longer clear just which goal the ball is supposed to be struck into'.[54] This seems roughly right to me, and it is helpful to explain my presentation of Bayle throughout this book. If there are several lines or threads or paths to follow through the *Dictionnaire*, lines that lead to different conclusions perhaps, then it seems warranted to choose to focus on one of these in particular, leaving the many others to one side (at least for now). This, briefly, is what my approach will be throughout this book. There is a specific reading of Bayle on which I will focus my efforts, a specific line through the maze that I have chosen to follow, and which *has* in fact been followed by many of Bayle's readers throughout the eighteenth century. This reading could be called 'Bayle the pessimist', and it is this version or voice of Bayle that will be encountered again and again in the writings of later thinkers featured in this book. This is not to say that this 'pessimistic Bayle' is the *real* Bayle, or that it represents my answer to the Bayle enigma, or even that it is the only version of Bayle worth having: far from it. But it is a view of Bayle that has had a profound influence on the Enlightenment, and that represents a philosophical tradition worthy of study in its own right, as I will argue throughout this book.

But how to pin down even this pessimistic Bayle? In my previous work, I have argued that in order to understand the *Dictionnaire*, readers first need to acquaint themselves with the work, and choose a way of making sense of it. It is not enough to read the whole thing from Aaron to Zuylichem, which is certainly not how the book was designed to be read: deeply discontinuous on the surface, the *Dictionnaire's* continuities always lie at least one level down. Even the alphabetical format invites the reader to browse casually before deciding where to take the plunge, and other

53. Jane Austen, *Pride and Prejudice*, 82.

54. John Robertson, in conversation and correspondence.

technical devices reinforce this stimulus of spontaneity on the side of the reader, as Bayle made the most of such 'information management' tools as were then available: above all, *the cross-reference*. Using as my test case the web of articles dealing with the problem of evil, I have shown that Bayle's marginal cross-references function almost like hyperlinks, continuing the discussion in a variety of contexts, so that a philosophical argument rarely stands alone.[55] To understand Bayle's treatment of evil, then, it is not enough to read just the seminal articles: we have to follow his signposts back and forth to map his considerations, as though we were continuing a conversation across the centuries. Based on my plotting of the 'Manichean web' in my previous work, I will here focus on just a few articles of that web, where Bayle develops his views on physical evil in particular, and we encounter full-fledged the voice of Bayle the pessimist.

XENOPHANES

First, a story. Imagine a London merchant who is deliberating whether to send his ten sons to Oxford or to Cambridge. By a special revelation, he knows that if he sends his sons to Cambridge, 'they will make considerable progress in the sciences as well as in virtue' and will acquire 'honourable occupations for the rest of their lives'. But the merchant also knows that if he sends his sons to Oxford, 'they will become depraved, they will become rascals, and they will pass from mischief to mischief' until they have to be punished by the law, though 'he will be able to obtain grace for one of them'. Thus Cambridge promises a life of virtue and happiness for all, Oxford a life of vice and misery for all but one. The fatherly course seems clear enough, and yet

> Never doubting the truth of this revelation, he still sends his sons to Oxford, and not to Cambridge. Is it not clear, according to our common notions, that 1) this merchant wants his sons to be wicked and miserable; and 2) that, consequently, he is acting in a way that is contrary to goodness and to the love of virtue? (*EMT*.I, ch. 8/*OD*.IV.24)[56]

This is not a passage from a Cambridge undergraduate prospectus: it is a version of the problem of evil, as presented in one of Bayle's later

55. See my *Bayle, Jurieu*, chapter 1.

56. My translation; though see Hickson's edition for an excellent English translation of the entire *EMT*.

works.[57] The point Bayle is trying to make has everything to do with the Christian narrative of Genesis, which is central to most positive strategies that reduce physical evil to moral evil, suffering to sin: what I have called the *reduction approach.* Because not all current sufferings can be explained by *particular* sins (for instance, the suffering of small children, or of righteous men such as Job), this strategy generally has recourse to original sin and to the narrative of the Fall: *we suffer now because we fell then.*

The question then remains, *why did we fall at all?*, and this is the question Bayle keeps asking, relentlessly, from the *Dictionnaire* to his last works (*EMT*, *RQP*). Human freedom does not suffice him as an answer: After all, if the gift of freedom were so wonderful, how could it have such devastating consequences, which God (being omniscient) must have foreseen and which God (being omnipotent) was able to prevent? Surely giving innocent man the gift of free will is like letting a small child play with a terrible weapon: something so inconceivably harmful that its consequences will echo down the centuries, hurting not only the child itself but all generations to come, in this life and the next.[58] Not much of a gift, this freedom; and not much of a parent, this God.

Bayle thus frames the problem of evil in the traditional way, as a conflict between the existence of evils and God's essential attributes. But the recurrent comparison to parenthood suggests that the divine attribute most crucial to Bayle's analysis is not, in fact, that of God's wisdom or power, but that of his *goodness.*[59] It is because our moral faculty gives us

57. These later works are sometimes seen as representing Bayle's considered position on evil, but are ambiguous enough to lead, *again*, to opposite conclusions as to what this position was: see, e.g., Hickson, 'The Message of Bayle's Last Title' (drawing on the *EMT* in particular); and McKenna, *Études sur Pierre Bayle* (drawing on the *RQP* and *Continuation des pensées diverses* in particular). In my view, both interpretations overstate the case: Bayle remains elusive to the bitter end.

58. On the question of damnation and the suffering of the damned, see chapter 2. The *Dictionnaire* too introduces several versions of this parable, the most notorious version of which is that of a mother wittingly sending her daughters to debauched ball (*Paulicians[1].E*).

59. Here, we can expand on Steven Nadler's helpful taxonomy of theodicies according to which of God's attributes is prioritised: while thinkers such as Arnauld and Jurieu prioritise God's power and sovereignty, and Malebranche and Leibniz are most concerned to safeguard God's wisdom and justice (if necessary, to the detriment of God's power), Bayle makes power and wisdom both subservient to the absolute exigency for God's goodness. See Nadler, 'Choosing a Theodicy', and *Best of All Possible Worlds*, chapter 6. But see also David Bentley Hart's recent defence of universal salvation, which hinges in part on a prioritisation of God's goodness over his sovereignty or omnipotence (*That All Shall Be Saved*, e.g. 170–1), and just as Bayle (and, indeed, as the Christian gospels) insists on the

a clear concept of what it means to be a good parent that the existence of evil in creation poses such an overwhelming problem to the goodness of God. Just as the London merchant would not have sent his sons to Oxford, so too a *truly good and loving God* would not have placed his children in a situation where he knew they would succumb to temptation and harm themselves *and* their offspring most dreadfully.

This is why, if we focus our attention to what *experience* tells us about the world, the Manichean hypothesis seems to make most intuitive sense: the notion that the divine principle must be twofold; that God's goodness is shadowed by the darker leanings of the demiurge, his evil twin. And this is why, at the centre of Bayle's discussion of evil in the *Dictionnaire* stand what I have called 'the Manichean articles': a triad of interlinked articles called *Manicheans*, *Paulicians*, and *Marcionites*.[60] Throughout these articles, and others besides, Bayle lets his hypothetical Manicheans pick apart the Christian narrative of Genesis, challenging any argumentation that would exonerate God from involvement with the introduction of sin—especially the free-will defence. Hence, in these articles, most attention is paid to moral evil: to the origins of sin.

However, if *moral* evil is at the centre of the Manichean web, *physical* evil receives an entire article of its own: namely, the article on the Greek Presocratic philosopher Xenophanes of Colophon (ca. 570–478 BC).[61] Here, Bayle addresses a factual–experiential question: whether there is more bad than good in human life. He begins by discussing how this matter has been viewed by a variety of poets and philosophers, especially the ancients, and groups the commentators into two camps, which we might (only *slightly* anachronistically) call optimists and pessimists.[62] Among the optimists, who believe the good surpasses the bad in human life, he ranks authors such as Euripides and Plato, later adding Seneca and Maimonides. Among the pessimists, who believe the bad surpasses the good, he ranks Pliny, Homer, Cicero, Plautus, and Diphilus, later adding

---

analogy between God and a *good parent* (ibid., e.g. 53–4). The analogy is also common in contemporary philosophy of religion: e.g. Trakakis, 'Anti-theodicy' (2), 101; Gleeson, 'God and Evil without Theodicy', 205–12.

60. For an excellent contextual presentation of these articles, see Hickson's introduction to Bayle, *Dialogues of Maximus and Themistius*.

61. *Xenophanes* was published in the first edition of the *Dictionnaire* (1696); then expanded for the second (1702). I maintain the later editions' (now standard) ordering of the Remarks. Unless otherwise stated, all citations are from the eighteenth-century translation by Pierre Des Maizeaux, though somewhat modernised and at times adjusted.

62. The terms *optimisme* and *pessimisme* were coined by the Jesuits in the wake of these debates; see chapter 2.

Aristotle, Empedocles, Holy Scripture (especially the Book of Job and the Psalms 'in various places'), the French philosopher François La Mothe le Vayer and Silenus—as well as Xenophanes himself.

Bayle then proposes to investigate whether Euripides or Pliny is right: Does evil or good surpass the other in human life? Straight away, Bayle launches his prognosis: if it were just a matter of *moral* good and evil—that is, of *malum culpae*—then the trial would quickly be decided in favour of Pliny and the pessimists.[63] After all, by far most people, especially in a Christian audience, would agree that the scale weighing human virtues and vices would tilt drastically in favour of the vices: the proportion would be something like 10 to 10,000, at best. To make this point more strongly, Bayle introduces an alternative history of mankind, told from the perspective of the devil, and argues (at some length) that history is basically a catalogue of the devil's victories, both in this life and the next, since the majority of souls are likely to be damned (*Xenophanes[1].E*).

Thus Bayle believes that the weighing of moral goods against evils is not a contentious question: most people will agree that moral evil outweighs the good.[64] But what about *physical* goods and evils? Here, Bayle suggests, Euripides and the optimists will gain some supporters (*partisans*), and he proposes to examine this more closely (*Xenophanes[1].E*). In doing so, he circles around several core issues. Behind the basic question of whether the bad surpasses the good in terms of human experience, lies the deeper, more philosophically charged, question of what this means for the value of existence itself. Aside from this, Bayle repeatedly raises a crucial methodological concern: How do we even determine whether goods or evils weigh out; how do we weigh the one against the other?

SICKNESS AND HEALTH

To begin to answer these questions, Bayle addresses some common thinking patterns—which, he argues, lead to various fallacies. For instance, says Bayle, those who argue that physical good outweighs physical evil in the world usually do so by analogy to sickness and health. Most people are generally healthy, not ill. In terms of duration, therefore, it seems that our healthy days generally outnumber our days of sickness; so too, it is often thought, does the good outweigh the bad (*Xenophanes[1].F*). But this, to

63. Bayle, *Xenophanes[1].E*; this is the only time in the *DHC* where Bayle himself uses the categories *mal de coulpe* and *mal de peine*.

64. It was, of course, contentious: both Leibniz and King would disagree.

Bayle's mind, is phenomenologically incorrect: health and illness are not symmetrical items of experience—

> health considered alone is rather an indolence than a sense of pleasure; it is rather a bare exemption from evil, than a good, whilst sickness is worse than a privation of pleasures: it is a positive state which plunges the mind into a sense of suffering [*un sentiment de souffrance*], and loads the patient with pain [*l'accable de douleur*]. (*Xenophanes¹.F*)

Instead, Bayle turns this comparison on its head, with sickness as the positive state, pushing health into the negative. The main problem with the analogy, says Bayle, is that it focuses purely on quantity, rather than on quality—but when it comes to weighing our experiences, we should attend primarily to their *intensity*. He explains this further, still staying with the contrast of sickness and health, which he likens to, respectively, dense and rare bodies (where *rare* signifies the opposite of *dense*):

> Sickness resembles the *dense* bodies, and health the *rare*. Health lasts many years successively, and yet contains but a small portion of happiness. Sickness continues but a few days, and yet comprehends a vast load of misery. If we had a scale adapted to weigh both a disease of fifteen days, and the health of fifteen years, we would observe the same difference that we find in the balance between a bag of feathers and a piece of lead. In one scale we would see a body which takes up a great deal of room, and in the other, one which lies in a very small compass; and yet one of them is not heavier than the other. Let us then beware of the illusion which the extension of health may draw us into, when it is paralleled with sickness. (*Xenophanes¹.F*; Bayle's emphasis)

Thus we could say that health tends to outweigh *extensively*, but sickness *intensively*, and the latter, for Bayle, is the more important measure when it comes to describing our experience.

He then considers an objection, and it is an important one, leading him to inquire more deeply into the nature of physical evil: 'But you will say that health is considerable, not only by reason it exempts us from a very great evil, but also by the liberty it affords us, to enjoy a thousand lively and very sensible pleasures' (*Xenophanes¹.F*). In other words: Is part of the great good of health not precisely that it opens up a world of other potential physical goods? Bayle grants this, but he immediately points out that there are in fact *two kinds* of physical evil, and so far we have only considered one of them: 'We are subject to pain and sorrow [*douleur, tristesse*], two such terrible afflictions, that it is not to be decided which is most dreadful' (*Xenophanes*[1]*.F*).

Thus we could say that Bayle differentiates the 'genus' of physical evil into two 'species': pain, or *bodily* physical evil (*douleur*), and sadness, or *psychological* physical evil (usually *tristesse* or *chagrin*). And while it is true that health exempts us from the first of these evils, Bayle argues, it leaves us fully exposed to the other (the psychological kind):

> The most vigorous health does not secure us from sorrow [*chagrin*]. For sorrow flows in upon us through a thousand channels, and is of the nature of *dense* bodies: it comprises a great deal of matter in a very small compass; evil is heaped up, crowded and pressed close in it. One hour's sorrow contains more evil, than there is good in six or seven pleasant days. (*Xenophanes*[1]*.F*)[65]

Hence, the same thing holds true for psychological as for physical suffering: it outweighs *intensively*. In fact, Bayle stresses repeatedly that 'the goods of this life are a good *to less extent* than the evils are an evil' (*Xenophanes*[1]*.F*; my emphasis).

PAIN AND SADNESS

At this point, the discussion moves away from health and illness, and more towards suffering (physical evil) in general. This leads Bayle to consider another objection, which arises at several points in *Xenophanes*, and represents a viewpoint deeply reprehensible to Bayle. There is a notion, widely spread among early modern as well as ancient philosophers (especially the Stoics), that pain is a state that can be controlled by reason or the will. If we suffer, therefore, this is due in large part to our own weakness: we could choose actively not to suffer or, at least, to suffer less. Thus Descartes, in a passage critiqued by Bayle in one of his later works, writes to Elisabeth of Bohemia that the true philosophy teaches us that 'even among the saddest accidents and the most pressing pains one can always be content [in life], so long as one knows how to use one's reason'.[66] Hence, it could be argued, as Bayle accuses Lactantius of having done, that man suffers

65. Hume's Philo in the *Dialogues* makes almost literally the same claim: 'One hour of [pain] is often able to outweigh a day, a week, a month of our common insipid enjoyments' (*DNR*.X.75). See chapter 5.

66. Descartes to Elisabeth of Bohemia, 6 October 1645 (*Correspondence*, 121).

inappropriately; that man complains of evils that objectively speaking aren't so considerable; 'that men are so delicate, that they complain of the least evil, as if it absorbed all the good things they have enjoyed' (*Xenophanes[1].F*). Or, as Maimonides had suggested, that the majority of human evils are self-inflicted; that man brings them 'upon himself'; that 'this is the cause of all corporeal and psychical diseases and ailments', for which man is wrong to blame God.[67] And if humans make themselves miserable—if suffering is a fault or weakness or even a choice—then neither kind of physical evil (neither pain nor sadness) can rightly pose a *problem* of evil.

But this, to Bayle's mind, would be to get things very wrong indeed. First, the specific *cause* of human suffering—for instance, whether it is self-inflicted—is completely irrelevant to the factual discussion (the 'matter of fact' [*point de fait*]; *Xenophanes[2].K*) of *whether* and *how much* man suffers:

> it would be departing from the state of the question to say, that man afflicts himself without cause. For it is not our business here to know whether his sorrows [*ses chagrins*] are reasonable, or the effect of his weakness; but the question is, to know whether he *has* sorrows [*s'il a des chagrins*]. This very thing, that a man vexes himself [*se chagrine*] without reason, and makes himself unhappy by his own fault, is an evil. (*Xenophanes[1].F*; my emphasis)[68]

Second, Bayle argues against Lactantius, it is equally irrelevant to discuss the objective or *absolute* quantities of good and evil in human life, since we are talking purely of human *experience*, which can only be measured in relative terms:

> it is to no purpose to consider here what the *absolute* quantity of good and evil dispensed to man, may be in itself; we are only to consider their *relative* quality; or, to express myself more clearly, we ought to consider nothing but *the feeling of the mind* [*sentiment de l'âme*]. A very great good in itself, which raises but a very moderate pleasure, ought not to pass for more than a moderate good; but an evil, though

67. Maimonides, *Guide*, 445–6.

68. A note on pronouns: where translating or directly paraphrasing early modern texts, I will retain the male pronoun as well as the generic 'man', since to do otherwise would be to over-modernise these authors, who often, in thinking of humanity, had only 'mankind' in mind. In other cases, I will use the singular 'they/them/their' for referring to indefinite nouns, in accordance with Amia Srinivasan's recent article 'He, She, One . . .'.

> very little in itself, which gives an uneasiness, sorrow, or pain, that are insupportable, ought to pass for a very great evil . . . (*Xenophanes*[1]*.F*; my emphasis)

In other words, physical evil is *exactly* identical to the (subjective) experience of that evil, just as physical good is exactly identical to the experience of that good. The human experience of good and evil is all that is relevant to the discussion of which weighs out in human life. Finally, against Maimonides, Bayle repeats this point, adding that not only is it irrelevant 'that we ourselves are the cause of our misfortunes, that we often afflict ourselves without any reason; and that the pleasures of life are numberless, and sometimes very long', but the very knowledge that we may suffer needlessly can make our suffering worse: 'No evil is small when it is felt and considered as a great one, and nothing troubles an uneasy man [*un homme chagrin*] more than to know, that he has no reason to be uneasy' (*Xenophanes*[2]*.K*).

This emphasis on subjective experience is at the essence of Bayle's phenomenology and his discussion of the problem of evil. It is also the point at which Bayle diverges from Malebranche. Both Malebranche and Bayle, as we have seen, make physical evil a significant part of the problem of evil. The main difference between their approaches is that Malebranche frames physical evil primarily as disorder, and as viewed from the perspective of the universe, rather than as experience: he does allow room for the positivity of pain, but the experiential aspect is not itself problematic, since it can be accounted for by sin. For Bayle, on the other hand, experience is all that matters: his account of physical evil is purely focused on subjective experience, regardless of the causes of this experience.[69]

While there is much to say for the common-sense clarity of this approach,[70] it is not an uncontroversial move: Bayle hereby incurs all the problems traditionally associated with hedonism. For one thing, if an evil is whatever is experienced as such, this seems to allow no room for error: Is it not possible for a person to be harmed without knowing it?[71]

69. This point is taken up explicitly by William Wollaston, who in the 1720s equates 'true pleasure and pain' with 'physical (or *natural*) good and evil' (*Religion of Nature Delineated*, 40; his emphasis).

70. There is a similarity here with the definition of pain espoused by 'many historians, anthropologists, sociologists, and even clinicians', as discussed by Joanna Bourke: 'Anyone claiming to be "in pain" *is* in pain; if a person describes her experiences as "painful", they are' (Bourke, *The Story of Pain*, 3).

71. For a recent discussion of this issue, see Cohen, *Toleration and Freedom from Harm*, 59.

To which Bayle might answer that while everything that is experienced as an evil is an evil, this does not mean that whatever is *not* experienced as an evil is *not* an evil. The *perception* of the 'evilness' may be a sufficient but not a necessary condition for the evilness of the thing. But it should be remembered that Bayle is not so much concerned about having a closing definition of evil as he is about arguing that life holds more evils than are generally accounted for. And so an even more Baylean response would be that if it is true that we can be harmed without knowing it, *this is itself another evil*, and this only strengthens the case for pessimism.

This experiential intervention has various striking results, one of which is that Bayle, unlike Malebranche, and unlike most other authors in the canon of evil, places sadness on an equal footing with pain.[72] It is not considered at all derivative or secondary or virtual, but as exactly symmetrical to pain: just as direct, intense, and violent. Thus in Bayle, physical evil is most commonly described as a conjunction of pain and sadness: of *douleur* and *tristesse/chagrin*. Physical evil is comprised of bodily and psychological suffering—and *of nothing aside from suffering*.[73] And, in fact, when Bayle offers examples of suffering individuals who despair at life, to the point of wanting to leave it altogether, these examples tend to revolve around psychological rather than bodily suffering: focusing on sadness, grief, *chagrin*.

BAD TASTE

Bayle's claim that the weighing of physical goods and evils in human life hinges on subjective experience leads him into seemingly insurmountable methodological problems. For instance, the consequence of his emphatic focus on the purely 'relative quality' of good and evil is that no one can

72. See, e.g., Malebranche (*Entretiens sur la métaphysique et la religion* (1688), *OCM*. XII.94), who argues that pain precedes knowledge of harm, while sadness follows it (and is pleasing to us). This idea seems to go back roughly to Augustine, who, in Susan James's words, 'argues that, with the exception of pains and pleasures caused by the body, emotions have their source in the soul itself and are essentially acts of will' (James, *Passion and Action*, 114). Though Descartes sees passions as perceptions, thus passive states (James, ibid.), he also frames sadness as rather a secondary phenomenon, a mental or virtual commentary on pain or other evils, whereas pain itself is portrayed as sensuous, violent, and direct (*Passions of the Soul*, articles 61 and 94).

73. This conjunction of 'pain and sorrow' is taken up by Hume—for example, in his essay 'Of Suicide'; see chapter 5, where I argue that Hume develops Bayle's intuitions on psychological suffering into a *dispositional problem of evil*.

appropriately judge the proportions between goods and evils in another's life, since we have no direct access to their experience:

> On this account no man is able to judge aright, either of the misery or happiness of his neighbour. We do not know what another feels, we only know the outward causes of evil and good: now these causes are not always proportioned to their effects; those which seem to us very small, frequently produce a lively sense; and those which appear to us great, very often occasion but a faint one. (*Xenophanes¹.F*)

All that we can know 'with full certainty' is that no life is entirely exempt from such evils (*Xenophanes¹.F*). Furthermore, even when judging our own lives, we run into difficulties. For one thing, age is an issue: Bayle grants that when a person is young, 'pleasures are predominant' and 'good turns the scale', which would lead to a positive evaluation of life at that moment—but the balance usually shifts in old age, which is when the greatest evils of life introduce themselves (*Xenophanes¹.F*). This suggests that one can only appropriately judge the value of one's own life as a whole at the very end. But even then, how does one go about the business of weighing the goods and evils of one's life? Bayle, in the attempt of finding some kind of procedure that aims at a level of objectivity, introduces a thought experiment: would you live your life again, if it meant reliving all past sorrows as well as joys?

Bayle knows that he cannot answer this question for all mankind, but he does offer his prognosis, and he does so through the example of two philosophers, one ancient and one modern, who prospered in life, and yet at the very end would have refused to live it over again. The cross-references lead to two articles (*Tullia* and *Vayer*), which suggest that, in both the case of Marcus Tullius Cicero (106–43 BCE) and the seventeenth-century philosopher François La Mothe le Vayer (1588–1672), it was grief that made them swear off life, for both lost a beloved child:

> I am sure that the dismal state to which Cicero was reduced by the loss of Tullia appeared to him such a weighty pressure that he would very willingly have quitted all the lustre of his glory, to be delivered from this insupportable sadness [*tristesse*]. I believe also that he would not have returned into the world, on condition of passing through the various states that he had gone through. (*Tullia¹.R*; see *Porcius².R*)[74]

74. Cicero himself does not have his own article in the *DHC*; his daughter Tullia does. La Mothe le Vayer too 'was extremely afflicted at the loss of his only son' and sought

And if this is so for Cicero and La Mothe le Vayer, whose lives were relatively prosperous, then 'we must believe that, upon the whole, *every one* finds the pleasures which he has enjoyed, have been unequal to the uneasinesses and pains [*les déplaisirs, et les douleurs*] with which he has been afflicted' (*Xenophanes¹.F*; my emphasis). According to Bayle, many would agree with his prognosis that, 'except some brutal wretches, *no old man* would return into the world on condition to be obliged to act the same part over again' (*Vayer¹.F*; my emphasis).

Bayle's thought experiment is not itself new: it goes back to earlier versions in Cicero and Erasmus, but after Bayle's reprise it becomes an obsession for thinkers following in his footsteps, and it is taken up by almost every philosopher engaging with questions of optimism and pessimism in the eighteenth and nineteenth centuries. As a result, we will encounter the thought experiment again in *every chapter* of this book. And while their conclusions may differ, the very fact that such a wide variety of authors took up Bayle's challenge shows that they considered the thought experiment valid in a meaningful way.[75] For Bayle, though, the point of the thought experiment is to make us rethink our intuitions regarding the general agreeableness of life. Again and again, Bayle represents the ability of even a small period of suffering to turn sour a longer period of happiness, or a mere 'grain of evil' spoiling 'a hundred pound [*degrés*] of good', just as a small portion of seawater can make a large amount of fresh water turn salt (*Xenophanes².K*). Sometimes, it is not even grief or bereavement that has this macabre ability—for they at least have a clear cause—but something approaching depression:

> The other day I was told of a man who killed himself, after an anxious melancholy [*chagrin*] of three or four weeks. Every night he had laid his sword under his pillow, in hopes that he would have courage enough to end his life, when darkness should increase his grief [*tristesse*]: but his resolution failed for several nights successively. At last, not being able to resist his uneasiness [*chagrin*], he cut the veins of his arm. I affirm, that all the pleasures which this man had enjoyed in thirty years, would not equal the evils which tormented him the last

---

consolation in a second marriage at old age, another sign for Bayle of the 'disorders' which grief can cause in us (*Vayer¹.G*).

75. Though they sometimes present it in an adjusted form, so as to produce either a more optimistic outcome (in the cases of Leibniz, King, Rousseau), or an even more pessimistic one (Kant!).

month of his life, if both were weighed on the right balance [*une juste balance*]. (*Xenophanes*[1]*.F*)

Thus Bayle, unlike most of his contemporaries, emphatically includes emotional dispositions (sadness, grief, *chagrin*) in the range of things that require theodicean explanation, to the point of making them central to the problem of evil itself.

This concern with specifically *psychological* suffering also feeds into Bayle's unusual attitude towards the urge for suicide or annihilation, which by most authors of the time was considered an emphatically irrational desire. In mild deviation from this tradition, Malebranche had argued that there are worse states than nothingness, *pire que le néant*, so that one can indeed desire (quite reasonably) to want to re-enter a state of nothingness, rather than continue in a state of misery and desolation.

Bayle went further. Not only is suicide understandable, but if the evils of one's existence greatly outweigh the goods, it is a perfectly rational response, perhaps the only rational response possible to one's existential situation. At least in some cases, therefore, suicide can be a courageous, even laudable, though also tragic act.[76] Conversely, if a person who suffers dreadfully still prefers to live rather than to die, this is not just irrational: it is a sign of bad taste. This is Bayle's verdict of Claudia Octavia (ca. 40–62 CE), the unfortunate first wife of emperor Nero, who was first exiled and later executed by her husband. Bayle describes her tragic life as a large bowl of misery with only 'two or three drops' of good: 'Such was the lot of our Octavia, and yet she had a mind to live: death was more frightful to her than all her calamities, for which ill taste [*mauvais goût*] her youth ought to plead her excuse' (*Octavia*[1]*.G*). Furthermore, in both *Xenophanes* and *Tullia*, Bayle mentions Silenus's dictum (via Pliny, Cicero, and Lactantius) that the best thing in life is not to be born at all, the second best to die as soon as possible (*Xenophanes*[1]*.D*; *Tullia*[1]*.R*; also *RQP*.IV.23/*OD*.III.1070).[77] We are left with the suggestion that not only are there many people for whom death would be preferable to life, but there are also

76. For Bayle's response to King on suicide, see chapter 2.

77. Bayle follows Lactantius in suggesting that Cicero cited 'this sentence of Silenus' in his *De Consolatione* (*Tullia*[1]*.R*). See also Epicurus, *Letters*, 55, who refers this dictum to Theognis of Megara. For recent proponents of the 'wisdom of Silenus', see Benatar, *Better Never to Have Been*, and Cioran, *The Trouble with Being Born*, 212: 'Not to be born is undoubtedly the best plan of all. Unfortunately it is within no one's reach.'

people (perhaps, even, the majority of people) for whom it would be better never to have been.[78]

A Theodicean Turn?

Now, this very pessimistic conclusion need not be a problem for the Christian narrative, as long as physical evil is still embedded in an Augustinian framework that connects suffering with sin. As we have seen in Malebranche, if the creature is ultimately responsible, the creature has no legitimate complaint. However, in Bayle, his discussion of physical evil is only one part of his discussion of evil: the other part, focusing on moral evil, calls into question precisely the Augustinian narrative that reduces suffering to sin—and this part strongly emphasises creaturely innocence in comparison to the absolute responsibility of the creator. Since sin is called into question, suffering becomes a problem again, in a way that it had not been before: the spectre of truly innocent or undeserved suffering, which Augustine had said was irreconcilable with God's justice, is firmly planted at the centre of the debate. It is this causal disconnect of suffering from both the past (as punishment) and future (as preparation for reward) that creates the space for a modern notion of truly meaningless suffering, which makes no sense in an Augustinian framework. The rejection of original sin as the fundamental explanation for the origins of evil means the reproblematisation of physical as well as moral evil. And this means that in Bayle, unlike in Malebranche (or most other authors), the creature does indeed have a legitimate complaint.[79]

That is, *if* we give credence to Bayle's hypothetical spokespersons, the Manicheans. Famously, having built up the case against any rational theodicy, including Malebranche's, and having suggested that heretical or

78. There are strong parallels here with the work of David Benatar; in fact, many of Benatar's arguments mirror Bayle's to an uncanny extent, with Benatar arguing on the ethics of *pro*creation in much the same way as Bayle did with regard to *divine* creation. Very briefly, Benatar combines a posteriori and a priori arguments (having to do with pessimism, but also with certain asymmetries between harms and benefits) to argue that coming into existence is always a harm, and that it is better for any sentient being never to have been. See his *Better Never To Have Been*, 'Anti-Natalism', and *The Human Predicament*.

79. This is my interpretation, which I believe is warranted by Bayle's repeated presentation of creaturely complaint in his many trial-like parables. For a different interpretation, see especially Hickson, 'Theodicy and Toleration', who argues that Bayle's argument on evil is essentially an argument for religious toleration. While I agree that there is a toleration impulse here, I don't think this is the whole story behind Bayle's entrenched philosophical pessimism, which he goes to such lengths to ground in both reason and experience.

pagan philosophers such as the Manicheans could utterly confound the arguments of Christians, Bayle abruptly steers his argument to a fideist conclusion that is as confusing as it seems unsatisfactory, and that has left his commentators in disagreement for centuries to follow. Since there can be no rational solution to the problem of evil, one must either choose reason over faith or faith over reason, and Revelation points us towards the second option; the first, however, remains intact.

Again, I will not venture to answer this vexed question, which does not require answering in order to consider some of Bayle's innovations in the debate on evil. For while moral evil remains central to Bayle's 'anti-theodicean' project, as a crucial threat to God's goodness if considered rationally, the parallel introduction of physical evil is perhaps even more striking. However, it should be noted that Bayle did not *have* to bring physical evil into the debate. Since the justification of moral evil is repeatedly posited as the foundation of any rational theodicy, if that part crumbles, the whole edifice falters. Physical evil, then, is technically superfluous to Bayle's argument, so that we could ask of Bayle what Al Alvarez asks of Dostoevsky: 'why this intensity, this need to nag away at the problem like a man enraged by a bad tooth?'[80] In Bayle's case, at least, the answer seems clear: if he emphatically focuses on physical evil, to the point of devoting an entire article to it, it is because he considers it philosophically important on its own account. For Bayle, the question of experiential pessimism is acutely relevant to the problem of evil, and to the evaluation of human existence as a whole. This relevance, furthermore, was implicitly recognised by Bayle's critics, even as they disputed his method, his premises, and his conclusions.

As we will see in chapter 2, Bayle's primary detractors, Leibniz and King, both take up the challenge of Bayle's pessimism, aiming to tip the balance in favour of the good. In Leibniz's case, as in Bayle's, this is technically unnecessary: Leibniz explicitly states that physical evils are 'the results of moral evil', and so the origins of the former can be explained by the latter (*EdT*, 241.276/*G*.VI.261).[81] And yet, just like Bayle, both King and Leibniz aim to support their arguments with a certain view of the cosmos and of human existence, which the Jesuits were quick to style 'optimism'. Both believed that Bayle exaggerated the evils of life, and argued

80. Alvarez, *The Savage God*, 239.

81. For King, the source of natural evils lies in the origin of all things from matter (*DOM*, 146); however, he also at times refers natural evils to punishment for sin (e.g. *DOM*, 203).

instead that human life contains much more good than evil—and, indeed, that there is more good than evil in the universe on the whole.

Perhaps most importantly, both King and Leibniz seem to concede a certain shift in the debate. Even in the course of disputing Bayle's conclusions, both authors incorporate experiential questions into their arguments and considerations—the door to which Malebranche, with his notion of the positivity of evils, had left ajar, but Bayle had pushed wide open. Unlike Bayle, however, Leibniz and King both focus on pain rather than on sadness, on bodily rather than psychological suffering, and offer their explanations in exactly the fashion to which Bayle had objected: making pain a matter of human responsibility and, ultimately, human guilt. And yet, in doing so, they implicitly acknowledge that pain and suffering have become part of what is *now* the problem of evil: a problem not only of disorder or imperfection, but of *experience*. The question arises, in King and Leibniz as in Bayle, whether existence is always worthwhile to the creature, whose perspective is now, to some extent, taken into account.

Hence, throughout this discussion, we can see the reinvention of the category of evil that is (at least initially) outside the moral order. Natural evil in the scholastic sense is dropped from the debate, to be replaced with physical evil, casually by Malebranche, then consistently by Bayle, who deliberately refurnishes the category to represent all kinds of experienced evils, of suffering in general. This novel category was picked up by Leibniz and also by King, whose category of natural evil corresponds to the earlier scholastic category only in name: in fact, this is Baylean *physical evil*—and so is the 'natural evil' of later anglophone writers such as Hume. The reinvention of physical evil was a major event in the history of philosophy, *and it was not turned back*: when Kant discusses the two categories of 'evil proper' or sin (*das eigentliche Böse*) and 'ill' or pain (*Übel*), he is using Baylean categories; so too are most philosophers discussing natural or physical evil (now generally considered synonymous) today.[82] Suffering was never a main issue for the scholastics: it becomes one only when

82. Thus the purpose of C.S. Lewis's *The Problem of Pain* is 'to solve the intellectual problem raised by suffering' (xii). The categories of moral and physical/natural evil are now standard in contemporary philosophy of religion, where the overwhelming emphasis tends to be on physical evils, with the result that in many cases animal suffering also becomes more central: a problem that in Bayle is recognised but not treated extensively (see chapter 2).

it receives a category of its own. For better or worse, suffering becomes a problem with Bayle.[83]

To sum up, for most of the seventeenth century, as in the ages before, the problem of evil is primarily a problem of sin. Evil is categorised primarily as privation; suffering is seen as punishment for sin. The complete excision by Malebranche and Bayle of the Augustinian privation approach—their argument for the symmetrical positivity of good and evil, of pleasure and pain—effectively reopens the debate on *physical evil*, which in Malebranche means disorder, and in Bayle means suffering *tout court*.

Bayle radicalises Malebranche's philosophy of physical evil in two ways. First, he interiorises or subjectivises it: he makes it all about experience, and the weighing of goods and evils *as we experience them*—a consequence of which is the new stress placed on psychological as opposed to merely bodily suffering. Second, he logically severs the crucial link to human responsibility, the Augustinian justification of evil by way of *culpa*.[84] The result is that both moral evil and physical evil are pushed to the centre of the debate. The critics, in resisting this, confirm it. In taking Bayle to task on subjective experience, and offering their counter-phenomenologies, their alternative outcomes of weighing the goods and evils of life, both Leibniz and King are effectively conceding an important point to Bayle: that all of this matters somehow. That it is indeed relevant to discuss whether life is generally happy or unhappy, in order to negotiate God's goodness. That the ratio between joy and suffering, pleasure and pain, goods and evils is part of the problem of evil. That *experience* is key.

By the time we reach Leibniz and King, the problem of evil has become a problem of pain, a problem of suicide, a problem of taxonomy, and,

83. As such, this chapter proposes one possible answer to the question posed by Thomas G. Long and paraphrased by N.N. Trakakis ('Anti-theodicy' (1), 131): 'Why does no biblical author or medieval theologian regard suffering as even posing *prima facie* evidence against the existence of God, whereas today philosophers and theologians routinely view suffering in this way?'

84. I agree with Neiman (*Evil in Modern Thought*, 39) that it is 'crucial' to a 'modern distinction between natural and moral evil' that 'natural evils have no inherent significance'—but in order for such a modern distinction to be possible, natural/physical evil must first be conceptualised in a secular way, which Bayle does by making it just about suffering; rather than starting from sin, he starts from experience. Neiman places the origin of distinction with Rousseau and the Lisbon earthquake (ibid., 3–4, 39–40, 217); I think the story starts with Bayle and Malebranche. For a parallel development with regard to 'privation theory', see Newlands, 'Evils, Privations'.

crucially, a *problem of suffering*: of experience. This turn to experience, hesitant at first, thickens and intensifies in the eighteenth century, with its revival of the Book of Job and new anti-theodicies such as Voltaire's *Candide* and Hume's *Dialogues concerning Natural Religion*, both of which inherit precisely Bayle's focus on the human experience. Terms such as optimism and pessimism were coined to great success in the course of this debate. This intensification of thinking about evil, combined with a growing tendency to think (sometimes grudgingly) about *experienced* evils, seems prominent and coherent enough to warrant its own designation, and we might consider calling it the 'theodicean turn'.[85] A turn that reaches a form of climax, perhaps, in Leibniz's *Theodicy*, with its justification of the goodness of creation, but that would be unthinkable without Bayle and Malebranche, and their argument for the positive reality of *all* parts of creation: the good, the bad, and the ugly.

Complaint and Consolation

This, then, is the creaturely complaint in its starkest form: Why do I suffer, I, who did not ask to be created? There are many questions still left unanswered concerning the complaint, and several of these will be addressed in chapter 2. For instance, wherein exactly lies the problematic part: Is it that there are more evils than goods in existence, or that there are any evils at all?—That there are many creatures who suffer, or that there is even one? For now, let me say a few things about some of the assumptions underlying such questions. As I will argue throughout this book, the point being made by 'pessimists' such as Bayle and 'optimists' such as Leibniz is not just a theoretical but also a practical one: it has everything to do with the moral valuation of complaint and consolation.[86]

The latter is one of the subtler threads woven through the Manichean web. It is no coincidence that Bayle's grieving fathers are also grieving philosophers: people who, like Bayle himself perhaps, tried to find consolation in philosophy, only to find that consolation is nowhere to be found. Little is known of Bayle's inner life, but we know that he was devastated after the death of his brother in 1685 in a French prison, where he had been tortured in response to Bayle's own anti-Catholic writings: a death, then, that was violent and far away, and for which Bayle may have felt at

85. Then again, perhaps there have been enough turns and moments in the history of ideas; and though I will make sporadic use of this term in the following chapters, I do not insist on it.

86. On 'optimism' and 'pessimism', see chapter 2.

least partly responsible.[87] We must tread carefully here, to avoid what I have earlier called the reduction to biography, but without going so far as to reduce philosophy to experience, we may yet acknowledge that experience can inform it. Scattered throughout Bayle's writings are the traces of a deep, dark pain that pervades his pessimism—and seems to drive his philosophy of consolation.[88]

The point is most strongly stated in the case of Cicero, who after the death of Tullia could not be consoled either by the kind words of his friends or by reading what past philosophers had written: 'my sorrow is too much for any consolation'.[89] If Cicero did end up writing a book, now lost, *On Consolation*, this in Bayle's view does not mean that Cicero was successful in consoling himself, for 'making books accomplished almost nothing against his sadness: he merely numbed a little the part that was afflicted' (*Tullia*[1]*.O*).[90] He cites Cicero's own words to this effect:

> I have done what certainly no one ever did before me—tried to console myself by writing a book, which I will send to you as soon as my amanuenses have made copies of it. I assure you that there is no more efficacious consolation. I write all day long, not that I do any good, but for a while I experience a kind of check, or, if not quite that—for the violence of my grief is overpowering—yet I get some relaxation, and I try with all my might to recover composure, not of heart, yet, if possible, of countenance. When doing that I sometimes feel myself to be doing wrong, sometimes that I shall be doing wrong if I don't. [91]

Bayle stresses 'the disorder into which [Cicero's] affliction had plunged him'. On the one hand, Cicero presented himself as inconsolable, but on the other, he did not want to be reproached for showing too much weakness, and so he tried to manifest both courage and despair: 'Sentiments

87. See Bost, *Pierre Bayle*, 277–84; Labrousse I, 198–200, who notes that Bayle's correspondence no longer makes personal reference to providence after 1685; a year that also saw death of Bayle's father, his patron Adriaen Paets, and the devastating Revocation of the Edict of Nantes, which revoked toleration of protestants under Louis XIV.

88. A pain that, furthermore, is nowhere counterbalanced by religious sentiment as it is in Pascal or Kierkegaard, who would still answer positively the question of whether or not they 'accept the universe' (see William James, *Varieties of Religious Experience*, 41, on Margaret Fuller), whereas in Bayle we see everywhere the signs of a no-saying ghost; and it is this ghost that I am following throughout this book.

89. Cicero to Atticus, 8 March 45 BCE, *Letters to Atticus* DXLV (*A*.XII.14).

90. My translation. While Cicero's *De consolatione* was lost, fragments have been preserved in Lactantius, who Bayle cites at length throughout *Tullia.*

91. Cicero to Atticus, 8 March 45 BCE, *Letters*, DXLV (*A*.XII.14); this passage is cited by Bayle in parts.

utterly incompatible' (*Tullia¹.O*). But Cicero's broken-heartedness is not a sign of weakness in Bayle's eyes: on the contrary, 'his affliction is the most convincing proof which he gave of his tender affection for Tullia' (*Tullia¹.O*).[92]

And indeed there is something touchingly sincere about the image of Cicero as Bayle paints it, which is that of a father struggling so desperately to make sense of his daughter's death that it led him to accept the Platonist doctrine of metempsychosis and the 'pre-existence of sin, which however false it was, might yet inspire patience':

> For he might very well say to himself, *My daughter's death hath overwhelmed me, and plunged me into despair; but about two hundred years ago or more, I committed some crimes which deserve this punishment. I hereby expiate them. I suffer for them in this organised prison, in which my soul was confined when I was born: It is just that I should be unhappy, since I sinned so long ago.* (*Tullia¹.R*; Bayle's italics)

The Cicero presented here is one searching everywhere for some kind of consolation, trying to convince himself that perhaps his suffering is the punishment for an earlier sin, and thus suggesting that this particular answer to the problem of evil has something in it that is itself consoling: we may still suffer, but at least we don't suffer *pointlessly*.

But Cicero's words, as channelled by Bayle, sound too desperate to offer more than the thinnest straw for a drowning man to cling to. If this is the consolation offered by philosophy, it serves only to prove that philosophy fails at consolation—a point that Hume will drive home more forcefully. The same, furthermore, may well apply to religion, for as Bayle points out, Cicero's view of transmigration is not so far removed from the Christian doctrine of original sin: both employ the reduction approach to make sense of suffering by reducing it to sin. And this is Bayle's deepest objection to the Stoics and optimists and other makers of theodicy: to be told that our suffering is somehow down to us, that we have deserved it or that we could prevent it if only we were strong enough, *only serves to make our suffering worse*.[93] This does not mean that there is no hope of consolation in human life, but that we may need to plot a different route to get there: a

92. Though Bayle cites other expressions of Cicero's fatherly love to show that even 'if he had died before her, we should not have wanted proofs of his extraordinary affection to her' (*Tullia¹*.O).

93. As we will see throughout this book, the recurrent objection to the pessimists is that they take away hope or consolation, but this is the same objection pessimists level against the optimists.

route that Bayle himself does not chart, though Hume will lead us a little on the way.

By presenting us with these images of grieving fathers, who happen to be philosophers, Bayle is not just indulging us in historical anecdote (though he is also doing this), but sketching a different moral character, a different *persona* for the philosopher—who need not confine himself to the strictures of manliness and fortitude and forbearance, but may prove himself (and, perhaps, *herself*) precisely through 'the sincere avowal that he has succumbed to his sadness' (*Tullia*^{1}.*O*).[94]

This rethinking of the ethics of grief and consolation is already an astounding intervention in the debate, and it is echoed by what is perhaps an even greater one: the revaluation of complaint. As will become clear in the chapters to follow, one of the recurring themes in the history of theodicy is what might be called the *presumption against complaint:* the idea that there is something fundamentally wrong, warped, and most of all ungrateful about the creaturely complaint. Few things could be more despicable to the early modern mindset than for a creature to grumble against its maker: a creature who should be grateful to exist at all, on the underlying assumption that existence is inherently a good thing.[95] As we will see, the recurrent objection raised against Bayle and other pessimists is that they are ungrateful: that it is presumptuous or narrow-minded or hard-hearted to complain of one's condition. This intuition that complaint is a sign of despair and ingratitude has a long lineage, going back to the Book of Job at least, which puts into relief the theme of patience precisely by contrasting it with Job's complaints. Nor is it confined to the Judaeo-Christian tradition, as Stoics such as Marcus Aurelius remind us by censuring those who are displeased with the universe.[96]

This is why Bayle's move is such a powerful and, I venture to say, even courageous one. It is through grieving figures such as Cicero and La Mothe le Vayer, through the depressed man on the verge of suicide, through the unfortunate Octavia, through countless examples of persons real and

94. On the persona of the philosopher, see Condren et al. (eds.), *The Philosopher in Early Modern Europe.*

95. Thus Bayle's eighteenth-century critic Pierre Alexandre d'Alès de Corbet (1715–ca.1770) argued that God can be said to do good by us, as long as 'the being that he bestows upon us, is worth more to us than Nothingness' [*le Néant*] (*De l'Origine du mal*, vol. 1, 51; my translation).

96. Marcus Aurelius, *Meditations*, especially book V, xviii–x, where he argues that such dissatisfaction is not only a sign of moral weakness, but compromises the integrity of the whole. Note that for all Nietzsche's fulmination against Christians and Stoics, there is something of this mentality in his ethos of radical affirmation.

imagined whose lives were in the end not worth living, that Bayle gives voice, force, and countenance to the creaturely complaint. Far from being a bad thing, complaint in Bayle's eyes is as morally unobjectionable as it is philosophically poignant: it should elicit our compassion and understanding, not our judgement and condemnation. This revaluation of complaint as well as consolation is a major innovation on Bayle's part, one that his detractors fail to recognise for what it is, which is why, a century onwards, Kant will have to make the same point all over again. That it is a point worth making, the pages of this book will aim to show.

CHAPTER TWO

The Optics of Optimism

LEIBNIZ AND KING RESPOND TO BAYLE

There is but one truly serious philosophical problem and that is suicide. Judging whether life is or is not worth living amounts to answering the fundamental question of philosophy.

ALBERT CAMUS[1]

SOME PASSAGES IN THE HISTORY of philosophy have been cited so often that they all but lose their meaning, becoming almost as trivial as they are seminal. The above words from Albert Camus are one such passage; something that, according to one philosopher, 'every sophomore knows, and every philosophy professor is tired of hearing'.[2] The idea is simple and, somehow, intuitively appealing: according to Camus, the decision on whether to commit suicide represents the ultimate judgement on whether one finds life worth living.[3] But if the idea is simple, so too is the obvious critique: for one thing, suicide is *not* the same thing as judging whether or not life is worth living. One might consider life not worth living and still not want to kill oneself, or even to die at all; conversely, there could be (and are) other reasons why people kill themselves. Thus, not only is suicide a 'failed test' for what makes a life worth living[4]—but to equate the phenomenon of suicide, in all its tragic complexity, with a flat-out intellectual

1. Camus, *The Myth of Sisyphus*, 1–2.

2. Smuts, 'Five Tests for What Makes a Life Worth Living', 442.

3. William James, in his essay 'Is Life Worth Living?', which aims to philosophically dissuade people from committing suicide, makes the same equation as Camus: 'That life is *not* worth living the whole army of suicides declare . . . '. James, *The Will to Believe*, 37.

4. Smuts, 'Five Tests', 442–3.

judgement on the worth or value of life is to trivialise and oversimplify an incredibly complicated feature of human existence, which, in many cases, defeats reason rather than responds to a rational calculation.[5]

Cogent as they are, the philosophical and psychological criticisms of the provocative first part of Camus's quote may cause us to miss something important expressed in the second part. This is the idea, deceptively intuitive perhaps, that the question of whether or not life is worth living is fundamental for philosophy: Indeed, what could be more fundamental for philosophy than the very value of existence? It is interesting, then, that the question of whether or not life is worth living is in fact a rather new one, at least in the Western tradition—becoming a philosophical topic in its own right only in the late seventeenth century, to be discussed at great length and in many varieties in the eighteenth and nineteenth, and up to the present day.[6] This chapter will look at some of the earliest posings of this question, in the competing philosophical traditions since known as *optimism* and *pessimism*.

Definitions

Here, we must pause for some conceptual clarification, for *optimism* and *pessimism* are terms that have shifted in meaning since their inception and all too easily lend themselves to misunderstanding. I will distinguish just two conceptions, which I will call *future-oriented* and *value-oriented*.[7]

The first of these represents the most common use by far. Nowadays, we mostly use *optimism* and *pessimism* for expectations about and attitudes towards the future. This is, overwhelmingly, the colloquial use: 'I'm

5. As the Dutch writer Joost Zwagerman, who studied depressions and suicide, wrote: 'This kind of knowledge did not bring me power. Now that I suffered from [depression] myself, all of this was useless. Nothing but armchair-wisdoms' (Zwagerman, cited in *De Volkskrant*, 8 September 2015; my translation). He eventually killed himself on 8 September 2015. Camus himself points out the 'relative character' of his essay (*Sisyphus*, 4). For some deeply sensitive and insightful studies of suicide, see Alvarez, *The Savage God*; Solomon, *The Noonday Demon*, chapter 7; Zwagerman, *Door eigen hand*.

6. For just a few examples, see Smuts, 'Five Tests', and *Welfare, Meaning, and Worth*; David Benatar, *Better Never to Have Been*.

7. Note that optimism and pessimism can also refer to mental or psychological attitudes—I am referring solely to philosophical opinions. See Dienstag, *Pessimism*, 4: 'philosophy and disposition should simply not be confused with one another'. This in contrast to some earlier treatments of the subject, e.g. Sully's *Pessimism* of 1877, which sees philosophical pessimism as coextensive with temperamental pessimism, but also Terry Eagleton's recent *Hope without Optimism*, which reduces optimism to 'simply a quirk of temperament' (2).

cautiously optimistic about our chances'; 'don't be such a pessimist, I'm sure it will work out'. It is also the way in which one of the few book-length studies of pessimism, Joshua Foa Dienstag's *Pessimism: Philosophy, Ethic, Spirit,* frames the concept of pessimism, as a philosophical outlook that is crucially future-oriented. Thus Dienstag opposes the Enlightenment's idea of *progress* to a counter-philosophy of *pessimism,* and links both to the modern concept of *time.*[8]

Alternatively, there is also a way of conceiving of both optimism and pessimism as not primarily time- or future-oriented, but as addressing something pivotal about the nature of human (and perhaps animal) experience, and what that means for the value of life and death, of being and not being. This is also closer to the way in which the terms were originally conceived: *optimism* was coined by the Jesuits as a pejorative term for Leibniz's notion that we live in 'the best of all possible worlds'; a few decades later, *pessimism* followed as a label for the opposing view, as expressed in Voltaire's *Candide.*[9] Conceived in this 'value-oriented' way, optimism and pessimism address questions such as: Is life worth living? Do the goods of life outweigh the evils? Is creation justified? Can it be better for any being not to be—or even, can it be 'better never to have been'?[10]

While I believe the terms optimism and pessimism can be appropriately used in both conceptions, I also believe the second conception to be the more essential one. This is so for two reasons, one conceptual and one historical. The *conceptual* reason is that the more future-oriented questions flow naturally from value-oriented ones, so that the first kind of pessimism (future-oriented) can be considered a sub-question or subcategory of the second kind (value-oriented). Having certain assumptions about the value of existence in general will tend to lead to matching expectations (or lack of expectations) about the future. The *historical* reason is that the more future-oriented traditions discussed by Dienstag follow, historically,

8. Dienstag, *Pessimism,* especially 8–19. Dienstag's work remains the only in-depth modern study of (mainly future-oriented) philosophical pessimism, but see also the older study by Sully, *Pessimism*; and, in a more specific context, Vyverberg, *Historical Pessimism.*

9. *Optimisme* was coined in a review of Leibniz in the Jesuit journal *Mémoires de Trévoux,* February 1737, *pessimisme* by Voltaire's critics in 1759. (See Wootton, editorial footnote to Voltaire, *Candide,* 1n.; Dienstag, *Pessimism,* 9). The *Oxford English Dictionary* cites a 1759 letter from William Warburton as the first appearance in English of *optimism* (though Warburton uses the French spelling; see his *Letters,* 289–90); *pessimism* seems to have had a slower arrival, only really coming into use in the course of the nineteenth century.

10. This is the title of Benatar's 2006 book, in which he makes the case for the immorality of procreation.

from the more value-oriented ones. This is not to make a claim of influence or even importance, but simply to assert chronological precedence: to borrow an expression from a different debate, if future-oriented pessimism constitutes second- or even third-wave pessimism, value-oriented pessimism, though perhaps less sophisticated, was certainly first-wave. It is this latter type of pessimism that this chapter will discuss: the type that focuses on questions concerning the value of existence.

In my view, any philosophy that runs along the axes of these questions can rightly be termed optimism or pessimism—but *only* if these matters are really in question. For centuries, the answers to such questions have been seen as self-evident: of course life is worth living, since we were created by a benevolent God.[11] Optimism does not apply where the questions and the answers are considered to be self-evident: it operates only if a real alternative is on the horizon; if there really is a challenge, and if rising to it really *matters*. This means that optimism can only truly emerge—as a coherent philosophical position—once pessimism is a real alternative. The story of pessimism is often supposed to begin with optimism, with Voltaire responding to Leibniz and Pope—but this is true only in the trivial sense that the term *optimism* was indeed coined before that of *pessimism*. In fact, optimism in its earliest varieties was a crucially *reactionary* attitude, formulated in response to the first coherently argued philosophical pessimism: that of Pierre Bayle.

Having introduced the problem (or problems) of evil in the early modern debate in chapter 1, here I will focus on the debate on pessimism specifically, as it flows from that part of the problem of evil that deals with *physical evil* (suffering in general). In particular, I will discuss the responses to Bayle as they were articulated by the famous polymath Gottfried Wilhelm Leibniz (1646–1716) and the lesser-known philosopher (and archbishop of Dublin) William King (1650–1729), especially with regard to misery, suicide, and damnation. Drawing out the background mechanics of their arguments, I will show how the earliest optimists and pessimists agree on many theoretical assumptions, but part ways when

11. Which is not to say there is no room for the acknowledgement of the misery of human life, as expressed in the Bible and in a variety of theological and religious tracts; however, in the Christian tradition these are combined with a reference to the *future* life, in which current misery will find justification (e.g. in the Christian interpretation of the Book of Job, esp. Job 19:25). Suffering, in traditional narratives, is tightly causally 'nested' in the past (as punishment) and the future (as preparation for reward); the innovation of pessimism is to sever these links and question suffering separately from such justificatory routes.

it comes to the actual qualifications of existence. I will point out a subtle recurrent rhetorical move on the part of the optimists who, when their answers threaten to fail, start answering a slightly different question. Consequently, I will designate the clash between optimism and pessimism as a conflict between two perspectives, which I will call *creaturely* and *cosmic*, and suggest that they are not only phenomenologically, but also ethically and epistemologically, divided. Finally, with some comments on Dienstag's work, I will offer my suggestions with regard to the conceptual framework in which to cast philosophical pessimism.

The Challenge of Pessimism

According to Dienstag, 'If pessimism can be said to have an identifiable starting point in the philosophical tradition, it must be found in the contradictory figure of Jean-Jacques Rousseau', '"the patriarch of pessimism"'.[12] Leaving aside for now the tricky question of whether Rousseau should be styled an optimist or pessimist (or, more probably, something in between),[13] I would suggest that if we are indeed speaking of 'identifiable starting point[s]', it is Bayle who should take Rousseau's place as pessimism's 'patriarch'.

Historically speaking, Bayle's work is at the origin of the very tradition of pessimism that Dienstag seeks to describe. While Voltaire, being the target of the first usage of the (derogatory) term 'pessimism', could be styled the first pessimist as such, the philosophical opinions for which he was derided *as* pessimistic were borrowed directly from Bayle. Similarly, it is precisely from Bayle's work that eighteenth-century varieties of pessimism, in Voltaire but also in Hume, are derived.[14] Philosophically speaking, furthermore, Bayle's pessimism was of the most extreme and uncompromising variety, leading to conclusions with which Rousseau would have been—indeed, *was*—deeply uncomfortable, but which are echoed by equally uncompromising pessimists today.[15] Finally, and crucially, it

12. Dienstag, *Pessimism*, 49; the latter characterisation is taken over from Walter Starkie (quoted in ibid.).

13. Note that Dienstag (*Pessimism*, 74), only 'insist[s] on [his] thesis for Rousseau's early period'. But see chapter 6.

14. Dienstag fails to mention Hume as well as Bayle. We may cautiously add Maupertuis, whose argument that the evils of life outweigh the goods might be drawn directly from Bayle, and who would in turn be critiqued by Voltaire and Rousseau. See chapters 3, 4, 5, and 6.

15. E.g. David Benatar, but also the Norwegian philosopher Peter Wessel Zapffe, discussed at length in Thomas Ligotti's *The Conspiracy Against the Human Race*.

was to *Bayle's* pessimism that the earliest formulators of optimism were responding: at the risk of over-stretching this terminology, if Voltaire's was second-wave pessimism, Bayle's was first-wave.

I have already discussed, at some length, Bayle's discussion of physical evil in particular in chapter 1. However, in order to fully appreciate Leibniz's and King's responses, I will here briefly summarise the central components of Bayle's argument, which together make up what I will call *the challenge of pessimism*.[16]

First, against the commonly accepted scholastic notion that evils are strictly *privative*—that is, they do not have being in themselves but exist only in a good that lacks some perfection due to it—Bayle (following Malebranche) argues that, on the contrary, evils do have positive being of their own. For instance, the experience of pain is not the same as the mere privation of pleasure: pain constitutes just as positive a reality as pleasure does. Evils are thus ontologically symmetrical with goods. (The corollary of this is that existence cannot be de facto a good, only neutral at best.)

Second, while evils are *ontologically* symmetrical with goods, Bayle argues that they are *phenomenologically* asymmetrical: evils offer a greater *experiential intensity* than goods.[17] According to Bayle, we each know this from our own lives, in which physical evils such as pain and sadness offer a much more intense experience than do the mirroring goods of pleasure and joy. Evils also resist our getting accustomed to them much more than goods do: we get used to the pleasures of life all too quickly, but a chronic pain hardly dulls down over time.[18] Hence, Bayle's pessimism is built upon the assumption that evils (moral *and* physical) outweigh goods in *quantity* but especially, and most significantly, in *quality*. Not only are there more evils than goods in life *on the whole*, but even a small amount of evil is capable of spoiling a great amount of good.

16. Throughout this chapter and the remainder of this book, I will generally be using Bayle's casual conceptions of moral and physical evil, which both Leibniz and King take up unaltered, though they each add a third category of metaphysical evil (Leibniz) or evil of imperfection (King). Bayle dismisses any such alternative category, since evils are only regarded as such by creatures capable of sensation; and so evil can only be placed in the categories of physical evil or moral evil; see *RQP*.II.75 (*OD*.III.653).

17. For similar ideas in Schopenhauer, Freud, and Rousseau, see Dienstag, *Pessimism*, 93–4.

18. 'Evils are generally more pure and unmixed than good things; the lively sense of pleasure does not continue long, it immediately grows flat and dull, and is followed by aversion [*dégoût*]. . . . What appeared to us a great good when we did not possess it, hardly affects us in the enjoyment . . .' (*Xenophanes*¹.*F*). See chapter 4 for Maupertuis's development of Bayle's argument.

Finally, with regard to the question of whether life is, on the whole, worth living, or *reliving*, Bayle answers that, for most people, the reasonable answer is presumably negative: perhaps it is even the case for all of us that it would have been better never to have been. The overall conclusion is that God's decision to create unhappy creatures (humans but perhaps also animals) cannot *rationally* be justified.

Rising to the Challenge

This, very briefly, is the challenge posed by Bayle's pessimism. Let us now turn to the most influential responses: William King's *De origine mali* of 1702 (English translation following in 1732), and Leibniz's *Essais de Théodicée* of 1710.[19] These days, the former is much less known than the latter—but this was not the case in the eighteenth century, when King's treatise was very widely read and considered, by some, 'a masterpiece'; its author 'a more thorough and more consistent philosopher than Berkeley'.[20] Arthur O. Lovejoy calls *De origine mali* perhaps 'the most influential . . . of eighteenth-century theodicies' and suggests that it was a major influence on Alexander Pope's *Essay on Man*.[21] If this is the case, then, through Pope, King probably exercised more influence on Voltaire than did Leibniz, who Voltaire only read cursorily and indirectly.[22]

Together, these texts constitute the first great philosophical reactions to pessimism, and are representative of the philosophical optimism of their age. Both works are produced in direct opposition to Bayle's argument that the problem of evil is rationally insoluble; that reason, if properly followed, will lead us to conclude that God is unjust; and so, if religion is to be saved, we must proceed by faith alone. Bayle himself died just between the publication of these two works, in 1706, and so was able to respond to King but not to Leibniz: however, he anticipated so many of his critics'

19. Citations to King's *De origine mali* (*DOM*) will be to the 1732 posthumous English translation by Edmund Law, *An Essay On the Origin of Evil*. Citations to Leibniz's *Essais de theodicée* (*EdT*) will be to the standard paragraph number, followed by the page number of the English translation by E.M. Huggard (e.g. *EdT*, 255.283); and the page number of the Gerhardt edition (*G*). See the bibliography.

20. Karl Gottlob Küttner, *Briefe über Irland* (1785), quoted in English translation (Mia Craig) in Joseph Richardson, 'William King', 121–2.

21. Lovejoy, *The Great Chain of Being*, 212. For some reservations on King's influence on Pope, see Mack, *Collected in Himself*, 206.

22. See chapter 3; and see Greenberg (who also mentions King's probable influence on Hutcheson and Hume), 'Leibniz on King', 207; Rutherford, *Leibniz and the Rational Order of Nature*, 1; Barber, *Leibniz in France*, chapter 12.

arguments that we can reconstruct his responses to Leibniz (and others) as well.[23]

The problem is, of course, that Leibniz and King didn't just offer arguments against Bayle; rather, they constructed entire systems.[24] And so I will here only focus on three particular arguments, in reverse order of importance, by which they responded to Bayle's *pessimism* specifically—of which the third (on the balance between goods and evils) is the most important in terms of answering the fundamental question that runs through these debates: the question, that is, of whether or not life is worth living.

PHYSICAL EVILS ARE UNDER OUR CONTROL (AND/OR ARE USEFUL)

The first argument springs from a strong Stoic impulse: this is the idea that we can learn to control physical pain; there are alternatives to suffering. The corollary of this, seldom stated but often implied, is that if we continue to suffer, this is ultimately our own choice.

In a passage quoted with concern by Bayle and with approval by Leibniz, Descartes had written that 'each person can make himself content by himself and without waiting on something from elsewhere just so long as he observes three things', namely, by making optimal use of his mind, by following the dictates of reason in all actions, and by accustoming himself not to desire things that are 'outside of his power'. According to Descartes, the true philosophy teaches us that 'even among the saddest accidents and the most pressing pains one can always be content [in life], so long as

23. Note that Bayle only read King second-hand, through the elaborate review and summary by Jacques Bernard (*Nouvelles de la République des Lettres* [*NRL*], May–June 1703), for which he is criticised by Bernard (*NRL*, January 1706, art. iv, 56–9, 69–70); Bayle motivates his decision in *RQP*.II, 'Préface' (*OD*.III.631), and again (after Bernard's critique) in *RQP*.IV.23/*OD*.III.1069.

24. I cannot go into the intricacies of King's and Leibniz's systems here; I will be discussing only particular arguments used by either or both in response to Bayle's argument for pessimism. The literature on Leibniz is vast: for a recent intricate analysis of Leibniz's treatment of the problem of evil, see Rateau, *Leibniz on the Problem of Evil*, as well as his *Leibniz et le meilleur des mondes possible*; see also the collected volumes by Jorgensen and Newlands (eds.), *New Essays on Leibniz' Theodicy*, and Leduc, Rateau, and Solère (eds.), *Leibniz et Bayle: Confrontation et dialogue*, as well as Lærke, *Les lumières de Leibniz*, 205–83 (on Leibniz's reception of Bayle's *DHC*). There is much less literature on King, but for some helpful articles, see Pearce, 'William King on Free Will'; Greenberg, 'Leibniz on King'; Antognazza, 'Metaphysical Evil Revisited'.

one knows how to use one's reason'.[25] To which Bayle had replied that this is not to say anything; it is to propose a remedy that hardly anyone is capable of (*RQP*.II.157/*OD*.III.831).[26] Leibniz, however, holds 'that the thing is not impossible, and that men could attain it by dint of meditation and practice' (*EdT*, 255.283/*G*.VI.268). As an example, he points to various indigenous American tribes ('the Hurons, the Iroquois, the Galibis') and remarks: 'one cannot read without astonishment of the intrepidity and well-nigh insensibility wherewith they brave their enemies, who roast them over a slow fire and eat them by slices' (*EdT*, 256.283/*G*.VI.268). Similar intrepidity, Leibniz argues, could be achieved by us through education, mortification of the flesh, and the right use of reason: nevertheless, 'the very fact that one has no need of that great remedy is a proof that the good already exceeds the evil' (*EdT*, 258.284/*G*.VI.269). The universe is not made for us alone, but it is 'nevertheless made for us if we are wise: it will serve us if we use it for our service; we shall be happy in it *if we wish to be*' (*EdT*, 194.248/*G*.VI.232; my emphasis).[27]

Similarly, King suggests that we have the power to change our attitudes to pain and draw pleasure from this choice, to the point that our pleasure in choosing to bear pain can overwhelm the pain itself:

> For instance, if one feel two Degrees of Pain from a Distemper, and receive six Degrees of Pleasure from an Election to bear it with Patience and Decorum; subtracting two Degrees of Pain from these six of Pleasure, he has four of solid Pleasure remaining: He will be as happy

25. Descartes to Elisabeth of Bohemia, 6 October 1645 (*Correspondence*, 121).

26. It is possible that Bayle is led here by Spinoza, who strenuously rejects this Stoic position of Descartes in part 5 of the *Ethics*: however, considering that Spinoza goes on to achieve a similar view on the possibility of joy in all circumstances along different lines (through the knowledge of God), it may be that he is objecting rather to Descartes's *route* to this position than to the position in itself—unlike Bayle, who rejects both. Spinoza's critique of Descartes, furthermore, is focused on *bodily* pain. I thank Alex Douglas for pointing this out. Malebranche, too, may have had Descartes in mind when he criticised the 'false view' of the Stoics: 'There are philosophers who try to persuade men that pleasure is not a good and that pain is not an evil; that we can be happy in the midst of the most violent pains and miserable in the midst of the greatest pleasure' (*SAT*, 307/*OCM*.II.76).

27. In an earlier text, Leibniz does acknowledge that physical evils such as pain can hinder the happiness of even the virtuous, but speaks of the possibility for any person whose 'mind is well-ordered' to create 'a great joy which overcomes these pains and misfortunes' ('On Wisdom' (ca. 1690–1700), in *Philosophical Papers and Letters*, 427/*G*.VII.89; for discussion, see Rutherford, *Patience sans espérance*, 74, 87n.). Malebranche's view is that humans lost the ability to end pain by an act of will after the Fall, as a punishment for sin; see Newlands, 'Malebranche', section 3.

therefore as one that has four Degrees pure and free from all Pain. (*DOM*, 364)[28]

Bayle had anticipated such criticisms and had explicitly said that the *cause* of suffering is to no purpose in trying to decide whether there are more goods or evils in life. If humans make themselves miserable, or suffer unduly, that itself is just another evil; in fact, pointing out to a suffering person that they are the cause of their own ills will serve to make their suffering even worse. More importantly, Bayle doubted that such Stoic control was possible for either physical or psychological suffering—the latter of which is hardly mentioned by Leibniz and King, though it was precisely in psychological pains that Bayle thought the greatest evils of life resided. It was psychological suffering (grief, sadness) that Bayle thinks is most likely to make life a burden to us; even to drive some men to suicide.[29]

Note that this argument is suggestive of an ethical drive on both sides of the debate. This drive, in Leibniz and King, is didactic: in the course of justifying evils, they are also attempting (clumsily, at times) to encourage and inspire hope in people who suffer physical pain.[30] On Bayle's side, something different is happening: Bayle objects to philosophers overemphasising the human ability to control pain and thereby playing down the very legitimacy of their suffering. Both sides think the other is making things worse, by overstating either suffering or the human ability to overcome suffering.

With regard to pain, King introduces a subsidiary (and also traditional) argument, according to which physical evils such as pain are useful to humans *and* animals.[31] For instance, pain makes us aware of illnesses that would otherwise go unnoticed and untreated; it warns us to avoid

28. See also *DOM*, 362: 'Whoever therefore has free Choice may make himself happy, *viz.* by choosing every thing which befalls him, and adapting his Choice to things.'

29. The reason why Leibniz and King offer their responses only with regard to physical pain may be because this argument kicks in all the more strongly for psychological evils: we can choose not to suffer, *especially* when suffering is inside our minds. I think this is supposed to be a self-evident point. But see chapter 5 for Hume's development of Bayle's view on psychological evils.

30. Joanna Bourke, in her book on pain, cites various reports of people subduing pain by willpower; e.g. Thomas Smyth, who wrote in his autobiography of 1914: 'Any man may subdue pain, if he only has the will to do it' (cited in Bourke, *The Story of Pain*, 20).

31. Thus offering an initial justification for animal suffering; see King, *DOM*, Rem. M (1732:173–82). For a similar argument on the usefulness of pain to animals, see Bayle's other critic, Isaac Jaquelot, *Conformité de la foi avec la raison* (1705), 210–14. On the debate between Bayle and Jaquelot, see Whelan, 'Reason and Belief'. Note that King also believes pain to be unavoidable to any ephemeral constitution endowed with sensory experience (*DOM*, 176).

things such as poisons and dangerous animals: 'And if the Preserving our Being be a greater Good to us than these Pains are a Mischief, then it is plain 'tis better we should have than want them' (*DOM*, Rem. M, 175).[32] According to Bayle, this argument is a dead end, since the supposed goals of pain could easily have been achieved by different means (especially by an omnipotent creator): for instance, by the addition or withdrawal of pleasure rather than the addition of pain.[33] Furthermore, Bayle points out specific instances where pain is demonstrably *not* useful: for instance, the torments at the end of a fatal disease, where pain cannot help us ensure our health. And what of 'the pains of childbirth', Bayle asks rhetorically, 'what use is there in them?'(*RQP*.II.77/*OD*.III.656).

On this point, Leibniz is half in agreement with Bayle: 'I also doubt, with M. Bayle, whether pain be necessary in order to warn men of peril.' However, he does suggest that 'pain itself makes us aware of the importance of health when we are bereft of it' (*EdT*, 259.285/*G*.VI.270). Furthermore, while pain is not strictly necessary to alert men to 'present peril', it might yet have other uses; 'it is wont rather to serve as a penalty for having actually plunged into evil, and a warning against further lapse' (*EdT*, 342.330–1/*G*.VI.318). It is this notion of pain as penalty that is at the heart of the second major argument deployed against Bayle's pessimism.

PHYSICAL EVILS ARE PUNISHMENT FOR (AND/OR AN EFFECT OF) MORAL EVILS

For this argument, we must return to Augustine's famous dictum, that 'under a just God no one can be miserable, unless they deserve to be'.[34] This premise was so widely accepted that it bolstered what was possibly the most influential strategy for answering the problem of evil, and the problem of *suffering* specifically: the idea that physical evils could be explained by reducing them to moral evils; that all suffering is punishment for sin (*the reduction approach*). Both Leibniz and King have recourse to the idea that we ourselves are the cause of the physical evils we suffer.

32. Technically, this answers a different question: not whether there are more evils than goods on balance, but how *any* evils (here, pains) can be justified. There is a constant slippage between these questions.

33. To which King (*DOM*, Rem. M, 177) objects: 'The withdrawing of pleasure or diminishing it, is a greater Evil to us than the pains we feel on such Occasions.' Hume's Philo makes the same argument as Bayle in *DNR*.XI.81. On useless pains, see also Hume, *DNR*.X.74.

34. Augustine, *Contra responsionem*, 1.39.

Thus Leibniz, having explained moral evil, thinks physical evil poses even less of a problem:

> Now at last I have disposed of the cause of moral evil; *physical evil*, that is, sorrows, sufferings, miseries, will be less troublesome to explain, since these are results of moral evil. . . . One suffers because one has acted; one suffers evil because one does evil. (*EdT*, 241.276/*G*.VI.261)

However, this traditional strategy also harbours some traditional problems: specifically, the case of animals and young infants, instances where there has been suffering without previous sin.[35]

To the problem of animal suffering, Cartesian dualism offered a controversial solution by seeming to deny animal sensation: if animals do not feel, neither can they feel pain. This, as Gordon Baker and Katherine Morris have argued, was not Descartes's own view: he explicitly wrote to Henry More that in 'denying thought to animals' he was speaking of 'thought, and not of life or sensation'.[36] But it was how he was widely interpreted by his contemporaries, possibly due in no small amount to Malebranche, who wrote that animals 'eat without pleasure, cry without pain, grow without knowing it; they desire nothing, fear nothing, know nothing' (*OCM*.II.394/*SAT*, 494–5).[37] This allows Malebranche and other theologically minded Cartesians to avoid the problem posed by Augustine's dictum cited above, but it faces obvious problems of credibility, and is not taken very seriously by Leibniz and King, neither of whom deny that animals experience pain. (Nor, contrary to Leibniz's impression, does Bayle.) Instead, both offer a restricted definition of what it means to be *miserable*.

According to Leibniz, animals feel pain but not misery or unhappiness, just as they feel pleasure but not joy. This is because they lack the crucial element of *reflection* (by which he possibly means something like apperception: the endured being of the subject in time):[38]

35. This is a problem especially for Leibniz, since King is more confident about the beneficial qualities of pain for all creatures: however, if he allows for *pain* in innocent creatures, he does not allow for *misery*. On Leibniz's rejection of the Augustinian–Jansenist doctrine that unbaptised children go to hell, see Kremer, 'Leibniz and the "Disciples of Saint Augustine"'. On young children, see also Jaquelot, *Conformité*, 205–9.

36. Descartes to Henry More, 5 February 1649; cited in Baker and Morris, *Descartes' Dualism*, 4; see also Morris, 'Bête-machines'.

37. See Jolley, *Causality and Mind*, 78, who notes rightly that Malebranche's reasons for stating the beast-machine doctrine so dogmatically has 'less to do with the philosophy of mind than with theological considerations', namely, the problem of innocent suffering.

38. See Jolley, 'Is Leibniz's Theodicy a Variation on a Theme by Malebranche?', 65–7. Jolley notes that 'this point cuts both ways': the addition of reflection can also provide

> I think that, properly speaking, perception is not sufficient to cause misery if it is not accompanied by reflection. It is the same with happiness: without reflection there is none. (*EdT*, 250.280–1/*G*.VI.265–6)

By this route, the Augustinian principle is saved: no innocent creature is *miserable*—though it may experience 'mere' pain.

King's definition of misery is even more narrow. According to him, misery is the exact state wherein evils outweigh the goods of existence; the point at which life becomes a burden to us, and non-existence would be preferable:

> He only therefore is to be denominated *miserable*, who is oppressed with more and greater Evils than his good can requite with Happiness. So that upon balancing the Conveniences and Inconveniences of Life, it were better for him not to be than to be. (*DOM*, 209)

Hence, in King's system, misery is the absolutely worst state of being imaginable. But does this state ever occur? In principle, the answer is no—and King provides two different arguments for why this is the case.

The first we could call neo-Platonic. In King's philosophy, existence is the first degree of perfection, whereas evils are mere absence or non-being: it will, therefore, always be better to be than not to be.[39] Like Leibniz, King characterised evils as strictly negative: evils do not possess being of their own, while existence is intrinsically a good.[40] If we represent the state of nothingness or non-existence as 0, existence brings us to +1, at the very least: for King, as for Leibniz, existence can never represent a state of −1, nor can evils (lacking in positive being) bring us below 0. Evils can indeed detract from our overall goods, bringing us from, say,

---

the 'comforting resource' of knowing that certain pains or discomforts are temporary (ibid., 67n.).

39. King, *DOM*, 133–4: 'Existence is, as we said, the Foundation, or first Degree of Perfection, and the next, as it were, to this, the second, is perception of Existence.' This view also arises strongly in Maimonides, according to whom God's 'bringing us into existence is absolutely the great good' (*Guide*, II.448). See Lobel, 'Being and the good'.

40. Leibniz's early rejection and later adoption of the privation theory has puzzled some scholars, but Newlands has recently delivered a convincing argument that the later Leibniz continues to depart from traditional privation theory 'in all but name', effectively reducing the 'Scholastic evil-as-privation view' to the 'Neoplatonic evil-as-negation view' (Newlands, 'Leibniz on Privations', 282, 304). This aligns Leibniz all the more closely to King, who does not even acknowledge the scholastic distinction between negation and privation, and makes evil strictly *negative* throughout. As Antognazza writes, ontologically speaking, 'Leibniz fully subscribes to a Neoplatonic conception of the nature of evil as non-being' ('Metaphysical Evil Revisited', 133); in their ontologies, then, Leibniz and King are fundamentally in agreement.

+10 to +9, but they can never bring us below 0, which is the point at which all being ends. Therefore, there is no state worse than non-existence; it can never be better for a being not to be.[41] This view stands in stark contrast to that of Bayle, according to whom existence is divided into things better than nothing and things worse than nothing, evils having at least the same degree of positivity (and possibly more) as goods do. For Bayle, existence is not intrinsically a good, and it can certainly be better not to be than to be.[42]

King's second argument why the state of true misery never comes into being is rather curious. According to King, at the very moment when evils begin to outweigh the goods of life, at the first threshold of misery, God's justice ensures that life is removed from the creature. Death is the mechanism that removes evils at the very point at which they become overwhelming:

> if this ever come to pass, as soon as the Evil preponderates, Life is taken away together with the Benefits of Nature. . . . Life then can be a burden to none; nor is it necessary that any one should withdraw himself from natural Evils by voluntarily putting an end to his Life. For if these Evils be such as take away the Benefits of Life, they also bring it to an end. (*DOM*, 209)[43]

Hence, there is no such thing as unendurable suffering: there can be no misery in God's creation, though there is pain. God's creatures can never be truly miserable, *whether or not they have sinned*.[44] As we will see, both King and Leibniz do, however, allow for an exception to this seemingly

41. None of these authors distinguish between no longer existing and never having existed; and so, like them, I will treat both options as equivalent (while acknowledging that this is philosophically problematic: see Smuts, 'Five Tests', 439–40; Benatar, *Better Never To Have Been*, 22–8). While Jacques Bernard does make this distinction in defence of King (*NRL*, January 1706, art. iv, 73), Bayle denies that it makes sense, since one cannot regret no longer existing as soon as one ceases to exist, and so one's own death cannot properly be called a loss or harm, any more than one's failing to come into existence can be; see *RQP*. IV.23/*OD*.III.1070.

42. See also Malebranche's comment, cited in chapter 1, that 'when we are unhappy and desperate in our misery, we can wish not to be' (*Traité de morale*, *OCM*.XI.82).

43. See also King's Appendix 'Concerning the Divine Law' (*DOM*, 501): 'God has framed all things and disposed them in such a manner, that nothing may repent of its having been made by him: for when it is come to this, that its Misery exceeds its Pleasure, the Being perishes, and is withdrawn from both.'

44. See King at the end of *DOM*, 477: 'I believe that there's no Evil in Life but what is very tolerable; especially to those who have hopes of a future Immortality.'

firm rule that *true misery*, as defined by King, can have no place in God's creation.[45]

GOODS OUTWEIGH EVILS IN HUMAN LIFE

The final argument, and the most important for this chapter, consists in what is perhaps the core tenet of optimism: the idea that the goods of life outweigh the evils. Proving the opposite of this claim was, as we have seen, Bayle's main enterprise in *Xenophanes*, which had argued that our *experience* tells us that the evils of life outweigh the goods, and had offered intricate phenomenological arguments in support of this claim. Mostly neglected by Bayle scholars, the article was read widely and intensely by Bayle's first audience: it is from *Xenophanes* that Hume draws most of his arguments in chapters 10 and 11 of the *Dialogues concerning Natural Religion*, and both Leibniz and King engage extensively with its pessimistic claims. This suggests that a lot is riding on this question, and that Bayle's opponents had reason to take his challenge very seriously—as, in fact, they did. This becomes clear if we reconstruct the argument that is active in the background of this debate.

Let's call this the main *pessimist premise*: under a just God, there can be no creature whose life is not worth living.[46] This can be unfolded into the following syllogism:

a. If there is *even one* creature whose life is not worth living, then God is not just (in having created it).
b. Our experience tells us that this is indisputably the case for some of us, probably for most of us, and *possibly* even for all of us (the latter, in Bayle, remains just a hint).
c. So the *rational* conclusion must be: God is not just (or, alternatively, there is no just God).

Note that there are actually two possible versions of the major premise (a): Does it require *one* creature or *most* creatures to be miserable? These are stronger and weaker versions of the pessimist premise; I will call them a.1 and a.2:

45. Note that though Leibniz has a different conception of misery (closer to suffering but distinct from animal pain), he is roughly in agreement with King on the impossibility of there being any creature for whom it would be better not to be.

46. I am not saying this is the *only* premise of pessimism: an alternative (also offered by Bayle) could be that there are more evils than goods in human life on the whole. Here, I am focusing on this specific point of contention.

a.1. If there is *even one* creature whose life is not worth living, then God is not just.[47]

a.2. If it is the case for *most* creatures that life is not worth living, then God is not just.

For Bayle, the distinction doesn't matter: a problem of evil arises in both cases. But it does matter for his opponents, since it is much easier to disprove the weaker version (a.2) than the stronger one: denying that *any* creature can be truly miserable seems like rather a stretch. Then again, there are strong theological reasons for wanting to preserve God's consideration of *every last* creature, and the optimists are confident or ambitious enough to want to try to refute the stronger version (a.1) too: it is only when this attempt threatens to fail that they shift to the weaker version instead. In fact, the 'optimists' seem to concede the major premise (a.1), but deny the minor (b), and therefore the conclusion (c).

This is particularly clear in King, who leads all kinds of evils back to creaturely imperfection: as long as a creature is not God, it will be limited, and from these limits evils (conceived as imperfections) necessarily flow in.[48] The crucial point is that the creation of such beings (in various degrees of imperfection) is justified *as long as it is better that they exist than that they do not exist*; 'the Divine Goodness providing that no Creature should be worse by its Existence than if it had not existed' (*DOM*, 'Appendix', 501). So the pessimist premise is, at the same time, the *minimal condition of optimism*: under a good God, the creature cannot be *truly miserable*—where the state of *true misery* is narrowly defined, *pace* King, as the condition in which the evils outweigh the goods, so it would be better for the being not to exist.[49] Leibniz also seems to assume that there can be no creature for whom it would be better not to exist. In an earlier text he argues, for instance, that a suffering creature can have no legitimate complaint against its creator, since the

47. Kant, in his essay 'The End of All Things' of 1794, raises this point as an objection against the doctrine of eternal damnation: 'for why, one could ask, were even a few created—Why even a single individual?—if he is supposed to exist only to be rejected for eternity? For that is worse than never having been at all' (8:329/*RRT*, 223). Hart makes the same point in his book on universal salvation, *That All Shall Be Saved*.

48. This is where King's third category, the evil of imperfection, comes into play.

49. The condition of true misery thus seems to be equated with (a) life's evils outweigh the goods, and/or (b) life is not worth living, and/or (c) it is better not to be. Throughout this chapter, I will hold to this equation, which, while philosophically problematic (one could think of cases in which evils outweigh goods and yet life *is* worth living), is true to the ideas of the philosophers in question.

alternative is that it would not have been created at all (rather, another creature instead of it).[50]

The basic assumption shared by Leibniz and King, and most of the Western philosophical tradition, is that *existence is better than non-existence*. Existence is considered a positive good, as opposed to which non-existence can never be a good, since it has no being. This is such a basic and supposedly self-evident point that it gets stated and restated without a lot of foundation. The problem is that Bayle, like many pessimists after him, does not share this assumption. On what basis can existence be called a good if it brings in so many (according to him) *positive* evils? For Bayle, existence is neutral at best, not intrinsically a *good*.

But however the optimists and pessimists differ on this point, it also means that both parties accept the strong version of the major premise (a.1): under a just God, there can be no creature who is truly miserable in King's sense; a creature for whom it would be better not to be. This means that much is riding on the minor premise (b): the actual value of existence to the existent; of creation to the creature. And the way in which Leibniz and King go about unravelling this syllogism, having conceded the major, is by weighing goods and evils; by countering Bayle's balances. In what follows, I will discuss a few of the arguments and mechanisms by which they do so.

The Thought Experiment

One way of opposing Bayle's pessimist assumptions is simply to offer a counter-phenomenology. As a sign of the overwhelming evils of human life, Bayle had pointed to the many prisons, hospitals, gallows, and beggars we see in the world (*Manicheans¹.D*). Leibniz objects that this is an exaggeration: 'there is incomparably more good than evil in the life of men, as there are incomparably more houses than prisons' (*EdT*, 148.216/G.VI.198). This may seem a trivial point, but it has to do with Leibniz's idea

50. For this early version of the non-identity problem, see also this comment by Leibniz: 'You will insist that you can complain, Why did God not give you more strength? I reply, if He had done that, you would not exist, for He would have produced not you but another creature' ['si hoc fecisset, tu non esses, nam non te, sed aliam creaturam produxisset']. Leibniz, *Mentes ipsae per se dissimiles sunt inter se* (written 1689/1690), *A*.IV.4B.1639; cited in English by Robert C. Sleigh in his introduction to Leibniz, *Confessio philosophi*, xl; see also Antognazza, 'Metaphysical Evil Revisited', 124–5. Compare King, *DOM*, 145: 'Nor can the Creature justly complain of its Condition, if it have not all, or equal Perfection with some others; since 'twas necessary that it should fill the Station wherein it was placed, or none at all.'

of a neutral state; the idea that the *neutrum* is itself a good. Following Bayle, Leibniz does allow for our experience of pain as something equally intense as that of pleasure. However, rather than placing goods and evils as symmetrical opposites on either side of a middle state of nothingness, Leibniz argues that the good also lies in this 'middle state'. For instance, when we are healthy, though both lacking in actual pleasures and actual pains, this neutral state is a good: health is not just the absence of evils but a good in itself (*EdT*, 251.281/*G*.VI.266). Similarly, humans for the most part are neither exultantly happy nor deeply miserable, but generally ok: there are more houses than prisons in the world.[51] In like manner, King had argued that most people do succeed in achieving a 'moderate Happiness' (*DOM*, 455–6).

This point concerning the neutral state is related to the problem of *bias*. According to Leibniz, we experience evils immediately but don't experience goods until we are deprived of them. Consequently, we tend to notice evils more than goods—but that's a perception bias for which we must correct (*EdT*, 251.281/*G*.VI.266–7). Similarly, we may be biased when judging *past* goods and evils if we are *presently* unhappy. This is one of Leibniz's main criticisms of Bayle's phenomenological approach, which is too subjective and leads to an exaggeration of the evils of life: on the contrary, if we examine things without prejudice, we will find that, in general, human life is passable and tending strongly to the (moral and physical) good. The bias critique, however, can cut both ways: Bayle had argued precisely that humans tend to overemphasise the *goods* of life and fail to take into account the evils still before them (*Xenophanes*[1]*.F*).[52] This is why he introduced the thought experiment discussed briefly in chapter 1, which asks us whether we would want to live our lives again, if it meant reliving all past sorrows as well as joys. According to Bayle, most persons *of a certain age* will answer negatively:

> most persons, when a little advanced in years, grow like La Mothe le Vayer, who would have refused to pass again through the same good and evil which he had felt in his life. If it be so, we must believe that, upon the whole, every one finds the pleasures which he has enjoyed

51. Leibniz says this explicitly with regard to moral evils (*EdT*, 148.216/*G*.VI.198: 'With regard to virtue and vice, a certain mediocrity prevails'), but the context suggests he means it of physical evils too.

52. See also Benatar, *Better Never to Have Been*, 64–9, on psychological biases towards optimism (e.g. the Pollyanna Principle).

> have been unequal to the uneasinesses and pains with which he has been afflicted. (*Xenophanes*[1]*.F*)

In the cases of both Cicero and La Mothe le Vayer, it was grief that upset the balance, making them feel life was a burden to them; not worth living or *re*living.[53] Bayle suggests that this is the reasonable response for most or all of us: this is the judgement we will make once we have reached a certain age and are in a due position to weigh the goods and ills of life.

This thought experiment comes up just briefly in two articles of the dictionary, but Bayle's formulation of it has great currency: it's picked up by King and Leibniz, and arises again in most other authors continuing the debate, as well as in later pessimists, such as Leopardi, Hartmann, and even (in the form of eternal recurrence) Nietzsche.[54] King discusses it at length in his later additions to *De origine mali*, criticising the thought experiment before offering his own alternative (*DOM*, Rem. Z [1732], 460–1). First, King argues that the experiment is purely hypothetical as well as anecdotal: it was never really performed, and even *if* La Mothe le Vayer answered as he did, he cannot speak for all of mankind. Second, King objects to the idea that old age places us in a better position to judge the value of life: on the contrary, in old age the pleasures of life are less present to us, so it makes us *worse* judges of life, not better ones (here, the problem of bias is turned around again). Third, and perhaps most importantly, the experiment doesn't work because it takes out the crucial element of *novelty*:

> The proposing to a Man to live his Life again is not a motive equivalent to what is past. . . . when we offer him to live the same Life over again, we cut off all his Hopes, destroy the agreeable Novelty of the good Parts, and give him only a prospect of the uneasy Passages that he must meet with in it: all which must make his Life a thing quite different from what it was when he first lived it. (*DOM*, Rem. Z, 460)[55]

53. Bayle thus equates living and reliving, and sees this as a successful test for what makes life worth living. For reasons why the test fails, see Smuts, 'Five Tests' (446–51), especially on the 'Extra Life Test' but also on the 'Recurrence Test': it is not clear whether Bayle wants us to live the same life or a similar life (equivalent in goods and evils) again. Both raise problems.

54. See Grandjean, 'Voudriez-vous revivre?'; Dienstag, *Pessimism*, 79–80; D'Iorio, 'Nietzsche et l'éternel retour'; Lovejoy, 'Rousseau's Pessimist', 451. Earlier versions of the thought experiment occurred in Cicero and Erasmus.

55. For a similar critique, see Smuts, 'Five Tests', 448–9.

Leibniz makes a similar point, suggesting that the idea of reliving one's life while conscious of the fact takes out the crucial element of *variety*, which is the spice of life:

> Had we not the knowledge of the life to come, I believe there would be few persons who, being at the point of death, were not content to take up life again, on condition of passing through the same amount of good and evil, provided always that it were not the same kind: one would be content with variety, without requiring a better condition than that wherein one had been. (*EdT*, 13.130/*G*.VI.109)[56]

Finally, King argues that, even if someone wants to die after a long and happy life, this only proves that the very *last* part was not worth living—the dregs of a good bottle of wine don't mean that the whole bottle was bad (*DOM*, Rem. Z, 461). Instead, he suggests a different version of the thought experiment:

> if we would propose to a Man of sixty Years to lengthen his Life for sixty more with the same strength and vigour he had at twenty, and let him take his Chance, I doubt if one in a million would refuse the offer. (*DOM*, Rem. Z, 461)

As a test for the value of life, however, this revised version is equally or even more problematic than Bayle's original: it is to propose a life both longer and better (in terms of physical health) than can be expected of normal lives. If Bayle's experiment, removing the element of novelty or variety, was biased towards pessimism, King's version is biased towards optimism. (Alternatively, Rousseau would say that it depends on who you ask: men of letters will not want to relive their lives, miserable creatures as they are, but ask a peasant or 'honest burgher', and they will be more than happy to live again.[57] Kant, on the other hand, thinks the experiment even works in a much stronger form: no 'human being of sound mind' would want to live again in *whatever* circumstances if it means living in the current world.[58])

56. See also *EdT*, 253.282/*G*.VI.267, and *EdT*, 124.198/*G*.VI.179: 'wisdom must vary'. Variety emerges as a veritable 'law of delight' (*lex laetitiae*) in his earlier *De rerum originatione radicali* of 1697: 'Pleasure does not derive from uniformity, for uniformity brings forth disgust and makes us dull, not happy: this very principle is a law of delight' (*Philosophical Essays*, 153/*G*.VII.307; see Lærke, 'The End of Melancholy').

57. Rousseau to Voltaire, 18 August 1756, *LV*, 235–6. See chapter 6.

58. Kant, 'Theodicy' (8:259); see chapter 7.

Thus Leibniz and King argue, against Bayle, that most people would consider their lives worth living, and *re*living, so that the experiment, *rightly framed*, would support the overall goodness of life. In fact, according to King, this judgement is not hypothetical: we actually make it *while* living *by* living; that is, by choosing to continue our lives rather than ending them.

The Argument from Suicide

This is a recurrent strategy in authors making the case for optimism in the eighteenth century: it can be called the argument from suicide—or, rather, from *no* suicide.[59] The idea is that all (or the vast majority of) creatures prove their ongoing desire for life—and thereby that they judge its goods to outweigh its evils—by striving to continue in their existence: by not killing themselves and not wanting to die. As such, it can be considered a version of Camus's intuition that the question of whether to commit suicide can be equated with the question of whether life is worth living. As King, who makes this point repeatedly, writes: 'though we complain of the Miseries of Life, yet we are unwilling to part with it, which is a certain Indication that it is not a burden to us' (*DOM*, 455–6; see also 212, 219).

This is a risky argument for the optimists to make, especially on King's part, since the fact that some people *do* commit suicide would suggest there are some intolerable evils in human existence; that some people do consider themselves to be miserable, and believe that it would be better for them not to exist. So the argument from suicide could easily be flipped around and used against King (and other optimists). And this seems to be exactly what Bayle tries to do in response to King. True, says Bayle, suicides are rare, but they wouldn't be if there weren't three great obstacles preventing men from killing themselves: the lack of courage, the fear of infamy and social disgrace, and the fear of eternal damnation (*RQP*.II.75/*OD*.III.653). First, not everyone possesses the courage that is required for such an 'expedition', especially not during 'the exhaustion of a black melancholy or languor', which is the state in which people are most likely to

59. As far as I know, Leibniz does not make this argument, but it comes up repeatedly in King as well as later authors, such as Bolingbroke, Voltaire, Rousseau, and Jeremy Bentham, who writes: 'The unfrequency of suicide is irresistible testimony to the fact that life is, on the whole, a blessing' (*Deontology*, 80). Kant argues against the argument from suicide: see chapter 7, *ZW.2.a*.

kill themselves (*RQP*.II.75/*OD*.III.653).[60] Second, people are aware of the dishonour and infamy to which their corpse and their families would be exposed. Third, people are afraid of eternal damnation; hence, suicides are more common among freethinkers and pagans (and nowadays, Bayle adds in the margin, among the Chinese; *RQP*.II.75/*OD*.III.653).

These obstacles aside, even people who don't want to die do not thereby prove that they are happy living: 'What about galley-slaves, prisoners, sick people—are they happy?'[61] It's true, says Bayle, that they would often still prefer life in their current state to death—but being able to envision a *worse* state doesn't make the current state a *happy* one. Hence, it is perfectly possible for a person to be miserable in life and still not want to die (*RQP*.II.86/*OD*.III.670). Furthermore, the fear of death is so deeply entrenched in us that it warps our judgements on the value of existence: 'There is perhaps nothing on which man makes more erroneous judgments than on life and death' (*RQP*.II.75/*OD*.III.653). In other words, the fact that few people commit suicide cannot serve as proof in favour of Kingian optimism—but the fact that some people *do* commit suicide (in the face of such great obstacles) does seem to count in favour of some version of pessimism: it hints at the existence of truly miserable creatures.

King responded to these criticisms in his posthumous papers, which were edited and added to *De origine mali* by Edmund Law in his English translation of 1732.[62] With regard to the lack of courage, King argues that, if so much courage is needed to commit suicide, this itself proves that life is considered a great good, from which we find it hard to part, courage being 'the Power of attempting hard, painful, and disagreeable things'. With regard to the fear of infamy, he (dodgily, for an archbishop) suggests that this could easily be avoided: 'A Dose of Opium will do the Business, and leave no room for Discovery.'[63] Finally, with regard to the fear of damnation, he argues that this wouldn't move atheists, who nevertheless are usually the fondest lovers of life; furthermore, that it is often precisely a kind of 'religious Melancholy' that drives men to suicide,

60. Bayle thinks suicides usually occur in a period of long depression or long illness ('au milieu d'un long chagrin, ou d'une longue maladie', *RQP*.II.75/*OD*.III.653); as in the case of the thirty-year-old man killing himself at the end of what sounds like a bout of depression, 'un chagrin de trois ou quatre semaines' (*Xenophanes*[1]*.F*).

61. This passage addresses Stoic ethics, but in a footnote is redirected against King (*OD*.III.671).

62. King, *DOM*, Rem. Z (1732), 456–61; on suicide, see especially 458–9.

63. King also suggests that people who kill themselves generally seem to be unconcerned with infamy, since they tend to be infamous already.

'which proves that the fear of Damnation is no such hindrance to it' (*DOM*, Rem. Z, 459).[64]

But if we think back to the above syllogism, it seems that King's replies fail to touch the main problem posed by the phenomenon of suicide: For if there is even *one* person who is miserable enough to kill themselves, doesn't this fly in the face of King's (and Leibniz's) philosophy?[65] Doesn't it mean that the minimal condition of optimism fails to be satisfied? Not necessarily. For King subscribes to the traditional view that suicide is strictly irrational, stemming from a corruption of the mind, and hence cannot be considered a sound judgement of the value of existence: 'No Person therefore, except he be corrupted in his Judgment and indulge himself in Error, can seriously prefer Non-existence to the present Life' (*DOM*, 214).[66]

The Misery of the Damned

. . . *the present Life*. But what of a future one? Could it not also be argued that any evils that would tend to outweigh the goods of this life are nevertheless compensated by rewards in a future life? Wouldn't such a future-life response be an easy way out of the whole conundrum?

This is indeed a formidable part of most theodicies of the age, and had been used to justify a variety of seemingly undeserved physical evils (for instance, those suffered by small infants), the intuition being that, while some evils have their justification in the past, as punishment for sin, others have their justification in the future, where patience and perseverance will be rewarded in the afterlife. Thus, according to Leibniz, while there is a misalignment between moral and physical evil (and moral and physical good) in *this* world, which is why good things happen to bad people and bad things to good people, these become perfectly calibrated in the afterlife, where virtue and vice will be exquisitely aligned with reward and

64. Bayle died long before these critiques were published (in 1732)—but some of his views on suicide and fear of death are developed by Hume in his essay 'Of Suicide' and *Dialogues concerning Natural Religion*. Like Bayle, Hume sees the fear of death as 'the secret chain . . . that holds us' (*DNR*.X.72), and believes that existence can be worse than non-existence (*EMPL*, 588). See chapter 5.

65. While Leibniz does not make the argument from suicide, in so far as he also seems to assume there can be no truly miserable creatures in King's sense (for whom it would be better not to be), the fact of suicide would raise similar questions.

66. See also *DOM*, 215, where suicide is represented as a depraved choice, which is why beasts don't kill themselves.

punishment.[67] Similarly, King suggests that the present life may be a kind of '*Prelude* to or *Preparation* for a better' (*DOM*, 198).

However, in the context of this particular debate, there are two problems with such a response. For one thing, from Bayle's point of view, the argument doesn't work: Future bliss cannot justify present suffering, for if God is all-powerful and all-good, why didn't he place his creatures in this state of bliss in the first place; or if he did (with Adam and Eve), why didn't he keep them there? But the more considerable problem is that as soon as we're taking into account the happiness of the blessed, we must also account for the misery of the damned. For if under a just God no creature can repent of its existence—what of the existence of the damned? Would it not be better for the *damned* that they did not exist?

Leibniz and King both struggle with this question, which they must answer because they both include in their justifications of evil an account of a future life.[68] Now, of this future life, both Leibniz and King have a rather rosier expectation than Bayle does (unsurprisingly). Bayle asserts that, according to Catholics and Protestants alike, the greater proportion of souls will be damned. We don't know the exact number: the ratio of damned to saved might be one million to one. In any event, a multitude of souls will suffer for all eternity (*Xenophanes¹.E*).[69] Both Leibniz and King deny this, on two grounds. First, as Leibniz stresses repeatedly, we don't know this for sure: perhaps more humans are saved than damned.[70] Second, even if more *humans* are damned than saved, 'that would not preclude the possibility that in the universe the happy creatures infinitely

67. E.g. *EdT*, 17.132/*G*.VI.111–2, *EdT*, 74.162/*G*.IV.142. As R.M. Adams rightly argues, Leibniz's concept of the *City of God*, whose 'membership includes all intelligent beings', is crucial for understanding what he means by 'the best of all possible worlds'; see Adams, 'Justice, Happiness, and Perfection in Leibniz's City of God', 201. According to Rateau, what is shocking to Leibniz is not 'the existence of suffering in itself', but its unjust distribution over the virtuous and the wicked ('Theoretical Foundations', 97–8).

68. Whether Leibniz actually believed in the doctrine of eternal punishment is a matter of debate; here, I am following Leibniz's suggestions in the *Theodicy*, and am sympathetic to Lloyd Strickland's interpretation 'that Leibniz held (and only ever held) the traditional view, i.e. that the wicked will suffer eternal punishment'. Strickland, 'Leibniz on Eternal Punishment', 308. On seventeenth-century discussions of eternal torment, see Walker, *The Decline of Hell*. For a recent attack on the doctrine on theological as well as ethical grounds, see Hart, *That All Shall Be Saved*.

69. See also *RQP*.II.144/*OD*.III.798; *RQP*.II.87/*OD*.III.671.

70. See *EdT*, 17–19.132–34/*G*.IV.111–14, 133.203–5/*G*.IV.184–7. King also seems to assume that the blessed outnumber the damned, especially in *DOM*, Rem. X (1732), 411, where the good of the many is contrasted with 'the fall of a few': 'Thus good Men here are happy, the blessed in Heaven, and all the Holy Angels, so far as we know of them.' King also believes there is more moral good than evil in the world (Rem.AA [1732], 473–7, at 473–4).

outnumber those who are unhappy': for both Leibniz and King assume the existence of angels and aliens ('the inhabitants of the other globes'; *EdT*, 133.205/*G*.VI.187).[71] And if all are taken into account, we must assume that the total sum of blessed souls (human, alien, and angelic) will be far greater than that of the damned.[72]

However, this still doesn't remove the principal problem: even *one* truly miserable creature, one being who would be better off *not* being, poses a problem for God's goodness—on the optimists' *own* principles (at least up to this point). They do respond to this problem, but both Leibniz and King seem rather more hesitant and uncomfortable than usual, in these, the darkest corners of their systems. Part of their discomfort possibly has to do with two verses of the Gospel, where Christ says of Judas that 'it had been good for that man if he had not been born'.[73]

King poses the problem in the following way: if *not to exist* is indeed 'the very worst Condition', as King had argued, how can eternal punishment be harmonised with God's goodness, since this would reduce sinners to a state worse than non-existence? (*DOM*, 'Appendix', 501). Again, King believes that this is not a question for *this* life, for as soon as evils outbalance the goods of life, these same evils will put an end to life itself. But this is not the case for the damned, who we know suffer eternally. As Bayle would write in response to King, annihilation is clearly preferable to eternal punishment, just as it is less cruel to kill someone quickly than to prolong their lives in order to make their pains and miseries last longer: 'This notion is so self-evident, that I could assert without temerity that it's

71. See also *EdT*, 219.264/*G*.VI.249. King is less outspoken on aliens than on angels, but he does suggest that humans only constitute a small portion of free agents in the universe (*DOM*, 472–3), and that the chain of being continues upward (from man via superior beings to God) as well as downward (from man via animals to inanimate nature); on which, see Lovejoy, *Great Chain*, 189–94. The possibility of *unhappy* aliens is not considered by either Leibniz or King.

72. Note that in making this argument, Leibniz and King are actually conceding an important point to Bayle: that it would indeed be problematic if it were otherwise; that God's goodness requires the blessed to outnumber the damned.

73. Matthew 26:24 (King James Version, KJV); see also Mark 14:21 (KJV): 'good were it for that man if he had never been born'. The verses are discussed by Bayle in particular (*RQP*.II.87/*OD*.III.672 and especially *RQP*.IV.23/*OD*.III.1070), who argues it would both be better for Judas never to have been born *and* to have been annihilated after his crime (but prior to his punishment) than to be punished eternally. King doesn't mention the verses in the original Latin edition of *DOM*, but Law adds a reference to them in the 1732 edition ('Appendix', 501). Malebranche seems to think Christ's words apply not just to Judas, but to 'all the damned, for whom it would be better . . . not to be than to be as evil as they are' (*OCM*.II.48/*SAT*, 288). Leibniz alludes to the verses in a different text from 1705 (see below, n. 77).

commonly shared not only by the learned, but also by all peoples of the world, in whichever country they live, known or unknown' (*RQP*.II.87/*OD*.III.672).

How, then, to solve the problem of the damned? First, King conjectures that perhaps the damned are like madmen, perverted in their minds so that they keep pursuing what harms them, 'as it were pleasing themselves in their Misery' (*DOM*, 'Appendix', 506). This notion springs from King's philosophy of free will, according to which we please ourselves primarily in the very act of choosing ('Elections').[74] We do not choose things because they are good; rather, we see them as good because we choose them. And there can be a specific pleasure in choosing the option one knows one is not supposed to, just because one can (*DOM*, esp. 324–49). This is similar to what we can see in this life, where people will continue in a downward spiral of harming themselves by pleasing themselves, spending their money and their very bodies for the pleasure of exercising their free will. What are these, says King, if not the '*Preludes* of the Misery of the Damned'? (*DOM*, 'Appendix', 507).

So King's first suggestion is that the damned choose to persist in their current state, and even that they may draw some pleasure from it: they please themselves in their misery, and would still prefer to be than not to be, if that is the question. But it isn't quite. The question was not whether the damned want to continue existing, but whether it is *actually* better for them to exist while miserable than not to exist. And here, in fact, King concedes the point: 'Tis better for them indeed not to be, than to be; but only in the Opinion of wise Men, to which they do not assent' (*DOM*, 'Appendix', 506).

Here it is then: here we have one instance, in King's system, of a creature so miserable that it would be better served by not existing. But if this would be better for the creature, it would not be better for the system as a *whole*. For if it had been necessary for God to avoid any miserable creatures in his system (i.e. creatures who bring misery upon themselves), he would have had to create nothing at all; and King considers it self-evidently better that there be a world, even with the inclusion of some true misery, than that there be no world at all:

> If God had made nothing at all, and been contented to have remain'd alone, there wou'd have been nothing that could sin, that could choose amiss, that could be miserable. . . . Now it was expedient, *for the Good*

74. On which, see Pearce, 'William King on Free Will'.

> *of the whole*, that some of these should have a Power of bringing Misery upon themselves by evil Elections. . . . He chose therefore that some should regret their having been made by God, viz. thro' the abuse of their Free-Will, rather than that none should be happy by using it aright. (*DOM*, 'Appendix', 510; my emphasis)[75]

Furthermore, as King suggests elsewhere (to Bayle's bafflement), the punishments of the wicked may help the good to make choices for the better—even in heaven, contemplating this misery of the damned may elevate the blessed.[76] So even *eternal* punishment can be attributed to the goodness of God.

Leibniz, in the *Theodicy*, leaves questions concerning damnation open, suggesting that God hasn't given us enough information to understand damnation, only to fear it (*EdT*, 272.294/G.VI.279–80). He does mention King's opinion that the damned still want to exist and even please themselves in their misery; in fact, he says that he himself has had similar opinions, but has not dared to judge decisively on the question ('Appendix on King', *EdT*, 27.441/G.VI.435–6). In another text, written around the same time, he is a bit clearer on the state of the damned:

> I would . . . say that for such a man himself it would be better not to be, as Christ too says explicitly that *for such a man* it would be better not to have been born. But it is *better for the universe* itself for the matter to be as it is.[77]

Note the shift between these two viewpoints, which I will call the *creaturely* and the *cosmic*. From the creaturely perspective, it is better for the damned not to exist: that is, it is better for *them* that they do not exist. From the cosmic perspective, it is better that the damned do exist: it is *worse* for them, but better for the universe as a whole.

75. Note that this contradicts King's earlier assertion that when life's evils outweigh the goods, existence is withdrawn from the creature.

76. This 'abominable fancy' has a long lineage, from Tertullian and Augustine to Thomas Aquinas and Peter Lombard; see Walker, *Decline of Hell*, 29–32. Bayle rejects it fiercely in *RQP*.IV.23/*OD*.III.1069; in a similarly indignant vein, see Hart, *That All Shall Be Saved*, 167–71.

77. My emphasis. This quote is from Leibniz's 1705 commentary on an anonymous text by one 'J.C.', *An Answer to the Query of a Deist, concerning the Necessity of Faith* (1687): 'Ego distinguendo dicerem melius fore ipsi homini tali ut non sit, quod etiam diserte Christus dixit melius tali homini fore non esse natum. Sed ipsi universe melius est rem sic esse ut est.' (Leibniz, *Textes inédits*, I, 252). The English translation cited here is from Adams, 'Justice', 211. On the admission into existence of Judas (the 'such a man', *tali homini*, referred to here), see also Leibniz, *Discourse on metaphysics* (1685–1686), 48–51/*G*.IV.454–6.

Now Leibniz and King make a concession *only* for the damned: only for them is it the case that they would be better off not being. They seem to take the misery of the damned as an exception that proves the rule. But this exception is enough for the creaturely perspective to collapse entirely: there *is* a creature for whom it would be better not to be, or perhaps even never to have been at all. And, considering the minimal condition for optimism, where does that leave the goodness of God? Yet the mechanics of optimism are such that when the creaturely perspective fails, it falls back immediately on the cosmic, bolstered by three recurrent points. First, most people are moderately happy; only a *very few* are truly miserable. Here, the optimists are subtly slipping from the stronger to the weaker version of the pessimist premise mentioned above—from a.1 to a.2. They are now responding to the *weaker* version of the premise: it is not the case that *most* creatures are miserable, even if some are. Second, even if there are (a considerable amount of) miserable humans, there are still more happy than unhappy creatures in the *universe* as a whole, which encompasses angels and aliens; whatever the tally of human misery, there is more good than evil on the whole. 'But *even though* there should have fallen to the lot of the human kind more evil than good,' writes Leibniz, 'it is enough where God is concerned that there is incomparably more good than evil in the universe' (*EdT*, 262.287/*G*.VI.272; my emphasis).[78] Third, it is necessarily better for the whole that things are arranged as they are.[79] It is this view from the whole that I will call the *optics of optimism*.

The Optics of Optimism

In using this term, I don't *just* mean the age-old idea that the beauty and goodness of the universe only emerge when we look at the whole rather than the parts.[80] This idea does become highly influential in the eighteenth century, to the point that it can be called a true cornerstone of optimism. '[I]f we could view the whole Workmanship of God,' says King, then 'it would appear that the World is as well as it could possibly be' (*DOM*, 219).

78. Leibniz and King seem to concede, throughout, that God's goodness requires there to be more goods than evils *on the whole*.

79. *Necessarily*: since we know we are created by a good God. The problem, and the recurrent threat of circularity, is of course that this very goodness of God is exactly what's in question—especially in the wake of Bayle.

80. See again Augustine, *De ordine* 1.1.2, for an example of the aesthetic approach discussed in chapter 1.

Or, in Leibniz's words, 'the apparent deformities of our little worlds combine to become beauties in the great world' (*EdT*, 147.216/*G*.VI.198). Or again, in Pope's, ''Tis but a part we see, and not a whole' (*EM*, I.2). The term *optics* seems particularly appropriate for this perspectival turn, since the focus on sight and the appearance of visual metaphors is striking throughout the optimist canon, not just in Leibniz and Pope, but also in Voltaire, whose ambivalence to such optics already shows cracks in the decade leading up to the Lisbon earthquake: his Memnon, for instance, is a one-eyed man, who questions providence because he does not see the whole picture, he does not have the right perspective—or does he?[81]

But here, what I am referring to specifically is a shift of perspective, not just from the parts to the whole, but from the *creaturely* to the *cosmic*: from the internal viewpoint, the particular experience of the creature, to an external God's-eye view on the universe. It is the recurrent effort to supplement, or even substitute, the creaturely perspective with the cosmic. As said above, this is a recurrent dynamic in Leibniz and King: whenever the creaturely perspective fails, it collapses into the cosmic. What is interesting is that they keep wanting to go back to the creaturely perspective nevertheless. King and Leibniz seem to want to have it both ways: on the one hand, there can be no *truly miserable* creatures (for whom it would be better not to be)—but on the other, if there are, then this must be better for the whole: God is still just.

The point of optimism is that the cosmic viewpoint is the one that matters. But the point of pessimism is precisely to prioritise the *creaturely* perspective. For optimism, this is the most uncertain perspective; for pessimism, the most certain one—all we have is (each our own) experience (there are strong sceptical elements here).

As Leibniz writes elsewhere, 'It is only with the eyes of the understanding that we can place ourselves in a point of view which the eyes of the

81. See the final lines of Voltaire's story *Memnon, ou La Sagesse humaine* (1749), *OCV*.30B, 267; cited in chapter 3. But compare Voltaire's criticism of Maupertuis's (and by extension Bayle's) pessimism in 1752: 'When one examines these commonplaces with attentive eyes, one sees that in effect there is much more good than evil on the world' (Voltaire, '"Extrait" de la Bibliothèque raisonnée', *OCV*.32B, 296; my translation). In Leibniz, see, e.g., *EdT*, 194.248/*G*.VI. 232: 'You have known the world only since the day before yesterday, you see scarce farther than your nose, and you carp at the world.' And again *EdT*, 147.216/*G*.VI.197: 'It is as in those devices of perspective, where certain beautiful designs look like mere confusion until one restores them to the right angle of vision or one views them by means of a certain glass or mirror.'

body do not and cannot occupy.'[82] But this, for Bayle, is to take the wrong perspective entirely. Granted, on the scale of the universe the imperfections of the parts don't count for much; a machine works even if it has stronger and weaker parts. But evils are only evils in so far as they are experienced, and experienced *as* evils. Nothing is an imperfection, according to Bayle, unless it is seen or felt as one (*RQP*.II.75/*OD*.III.653). And when it comes to weighing the goods and ills of life, we are speaking precisely of our experience, to which the cosmic viewpoint, mediated by the understanding, cannot grant us access. With equal philosophical foundation, Bayle could invert Leibniz's dictum: it is rather with the eyes of the *body* that we are able to occupy a point of view that the eyes of the understanding do not and cannot occupy.[83]

This seems to be part of the reason why these two philosophies clash so spectacularly, operating not just with different assumptions, but in different paradigms altogether, ethically and epistemologically divided. Ethically, because the optimists place their focus on the duty of the creature to the creator: the duty of gratitude, but also, the duty to take the cosmic point of view (the optics of optimism is also its ethics). But since pessimism focuses on the creaturely perspective, the problem of gratitude or ingratitude doesn't come up. It's not the duty of the creature to the creator that's central, but the duty of the creator to the creature; the *ethics of creation*. And they are epistemologically divided, because they differ in their estimation of what constitutes the most certain source of knowledge: the quality of our experiences, or our conception of God. This is why, just as the optimists keep trying to shift back to the cosmic perspective, so too the pessimists keep going back to the creaturely.[84]

This taking of a point of view, then, is not a passive thing—it is a course of action, it has ethical force: we *ought* to take the cosmic point of view. On the part of the optimists, this is informed by what we might call the politics of gratitude: to take the cosmic point of view and accept that things are on the whole good or right or for the best is to exercise gratitude for one's creation; conversely, to take the creaturely perspective and focus on

82. 'Allein wir müßen uns mit den Augen des Verstandes dahin stellen, wo wir mit den Augen des Leibes nicht stehen, noch stehen können.' Leibniz, 'On Destiny or Mutual Dependence' (*Selections*, 572/G.VII.120). See Rutherford, 'Leibniz and the Stoics', 139.

83. If the eyes of the body are here taken to represent psychological as well as physical experiences.

84. See again Bayle, *RQP*.II.75/*OD*.III.653, where he dismisses King's evils of imperfection as well as the relevance of the viewpoint of the universe: only experienced evils count as evils, and so only the experience of the creature is relevant.

the particular wrongs of existence (especially, one's *own* existence) is to be ungrateful. This point is repeated by the optimists time and time again. As life 'has more Good than Evil in it,' says King, ''tis plain we are obliged to him that gave it; and it is a very wicked and ungrateful thing for anyone to pretend the Contrary' (*DOM*, Rem. Z, 416).[85]

Yet there is also a concern here with the human condition: with the condition of the individual sufferer. One of Leibniz's criticisms against books that listed human misery (among which he presumably counted Bayle's) was that this only increases suffering: 'evils are doubled by being given an attention that ought to be averted from them, to be turned towards the good which by far preponderates'. It is better 'to be well satisfied with Nature and with fortune and not to complain about them': to be grateful that we exist at all (*EdT*, 15.131/*G*.VI.110).[86] The same point will emerge in more crystallised form in Rousseau's criticism of Voltaire's poem on the Lisbon earthquake, where he accuses Voltaire of intensifying our miseries by painting so vivid a picture of them, as opposed to which the 'optimism' of Pope and Leibniz 'allays my evils and inclines me to patience'.[87] This too is the sentiment of Shaftesbury's 'Inquiry Concerning Virtue or Merit' (1711):

> Nothing indeed can be more melancholy than the thought of living in a distracted universe, from whence many ills may be suspected and where there is nothing good or lovely which presents itself, nothing which can satisfy in contemplation or raise any passion besides that of contempt, hatred or dislike. Such an opinion as this may by degrees embitter the temper and not only make the love of virtue to be less felt but help to impair and ruin the very principle of virtue, namely, natural and kind affection. (*CMM*, 189)

The optics of optimism here arises as a moral duty, not only to God, but also to oneself and others. But this sense of moral responsibility also exists on the other side. Voltaire's problem with optimism (as perceived by him) is that it makes us passive and takes away the possibility of hope: If all is

85. See also *DOM*, 193, 214, 215, 387, 416.

86. See also *EdT*, 148.216–7/*G*.VI.198 (explicitly criticising Bayle, though here speaking of moral evil in particular): 'I find it a great fault in historians that they keep their mind on the evil more than on the good.' Note, however, that Leibniz remained an admirer of Bayle, who he called 'l'auteur du plus beau des Dictionnaires' (cited in Lærke, *Les lumières de Leibniz*, 219).

87. Rousseau to Voltaire, 18 August 1756, *LV*, 232–3.

well now, how can we hope for something better? The last word of the poem on the Lisbon earthquake is, famously, *espérance*.[88]

This emphasis on hope is not present in Bayle, who feels he must, as a historian and philosopher, describe reality as he sees it—but there is certainly a concern with the perspective of the sufferer. For Bayle, to play down suffering is precisely to increase it. To suggest that one's suffering is unnecessary, or self-inflicted, or that one is complaining wrongly—all of this is to make one's suffering greater (*Xenophanes*^{2}.*K*). I think there is a drive here to open up a space that allows for the full expression of experienced suffering—something not at all self-evident in a tradition thick with Stoic–Christian assumptions that the best way to suffer is to suffer quietly, and patiently.[89]

Hence, behind both the optimistic and pessimistic perspectives there is a strong sense of moral and social (as well as, in the optimists, theological[90]) responsibility: How ought we look at creation; how should we speak of goods and evils; what gives hope, what fosters despair? And above all: How are we to speak of creaturely suffering?

Considering this moral background to the debate, it is somehow unfortunate that neither side seemed to recognise the other's ethical orientations. Voltaire's fiery indignation at what he perceived to be an inhumane 'optimism' (and the venom, here, is in the -*ism*), is understandable, but perhaps also unfair, which is what Rousseau, in his muted disappointment, seemed to be getting at. King, Pope, Leibniz—theirs too were hope-driven philosophies, especially in their expectations of a future life.

88. Note that Voltaire's objections to optimism are founded, in part, on a misunderstanding of this doctrine, which does not deny that we can hope for better states than the current one: on the contrary, the expectation of a future life is crucial for both Leibniz and King. Leibniz's system of optimism, furthermore, need not be interpreted as one of 'optimalism', according to which 'we already enjoy the best of all possible cosmic arrangements' and so cannot hope for progress or improvement (Eagleton, *Hope without Optimism*, 4). In fact, we could also take the 'best of all possible worlds' as applying to the *whole* system, stretched out in *time* as well as space, which would allow for temporal improvement (as well as temporary deterioration), as long as the system in its entirety is preferable to any other. For a discussion of various conceptions of progress in Leibniz, see Rateau, 'L'univers progresse-t-il?'

89. Though there are again different interpretations of what such patience would look like. Thus Leibniz objected to the Stoic tenets in Descartes's ethics: 'Patience without hope cannot last and scarcely consoles' (Leibniz to Molanus (?), ca. 1679, in *Philosophical Essays*, 241/G.IV.298). On this passage and Leibniz's wider views on hope and patience, see Rutherford, '*Patience sans espérance*'.

90. There is no reason why there should be no sense of theological responsibility in pessimism (Pascal?); but it is, to my mind, not present in Bayle (or Hume).

Yet they in turn were too easily dismissive of Bayle's tortuous attempts to make room, within philosophy, for a non-reductive concept of suffering, of evil. Both sides might have worked harder to acknowledge the other's sincerity and moral motivations as well as philosophical attitudes, rather than brushing aside the latter with the former, each side decrying the other as inhumane.

This may serve as a caution for contemporary debates, where optimism and pessimism (especially in their *future*-oriented sense) are all too often described as, respectively, a philosophy of *naïveté*,[91] and a philosophy of passivity, of giving up.[92] Such simplistic characterisations are themselves a choice: not to engage truly and deeply with the other side. 'Optimism' and 'pessimism' originated as pejorative terms and the latter remains so still, despite Dienstag's important efforts to strip pessimism of its overly negative associations (as passive and passive-making, nihilistic, depressed). Pessimism, Dienstag argues, can be deeply life-affirming, politically, artistically, and ethically motivating; as he cites Cioran: 'The more I read the pessimists, the more I love life.'[93]

Seeing the wider historical and philosophical backgrounds and motives behind the debates in question may, then, serve as a caution against the casually dismissive use of terms such as 'optimist' and 'pessimist', where merely to say these words is enough to discredit a philosophy. Properly developed, the ideas associated with either optimism or pessimism are neither trivial nor self-serving, and nor are they superficial (though they can be), but rather, they are sophisticated and morally driven philosophical opinions, born from a deep engagement with the reality of life's brighter and darker sides.

91. See Steven Pinker's objections to such representations in *Enlightenment Now*, chapter 4; also Francis Fukuyama's comments on the ridicule awaiting 'naive optimists' (cited in Raymond Tallis, *Enemies of Hope*, 358). Eagleton associates both optimism and pessimism with fatalism (*Hope*, 2–3), while Roger Scruton strangely equates optimism with anything but his own 'pessimistic' conservatism (*The Uses of Pessimism*). Note, however, that all of these authors are speaking primarily of the *future-oriented* kinds.

92. See Chomsky, *Optimism over Despair*, 196 (cited fully in chapter 3) on pessimism as a form of despair and resignation; also Tallis, *Enemies of Hope* (attacking a specific kind of pessimism, namely that of an irrationalist anti-humanist 'Counter-Enlightenment'). Again, these are critiques of future-oriented pessimism; for criticism of which, see Dienstag, *Pessimism*, ix–x, 3–4.

93. Cioran, *On the Heights of Despair*, quoted in Dienstag, *Pessimism*, 121. For criticism in turn of the 'healthy, heroic pessimism' of Dienstag, Unamuno, and Camus, see Thomas Ligotti, *Conspiracy*, 30–33.

Pessimism

As has transpired from this discussion, there is a sense of urgency to these debates—the questions raised by the challenge of pessimism are seen as a matter of life and death, of the value of being versus not-being. The responses of optimism go back and forth between two competing strategies. Initially, they do not want to concede to pessimism any of its assumptions: that there are beings for whom it would be better not to be, or that there is more that is bad than good in human life. They seem to want to defeat pessimism on its own turf: from *within* the creaturely perspective. But in doing so, in building the case for experiential optimism from the creaturely perspective, they seem to be conceding to pessimism its fundamental premise: that, indeed, there cannot be truly miserable creatures in a just God's creation; that it cannot be the case that the evils of a God-given life outweigh its goods. However, if this is a point that can perhaps be maintained for life in this world, it falters when confronted with the next: with the misery of the damned, the presumed fact of existence that is worse than non-existence, *pire que le néant*. And so these thinkers need to build their case for optimism on an alternative foundation: the cosmic perspective is appealed to whenever the creaturely perspective fails. It is in this failure, in this inability to square the goodness of any creation with the misery of the damned, that the project of optimism seems to waver, and pessimism has an unacknowledged victory.

By way of conclusion, let us return to pessimism for a moment. As argued at the beginning of this chapter, contemporary definitions of pessimism (and optimism) seem to overemphasise its temporal orientation, when time-oriented pessimism is just a subspecies of a more general philosophy that focuses broadly on the value of life in all its aspects. It is this latter kind of pessimism that is at the origins of the former kind; indeed, that carries the former within itself. It is this 'value-oriented' pessimism that is introduced into the philosophical scenery by Pierre Bayle; it is this type of *pessimism* to which Leibniz (the first to be called 'optimist') and King are responding; and, conversely, it is this type of *optimism* to which Voltaire (the first to be called 'pessimist') objects.

It should perhaps be stressed what a momentous phenomenon this is, which somehow tends to be overlooked or understated, by scholars of Bayle (less interested in pessimism) and scholars of pessimism (less interested in Bayle) alike. With regard to pessimism, I agree with Dienstag that it is a crucially modern phenomenon—but I disagree on the reasons for this qualification. For Dienstag, the rise of pessimism (as well as of the idea of progress) has to do with the rise of the modern sense of time, and the invention of clock time in the West. Dienstag's pessimists (among which he counts Schopenhauer and Leopardi but also, more controversially, Rousseau), all include in their accounts of the tragic condition of life a crucial distinction, and separation, between humans and animals. Pessimism is defined as an inherently *human* question, since animals lack time, or reason, or reflection; there is something that makes life a burden to us but not to them.[94]

I fully agree with Dienstag that this distinction does exist, and is important for the debates at hand, with this qualification: that in these debates, it is not the *pessimists* who keep emphasising it, but rather, the *optimists*.[95] Leibniz, King, Pope, Rousseau (who I here, for his opposition to Voltaire, rank among the optimists[96])—they all explain the suffering of animals by distinguishing their condition from ours, and arguing that either they do not suffer, or at least they do not suffer as we do—a common argument being that animals have neither the knowledge nor fear of death.[97] Contrast with this the following passage from Bayle on the suffering of animals:

> The war they wage against each other, and the war man wages against them, and the troubles he imposes on them, are they not a source of unhappiness? Are they exempt from affliction when one takes their little ones from them? Are they exempt from the fear of death? A poor hare, what won't it do to save its life? And most of the time, after so many efforts, doesn't it die a deeply violent and deeply painful death? (*RQP*.II.78/*OD*.III.657)

Similar passages can be found in other pessimists following Bayle's footsteps, such as Hume and Schopenhauer, and in pessimists such as David

94. Dienstag, *Pessimism*, especially 19–25. This leads Dienstag to some questionable value judgements, for example: 'I will believe the animals have an inner life worth respecting when I see one of them disrespect it, that is, when I see one commit suicide' (249).

95. I fully acknowledge that Dienstag's *later* pessimists do emphasise this distinction, but in this they should be set apart from the earlier, Baylean varieties, as well as from even later ones (e.g. Benatar, *Better Never To Have Been*, 89, 223–4; John Gray, *Straw Dogs*).

96. But not unequivocally: see chapters 3 and 6 for complications in both Voltaire and Rousseau. On the partial convergence between Leibniz and Voltaire, for instance on the idea of progress, see Phemister, *Leibniz and the Environment*, 170.

97. See Pope, *EM*, I.81–6: 'The lamb thy riot dooms to bleed to-day, / Had he thy Reason, would he skip and play? / Pleas'd to the last, he crops the flow'ry food, / And licks the hand just rais'd to shed his blood. / Oh, blindness to the future! kindly giv'n, / That each may fill the circle, mark'd by Heav'n'.

Benatar today—their pessimism being all the greater for not being an exclusively human category or question.[98] We are not even uniquely tragic or special in our tragic condition, which we share with all beings capable of sensation; with the result that their situation too must be explained by any project of theodicy—or optimism.

To my mind, the modern quality of the project of pessimism resides not in the exceptionality of the human experience, but rather in these four elements. First, the prioritisation of the creaturely over the cosmic perspective.[99] Second, the emphasis on experience. What matters is not the objective quantity of goods or evils in the world, somehow abstracted from our experience, but *how we experience them*. We have nothing beyond our experience to answer these questions, and any answer to the problem of evil that tries to sideline our experience is missing the point entirely. Third, the widening of the category of tragic existence to include all sentient beings. And fourth, the reconsideration of the moral and experiential background of suicide and desire for death. For Bayle, suicides share in the condition of the damned—but so too do many others for whom death is not an option, or not an acceptable one. People who want to die but cannot,[100] or who suffer dreadfully but fear death even more. The truly tragic, truly miserable live among us; we should not seek them among the damned. The cosmic perspective is irrelevant to this situation, since God, if he is responsible at all, is responsible for each and every creature, and any theodicy must address this. The creature, for Bayle, taking the creaturely perspective, has just cause for complaint.

It remains for me to say that the project of theodicy may have been declared dead by Kant, but the question of whether life is worth living remained very much alive and remains so still—to the point of Camus declaring it the 'fundamental question of philosophy'. To which I will only add that the earliest optimists and pessimists would probably have agreed.

98. See Hume, *DNR*.XI.85: 'Were *all* living creatures incapable of pain . . . , [natural] evil never could have found access into the universe' (my emphasis).

99. The latter, in Bayle, disintegrates almost entirely (at least in discussing the origins of evil); in Hume, it has already disintegrated. In Voltaire, the perspective shifts gradually from the cosmic to the creaturely: see chapter 3.

100. See *RQP*.II.87/*OD*.III.671: the saddest condition in which we can find ourselves on earth is 'that of wanting to die, and finding no one who will relieve us of life'.

CHAPTER THREE

Of Hope and Consolation

VOLTAIRE AND THE DEISTS

The affair of Lisbon has made men tremble, as well as the Continent shake from one End of Europe to another; from Gibraltar to the Highlands of Scotland. To suppose these desolations the scourge of Heaven for human impieties, is a dreadful reflection; and yet to suppose ourselves in a forlorn and fatherless world, is ten times a more frightful consideration.

WILLIAM WARBURTON[1]

Optimism leads to despair. It is a cruel philosophy hiding under a reassuring name.

VOLTAIRE[2]

THE STORY OF OPTIMISM and pessimism does not end here, of course: on the contrary, it has hardly even begun. By this time, however, the structure of the debate on evil has been mapped out, the lines of argument established, and the most original points made. From this point onwards, thinkers will fall almost naturally into the modes of thought established by either Bayle, with his strong ethical objection to rational theodicy and its supposed consolations, or Leibniz and King, with their suggestions of equally morally charged strategies. But this is not how the story tends to be told.

1. William Warburton to Richard Hurd, in Warburton, *Letters*, 203.

2. Voltaire to Élie Bertrand, 18 February 1756 (*D*6738/*CRT*, 134). References to Voltaire's works are to the Voltaire foundation edition (*OCV*, or '*D*' for letters according to the standard organisation, e.g. *D*6738), followed or preceded by the translation used, except where translations are my own.

According to a common historical narrative, the problem of evil erupts into European consciousness in the mid-eighteenth century, around the time of the Lisbon Earthquake of 1755. According to the same narrative, Voltaire is a key figure in effecting the Enlightenment's change of heart with regard to evil; in fact, the narrative tells us that Voltaire himself changed his mind about optimism when faced with the horrors that Lisbon represented, not to mention his own unhappiness. We all enjoy a good volte-face.

Part of this story is certainly true. Lisbon and Voltaire *were* influential in redirecting the philosophical debate, and a background shift in the wider cultural mood *was* brought into focus by Voltaire's *Candide*. But as I will argue in this chapter, by the time the earthquake struck Lisbon and inspiration Voltaire's pen, most of the debate had already been carried out, most available avenues explored, and most arguments delivered, especially the ones that Voltaire would bring to bear on the question of optimism. Furthermore, while it is true that Voltaire, in his powerful challenge to the more nonchalant varieties of optimism, was responding to a growing cultural tendency to opt for this philosophy, it should not be forgotten that pessimism also had its adherents in the eighteenth century, on various sides of the debate.

The picture painted of the eighteenth century is all too often a dichotomous one, and the history of philosophy is perhaps not best served by such clear-cut oppositions as that between optimism and pessimism. Hence, having contrasted the views of the optimists with those of the pessimists in chapter 2, I now want to suggest that we should envision the eighteenth-century debate not as a dichotomy, but rather as a triangular relationship, or something more complex still. For it is in the course of this century that *the two strategies of optimism*, sketched in chapter 2, begin to part ways, causing a division between those who deny the pessimist premise and seek to prove that existence is (broadly or radically) good, and those who incorporate pessimism's points and seek to prove the goodness of creation by a different route (typically, by the prospect of a future life). Opposed to both strategies is a darker countercurrent, continuing on the Baylean line, which pushes pessimism to its most radical conclusions: that life is not worth living for some or most or all of us; that a creature destined to suffer has just cause for complaint.[3]

3. Spoiler: we do not really find the Baylean position restated until Hume, with inklings in Voltaire.

To the extent that we can speak of a tradition, this is one that can only be fragile, fractured, and fraught with misunderstandings, as Bayle continues to be read, published, and circulated, his arguments reprised often without attribution.[4] Perhaps the crucial notion is that of timeliness, or momentum: that elusive decider of what makes some philosophies 'catch on'. Leibniz has it, as do King and Pope, as do all the varieties of optimism they represent. But pessimism does not have it, at least not until Voltaire turns Lisbon's earthquake into the fertile soil that Bayle's arguments need to take root in more than a philosopher's imagination. By this time, however, most of the *philosophical* groundwork had already been done: in so far as we can speak of theodicy as a cultural and intellectual battleground, the war was more or less over by the time Voltaire decided to join the action.

The effort in this chapter, and in the chapters to follow, will not be to offer a single linear narrative of the eighteenth-century debate on pessimism and the problem of evil, but precisely to complicate this history, offering a kind of Grand Tour of the debate. This chapter will trace the discussion in three sets of authors—Wollaston and Bolingbroke, Pope and Prior, and Jenyns and Johnson—before pausing to re-examine Voltaire's intervention following the Lisbon earthquake. These contexts—Voltaire and the British deists—may seem separate, but they are linked in curious ways. Voltaire associated optimism consistently with Leibniz on the one hand (whose work he probably knew mostly through his companion and fellow philosopher Émilie du Châtelet) and with the British deists on other, by whose writings he was initially convinced: especially Shaftesbury, Bolingbroke, and Pope, all three of whom were themselves influenced strongly by King.[5] His allusions to Leibniz to the contrary, Voltaire seems to have been responding to the British intellectual context specifically, and it was here that eighteenth-century optimism had its strongest, if not its finest, hour.

None of these thinkers, it should be noted, introduce any radically new arguments into the debate, instead offering recombinations and elaborations of earlier ones, drawing in particular from what has already become

4. On the eighteenth-century reception of Bayle, see Rétat, *Le dictionnaire de Bayle*.

5. Voltaire consistently associated Shaftesbury, Bolingbroke, and Pope with optimism, both when he approved of it and when he attacked it. The association of these three thinkers with Leibniz and optimism is enduring; see, e.g., Schopenhauer, *WWR*.II. 584. I will not give a separate exposé of Shaftesbury here, whose views on the question of optimism are generally aligned with those of King, Pope, and Bolingbroke; see especially Shaftesbury's *An Inquiry Concerning Virtue or Merit*, book I, and *The Moralists*, part I.

the canon of theodicy: Bayle, Leibniz, and King. Indeed, if there is any novelty to be found in this chapter, it resides in other things: in the way in which arguments are now made poetically, as well as philosophically; in the tactical decisions on which strategy of optimism to prioritise; in the moral objections raised to optimism as well as pessimism; and in the ways in which the debates on evil and pessimism intersect with yet *other* debates, such as the great chain of being (King, Bolingbroke, and Pope), the immortality of the soul (Bolingbroke and Wollaston), and the question of Stoicism (Maupertuis and La Mettrie). First up: the deists.

Wollaston and Bolingbroke

In the final years of his life, the reclusive scholar and school teacher William Wollaston (1659–1724) had his book *The Religion of Nature Delineated* printed privately, then published just before his death in 1724. In this book, a work of moral philosophy as well as of natural theology, Wollaston attempts to found natural religion and moral rationalism without having recourse to revelation, and does so combining 'deistic and Jewish concepts'.[6] Little read now but for its influence on writers such as Hume, Wollaston's work has been described as 'one of the most original and debated versions of natural religion in eighteenth-century Britain', and was well read on the continent, by authors such as Voltaire and Diderot.[7] He was also read by Henry St John, the first Viscount Bolingbroke (1678–1751), who spends many pages of his *Fragments or Minutes of Essays* (1754) trying to refute Wollaston's pessimism as well as his solution to the problem of evil, which is actually rather a strategy of *using* the problem of evil in order to make a rational argument for the immortality of the soul. It is on this lesser-known aspect of Wollaston's book that I want to focus: the part where Wollaston develops a case for pessimism along highly Baylean lines, with the express purpose of making the rational case for a future state as the only way to solve the problem of evil (the part, that is, that so bothered Bolingbroke).

In the final section of the work, Wollaston steers the discussion towards the problem of evil and, more specifically, the ethics of creation. Wollaston sees it as a clear principle of reason that to produce a being in a condition of happiness, either pure or mixed, is not to harm that being; in fact, even

6. Lucci, 'William Wollaston's Religion of Nature', 121.

7. Ibid., 119–20; Hume criticises Wollaston's ethics in his *Treatise of Human Nature*, though possibly misinterpreting him: see Lucci, ibid., 127–8.

to produce it in a condition of misery is not to harm it *so long as* that being has the capacity to avoid at least *part* of that misery by its own power. But reason also tells us that creation becomes immoral when it *destines* the creature to unhappiness: 'The only case then, by which wrong can be done in the production of any being, is, when it is *necessarily* and *irremediably* to be *miserable*, without any recompense, or balance of that misery' (*RND*, 200; his emphasis throughout). This certainly seems to be the case in creation as we know it: thus we have an insurmountable problem of evil *unless* our miseries are compensated in a future state. According to Wollaston, those who do not believe in a future state must *either* indict God for cruelty *or* claim that *no man who ever lived* 'has a greater share of misery, *unavoidable*, than of happiness' in this life (*RND*, 200).[8] The first road is clearly unacceptable, but to take the second road 'is to contradict the *whole story* of mankind, and even *one's own senses*' (*RND*, 200). Like Bayle in *Xenophanes*, Wollaston lists countless examples to prove this: from historical accounts of corporal punishment, torture, execution, and religious persecution, to contemporary evils, such as wars, tyrants, slavery, diseases, poverty, and social injustice, and concludes that 'the *history* of mankind is little else but the history of uncomfortable, dreadful passages' (*RND*, 200–2).[9]

Even those of us fortunate enough to have lived comfortably suffer things like 'hunger, thirst, heat, cold, and indispositions' (*RND*, 205), the ills associated with the various stages of life, and finally old age, at which point man loses his loved ones while 'wants and *pains* all the while are multiplying upon him: and under this *additional load* he comes melancholy behind, tottering, and bending toward the earth; till he either stumbles upon something which throws him into the grave, or fainting falls of himself' (*RND*, 206). At this point, Wollaston introduces a familiar thought experiment, in wording very similar to Bayle's:

> I am apt to think, that even among those, whose state is beheld with envy, there are *many*, who, if at the end of their course they were put to their *option*, whether, without any respect to a *future state*, they would repeat all the pleasures they have had in life, *upon condition* to go

8. Wollaston does not include animals in the pessimistic condition, though he does discuss animal suffering and argues that while animal lives are worth 'little more than nothing', humans should nevertheless take care not to make them suffer unnecessarily (*RND*, 34–5).

9. Wollaston was presumably aware of Bayle, if not first-hand then certainly through King; his argument here is strongly suggestive of a close reading of the *DHC*.

> over again also all the same disappointments, the same vexations and unkind treatments from the world, the same secret pangs and tedious hours, the same labors of body and mind, the same pains and sicknesses, would be *far from accepting* them at that price. (*RND*, 207)[10]

In a cascade of rhetorical questions, Wollaston asks whether a good God would send man on such a terrible journey, '*only* that the man might faint and expire at the end of it, and all his thoughts perish' (*RND*, 206). Again, the point is that we cannot explain this without having recourse to a future state, unless we accept one of various supposedly repugnant conclusions, such as atheism:

> So that the argument is brought to this undeniable issue; if the *soul* of man is not *immortal*, either there is *no God*, upon whom we depend; or He is an *unreasonable Being*; or there never has been *any man*, whose sufferings in this world have exceeded his enjoyments, without his being the cause of it himself. But surely *no one* of these three things can be said. *Ergo* — (*RND*, 203)

Ergo, there has to be a future state in which man's sufferings are compensated, not because reason has given us a clear conception of it, but because it is the only remaining option that is remotely palatable to a natural theologian.

All of this was very annoying to Bolingbroke, who in his posthumously published *Fragments* took on Wollaston, together with Samuel Clarke, as his favoured targets, the former featuring as the 'whining philosopher', the latter as the 'presumptuous divine' (*FME*, 388). He presents his main problem with both authors as one of *method*, since both start from abstract reason instead of the phenomena. This is where they begin to go wrong: 'the Clarkes and Wollastons of the age' accuse God's providence by arguments drawn from his nature and the 'eternal reason of things', while knowing as little of this as anyone else. Bolingbroke, on the other hand, proposes to defend God's providence 'by arguments, drawn from the nature of man, and the actual constitutions of the world, both equally well known to them and to us' (*FME*, 365; also 367).

This methodological point is itself intriguing, since it is precisely about the characterisation of the *phenomena* that Bolingbroke and Wollaston are in disagreement. Wollaston had argued, like Bayle, that the phenomena reveal to us a creation fraught with unavoidable miseries, and there's no

10. Wollaston refers the claim to Seneca, though the wording again is similar to Bayle's.

denying the phenomena: hence, we have a problem of evil. The power of this argument, as of pessimism in general, lies very much in its a posteriori force, and the traditional way of countering it is to *deny* that appearances should guide our inquiry: rather, it is reason that should correct our observation and lead us to a higher perspective (what I have called *the optics of optimism*). Bolingbroke will soon make this move as well, but at the same time he seeks to turn the tables on Wollaston and pessimism in general, claiming that it is not Wollaston but Bolingbroke himself who takes as his starting point 'the actual constitutions of the world' as we experience it. This is perhaps a rhetorical point rather than a philosophical one, but it does say something about the shifting assumptions of the time, and the changing status of the phenomena or appearances, especially in the more empiricist climate of British deism. Bolingbroke is anticipating the Baylean accusation of not having done justice to what *experience* tells us about the world—clever!

Having scored this initial point, Bolingbroke goes on to dismantle Wollaston's pessimism by a mixture of experiential and conceptual arguments. He accuses Wollaston of exaggerating man's condition in a 'delirium of metaphysics' (*FME*, 374): this is a standard refutation of experiential pessimism, but it is effective in its way, since there is no way to judge experience except by reference *to* experience. But Bolingbroke also makes a more refined point when he argues that Wollaston has failed to distinguish real and enduring *misery* from things that are mere 'inconveniencies at most, to which every man is liable', such as catching a cold or being worried about things in day-to-day life (*FME*, 378).[11] Unpleasant, yes: But is this *misery*? According to Bolingbroke, the bar for speaking of misery should be higher; and once it is, we will find that no man suffers misery 'necessarily, and unavoidably':

> As I take happiness to be a continued permanent series of agreeable sensations or of pleasure, so I take misery to be a continued permanent series of the contrary: and *such misery has never been brought, I believe, on any man necessarily, and unavoidably*, as a consequence of the general state wherein God has placed mankind. (*FME*, 387–9; my emphasis)

11. A similar objection has often been raised against David Benatar, who grounds his pessimism not *only* in cases of horrendous suffering, but also in day-to-day discomforts, such as 'hunger, thirst, bowel and bladder distension . . . , tiredness, stress, thermal discomfort (that is, feeling either too hot or too cold), and itch' (*Better Never to Have Been*, 71). For criticism see, e.g., DeGrazia, 'Is it wrong', 325–6; Wasserman, 'Pro-Natalism', 156–7.

The second part of this statement rather deflates the cogency of the first part, as Bolingbroke feels he has to take the Kingian–Leibnizian line that there is no *real* misery in existence, adding only the clause: *unless deserved*.[12] Bolingbroke goes on to develop this argument at some length and in familiar ways, trying to demonstrate that many evils are not as bad as we often make them out to be, and that in most cases of human suffering 'their greatest evils are from themselves, not from God' (*FME*, 380). Physical evils, he argues, generally pass quickly and are seldom renewed, whereas moral evils are frequent but not *fated*:

> God has given us means, as I said above, to avoid, or to palliate, or to cure these evils in many cases. But men court them. The evils, that may be said to come from God, are, for the most part, soon over. The greatest of these calamities are seldom renewed; and few men have been, I suppose, exposed to the plague twice, or involved twice in the ruines of an earthquake. But ambition, avarice, and other ruling passions, are never fated: and the same persons expose themselves anew and continually to all the evils that accompany the pursuit of them. (*FME*, 343)

He also restates the familiar point of optimism that the seeming imperfection of parts contributes to the real perfection of the whole: 'the general state of mankind in the present scheme of providence is a state not only tolerable, but happy'; 'there is much more good than evil in it' (*FME*, 382). The simplest and most elegant proof of this, for Bolingbroke, is the argument from suicide (in all likelihood, again drawn from King):

> It is plain that every man has more good than evil in actual enjoyment, or in prospect, since *every man prefers existing as he is to non-existence*, and since none of them, not those who suffer the worst accidents in life, are willing to abandon it, and to go out of the state these declaimers represent to be so miserable. (*FME*, 382; my emphasis)

Bolingbroke goes on to direct this argument ad hominem to Wollaston himself, concluding triumphantly that Wollaston defeats his own argument by not wanting to die himself:

> What our author's circumstances were of any kind I am ignorant. But whatever they were, I am persuaded, you will be of my opinion, that any charitable person who had offered to cut his throat, in order only

12. This clause is a new addition: King doesn't really mention it, since he sees any *real misery* as problematic.

> to deliver him from the miseries he complained of in such lamentable terms, would have been very ill received. (*FME*, 382–3)[13]

There are times, reading the optimists and pessimists alike, when one wishes they would just stop writing, and quit while they're ahead. But there's something in the topic that tends to run away with its authors, and so it is with Bolingbroke. He continues, *at length*, to try to demonstrate the goodness of the world, and spends many pages refuting historical examples of misalignment: that is, of bad people who prospered and good people who suffered (*FME*, 404–14). If someone dies before their time, for instance, how do we know they were not spared greater miseries to come (*FME*, 407–8)? He even goes so far as to argue that there can be no political corruption or injustice suffered by any people without them somehow having had it coming: 'we are to consider that they who suffer deserve to suffer', since it is impossible for good government to turn excessively bad 'unless the body of a people co-operate to their own ruin' (*FME*, 388). This is surely optimism of the crassest kind, and it is precisely this mentality that ended up giving optimism such a bad name in the decades to follow. *With friends like that*, a Bayle or Voltaire might well have commented, *who needs enemies?*

But perhaps it is misleading to represent the confrontation between Wollaston and Bolingbroke as one of pessimism versus optimism. After all, Wollaston sets up the problem of evil only in order to solve it by way of a future state: pessimism may hold for our current condition, but the view offered us by the prospect of immortality is, for Wollaston, an optimistic one. Bolingbroke is aware of this, and more than that: it is precisely why he takes such issue with Wollaston's argument, which makes God's goodness hinge entirely on the existence of a future state and the immortality of the soul—both points of contention among deists at the time. Wollaston's 'optimism', for Bolingbroke, represents the *wrong kind* of deism, and so is possibly even more important to refute than traditional views of 'divines' such as Clarke.

Perhaps the most interesting aspect of the discussion between Wollaston and Bolingbroke is that here we see again the *two strategies of optimism*, which sit so uncomfortably together and yet were so optimistically combined by both Leibniz and King. In Wollaston and Bolingbroke, as also in later authors, the two strategies begin to part ways. Authors such as Wollaston (but also someone like Samuel Johnson) are happy to accept the

13. This passage is cited approvingly by the Scottish philosopher Dugald Stewart in his *Philosophy of the Active and Moral Powers of Man* (1828), II, 103–4.

premise of pessimism, and acknowledge that life is indeed more marked by miseries than happiness, but argue that God's justice is nevertheless saved by the assumption of a future state. Authors such as Bolingbroke believe that this is a fatal mistake: to accept the pessimistic premise is to be set ourselves up for failure; instead, we should deny the premise and prove that even *this-worldly* existence is a good thing, *whether or not* we allow for a future state as well.[14] We will encounter these two strategies again in Hume's *Dialogues*, where Demea voices the first strategy and Cleanthes the second. But as Bolingbroke himself demonstrates, the second strategy too is flawed, since it inevitably tries to prove too much. Rather than admitting *some* undeserved suffering in creation, this strand of optimism seeks to cleanse the parts as well as the whole of any residue of *hard misery*: the kind that can neither be avoided nor attenuated. The problem for authors such as Bolingbroke is that they are ultimately unable to defeat the intuitive force of the pessimist challenge: their argument, by trying to dismantle *any* pessimistic description of existence, ends up dismantling itself, and fails by its own ambition.

Pope and Prior

While Bolingbroke's *Fragments* were published posthumously in 1754, he began writing them in the 1730s, at around the same time as Alexander Pope (1688–1744) was working on his *Essay on Man* (1733–1734), which was addressed to Bolingbroke.[15] Both works stand firmly in the Kingian line, and, considering the closeness in both timing and topic, it is understandable that the *Fragments* and the *Essay* were seen as two strands of the same project from early on: one offering the philosophical backbone, the other the poetic flourish. As a result, the question of who influenced who has been a controversial one ever since the eighteenth century, and it has impacted how Pope's *Essay* was received in different times and places. As Maynard Mack notes, continental readers favoured Leibniz as Pope's main source, so that 'the poem there became the battlefield for a struggle between pro- and anti-Leibnizians which had very little to do with

14. But note that Bolingbroke himself combines the two strategies, arguing that *even if* there were as many evils in *this* world as some suggest, then we could draw no conclusions from this with regard to God's moral attributes, since this world is only part of the greater system of the universe (*FME*, 392).

15. The four epistles of *Essay on Man* were written between 1729 and 1733, published separately and anonymously in 1733–1734, then together in 1734, and under Pope's name in 1735 (Jones, 'Introduction', xlvii–xlix).

its actual contents'.[16] This connection had consequences for the reception of Leibniz as well, who for centuries to come would be overwhelmingly read through a Popean lens, which is all the more curious since 'Pope said himself that he had not read the *Théodicée*.'[17] Translation seems to have confused things further, as Pope's famous dictum 'Whatever is, is RIGHT' (*EM*, I.294; IV.394) was rendered into French as *Tout est bien*, thus suggesting that Pope had written that *all is well* or *all is good*.[18] While Pope may well have meant this, Leibniz certainly did not: Leibniz had not said that 'everything is as good as could be' (*Candide*, 4/*OCV*.48.122), or that 'everything is for the best' (*Candide*, 10/*OCV*.48.133), or that optimism entails that there is no room for improvement over time in our current states of affairs (*tout est au mieux*: *OCV*.48.120); nor had he denied the reality of evils in existence.

The Leibnizian link, however, seems not to have been as strong in England, where the favourite source for Pope's *Essay* was considered to be Bolingbroke, at least after the posthumous publication of his *Fragments* in 1754; while later critics added Shaftesbury and King, whose *De origine mali* was 'probably the most influential of eighteenth-century theodicies in prose'.[19] The case for Bolingbroke (who may have shared some of his ideas with Pope in conversation and writing) has been discredited by scholars such as Mack, who argues that the line of influence is more likely to have gone the other way round, with Pope influencing Bolingbroke.[20] At the same time, Lovejoy's suggestion that King was the main source for *both* authors remains a very likely one, regardless of whether Bolingbroke and Pope also influenced each other, and I will take this as my working assumption as I turn to some of the more specific aspects of the *Essay* in relation to the wider theodicean debate.[21]

Famously, Pope popularises and poeticises Kingian optimism, offering readers a loose *mélange* of its central tenets, polished up into gems of philosophical aphorism, such as its most notorious catchphrase: 'Whatever is, is RIGHT.' In a looser interpretation of the optics of optimism, the work urges us to take a wider viewpoint, continually referring us to the

16. Mack, *Collected in Himself*, 205.

17. Ibid.; the same may well be true for Voltaire at the time of writing *Candide* and the Lisbon Poem (see below, n. 97).

18. See Gourevitch, 'Rousseau on Providence', 567. Rousseau will object that the phrase should rather be rendered *Le tout est bien*; see chapter 6.

19. Mack, *Collected*, 205.

20. Ibid., 206–8. See Erskine-Hill, 'Pope on the Origins of Society', 91.

21. Lovejoy, *Chain of Being*, 212, 359n.

whole rather than the parts: ''Tis but a part we see, and not a whole' (*EM*, I.60). Philosophically, it is built on the notion of a 'Vast chain of being' (*EM*, I.237), which sees the universe as an elaborate system of interlocking causes, the ultimate design of which is both beautiful and benevolent; it denies that our experience of evils poses a problem to this benevolence; and hints that any appearance of misalignment will be reconciled in the afterlife (*EM*, IV.67–72). In the light of the wider theodicean debate, and its wavering stance with regard to moral and physical evils, one much-cited passage is particularly striking. Pope suggests that while there is a tendency to see *moral evils* as the more problematic kind, in fact they can be accounted for in the same way as *physical evils*, and so we should place them on the same footing:

> If plagues or earthquakes break not Heav'n's design,
> Why then a Borgia, or a Catiline?
> . . . From pride, from pride, our very reasoning springs;
> Account for moral, as for nat'ral things:
> Why charge we Heav'n in those, in these acquit?
> In both, to reason right is to submit.
> (*EM*, I.155–64)

The irony is that rather than making moral evils *less* problematic, Pope's argument can also be used to make physical evils *more* problematic. His point is one of equivalation: Why acquit the one and not the other? But this premise can lead to two opposite conclusions, and both conclusions were drawn by the eighteenth century: Rousseau would follow Pope in thinking that both kinds of evils should be acquitted, while Voltaire (at least in his Lisbon writings) would follow Bayle in concluding that neither kind should be.[22] As for *why* physical evils are not problematic in Pope's view, he gives us the sketches of various lines of argument: either they are somehow good for the whole (Jenyns's point), or they are not unavoidable (Bolingbroke's point), or they are brief and rare in nature (Bolingbroke's and Johnson's point):

> What makes all physical or moral ill?
> There deviates Nature, and here wanders Will.
> God sends not ill; if rightly understood,

22. Soame Jenyns takes Pope's point the furthest: 'If natural Evil owes its existence to Necessity, why may not moral? If Misery brings with it its Utility, why may not Wickedness?' (*FIN*, 109).

Or partial Ill is universal Good,
Or Change admits, or Nature lets it fall,
Short, and but rare, 'till Man improv'd it all.
(*EM*, IV.111–16)

Animal suffering, meanwhile, is not even considered: Pope believes the happiness of animals to be self-evident, since they have no awareness of time (*EM*, I.81–6).[23] As for our passions, pleasures and pains, they are like 'lights and shades' that together make up 'the balance of the mind' (*EM*, II.120–1).

None of this should strike us as particularly original: nevertheless, the *Essay on Man* has been taken by some as a pivotal moment in the history of theodicy. As Susan Neiman writes:

> With his very title, Pope signaled a shift of focus from God's nature and responsibilities to our own. In so doing, he began to push the problem of evil out of the realm of metaphysics and theology into the world of ethics and psychology, and therewith to a set of questions we can recognise as our own. Pope directs us to understand ourselves, our passions, and our possibilities, for only these have bearing on any problem of evil we may hope to affect.[24]

But there was nothing particularly novel about emphasising human responsibility for the evils befalling us. On the contrary: reducing physical evil to moral evil was one of the oldest theodicean tricks in the book, going back to Augustine's dictum that *under a good God no creature can be miserable unless it deserves to be*. There is indeed an innovation in the eighteenth century's excision of original sin from this schema, but this was not Pope's invention, and he was hesitant in carrying it out. Furthermore, the excision itself cannot unproblematically be seen as a modern moment, an example of progress in philosophy: for it is precisely this excision that requires authors such as Pope, Bolingbroke, and Jenyns to opt for a *hyperbolic optimism*. If we cannot refer the majority of evils of existence to a fallen condition, we have to either assume radical responsibility for them, or push them under the carpet and maintain that all is well in the Panglossian way. Original sin had its limitations as a doctrine, but one thing

23. See also Jenyns: 'Brutes are exempted from numberless anxieties, by that happy want of reflection on past, and apprehension of future sufferings, which are annexed to their inferiority' (*FIN*, 34–5). Johnson notes that animals, through their restricted time consciousness, 'feel few intellectual miseries or pleasures' (*Rambler* 41, *SJW*, 3.222).

24. Neiman, *Evil in Modern Thought*, 35.

it did have was great explanatory and imaginative force, and it is the main reason why pre-modern Augustinian theology did not have as much of a problem with pessimism as the eighteenth century did.[25]

Philosophically, then, Pope's *Essay* does not do much that authors such as King, but also Shaftesbury and Hutcheson, had not done before him. This was Samuel Johnson's main criticism of the work, which according to him offered little in intellectual depth, clarity, or novelty:

> Never were penury of knowledge and vulgarity of sentiment so happily disguised. The reader feels his mind full, though he learns nothing; and when he meets it in its new array, no longer knows the talk of his mother and his nurse. ('Life of Pope', *SJW*, 23.1219)

Other readers, too, remained dissatisfied. As Maynard Mack notes, by 1733 Pope 'may have wished to have it both ways', sympathising both with more traditional Christian views and with the new 'liberal theology' of the deists. The result was that the poem ended up satisfying neither free-thinkers such as Bolingbroke nor orthodox readers such as Jean-Pierre de Crousaz: it 'did not unequivocally embrace explicit Christian doctrines, but it did not unequivocally oppose them'. This ambiguity, however, may itself be significant: 'the duality of his poem expresses the duality of his age, and in all likelihood . . . of his mind'.[26]

It is perhaps precisely the duality that explains the *Essay*'s reach in the eighteenth century. This century, again, came to be deeply divided over the two strategies of optimism: the kind that denies that existence is full of evils, and the kind that admits evils but looks to a higher prospect for their resolution (for instance, in a future life). Leibniz and King had combined the two; later authors are not so comfortable. A sense seems to be rising that a choice needs to be made, one's allegiances declared one way or another; and that much depends on this. Wollaston was so obnoxious to Bolingbroke by falling into the second line of argument, which

25. Voltaire made this point several times, arguing that the British deists excised original sin to their detriment, since it left them with no way to explain evils: 'their system saps the very foundation of Christianity but explains nothing' ('All is Good', *Dictionary*, 48/ *OCV*.35.426). In his letter to Bertrand, he argued that while Pope's *Essay* attacked original sin, his Lisbon Poem defended it (*D*6738).

26. Mack, *Collected*, 205. Crousaz published two critiques of Pope's *Essay*, accusing Pope of what he considered to be a Leibnizian fatalism: *Examen de l'Essai de M. Pope sur l'homme* (1737) and one year later (following the *very* liberal French translation of the *Essay* by the Abbé du Resnel) *Commentaire sur la traduction en vers de M. l'abbé du Resnel, de l'Essai de M. Pope sur l'homme* (1738); the latter was in turn translated into English by Samuel Johnson in 1739 (*SJW*.17.xxii).

concedes much to the pessimists: too much in the Viscount's eyes. Pope on the other hand, like Bolingbroke himself, falls mainly into the first line of argument, which can be properly called optimistic in its efforts to play down the evils of existence and thereby demonstrate (with poetic, intuitive force) the goodness of both creation and creator. The innovative power of Pope's restatement of optimism lies not so much in its theoretical underpinnings but in the poetic, intuitive force of his demonstration: in what it does *poetically* with these fragments of philosophy. Had the *Essay* really been just that (an *essay*), it is unlikely to have had the effect that it did. It is not surprising, then, that Voltaire—the same Voltaire who in his youth wrote his own alternative to Pope's *Essay on Man*—would later seek to refute Pope (and perhaps that earlier version of himself) not in an essay or treatise, but in a poem and a story.

But Pope and Voltaire were not the only ones to use poetry in this way. Matthew Prior's poetic work *Solomon* is as opposed to Pope's *Essay* as Voltaire's 'Poem on the Lisbon Earthquake', but it is a different kind of opposition, since Prior falls into the second line of argument mentioned above: that which concedes the premise of pessimism while steering it towards a pious conclusion.[27] Opening with Cato's dictum, reported by Cicero and repeated by Bayle, that he would not want to relive his life from the beginning, *Solomon* consists of three books demonstrating the impossibility of this-worldly happiness by any road, whether by knowledge, pleasure, or power. As Prior summarises the pessimistic point of his book in his preface: 'The Pleasures of Life do not compensate the Miseries: Age steals upon Us unawares; and Death, as the only Cure of our Ills, ought to be expected, but not feared' (*Solomon*, 308).[28] The final part is especially glum, listing the evils of life and futility of improvement, the evils of body and soul, the misfortunes and betrayals that befall even the happiest lives, which

> Can fright, can alter, or can chain the Will;
> Their Ills all built on Life, that fundamental Ill.
> (*Solomon*, 367)

27. See also Albrecht von Haller's poem 'Über den Ursprung des Übels' ['On the Origin of Evil'] of 1734, where he emphasises the moral evils of creation in particular, but justifies these along broadly Leibnizian and Kingian lines. On the Book of Job, much translated in the eighteenth century, see chapter 7.

28. Unsurprisingly, Prior's *Solomon* is cited by Hume's Philo: specifically the lines 'Not satisfy'd with Life, afraid of Death' (*Solomon*, 379; Hume, *DNR*.X.72).

Paraphrasing the wisdom of Silenus, as Bayle had, Solomon calls happy those who have lived their lives and are about to die, happier still those who die just after birth, happiest of all those who have never seen the light of day:

> Who breathes, must suffer; and who thinks, must mourn;
> And He alone is bless'd, who ne'er was born.
> (*Solomon*, 367)

At the end of his dour complaint, however, Solomon turns to the heavens for enlightenment and is visited by an angel, who predicts even more sorrows in store for him and his progeny, but also predicts the coming of Christ, to whom it is given 'Passion, and Care, and Anguish, to destroy' (*Solomon*, 384). The angel counsels Solomon to endure his trials with patience and forbearance, which is the moral of the poem.[29]

Arthur Lovejoy mentions Prior's *Solomon* as one of two examples of the eighteenth-century 'pessimist—a type by no means unknown in the period'.[30] This characterisation should be qualified by the fact that *Solomon* actually represents one of optimism's strategies, albeit the one that gives most credence to pessimism's claims. It should also be noted that the context of *Solomon* is not a firmly theodicean one except in so far as it speaks to hope and consolation; it is more closely related to enlightened elaborations of the Book of Job, the plot and pathos of which it mirrors (at least to an eighteenth-century eye). As a philosophical poem, furthermore, it was not very successful, especially if compared with Pope's *Essay* or Voltaire's Poem. This mostly has to do with Prior's abilities as a poet,[31] but it may also have had something to do with a turn in precisely the philosophical tastes of the age. Above all, Pope's poem was *timely*: it had momentum in a way that pessimism did not, catching a wave on the tide of deism and linking into the great chain of being, which was so appealing to the eighteenth-century imagination in its sidelining and eventual erosion of the idea of original sin, while remaining controversial for precisely the same reason.

29. Thus aligning Prior with Johnson's comment that the point of thinking about evil must be to help us bear it (see below, p. 124). Note that Prior lays little emphasis on expectations of a future life.

30. Lovejoy, *Great Chain*, 209, 358n.; his other example is 'Rousseau's Pessimist', on which, see chapter 6.

31. Thus Johnson convicts Solomon of 'tediousness' ('Life of Prior', *SJW*, 22.727–8).

This variety of optimism is initially as convincing to Voltaire as it was to Bolingbroke, Shaftesbury, Jenyns, and Francis Hutcheson, the latter of whom saw nothing very problematic about 'the present Order of Nature, in which *Good* appears far superior to *Evil*'.[32] Thus the problem of evil seems to have been defused for now; the pessimist challenge defeated or at deflected; the first strategy of optimism victorious. But appearances can be deceiving. *Solomon* should remind us that Pope's was not the only road available to those seeking to justify God's ultimate goodness or to contemplate the trials of existence in a way that did not run counter to piety and faith. Prior's more traditional line of thought remains influential throughout the eighteenth century, rising in its interpretations of the Book of Job as well as in the more 'pessimistic' theodicies of authors such as Wollaston. This is important to note, for if Voltaire's later challenges strike home against authors such as Pope, *they are not even aimed* at the more understated variety of optimism (if it deserves the name) represented by Wollaston, Prior, and Samuel Johnson.

Jenyns and Johnson

What if the problem with Pope and Bolingbroke was not that they were *too* optimistic, but that they were *not optimistic enough*? There may not be much that is original in *A Free Inquiry into the Nature and Origin of Evil* by the English MP Soame Jenyns (1704–1787), but there is something refreshingly bold in his attempt to out-Pope Pope himself, and indeed to upstage the entire history of theodicy, a subject that 'has never been attended to with that diligence it deserves, nor with that success, which might have been hoped for from that little that has been bestowed upon it' (*FIN*, 2). Lovejoy calls the book 'one of the typical theodicies of the middle of the century', but this is right only in so far as it stands directly in the Kingian–Popean tradition, closely knit together with the notion of a 'great chain of being'.[33] I will here focus only on Jenyns's discussion of natural evil, which presents a curious *mélange* of the typical, the idiosyncratic, and the downright silly.

Conceptually, Jenyns takes over the Kingian tripartite division of evils of imperfection, natural evils, and moral evils (though he expands the latter category with two chapters on political and religious evils), while

32. Hutcheson, *An Essay on the Nature and Conduct of the Passions and Affections* (1728), 182.

33. Lovejoy, *Chain of Being*, 209.

taking a very Baylean line on natural (i.e. physical) evils specifically, which he defines as 'the sufferings of sensitive Beings only'.[34] What that means concretely is that an earthquake, for instance, is not an evil in itself, but only in so far as it is *experienced* as an evil: 'tempests, inundations and earthquakes, with all the disorders of the material World, are no farther Evils than as they affect the sensitive: so that under this head can be only comprehended pains of body, and inquietudes of mind' (*FIN*, 45). This is precisely the Baylean conception, in so far as it includes animal suffering as well as psychological suffering, both of which were often excluded or sidelined in traditional discussions of evil. Furthermore, Jenyns is adamant in resisting any attempt to deny the reality of such natural evils: 'That these are real evils, I readily acknowledge; and if anyone is philosopher enough to doubt of it, I shall only beg leave to refer him to a severe fit of sickness, or a tedious law-suit, for farther satisfaction' (*FIN*, 45–6).[35]

Such natural evils include psychological suffering, at least for humans, whose grievances include 'poverty, labour, inquietudes of mind, pains of body, and death', but Jenyns justifies such evils by an argument of necessity: man could not have been exempted from these 'so long as he continued to be Man' (*FIN*, 49). This again is the Kingian–Popean line, also taken by Bolingbroke, having to do with the great chain of being: the 'evils' of existence could not have been avoided without the loss of greater goods or the admission of greater evils; the only alternative would have been for God not to have created us at all (*FIN*, 49). All of this is, as Lovejoy notes, a move 'typical' of the mid-eighteenth century; if only Jenyns had left it there. But it seems to be an indefeasible instinct of these optimists, having made the initial point that evils are unavoidable, to want to try to efface them after all, almost as an afterthought, sensing perhaps the intuitive strength of the pessimist challenge, which rides on the apparent disjunction between the perfect goodness attributed to God and the horrors experienced as part of his creation.

Pope counters this intuitive force with poetry (a move that will be countered by poetry in turn); other authors are not so poetically endowed.

34. From Bayle and Leibniz onwards, the terms 'physical evil' and 'natural evil' are mostly equivalent, with francophone writers tending to prefer the former and anglophones the latter: thus when Jenyns and others speak of 'natural evil', this is the same as Bayle's *mal physique*.

35. But he later qualifies that while the maxim that 'Pain is no Evil' is 'downright nonsense' in so far as it applies to individual sufferers, it is 'an undoubted truth' in so far as it 'affects the universal System' (*FIN*, 20). The same points are made by Shaftesbury, *Moralists*, *CMM*, 253; and *Inquiry*, *CMM*, 169.

Jenyns gratefully cites Pope from time to time, but mostly he repeats the familiar point that many so-called evils are necessary for our well-being: we need things like fear, anger, and pain for our self-preservation, and so forth. At the same time, Jenyns also seems to sense that this is not enough. After all, what about all the other 'innumerable miseries' of human life in particular, such as 'diseases of the body, and afflictions of the mind, in which Nature seems to play the Tyrant'? In a free flow of passages thick with pessimistic pathos, Jenyns writes that we cannot 'avoid seeing every moment with horror numbers of our fellow-creatures condemned to tedious and intolerable miseries, some expiring on racks, other roasting in flames, some starving in dungeons, others raving in mad houses; some broiling in fevers, others groaning whole months under the exquisite tortures of gout and stone' (*FIN*, 58–9). But Jenyns thinks that the very fact of such horrors suggests that there is a pivotal *connection* between pain and pleasure, and that there is something abstractly positive about pain even when it serves no perceptible purpose to the sufferer:

> From hence therefore I am persuaded, that there is something in the abstract nature of pain conducive to pleasure; that the sufferings of individuals are absolutely necessary to universal happiness; and that, from connections to us inconceivable, it was impracticable for Omnipotence to produce the one, without at the same time permitting the other. . . . This universal connection of pain with pleasure seems, I think, strongly to intimate, that pain abstractedly considered must have its uses . . . (*FIN*, 60–2)

If King and Leibniz had tentatively mentioned the possibility of beneficent aliens somehow raising the level of happiness in the universe of a whole, Jenyns takes this hypothesis to the next level. Maybe, he philosophises, the sufferings of humans on earth somehow affect those living on another planet, so that even the miseries of particular beings are conducive to the happiness of the whole; maybe, just as we draw benefits and even enjoyment from animal suffering, there are superior beings benefiting similarly from ours, either by watching our sufferings or even by manipulating and exacerbating them (*FIN*, 62–66). Our individual sufferings, he concludes, should be seen as a kind of 'necessary taxes, which every member of this great Republic of the Universe is obliged to pay towards the support of the Community' (*FIN*, 71–2).

All of this is rather baffling to read: one cannot help but wonder what on earth Jenyns thought he was doing, and many optimists must have read him wincingly. After all, the strange hypothesis of superior beings delighting in torturing humans surely makes the theodicean problem *worse*: How could God have created a system hinging not on universal love but on angelic *schadenfreude*? Jenyns, however, is pleased with his solution, which he sees as the first real answer to the problem of evil—one, furthermore, that makes no reference to the doctrine of original sin (which he finds nonsensical), and that includes the possibility of transmigration as more consistent with God's wisdom and goodness than the Christian doctrine of heaven and hell (*FIN*, 74).

Among those bemused by Jenyns's book was Samuel Johnson: rarely, if ever, was the Doctor so annoyed by a piece of writing as he was by the *Free Inquiry*. In general, when reviewing other people's work, Johnson took care to be restrained in his criticism, but he made an exception for Jenyns, whose book he reviewed in three instalments of the *Literary Magazine* in May–July 1757.[36] As Brian Hanley notes, Johnson seems to find Jenyns to fit the category of authors who should be exempted from 'critical reticence':[37] authors, that is, who 'attack . . . those truths which are of importance to the happiness of mankind'.[38]

Part of Johnson's critique boils down to an accusation of unoriginality: he accuses Jenyns of taking most of his arguments from Pope and asks dismissively, 'Why he that has nothing to write, should desire to be a writer?' (*SJW*, 17.399–400).[39] But he also calls Jenyns out on some specific philosophical inconsistencies. For instance, Jenyns defines natural evil as any evil that is experienced by a sensitive being, and Johnson agrees with this: but this definition also means that some of Jenyns's other arguments, borrowed from Pope and others, don't work, such as the *aesthetic strategy*. Jenyns had used the example of harmony being formed by trebles, tenors, and basses, which Johnson says is an elaboration of Pope's metaphor of oaks and weeds.[40] But, as Johnson points out, it makes no sense to speak of imperfection in any of these unconscious parts, if evil can only inhere in our experience:

36. Johnson, 'Review of Soame Jenyns' *A Free Inquiry Into the Nature and Origin of Evil*', in *SJW*, 17.387–432.

37. Hanley, *Samuel Johnson*, 121.

38. Johnson, *Rambler* 93, 5 February 1751 (*SJW*, 4.133).

39. Johnson also cannot see much sense in the entire notion of chain of being, which left him with nothing but 'doubt and uncertainty' (*SJW*, 17.403).

40. Pope, *EM*, II.39–40: 'Ask of thy mother earth, why oaks are made / Taller or stronger than the weeds they shade?' See also Shaftesbury, *The Moralists* (*CMM*, 239, 241, 244) for the aesthetic strategy.

> Perfection or imperfection of unconscious beings has no meaning as referred to themselves; the bass and the treble are equally perfect; the mean and magnificent apartments feel no pleasure or pain from the comparison. . . . *There is no evil but must inhere in a conscious being, or be referred to it; that is, evil must be felt before it is evil.* (*SJW*, 17.401; my emphasis)

The criticism may not seem entirely fair, since Jenyns was speaking of evils of imperfection specifically, not of natural evil (he identifies only the latter with our experience), but Johnson's point seems to be precisely that the very category of 'evils of imperfection' is nonsensical: the only concept of evil that can have any real meaning for us has to refer to our experience. For what is evil that has no relation to *any* kind of experience? This, again, is precisely the Baylean line of argument, which would also be taken up by Hume.[41]

Johnson takes issue in particular with the efforts, by Jenyns as well as Pope, to alleviate 'those evils which we are doomed to suffer' (*SJW*, 17.405). He goes through Jenyns's examples one by one, from the benefits of poverty and secret gratifications of sickness to the pleasures of madness, pausing at length on the idea that the poor are compensated for their suffering by being free from other 'little vexations': if this is happiness, it is like 'that of a malefactor who ceases to feel the cords that bind him when the pincers are tearing his flesh.'[42] Anyone who writes in this way of other people's suffering proves nothing but the limits of philosophy: 'Life must be seen before it can be known. This author and Pope perhaps never saw the miseries which they imagine thus easy to be borne' (*SJW*, 17.407). As for Jenyns's suggestion that, just as we use animals for food and diversion, maybe higher beings use us in the same way, Johnson's mockery is undisguised: 'Some of them, perhaps, are virtuosi, and delight in the operations of an asthma, as a human philosopher in the effects of the air pump. To swell a man with a tympany is as good sport as to blow a frog' (*SJW*, 17.419). Such conjectures may be 'entertaining' enough, says Johnson, but they are not helpful; indeed, they are anathema to any valuable discussion of the

41. Johnson himself owned the 1702 edition of Bayle's *Dictionnaire*, which he called 'a very useful work for those to consult who love the biographical part of literature, which is what I love most' (Boswell, *Life of Johnson*, I.425). See Donald Greene, *Johnson's Library*, 34–5.

42. Probably an allusion to the gruelling torture and execution by drawing and quartering of Robert-François Damien, the would-be assassinator of Louis XV, earlier that year: see Schwartz, *Samuel Johnson and the Problem of Evil*, 34; Greene, '"Pictures to the Mind"', 141–2.

problem of evil, where the whole point is to offer consolation or at least 'patience' in the face of suffering: 'The only reason why we should contemplate evil is, that we may bear it better, and I am afraid nothing is much more placidly endured, for the sake of making others sport' (*SJW*, 17.421).

So the core problem is twofold: not only does Jenyns's argument fail to help us, but it also fails to explain anything. In the end, everything is brought back to natural evil, which is supposed to be useful to the universe 'by some inconceivable means'. This, Johnson tells us, does not help us any further: 'There was enough in this question inconceivable before, and we have little advantage from a new inconceivable solution' (*SJW*, 17.418).[43]

But if this conclusion explains the *theoretical* point of Johnson's review, it does not perhaps explain his vehemence. For one thing, Jenyns's was surely not the first unoriginal or uninstructive intervention in the muddy waters of theodicy.[44] For another, Johnson himself was far from being a pessimist in the Baylean sense: his pessimism does not serve a deeper anti-theodicean argument.[45] On the contrary: like Wollaston, Johnson accepts a pessimist description of reality in this world, but seeks to ward off any inference from this to an impious conclusion. He does this not just by referring us to a future life (though he does this too),[46] but especially by again trying to close the gap that had been growing, in the first half of the eighteenth century, between moral evil and physical evil. These, he argues in his fifth *Sermon*, are 'for the most part so closely united, that, to avoid misery, we must avoid sin, and that while it is in our power to be virtuous, it is in our power to be happy' (*SJW*, 14.55). Very 'few of the evils of life can justly be ascribed to God,' he continues, since most of them are 'either imaginary, or the consequences, either of our own faults, or the faults of others' (*SJW*, 14.57–9). Even these evils, furthermore, can be assuaged by the practice of piety and patience, which will foster our happiness even in this world, while preparing us for the next (*SJW*, 14.59–64).

This argument seems a little curious when juxtaposed with Johnson's scathing review of Jenyns. Johnson may have been more willing than

43. This is exactly Bayle's point in his article *Rufinus*: If we are going to end with inconceivability, why not start there? See my *Bayle, Jurieu*, chapter 4.

44. Johnson offers a similar criticism of Pope's *Essay* in his 'Life of Pope' (*SJW*, 23.1217–21).

45. But let us be equally wary of reducing Johnson's pessimism to his tendency to depression.

46. Though not emphatically: Johnson does not seem to want his argument to hinge on this point (*SJW*, 14.62). But see, e.g., *Adventurer* 120 (29 December 1753), where he sounds much like Wollaston: 'The miseries of life, may, perhaps, afford some proof of a future state, compared as well with the mercy as the justice of God' (*SJW*, 2. 469).

Jenyns to admit that 'the world [is] full of misery and disorder' (*SJW*, 14.55),[47] but even Jenyns had emphatically listed the evils of existence: he had certainly not *denied* them. Furthermore, in trying to show that the things we customarily think of as evils are often imaginary, or are not as bad as we make them out to be, Johnson is himself not far removed from what Jenyns and other optimists (such as Bolingbroke) had been trying to achieve. Johnson's theoretical objections, then, seem to have less to do with the project of optimism itself (that is, the attempt to prove that existence is a good thing and we should be grateful for it) than with the *way* in which optimism is defended by authors of 'typical theodicies' such as Jenyns. Johnson's problem with Jenyns and others following in the wake of Pope is that they are trying *to prove too much* in their rather forceful demonstration of the *entire system's* happiness, and in linking the miserable parts too adamantly and concretely to the beatific whole; the last straw being Jenyns's conjecture of superior life forms profiting from our earthly sufferings.[48] We also seem to see, in Johnson's review, the beginnings of a concern with fatalism that will haunt optimism (*and pessimism*) for centuries to come: if everything is good as it is, including all our pains and passions and sufferings, then surely this will demotivate us from aiming for improvement, whether by cultivating a practice of patience and piety, or by battling social injustices such as poverty and inequality.[49]

Finally, the biting tone of Johnson's review seems to be at least partly rooted in a different concern, having to do with *sensitivity*. As several commentators have noted, Johnson was particularly outraged by 'the disparity between the enormity of the subject and the shallowness of Jenyns's treatment of it': the disparity, that is, between Jenyns's light touch and the gravity of the topic under consideration.[50] Johnson's deepest objection seems to be the one phrased in his opening lines: that Jenyns 'decides too easily upon questions out of the reach of human determination, with too

47. See also *Rasselas*: 'Human life is everywhere a state in which much is to be endured and little to be enjoyed' (*SJW*, 16.50; see Gwin Kolb's footnote for other versions of this remark).

48. Recall that Leibniz also made reference to hypothetical higher beings, but he did so more tentatively, in order to raise the happiness of the universe *as a whole*, not to justify our particular sufferings.

49. See *SJW*, 17.409 (on poverty), and see below, p. 135, on 'the hope objection'.

50. Schwartz, *Samuel Johnson*, 35; see Hanley, *Samuel Johnson*, 119, who adds that Johnson was also objecting to Jenyns's hubris. Perhaps a similar sentiment is expressed in Johnson's critique of Pope's *Essay*: 'The subject is perhaps not very proper for poetry, and the poet was not sufficiently master of his subject' ('Life of Pope', *SJW*, 23.1217–18).

little consideration of mortal weakness, and with too much vivacity for the necessary caution' (*SJW*, 17.397).

This is a criticism that is paradigmatic for the age, and striking in its novelty: no such objections were made to theodicies in the seventeenth or even early eighteenth century—at least, by no one but Bayle. Traditional treatments of the origins of evil were lodged firmly in an intuitive sense that the very notion that there might be anything problematic about creation ('complaint') is ungrateful and immoral in its way; an intuition that could be called *the moral objection to anti-theodicy*. Bayle, as we have seen, turns this around and argues that there is something insensitive and even immoral about the way certain theodicies try to explain away the evils of existence; we could call it *the moral objection to theodicy*. It is this objection that will arise again in Voltaire and Hume, just as it arises now in Johnson: strikingly so, since Johnson is not even on Bayle's side. Like the traditionalists, Johnson thinks complaint is ungrateful and contrary to fostering patience, which is (he repeats in both the Sermon and the Review) the entire point of thinking about the origins of evil. Nevertheless, he also recognises that if complaint is problematic, it is not quite so problematic as the alternative, if the alternative is Jenyns's inflated hyper-optimism.

What Johnson's confrontation with Jenyns suggests, therefore, is that while the arguments on evil have not significantly changed, the moral and emotive background has. This goes to show that much of the work to turn the early modern consciousness with regard to pessimism and the problem of evil has already been done by the mid-eighteenth century; and this is why the time is so very ripe for Voltaire, and for *Candide*.

Voltaire's Volte-Face?

Lionel Trilling, in his book *Sincerity and Authenticity*, makes an important comment about the effect of Rousseau's *Confessions* on our reading of his other works: 'Anyone who responds to Rousseau's ideas in a positive way must wonder whether they would have made an equal effect upon him if they had not been backed by the *Confessions*.'[51] We could ask a similar thing about Voltaire's writings on optimism: Would they have made a similar effect if they had not been backed by the Lisbon earthquake? Both *Candide* and the 'Poem on the Lisbon Disaster' lean heavily on their

51. Trilling, *Sincerity and Authenticity*, 24.

a posteriori force, their ability to make the doctrine of optimism be *felt*, almost viscerally, as something deeply out of touch with the way things 'really' are. As an exercise in counter-optimism, it is an exceptionally effective one, but we might ask ourselves how well it would have worked had 'Lisbon' never occurred.

So was Lisbon *the* paradigmatic event of the eighteenth century? Many scholars seem to assume that it was, and focus their efforts on explaining *why* it was. 'The Lisbon earthquake had an unprecedentedly large intellectual impact in the eighteenth century precisely because it conflicted so grievously with the upbeat picture of benevolent order', writes Charles Taylor.[52] And Susan Neiman juxtaposes Lisbon and Auschwitz as pivotal events that were each 'seen by its era as paradigmatic' of natural and moral evil, respectively: 'The eighteenth century used the word *Lisbon* much as we use the word *Auschwitz* today.'[53] To some extent, such sweeping statements may seem justified: Lisbon did devastate, as 'the largest documented seismic event to have affected Europe', perhaps even 'the first modern disaster'.[54] But the comparison with Auschwitz is unhelpful. Some of the literature makes it sound as though the earthquake was physically and isolatedly responsible for effecting a sea change in the European consciousness, not to mention in the mind of Voltaire himself. In recent years, scholars have grown uncomfortable with the picture thus presented, which is a decidedly high-brow interpretation of events: the day-to-day devout did not adhere to the deistic hyper-optimism of Pope and Bolingbroke, and had no reason to see Lisbon as its prima-facie refutation. Optimism was the province of intellectuals, and it was a small group of intellectuals who made such a *philosophical* fuss over Lisbon.[55] The mainline response was perfectly traditional: theologians reinforcing

52. Taylor, *Sources of the Self*, 559.

53. Neiman, *Evil*, 239, 1. She later specifies: 'Lisbon revealed how remote the world is from the human; Auschwitz revealed the remoteness of humans from themselves' (239–40).

54. Chester, 'The 1755 Lisbon Earthquake', 363; Dynes, 'The Lisbon Earthquake of 1755', 34.

55. See, e.g., Gisler, 'Optimism and Theodicy', who believes the influence of the Lisbon earthquake (and especially Voltaire's interpretation of it) has been overemphasised by eighteenth-century studies; and Pearson, *Fables of Reason*, 112, who thinks it has been overemphasised by Voltaire scholarship, especially with regard to *Candide*. See also the essays in Braun and Radner, *The Lisbon Earthquake of 1755*; and Lauer and Unger, *Das Erdbeben von Lissabon*.

traditional providential explanations to a wider audience emotionally but perhaps not '*conceptually* devastated' by the tidings of disaster.[56]

It is true that Lisbon provoked a cascade of responses, but it was precisely that: a *cascade*. Philosophers reacting to Lisbon were often reacting rather to each other, and to one man most of all. It was Voltaire who turned Lisbon into *the philosopher's earthquake*, with the result that this particular sample of physical evil came to be seen as a problem for God's goodness in a way that earlier disasters were not. And so we could also pose the counterfactual question the other way round: Would Lisbon have made an equal effect on the eighteenth century if Voltaire had not taken up his pen when he did? I ask this purely as a moment of caution, and in recognition of the fact that a very powerful narrative or even mythology has sprung up around Lisbon and Voltaire, which other scholars are painstakingly trying to unpick. I do not want to deny that there is an important moment here, but I do wish to place this moment in a wider, deeper context, for while the earthquake may have come out of nowhere, the writings that followed certainly did not. It is worth at least considering the possibility that Lisbon was over-appropriated by the philosophers, and over-interpreted by historians in their wake.

Similar questions can be raised with regard to the equally pervasive narrative of Voltaire's 'volte-face', according to which the playwright and philosopher changes his mind about optimism over the Lisbon earthquake. It is, in the works of some scholars, almost as though we could speak of a *pre-Lisbon Voltaire* as we do of a pre-Critical Kant. Here too there seems to be good reason. It is true that in his early works Voltaire seems more amenable to optimism and providence, even writing his own version of Pope's *Essay* (in which both Pope and 'le grand Leibniz' are mentioned approvingly),[57] and later introducing angelic characters into his stories commenting that 'if all is not well, all is tolerable'.[58] Indeed, we can catch him criticising Pas-

56. Neiman, *Evil*, 240. For examples of the mainline theological responses, see the articles by, e.g., Georgi, Ingram, and Gisler in Braun and Radner's volume *The Lisbon Earthquake of 1755*.

57. Voltaire, *Discours en vers sur l'homme* (published 1738–1742), *OCV*.17.513. Voltaire admired both Shaftesbury and Bolingbroke, and wrote two works in defence of the latter: *Défense de milord Bolingbroke* (1752) and *Examen important de milord Bolingbroke* (1766), though these mostly discuss toleration and biblical criticism.

58. Voltaire, *Le Monde comme il va* (1748): the point is that the higher powers realise they must 'laisser aller *le Monde comme il va*'; since '*Si tout n'est pas bien, tout est passable*' (*OCV*.30B.63). The same point is repeated in his essay 'Si l'homme est né méchant et enfant du diable' (1768); see Wootton, 'Introduction', xvi–xvii. For a wider discussion see Barber, *Leibniz in France*, chapter 12; Pearson, *Fables of Reason*.

cal for precisely his pessimism and misanthropy in the twenty-fifth of his *Lettres philosophiques* (also known as the *Letters on England*):[59]

> It seems to me that, in general, the spirit in which Pascal wrote these *Pensées* was to portray man in a hateful light. He is determined to depict us all as evil and unhappy. . . . He vilifies the human race eloquently. I venture to champion humanity against this sublime misanthropist; I venture to assert that we are neither so wicked nor so wretched as he says. (*Letters*, 120)[60]

However, as David Wootton has argued, the story can also be told in a different way, 'so as to emphasize continuity rather than change'. He notes that the early Voltaire repeatedly makes arguments similar to those of the dervish at the end of *Candide*, suggesting that God is not concerned with human happiness.[61] Voltaire's philosophical *contes* or stories of the 1740s meanwhile increasingly contrast the optics of optimism with what might be called *poetics of pessimism*, charged as they are with heated descriptions of evils, and especially (at this stage) of *moral* evils. Thus *Memnon, ou La Sagesse humaine* (1749) concludes with a dialogue between a one-eyed human sufferer and an alien or angelic spokesperson:

> 'But are those poets and philosophers wrong, then, who tell us that everything is for the best?' said Memnon.
>
> 'No, they are right, when we consider things in relation to the gradation of the whole universe,' said the spirit.
>
> 'Oh! I shall never believe it till I recover my eye again,' said the unfortunate Memnon. (*Memnon*, 394/*OCV*.30B, 267)[62]

59. Voltaire first published his *Letters concerning the English Nation* in English in 1733 (though he had written them in French: see Nicholas Cronk's notes in his edition of the work, xxxvi); however, the twenty-fifth letter first appeared in French in the *Lettres philosophiques* of 1734.

60. Thus Voltaire writes to Pierre Robert Le Cornier de Cideville (20 September 1735, *D*915), that Pope's *Essay* constitutes 'la paraphrase' of Voltaire's remarks on Pascal in the twenty-fifth *Lettre philosophique*. See also Voltaire's poem *Le Mondain* of 1736, which grew out of the twenty-fifth *Lettre* and develops its argument on the possibility of human happiness in this world (Wade, *The Intellectual Development of Voltaire*, 355).

61. Wootton, 'Introduction', xvi. See also the sixth *Discours en vers sur l'homme* (*OCV*.17.513–21).

62. Translation (Peter Eckler) adapted slightly. See also *Zadig*, where the angel Jesrad gives a little exposition of optimism (blending Pope and Leibniz loosely); Zadig begins to ask questions ('But . . .'), but the angel flies away. The story ends well, almost *too* well, in the original version, but Voltaire rewrites it to tone down what Pearson calls its 'fairy-tale' ending (Pearson, *Fables*, 79).

After *Candide*, furthermore, 'Voltaire was perfectly prepared to revert to optimistic arguments'[63]—for instance, in his *Histoire de Jenni* of 1775, which 'bears the marks of an enduring sympathy with the Leibnizian conception of a benevolent and rational God who has done His best'.[64] This did not, however, prevent him from sounding overtly pessimistic at other times, especially in his letters, which is why Schopenhauer so liked to cite passages such as the following:

> Happiness is but a dream, and pain is real; I have experienced it now for eighty years. All I know is to resign myself to this and to tell myself that flies are born to be eaten by spiders, and humans to be devoured by sorrows [*chagrins*].[65]

Thus Voltaire seems to go back and forth on the question of optimism, much as Candide does, never quite opting for pessimism but ending up in an in-between position, which is as interesting for what it tells us about Voltaire as it is for what it tells us about the complications of these very categories in the early modern period.

I will not untangle the question of Voltaire's volte-face in much detail: the existing literature is rich and vast, and I won't go over all of this much-covered ground again. But no discussion of pessimism and the problem of evil in the eighteenth century can be complete without some reference to Voltaire, whose intervention in these debates was one of the most influential ones, culminating in the popularisation of the terms 'optimism' and 'pessimism' alike. There was apparently something in Voltaire's Lisbon writings that fitted the wider cultural feeling, in possession of enough 'momentum' to suggest that the world was ready for *Candide*, as it was not quite ready for *Xenophanes*. It seems we have to go back to Lisbon after all.

63. Wootton, 'Introduction', xvi–xvii.

64. Pearson, *Fables*, 72. See especially the 'Dialogue de Freind [*sic*] et de Birton sur l'athéisme' (chs. 8–11; *OCV*.76.93–122), especially chapter 9, where natural disasters such as earthquakes are explained as 'accidents that have attacked certain wheels of the machine of this universe' (*OCV*.76.103; my translation).

65. To the marquis de Florian, 16 March 1774 (*D*18857; my translation), which is cited by Schopenhauer twice (*WWR*.II.576 and *PP*.I.356). See also Voltaire to the comtesse de Lutzelbourg, 19 March 1760: 'nous laisserons vous et moi madame ce monde-ci aussi sot, aussi méchant que nous l'avons trouvé en y arrivant' (*D*8811; cited by Schopenhauer in *PP*.I.274). But earlier letters sometimes manifest a similar pessimism; for example, to the marquis d'Argenson, 19 July 1748 (*D*3723).

The Philosopher's Earthquake

The Lisbon earthquake occurred on All Saints' Day, 1 November 1755.[66] Voltaire was in Geneva at the time, where the first reports reached him in the course of that month. These were all the more shocking for having been exaggerated, estimating 100,000 dead instead of a more likely 15,000–20,000, as Voltaire commented a few weeks later: 'we are now told that half that city is still standing'.[67] But the first shock, at least, was terrible. As Voltaire would later write to his friend, the duchess of Saxe-Gotha, while sending her a copy of the Lisbon Poem, he had been angry (*fâché*) at earthquakes while writing it.[68] Other letters too bring out this sense of cosmic outrage, which for Voltaire was directed, early on, not just at the earthquake but at those philosophers he associated with optimism, especially Leibniz and Pope, but also Shaftesbury and Bolingbroke.[69] 'It would be really be quite difficult to work out how the laws of physics create such horrendous disasters in the best of all possible worlds,' Voltaire wrote to one of his correspondents on 24 November 1755.[70] And a few days later, to another: 'If Pope had been in Lisbon would he have dared to say, all is well?'[71] And again, to the same: 'The city of Lisbon swallowed up by an earthquake; a hundred thousand souls buried under the ruins: . . . see there a terrible argument against *optimism*.'[72]

By early December, drafts of the 'Poem on the Lisbon Disaster' were circulating or being read out by Voltaire himself; after revision, he published it in March 1756, together with another philosophical poem, 'La Loi naturelle', which he had written some years earlier (he would refer to both poems as his 'sermons').[73] Part of the reason for the Lisbon Poem's early circulation seems to have been to test whether the verses were 'orthodox'

66. On the geological and practical aspects of the earthquake, see Mendes-Victor et al., *The 1755 Lisbon Earthquake.*

67. To François-Louis Allamand, 16 December 1755 (*D*6629/*CRT*, 132). Estimates of the death toll continue to vary widely; here, I am following Martínez Solares and López Arroyo ('The Great Historical 1755 Earthquake', 279), who estimate 15,000–20,000 casualties overall, with up to 10,000 in Lisbon alone.

68. To the duchess of Saxe-Gotha, 1 January 1756 (*D*6666).

69. Recall that the term optimism, coined by the Jesuits, at this time was strongly pejorative; see chapter 2. Voltaire groups these four authors together in his letter to Bertrand (*D*6738).

70. To Jean-Robert Tronchin, 24 November 1755 (*D*6597/*CRT*, 132).

71. To Bertrand, 28 November 1755 (*D*6603; my translation).

72. To Bertrand, 30 November 1755 (*D*6605; Voltaire's emphasis, my translation).

73. Originally titled 'La religion naturelle', this poem was written in 1752 in refutation of La Mettrie's moral relativism (Pearson, *Voltaire Almighty*, 225).

enough: 'I think they are; but I'm afraid of being a bad theologian.'[74] Voltaire's doubts are confirmed when some of his early readers criticise the Poem for not explicitly mentioning a future state, and thus abandoning the reader 'in depression and in doubt'.[75]

Voltaire himself thinks this criticism is misplaced, since the Poem is only directed at those who think all things are as good as they can be in *this world* (the position he associates with optimism):

> The question at issue is not this one of hope. The sole question concerns the axiom, or rather the joke, that all is well as it is, everything is as it ought to be, and universal happiness here and now is the consequence of the miseries suffered right now by each creature.[76]

He defends his own orthodoxy by pointing out that it is Pope who should be criticised for attacking the notion of original sin, which Voltaire's 'sermon' effectively defends: the very experience of human unhappiness suggests that God's work must have been altered from its original conception. Nevertheless, Voltaire is ready to make some concessions in the Poem, integrating the element of hope in particular. But he will not deny the Poem's core message, which is a profoundly Baylean one:

> the heart of the work remains unhappily the presentation of an incontestable truth. There is evil on earth. And you're laughing at me if you say that a thousand miserable lives are the embodiment of happiness. Yes, there is evil, and few people would want to start their lives over again, perhaps not one in a hundred thousand.[77]

Thus Voltaire takes issue with the optimists' rejection of the pessimist premise, and with their playing down or denial of the evils of existence.

74. To the comte d'Argental, 15 February 1756 (*D*6734; my translation). Later, however, Voltaire will express the fear that he is being *too orthodox* ('trop orthodoxe') to d'Argental (22 March 1756, *D*6798); and write to Cideville (12 April 1756, *D*6821) that he seeks to offend 'ni les esprits trop philosophes ni les esprits trop crédules'.

75. To Élie Bertrand, 18 February 1756 (*D*6738/*CRT*, 133).

76. Ibid. See David Bentley Hart, *The Doors of the Sea*, 22, who notes that 'Voltaire's poem is not directly concerned with the God of Christian doctrine', with its narrative of a 'wounded creation' and the promise of redemption, but 'concerns a God who directly governs a cosmos that is exactly as he intended it': the doctrine of optimism.

77. Ibid. If this sounds like Bayle's thought experiment, that's because it is, and it appears again in the Poem itself ('nul ne voudrait renaître'), where Voltaire adds a very Baylean footnote: 'It is difficult to find anyone willing to live the same life over again, and experience again everything they experienced the first time' (*CRT*, 107/*OCV*.45a.347).

But his main objection to optimism is a *moral* one, and it is precisely that optimism is depressive or 'désespérant':

> We need a God who speaks to the human species. Optimism leads to despair. It is a cruel philosophy hiding under a reassuring name.[78]

This may seem counter-intuitive to modern readers, especially to those familiar with titles such as Noam Chomsky's *Optimism over Despair*. After all, what could be *less* despairing and *more* hopeful than *optimism*, the view that existence is crucially a good thing?

THE CONSOLATION OBJECTION

There are two reasons why optimism fosters despair according to Voltaire. One we have already encountered (and will encounter again): it is the moral objection that optimism, in so far as it denies or plays down the evils of existence, is deeply unconsoling and uncompassionate; that it makes our suffering worse. We could call it *the consolation objection*, and it is what explains the fierceness of Voltaire's words: that optimism is not just an unsatisfying philosophy, but an outright *cruel* one. By drawing us into the realities of suffering, the Poem offers a kind of touchstone for different kinds of consolation. Would the victims of Lisbon, for instance, be consoled [*consolés*] by being told that their sufferings are good for the whole, or that they are of no concern to God? 'Cruel ones! do not add outrage to my pains' (*OCV*.45a.340).[79] This is not consolation but its very opposite: 'Sad calculators of human misery / Do not console me, you only make my pains worse' (*OCV*.45a.340).[80]

This is the crux of the Poem, which combines a Baylean appeal to experience (and especially to physical evils) with an equally Baylean appeal to compassion and consolation. If the universe is not enough to refute optimism, then the heart surely must be: 'The universe belies you, and

78. Ibid. (*D*6738/*CRT*, 134). See 'All is Good': 'Far from consoling us, the opinion of the best of possible worlds is unhopeful [*désespérante*] for the philosophers who hold it' (my translation). 'Désespérant' is untranslatable; Fletcher renders it as 'depressive' (*Dictionary*, 49); Wootton as 'drives' or 'leads to despair' (*CRT*, 142, 134/*OCV*.35.427).

79. 'Cruels! à mes douleurs n'ajoutez point l'outrage.' I am at times replacing McCabe's poetic translations with more literal ones; I have also corrected his use of italics throughout.

80. 'Tristes calculateurs des misères humaines, / Ne me consolez point; vous aigrissez mes peines.' Note that this objection works both ways: if Voltaire was right in objecting to providential explanations of Lisbon, surely David Bentley Hart is equally right in calling out the callousness of those who proclaimed the vindication of atheism in the wake of the 2004 tsunami (Hart, *The Doors of the Sea*, 7–8).

your heart / Refutes a hundred times your mind's conceit' ('Lisbon', 4/*OCV*.45a.341).[81] This juxtaposition between *cœur* and *esprit*, and the accompanying accusation of heartlessness on the part of the optimists, is a very deliberate move on Voltaire's part, one that matters a lot to him. The right kind of consolation, the right kind of speaking about suffering, must come out of a sense of *generosity*, an awareness of the fragility of life, to which even the happiest of us are bound by our humanity. As Voltaire wrote to Nicolas Claude Thieriot, not long after the Lisbon Poem:

> When I spoke in verse about the miseries of my fellow human beings I did so out of pure generosity, for, having made allowances for my uncertain good health, I am so happy that it makes me feel ashamed.[82]

The intuition behind this statement may well be a crucial one: as Wootton notes, Voltaire 'constantly declares both that he is happy and that others suffer', but 'he objects to those whose optimism leads them to belittle or dismiss the sufferings of others'.[83] The background question is one that aligns Voltaire with thinkers on both sides of the increasingly unstable optimist/pessimist divide: How can we speak most meaningfully of and to suffering, in a way that does not make it worse, and perhaps helps us to 'bear it better' (Johnson); in a way that is able to offer consolation? The problem is that thinkers of the age are deeply disagreed about what constitutes *the right kind of consolation*; and as we will see, Rousseau for one thinks that Voltaire gets something fundamentally, and dangerously, wrong.

So what, for Voltaire, is the right way of offering consolation? Mere sympathy, perhaps, or generosity, or compassion. It is certainly not by philosophy, as he writes in 1758 in a letter of condolence to George Keith, who had just lost his brother as one of the casualties of the Seven Years' War (an event more devastating to Voltaire than the earthquake ever was):

> All your philosophy cannot remove your grief. Philosophy assuages the wound and leaves the heart wounded. . . . Let the happy madmen who say that all what is, is well, be confounded. (*D*7931; Voltaire's English)

81. 'L'univers vous dément, et votre propre cœur / Cent fois de votre esprit a réfuté l'erreur.' The Baylean influence is explicit at times: Bayle is mentioned in the Poem and defended in a long footnote; aside from which Voltaire makes use of the Baylean thought experiment.

82. To Nicolas Claude Thieriot, 27 May 1756 (*D*6875/*CRT*, xxv).

83. Wootton, 'Introduction', xxvii.

Optimism is depressive because it offers but a false consolation. Time, not philosophy, is 'the great healer'.[84]

THE HOPE OBJECTION

The second reason why optimism is *désespérant* for Voltaire is more original, having to do rather with hope, something to which Voltaire, like many of the more outspoken pessimists, has a complicated attitude. In order to understand what might be called *the hope objection*, we need to take a closer look at Voltaire's conception of optimism, which he sees as a deeply static philosophy. Voltaire defines optimism loosely as the doctrine that all is well in the world as it is, which he sees as equivalent to saying that all is as good as it can be: *nothing could be better* (see *Candide*, ch. 1). According to Voltaire, this static quality is optimism's weakness: if all is as good as it gets, then the concept of progress or betterment makes no sense; if nothing could be better, then there is no reason for humanity to hope for improvement, whether in this world or the next. Conversely, if we do have an idea of a 'better world', then this itself suggests all is not as good as it can be: 'This idea of a better world, is it not proof in itself that all is not well?'[85]

It should be noted that this critique does not work as a refutation of Leibniz, since it rests on a common misunderstanding of his philosophy. In fact, Leibniz's optimism also allows for a dynamic or diachronic interpretation: if the 'best of all possible worlds' applies to the entire system of existence, stretching out across time as well as space, then the best system allows for change and improvement or progress (and, indeed, even deterioration and regress), as long as the entire system represents an *optimum*. This is precisely why Leibniz emphasises the cosmic perspective: we need to zoom out in terms of time as well as space to understand which system, *as a whole*, is best.[86] Nevertheless, Voltaire's objection is valid for a specific interpretation of optimism, which he associates crucially with fatalism (against which Leibniz himself had warned in the preface to the

84. The latter phrase is drawn from Wootton's translation of Voltaire's story *Les Deux Consolés* of 1756 (*CRT*, 131/*OCV*.45b.56); see also Voltaire's *L'Ingénu*: 'Time softens everything' ('Le temps adoucit tout'). (*OCV*.63c.326; my translation), and Voltaire's criticism of Job's unconsoling friends in his dictionary article 'Job' (*OCV*.36.247). On the (impossibility of) consolations of philosophy, see also chapters 1 and 5 (on Bayle and Hume); and Samuel Johnson, *Rasselas*, chapter 18.

85. To Bertrand (*D*6738/*CRT*, 134).

86. See chapter 2; and see again Rateau, 'L'univers progresse-t-il?'

Theodicy).[87] In fact, it is a criticism that may be familiar to us, albeit not in this context: for we are used to seeing the hope objection raised against *pessimism* rather than optimism. This is the point implied by Chomsky's title: we must opt for optimism over despair or pessimism, which he sees as the same as giving up.[88]

Interestingly, Voltaire himself has formulated this same objection before, criticising not optimism, but *pessimism*. In his twenty-fifth *Letter on England* (cited above), Voltaire censured Pascal's pessimism on exactly the same grounds as he would later censure optimism, its removal of hope:

> Man's most precious treasure is this hope which softens our sufferings and depicts pleasures for us in the future in terms of those we possess at present. If men were unfortunate enough to be concerned only with the present, they would not sow, they would not build, they would not plant or provide for anything, and in the midst of this false enjoyment they would lack everything. (*Letters*, 132)

Is this a contradiction? Not necessarily. Both versions of the same objection are directed at the idea of fatalism, which takes away our hope of change and progress, so that we see no reason to work to improve ourselves or the world around us. It is the very same problem that Voltaire diagnoses in (certain versions of) pessimism and optimism. Victor Gourevitch nicely identifies and resolves the apparent contradiction:

> [Voltaire] attacks *what was then called optimism*—the reasoned trust that this is the best world possible—in the name of *what is now called optimism*: the belief that things can and do keep getting better and better, and that the evils of this world can be reduced or even eliminated altogether.[89]

Thus Voltaire's writings against optimism signal a crucial shift in orientation, pushing the debate towards the future-oriented meaning of optimism as the more important kind, and paving the way for the modern-day conceptions of optimism and pessimism as saying something about the future. Voltaire, it seems, can indeed be called an optimist, but only in the modern future-oriented sense.

87. Leibniz distinguishes different conceptions of fate and argues at length against the kind of determinism that renders us passive and resigned (i.e. fatalism) in his Preface to *EdT*.

88. Chomsky, *Optimism over Despair*, 196.

89. Gourevitch, 'The Religious Thought', 200 (my emphasis).

But hope can have different objects, and the hope objection can be developed in different ways: Does Voltaire mean *this-worldly* hope or *other-worldly* hope? In its final published version, the Poem seems to emphasise the latter, and Voltaire's preface brings the point home:

> the saying 'All is well,' taken in an absolute sense and without any hope for a future life, is nothing but an insult to the sufferings of our lives. . . . the hope of a development of our being within a new order of things can alone provide a consolation for our present miseries . . . (*CRT*, 98/ *OCV*.45a.326–7)[90]

The Poem itself also speaks of other-worldly hope, such as in this passage:

> *All will be well one day*— so runs our hope.
> *All now is well*, is but an idle dream.
> ('Lisbon', 7/*OCV*.45a.348)

Following feedback from his correspondents about the bleak ending of the poem in particular, Voltaire famously added six additional lines, in which a caliph brings to his God all the things that God lacks ('faults, regrets, evils, and ignorance'). The final line comments: 'He might have added one thing further—*hope*' ('Lisbon', 7/*OCV*.45a.349).[91]

However, as George R. Havens stressed in 1929, 'it would be entirely unsafe to quote Voltaire's final published lines as representing accurately his real opinion'.[92] A chance discovery in what was then the Leningrad archive brought to light Voltaire's own copy of the published Poem, in which the author had made some revisions—perhaps for a new edition—in particular, to the lines addressing hope:

> *All will be well one day*, what a fragile hope!
> *All now is well*, what an illusion![93]

And in fact, the revisions extend even to the famous final line, which Voltaire now turns into a question: 'But might he have added one thing

90. The Preface also stresses revelation and providence, and is much more lenient towards Pope than in, for example, the correspondence, emphasising, for instance, that Voltaire is taking issue only with certain *interpretations* of Pope.

91. 'Mais il pouvait encore ajouter l'espérance.'

92. Havens, 'Voltaire's Pessimistic Revision', 491.

93. My translation, adjusted from McCabe. In the original: '*Un jour tout sera bien*, quelle frêle espérance! / *Tout est bien aujourd'hui*, c'est quelle illusion!' (Havens, 'Voltaire's Pessimistic Revision', 492).

further—*hope*?'[94] As Havens writes of his discovery, this appears to have been 'Voltaire's final word on the conclusion of this important poem',[95] which still ends with the word *hope*—but also ends with a question mark. Though we should be equally cautious about overinterpreting these never-published remarks, they do suggest that Voltaire was less than comfortable with his own emphasis on hope in the published version of the poem. Having boosted the level of hope in response to his critics, he now tones it down again, adding instead a dimension of uncertainty as well as fragility: 'quelle frêle espérance!'

Voltaire's wavering stance with regard to hope, however, applies specifically to *other-worldly hope*, and understandably so: his letters and other works suggest he had little expectation of an afterlife. While the Poem tells us little about the possibility of *this-worldly* hope, we know from the hope objection that Voltaire, like Johnson, was deeply concerned to preserve a perspective of progress or improvement: something that will motivate us to keep working or striving for our betterment.[96] It is this kind of hope that we would nowadays associate with optimism, and it is this kind of hope that provides the equivocal background to *Candide*.

Candide, or Optimism

The story is well known. Candide grows up a blessed child, with no reason not to believe the doctrines of philosopher Pangloss, according to whom everything is as good as it could be in this, 'the best of all possible worlds'. The phrase points to Leibniz, as it's supposed to, but in fact Pangloss's expressions are aimed rather at certain unsophisticated interpreters of Leibniz, possibly mediated through Pope: those who had taken up the catchphrases without a deeper grasp of the underlying philosophy.[97] In

94. 'Mais pouvait-il encore ajouter *l'espérance?*' (Havens, 'Voltaire's Pessimistic Revision', 492).

95. Havens, 'Voltaire's Pessimistic Revision', 492.

96. Compare Johnson's comments on this-worldly hope, e.g. *Rambler* 67: 'Hope is necessary in every condition' (*SJW*, 3.533–4), and letter of 8 June 1762 to an unidentified female correspondent: 'Hope is itself a species of happiness, and perhaps the chief happiness which this world affords', though he warns against its excesses (Johnson, *Letters*, I, 203–4).

97. See Barber, *Leibniz*, 228, who claims that Voltaire was mainly attacking the French followers of Pope as well as the hyper-optimistic deists who denied any possible discord in God's creation. Voltaire had probably not read Leibniz's *Theodicy* first-hand until the 1760s, when he claims to have read it twice (Barber, *Leibniz*, 214); King, too, he seems only to have known secondarily (Wade, *Intellectual Development*, 642).

fact, some of Pangloss's representations of optimism bring to mind the more exaggerated tendencies of later optimists, such as Jenyns and those *chain-of-being* deists who were dead set on explaining not only general but also *particular* evils: 'the misfortunes of individuals go to make up the welfare of the whole, in such a way that the more personal misfortunes there are, the more everything is for the best' (*Candide*, 10/*OCV*.48.133). It is clear from the start that Pangloss is being set up for failure, and in the remainder of the story almost every kind of misfortune is thrown at Candide and his companions as they travel the world, leading to Candide's famous outburst of exasperation: 'If this is the best of all possible worlds, what on earth are the others like?' (*Candide*, 13/*OCV*.48.139).

Voltaire was an avid reader of Bayle, and the Baylean echoes in *Candide* are well documented.[98] The old woman (*la vieille*) comes close to paraphrasing Bayle sometimes, especially when she discusses man's irrational love of life even in the face of overwhelming evils, a passage that calls to mind Bayle's comments on the 'bad taste' for life in *Octavia*, and his responses to King's argument on suicide:

> A hundred times I wanted to kill myself; but I was still in love with life. This ridiculous weakness is perhaps one of our most disastrous attachments; for is there anything more stupid than to choose to carry continuously a burden that at the same time one constantly wants to let drop to the ground? To hate one's existence, and to cling to it? To stroke the serpent that bites us, until it has eaten our heart out? (*Candide*, 25/*OCV*.48.162)

The old woman and Martin the Manichean both represent Bayle's pessimism, and in both cases, it is their *experience* of life that reinforces their bleak view of it. As Martin says, having just listed some of humanity's sufferings: 'In a word, I have seen so much, and experienced so much, that I am a Manichean' (*Candide*, 47/*OCV*.48.202).[99] In fact, he is not so much a Manichean as he is a downright pessimist, if Candide is right in attributing to him this opinion: 'There is nothing to life except illusion and calamity'

98. On Voltaire and Bayle, see, e.g., Mason, *Pierre Bayle and Voltaire*; Haxo, 'Pierre Bayle et Voltaire Avant Les Lettres Philosophiques'; Wade, *Intellectual Development*, 632–51; Rétat, *Le dictionnaire*.

99. See also *Candide*, 62/*OCV*.48.229. Voltaire has little eye for the suffering of animals, which, if it is mentioned at all (as in the passage on vivisected dogs in his essay on happiness for the *Encyclopédie*) typically serves to emphasise *human* suffering; see the lemma 'Heureux, heureuse, heureusement' (*Encyclopédie*, ed. Diderot and d'Alembert, 8:194); on this passage, see also Wootton, 'Unhappy Voltaire', 150.

(*Candide*, 60/*OCV*.48.225). Throughout the story, Martin stands for pessimism as Pangloss stands for optimism, and Candide swings back and forth between the two. Neither Martin nor Pangloss gets the final word, but it is hinted that there is something in pessimism that is consoling in its own way, since hope (here juxtaposed to pessimism) can be a blessing as well as a burden. Early on, Candide knows that he is in a better situation than Martin, since Candide still has something to hope for (*Candide*, 46/*OCV*.48.201), but by the end, once the company has arrived in Constantinople and everyone is miserable with the day-to-day drudgery of life, Martin is least miserable of all, since 'he was convinced that one is equally badly off wherever one is, and he put up with everything patiently [*il prenait les choses en patience*]' (*Candide*, 76/*OCV*.48.255).

By its sweeping enumerations of the evils of existence, *Candide*'s deeper concern seems to be to provide an a posteriori argument for pessimism and against optimism, which is associated (through Leibniz in particular) with theodicy. In a sense, the *conte* represents a subversion of the aesthetic strategy in theodicy, according to which the evils of life, as Candide himself says, 'are like shadows that form part of a beautiful painting', to which Martin reliably replies: 'What you call shadows are horrible smudges and stains' (*Candide*, 55/*OCV*.48.217). Just as Pope's *Essay* made a mainly aesthetic and poetic case for optimism, so *Candide* seems to offer a kind of aesthetic pessimism in refutation, and this is why Friedrich Schlegel argued that any response to *Candide* would have to operate along the same lines: 'Against *Candide* one can counter with only an aesthetic optimism: that this world is the most beautiful.'[100] And yet it is not clear that *Candide* makes the case for pessimism as Pope's *Essay* did for optimism. The famous final lines have triggered many discussions: 'Il faut cultiver notre jardin' ('we must cultivate our garden'—or, in Wootton's translation, 'we must work our land'). Whatever Voltaire, a gardener himself at this time, precisely meant by this, it is clear that he did not want the story to end on an overtly pessimistic note. Nor is it all's well that ends well, as in the final lines of the earlier philosophical poem *Le Mondain*: 'The earthly paradise is where I am.'[101] Instead, we seem to see a tentative and fragile ethic of trying to live in an unreliable world; a careful inching

100. Schlegel, *Philosophical Apprenticeship*, 162. Schopenhauer mentions Schlegel's critique of *Candide* (and of Byron) in *WWR*.II.585.

101. 'Le paradis terrestre est où je suis' (*OCV*.16.303; my translation). See also Voltaire's *Discours en vers sur l'homme*, especially the second letter, on man's ability to achieve (if not perfect, then certainly relative) happiness in this world, on which topic *Candide* is markedly less confident.

towards this-worldly hope but without expectation or certainty.[102] Like Johnson's novel *Rasselas, Prince of Abyssinia* of the same year (1759), which one nineteenth-century edition printed together with *Candide*, the story ends with a 'conclusion, in which nothing is concluded', but where hope is yet made possible again.

It is, then, not entirely helpful to want to define Voltaire as either an optimist or a pessimist, since (like Rousseau and others) he manifests aspects of both strands, thus showing the limits of the very categories that he is so instrumental in establishing. But it may be worth noting that there are objections that can be made to *Candide* following the lines of argument associated with pessimism thus far, and especially according to what I have called the *moral objection to theodicy*. If there is an ethic that unites the pessimists, it is that we have to find a way to speak of suffering that is sensitive to our experience and to the gravity of the subject (an intuition that also arises in Johnson's objection to Jenyns). The result of this intuition is a bleak legacy: the most convinced pessimists offer their readers page upon page describing the sufferings of existence. From Bayle and Hume's Philo to Schopenhauer and Benatar, all are steeped in such gravity: dark matters, indeed. Voltaire's Lisbon Poem can be placed squarely within this tradition: *Candide*, written but a few years later, cannot.

The reason has much to do with tone, with style. One of the strengths of *Candide* lies in its *chiaroscuro* touch, in its mixture of light and dark, the comic and the tragic. Had it just been a dreary enumeration of the trials of Candide and his friends, the story would have been as tedious as Johnson thought Prior's *Solomon* was. But questions might be raised with regard to the appropriateness of this comic touch, and with regard to the entire premise of *Candide*, questions that are still relevant today: Do creators of fiction have the moral right to avail themselves of endless imaginings of suffering in order to prove a point, and to entertain? Fiction offers opportunities that history and philosophy do not—but it may also come with certain obligations.[103] When Voltaire has Candide's

102. On the semantic contexts behind these final lines, see Langdon, 'On the meanings of the conclusion of Candide', Murray, *Voltaire's Candide*. Starobinski (*Blessings in Disguise*, 99) offers cautiously: 'Perhaps Voltaire's intention was to make us aware of the fragility, the eccentricity intrinsic to anything that might seem to offer hope of stability.'

103. As Neiman notes, the evils listed in *Candide* are things that really happened at the time: 'The characters may be invented, but what they experience is not' (*Evil*, 133; see also Starobinski, *Blessings*, 84–5). This is true only on the general level (there were and are things like torture, rape, and murder), and is equally true of most sufferings represented in all of fiction, which does not mean we cannot look critically at *the ways in which* they are represented.

beloved Cunégonde raped and disembowelled, or when he has the old woman remember her mother being quartered and herself waking up on a pile of dead bodies when she was still a girl, only to finish the chapter with a smutty joke before moving on to the rest of the girl's sufferings, we may begin to grow uncomfortable: not only with the mixture of horrific descriptions and one-liners for comic effect, but with the general use of moral evils in particular (rape, torture, murder, slavery) in order to move the story forward.

In contrast to the Lisbon Poem, *Candide* displays an unsettling mixture of humour and horror, as well as a certain nonchalance: Voltaire does not seem to really care what happens to his characters, just as Candide does not really care about the sufferings he sees around him. It is true that Candide weeps when he hears a slave recount the story of his suffering, and that his compassion with the slave is what makes him feel he has to give up his 'optimism' after all.[104] But it is also the case that Candide, still weeping, leaves the slave behind and goes on to Surinam, and so his tears cost him nothing: he and Voltaire go on with the story, and we go with him (*Candide*, 43/*OCV*.48.196).[105] This line of criticism may well be controversial: *Candide* seems universally considered a moral triumph, one that still has relevance for us today, as Julian Barnes writes: 'we . . . shall have need of *Candide* for some centuries to come'.[106] In fact, I believe *Candide's* message may be even more relevant today than it was in Voltaire's time, to counter those modern versions of hyper-optimism that place human happiness entirely in our own hands. But I do not think the charms and importance of *Candide* should blind us to the ways in which it is limited, especially since Voltaire himself points the way towards such a critique.

I cannot help but wonder what an author such as Bayle, or Hume, or even Samuel Johnson would have made of *Candide*, though we know that Schopenhauer loved it, and that David Benatar cites the old woman approvingly.[107] Perhaps it does not matter what Bayle would have thought, since we can reconstruct a critique along Baylean lines. Just as Johnson criticised Jenyns for too little gravity and 'too much vivacity' in his treatment of a

104. As Wootton notes: 'This is the only time the word "optimism" appears in the text of *Candide*, and this section is a late addition' (*CRT*, 43n.).

105. Much has been made of this episode (which stands out in its absence of burlesque humour) as representing Voltaire's objections to either slavery in general or to specific colonial abuses. I won't comment on this tricky question: for discussion, see, e.g., Kjørholt, 'Cosmopolitans, Slaves, and the Global Market', who notes that 'neither Candide nor the narrator shows the same compassion towards all cases of slavery' (77).

106. Barnes, 'A Candid View of *Candide*'.

107. Schopenhauer, *WWR*.II.582; Benatar, *Better Never to Have Been*, 93, 219–20.

subject of this magnitude; just as Bayle criticised authors playing down the sufferings of others; just as *Voltaire himself* criticised the optimists for refusing to give due weight to evils—so too Voltaire could be criticised for the lack of gravitas owed to the topic, for painting in light tones where darker ones are due.[108] With regard to *Candide*, at least, I agree with Cassirer's assessment of Voltaire: 'Even his pessimism remained playful, while Rousseau's optimism was filled with and sustained by tragic seriousness.'[109]

VOLTAIRE UNHAPPY?

Then again, Voltaire is not Candide. This was no armchair philosopher, but someone who has been called 'the first modern politically engaged intellectual', and 'the first human-rights campaigner of the modern era'.[110] Someone who could not get the image of public executions out of his head, and wrote to his friends that the victims of injustice 'sometimes present themselves to me in my dreams'.[111] Someone who 'trembles with the world's suffering'.[112] After *Candide*, Voltaire's campaigns against injustice suggest that he at least was not content to walk away from suffering and 'simply to cultivate his land'; indeed, it has been suggested that *Candide* was instrumental in turning Voltaire's efforts to fighting injustice.[113] This is the interpretation of David Wootton, who objects to the common notion that Voltaire's turn from optimism can be explained by his unhappiness at the time, when in fact, by 1758 Voltaire had 'found relative contentment'.[114] In Wootton's view, this contentment, or even happiness, is crucial:

> The origins of *Candide* are to be found rather in Voltaire's happiness than his despair. . . . Crucially, becoming happy freed Voltaire to admit that he had not been happy in the past and that most human beings

108. For a different view see Starobinski, *Blessings*, 84–100; and indeed most of the existing literature.

109. Cassirer, *Question of Jean-Jacques Rousseau*, 81. Note that this is not the case for the Lisbon Poem, which Voltaire himself called 'des vers tragiques' (Voltaire to d'Argental, 15 February 1756; *D*6734).

110. Neiman, *Evil*, 142; Pearson, *Voltaire Almighty*, 32.

111. To d'Argental, 30 August 1769 (*D*15855); see also various letters following the execution of La Barre in 1766, e.g. to Étienne Noël Damilaville, 7 July 1766 (*D*13394): 'mon cœur est flétri, je suis atterré'; see Pearson, *Voltaire Almighty*, 402.

112. Starobinski, *Blessings*, 85.

113. Wootton, 'Introduction', xxvii; Wootton, 'Unhappy Voltaire', 150. Consider also the late addition of the slavery episode mentioned above (p. 142).

114. Pearson, *Fables of Reason*, 112; cited by Wootton, 'Introduction' xv.

live lives that are painful and miserable. It was happiness, not misery, that led Voltaire to abandon optimism.[115]

Wootton suggests that through *Candide*, Voltaire was writing his way out of his own suffering, or finding a way to transform himself through story-telling. And of this suffering, Wootton takes a very specific view. Unlike the majority of Voltaire scholars and biographers, Wootton believes we should take literally Voltaire's comment to Pope's mother that he had been sexually abused by the Jesuits as a schoolboy and would 'never get over it as long as I live'.[116] According to Wootton, this history of child abuse informs the crucial background to both *Candide* and Voltaire's later 'campaign[s] against injustice': 'it is his own fictional character, *la vieille*, who, by talking about the past, showed him how to come to terms with what had happened to him'.[117] If this interpretation is correct, then it is suggestive of a deeper transformative potential of pessimism itself, both on a personal and political level: pessimism as an act of healing, and as a principle of change. But let's not go there yet.[118]

As Wootton himself notes, he is not the first to draw a connection between the Lisbon writings and the question of Voltaire's personal (un)happiness; in fact, such efforts have shadowed these writings from the start. Thus Voltaire's doctor Théodore Tronchin wrote to Jean-Jacques Rousseau (with regard to the Poem) that Voltaire 'laid claim to more happiness than he had a right to expect'.[119] In Wootton's words, both Tronchin and Rousseau thought that Voltaire abandoned optimism precisely 'because too many things had gone right' for him.[120] In Rousseau's case, as we will see, this reduction of thought to temperament serves to prove a philosophical point. Rousseau is able to discredit Voltaire's Poem by arguing that Voltaire has no right of speaking: he has not suffered enough to speak of suffering—that is, he has not suffered as Rousseau has. The Genevan philosopher Charles Bonnet (1720–1793) took a different view, writing to Albrecht von Haller that it was Voltaire's bleak outlook on life that explained his writings on Lisbon and discredited them:

115. Wootton, 'Introduction', xxvi.

116. Cited in Wootton, 'Unhappy Voltaire', 137; most commentators think Voltaire's comment was exaggerated, see, e.g., Pearson, *Voltaire Almighty*, 23.

117. Wootton, 'Unhappy Voltaire', 150.

118. Dienstag has written extensively on pessimism's potential for political energisation; see again his *Pessimism*.

119. Théodore Tronchin to Rousseau, 1 September 1756 (*D6985*/*CRT*, viii): 'il a voulu plus de bonheur qu'il n'en pouvait prétendre'.

120. Wootton, 'Introduction', xxii.

> [Voltaire] is in my opinion one of the most miserable beings on the surface of the Globe. . . . A man who paints the Universe as it is painted in the Poem on Lisbon and in *Candide*, sees all of Nature cast in black. But that which I can't forgive him is that he shows it to us thus.[121]

In contrast, Wootton, by drawing attention to the dual facts of Voltaire's *past* suffering and concurrent happiness (at the time of *Candide*), aims precisely to deepen the story's credibility and its moral force, thereby defending Voltaire against what seems to be the accusation most to be avoided: that of complacency.[122]

But we might also be asking different questions. Is it entirely appropriate to seek the origins of Voltaire's Lisbon writings in *either* his happiness or misery? Should the question of whether or not an author has suffered—and if so, how much—guide us in our interpretation and evaluation of their texts? Is Rousseau right that, had Voltaire himself *not* suffered, he would have had no right to speak of other people's suffering? And if he had suffered, would this somehow lend more credibility to his pessimism? Or is it precisely the other way around: Does personal happiness bestow an aura of credibility on pessimism just as unhappiness does on optimism? I mention these questions not to answer them, but to show there is something in the topic, from early on, that seems to call for biographical explanation: what I have called a *reductio ad biographiam*. This tendency to explain authors' ideas by their experiences may well be appropriate at times, but it should be accompanied by great caution, for it is precisely this temptation to psychologise that has led to the trivialisation of many of these thinkers, and especially the pessimists. As such, the new sensitivity about the *right way of speaking about suffering* signals both the deepening of this debate as well as its eventual shallowing, as optimism and pessimism will increasingly be reduced to psychological states of mind.

The Complications of Hope

It is precisely this background shift in intuitions that indicates a wider development in the debate on the origins of evil, as the moral objection to optimism grows out to be the self-evident one. Even as optimism gains currency in the eighteenth century, it loses its intuitive appeal and

121. Bonnet to Haller, 27 March 1759 (my translation), cited in Gisler, 'Optimism and Theodicy', 257.

122. See also Neiman (*Evil*, 135), who suggests: 'Voltaire was fighting his own tendency to be complacent.'

provokes increasing indignation, and this is due mainly to the deep disagreement *internal to optimism* over its two strategies. It is this disagreement that pushes authors such as Bolingbroke and Jenyns to try (too ambitiously) to explain away all particular evils, in contrast to which Leibniz's approach (in spite of Voltaire's view of it) is actually much more subtle and refined. Catchphrases aside, it is in fact the hyperbolic optimism of Pope's and Leibniz's followers to which Voltaire objects—doing so, as Gourevitch notes, on terms we would now call 'optimistic'. Hence the introduction of the hope objection against *optimism*, which originally was an objection against *pessimism*, and which now begins to indicate not just other-worldly but *this-worldly hope*. At the same time, the consolation objection, not itself new, gains widespread appeal, though it continues to be interpreted in different ways, as we will see in Rousseau, who views pessimism with the utmost seriousness but believes that optimism provides the appropriate consolatory response.

As for the problem of evil itself, it is now almost identified with the problem of pessimism, and particularly, with the a posteriori question of weighing the goods and evils of existence. It is also focused mainly on the problem of physical evil: that is, the problem of suffering. This is why Voltaire's Lisbon Poem could have such force, as an exercise of indignation relying heavily on a posteriori descriptions of physical evils. At the same time, Voltaire does not quite fit this development, for while it is true that the Poem is centred on physical evils, *Candide* focuses on moral ones, as does the rest of Voltaire's oeuvre.[123] In fact, even as the first versions of the Poem were circulating, Voltaire wrote to one of his friends that he believed moral evils to be the worse kind:

> Like you, I mourn the Portuguese; but human beings do more harm to each other on their little mole hill than nature does harm to them. Our wars murder more people than are swallowed up in earthquakes. If there was nothing in this world to fear but the Lisbon disaster, we would be in a reasonably good situation.[124]

But if moral evils are the worse kind, they are also the kind that are remediable, and so we have all the more reason to focus on them. Thus, if *Candide* can be seen as an exercise in a posteriori pessimism, it can also be seen

123. See Haydn Mason, 'Voltaire's "Sermon" against Optimism', 191: 'Within the whole corpus of the *contes* the earthquake in *Candide* stands out by its exceptionality; and even there the author is more concerned with the human reactions . . . than with the disaster itself.'

124. To François-Louis Allamand, 16 December 1755 (*D6629*/*CRT*, 132).

as an exercise in optimism in the modern sense of the term, which insists on the possibility of progress and improvement and resists any philosophy that risks our losing heart and losing hope. Against the background of chaos and uncertainty, we can still 'work our land'. There can be little doubt that Voltaire would have agreed wholeheartedly with Chomsky:

> We have two choices. We can be pessimistic, give up, and help ensure that the worst will happen. Or we can be optimistic, grasp the opportunities that surely exist, and maybe help make the world a better place. Not much of a choice.[125]

The question remains, then, what *are* the opportunities that 'surely exist'? Which evils of life are avoidable, which unavoidable? If fatalism is the outcome repugnant to optimists and pessimists alike, how do we steer clear of it; wherein resides our power, wherein our hope? Is it true that, as Johnson writes, 'while it is in our power to be virtuous, it is in our power to be happy, at least to be happy to such a degree as may have little room for murmur and complaints'?[126] Has the time 'already come, when none are wretched but by their own fault'?[127] Or is this precisely the kind of 'cruel' consolation to which Voltaire so objected?

The question of optimism and pessimism, having been lifted out of the debate on evil, is now drifting increasingly towards a different question: that of the (im)possibility of human happiness. Before we move on to Hume and Rousseau, therefore, it is worth paying a visit to one of Voltaire's friends and one of his rivals, who will show us what happens when Stoicism meets pessimism.

125. Chomsky, *Optimism over Despair*, 196.

126. Johnson, Sermon 5 (*SJW*, 14.55).

127. Johnson, *Rasselas* (*SJW*, 16.85); the speaker is one of various philosophers in the novel: this is not Johnson's view.

CHAPTER FOUR

When Stoicism Meets Pessimism

LA METTRIE AND MAUPERTUIS

The happiest constitution does not lead to perfect happiness; there is no such thing in nature: it is the island of Ithaca that always flees before Ulysses.

JULIEN OFFRAY DE LA METTRIE[1]

The tip of a finger or a single tooth is able to torment us more than the organ of the greatest pleasures can render us happy.

PIERRE DE MAUPERTUIS[2]

NOT UNLIKE OUR CURRENT AGE, the eighteenth century was a little obsessed with happiness. As the mere proliferation of treatises and discourses *On Happiness* suggests, this was a hot topic for the eighteenth century in a way and to an extent that was perhaps unprecedented: 'No previous age,' writes Darrin McMahon, 'wrote so much on the subject or so often.'[3] What is happiness? Is there a right road to happiness and if so, how do we make sure we are on it? Questions like these were high on the agenda, and texts proposing to answer them seemed to cater to an appetite as insatiable as that for self-help books today. This trend, though not limited to philosophy, was spurred by and in turn reinforced a deep

1. La Mettrie, *Anti-Senèque/Discours sur le bonheur*: *DB*, 209.
2. Maupertuis, *Essai de philosophie morale*: *EPM*, 35–6.
3. McMahon, *The Pursuit of Happiness*, 200; Mauzi, *L'Idée du bonheur*, 9–10.

engagement with those ancient philosophers in whose writings happiness had become a topic of philosophy: Plato and Aristotle, the Stoics and Epicureans. Of those four pillars of the canon of happiness, one was singled out for particular examination, not just by individual philosophers but by an entire culture. For the eighteenth-century debate on happiness was also a debate on Stoicism, and on a very specific question associated with Stoicism in particular: to what extent is it up to us to control our flourishing in this world? Are we in charge of our own happiness?[4]

Darrin McMahon writes with verve on the shift that takes place in the eighteenth century, when happiness becomes something that is in our control and for which we bear personal responsibility, a shift that he claims has had a huge influence on how we think about happiness today.[5] But happiness necessarily also has to do with unhappiness, and the question of whether we can control happiness is also a question of whether we can control our pain and suffering: as such, it relates directly to the debate on pessimism and, in a subtler way, to that on the problem of evil.

Stoicism has crossed our path at several points in the past chapters. Descartes's assertion to Elisabeth of Bohemia, that 'even among the saddest accidents and the most pressing pains one can always be content, so long as one knows how to use one's reason', was cited with concern by Bayle and with approval by Leibniz, both of whom reprise this passage in the context of the problem of evil.[6] Here and in many other places, we have caught glimpses of a high Stoicism running through these debates, intersecting with the questions of pessimism and the problem of evil again and again. This Stoic strand intensifies as we travel more deeply into the eighteenth century, but it also becomes more complicated. On the one hand, the eighteenth century continued on the Stoic revival of the seventeenth, and updated neo-Stoic texts such as Shaftesbury's *Characteristics* were capable of exercising a dramatic hold on the imagination, as they did on the young David Hume. On the other, Stoicism came repeatedly and increasingly under attack from various angles, and these attacks in

4. While such questions apply equally to Epicureanism, they were less discussed in this context, possibly because the moral philosophy of Epicureanism tended to be misinterpreted as hedonism, both by its proponents and its attackers. Throughout this chapter, 'Epicureanism' signifies the school of thought as perceived through this particular eighteenth-century lens (as in La Mettrie and Maupertuis).

5. McMahon, *Pursuit of Happiness*, especially chapters 4 and 8; see also Hazard, *European Thought*, 14–25; and on the French context specifically, Mauzi, *L'Idée du bonheur*.

6. Descartes to Elisabeth of Bohemia, 6 October 1645, *Correspondence*, 121. Recall that Leibniz is also critical of the Stoics; see Rutherford, 'Leibniz and the Stoics', '*Patience sans espérance*'.

turn spurred new defences that approached the Stoic question in startling new ways. The result, throughout this dynamic exchange of attacks and defences sharpening each other with every round, is a kind of crystallisation not just of what Stoicism was, but what it *meant*, and what it meant for this age in particular.

Bayle, as we have seen, features as a forerunner of this anti-Stoic challenge, and his objection operates on several levels. Most crucially, he argues that the Stoic project asks too much of us, and in so doing is more likely to deepen our misery than to alleviate it, since aside from our unhappiness, we now have to bear *the burden of responsibility* for that unhappiness. Furthermore, against the assumption common to both sides of the debate, that physical pain is harder to control than psychological suffering, Bayle holds that the latter is just as resistant to our efforts as the former, and possibly more so: in his examples of deep suffering, it tends to be psychological evils that drive us to despair. In contrast, most authors of the era seem to assume that the sharpest refutation of Stoicism is provided by the blunt fact of physical pain, with gout and toothache featuring as common examples. In the words of Shakespeare's Leonato, 'there was never yet philosopher / That could endure the toothache patiently'.[7] Bayle would surely not disagree, but the point he is making is a deeper one: we have at least as little control over our mental miseries as we have over our physical pains, and by extension over our happiness itself.

Bayle, at the time of writing, is in a minority: this is not where the cultural trend is headed. But the eighteenth century finds others formulating similar objections, often in the very treatises flagging happiness in their titles, such as in Bernard de Fontenelle's treatise *Du Bonheur*:

> Whatever the proud Stoics may say, a large part of our happiness does not depend on us. If one of them, afflicted by gout, were to say to it: *Nevertheless I won't admit that you're an evil*, he will have spoken the most extravagant word that ever left the mouth of a philosopher. . . .

7. Shakespeare, *Much Ado About Nothing*, act 5, scene 1, v. 36–7. For a more recent exponent of the view that 'the body can suffer twenty times more than the mind', see C.S. Lewis, who, deep in grief, wrote that: 'Grief is like a bomber circling round and dropping its bombs each time the circle brings it overhead; physical pain is like the steady barrage on a trench in World War One, hours of it with no let-up for moment. Thought is never static; pain often is' (*A Grief Observed*, 33).

> Let's not add to all the evils that nature and fortune can send to us the ridiculous and useless vanity of believing ourselves invulnerable.[8]

These questions, then, are high on the European mind throughout the eighteenth century, suggesting something about the philosophical climate of the time, and perhaps allowing us to take the temperature of some of these thinkers. As we will find in this and the chapters to follow, the wider cultural re-engagement with the Stoic legacy, though distinct from the debates on pessimism and theodicy, nevertheless intersects with them at several crucial turns. In so doing, it reconfigures what might seem to be a set opposition of optimists versus pessimists and creates new alignments and constellations, which can only awkwardly be named, such as 'optimistic pessimism' or 'pessimistic optimism'.

This encounter between Stoicism and pessimism, which takes place on a much wider scale (as we will see in Hume and Rousseau), comes to the fore in a very distinct way in the decade preceding the Lisbon earthquake, when two philosophers cross pens over the question of happiness: La Mettrie and Maupertuis. Both names, little known now, were famous in their own day. A scientist and explorer as well as a philosopher, Pierre Louis Moreau de Maupertuis (1698–1759) was director of the *Académie des Sciences* in Paris before Frederick II appointed him the president of the Berlin equivalent. As such, he was an influential man, whose pessimistic essay on moral philosophy may well have spurred the topic of the 1755 prize contest of the Berlin Academy on whether Leibnizian–Popean optimism is tenable—which Kant considered entering, and which itself forms part of backdrop to Voltaire's poem on the Lisbon earthquake. Maupertuis was read by Kant and Schopenhauer for his scientific theories, and by Rousseau and the young Bentham for his 'arithmetic of happiness'. He also travelled to Lapland to measure the shape of the earth.[9]

As esteemed and influential a figure as Maupertuis was, so notorious and controversial was his friend and fellow philosopher Julien Offray de La Mettrie (1709–1751). When La Mettrie received an invitation to

8. Fontenelle, *Du Bonheur*, 246 (his emphasis); compare Maupertuis, *EPM*, 32: 'the philosopher who said that gout is not an evil spoke a stupidity [*une sottise*]'. Fontenelle makes a similar point as Hume will make in 'The Sceptic': that the only people susceptible of having philosophy increase their happiness are those people who are, by virtue of their moderate temperament, already happy (*Du Bonheur*, 248).

9. For details of Maupertuis's scholarly and scientific pursuits, see Beeson's intellectual biography, *Maupertuis*. The term 'arithmetic of happiness' is Beeson's (ibid., 197).

Frederick's court in 1748, allowing him to flee prosecution and possibly persecution in Holland for his treatise *Machine Man* (*L'Homme machine*), this was probably orchestrated by Maupertuis, the only one of La Mettrie's friends to help him in his time of need.[10] At the court of Frederick II, the two men seem to have remained on good terms, though their writings of these three years (1748–1751) provide evidence of a fascinating clash between two authors challenging each other in an inspired, but also tortured, intellectual relationship. The main battleground in their debate is over the attainability of happiness and the 'up-to-usness' of suffering, but hiding just beneath the surface, the dark matters of pessimism are never far away.

'But We Shall Be Anti-Stoics!': La Mettrie

'Write, as though you were alone in the Universe . . .'[11] A physician and philosopher as well as an outspoken libertine, La Mettrie was not one to eschew provocation. Descartes's famous conception of the animal body as mere machine (*la bête machine*) had always raised concerns that the next step would be to extend this deterministic model to humans as well, concerns that generations of Cartesians had struggled to lay to rest and that La Mettrie delighted in proving well founded, giving his books titles such as *L'Homme machine* and even *L'Homme plante*.[12] Some of these doctrines were so controversial that soon even the *philosophes* (such as the marquis d'Argens and Voltaire, but also fellow materialists such as the baron d'Holbach and especially Diderot) began to keep their distance and even to mount a counter-attack, in an ongoing but apparently futile attempt to dissociate themselves from La Mettrie.[13] The problem for them was not La Mettrie's mechanistic and deterministic world-view itself, but the fact that he was unafraid to draw from this a stark moral relativism, thus

10. Thomson, *Materialism*, 11. While Maupertuis later denied helping his friend, this was probably in order to dissociate himself from La Mettrie's increasing outrageousness (Thomson, *Materialism*, 10–14).

11. La Mettrie, Discours préliminaire, 247.

12. These provocative titles are somewhat deceptive: La Mettrie did not think humans and animals are devoid of feeling, rather that their conditions are similar in that both are machines endowed with feeling but not freedom; see Thomson, *Materialism*, 36–41, and her introduction to *Machine Man*.

13. This attack intensifies after La Mettrie's death, as the *Anti-Seneca* continues to appear in new editions of La Mettrie's *Œuvres philosophiques*, and as more and more apologists start to quote him in conjunction with the *philosophes*; see Falvey, 'Introduction', 87–95; Thomson, *Materialism*, 175–86.

making the very association between materialism and (im)morality that the *philosophes* had been so very anxious to avoid.

The reasons for their discomfort can be felt keenly from a little work written in La Mettrie's final years. The physician had been engaged in a new translation of Seneca when he began to write a short treatise on happiness, which started out as an introduction to his translation, then turned into more of a refutation, unsubtly titled *Anti-Seneca, or the Sovereign Good* (1748–1751).[14] Here, he takes head on the Stoic notion of the sovereign good, recapping its central tenets only to brush them briskly to one side:

> But we shall be Anti-Stoics! Those philosophers are sad, strict and unyielding; we shall be cheerful, sweet-natured and indulgent. They are all soul and ignore their bodies; we shall be all body and ignore our souls. They appear impervious to pleasure or pain; we shall glory in feeling both. (*MM*, 119)

In contrast to the Stoics, La Mettrie defines the sovereign good purely in terms of happiness and pleasure, which he describes in strongly physiological terms:

> Our organs are capable of feeling or being modified in a way that pleases us and makes us enjoy life. If the impression created by this feeling is short, it constitutes pleasure; if longer, sensuality [*volupté*] and if permanent, happiness. It is always the same feeling; only its duration and intensity differ. (*MM*, 120)

In other words, the different kinds of positive feelings we experience are modified only by this duration and intensity: the shorter and 'more intense' the feeling, the closer it is to pleasure; the 'longer-lasting and calmer', the closer it is to happiness (*MM*, 120). As for the *causes* of happiness, La Mettrie distinguishes two kinds: the first kind are 'external'

14. A note on editions: the *Anti-Seneca* first appeared in 1748 as an introduction to La Mettrie's translation of Seneca's *De vita beata* and was titled 'Discours sur le bonheur'; it was then reworked and published separately in a very limited edition of twelve copies in 1750, now bearing the definitive title *Anti-Senèque ou Le Souverain Bien*. It was then reworked yet again and published in 1751, with a new preface and an alternative ending. The renaming has given rise to some confusion, and the *Anti-Seneca* is often referred to as the *Discours sur le bonheur*, but as Ann Thomson notes, this is not the title La Mettrie chose himself (*MM*, 118; see also Falvey, 'Introduction', *DB*, 11). To add to the confusion, I am using three different editions as a basis for my discussion: *MM*, *AS*, and *DB*; all English translations are mine except for *MM*, which is translated by Ann Thomson (see the bibliography).

or 'accessory' causes, which have their origin outside us, such as education, sensual pleasure, wealth, and reputation, but also learning and, crucially, even virtue. The other kind are 'Internal or intrinsic causes': these are often believed 'to depend on ourselves', but in fact they arise purely from our internal 'organisation'; that is, from our physiological constitution (which on La Mettrie's mechanistic model includes the fibres of the nerves and brain). It is this latter kind of cause that produces both 'the steadiest' forms of happiness and the most irremediable forms of *un*happiness (*MM*, 120–1). Again, the point is that these most powerful causes of happiness and unhappiness are entirely out of our control; and that there is, therefore, no right road to happiness, as the Stoics would have it. Virtue and learning are not natural to man and not intrinsically linked to happiness: 'It is natural for man to feel because he is an animate body, but it is no more natural for him to be learned and virtuous than to be richly dressed' (*MM*, 121). This is why there are as many 'happy ignoramuses' as there are unhappy intelligent people (*MM*, 123).[15]

The central notion here is that differences in happiness spring from differences between persons, and more specifically, between their physiological constitutions:

> All things being equal, some people are more subject to joy, vanity, anger, melancholy and even remorse than are others. What is the cause of this if not that particular organic disposition which produces mania, idiocy, vivacity, slowness, calm, perspicacity, etc.? Well, I dare to include organic happiness [*le Bonheur organique*] among those effects of the human bodily structure. (*MM*, 122)

This kind of organic or constitutional happiness is the reason why some 'blissful people' are blessed with 'happy temperaments': 'Their constitution is such that sorrow, misfortune, illness, minor pains, the loss of what is held dearest . . . slide over their souls, hardly touching them.' The gift of this happy constitution is most unevenly distributed, but when it is given, it is the surest road to happiness: 'How fortunate is he who carries happiness in his veins!' (*MM*, 122).

La Mettrie calls this kind of happiness 'organic, automatic or natural, because the soul is not involved at all and can claim no credit for it, as it

15. He also remarks on the capacity of reflection for making us unhappy—'It seems that thought tortures feeling' (*MM*, 123)—and contrasts human suffering with animal happiness, in which we may see a link to Dienstag's notion of the pessimist tradition (see chapter 2).

is independent of the will' (*MM*, 123). He compares it to states of bliss induced by opium or even by delirium and dreams; in fact, he denies that the chemical source of the one and the illusory nature of the other is any reason to see their effects as lesser forms of happiness. Better a happy illusion, he argues against Descartes, than an 'unpleasant reality' (*MM*, 125). Echoing Bayle's definition of suffering, La Mettrie holds that if something is *experienced* as happiness, then happiness is what it is. So, on the one hand, happiness is all that matters: 'He who has found happiness has found everything.' But, on the other, actually *achieving* happiness is not in our control: 'he who has found happiness has not sought it. We do not seek what we have, and if we do not have it, then we will never have it' (*MM*, 125). Happiness, in other words, is fundamentally not something that is up to us at all.

UNHAPPY HAPPINESS

What does this have to do with the Stoics? On the most basic level, La Mettrie is opposed to the idea that certain kinds of pleasures are more conducive to happiness than others: that there is a right road to happiness that can be formulated on the basis of intrinsic qualities of pleasures (for instance, the idea that greater happiness is won through intellectual than sensual pleasures, or vice versa). In fact, he argues, there is no qualitative difference between pleasures except for their *degree* and *intensity*: aside from this difference, whether or not something is more or less likely to make us happy depends purely on the *temperament* and *constitution* of the person in question. His objection to those philosophers (read: the Stoics) who place happiness in either intellectual pleasures or literary glory is that they have made two mistakes in one: not only have they generalised the particular (by turning their particular pleasure into a universal one), but they have also hedged in something that is in fact given to 'all animated creatures', namely: 'the faculty of being happy, and of being happy each in their own way and according to their own whims' (*AS*, 192).[16] Placing happiness only in literary culture or in reputation and glory is like a child putting it in a single toy: after all, many people are happy without

16. This confidence about all creatures' innate capacity for happiness is a kind of optimism and sets La Mettrie apart from, for example, Hume, with whom he otherwise has much in common.

riches and without science or reputation, living in 'an obscure and tranquil mediocrity' (*AS*, 193).[17]

The same holds true of virtue: 'We can immerse ourselves with the sovereign good as much as we like, and envelop ourselves in all virtue; but neither virtue nor philosophy with all their oars can conduct us to the desired port' (*AS*, 194). Furthermore, not only is happiness completely independent from virtue, it is also separate from notions of good and evil. La Mettrie argues 'that in relation to felicity, good and evil are totally indifferent in themselves, and that he who has greater satisfaction in doing evil will be happier than whosoever has less satisfaction in doing good'. This suggests 'the existence of a particular individual happiness without virtue and even in crime' (*MM*, 141–2).[18] This is the point at which we can imagine La Mettrie's readers beginning to grow uncomfortable. Surely he is not saying that the wicked can be just as happy as the virtuous? Yes, this turns out to be exactly what he is saying, on one condition: 'They can be happy, if they are able to be wicked without remorse' (*AS*, 206). In fact, a moral monster such as a remorseless criminal may well be happier than someone who does a good deed and regrets it afterwards.

Not satisfied with making this already controversial point, La Mettrie goes on to address the wicked directly, telling 'parricides, committers of incest, thieves, and scoundrels' that as long as they are able to quell remorse and escape punishment by the state, they have no reason to be unhappy (*AS*, 207–8). A similar address is made to a hypothetical tyrant, 'a cruel and cowardly Prince', who finds his pleasure in tormenting others:

> The only good that is in your power is to do evil: to do good would be your agony. I do not tear you away from the accursed inclination that

17. In fact, La Mettrie argues that reason and learning can even be counterproductive to our happiness, which he illustrates by pointing to Bayle's example of La Mothe le Vayer (suggesting that La Mettrie too had entered into the 'Manichean web'): 'The mind, learning and reason are most often useless in creating bliss, and sometimes even fatal and murderous, as La Mothe le Vayer proved by his own example; for although he was tutor to a prince, laden with literary honours and very rich for a man of learning, he would not have wanted to begin his career again. Such a rare creature is happiness!—as Bayle concludes rather flippantly on this subject!' (*MM*, 126; passage added in the second edition). La Mothe le Vayer appears again in La Mettrie's *System of Epicurus*, LXXVIII (*MM*, 110–11), and in the new preface added to *Anti-Seneca* in 1751 (*DB*, 117). On Bayle's overall influence on La Mettrie (who often refers to the *Dictionnaire* and *Pensées diverses*), see Thomson, *Materialism*, 155–61.

18. Compare Bentham's suggestion that the pleasure felt by a criminal is morally good *qua* pleasure (Baumgardt, *Bentham*, 211–15).

> drives you. How could I? It is the source of your *unhappy happiness*. Bears, lions, tigers, they love to tear apart other animals: since you are ferocious like they are, it is only just that you should cede to the same inclinations. (*AS*, 208–9; my emphasis)

Finally, he addresses that spectre of the age, the libertine [*voluptueux*], in a passage later read by the marquis de Sade as advice to all mankind:

> since you cannot attain the happy life without vivacious pleasures, leave your soul and your Seneca behind; all these Stoic virtues are just songs to you! Think of nothing but your body. . . . Have a good time whenever and wherever it comes to you; enjoy the present; forget the past which no longer exists, and don't fear the future. . . . Since you have no other resources, make the most of them: Drink, eat, sleep, snore, dream; and if you're going to think from time to time, let it be in between two wines . . . if filth and infamy are more your thing; wallow in it as pigs do, and you'll be happy in the same way as they are. (*AS*, 210)[19]

As for the objection that seems to present itself, that La Mettrie is inviting crime, he denies the charge: 'I only invite *repose* in the crime' (*AS*, 211; my emphasis). He stresses that he is writing not as a preacher or even as a citizen, but as a *philosopher*, and as a philosopher he sees that some people are born to steal and kill: 'Counsels are useless to those who are born with the thirst for carnage and for blood' (*AS*, 212).[20]

The idea, then, seems to be that we are radically powerless to control our actions as well as our temperaments: if we have the misfortune (and La Mettrie *does* consider it a misfortune) to be born a thief or murderer or tyrant, then this is our lot, but we need not add to this lot the burden of remorse and misery. 'I do not embolden the wicked,' says La Mettrie, 'I pity them from humanity, and I calm them by reason. If I relieve them of a heavy burden, this does not mean I don't acknowledge that they are themselves a much more onerous burden for society' (*AS*, 213). He does not, however, shy away from the conclusion that 'happiness is, like sensuality, in the reach of all the world; the good as well as the wicked' (*AS*, 215). Since happiness depends crucially on modifications in the nervous system, it is as possible for the good to be unhappy as it is for the wicked to be happy:

19. De Sade paraphrases this passage in *Juliette* (*Justine*, viii, 198); see Falvey, 'Introduction', 97–8.

20. On the *citoyen*/*philosophe* distinction, see also *DP*, e.g. 233.

> I conclude that everyone has his portion of felicity, beggars as well as the rich, the ignorant as well as the learned, animals as well as men (for the time of making them machines devoid of feeling is over), and that every individual attains his own degree of happiness, as it is with health, with gaiety, with intellect, with strength, with courage, and with humanity; and that, consequently, *we are built to be happy or unhappy*, almost to an exact point, just as we are built to die young or old from this or that cause, surrounded by physicians. (*AS*, 216; my emphasis)

Not only, then, is happiness attributed entirely to factors outside our will (our internal constitutions in combination with external circumstances), but La Mettrie provides here a physiological, determinist, and naturalistic explanation of the theodicean problem of *misalignment*: the question of why the wicked prosper while the righteous suffer. Theodicy, all the while, is not in question here: it is not even a factor taken into consideration by a materialist such as La Mettrie.

MISERY AND SUICIDE

Thus La Mettrie's *Anti-Seneca* provides us with a neo-Epicurean attack on Stoicism, where the main argument is not just that Stoicism doesn't work, but that it gets some fundamental things wrong about the nature of happiness and the extent to which we are in control of our this-worldly flourishing.[21] If we are unhappy, that is not due to a failure of the will, but to the fact that not everyone is made for happiness—and certainly not everyone is made for the kind of high-brow happiness that the Stoics espouse. This is not to say, however, that La Mettrie makes happiness dependent on sensual pleasures instead: in fact, he believes that these are often too brief and too infrequent in nature to provide us with a permanent state of happiness. Nevertheless, he argues, we should consider them as 'lightning flashes of happiness [*des éclairs de Bonheur*], which cannot be lacking without rendering the joys of life imperfect and truncated' (*AS*, 202).

But what about misfortunes? The strength and enduring appeal of the Stoic project, especially in the early modern age, may have had more to do with its promise to help us cope with adversity than in paving the road to happiness itself. The question to which the Stoics provided such a persuasive answer was not just *How to be happy?*, but also *How to respond to misfortune?*

21. This, again, is not originally an Epicurean point: La Mettrie's neo-Epicureanism (where the emphasis is very much on the *neo*) is at times rather a form of scepticism.

In considering the latter question, La Mettrie ends up supporting a large part of the Stoic solution. It is with great appreciation that he refers to Seneca, Epictetus, and Marcus Aurelius, aside from Epicurus and Montaigne, as 'my physicians in adversity; their courage is its remedy' (*AS*, 169). If the Stoics excel in one thing it is in helping 'us' (that is, 'gens de Lettres') to cope with our afflictions; for instance, by teaching us to detach ourselves from certain things so we will not be too devastated if we end up losing them (*AS*, 170). However, La Mettrie parts ways with the Stoics when it comes to their attitude to another possible 'remedy' to our misfortunes: that of suicide.

The problem for La Mettrie is not that the Stoics do not condemn suicide. In some cases of truly unbearable suffering, La Mettrie agrees that suicide is the best (essentially, the *only*) way out. Sometimes nature accosts us with ills such as 'poverty, misery, pain, chains', which are followed by horror and despair, so that the soul thus afflicted has no more hopes and no more desires than to die: now seeing 'nothingness as a good, because its being is an evil, [the soul] tries to hasten itself towards it'. Not only is this flight into *le néant* permitted, but the alternative becomes a kind of transgression in itself: 'Without doubt it is a violation of nature to conserve it for its own torment.' As soon as life is 'absolutely destitute of any good, and on the contrary afflicted by a host of terrible evils', there seems to be little reason why anyone should wait for 'an ignominious death' (*AS*, 171–2). The Stoics are not wrong to condone suicide in such cases. Their mistake lies, rather, in carrying their lenient attitude too far, which leads them into several contradictions. It is one thing to allow for suicide in cases of extreme suffering, La Mettrie argues, but it is quite another to recommend it whenever someone complains of *any* misfortunes:

> 'You cry', says my Stoic, 'because you lack bread! and why do you care, since you do not lack means of dying? For one way of coming into the World, Nature, which does not retain anyone, offers you a hundred of leaving it.' (*AS*, 171–2)

La Mettrie criticises the Stoics for first saying that poverty and illness are not real evils, then suggesting that we kill ourselves to free ourselves from them; and for first saying that no one can be unhappy as long as they have virtue, then recommending suicide at the first sight of misfortune. The fact that Stoics, like La Mettrie himself, do not believe in an afterlife does not mean they should cast aside *this life* so lightly:

> it is equally ridiculous for a person who only believes in one life (which he believes to be beautiful and good, if he is not a hypochondriac) to

prepare himself to receive a blow which he does not fear as to accelerate it, as long as life is not only bearable but full of charms. (*AS*, 174)

So, on the one hand, La Mettrie accepts that suicide might be a due response to *extreme* misery or misfortune, but on the other, he rejects it as a response to *any* misery whatsoever. The Stoics should have focused on helping us bear our 'chains of flowers', rather than on emphasising this last resort (*AS*, 174).[22] 'It is less glorious to know how to die than to know how to live with pains and setbacks' (*AS*, 199).

Thus La Mettrie combines a basic anti-Stoic argument, according to which we have little control over our own happiness—and, anyway, happiness does not reside in virtue—with a kind of mitigated Stoicism that opts *against* Seneca with regard to happiness and suicide but *for* him with regard to suffering, misfortune, and death. As he would write shortly afterwards in his *System of Epicurus* (1750): 'Such are my *Projects for Life and Death*: a voluptuous Epicurean in the course of life until my last breath, and a steady Stoic at the approach of death' (*MM*, 114; his emphasis).[23] La Mettrie never did make a secret of his 'voluptuous Epicurean' lifestyle, and in fact he died shortly afterwards with the unflattering, though probably ungrounded, reputation of having eaten himself to death.[24]

All in all, there is a lot here for any eighteenth-century philosopher to take issue with, and the first reply to La Mettrie's *Anti-Seneca* appeared almost before the ink was dry, penned by the very person who had given him the idea of writing it in the first place: his friend Pierre de Maupertuis.

Calculating Evils: Maupertuis

In the article *Xenophanes*, as we have seen, Bayle tried to find 'the right scale' for weighing life's goods and evils, and in calibrating this scale he appealed to history and literature as well as to everyday experience and

22. More deeply, La Mettrie seems to be criticising the Stoic assumption that nothing is lost in death from an atheist viewpoint, and the old Epicurean argument that death cannot be bad for the person who dies, which is all the more striking since such views tended to be seen as the only available alternative to the religious paradigm.

23. This self-representation of La Mettrie as an Epicurean *and* a Stoic occurs at several points, such as in this passage added in the second edition: 'I am not so Epicurean that I'm not a Stoic at the same time, since I want to reduce the sum of evils even before I try to augment the sum of goods' (*DB*, 231). It is not clear that this reflects a deep understanding of what Epicureanism as a *moral* system entails.

24. La Mettrie's death seems to have had something to do with indigestion but was sumptuously overcooked by posterity as something resembling Monty Python's Mr Creosote; see Falvey, 'Introduction', 92, McMahon, *Pursuit*, 222; Wellman, *La Mettrie*, 6.

thought experiment (*would you live your life again?*). He fully conceded a methodological problem: we cannot objectively evaluate other people's experiences and even tend to misjudge our own situations. While it may therefore be possible to weigh goods and evils against each other, it is not possible to calculate or quantify them absolutely: the most we can achieve is probability. That being said, Bayle argues that it is highly probable that pessimism is true, and that the burden of evidence lies on the side of optimism.[25] As we will see in chapter 5, Hume, following in Bayle's footsteps, expresses even greater methodological caution: 'For who is able to form an exact computation of all the happiness and misery, that are in the world, and to compare them exactly with each other?' (*FE*, 110).[26]

Writing at about the same time as when Hume was composing his *Dialogues concerning Natural Religion*, Pierre de Maupertuis, armed with all the confidence of the Enlightenment *philosophes*, seems to think he is able to do just this. In a curious little treatise, *Essai de philosophie morale*, he offers a computation or calculation of the goods and evils of existence, coming down firmly on the side of pessimism, and in the course of this supplying what seems to be an argument in defence of suicide. But lest we mistake Maupertuis for an unadulterated pessimist making neo-pagan arguments for suicide and taking a Baylean stance on the problem of evil, we should bear in mind the immediate context in which it was written. What occasioned the treatise was the appearance of La Mettrie's unexpected attack on Seneca, an attack all the more unwelcome since it seems to have been triggered by Maupertuis himself: La Mettrie apparently got the idea of translating Seneca's *De vita beata* when he saw a copy of the work on Maupertuis's desk, and Maupertuis heartily encouraged this project until he knew what it entailed. Having read the *Anti-Seneca* in its earliest version, the one first published in 1748 as an introduction to La Mettrie's translation, Maupertuis immediately penned a treatise in response, which was pirated soon after he sent the manuscript to one

25. Note that it is the theodicean context of justification that places the burden on optimism here.

26. Hume also offers an interesting analogy: we couldn't decide whether more boys or girls are born just by asking the people we know; we'd need proper data (such as the 'bills of mortality') to 'bring the matter to a certainty' (*FE*, 111). Thus the calculation of goods and evils would seem to require a proto-sociological approach, like the one suggested by William Petty, who thought he knew a way of quantifying sin and vice: 'By the number of people, the quality of inebriating liquors spent, the number of unmarried persons of between 15 and 55 years old, the number of Corporal sufferings & persons imprisoned for Crimes, to know the measure of Vice & Sin in the Nation' (William Petty, *Of Lands and Hands*, cited in Sivado, 'The Ontology of Sir William Petty's Political Arithmetic').

of his friends.[27] Following this first pirated edition of 1749, Maupertuis rushed to prepare a corrected and approved version of his *Essai de philosophie morale*, which contained a new preface and several new passages, and was published in the autumn of 1750.

It incurred something of a reputation. 'Mr Maupertuis, who has believed all his life and has perhaps proven that he is not happy, just published a small text on happiness,' wrote Montesquieu gleefully,[28] while Madeleine de Puisieux commented that 'after reading Maupertuis, you would almost wish you were dead'.[29] But while the *Essai* is best known for its calculation of goods and evils and the resulting pessimist conclusions, this is only part of the story Maupertuis is trying to tell. The background to this treatise is filled up with the spectres raised by La Mettrie: the question of whether there is a right road to happiness and whether we are even capable of achieving happiness by self-determination; whether happiness is even something that is really *up to us*. In responding to La Mettrie, Maupertuis does supply some very Baylean weighing exercises *and* makes the case for pessimism, but he does this in order to argue that we are *to some extent* empowered to control our levels of happiness, and that the very 'fact' of pessimism provides a principal argument in favour of Stoicism over Epicureanism. The point of the treatise, therefore, is not just to argue that pessimism is true, but to demonstrate how we can try to be happy nonetheless. At the risk of making Maupertuis sound a little too much like a self-help book, I will reconstruct his hedonic calculus in four steps.

STEP ONE: WHAT IS HAPPINESS?

First, some definitions. What are pleasures and pains; goods and evils; happiness and unhappiness? Maupertuis defines *pleasure* as 'any perception that the soul would rather experience than not experience'; *pain* as 'any perception the soul would rather not experience than experience' (*EPM*, 1–2).[30] These pleasures and pains create happy and unhappy

27. Maupertuis probably read La Mettrie's work in May 1749; by late December, he was complaining of a pirated edition of his *Essai* (Beeson, *Maupertuis*, 193–4).

28. Quoted in Beeson, *Maupertuis*, 204 (my translation).

29. Madeleine de Puisieux, *Les Caractères* (1750), 174; my translation. In this work, Puisieux (French writer and early feminist, 1720–1798) criticises Maupertuis for having submitted all of humanity to a 'moral arithmetic that is particular to him' and to people like him (ibid., 175). His thought experiments, then, lack universality.

30. Maupertuis mostly uses the more neutral term *peine* in the conjunction of *plaisirs et peines*, reserving *douleur* for physical pain specifically. Bentham thinks it is in his

moments, which last as long as the corresponding pleasures and pains do. But in weighing these happy and unhappy moments, we should take into account not just the *duration* but also the *intensity* of the pleasure or pain in question. This intensity can be so great that a brief but intense happy (or unhappy) moment could be equivalent to a very long but much less intense one, and vice versa: duration, if it lasts long enough, could outweigh a powerful intensity (*EPM*, 3–5).[31] The problem is that while durations are easy to compare, respective intensities are not. Nevertheless, we have a strong intuitive sense of which are stronger or weaker, and we constantly make judgements with regard to both the duration and intensity of our pains and pleasures throughout our daily lives. From these off-the-cuff judgements result our confused daily estimations of happy moments and unhappy ones (*EPM*, 6–7).

Moving on to what constitutes goods and ills (or evils), Maupertuis's answer is a firmly hedonistic one: the good (*le Bien*) equals the sum of happy moments, whereas the bad or ill (*le Mal*) equals the sum of unhappy moments in our lives. So far, the sums in questions are purely the result of addition: of adding up the amount and weight of happy moments (in one case) or unhappy moments (in the other). But to arrive at a calculation of *happiness* and *unhappiness*, another sum has to be made, one that features subtraction as well as addition: since there are always intervals of happy moments between unhappy moments, and vice versa, we have to subtract the one from the other. Happiness can thus be defined as 'the sum of goods that remain once the ills have been subtracted from them', and unhappiness as 'the sum of ills that remain once the goods have been subtracted from them' (*EPM*, 8–9).

Happiness and unhappiness depend, therefore, on the *relative proportion* of goods and evils in our lives. The happiest person is not always the person who has the greatest overall sum of goods, since this says nothing about the evils in that person's life: evils that may have detracted from these goods to such an extent that they could have diminished this person's happiness even more than the goods have augmented it. The happiest person, therefore, is the person left with the greatest sum of goods remaining *after* the evils have been subtracted: what we might call the

definition of pleasure that Maupertuis goes wrong, since it 'is so constructed as to exclude from any title to that appellation, every degree of pleasure that falls short of being the highest' (Bentham, manuscript of ca. 1782, cited in Baumgardt, *Bentham*, 557; see also another manuscript from ca. 1776; ibid., 567).

31. This is all very similar to Bayle, with the qualification that Bayle thinks (like Schopenhauer and Benatar after him) that pains are intrinsically more intense than pleasures.

'net value' of happiness (*EPM*, 10).[32] What of a person for whom the sum of goods is exactly equal to the sum of evils? Such persons, for Maupertuis, are neither happy nor unhappy; their existence is worth as much as nothing: 'Le Néant vaut son Être.' Furthermore, as soon as the sum of evils begins to surpass the sum of goods, such persons can be called *unhappy*; and the more the evils outweigh the goods, the unhappier they are. Their existence, then, is not even worth as much as nothing: 'Son Être ne vaut pas le Néant' (*EPM*, 11).[33]

This latter point in particular may give us some pause. Many of us may well agree that once there are more pains than pleasures in a person's life (in terms of intensity as well as duration), that person can be called unhappy (and, indeed, this does seem to be the leading conception in modern happiness research). But even if we were to concede this point, it is quite another to say that the existence of an unhappy person is not just worth nothing, but is *not even* worth nothing; is worth *less* than nothingness. Is this not the same as suggesting that it would be better for such persons to stop existing altogether, even though the tide may turn on their unhappiness, and even though they might have other reasons to continue living? I return to this question in step four below.

STEP TWO: WHY EVILS SURPASS THE GOODS

Maupertuis's next step is to prove that 'in ordinary life the sum of evils surpasses the sum of goods' (*EPM*, 17). If this sounds very much like Bayle, that's because it probably is; this part of Maupertuis's project reads very much like a remake of *Xenophanes*, including the thought experiment that featured so prominently there. Maupertuis may not refer explicitly to Bayle, or to any other modern author in this treatise, but that does not mean Bayle is not in the background here as much as he is in Hume's *Dialogues concerning Natural Religion*, and in much the same way.[34] In fact, there is little that Maupertuis contributes to this discussion that had not already been said by Bayle. Considering Maupertuis's mathematical

32. The term 'net value' is mine, though Wollaston in his calculus of pains and pleasures also speaks of a 'net' or 'true quantity of pleasure', which is identical to happiness (Wollaston, *RND*, 36).

33. A drastic conclusion, since it would suggest that even the slightest outweighing of evils over goods would render life not worth living; which is, in fact, the conclusion reached in an anti-natalist context by Benatar, *Better Never to Have Been*.

34. See Wootton, *Power, Pleasure, and Profit*, 122: 'It was presumably from Bayle (although he never mentions him) that Maupertuis got the key arguments of his essay on morality.'

language of calculating or counting pains and pleasures (*calculer*, *compter*, *tenir compte*), we might expect a more scientific or at least quantitative analysis than Bayle's fluid phenomenological approach. In fact, Baylean intimations are exactly what we're in for.

First, Maupertuis again separates the duration of pains and pleasures from their intensity, as Bayle too had distinguished the quantitative and qualitative aspects of our experience. According to Maupertuis, most people, if they considered their happy and unhappy moments purely in terms of *duration*, would agree that their lives consisted of more unhappy than happy ones (*EPM*, 20). He assumes this to be a commonsense assumption, based on what we observe in our lives and the lives of others,[35] but he also adds a more technical point, one that foreshadows later pessimists' reflections on the nature of longing or striving. To desire something, says Maupertuis, is to wish for the span of time between ourselves and the attainment of that desire to be annihilated; longing, as long as it is unsatisfied, is mere frustration. The result is that we desire days or months or even entire years to be suppressed from our lives, so that, in an entire lifetime, there are maybe just a few hours that remain unbegrudged: that is, just a few hours in which we do not desire for that time to be annulled. As for all the other time, since we would wish it gone from our lives, it can be composed only of unhappy moments (*EPM*, 19–20).[36] Schopenhauer *avant la lettre*, indeed: here, we see the beginnings of exactly the kind of a priori pessimism that the later thinker would attempt to establish in its own right.[37]

Furthermore, Maupertuis continues, if people also considered the *intensity* of their pains and pleasures, then the sum of evils would be all the greater, and the pessimistic proposition (according to which evils outweigh goods) all the more true (*EPM*, 21). 'All the pastimes of men prove the unhappiness of their condition', writes Maupertuis: occupations such as chess and hunting are invented purely to avoid disagreeable

35. The fact that Maupertuis, like Bayle and Hume, sees this as a common-sense assumption is itself significant.

36. To which Bentham (who argues that well-being indisputably outweighs ill-being) would object that there is a pleasure in anticipation itself: 'Pleasure may be springing from a thousand sources, while anticipation is looking to the opening of many more. The present may be bright with enjoyment, while the door of a brighter future is unlocked; and to the pleasures of possession may be associated the pleasures of hope' (*Deontology*, 79–81). Compare also Fontenelle (*Du Bonheur*, 263) on the 'intervalles languissants' between happy moments.

37. For the most part, however, Maupertuis conducts his glossary of evils purely on (Baylean) a posteriori terms.

perceptions, and if these distractions don't suffice, then other resources such as liquors and opiates take their place (*EPM*, 21–2). This condition, furthermore, is universal: 'In Europe, Asia, Africa, and America, all men, otherwise so distinct, have sought out remedies for their unhappiness (*Mal de vivre*)' (*EPM*, 22–3). To drive this point home, Maupertuis has recourse to a certain thought experiment that by now should sound very familiar indeed:

> Just ask them; you will find very few people, in whatever condition, who would want to recommence their life just as it had been, who would want to pass again through the same states in which they had found themselves. Isn't this the clearest avowal that they have experienced more evils than goods? (*EPM*, 23)[38]

Maupertuis's case for pessimism ends here. For all his confidence, he has not done anything that Bayle had not done before: the chapter on pessimism is a kind of *Xenophanes* revisited, but lacking in Bayle's subtlety or caution. It would be a mistake, however, to stop reading here, for the main interest of this text resides not so much in Maupertuis's statement of pessimism itself, but rather in what he does next. Again, the philosophical context here is not the problem of evil but the problem of happiness, and it seems that Maupertuis is making things rather difficult for himself by prefacing his theory of happiness with an argument that pessimism is objectively true. Yet he concludes this chapter by asking whether this proportion between goods and evils cannot be changed; whether it isn't the bad usage man makes of his reason that makes this proportion so *funeste*; whether man could not somehow attain a happier life after all (*EPM*, 24). In other words: If life is indeed miserable, how can we be happy nonetheless?

STEP THREE: BODY AND SOUL

Maupertuis goes on to discuss the nature of pleasures and pains in more detail, focusing specifically on two overall categories: pains and pleasures *of the body*, and pains and pleasures *of the soul* (*EPM*, 29–31). Here, I will

38. Similarly familiar is Bentham's response, which is a version of King's argument from suicide: 'The unfrequency of suicide is irresistible testimony to the fact that life is, on the whole, a blessing' (*Deontology*, 80). Puisieux argues that nothing general can be concluded from these and similar thought experiments, since other motives (such as the fear of death) may influence the answer (*Caractères*, 178–9).

call these *physical* and *spiritual* pleasures and pains.[39] We are moving more clearly to ground covered by La Mettrie, with whom Maupertuis is partly in agreement. Like La Mettrie, Maupertuis argues that there is no difference *in principle* between spiritual and physical pleasures: the one kind is not more or less noble than the other. All that matters for our evaluation, again, is intensity and duration: 'the most noble pleasures are those that are the greatest' (*EPM*, 29). Like La Mettrie, furthermore, Maupertuis rejects those philosophers who would overemphasise one kind of pleasure at the expense of the other, when in fact both kinds need to be taken into account in our calculation of goods and evils (*EPM*, 33). Having said this, Maupertuis goes on to address certain background asymmetries between pains and pleasures, noting for instance that while the intensity of pleasure tends to diminish by duration, the intensity of pain tends rather to increase (*EPM*, 33). He then moves to highlight more specific asymmetries between spiritual and physical pains and pleasures.

First, with regard to *physical* pains and pleasures, Maupertuis argues that physical pleasures tend to last only briefly, and if they do last longer, they become fainter or even uncomfortable. Physical pain, on the other hand, 'can last as long as life itself; and the longer it lasts, the more unbearable it becomes' (*EPM*, 34). He suggests that this point is easily confirmed by experience: the most delightful sensual pleasures fade with overexposure, while bodily pain caused by sword or fire only intensifies the longer it lasts (*EPM*, 35). Second, there are only a few body parts that can procure pleasures for us, while all of them can make us feel pain: 'The tip of a finger or a single tooth is able to torment us more than the organ of the greatest pleasures can render us happy' (*EPM*, 35–6).[40] Third, the overuse of objects inducing bodily pleasures will lead to infirmities, 'whereas the amount of pains [we can suffer] is without boundaries, and even the pleasures themselves contribute to filling it' (*EPM*, 36–7). Hence, there exists a qualitative phenomenological difference between physical pains and physical pleasures. The point tacitly being made here is that we cannot expect physical sensation to contribute meaningfully to our happiness, considering that the associated pleasures are in such a disadvantaged position with regard to the associated pains.

39. I use the term *spiritual* because this represents a narrower category than all mental or psychological pleasures and pains (see below, p. 168).

40. Compare David Benatar: 'The worst pains are also worse than the best pleasures are good. Those who deny this should consider whether they would accept an hour of the most delightful pleasures in exchange for an hour of the worst tortures' (Benatar, 'Anti-Natalism', 49).

What of *spiritual* pains and pleasures? It should be noted here that Maupertuis, in speaking of pains and pleasures of the soul, does not employ a Baylean conception. Bayle, as we have seen, holds that *any kind* of psychological suffering can rightly be considered an evil of the soul, be it grief, sadness, regret, general malaise, or 'chagrin'. In contrast, Maupertuis takes a more Augustinian or even neo-Platonist view, according to which true spiritual pleasures are defined by either truth or justice, and spiritual pains by the lack or transgression of either good. Consequently, base mental or psychological pleasures having to do rather with avarice or worldly ambition do not qualify: these are just 'pleasures of the body seen from a distance' (*EPM*, 39). Similarly, Maupertuis does not count the loss of riches or power as pains of the soul, since such regrets have to do rather with the loss of bodily pleasures; as such, his conception of physical and spiritual pains is lodged firmly in Augustinian associations of sin with the body, even though the body may not be directly involved. In the preface added to the first authorised edition of the *Essai*, he even extends this distinction to the pain of grief. The idea is that if I mourn a friend who benefited and pleased me, then grief belongs to the body, but if I mourn someone who helped me on the way to truth and justice, then what I experience is a grief of the soul (*EPM*, xxvii).[41]

Spiritual pleasures, then, are associated with either 'the practice of *Justice*' or 'the view of *Truth*', and spiritual pains with the loss of either one (*EPM*, 40–1; his emphasis).[42] Using this conception, Maupertuis argues that spiritual pleasures have certain advantages over bodily pleasures—*not* because they are intrinsically more noble, but because they are generally more effective to our happiness. First, 'far from passing away quickly, or weakening by enjoyment, the pleasures of the soul are sustainable; they are augmented by duration and repetition'. Second, the soul experiences these pleasures throughout its being ('dans toute son étendue'). Third, the enjoyment of these pleasures does not weaken the soul (as bodily pleasures do the body), but strengthens it (*EPM*, 42). A further distinction has to do with the nature of spiritual pains. While it is true that such pains (such as the awareness that 'we have not followed

41. This stands in sharp contrast to the more neutral or amoral representations of grief in Bayle and Hume; see chapters 1 and 5.

42. Bentham objects to the separation of these lofty pleasures from the others: 'I think it will not need many words to shew that these pleasures, great and real as they are, (or, to speak more accurately sources of pleasures) depend as entirely upon the pleasures of the body, as those which he has allow'd to do so' (manuscript ca. 1776, cited in Baumgardt, *Bentham*, 568).

justice or have not been able to discover the truth') are deeply painful, it always depends on us to avoid them, so that the pain itself is its own 'préservatif': the more keenly we feel it, the more it distances us from the danger of feeling it (*EPM*, 43).

Thus Maupertuis argues that spiritual pleasures are more effective to our happiness than bodily pleasures. But lest this is taken to suggest that life is not so bad after all, he is quick to point out that even those rare sages who manage to devote their lives to justice and truth are still exposed to pains of the body, so that the overall proposition remains valid: in ordinary life, the sum of evils surpasses the sum of goods (*EPM*, 44–5).

STEP FOUR: HOW TO BE HAPPY NONETHELESS

So much for the philosophical groundwork: In concrete terms, what does this mean for our chances of happiness? Isn't Maupertuis rehearsing the same old Stoic–Christian refrain criticised by La Mettrie, that we should reject sensual pleasures in order to strive solely for those associated with the virtues, with justice and truth? Maupertuis's point is subtler than that. He does not want to argue that sensual impressions are bad or should be avoided altogether, which would be impossible anyhow, since we live in a physical world (*EPM*, 47). But he does want to argue, against La Mettrie's hard determinism, that we have *freedom* by which we can arm ourselves against the effects of external objects: either by fleeing them or by diminishing their force upon us (*EPM*, 49–50). By virtue of this freedom, we can triumph entirely over the pains of the soul, and even exercise some control over the pains of the body: 'Even in the cruellest states [of being], there is no one who does not feel within himself a certain power that he can exert even against physical pain [*Douleur*]' (*EPM*, 50).[43]

Now, finally, Maupertuis is ready to come to his point. Considering that happiness depends entirely on the sums of goods and evils in our lives, there are only two ways to improve our condition: 'One consists in augmenting the sum of goods; the other in diminishing the sum of evils. It is to this calculation that the life of the sage ought to be devoted' (*EPM*.52). Accordingly, the ancient philosophers can be divided into two categories. One group (the Epicureans) believes that in order to improve our condition we have to accumulate as many pleasures as possible, while the other

43. Here again, we meet the neo-Stoic point made by Descartes and Leibniz: that through willpower and/or the right use of reason all are capable of conquering physical pain; see chapter 2.

group (the Stoics) only seeks to diminish our pains.[44] La Mettrie's judgement, as we have seen, comes down mostly on the side of the (neo-)Epicureans; Maupertuis, it may be clear by now, wants to opt rather for the Stoics. After all, 'If we had as many goods to hope for as evils to fear, both systems would be equally well founded.' But considering what has been said about the nature of pleasures and pains and their relative proportions, we know 'how much more reasonable it is to try to improve our condition by the diminution of the sum of evils than by the augmentation of the sum of goods' (*EPM*, 56).

Having examined the Stoic method (mastering our desires, distancing ourselves from exterior objects, choosing death when life's evils become overwhelming) in more detail, Maupertuis considers a possible objection: Isn't what the Stoics propose simply impossible? He replies that if we take a look at the lives of Stoics such as Seneca and Marcus Aurelius, it seems they have indeed approached the Stoic ideal; furthermore, if we consider the nature of man, we will believe him capable of everything as long as he is sufficiently motivated: 'capable of braving sadness, capable of braving death' (*EPM*, 66–7). As Leibniz did in the *Théodicée*, Maupertuis points to the example of the intrepid natives of North America, compared to whom people like Socrates were 'mere women': 'Amidst the cruellest torments you will find them unshaken; singing and dying' (*EPM*, 67). Other peoples have recourse to suicide as soon as 'the ennui of life takes over', or even for the smallest affront or *chagrin*. Thus there seem to be entire nations practising the most terrible parts of what the Stoics prescribed (*EPM*, 68–9).

There are, of course, those who believe that suicide, 'far from being a generous action, is nothing but a true cowardice', but such people insufficiently distinguish between 'the different positions in which man can find himself' (*EPM*, 70–1). If a person kills himself in the belief that he will suffer eternal torments, he is indeed neither courageous nor cowardly but insane (*un insensé*). But Maupertuis is only considering man 'in the natural state, without fear and without hope of another life; trying only to improve his condition' (*EPM*, 71–2). And if we reason from this natural state alone, we find that suicide is permissible in certain cases:

> it is evident that there is neither glory nor reason in remaining prey to evils that can be avoided by the pain of a single moment. As soon as the sum of evils surpasses the sum of goods, Nothingness [*le Néant*] is

44. Note again the misrepresentation of Epicureanism, which stood much closer to Stoicism in its 'strict regulation of desire' (McMahon, *Pursuit*, 55).

> preferable to Being: and the Stoics reasoned correctly when they considered death as a useful and permitted remedy. (*EPM*, 72)[45]

As soon as life's evils begin to outweigh the goods (even slightly, it seems), suicide is thus considered a reasonable action, so long as it is not forbidden by that person's religious beliefs: 'this question, of the right that a man has to his life, depends on the ideas he has of a divinity who permits or forbids him to dispose of it; on the mortality or immortality of the soul. It is therefore clear that the religion of the Stoics left them free in this regard' (*EPM*, 76).

Having said this, Maupertuis notes that while Stoicism is indeed more effective than Epicureanism for our happiness, another road is more effective still, one suggested not by reason but by revelation: the road of Christianity. Against contemporary tendencies to exaggerate the similarities between the morality of the Gospels and that of the Stoics, Maupertuis emphasises the contrast between the two: while Stoic morality tells us to think only of ourselves and to sacrifice everything to our own peace, Christianity tells us to love God with all our hearts and other people like ourselves (*EPM*, 88). He argues that accomplishing these two precepts is the source of the greatest possible happiness that can be found in this life: 'Not only will this universal devotion lead to tranquillity; but love will spread a sweetness through it which the Stoic does not know' (*EPM*, 90). This sweetness (*douceur*) has to do with the *kind of world* that Stoics and Christians inhabit: while the Stoic sees nothing but an inflexible fate and human beings he despises, the Christian sees everywhere the signs of providence and of 'an infinitely good Being [who] arranges all things'; furthermore, he respects other men as the work of God and loves them as brothers (*EPM*, 92–4). Thus the Stoics' beliefs fill their lives with sadness, while the Christian's life is filled with sweetness: 'he loves, he adores, he blesses constantly' (*EPM*, 94).[46] Furthermore, while the goods promised by the Stoics are limited to the present life, after which only nothingness awaits us, Christianity offers goods in the present *as well as* the future life (*EPM*, 95–6).[47]

45. Litwin ('"Le principe nécessaire"', 209n.) sees in the middle part of this passage, and in Maupertuis's weighing of goods and evils more generally, a reprisal of Malebranche.

46. Compare Schopenhauer, *WWR*.I.374, '[t]he good person lives in a world of friendly phenomena', as well as Wittgenstein, *Tractatus*, 6.43, 'The world of the happy man is a different one from that of the unhappy man'.

47. Perhaps as a sign of the times, Maupertuis fails to discuss the obvious objection: that Christianity also offers significant evils in the form of (eternal) damnation.

It is crucial for Maupertuis that the goods offered by Christianity do not reside *purely* in the hopes of other-worldly happiness, and that we do not draw too crude a distinction between the kind of happiness we can expect in this life and in the next. It would be an error to believe that there must be different means to the same end (happiness) in this and the next life, just as it would be an error to believe that we have to live in sadness and bitterness in order to be eternally happy. More than this, Maupertuis argues, in what is perhaps the only theodicean moment of the *Essai*: 'It is an impiety to think that the Divinity would have turned us away from the true happiness while offering us a happiness incompatible with it' (*EPM*, 124). And, in fact, it is precisely Christianity's claim to ensuring our happiness that Maupertuis cites as the strongest reason to believe, a move that Arthur O. Lovejoy compares to the kind of 'pragmatism' espoused in William James's *The Will to Believe*: 'Should I not believe that [the system] that leads me to happiness is the one that cannot deceive me?' (*EPM*, 123).[48] This happiness, furthermore, belongs equally to this life and the next, as Maupertuis writes in the closing words of his treatise: '*All that we have to do in this life to find the greatest happiness of which our nature is capable is the same that will lead to eternal happiness*' (*EPM*, 124–5; his emphasis).

Optimistic Pessimism?

In this curious dialogue between La Mettrie and Maupertuis, we see the intersection of two debates: that on pessimism with that on Stoicism. The context, again, is decidedly not a theodicean one: the question at the heart of these debates is whether any happiness is to be found in human life, and if so, *how*. It is here, then, that pessimism, for the first time in the modern era, has its own debate, emancipated as it were from the debate on the origins of evil and justification of God's goodness. In Maupertuis's essay in particular, the questions posed by Bayle in the context of the problem of evil are lifted out of that much older debate and become topics in their own right, in a way that allowed them to be discussed by later authors still less interested in providence and justification, and all the more in happiness, suffering, and ways of weighing them. (One such reader was Jeremy Bentham, who read Maupertuis in his early twenties, and cited

48. See Lovejoy, 'Rousseau's Pessimist', 451–2.

Maupertuis as one of the influences for his own attempt of establishing a hedonic calculus[49]).

If nothing else, this is a defining moment in the history of pessimism, and it is marked by several crucial concerns that will haunt later pessimists and can here be seen subtly coming to the fore. One of these concerns is the effort of authors to distance their personal characters from the dark subject matter of their books. It is with good reason that Maupertuis anticipates the objection (well-known to later thinkers in this tradition) that his pessimism is simply the effect of his personality; that it cannot be taken seriously as a philosophy since it probably derived rather from a pathology or idiosyncrasy.[50] In the preface added to the first authorised edition of the *Essai* (1751), Maupertuis writes that some people attacking his work have represented it as 'the bitter fruit of melancholy', and is quick to point out that it was written 'neither in exile or in chagrin, but in my most beautiful days, at the centre of a dazzling court' (*EPM*, xiii–xiv).[51] Here, we can already see the need for a justification of pessimism, which seems to gain in credibility the more the author is able to distance it from his personality. As we will see, a similar concern presents itself in the writings of optimists such as Rousseau, who feels the need to emphasise his hardships in order to give credibility to his optimism.[52]

Another striking feature of Maupertuis's pessimism is his sense that this philosophy entails a specific moral responsibility, one that we might almost call *an ethics of pessimism*. Again in the preface, Maupertuis defends himself against the charge that by way of his pessimism he meant to 'make people hate life'. For one thing, he points out that he is not a poet or orator depicting more sadness than there is: he is a 'Philosopher who counts and weighs pains and pleasures' (*EPM*, xv). For another, while he concedes that his work would be pernicious if it painted evils too vividly *without* offering ways to bear them and even remedies against them, this is not a case that can be made against Maupertuis (*EPM*, xvii). Pessimism, for Maupertuis, *ought not* to have a place in the philosophical

49. Halévy, *Jeunesse de Bentham*, 288–9; on Bentham and Maupertuis see also Guidi, 'Jeremy Bentham's Quantitative Analysis', and 'Pain and Human Action'.

50. On which, see Dienstag, *Pessimism*, 3–5.

51. Maupertuis's choice of words here is noteworthy, since La Mettrie was himself an exile at Frederick's 'dazzling' court and, despite his assertions to the contrary, 'extremely unhappy in exile' (Thomson, *Materialism*, 247n., 12–15). La Mettrie points out the contrast between Maupertuis's life and writings in *DP*, 230.

52. See chapter 6; note that I use the label 'optimist' most hesitantly here.

debate without a practical counterpart that offers something in the way of hope and consolation: rather than standing still at the predicament, writers of pessimism ought to offer us ways of bearing it. This, furthermore, is something philosophy is more than capable of doing, since philosophers have been more successful in making progress in the quest for happiness than in any other science (*EPM*, 25–6).

A final element by which Maupertuis foreshadows later pessimists has to do with the question of style:

> Some have found [the style of this work] sad and dry; I admit that it is so: but I do not believe it should be otherwise. Even if I would have been able to adorn it with flowers, the severity of the subject did not allow it. (*EPM*, xxx)

While it is not the case that all later pessimists would agree that their philosophy should be 'sad and dry', thinkers such as Schopenhauer would certainly agree that there is a special need for awareness here: that pessimism requires a style of its own.[53]

Then again, we should not overemphasise Maupertuis's place in any pessimist tradition. As we have also seen, towards the end of the *Essai*, Maupertuis's pessimism seems to have run its course, flowing out into what looks to be a muted providential optimism: while the evils of *this life* outweigh the goods, Christianity offers a wider perspective and another life, in which eternal happiness awaits us. This is the hope and consolation offered to those who live in this-worldly misery, which can itself be softened and even transformed once Christianity changes, with our perspective, the kind of world we live in. The optimistic turn of the *Essai*, then, does not reside solely in its reference to the next life (where so many critics of pessimism would place our hope and consolation). Behind the technical arguments on pains and pleasures, Stoics and Epicureans, lies a deeper objection that Maupertuis struggles to articulate: that the view afforded on human life by La Mettrie's uncompromising determinism is not just mistaken, but morally compromised, not so much because it encourages us to crime, but because it discourages us from striving for improvement. If it is true, as La Mettrie argues, that we dramatically lack control over our happiness, then we have no hope of bettering our condition, and it is even more the case that we live in a deeply unfriendly world. This, Maupertuis seems to be saying, this is *real* pessimism, not his own view,

53. On the style of pessimism, particularly the aphorism, see Dienstag, *Pessimism*, chapter 7.

which offers such hopes of improvement, even if we choose not to adopt the Christian stance (in which case, Stoicism features as second best). As such, the critique he formulates against La Mettrie is of exactly the same kind as the one Leibniz presents against Bayle and Rousseau against Voltaire: that pessimism (of any of these varieties) is discredited by its failure in hope and consolation. What we find in Maupertuis, then, is less a Baylean pessimism than a Christian pessimism, a hopeful pessimism, or even, paradoxically, an *optimistic* one.

Pessimistic Optimism?

This is where we may begin to be confused: Who is the optimist here, who the pessimist? After all, unlike Maupertuis, La Mettrie believes that life is generally pretty good: unless you're actually overwhelmed by horrific suffering (in which case he does recommend suicide), then most afflictions are bearable, and only a 'hypochondriac' would fail to believe that life is 'beautiful and good' (*AS*, 174). So surely he was the optimist and Maupertuis the pessimist? But the reason why the encounter between these two thinkers is so interesting is precisely *because* it disturbs these common categories. La Mettrie may well have taken a more positive view of life in general, but he also believed that we are not in control of our own happiness: that humans are born to happiness or unhappiness as they are born to die at a young or old age. If we are unlucky enough to enter this world with the wrong constitution, then there is nothing we can do, except make things worse by trying to fight against our lot or feeling guilty about it. (Like Bayle and especially Hume, La Mettrie is sceptical about the power we have to shape our attitudes in response to misfortune.)

As we have seen, La Mettrie is prepared to take this argument very far indeed, sounding positively immoral rather than amoral when it comes to his plea for the wicked and depraved to embrace their specific varieties of 'happiness'.[54] There is plenty to make us feel uncomfortable here, and yet it seems that La Mettrie is trying to offer a consoling and even hopeful message, which seeps into his very conception of the philosophical exercise. Unlike 'false philosophy', which fills our minds with false promises of eternal happiness, 'True philosophy . . . only admits temporal bliss; it casts roses and flowers in our path and teaches us to

54. One can imagine the marquis de Sade reading along in such passages, and he does cite La Mettrie on several occasions, though he may not have read his work 'other than in extracts' (Falvey, 'Introduction', 97).

gather them' (*MM*, 127).[55] While the true philosophy may deprive us of the consolation of an afterlife, it also frees us from many 'cruel fears' and worries about the future, allowing us to make the most of our short lives (*MM*, 128). This is a consolation, furthermore, that La Mettrie means to extend not only to the lower classes, but also to the depraved: 'In the system based on nature and reason, happiness is open to the ignorant and poor as much as to the learned and rich; there is a happiness for all classes—and this will revolt prejudiced minds—for the wicked as well as the good' (*MM*, 121).[56]

What La Mettrie is doing thus goes beyond a nonchalant defence of depravity, which was how many of his contemporaries interpreted his ideas (though Maupertuis and Voltaire both believed his character to be beyond reproach).[57] There is a curious and often clumsy plea here for compassion, which goes hand in hand with La Mettrie's rambunctious provocations and yet stands firmly apart from them.[58] Whether or not we are made for happiness, he repeats again and again, is just not up to us, and in fact 'it is not even in our power to take as much advantage of the best education as we would like, for the good of society. *We degenerate despite ourselves*' (*MM*, 143; my emphasis). In the same passage, he stresses the importance of these ideas, precisely from a moral point of view:

> This materialism deserves esteem; it should be the source of indulgence, excuse, pardon, reprieve, praise, moderation in punishment, which should only be decided regretfully, and the reward due to virtue, which cannot be accorded too wholeheartedly, as virtue is a sort of afterthought, an extraneous decoration, always ready to flee or to fall off for lack of support. (*MM*, 143)

Even if someone is found guilty of a crime and needs to be punished (which La Mettrie concedes is necessary for the public good), then such punishment should be exercised with due compassion and regret: 'For,

55. The question asked by Hume will be whether philosophy *can* in fact teach us to gather these flowers.

56. La Mettrie's attitude to the poor is a complicated one; on the one hand, he seems anxious to offer consolation by emphasising that happiness is in reach of even the poorest beggars, but on the other, he also represents poverty as a kind of life choice, a personal preference of laziness over activity (*DB*, 203–4).

57. Beeson, *Maupertuis*, 192: 'Like Voltaire, and unlike many *philosophes* who were unacquainted with La Mettrie personally, Maupertuis refused to condemn the man with his works.'

58. Falvey ('Introduction', 25–6) thinks there may be some truth in the reports that La Mettrie sometimes wrote while drunk.

Good God, what equity is there to take the life of a miserable wretch, who is the slave of the blood galloping in his veins, as the hand of a watch is the slave of the works which make it move?' (*MM*, 143).[59] La Mettrie's perspective, it should be remembered, is that of a physician, and so is his philosophy: 'we shall . . . start calmly along this new path, where we are led by *the best philosophy, that of physicians*' (*MM*, 135; *AS*, 153; my emphasis).[60] As a physician, La Mettrie feels bound to the conclusion that man is completely determined even to evil actions; as a philosopher, he believes the only possible response to this view of human nature is one of uncompromising compassion, not just for the miserable or the righteous who suffer under the wicked, *but for the wicked themselves*. As he wrote in a new preface to the *Anti-Seneca*, 'man is no more culpable for his perfidy or his wickedness than the tree is for its corrupted fruits. The germ of all things lies in character, and I know of no Philosopher Physician [*Médecin Philosophe*] who disagrees' (*DB*, 117).[61]

This is fatalism indeed, explicitly so, but it is a kind of fatalism that is thought not to be entirely without consolation.[62] The idea seems to be that the wicked, by being punished for their crimes, are actually being punished *twice* or even *three times*: having already been punished once by their very *constitutions*, which force them to strive for happiness in ways that run counter to the good of society, they are punished again by their conscience, which few are able to suppress completely, and a third time by the state, often in gruesome ways.[63] La Mettrie, motivated in this by what looks to be a real sense of concern and compassion, wants to remove from this machine of retribution the few cogs that can be eliminated: the feeling of remorse on the part of the criminal on the one hand, and the callousness of state punishment on the other, which should never be executed without an element of sadness and regret—

> When I see our executioners hanging, breaking on the wheel, burning and torturing their fellow beings, I can feel inside myself something which is in revolt; I seem to hear a voice groaning in the depths of my heart: 'Oh nature, Oh humanity, you are only an empty word if by

59. La Mettrie thinks 'legal punishment is as absolutely unjust as it is relatively necessary' (*MM*, 143).

60. Being a physician was important to La Mettrie, as Thomson notes (*Materialism*, 7; and ch. 2): 'La Mettrie was first and foremost a doctor.'

61. This preface was added in the third edition of 1751 (*DB*, 111–19).

62. La Mettrie explicitly endorses fatalism in the 1751 preface (*DB*, 116).

63. See also his comments in *Machine Man* (*MM*, 21–2).

> these actions you are not violated—no that is not enough—if you are not torn apart while obeying the law.' But no, criminals have executioners and the executioners have none; their hearts are closed to remorse and repentance. And yet they are murderers! (*MM*, 136)

If this can still be called optimism, then it is an optimism of the most pessimistic kind, and one that is aligned with the pessimist tradition in several crucial ways: in its resistance to any neo-Stoic attempt to overburden the will, and in its seeking out of different attitudes to suffering and different avenues of consolation. Bayle had already taken issue with the Stoic view dusted off by Descartes and Leibniz (and repeated by Maupertuis) that we can conquer pain by an effort of reason or the will, but La Mettrie goes further still, agreeing with Bayle that we have no control over our physical evils, and adding to this that we have no control over our *moral* evils either. Here, the Augustinian notion of radical and universal guilt is replaced by a radical and universal *innocence*: none of us are able to help the evils, moral *or* physical, that we are born with. This is certainly problematic in many ways, but our discomfort should not prevent us from seeing that there is a morality at play here, however ill-considered in its development: that the argument La Mettrie was articulating was not an *amoral* but, crucially, a *moral* one.[64]

And the morality in question, however this is belied by La Mettrie's more blustering statements, is ultimately one of fragility. We may strive to be as good and virtuous and self-determined as we can, says La Mettrie, and still be overwhelmed by misery: 'Without this modification of the nerves (so true is it that all depends on temperament) the good can be plunged into an abyss of evils' (*DB*, 203).[65] But La Mettrie struggles with the question of how much weight to give to this darker, uncontrollable side of life, at the expense of the more upbeat picture he also wants to paint, and this tension will mark the last years of his life, years in which he seems to be writing with two hands, as it were, trying to mollify Maupertuis with the one while, with the other, striking back.

64. Note, however, that La Mettrie later writes (in the 1751 preface) that he thinks his ideas will not be very effective in excising remorse from either the weak of mind or criminals: his arguments cater mainly for the philosophically oriented *voluptueux* (*DB*, 118). (For a similar point, that normal people aren't swayed by philosophy, see *DP*, 216–23.)

65. This passage was added in the second edition. For a similar point, again see chapter 5.

La Mettrie Strikes Back

In the years that separate the first edition of the *Anti-Seneca* from his death in 1751, La Mettrie managed to rewrite the conclusion of the *Anti-Seneca* not once but twice, first becoming more pessimistic (in the Maupertuisian sense), then more optimistic and contrarian, going back and forth between different viewpoints. This was not a careless exercise: in the course of collecting his philosophical works into the *Œuvres philosophiques*, La Mettrie 'seems to have come to realise that the [*Anti-Seneca*] was really the culmination of his philosophical thinking . . . , giving point to his materialism by binding it to a theory of morality'.[66] The fact that La Mettrie continued to work on the *Anti-Seneca*, while never abandoning the main tenets of its original version, suggests something not only of its importance to him, but also to the tensions inherent in any 'pessimistic optimism' of this kind. Let's take a quick look.

In the second edition of 1750 (the first to be titled *Anti-Sénèque, ou Le Souverain Bien*), La Mettrie, ticked off by Maupertuis as well as Frederick for writing as if he were alone in the universe, tries with some awkwardness to align himself with the former. Fundamentally, he suggests, Stoics and Epicureans are agreed that it's always the sentiment of well-being that propels us to action, and by extension so too are he and Maupertuis: 'Say, if you like, that it's the desire to *augment the sum of goods and to reduce the sum of evils*, you will be speaking as a geometer, but really you won't be saying anything else [than I]' (*DB*, 202; his emphasis). As for the question of whether happiness or unhappiness weighs out, which Maupertuis turned into a philosophical topic on its own account, La Mettrie now wants to agree with him that man's need for distraction and diversity proves our general unhappiness:

> So many and so frequent needs of diverse pleasures prove sufficiently that men are generally more unhappy than happy in themselves, or organically [*en soi, ou organiquement*]; but especially those who, eaten up by avarice, ambition, vanity, and envy, have very limited talents but unlimited pretentions. It makes me sorry for Nature [*J'en suis fâché pour la Nature*]; a contrary truth would have done her a greater honour. It makes me even more sorry for men, who are my brothers: I see

66. Falvey, 'Introduction', 29 (and ibid., 12); he points to La Mettrie's 'Discours préliminaire', which 'makes this clear'.

> with sadness that the majority of them do not have the faculty of being happy, unless it is infrequently and at great costs. (*DB*, 230)[67]

While there are some who have an easy capacity for happiness, 'they are so rare that they could be counted, while the number of those for whom the sum of evils surpasses the sum of goods is infinite' (*DB*, 231). And it was precisely in response to this sad truth that La Mettrie had attempted to make this reality more bearable, by liberating mankind from prejudice and remorse, and by being not just a physician of ailments of the body, but of the mind: 'le médecin des maladies de l'esprit' (*DB*, 231).[68] The treatise now concludes with several paragraphs explicitly praising Maupertuis and his *Essai de philosophie morale* (*DB*, 233).

This attempt at realignment seems not to have been very welcome to Maupertuis, who was already concerned about the direction La Mettrie's thought was taking, and possibly objected, after which La Mettrie rewrote his conclusion yet again, omitting any direct references to Maupertuis or the *Essai* while once more changing his mind on the question of pessimism.

True, writes La Mettrie in the third edition of 1751, there is no such thing in nature as perfect happiness (or unhappiness): 'The happiest constitution [*Organisation*] does not lead to perfect happiness; there is no such thing in nature: it is the island of Ithaca that always flees before Ulysses' (*DB*, 209). But this should not be a cause to despair or complain about the human condition, since it is clear that 'there are more happy than unhappy moments in life' (*DB*, 211). The reason why we take little notice of the first and much of the latter is because the most natural movements are those we sense the least, and because we tend to be distracted during all our happy moments, which generally accompany a state of good health (and therefore many occupations). Without mentioning Maupertuis by name, La Mettrie takes issue with his computation of happiness on methodological grounds, as Leibniz had done in his response to Bayle: 'Not to take into account the happy moments that Nature gives us, and only to pay attention to the unhappy moments, which are so much rarer than the others, is an unjust calculation [*un Calcul injuste*]' (*DB*, 211).[69]

67. This passage is rewritten in the third edition; see below, p. 181.

68. See Falvey ('Introduction', 82, 86), who connects La Mettrie, and especially the *Anti-Seneca*, with the rise of the disciplines of psychology and psychiatry.

69. This is a methodological objection to Maupertuis similar to those kinds raised against Bayle and (much later) Benatar.

Another interesting thing occurs with the pessimistic passage from the second edition, where La Mettrie lamented the evils of life on behalf of nature as well as men. In the drastically rewritten new version of this passage, this element of lament is retained and even deepened:

> I certainly regard as unhappy, and as very justified in complaining, those who habitually suffer great pains; those who are penetrated by the magnitude of their loss, or by the enormity of their fall; those for whom the cruellest condition of the soul makes them imagine, despite contrary experiences, that they will never escape from it; those who can no longer remember their pleasures [*Voluptés*] or the splendour in which they have lived without being plunged into their current misery. I find worthy of pity those whose avarice, ambition, vanity, envy, and love pursue them like so many furies; those who with very limited talents have unlimited presumption and pretentions; those who while captivated by honest pleasures whose charms they cannot resist are continually torn apart by these tormentors of which I have spoken [i.e. remorse]; finally, those deplorable criminals condemned to the galleys, or those miserable enough to be galley slaves to themselves, who have as many indomitable passions in their heart as they have illusions and ineffaceable prejudices in their mind. (*DB*, 211–2)

I quote this passage in full because it presents a kind of climax of La Mettrie's moral concern and the general theme of compassion, which here surfaces in all its breadth, and is reminiscent of the pessimists' powerful evocations of the evils of existence, as we have seen in Bayle and will see again in Hume and Schopenhauer. But La Mettrie no longer wants to be a pessimist and is setting up an important caveat: For aside from the very small number of people who suffer like this, he asks, who has so many pains and evils in their lives? As long as you have the necessary things to live, as long as you have your health, then many pleasures are open to you, such as eating, drinking, walking, reading, going to the theatre, enjoying friendship and, above all, enjoying the pleasures of love (*DB*, 212).[70] This again is a kind of optimism, but one that feels no need to explain away life's evils or to justify them: La Mettrie's atheism absolves him from concerning himself with the question of divine justice; in fact, it has reached the point at which he does not even feel the need to make the case against theodicy. The battleground has shifted, for him at least: once providence has been excised from metaphysics, the problem of evil seems to have disappeared.

70. In the course of which, La Mettrie explicitly condones homosexuality (*DB*, 213).

Or has it?

While La Mettrie's motivation for 'optimism' clearly does not lie in the realm of theodicean justification, nevertheless there is a *kind* of justification subtly in play, especially in the later editions, where certain moments in the text seem to manifest a desire to justify nature and existence on their own terms. In another passage rewritten from the first edition, La Mettrie argues that nature would not close the door to happiness to any being she had endowed with feeling:

> The devout, the impious, the debauched, the sensuous [*voluptueux*], the chaste, the sober, the gluttonous, the foolish, the intelligent, animals, humans; all animate bodies have just pretentions to happiness. . . . Why would a being who has the same organs and the same faculty of sensation not enjoy the same privileges? *There is no such injustice for which to reproach Nature.* She has not closed the door of happiness to any being: even less has she gratified it like a stepmother, by a sentiment that would crucify anyone who was endowed with it or could not lead them to pleasure as it could to pain. (*DB*, 204; my emphasis)[71]

'On n'a point cette sorte d'injustice à reprocher à la Nature': the suggestion here is that the complaint that could be made against a divine creator cannot be made against nature, but the reason, it seems, is not because nature acts without intentions, but because nature *would not be that cruel.* The theodicean theme is faint here, since the context is a firmly materialist one, and yet we may glean the traces of a kind of secular theodicy: justification does seem to be a concern for La Mettrie after all, and it is not quite clear why. Why would nature not close the door to happiness to certain beings; how do we know that nature would not be that cruel? (As we will see, a similarly curious theodicean moment will occur in Schopenhauer, the very philosopher who would bind pessimism into a tradition.)

There may be deeper reasons for this metaphysical optimism, but part of the point of it, for La Mettrie at least, seems to be to offer an antidote to despair. Happiness is indeed a rare dish that is never served in its entirety, but it is one of which all creatures can partake unless they are deeply miserable (*DB*, 215). *All creatures*: La Mettrie again aligns himself with the pessimists in his emphatic inclusion of animals in any consideration of the goods or ills of existence, since animals, according to the best of our

71. The passage appears in the second and third editions; note again the inclusion of humans and animals in a single system.

knowledge, are as capable of happiness and unhappiness as humans are, even though their delights and sufferings may take different forms from ours. The point, for La Mettrie, is to highlight our innate capacity for happiness while at the same time reminding us, again and again, of the extent to which this happiness is not in our control: try as we might, we may still end up the most miserable of wretches. This precarious balancing act, in which La Mettrie strives to give due weight to life's evils while at the same time offering a hopeful outlook to all creatures, leads him into tensions that are themselves telling of the moral background of this debate, and I emphasise them in order to draw out, not for the last time in this book, the underlying themes of hope and consolation.

These are, after all, things of which La Mettrie is conscious: there is an ethics of pessimism that runs through precisely his most optimistic passages. In a passage present only in the second edition, he proposes that we concentrate on the good aspects of life rather than the bad aspects, in a kind of psychological and materialist version of the optics of optimism:

> By this very reason, let us gloss over our pains and only deepen our pleasures; let us refrain from entering into any sinister detail . . . ; let us efface the gloomy colours of the picture of life and replace them by green and merry ones. The blacker the background, the more necessary it is to sow flowers upon it. In the absence of natural ones, let us employ artificial ones. One agreeable error is worth more than a hundred sad truths. (*DB*, 232–3)

This passage, which goes against the grain of pessimists (like Bayle) who want a due appreciation of the evils and fragility of life and *through* this right representation offer consolation, is removed by La Mettrie in the third edition, and perhaps it is meaningful that he does so. But it may be equally meaningful that he does not remove another passage: on hope itself.

Everything is always changing in nature, writes La Mettrie; everything is subject to the vicissitudes of fate. Suddenly, the clouds can obscure the warmth of the sun, but also, conversely, in the darkest night a star can appear at the horizon to bring joy to us mortals: 'It is hope, whose soft rays sometimes pierce adversity itself, and come to raise up within the downcast soul a dismayed and withered courage' [*DB*, 209 (third edition); *DB*, 227 (second edition)]. If everything is subject to change, then so too is adversity. Things can always get worse, but also, things can always get better, and it is in this knowledge that we may find our hope. That which makes life tragic is also what makes it comic; that which takes away our hope is also what gives it back to us. This kind of hope may seem but a feeble one, it is true, but from La Mettrie's point of view at least it is a solid hope, a true hope (like many pessimists, he is averse to 'false' hope), which it can only be for him because it is also, crucially, a secular hope. And it is this notion of hope as well as consolation that makes La Mettrie not only a pessimistic optimist, but also a hopeful pessimist.

Stoicism and Suicide

As we have seen, the context of Maupertuis's computation of goods and evils is not an explicitly theodicean one: it has to do rather with an attempt to establish a theory of happiness, and is lodged in a deeper debate about the extent to which we have control over our happiness and our suffering. Similarly, La Mettrie's challenge to Stoic self-determination is part of a wider cultural countercurrent opposed to Stoicism, itself strongly on the rise in the eighteenth century, which is part of the reason why the age was so deeply preoccupied with so many rival notions of happiness, and with the extent to which we even have power over our happiness. This debate, in La Mettrie and Maupertuis, may be one step removed from the debate on the problem of evil, but never more than one step: as we have seen in Bayle and Leibniz and will see again in Hume and Rousseau, the question of how much control we have over our happiness is deeply entangled with the question of how the universe has been providentially arranged by a good and all-knowing God.

As Charles Taylor writes in his *Sources of the Self*: 'A basically Stoic theodicy, explaining away suffering and loss as a necessary and integral part of a good order, is always creeping back, with Leibniz, for example, and is always being vigorously combated, as by Kant and even more sharply by Kierkegaard.'[72] The fact that the debate on Stoicism and happiness was not explicitly inscribed into theodicy, therefore, does not mean that these debates were entirely separate or unrelated. The same set of concerns arises again and again, providing a coherence and continuity to the intersecting debates of Stoicism, happiness, pessimism, and the problem of evil. How to speak meaningfully and compassionately to human suffering? And how to offer hope and consolation in the face of that same suffering? From now on, these three debates (pessimism, Stoicism, and theodicy) will be almost inseparable: where one occurs, the other two

72. Taylor, *Sources of the Self*, 220.

generally follow not far behind. And nowhere do they intersect more sharply than in the vexed question of suicide.

Some final words, then, on this darkest matter. As we have seen, both La Mettrie and Maupertuis evaluate the morality of suicide by way of a kind of calculation: once the evils outweigh the goods of life, then it seems justified to seek a way out of the burden that existence has become. Of the two, however, La Mettrie is more equivocal, rejecting with great fervour any Stoic nonchalance with regard to suicide. His suggestion seems to be that it is not enough for evils to outweigh a little or even a lot: they have to outweigh *terribly*. Only in the case of horrendous and insurmountable suffering (which he considers to be an extremely rare thing) does he accept suicide as an acceptable alternative; the lesser of two evils. Maupertuis is much less cautious, calling suicide a useful remedy as soon as life's evils begin to outweigh the goods, and as long as it is not prohibited by that person's religious beliefs. There is little awareness here of either the tragic background of suicide, the possible effects it may have on those left behind, or the danger of stating this argument too boldly, and it seems to have left La Mettrie uncomfortable, since he responded to Maupertuis's views on suicide in one of his final works.

In 1750, just a year before his death, La Mettrie published a *System of Epicurus*, which includes a long section describing his views on death, and one paragraph that seems to be responding specifically to Maupertuis.[73] Here again, he takes issue with the kind of Stoicism that dulls down life's pleasures as well as its pains, but he also proposes to dissuade any miserable humans from suicide by whatever means necessary:

> I shall try to blunt life's thorns if I cannot reduce their number, in order to increase the pleasure of gathering its roses. And I pray those who, due to a deplorably unfavourable organisation, are dissatisfied with the world's splendid spectacle, to stay here, for religion's sake if they have no humanity or, which is grander, for humanity's sake if they have no religion. (*MM*, 109)

La Mettrie believes that 'simple minds' can be dissuaded from suicide by the prospects of rewards and punishments in the afterlife. As for those to whom 'religion is only what it is, a fable', he will 'try to seduce them with generous feelings and inspire in them that greatness of soul which defeats

73. The *Système d'Epicure* was originally entitled *Réflexions philosophiques sur l'origine des animaux* (published anonymously in 1749 or 1750) and was then published under a new title and in a slightly expanded version in La Mettrie's *Œuvres philosophiques* of 1750 (see *MM*, 90). Paragraph LXXIV discusses suicide.

everything'. More specifically, he will point to the devastating effect suicide will have on those who are left behind:

> I shall show a wife or a mistress in tears, and heartbroken children who will be left by their father's death without education on the face of the earth. Who would not listen to such cries from the graveside? Who would not reopen his dying eyes? What coward refuses to carry a burden that is useful to several people? What monster sees his only aim as freeing himself, thanks to a momentary pain, from the most sacred of duties, by tearing himself from his family, his friends and his country! (*MM*, 109–10)

What is so striking about this passage is that arguments *against* suicide were usually framed in explicitly religious terms, while arguments *for* the permissibility of suicide tended to focus solely on the advantages and disadvantages for the prospective suicides themselves. What we see here, then, is one of the first arguments against suicide that is both formulated in purely naturalistic terms *and* takes into account the effects on those left behind, thus broadening the moral background of the ethics of suicide.[74] It features here as a refutation of Maupertuis and the Stoics, but it could just as easily have been written as a response to another Baylean pessimist, who was writing his *Dialogues concerning Natural Religion* at around the same time that La Mettrie drew his final breath. I speak, of course, of David Hume.

74. Note, however, that the mention of duties to one's country represents a slippery slope, lest it evoke the deeply problematic suggestion (raised by Hume, not to his credit) that some persons are more likely to be a 'burden' to society than others; as though this would render their suicides less tragic.

CHAPTER FIVE

The Dispositional Problem of Evil

DAVID HUME

. . . having read many Books of Morality, such as Cicero, Seneca and Plutarch, and being smit with their beautiful Representations of Virtue and Philosophy, I undertook the Improvement of my Temper and Will, along with my Reason and Understanding. I was continually fortifying myself with Reflections against Death, and Poverty, and Shame, and Pain, and all the other Calamities of Life.

DAVID HUME[1]

'Sir,' said the prince, 'mortality is an event by which a wise man can never be surprised: we know that death is always near, and it should therefore always be expected.' 'Young man,' answered the philosopher, 'you speak like one that has never felt the pangs of separation.'

SAMUEL JOHNSON[2]

AMONG THE MANY EXPERIMENTS of youth, Stoicism is surely not a common one—but it was Stoicism to which the young David Hume turned, reading Shaftesbury in his teens or twenties,[3] and closely follow-

1. Hume, letter to unknown physician (1734; possibly never sent), *Letters*, vol. i, 14. For discussion, see Wright, 'Dr. George Cheyne'.

2. Johnson, *Rasselas*, *SJW*, 16.75.

3. Hume acquired a copy of Shaftesbury's *Characteristics* in 1726, when he was 15: see D.F. Norton and M. Norton, *The David Hume Library*, 16; Harris, *Hume*, 26.

ing 'Shaftesbury's instructions as to how taste, and character, should be formed. Hume seems to have done his best to turn himself into a kind of Stoic', writes Hume's most recent biographer James Harris. But, he continues: 'The experiment was not a success. It helped to bring on a physical and mental breakdown in the autumn of 1729', a breakdown from which Hume was still recovering five years later.[4] The experiment may not have been successful, but it seems to have had its impact, and in more ways than one. It may not have turned Hume into a Shaftesburean Stoic, but it did offer him a privileged glimpse into the moral background of an age-old debate: for all the arguments of ancient and modern philosophers, Hume believed that he had seen, from personal experience, what Stoicism was worth.

Meanwhile, on the road to recovery, the young Hume started reading Bayle—and reading Bayle was quite a different thing, spurring a lifetime of deep engagement with Bayle's thought and writings.[5] A few decades on, Bayle is one of the authors most referenced in Hume's 'memoranda', a collection of handwritten notes, or 'notes taken from notes',[6] based on Hume's readings. A fragment probably written around the time of the completion of the *Treatise on Human Nature* shows Hume engaging with the problem of evil on closely Baylean lines. His published writings, furthermore, reveal not only an extensive but an intensive reading of Bayle's major works.[7] Bayle's *Dictionnaire* was included in a list of books Hume suggested to his friend Michael Ramsay if he wanted to understand the *Treatise*,[8] and most of Hume's treatment of Spinoza is borrowed directly from Bayle's article *Spinoza*. As for the problem of evil, many of Hume's arguments in the *Dialogues concerning Natural Religion* are drawn deeply from the pages of the *Dictionnaire*, suggesting that Hume pored over not only the famous Manichean articles

4. Harris, *Hume*, 26, 36–7; see again Hume's letter to a physician.

5. At twenty-one years old, Hume was reading either Bayle's *Dictionnaire* or his *Œuvres diverses*, possibly both; but, as Harris notes (*Hume*, 62), 'it seems likely that, on Hume as on Mandeville, it was the *Dictionnaire* that had the most immediate and dramatic impact'.

6. Harris, *Hume*, 146, who follows M.A. Stewart in attributing the memoranda to the early 1740s, against some earlier and later datings (Harris, *Hume*, 509n.). For an examination of the Baylean presence in the memoranda in particular, see Pittion, 'Hume's Reading of Bayle'; Mori, 'Bayle et Hume devant l'athéisme'.

7. Bayle's influence on Hume's scepticism is well documented; see, e.g., Richard Popkin, 'Bayle and Hume'; John Wright, 'Skepticism and Incomprehensibility'; Todd Ryan, 'Hume's Reply to Baylean Scepticism'; see also Mazza and Mori, 'Hume's Palimpsest'.

8. Specifically, 'the more metaphysical Articles' such as 'Zeno' and 'Spinoza' (Hume to Ramsay, 26 August 1737, cited in E.C. Mossner, *Life of David Hume*, 104).

but also *Xenophanes* and other lesser-known articles from what I have earlier styled the 'Manichean web'.

While Hume's treatment of the problem of evil has been excavated and analysed in considerable detail, both by historians of philosophy and by contemporary philosophers of religion, less attention has been paid to the role played by pessimism in the Humean discussion of evil, and to the connection of this discussion with the wider philosophical debate.[9] Hence, while my focus in this chapter is similar to that of a wide body of scholarship, my emphasis lies elsewhere: I am concerned less with the technicalities of Hume's argument than with the latent tendencies implied and developed therein, such as the juxtaposition of physical and psychological misery, and the central role accorded to philosophical pessimism. What kind of 'problem' is evil posing here; and what kind of 'evil' does it presuppose?

In what follows, therefore, I will set out Hume's problem of evil with a particular focus on Bayle's influence, often understated, both with regard to Hume's pessimism and his counter-theodicean arguments. This is not just to reiterate the point that Bayle was big in the eighteenth century, or that Hume borrowed from Bayle (who didn't?), but to tease out the contours of a continuing line of argument, which begins to resemble something like a 'tradition'. The Hume that will be encountered here is one who ranks among the foremost early modern formulators of the problem of evil and contributors to the pessimist challenge: that is, someone who framed the problem of evil without pretending to answer it, and who did so on strongly pessimist terms. My interest lies in the shifting preoccupations and background assumptions that are at work here: the kinds of problem that the problem of evil morphs into, and the role played by pessimism throughout this debate.

I will trace these elements by looking at some of Hume's central writings: the more obvious ones, such as the *Dialogues*, but also some less commonly discussed in this context, such as various essays. In doing so, I hope to show that Hume's primary innovation in the problem of evil lies elsewhere than is generally assumed: in formulating, for the first time, what might be called a *dispositional problem of evil*.

9. For just a sample of writings on Hume and the problem of evil, see Pike, 'Hume on Evil'; Newlands, 'Hume on Evil'; Pitson, 'The Miseries of Life'; Wykstra, 'The Humean Obstacle'; Holden, *Spectres of False Divinity*, chapter 6. Bayle's influence in this context is generally acknowledged but little explored in detail: for a specific exception, see Ryan, 'Pierre Bayle and the Regress Argument'.

A Fragment on Evil

To begin at the beginning, let us turn to the early manuscript fragment mentioned above, probably written in the late 1730s or early 1740s and 'tantalizingly' headed 'Sect. 7 Fourth Objection'.[10] Section 7—but of what? It is not clear whether the fragment was intended to form part of Hume's published works, such as the *Treatise* (as M.A. Stewart tentatively suggests), or as preparation of another work entirely. In terms of its content, it is most closely related to the discussion of the problem of evil in the *Dialogues*; as such, it manifests some of Hume's ongoing reflections on evil and pessimism, while at the same time flagging some central methodological concerns.

Bayle looms large throughout the text. As in the *Dialogues*, Hume introduces a sharp distinction between God's natural attributes (his intelligence) and his moral attributes (his benevolence), in order to argue that the latter cannot be inferred from the former.[11] Even if we allowed that God's intelligence could be proved by certain 'phenomena' (such as the order in nature), we would need a 'new set of phenomena' to prove his benevolence as well (*FE*, 109–10). That these phenomena have everything to do with the question of value-oriented pessimism, Hume shows by bringing to the fore that most Baylean of questions: Do the evils of life outweigh the goods?

> Whether the author of nature be benevolent or not can only be proved by the effects, and *by the predominance either of good or evil, of happiness or misery, in the universe.* If good prevail much above evil, we may, perhaps, presume, that the author of the universe, if an intelligent, is also a benevolent principle. If evil prevail much above good, we may draw a contrary inference. (*FE*, 110; my emphasis)

The problem, however, is that this question is methodologically deeply problematic and seems to allow for no objective answer or solution:

> we find that it is very difficult, if not absolutely impossible, ever to ascertain [the facts]. For who is able to form an exact computation

10. Harris, *Hume*, 147, 68; this dating would place it near the completion of the *Treatise of Human Nature*. See also M.A. Stewart, 'An Early Fragment on Evil', 163–4.

11. The same argument (blocking the inference of God's moral attributes from either his natural attributes or the phenomena) is made in parts X–XI of the *Dialogues*, while the earlier parts (I–IX) focus on God's natural attributes. The distinction between God's natural and moral attributes introduced here is thus central to the structure of the Dialogues; I thank an anonymous reviewer for pointing this out.

of all the happiness and misery, that are in the world, and to compare them exactly with each other? (*FE*, 110)[12]

Like Bayle, Hume assumes the 'common opinion' to be 'that evil prevails very much above good', even among mankind, though some dispute this 'popular opinion'. More so than Bayle, however, Hume is very sceptical about the possibility of pronouncing judgement on the question of optimism (life's goods outweigh the evils) versus pessimism (life's evils outweigh the goods), but he *does* believe we can ascertain some things with regard to the nature of our pains and pleasures. In a passage that summarises Bayle's findings in *Xenophanes*, Hume distinguishes two ways of considering pains and pleasures: degree and frequency, or what we might also call quality and quantity. Considering what we know from our experience, this allows us to make certain phenomenological claims:

> What one may safely pronounce on this head, is, that if we compare pains and pleasures in their *degrees*, the former are infinitely superior; there being many pains, and even durable ones, extremely acute; and no pleasure, that is at the same time very intense and very durable. (*FE*, 110; Hume's emphasis)

The only example of 'an exquisite and intense pleasure' is that of sexual love, and for some perhaps the scholarly exercise would also qualify but, asks Hume, 'what is all this in comparison of those many cruel distempers and violent sorrows, to which human life is subject?'[13]

In terms of *degrees*, therefore, Hume thinks that the pains tend to preponderate; in terms of *frequency*, however, he believes the pleasures to 'have the advantage', since 'small pleasures, to the greatest part of mankind, return oftener, than pain or uneasiness' (*FE*, 110).[14] Picking up a point refuted by Bayle in *Xenophanes*, that health allows for an infinity of pleasures or goods, Hume writes that

> When a man is in good health and in good humour, every common incident of life affords him satisfaction; to go to bed; to rise again; to

12. As Harris notes (*Hume*, 84), Hume is generally methodologically self-conscious. Compare also Maupertuis's attempt at a computation or calculation of evils (chapter 3).

13. A similar comparison between scholarly and sensual pleasures occurs in Bayle's article *Mahomet*. See also Hume's essay 'The Sceptic' (*EMPL*, 166), where it is argued that intellectual pleasures are only superior to sensual ones if they afford a greater enjoyment.

14. Bayle makes a similar point in *Xenophanes.F*, but adding that intensity or degree is the more important factor here (quality over quantity).

> eat; to drink; to converse; to enjoy the weather; to perform his business; to hear news; to retail them. (*FE*, 110)

But whether or not these pleasures 'compensate the acuteness of our pains', Hume says he is 'not able to determine with any certainty' (*FE*, 111). *Personally*, he is inclined to opt for pessimism:

> When I consider the subject with the utmost impartiality, and take the most comprehensive view of it, I find myself more inclined to think, that evil predominates in the world, and am apt to regard human life as a scene of misery, according to the sentiments of the greatest sages as well as of the generality of mankind, from the beginning of the world to this day. (*FE*, 111)

But Hume is aware that it is impossible to achieve complete impartiality on this score: 'there are many circumstances, which are apt to pervert my judgment in this particular, and make me entertain melancholy views of things'. For one thing, he writes, echoing a point that Leibniz had also made, evils in their intensity make a greater impression on us than pleasures do, so that 'it is almost impossible for us to make a just compensation betwixt them'. Rhetorically, furthermore, pessimism has a natural advantage: if one were to list all evils 'and display them, with eloquence, in their proper colours', then one could probably convince most people that pessimism is true, considering the experiential contrast between the goods and ills of life: 'Victuals, wine, a fiddle, a warm bed, a coffee-house conversation make a pitiful figure, when compared with racks, gravels, infamy, solitude, and dungeons' (*FE*, 111). But this would indeed be to make a rhetorical rather than philosophical point, and so Hume sets it aside, coming instead to a more sceptical conclusion:

> I shall only infer, from the whole, that the facts are here so complicated and dispersed, that a certain conclusion can never be formed from them, and that no single convert will ever be made by any disputes upon this subject; but each disputant will still go off the field with a stronger confirmation of those opinions and prejudices, which he brought to it. (*FE*, 111)

However, it is not necessary for Hume's purposes in this section to show that evil is predominant: even if good preponderates, the fact that it 'prevails in so small a degree, and is counterbalanced by so many ills', suggests that 'it can never afford any proof' of the divine attribute of benevolence (*FE*, 111–12).[15] This is, in essence, the same point to be developed by

15. Technically, Hume could have gone one step further and argued that even the *smallest* degree of suffering poses a problem for the inference of divine goodness. Here, Hume

Philo in the *Dialogues*: God's goodness may be logically *compatible* with the fact of evil, but it cannot be *proven* on the basis of the phenomena, in which the many evils of life are necessarily included.[16]

With regard to pessimism, the 'Fragment' thus reveals a Hume much more reticent about making the argument for pessimism than Bayle was, though appearing personally inclined to take a Baylean view of things. The main point to be taken away here is the extent to which Hume was immersed in Baylean arguments with regard to pessimism and the problem of suffering, especially those gleaned from *Xenophanes*. Hume's voice here, furthermore, appears to be his own, which gives us some reason to suppose that at least some of the pessimistic arguments in the *Dialogues* as uttered by both Philo and Demea reflect his own intuitions on this score. At the same time, it should be noted that Hume never published this fragment (though neither did he burn it), and we should be cautious about drawing too many conclusions from it. 'Sect. 7 Fourth Objection', whether excised or undeveloped, does not represent Hume's closing statement on pessimism or even his considered view. But read in conjunction with his later writings, it does tell us something about the development of his thoughts, his engagement with Bayle, and his interest in these dark matters from early on.

Dialogues concerning Natural Religion

Originally drafted in 1751 but not published until three years after Hume's death, in 1779, the *Dialogues concerning Natural Religion* remain a classic in the modern philosophy of religion.[17] In a series of twelve dialogues between a group of philosophical friends, Hume combines a deeply tolerant, companionable, and polite mode of argumentation with what turns out to be a devastating excavation of the rational foundations of belief.[18]

---

is already edging towards the stronger version of the pessimist premise (see chapter 2); to which he will move completely in the *Dialogues*.

16. Here we find the origins in inchoate form of the now standard distinction between 'logical' and 'evidential' problems of evil; early modern authors did not tend to distinguish between the two.

17. On the circumstances of publication, see Harris (*Hume*, 444–5), who also mentions that, despite the apprehensions on the part of both Hume and his editors, in fact 'very little stir was caused by the appearance of the *Dialogues*' (ibid., 445).

18. The tolerant and polite mode of discourse in the *Dialogues* (which is only disrupted at the point of Demea's sudden departure) suggests a kind of ideal 'intellectual world', reflecting Hume's belief that 'intellectual disagreement was not a personal matter' (Harris, *Hume*, 443, 442).

At the centre of the dialogues stands the question, much debated at the time, of how we can come to a natural religion; that is, how we might find religion through reason alone, separately from revelation. The main issue at stake is not so much the existence of God, which none of the contestants seem to dispute, but the *nature of God*, and how we could possibly infer the divine attributes, such as intelligence and especially benevolence, from the phenomena of nature.[19] In approaching these questions from different angles and through different voices, Hume interacts with deist, theist, sceptic, and atheist arguments, drawing from a wealth of sources, such as Shaftesbury, Clarke, Hutcheson—and Bayle.[20] The latter provides the main elements for Hume's presentation of the problem of evil in the tenth and eleventh dialogues, where Hume shows himself to be both a creative and highly attentive reader of Bayle.

Briefly, recall Bayle's core argument in the *Dictionnaire*. In *Manicheans*, Bayle's Manichean argued that while the 'heavens and the whole universe declare the glory, the power, and the unity of God', 'man alone' poses a problem of evil, through his wickedness and misery (*Manicheans*[1].*D*/ *Selections*, 146).[21] In *Xenophanes*, Bayle supplied a more formal phenomenological argument to prove that both moral and physical evils outweigh the corresponding goods. With regard to physical evils, which he equated with suffering in general, Bayle distinguished two kinds—bodily and psychological suffering—and argued that it is especially the latter that is capable of making life not worth living, thus creating a problem for the justness of God. Through a thought experiment developed in other articles, Bayle came to the dark conclusion that most of us would not want to live our lives again, if we evaluated them properly; nevertheless, the fear of death often outweighs even our suffering in life, thus impeding even some of the most miserable among us from taking their own lives.

Together, these discussions form a crucial backdrop to Hume's tenth and eleventh dialogues, where, as we will see, the sceptical character Philo (and, to some extent, Demea) repeats many of Bayle's core arguments, developing some of them in ways that Bayle would surely have adored. As with Bayle's voices, Hume's use of the dialogue format complicates

19. As such, it was possibly modelled on Cicero's *De natura deorum*, which is certainly in the background of the *Dialogues*; on which, see Christine Battersby, 'The *Dialogues* as Original Imitation'; Harris, *Hume*, 446. Note that this work by Cicero also played an important part in Bayle's discussion of the problem of evil; see my *Bayle, Jurieu*, 59–61.

20. As well as other French sources: see Mazza and Mori, 'Hume's Palimpsest'.

21. Recall that Bayle elsewhere includes animals among the suffering beings whose existence suggests a conflict with God's goodness (see chapter 2).

interpretation, and much has been written on the extent to which we can identify Hume with any or several of his 'voices', and what to make of certain internal inconsistencies.[22] I think there can be little doubt that Hume leaned towards many of the pessimistic musings of these dialogues, and agreed with many of Philo's arguments, which are often consistent with points made elsewhere in Hume's oeuvre. Nevertheless, there are reasons for exercising restraint in attributing specific positions to Hume. As Harris writes: 'The point of the *Dialogues* was not for Hume to establish a position of his own, for, properly speaking, he had no position to advocate. It was, rather, to present the best possible case for theism, and to show how it crumbles almost into nothing under rational examination.'[23] As a matter of caution, therefore, I will specify who is speaking throughout, and do my best not to overinterpret Hume's voices as his own.

THE CASE FOR PESSIMISM

In Part X of the *Dialogues*, the three friends—Philo, Demea, and later Cleanthes[24]—discuss the question of pessimism, which eventually leads into a discussion of the problem of evil. But the dialogue doesn't begin this way: the problem of evil is not introduced by Philo until the very end, after the case for pessimism has been made on its own account, especially, and naïvely, by the more orthodox Demea, who is not at all aware that Philo is setting up a problem for religion. The rhetorical value of this sequence is that pessimism is (at least cosmetically) discussed on its own merits, rather than as part of the problem of evil, which might have predisposed Demea to take a different or at least more muted stance on the question of pessimism. Meanwhile, Cleanthes sits back and lets his two friends paint a deeply pessimistic picture of human *and* animal life, interjecting only towards the end, when matters are beginning to get out of hand.

Initially, then, Philo and Demea join forces in laying out the case for pessimism, which Demea thinks is a psychological source or even a

22. Especially with regard to Philo's apparent change of heart in dialogue XII. For some recent commentaries, see Newlands, 'Hume on Evil'; Pitson, 'Miseries of Life'; Dees, 'Morality above Metaphysics'. On Hume's use of the dialogue form, see Michel Malherbe, 'Hume and the Art of Dialogue'.

23. Harris, *Hume*, 447.

24. Dorothy Coleman, in her introduction to *DNR*, calls Philo a sceptic, Demea 'an orthodox theist', and Cleanthes 'an empirical theist', i.e. someone who believes the nature of God can be inferred from empirical observation ('Introduction', xii). Harris (*Hume*, 451) emphasises that '[w]hat Demea wants above all is certainty. It does not matter to him what the source of that certainty is, whether it is rational or a matter of emotional attachment'.

justification of religious belief: for it is our despair at our current condition and hope for a better future one that drives us to devotion. 'Wretched creatures that we are!' says Demea. 'What resource for us amidst the innumerable ills of life, did not religion suggest some methods of atonement, and appease those terrors, with which we are incessantly agitated and tormented?' Philo, perhaps cunningly, agrees with Demea that 'the best, and indeed the only method of bringing everyone to a due sense of religion is by just representations of the misery and wickedness of men' (*DNR*.X.68).[25] Together, they argue that the 'vulgar' and the 'learned' are agreed on this. With regard to the former, Demea notes:

> The miseries of life, the unhappiness of man, the general corruptions of our nature, the unsatisfactory enjoyment of pleasures, riches, honours; these phrases have become almost proverbial in all languages. And who can doubt of what all men declare from *their own immediate feeling and experience*? (*DNR*.X.68–9; my emphasis)

To which Philo adds the authority of 'all letters, *sacred* and *profane*', and poets from Homer to Edward Young.[26] Demea again points to the entire library of Cleanthes; aside from some scientists, 'there is scarce one of those innumerable writers, from whom the sense of human misery has not, in some passage or other, extorted a complaint and confession of it'.[27] At the very least, he continues, 'no one author has ever, so far as I can recollect, been so extravagant as to deny it'. Here, Philo disagrees: '*Leibniz* has denied it; and is perhaps the first who ventured upon so bold and paradoxical an opinion; at least, the first who made it essential to his philosophical system.' In a footnote, Hume adds that this 'sentiment' (of denying the doctrine of pessimism) 'had been maintained by *Dr. King* and some few others before *Leibniz*; though by none of so great a fame as that German philosopher' (*DNR*.X.69; Hume's emphases).[28]

25. See also Hume's *Natural History of Religion* (e.g. *NHR*, 143). Newlands ('Hume on Evil', 631) emphasises the particular context of this opening move: Philo and Demea are 'trying to stir up a particular sentiment via rhetoric', not 'offering straightforward premises in an argument'.

26. Hume probably had in mind Edward Young's influential *The Complaint: or, Night-Thoughts on Life, Death, & Immortality* (1742–1745).

27. Such a list of authorities was, of course, precisely what Hume had found in Bayle's *Xenophanes*; see chapter 1.

28. Is this an accurate representation of Leibniz and King? Tony Pitson ('Miseries', 108n.) does not think so: 'Philo here mistakenly ascribes to Leibniz the view that evil in the form of human misery does not exist.' This would indeed be mistaken. But I think the doctrine ascribed to Leibniz and King here is not the denial of misery itself so much as the

Demea continues, with Philo's approval, to extend the miserable condition of humanity to *all creatures*:

> And why should man, added he, pretend to an exemption from the lot of all other animals? The whole earth, believe me, *Philo*, is cursed and polluted. A perpetual war is kindled amongst all living creatures. Necessity, hunger, want, stimulate the strong and courageous: Fear, anxiety, terror, agitate the weak and infirm. The first entrance into life gives anguish to the new-born infant and to its wretched parent: Weakness, impotence, distress, attend each stage of that life: And it is at last finished in agony and horror. (*DNR*.X.69–70)

Let me pause here to highlight the starkness of this juxtaposition of bodily and psychological evils, which are already placed on an equal footing, and the extension of the tragic condition to *all* living creatures. Seen in isolation from the wider debate, these may seem almost trivial points, and indeed both Philo and Demea suggest that these are not contentious matters; that all are agreed on the miseries of life. But if we compare this presentation of the creaturely predicament to others of its time, we find that it is strikingly different, aligned only with Bayle. Instead of presenting either psychological suffering or animal suffering as part of the *question*, Hume has his characters place these within the very premises of the debate, as the blunt *facts of the matter*. This is a double innovation in the very texture of the theodicean argument, building boldly on Bayle's groundwork; and it goes to show that Demea is not simply a foil for Philo's wit.

The discussion goes on to focus on man in particular, who (says Demea) may seem to be stronger than the other animals in his ability to conquer them, but (Philo adds) once the 'real enemies' have been defeated, conjures up 'imaginary enemies, the demons of his fancy', through the evil of superstition, which ruin his pleasures and increase his pains and fears (*DNR*.X.70).[29] Demea then lists the moral and physical or natural evils besetting man, though these are not yet denoted by these terms. With regard to *moral evils*, he takes a Hobbesian tone:

> Man is the greatest enemy of man. Oppression, injustice, contempt, contumely, violence, sedition, war, calumny, treachery, fraud; by these

---

denial that *the evils of life outweigh the goods*; which is indeed what the optimists held, arguing instead that life is worth living *for all living beings*, except maybe the damned. Note that Hume's memoranda reflect his reading of King's *De origine mali* (*Mem.*, 501–2).

29. On superstition, see also Hume's essay 'Of suicide'.

> they mutually torment each other: And they would soon dissolve that society which they had formed, were it not for the dread of still greater ills, which must attend their separation. (*DNR*.X.70–1)

With regard to *physical* or *natural evils*,[30] or evils that 'arise within ourselves, from the distempered condition of our mind and body', Demea takes up the Baylean distinction, citing Milton's grim list of diseases in *Paradise Lost* for ills of the body,[31] then turning specifically to ills of the mind, which, 'though more secret, are not perhaps less dismal and vexatious. Remorse, shame, anguish, rage, disappointment, anxiety, fear, dejection, despair; who has ever passed through life without cruel inroads from these tormentors?' (*DNR*.X.71).

Demea concludes from this that the evils preponderate over the goods to such an extent that *a single significant evil*, or the absence of *a single significant good*, can be enough to 'render life ineligible' (that is, turn the scales to such an extent that it would be better never to have been):

> All the goods of life united would not make a very happy man: But all the ills united would make a wretch indeed; and any one of them almost (and who can be free from every one?) nay often the absence of one good (and who can possess all?) is sufficient *to render life ineligible*. (*DNR*.X.71; my emphasis)[32]

This, again, is the Baylean line, more strongly and explicitly articulated; and it calls to mind the stronger version of the pessimist premise (as outlined in chapter 2).

Drawing ever more deeply from Bayle, and with ever clearer echoes from the *Dictionnaire*, Demea then asks how a stranger from another world would look upon the hospitals, prisons, and battlefields; as opposed to which we would have only trifling pastimes to show him:

> Were a stranger to drop on a sudden into this world, I would show him, as a specimen of its ills, a hospital full of diseases, a prison crowded with malefactors and debtors, a field of battle strewed with carcasses,

30. Hume categorises evils as Bayle does, into a moral and physical/natural category: like other anglophone writers, he mostly uses the term 'natural evil', whereas the francophones prefer to speak of *mal physique* (but see EHU.8.2:90, where Hume speaks of '*physical* ill'). Note that Hume does not take up a third category of either 'metaphysical evil' (Leibniz) or 'evil of imperfection' (King and Clarke).

31. Hume partly cites John Milton, *Paradise Lost*, book XI, verses 484–93.

32. Like most authors of the time, Hume does not distinguish between a life not worth starting and a life not worth continuing (see chapter 2).

> a fleet foundering in the ocean, a nation languishing under tyranny, famine, or pestilence. To turn the gay side of life to him, and give him a notion of its pleasures; whither should I conduct him? To a ball, to an opera, to court? He might justly think, that I was only showing him a diversity of distress and sorrow. (*DNR*.X.71–2)[33]

This passage recalls, of course, Bayle's famous riff, reprised by Leibniz, on the 'prisons, hospitals, gallows, and beggars' of the world; but it may also bring to mind Hume's earlier reflections in the 'Fragment' that such illustrations amount to mere rhetoric and are philosophically unconvincing as well as methodologically problematic.[34] Has Hume changed his mind? Not necessarily. For one thing, these theoretical limitations are not as problematic in the *Dialogues*, which constitute an entirely different context from the 'Fragment' (whatever that context was): rhetoric is surely better placed in a dialogue between opposing philosophers than in a detached philosophical treatise. For another, it is *Demea* who is speaking here, and we should bear in mind that, unlike Philo, Demea is *not* trying to formulate a philosophical argument so much as to appeal to the psychological sources of belief and, by bringing to mind the sorrows of existence, to awaken religious sentiment. Technically, furthermore, nor does Philo require theoretical certainty on this matter in order to make his point, which is that even a small amount of evil is enough to complicate the inference of God's attributes from our experience. But that this is in fact what Philo is after, only gradually becomes clear.

JUSTIFICATION

At this point, Philo takes over and begins to steer the dialogue subtly in the direction of justification, though without reference (as yet) to divine ordinance. Following Demea's illustration of the ills of life, Philo adds force to this off-the-cuff pessimism by arguing that any attempt to try to

33. Peter Kivy sees in this 'an echo of Voltaire's strategy', which tries 'to "overwhelm" the Leibnizian with the palpable pain and suffering in the world, in the hope of straining his belief system to the breaking point' ('Voltaire, Hume, and the Problem of Evil', 210). To which Catherine Wilson objects that Demea is surely *not* objecting to 'theological optimism', as Kivy seems to suggest ('Leibnizian Optimism', 766n.). Both are valid points: the solution is that Demea, in defending one kind of optimism, is rejecting another kind (Cleanthes's kind).

34. Bayle, *Manicheans*[1]*.D* (*Selections*, 146–7): 'Monuments to human misery and wickedness are found everywhere—prisons, hospitals, gallows, and beggars.' Bayle had also employed a thought experiment invoking the viewpoint of 'people from another world' in his earlier *Pensées diverses* (section 134; *Various Thoughts*, 167).

explain or justify these evils only serves to make the problem worse, to 'aggravate the charge':

> There is no evading such striking instances, said *Philo*, but by apologies, which still further aggravate the charge. Why have all men, I ask, in all ages, complained incessantly of the miseries of life? . . . They have no just reason, says one: These complaints proceed only from their discontented, repining, anxious disposition . . . And can there possibly, I reply, be a more certain foundation of misery, than such a wretched temper? (*DNR*.X.72; Hume's ellipses)

In other words, explaining away the tendency of some humans to complain or despair of life by pointing to their discontented disposition does nothing to defuse or dismantle pessimism: it just displaces the problem to that disposition itself.[35] This ties into a deeper argument with regard to dispositions, to which I will return.

Next, Philo briefly raises the argument based on suicide that King also brought against Bayle: 'But if they were really as unhappy as they pretend, says my antagonist, why do they remain in life?'[36] Which Philo then answers, again, on Baylean terms: 'This is the secret chain, say I, that holds us. We are terrified, not bribed to the continuance of our existence' (*DNR*.X.72). That is, it is the fear of death, not love of life, that binds us to existence. Like Bayle, moreover, Philo firmly rejects any attempt to attribute the evils suffered by man to man's own will; or to argue that men are 'willing artificers of their own misery'. In fact, says Philo, there is no escaping the human condition and the evils that beset it: if humans act, they end up troubled or disappointed; if they do not act, 'an anxious languor follows their repose' (*DNR*.X.72).[37]

At this point Cleanthes, silent so far, interposes that he has observed some of this experience in others, but 'I feel little or nothing of it in myself; and hope that it is not so common as you represent it.' To which Demea replies that Cleanthes is the exception, not the rule; many of even the most prosperous persons have nevertheless expressed their unhappiness in life. The three examples he employs to illustrate this are each drawn from

35. This is at core again a Baylean point: in fact, Bayle would have added that such explanations even serve to *increase* our suffering.

36. Philo quotes Matthew Prior's *Solomon* (book 3, line 683): 'Not satisfied with life, afraid of death.'

37. Schopenhauer, who adored Hume's *Dialogues*, may well have drawn on this for his 'pendulum' of pain and boredom; see chapter 8.

Bayle's *Dictionnaire*; specifically, from articles connected with the Manichean web.[38] First, 'the fortunate emperor, *Charles* the fifth', who despite his great fortunes '*had never enjoyed any satisfaction or contentment*' (*DNR*.X.72–3; Hume's emphasis).[39] Second, and analogously, Cicero's suffering despite his good fortunes, which he illustrated by introducing 'the great, the fortunate *Cato*, protesting in his old age, that had he a new life in his offer, he would reject the present'.[40] Third, Demea returns to the thought experiment Bayle mentioned in *Xenophanes* (and developed in *Tullia* and *Vayer*): Would you want to live your life again if it meant reliving all past sorrows as well as joys? But Hume, through Demea, delivers a different version of the experiment, asking not whether someone would want to live their *entire* life again, but just the last few decades. Most people, according to Demea, will decline this offer, while nevertheless hoping for better fortune in the future: 'Ask yourself, ask any of your acquaintance, whether they would live over again the last ten or twenty years of their life. No! But the next twenty, they say, will be better' (*DNR*.X.73).[41] The suggestion is that most people have a bias towards optimism, since they continue to hope for improvement, even against their better judgement and previous experience.

It is only at this point, towards the very end of the dialogue, that Philo comes clean about his real agenda: How can Cleanthes maintain 'the moral attributes of the deity' considering that 'neither man nor any other animal is happy' (*DNR*.X.73)? He restates Epicurus's question, *Whence evil?*, again lifted from the *Dictionnaire* (*Paulicians*[1].*E*). Like Bayle's Manichean, Philo is happy to concede that the order and beauty of the universe suggests there is 'a purpose and intention to nature' (*DNR*.X.74; see also *DNR*.X.77). But the problem arises on the level of animals and humans ('all animals'), who

38. Thus the *Dialogues* may also tell us something about how Hume read Bayle, following the cross-references connecting Bayle's articles into the darker corners of the *Dictionnaire*, and thereby coming to a more sophisticated and layered view of Bayle's arguments than many of his contemporaries.

39. The quotation (in italics) is taken by Hume from Bayle's article on Charles V (*Charles V*[1].*L*): one of several 'royal' articles in which Bayle had illustrated the ubiquitous nature of suffering by pointing out how many of the most prosperous rulers had yet been miserable (see my *Bayle, Jurieu*, 38–9).

40. Cicero's *De Senectute* is discussed in Bayle's *Tullia*, to which *Xenophanes* cross-refers.

41. Note that towards the end of his life, the ailing Hume himself commented that 'were I to name the period of my life, which I should most choose to pass over again, I might be tempted to point to this later period' (cited in Harris, *Hume*, 464).

suffer terribly and inexplicably. Again, Hume proves to be even more adamant than Bayle about including animals in the suffering condition.

The problem of evil, in its bluntest form, thus turns out to be a problem of pain. But we have encountered justifications of pain before, in both King and Leibniz, and Hume shows himself to be aware of such justifications. Against the Kingian idea, reprised by Hutcheson and others, that pain is *useful* to the creature, Philo, like Bayle, offers counter-examples of clearly useless pains: from the 'racking pains' that 'arise from gouts, gravels, megrims, toothaches, rheumatisms, where the injury to the animal machinery is either small or incurable', to the psychological ills, such as 'spleen, melancholy, discontent, superstition' (*DNR*.X.74).[42] The only way to account for 'this strange mixture of phenomena' is to take the way of the 'mystics', and interpret the phenomena according to the attributes ('infinitely perfect, but incomprehensible'), rather than inferring the attributes from the phenomena (*DNR*.X.74).[43]

THE TWO STRATEGIES OF OPTIMISM

At this point, Philo and Demea part ways, since it is now clear that Philo was making the case for pessimism only in order to pose a version of the problem of evil, which Demea and Cleanthes now try to answer along two different routes. In doing so, they manifest the two strategies of optimism that were combined by Leibniz and King but began to part ways in the eighteenth century: strategies that turned out not to be as complementary as the optimists assumed. Each involves making a specific concession to the pessimists—but if too much is conceded, then both are doomed to fail.

Cleanthes's strategy is, initially, to deny pessimism, full stop: to deny that the evils of life outweigh the goods (as Bolingbroke had done in response to Wollaston). But it involves the potentially fatal concession that *if* pessimism is true, then religion is done for:

> If you can make out the present point, and prove mankind to be unhappy or corrupted, there is an end at once of all religion. For to what purpose establish the natural attributes of the deity, while the moral are still doubtful and uncertain? (*DNR*.X.74)

42. One of Bayle's examples is the pain of childbirth; *RQP*.II.77 (*OD*.III.656).

43. This again recalls Bayle, who had argued in the article *Rufinus* that if we are going to end up appealing to incomprehensibility, it is better to start with it, and not to argue about such things at all. The path left open, in Philo as in Bayle, is of course the more controversial option of letting go of either God's attributes or his existence.

Demea's strategy, on the other hand, is to acknowledge the existence of overwhelming this-worldly evils from a *creaturely* perspective, but to respond to the problem this creates with an appeal to the *cosmic* perspective, as well as to a future life (just as Wollaston had done):

> This world is but a point in comparison of the universe: This life but a moment in comparison of eternity. The present evil phenomena, therefore, are rectified in other regions, and in some future period of existence. And the eyes of men, being then opened to larger views of things, see the whole connection of general laws, and trace, with adoration, the benevolence and rectitude of the Deity, through all the mazes and intricacies of his providence. (*DNR*.X.75)[44]

But this second strategy involves, again, the perilous concession that pessimism has a point; and it is this to that Cleanthes heatedly objects ('No! replied *Cleanthes*, No!'). Demea's optical points are merely 'arbitrary suppositions' that go flatly against 'matter of fact, visible and uncontroverted'. A hypothesis can only be proved by the 'apparent phenomena', whereas Demea is 'building entirely in the air', on 'conjectures and fictions' (*DNR*.X.75).

The reason why Cleanthes is so concerned to argue against Demea specifically is that, in conceding the point of pessimism, Demea's strategy threatens to weaken his own. The spectral argument looming in the background is at heart a simple one:

i. If pessimism is true, then it is the end of religion.
ii. Pessimism is true.
iii. Therefore, it is the end of religion.

While Demea's strategy is to concede the minor premise (that pessimism is true) but reject the major (that this is a problem for religion), Cleanthes's strategy is precisely the converse: to concede the major premise (*if* we're all so miserable, then religion is doomed) but deny the minor (that pessimism is true). The more they strengthen their own strategies, the more they weaken the other's. I emphasise this because Leibniz and King saw no harm in combining both strategies, arguing on the one hand that pessimism is not a problem for religion, but on the other, that pessimism is not true—and in trying to disprove pessimism, ended up conceding

44. Here, we see Demea aligned with authors such as Wollaston and Johnson, who conceded certain points to pessimism while appealing crucially to a future life, while Cleanthes is aligned with more outright optimists such as Bolingbroke and Jenyns (see chapter 3).

more and more ground to the pessimists. As Cleanthes rightly seems to observe, the strategies don't sit well together: in opting for one strategy, he and Demea end up discrediting or even deflating the other. But the real problem is that they are now holding the debate on pessimism *on the pessimists' terms*. In bringing out this argumentative collapse, Hume shows that he had a better understanding of the internal mechanics of optimism than he is often credited with, and it is why his challenge to optimism turns out to be more convincing *philosophically* than Voltaire's more rhetorical, ad hominem approach.[45]

Cleanthes now turns to Philo again in an attempt to override Demea, and quickly (hurriedly) tries to disprove the pessimism that he has so far allowed to go unchecked; he does so using all the optimist arguments refuted by Bayle in *Xenophanes*:

> The only method of supporting divine benevolence (and it is what I willingly embrace) is to deny absolutely the misery and wickedness of man. Your representations are exaggerated: Your melancholy views mostly fictitious: Your inferences contrary to fact and experience. Health is more common than sickness: Pleasure than pain: Happiness than misery. And for one vexation which we meet with, we attain, upon computation, a hundred enjoyments. (*DNR*.X.75)[46]

Philo is just as quick to reply, and does so by echoing Hume's early fragment on evil as well as *Xenophanes*. Even *if* pleasures are more frequent (which Philo doubts[47]), pains are clearly 'infinitely more violent and durable', as he explains in an almost direct quote from Bayle:

> One hour of it is often able to outweigh a day, a week, a month of our common insipid enjoyments: And how many days, weeks, and months, are passed by several in the most acute torments? (*DNR*.X.75; see Bayle's *Xenophanes.F*)

Repeating the point made in the 'Fragment', Philo states that there is a fundamental asymmetry between pleasure (which is often tepid and evanescent) and pain, which is able both to maintain great intensity and long duration:

45. It is not clear that Hume had read Leibniz's *Théodicée* as he had King's *De origine mali*, but he seems to have been familiar with its overall argument.

46. See chapter 1 on Bayle's health analogy in *Xenophanes.F*. Exaggeration was one of the criticisms made against Bayle by, for example, Leibniz.

47. Note that Philo is here closer to Bayle than to Hume's early 'Fragment', which conceded that pleasures predominate in frequency.

> Pleasure, scarcely in one instance, is ever able to reach ecstasy and rapture: And in no one instance can it continue for any time at its highest pitch and altitude. . . . But pain often, good God, how often! rises to torture and agony; and the longer it continues, it becomes still more genuine agony and torture. (*DNR*.X.75–6)

Philo then challenges Cleanthes's strategy specifically, which would make religion entirely dependent upon maintaining the predominance of human happiness in the face of all life's miseries, which is manifestly (says Philo) contrary to experience:

> What! no method of fixing a just foundation for religion, unless we allow the happiness of human life, and maintain a continued existence even in this world, with all our present pains, infirmities, vexations, and follies, to be eligible and desirable! But *this is contrary to every one's feeling and experience*: It is contrary to an authority so established as nothing can subvert . . . (*DNR*.X.76; my emphasis)

Furthermore, Philo makes it clear that while Cleanthes has so far been taking into account only the *weaker* version of the pessimist premise (God's goodness is challenged only if there are *more* evils than goods), he should be focusing on the *stronger* version (God's goodness is challenged if there are *any evils at all*):

> But allowing you what never will be believed; at least what you never possibly can prove, that animal, or at least, human happiness in this life, exceeds its misery; you have yet done nothing: For this is not, by any means, what we expect from infinite power, infinite wisdom, and infinite goodness. Why is there *any misery at all* in the world? (*DNR*.X.76; my emphasis)

Thus pessimism seems to be upheld with significantly more confidence by Philo in the *Dialogues* than by Hume in the 'Fragment', but this confidence should not mislead us into thinking that here Philo is trying to score a positive philosophical point, rather than a negative rhetorical one. For Philo does not, in fact, need to establish pessimism: the mere fact that there is *some evil*, and indeed *considerable* evil in the world, is enough to prove the same point as made in Hume's early fragment: that you can't infer God's moral attributes on the basis of the phenomena. Thus Philo is happy to concede to Cleanthes that 'pain or misery in man is *compatible* with infinite power and goodness in the deity'—but this is not enough to *infer* the attributes from the phenomena, which was the point of contention: how to prove, philosophically, the moral nature of God with the attributes of intelligence and benevolence (*DNR*.X.77).

This specific 'defensive' argument,[48] which uses the 'fact' of evil to block the inference of God's attributes from the phenomena, is further discussed in Part XI by Philo in particular, while Demea's sudden silence seems to reflect his increasing discomfort with the turn that the conversation is now taking.[49] Deepening his case against God's moral attributes (even considering Cleanthes's suggestion that God might not be *infinitely* perfect[50]), Philo drives home his point that, unless you're already convinced God is 'very good, wise, and powerful', you won't arrive at this conclusion on the basis of the phenomena (*DNR*.XI.79).[51] The problem is not simply that there are many evils in creation, but that almost all of these evils seem to us far from 'necessary or unavoidable', particularly from the perspective of a divine creator (*DNR*.XI.80). This is brought out by the four 'circumstances' on which 'all, or the greatest part of natural evil depend' (*DNR*.XI.85): namely, that pains as well as pleasures are installed in us to incite us to action; that the world is conducted by general laws; that 'powers and faculties' are so sparingly distributed; and that the machine of nature is so inaccurately put together (*DNR*.XI.80–5).[52] The main problem, Philo stresses again, is not just that there are many evils or that they outweigh the goods, but that there are *any evils at all.* Nevertheless, Philo continues to make the rhetorical case for pessimism, turning the optics of optimism upside down and directing it towards a pessimist conclusion; for even if we look at the whole rather than the parts, as Demea suggested, it is precisely this view from the whole that serves to bolster a deeply pessimistic perspective:

> Look round this universe. What an immense profusion of beings, animated and organised, sensible and active! You admire this prodigious

48. Newlands, 'Hume on Evil', 629.

49. Demea's silence seems to anticipate his departure at the end of this part XI.

50. This suggestion anticipates that offered by Rousseau, who is willing to compromise on God's omnipotence in order to save his benevolence; see chapter 6.

51. See chapter 6 for Rousseau's 'hermeneutical' objection to Voltaire on the impossibility of philosophically interpreting the phenomena *in either direction.*

52. Philo says that his arguments on natural evil apply also to moral evil, 'with little or no variation' (*DNR*.XI.87). These four circumstances are not as such in Bayle, but there are Baylean elements active here, especially with regard to pains and pleasures, which was a point Hume copied out from Bayle (*Mem.*, 501, no. 19). The most original element here has to do with the uneven distribution of powers and forces, and especially the role played by laziness, which is not something I find in Bayle.

> variety and fecundity. But inspect a little more narrowly these living existences, the only beings worth regarding. How hostile and destructive to each other! How insufficient all of them for their own happiness! How contemptible or odious to the spectator! *The whole presents nothing but the idea of a blind nature,* impregnated by a great vivifying principle, and pouring forth from her lap, without discernment or parental care, her maimed and abortive children. (*DNR*.XI.86; my emphasis)[53]

Of the various hypotheses concerning the nature of the 'first causes of the universe', therefore, Philo considers the most probable one to be that they 'have neither goodness nor malice' (*DNR*.XI.86).[54] At the end of the dialogue Demea, who 'did not at all relish the latter part of the discourse', takes leave 'on some pretence or other', and so the discussion ends abruptly and unresolved, though Philo has had the last word.

HUME AND BAYLE

So far, we have seen that Hume unfolds the *rhetorical* case for pessimism mostly along Baylean lines, with Philo and Demea sharing the dubious task of demonstrating the miserableness of things. As far as the *philosophical* case goes, Hume seems markedly more cautious than Bayle, allowing only for the briefest phenomenological reflection that (i) there are many evils in existence (Philo and Demea), and (ii) pains have a greater capacity for intensity than pleasures (Philo). The methodological scruples first expressed in the 'Fragment' thus still appear to be active. With regard to the problem of evil, Hume's approach seems to be generally aligned with Bayle's, while nevertheless diverging in several ways. For Bayle, the main question under scrutiny was one of *compatibility* (of God's existence *and* his attributes with the experience of evil); for Hume's contestants, it's rather one of *inferrability* (whether we can infer God's attributes from our experience). At the same time, this central issue bleeds out into other questions and contexts, so that Philo and Demea in fact supply the materials for a number of different 'problems' of evil.

53. The point on 'variety and fecundity' reflects Leibniz as well as other aficionados of a 'great chain of being': I wonder whether the last line may not also echo Malebranchean concerns over 'monsters'.

54. Philo also discusses and rejects Manicheism in this context (*DNR*.XI.86). As Pitson notes, 'Philo's assent to one of these hypotheses . . . is a result of eliminating the remaining alternatives on the basis of the available evidence' ('Miseries of Life', 100).

The gist of the Humean problem of evil, therefore, is indeed mainly 'defensive' in nature, and can be characterised primarily as an evidential argument from evil.[55] But as Philo himself declares at several points, it is in fact not necessary for him to make the case for pessimism at all, let alone to make it quite so strongly, since he is really trying to prove an essentially modest claim: that the fact that there are *some evils* is already a problem for those who would seek to infer God's benevolence from the phenomena. Why, then, this emotionally invested discourse; why then the heated speeches made by both Philo *and* Demea?

My sense is that the question of pessimism here begins to transcend the problem of evil and to live a life of its own, reflecting a deeper commitment of Hume with regard to how we go about speaking and thinking about evils. As James Harris observes, 'Hume's writings . . . are marked by a general refusal to accept the usual ways of explaining away the existence of evils natural and moral.'[56] This is a deeply Baylean commitment, and it is strongly suggestive of the manner in which Hume must have read Bayle as a kindred spirit, in more ways than one. Hume's Bayle made an impression on him not just as a sceptic but also as a *pessimist*, in a very specific and strongly moral sense of the term: a pessimism marked by this entrenched refusal to allow for the evils of life to be dulled down or explained away. This moral imperative returns repeatedly throughout the *Dialogues*, and it is also what flows through Hume's emphatic inclusion of *psychological* suffering next to the more commonly noted *bodily* kinds. From the early fragment on evil to the essay on suicide, this is another theme that marks Hume's writings, and one in which Bayle's influence is especially strong.

But these Baylean motifs also mean that Hume is vulnerable to some of the same objections. One is the question of hedonism: Hume seems to

55. Samuel Newlands argues that Hume mainly focuses 'on a problem of evil that is (a) *defensive* in force, (b) *distributive* in scope, (c) *natural* in kind, (d) and *third-person* in perspective' ('Hume on Evil', 629). In more general terms, most scholars see Hume mainly delivering an evidential argument from evil, which is surely right, especially for part XI—but it is also the case that the *Dialogues*, in their open-ended and fluid presentation of overlapping questions, engage with various wider concerns of theodicy (a debate of which Hume seems to have been acutely aware). I would caution against hedging in Hume's arguments too tightly.

56. Harris, *Hume*, 451. He continues: 'In the *History of England* there is unspoken contempt for the idea that the horrors he often describes admit of some kind of providential explanation. Unnecessary pain and suffering is a real and undeniable feature of the human condition.' He suggests there may be 'something Calvinist' in this, as in Demea's appraisal of misery as source for religion; if so, then this again brings Hume closer to Bayle.

identify goods and evils with pleasures and pains according to 'a hedonist value theory that is now widely rejected'.[57] As Tony Pitson notes, there are some reasons to modify this critique, since Hume's 'catalogue of evils . . . comprises many different sources of unhappiness, reflecting not only disorders of mind and body but also the external threats to survival posed both by nature itself as well as the violence and injustice of fellow human beings'.[58] This would suggest that far from equating pains and pleasures with evils and goods, Hume employs the former set mainly in a pedagogical way, as easily understandable *examples* or *instances* of goods and evils, not as their identical twins.

Furthermore, with regard to suffering in particular, there is also a more specific value to the Baylean–Humean approach of defining suffering as whatever is experienced or expressed as suffering; and an ill or evil as whatever is experienced as such. Granted, this approach may be problematic in some cases: for instance, when a person is mistaken about whether something is bad for them, or interprets an event as worse than it is.[59] But if we see this emphasis on the individual experience in light of the predominant notions at the time, we find that it is connected with a deeper impulse, as strong in Hume as it is in Bayle, *to resist the downplaying of evils*, especially when these are evils experienced by others. Far from being a casual sceptical invention, the 'hedonism' of Bayle and Hume, if it deserves the name, features as an antidote against a specific philosophical tendency in vogue at the time: namely, the tendency to argue that certain kinds of suffering are not *real evils*, because they are deserved or could have been avoided or are simply exaggerated. Against this, Hume (like Bayle) firmly prioritises the first-person perspective, which, as Samuel Newlands remarks, 'can provide indefeasible authority',[60] as appears from Philo's suggestion that something that 'is contrary to every one's feeling and experience' is 'contrary to an authority so established as nothing can subvert: No decisive proofs can ever be produced against this authority' (*DNR*.X.76).

Considering this prioritisation of the first-person perspective in both Hume and Bayle, it is particularly interesting that both authors emphatically include animal suffering in their discussions of pessimism and evil—the very *existence* of which was contentious in the seventeenth century.

57. Newlands, 'Hume on Evil', 643; see Yandell, *Hume's 'Inexplicable Mystery'*, 244–5.

58. Pitson, 'Miseries of Life', 109n.

59. This ties into the question of whether there can be cases of mistaken or misguided suicide, for which Hume does not seem to allow (see below, pp. 222ff).

60. Newlands, 'Hume on Evil', 629.

There is no dismissal of animal suffering on the grounds that animals, unlike humans, are unable to use words to express their first-person perspectives: on the contrary, both authors seem to assume that we can have access to animal suffering by observing their behaviour; the cries and whimpers by which animals express their pain and fear. There is more at stake here than simple hedonism. What we see here is a deeply felt attempt to formulate a kind of phenomenology and epistemology that is at same time an ethic, and that poses a question believed to be understated: How can we do justice, in our language and moral theories, to the suffering of other creatures?

These are all important innovations, in which Bayle's and Hume's efforts can be seen as two parts of a communal exercise, through which something like a tradition is beginning to take shape. However, in my view, Hume's particular innovation with regard to the problem of evil lies not in these considerations but elsewhere, in his treatment of dispositions and temperaments, and his tentative formulation of what might be called a dispositional problem of evil. This is a theme hinted at by Philo in the *Dialogues* (*DNR*.X.72), but for its development we must turn to an earlier essay of Hume's that is usually not associated with the problem of evil whatsoever: 'The Sceptic'.

'The Sceptic'

Published in 1742, in the second volume of his *Essays, Moral and Political*, 'The Sceptic' forms part of a curious quartet of essays modelled on four types of ancient philosopher: 'The Epicurean', 'The Stoic', 'The Platonist', and 'The Sceptic'. Together, they form the exception to Hume's general insistence that his essays should be read on their own, disconnectedly from each other and from the rest of his work.[61] In contrast, these four essays are to be read together.[62] But read how, exactly? As Hume himself notes, in these essays 'a certain Character is personated; and therefore no Offence ought to be taken at any Sentiments contain'd in them'.[63] The intention of the quartet, he writes elsewhere, is 'not so much to explain accurately the sentiments of the ancient sects of philosophy, as to deliver the sentiments of sects, that naturally form themselves in the world, and

61. Harris, *Hume*, 145.

62. See Hume's footnote added to 'The Epicurean' in 1748 (*EMPL*, 138n.); Harris, 'Hume's Four Essays', 223.

63. Hume, Advertisement to the second volume of *Essays, Moral and Political* (1742, but removed from the 1748 edition); quoted in Harris, 'Hume's Four Essays', 223.

entertain different ideas of human life and of happiness' (*EMPL*, 138n.). Written in the first person, each of the first three essays presents a distinct view of the right road to happiness, according to the modern versions of ancient philosophies, while commenting on each other's views in such a way as to form a kind of conversation. As James Harris notes, 'The Epicurean' sounds like a libertine, the Stoic like Shaftesbury, and the Platonist like 'a latitudinarian divine', while many think the Sceptic 'sounds very like Hume himself'.[64]

Thus we seem to have yet another dialogue on our hands. But there is something different about the fourth essay, 'The Sceptic'. For one thing, this essay is as long as the other three combined. For another, while the first three essays present specific views on happiness, the fourth does something else entirely. In M.A. Stewart's words: 'The first three express attitudes whereas the fourth develops an argument, and it is an argument directed against an assumption which lies behind those attitudes.'[65] The fourth essay argues that there is something deeply misguided about the first three, and about what might be called the 'happiness project' of ancient philosophers in general. Philosophy, Hume's Sceptic argues, is not able to lead us to happiness, or to show us the right ends in life; it is simply not a '*medicine of the mind*' (*EMPL*, 169; Hume's emphasis).[66] This is a point consistent with Hume's other writings, and as such the Sceptic largely seems to express Hume's own point of view; a view that gains particular force when we recall Hume's own youthful Shaftesburean project and the breakdown that ensued.

While much has been written on the four essays, and especially the Sceptic, less noted is the theodicean theme that runs through the final pages of the latter in particular, and the way it connects with Hume's more explicit writings on the problem of evil. As I have hinted, I believe one of Hume's most striking theodicean innovations is articulated precisely

64. Harris, 'Hume's Four Essays', 224; M.A. Stewart, 'The Stoic Legacy', 282 (on latitudinarianism).

65. Stewart, 'The Stoic Legacy', 277; Harris agrees ('Hume's Four Essays', 228).

66. I follow the interpretation of Stewart and Harris here in seeing 'The Sceptic' as an argument against philosophy's capacity for procuring or revealing happiness; but for other views, see, e.g., Immerwahr, 'Hume's Essays on Happiness', who believes that 'none of the speakers represents Hume's own position', and that the 'purpose of these essays is therapeutic rather than analytic' (308). Stewart and Harris disagree in how to connect 'The Sceptic' with a wider philosophical view: according to Stewart, Hume leaves philosophy no practical role whatsoever; while Harris reads 'The Sceptic' as effecting a move from morality towards politics, suggesting that political philosophy may have a practical role that moral philosophy does not.

in this essay. If this contribution escaped notice by his contemporaries, this was possibly because the field of theodicy was preoccupied elsewhere, focusing rather on the kinds of providential arguments that Hume would go on to anatomise in the *Dialogues*.[67] But influence can be deceptive, and it is precisely by evaluating Hume's arguments on his own terms, and not purely in terms of influence, that we can recognise a very modern moment; too modern, perhaps, to have been picked up by his contemporary readers. This is not to say there was no question of influence, only that this influence took on much subtler forms, working slowly through a deepening reflection on psychological suffering, and on suffering itself.

THE LIMITS OF PHILOSOPHY

Coming on the heels of the sweeping statements made by the first three philosophers, the Sceptic objects that philosophers who suggest there is a single road to happiness fail to take into account 'the vast variety of inclinations and pursuits among our species' (*EMPL*, 160). Since there is nothing in itself 'valuable or despicable' (*EMPL*, 162) and objects 'derive their worth merely from the passion' (*EMPL*, 166), the Sceptic argues: 'All the difference, therefore, between one man and another, with regard to life, consists either in the *passion*, or in the *enjoyment*: And these differences are sufficient to produce the wide extremes of happiness and misery' (*EMPL*, 167; Hume's emphasis). This point is then linked to the question of life's goods and evils, which the Sceptic, in good Baylean fashion, interprets entirely in terms of our subjective human experience:

> Good and ill, both natural and moral, are entirely relative to human sentiment and affection. No man would ever be unhappy, could he alter his feelings. PROTEUS-like, he would elude all attacks, by the continual alterations of his shape and form. (*EMPL*, 168)

The problem is that we lack this capacity, since nature has largely 'deprived us' of this 'resource': 'The fabric and constitution of our mind no more depends on our choice, than that of our body.' The point the Sceptic is trying to make is twofold. On the one hand, he wants to argue 'that all dispositions of mind are not alike favourable to happiness, and that one passion or humour may be extremely desirable, while another is equally disagreeable' (*EMPL*, 168). On the other, he wants to stress that this is not really *up to us*: we may well understand that 'the happiest disposition

67. Such as natural theology and the argument from design.

of mind is the *virtuous*' (*EMPL*, 168), but understanding this *cognitively* does not mean we are also able to attain this disposition. It is not always 'in a man's power, by the utmost art and industry, to correct his temper, and attain that virtuous character, to which he aspires. The empire of philosophy extends over a few; and with regard to these too, her authority is very weak and limited' (*EMPL*, 169). In alignment with both Bayle and Mandeville, the Sceptic comes to the following conclusion: 'Whoever considers, without prejudice, the course of human actions, will find, that mankind are almost entirely guided by constitution and temper, and that general maxims have little influence, but so far as they affect our taste or sentiment' (*EMPL*, 169).

These, then, are *the limits of philosophy*.[68] If we have a disposition that makes us insensitive to sympathy, esteem, or other moral sentiments, then no argument will serve to make the virtues desirable to us: philosophy is powerless when faced with a contrary disposition. The only effect that can be expected is an *indirect* one, similar to the effects gained from studying the other sciences and liberal arts, which help to soften the temper and to form certain beneficial habits (*EMPL*, 170). But the resolutions that come out of such an exercise are usually only effected if the person in question is already 'tolerably virtuous' from the start (*EMPL*, 171). The Sceptic is deeply doubtful that philosophy can have any effects beyond this very modest one of further converting the already converted. He illustrates this by turning to various traditional Stoic consolations of philosophy, to which I will return shortly.

How does all of this relate to the problem of evil? Towards the end of the essay, the Sceptic comes to the following conclusion: 'such is the disorder and confusion of human affairs, that no perfect or regular distribution of happiness and misery is ever, in this life, to be expected'. There is an uneven distribution not just of 'the goods of fortune, and the endowments of the body' between the virtuous and vicious, but even of the endowments of the wise: 'the most worthy character, by the very constitution of the passions, enjoys not always the highest felicity' (*EMPL*, 178). This may appear to be just another restatement of the well-known theodicean theme of *misalignment*: between moral and physical goods on the one hand, and between moral and physical evils on the other. Traditionally, however, misalignment tended to be represented purely in terms of vices and virtues on the one hand, and external prosperity or misfortune on the other: the examples used were those of the virtuous who suffer (such

68. I borrow the phrase from Williams, *Ethics and the Limits of Philosophy*.

as Job) and the wicked who prosper (such as Claudian's Rufinus). In contrast, Hume's Sceptic introduces the passions and dispositions into the mix, and rather than placing these under *moral* goods and evils, he classes them under the *physical or natural* kinds: things that befall us, or that we are born with; the goods and ills that are unevenly (and, it seems, undeservedly) distributed. This is a radical innovation, since the passions and dispositions were generally seen as more 'up to us' than external events that happen to us. Not so for Hume: misalignment, according to the Sceptic, prevails not only in external states of affairs but in the passions and dispositions themselves.

Through the dispositions, Hume's Sceptic is able to extend this feature of unevenness or randomness of distribution to all kinds of *psychological* suffering, so that even a 'gloomy and melancholy disposition', of the kind we would nowadays associate with depression, need not at all be indicative of a warped mind, or of anything other than blunt bad luck:

> A gloomy and melancholy disposition is certainly, *to our sentiments*, a vice or imperfection; but as it may be accompanied with great sense of honour and great integrity, it may be found in very worthy characters; though it is sufficient alone to imbitter life, and render the person affected with it completely miserable. (*EMPL*, 179; Hume's emphasis)

It is hard not to read such passages with the young Hume's own breakdown in mind; a breakdown that would have been all the more difficult for him to accept considering the widespread Stoic supposition, held by him at the time, that human flourishing is mostly a matter of the will. But the contrary supposition, that our dispositions too are a matter of fortune, turns out not to have been a passing or incidental view, but a deeply held belief that Hume took even to his grave. As Harris writes, Hume's 'confidence in the inapplicability of ancient philosophy to modern life did not desert him at the end'.[69] In his late autobiographical text 'My Own Life', written shortly before his death, Hume did 'emphasise his good fortune in the mildness of his temper, the cheerfulness of his humour, and the moderateness of his passions', but the main point was that he really considered these, as well as his equanimity in the face of death, as matters of sheer good fortune, *not* as matters of willpower or 'the fruit of years of learning'.[70] This is exactly the view voiced by the Sceptic, who concludes that 'human life is more governed by fortune than by reason; is to be

69. Harris, *Hume*, 465.
70. Ibid.

regarded more as a dull pastime than as a serious occupation; and is more influenced by particular humour, than by general principles' (*EMPL*, 180). The lesson to be drawn by philosophers is therefore as follows: 'To reduce life to exact rule and method, is commonly a painful, oft a fruitless occupation' (*EMPL*, 180).

THE DISPOSITIONAL PROBLEM OF EVIL

The main point Hume seems to be making in 'The Sceptic' thus has to do with the limits of philosophy and the proper nature of the philosophical exercise. But while this is certainly a very important part of what Hume is doing, it is not the whole story to be told here: in fact, I think we miss something important if we confine the Sceptic's argument to the philosophers' quartet rather than linking it to some of Hume's other writings, such as the *Dialogues*. There, after all, we see that Philo, that other voice of Hume, extends the creaturely complaint not only to external circumstances (the things that happen to us) but also to our internal *dispositions*:

> But it is hard; I dare to repeat it, it is hard, that being placed in a world so full of wants and necessities; where almost every being and element is either our foe or refuses its assistance; *we should also have our own temper to struggle with*, and should be deprived of that faculty which can alone fence against these multiplied evils. (*DNR*.XI.84; my emphasis)

The same point, in different wordings, is made by the Sceptic, suggesting that some of the Sceptic's musings are also connected with Hume's development of the problem of evil. The extent to which this is so may be easily missed, since it is so subtly articulated, but this subtlety should not blind us from the fact that Hume's turn to the dispositions is a drastic innovation when considered in the light of the wider theodicean tradition. Unlike almost any other thinker of the time, none of whom took the question of dispositions and temperaments into account in any deep or serious way—unlike even Bayle, whose intuitions on the score remain under-articulated—Hume integrates the question of pessimism into a deeper theory of human nature,[71] and in doing so reinvents the problem of evil entirely.

71. Note that Bayle and Hume, for all their agreements, were not so aligned in their moral philosophy, which Hume bases on sentiment and sympathy, and Bayle (for all his scepticism with regard to moral motivation) bases on reason, especially in his later works (see McKenna, *Études sur Bayle*, chs. 7 and 8).

To see the extent of the Humean innovation, let's briefly reconstruct the clash between the optimists and pessimists with regard to physical evil (i.e. suffering) in particular. A recurrent point of contention throughout this debate, as we have seen, was the Stoic idea, emergent in Leibniz as well as King, that we can learn to suffer well, and that the extent of our sufferings is somehow *up to us*. The Baylean objection was at heart an ethical one: to say this is just to make our suffering worse, adding to it a consciousness of guilt. The Humean objection goes further and argues that the Stoic point gets something fundamentally wrong: namely, *what we are talking about when we are talking about evils*.

According to Bayle, again, supported in this by Hume's Sceptic, an evil is whatever we experience as an evil. The objection to this definition is that while some people experience event x as a terrible evil, others may experience the same x as a mere nuisance, or even with indifference. The argument could then be made that event x cannot properly be called an evil, since the reaction of the first group was exaggerated or at least unnecessary: we are, on the Stoic line, able to control our responses to the things that happen to us. Bayle, as we have seen, is already sceptical about the extent to which we are in control of our responses, but it is Hume who drives this point home. Evil, on the Humean view, is not just the mere *experience* of x, but *the fact that* we experience x *as* an evil, as well as the very disposition or temperament that makes us experience x's as evils in general. In other words, we are not in charge of our dispositions in any meaningful way. The fact that some are better suited than others to the task of coping with misfortune, *this itself is an evil* to those people who are less suited. This is not just a question of education and the will: dispositions too are part of the evils to be explained in any meaningful theodicy.

As we have seen in chapter 4, this is a point rejected by Maupertuis, who uses pessimism precisely to defeat it, thus demonstrating again the eclecticism of these lateral pessimists.[72] It is, furthermore, a point missing completely from Rousseau, who will show the persistence of what is ultimately a Stoic point: that the way we deal with suffering is very much *up to us*. For the remainder of the eighteenth century, the question of the 'up-to-usness' of suffering will continue to shadow the pessimist debate, and it is precisely with regard to this question that Hume's dispositional turn is so very striking: no move could be more effective to deflate it.

72. Here, Hume is aligned rather with La Mettrie, who similarly argues that we are not in control of our passions, let alone our capacity for happiness (see chapter 4).

The Consolations of Philosophy

But what, then, of consolation? This will be Rousseau's sweeping objection against Voltaire, as it was Leibniz's against Bayle: that such a pessimistic view of things offers nothing in the way of consolation, whereas the value of true religion and the right philosophy lies at least partly in its ability to console us. Far from making us more miserable, a belief in the 'up-to-usness' of suffering is able to make us less so, since it offers us a hopeful perspective for the future: that we need not suffer as we do. At the very least, therefore, the Stoic line is *consoling*. What do the pessimists have to offer us instead?

As we have seen, while Bayle does not explicitly deny that there is such a value to be found in religion or even philosophy, he is deeply sceptical about the ability of philosophers to offer anything like real consolation: even Cicero, who believed he could philosophically console his friends, was himself unable to be thus consoled. In matters of consolation, philosophy is bound to fail, and to fail most dreadfully. Hume takes the same line, and takes it further, arguing that *neither religion nor philosophy* are properly placed to console us in this life. This, however, is not a single coherent argument, but must be pieced together from different corners of his works.[73]

With regard to the consolations of *religion*, it is again Philo who makes this claim. In the concluding part of the *Dialogues*, after Demea's departure, Philo and Cleanthes continue their conversation on the order of nature and the analogy between the human and the divine. Initially at least, Philo sounds much more conciliatory than before, but he resumes his contrariness when he lists the many evils of superstition and false or popular religion (*DNR*.XII.94ff).[74] Cleanthes then warns him not to let 'your zeal against false religion . . . undermine your veneration for the true', and emphasises the comforts offered by the latter: 'Forfeit not this principle, the chief, the only great comfort in life; and our principal

73. As such, my argument cannot be more than tentative and does not represent any overall interpretation of Hume's work: my aim is to show how these considerations are at least as active in Hume as they are in Bayle and the optimists; and, furthermore, that they form an important interpretive background against which to read Hume.

74. See Richard Dees, 'Morality about Metaphysics', who argues that Philo's conciliatory shift is motivated by 'an attempt to maintain a friendship with Cleanthes that might [otherwise] have been damaged' (132). On Demea's reasons for leaving, see, e.g., Dye, 'Demea's Departure'. Newlands in turn 'sympathize[s] with Demea's decision to quit the discussion; it was no longer a genuine inquiry' ('Hume on Evil', 639). On the alternative endings of the *Dialogues*, see Mazza and Mori, 'Hume's Palimpsest'.

support amidst all the attacks of adverse fortune.' Philo concedes this only to some extent, arguing instead that 'the terrors of religion commonly prevail above its comforts' (*DNR*.XII.99). In general, he continues, it is the suffering of mind or body that brings men to religion, and this dark spring of religious belief leads to the gloomiest depictions of God as well as the afterlife. Happy people don't have much reason to turn to religion, but unhappy people, who do, often become all the more miserable by doing so: 'as terror is the primary principle of religion, it is the passion which always predominates in it, and admits but of short intervals of pleasure' (*DNR*.XII.100). The suggestion we are left with is that far from consoling us, religion is only likely to make us all the more miserable.[75]

Thus Hume's Philo argues against the consolation of religion—or at least of *popular* religion. It is true that he admits the consolations of true or philosophical religion, but it is unclear what this consolation consists of, or even whether it is really needed here: whether such a philosophical religion should not rather take away the fear of death entirely.[76] In any event, it is clear that this modest consolation has nothing to do with expectations of an afterlife, the rosy perception of which is just another notion punctured by Philo: it is hard to consider the afterlife as intrinsically a consoling thing if we take into account not only the minority of the blessed as opposed to the majority of the damned, but also the terrors we are told to expect in hell (*DNR*.XII.100).[77] Is Philo, in his efforts to place these justificatory themes outside the debate, edging towards a modern conception of philosophy as a discipline that should not be concerned with either hope or consolation?[78] Not quite, for Philo dismisses these questions only to some extent: here, popular religion is discredited precisely by its failure

75. Here again, Philo's position is likely close to Hume's own views, considering his deep resistance to religious superstition. Note, however, that religious authors such as C.S. Lewis and Hilary Mantel have similarly taken issue with the idea of 'the consolations of religion': e.g. Lewis, *A Grief Observed*, 21: 'Talk to me about the truth of religion and I'll listen gladly. Talk to me about the duty of religion and I'll listen submissively. But don't come talking to me about the consolations of religion or I shall suspect that you don't understand.' See Mantel's commentary in the same volume, 65–6: 'you wonder how the idea began, that religion is a consolation'.

76. As Harris rightly notes, Philo's final concession that '*the cause or causes of order in the universe probably bear some remote analogy to human intelligence*' (*DNR*.XII.101; Hume's emphasis) amounts to a conception of 'true religion' that 'is almost completely empty of content' (Harris, *Hume*, 454–5).

77. That is, by the mainstream theologies available at the time. Note that the terrors of hell can also function as the kind of 'repugnant conclusion' that militates against the doctrine of (eternal) damnation; see Hart, *That All Shall be Saved*.

78. On which, see Douglas, 'Philosophy and Hope'.

in consolation, or rather, by its opposite quality of being positively *unconsoling*. Religion, in Philo's view, only serves to make matters worse: we thought we were only suffering here and now, and to this is added the prospect of an eternity of future suffering. But what then of the consolations of *philosophy*?

It will hardly come as a surprise that Hume, like Bayle before him, deeply questions the efficacy of philosophy in matters of grief and consolation. Unlike Bayle, however, Hume also supplies a positive counterpart to this argument, by offering a reflection on *what consolation should really look like*, if it is to take hold on our hearts and imaginations. For the negative part of this argument, we have to go back to 'The Sceptic', which closes with a kind of dialogue between the Sceptic and a variety of Stoics, some of a more optimistic, some of a more pessimistic bent. Thus a modern-sounding Stoic with Popean leanings (indeed, he quotes Pope's *Essay on Man*[79]) argues that: '*All ills arise from the order of the universe, which is absolutely perfect. Would you wish to disturb so divine an order for the sake of your own particular interest?*' But, replies the Sceptic, if even our moral evils are included in this order, as the Stoic admits, this means that 'my own vices will also be a part of the same order', and there would be no reason to reject them or to feel remorse (*EMPL*, 173).[80]

A more pessimistically inclined Stoic then argues that suffering is intrinsically a part of the human condition, so that no human has a ground for complaint:

> Man is born to be miserable; and is he surprised at any particular misfortune? And can he give way to sorrow and lamentation upon account of any disaster? (*EMPL*, 174)

To which the Sceptic replies, in a very Baylean vein:

> Yes: He very reasonably laments, that he should be born to be miserable. Your consolation presents a hundred ills for one, of which you pretend to ease him. (*EMPL*, 174)

This is not just a riposte to Stoic consolation: it is a defence of the creaturely complaint, suggesting that on the Humean view, it can be reasonable

79. Specifically the famous lines: 'If plagues or earthquakes break not Heaven's design, / Why then a Borgia, or a Catiline?' (Pope, *EM*, I.155–6).

80. See also Hume's *Enquiry concerning Human Understanding*, which contains a similar reflection on the inefficacy of rational philosophical consolation; in particular, the optimistic variety (EHU, 8.2:89–90).

for miserable creatures to lament their creation. As with Bayle, for Hume the creature does have a ground for complaint.

The Stoic (possibly the same one) then continues to argue that by meditating on the existence of evils and the likelihood of evils striking us, we will better prepare ourselves:

> You should always have before your eyes death, disease, poverty, blindness, exile, calumny, and infamy, as ills which are incident to human nature. If any of these ills falls to your lot, you will bear it the better, when you have reckoned upon it. (*EMPL*, 174)

The Sceptic replies that if this reflection is abstract, it is ineffective; if it is focused on particular evils, then it only makes things worse:

> I answer, if we confine ourselves to a general and distant reflection on the ills of human life, *that* can have no effect to prepare us for them. If by close and intense meditation we render them present and intimate to us, *that* is the true secret for poisoning all our pleasures, and rendering us perpetually miserable. (*EMPL*, 174)[81]

The Stoic, now sounding exasperated, continues: '*Your sorrow is fruitless, and will not change the course of destiny.*' To which the Sceptic responds: 'Very true: And for that very reason I am sorry' (*EMPL*, 174; Hume's emphasis throughout).[82]

Thus the Sceptic is constantly shifting the discussion to a wider viewpoint. As Bayle had also said: it is not at all relevant that our sorrows are pointless; this very fact (*of* their pointlessness) is an evil. To this, Hume adds that the more we try to offer these kinds of consolations, the less we end up actually consoling, and the worse a picture we paint of our existence. Far from alleviating our complaint by pointing to the inevitability of suffering, such consolation only ends up adding new grounds for complaint (namely, the fact of this inevitability). This is not quite a refutation of the Stoic theme, but rather, a kind of *reductio ad absurdum* of philosophical consolation. As the Sceptic finally concludes: 'Such is the imperfection, even of the best of these philosophical topics of consolation' (*EMPL*, 177).[83]

81. Note that this echoes the recurrent critique made by optimists that pessimism increases our misery.

82. The Sceptic goes on to cite some of Cicero's consolations for deafness and blindness and Plutarch's for exile, etc. (*EMPL*, 174–5).

83. A very long footnote follows in Hume's own voice, suggesting again that Hume subscribes to the Sceptic's conclusions (*EMPL*, 177–9). For similar views on philosophy

But if philosophical consolation is so imperfect, this does not mean that *all* consolation is bound to fail. So what is consolation supposed to look like? For the positive side of this argument, we have to turn to another essay, 'Of Moral Prejudices', published (like 'The Sceptic') in 1742, but withdrawn from later editions.[84] Here Hume (or the 'I' of the essay[85]) critiques two widespread moral or philosophical trends: one that ridicules everything, while another takes too grave and Stoic a view of life: 'I mean that grave philosophic Endeavour after Perfection which, under Pretext of reforming Prejudices and Errors, strikes at all the most endearing Sentiments of the Heart, and all the most useful Byasses and Instincts, which can govern a human Creature' (*EMPL*, 539). For one example of such Stoic advice, the essayist points to Epictetus's advice on giving consolation to a grieving friend: 'you may counterfeit a Sympathy with him, if it give him Relief; but take Care not to allow any Compassion to sink into your Heart, or disturb that Tranquillity, which is the Perfection of Wisdom' (*EMPL*, 540).[86] For another, he mentions Diogenes's request for his body to be thrown out into the fields after his death, since he would be devoid of feeling anyhow.

With this, Hume contrasts a story (in all likelihood fictional) of one Eugenius, who as a young man studied philosophy, but later married and had children, and was deeply afflicted after the loss of his wife. The only thing that could console him was his family: 'Nothing could have supported him under so severe an Affliction, but the Consolation he received from his young Family, who were now become dearer to him on account of their deceased Mother.' In the aftermath of this loss, Eugenius secretly treasures one daughter because she resembles her mother; he keeps his wife's picture, and he wants his body to be placed in the same grave after his death, where 'a Monument shall be erected over them, and their mutual Love and Happiness celebrated in an Epitaph, which he himself has composed for that Purpose' (*EMPL*, 541).[87] All things that, considered

---

and consolation, see Voltaire's story *Les Deux Consolés*, and Johnson's *Rasselas*, chapter 18 (quoted at the beginning of this chapter).

84. 'Of Moral Prejudices' appeared only in vol. 2 of *Essays, Moral and Political* (1742), but was withdrawn in next edition of 1748 (and subsequent ones) with several others Hume deemed 'too frivolous for the rest' (Hume to Adam Smith, cited in Harris, *Hume*, 166); see Norah Smith, 'Hume's "Rejected" Essays'.

85. As Harris notes (*Hume*, 156), it is not clear that the 'I' of the essay is to be 'straightforwardly identified with Hume himself'.

86. See Epictetus, *Encheiridion*, section 16.

87. This anecdote is followed by a letter, probably also fictional, of a woman rationally and coldly manoeuvring in order to fulfil her desire to have a child outside of marriage,

from the cold perspective of the Stoic philosophers, are not just irrational but counterproductive, since they serve to deepen our attachments rather than distancing us from them.

The Hume of this essay is not openly setting out an argument against philosophical (that is, Stoic) consolation, and yet it seems there is an argument being made. The idea being suggested to us is that the unreflected response of grieving Eugenius, which lends itself so easily to Stoical derision, is in fact a more natural and indeed a healthier way of mourning than Epictetus's heartless consolation or Diogenes's sweeping nonchalance. It is suggested, furthermore, that there can be beauty in such acts of mourning: that grief need not be purely negative, something to be avoided at all cost, but can be a celebration and even a continuation of that love (those of us who have lost someone can surely sympathise).[88] This may not be a downright philosophical argument, but that does not mean it is devoid of philosophical worth; it comprises, in fact, an important supplement to Bayle's argument against Stoic consolation which is purely negative, not to say depressing.[89]

Kant writes of the failure of all philosophical attempts at theodicy; in like manner, Hume and Bayle seem to be demonstrating the failure of all philosophical attempts at consolation. To which Hume adds that consolation works only if it is *not* philosophical. So far, many of his contemporaries might well have agreed: philosophy is simply not where we should look for consolation. But, as Hume's Philo also adds, neither is religion.

'Of Suicide'

Together, these essays paint a picture of a Hume deeply sceptical with regard to the power of philosophy to help us become better persons or even to console us ('The Sceptic'); and deeply compassionate with regard to our moral sentiments, which comprise a warm realm in which cold philosophy ought not to intrude ('Of Moral Prejudices'). And yet we

which the essayist raises as another 'Instance of a Philosophic Spirit' that has got out of hand (*EMPL*, 542–4).

88. See also Hume's comment in the *Treatise of Human Nature* that grief itself tells us something about 'the peculiar merit of benevolence': 'a person, whose grief upon the loss of a friend were excessive, wou'd be esteem'd upon that account. His tenderness bestows a merit, as it does a pleasure, on his melancholy' (*THN*, 3.3.3.6).

89. As a biographical note, I would mention here that Bayle's more embittered resistance to consolation is understandable considering that he had suffered a very different kind of loss in the violent faraway death of his brother than Eugenius did in his wife; see chapter 1.

encounter an entirely different Hume in the devastating essay 'Of Suicide', which brings us closer to the philosophical mood associated with Philo in the *Dialogues*: an uncompromising interrogation of superstition and religion alike. Withdrawn from publication in Hume's *Four Dissertations* of 1757 following the advice of Hume's friends, 'Of Suicide' nevertheless circulated, and appeared in French in 1770, without Hume's knowledge; it was eventually published posthumously and anonymously in 1777.[90]

Having heard so much about the things that philosophy *can't* do, we might be relieved to hear the essay open with a very specific benefit of philosophy: 'One considerable advantage, that arises from philosophy, consists in the sovereign antidote, which it affords to superstition and false religion' (*EMPL*, 577). This, then, is the right provenance of philosophy, which, though not able to correct things like '[l]ove or anger, ambition or avarice', is the most effective remedy against superstition, which after all is 'founded on false opinion' (*EMPL*, 579). It is by virtue of this efficacy that philosophy can exert an influence, albeit an indirect one, on both morality and happiness. We have learned that our happiness depends mostly on our dispositions, on which philosophy has little to no effect; but it *can* affect other elements of our mental lives, such as false opinion, which has the power to make us miserable. As Philo also told us in the *Dialogues*, there are various ways in which superstition can make us unhappy, but this essay is directed against a very specific way in which it does so: namely, by instilling in us the fear of death, thereby closing the door to the only way out of our miseries, the only 'refuge' or 'remedy' against the miseries of life, 'the regions of pain and sorrow' (*EMPL*, 579). The refuge in question is suicide, and Hume will spend the rest of the essay arguing against the widespread notion that suicide is 'criminal' or even just unethical. In Hume's words:

> Let us here endeavour to restore men to their native liberty, by examining all the common arguments against Suicide, and shewing, that That action may be free from every imputation of guilt or blame; according to the sentiments of all the ancient philosophers. (*EMPL*, 580)[91]

90. Together with that other withdrawn essay, 'Of the Immortality of the Soul'. Hume told William Strahan that he suppressed both essays 'from my abundant prudence' (quoted in Harris, *Hume*, 361), possibly persuaded in this by his friends (as argued by Mossner, 'Hume's "Four Dissertations"'). For an alternative argument, see Beauchamp, 'An Analysis of Hume's Essay "On Suicide"', who believes Hume withdrew the essay on suicide 'because of internal inadequacies in content' (95).

91. Hume later extends his attack to Christian arguments against suicide, in a long footnote towards the end of the essay, where he notes that suicide is not prohibited by 'a

'If Suicide be criminal,' Hume continues, 'it must be a transgression of our duty, either to God, our neighbour, or ourselves' (*EMPL*, 580). He goes on to argue that suicide does not comprise a transgression in any of these senses, dwelling in particular on the first kind (suicide as a transgression of divine duty) by arguing that suicide does not and *could not* disrupt the providential order.[92]

However, I want to focus here on a basic assumption made, or rather *presupposed*, throughout the essay: which is the basic point that it is possible for existence to become a burden to us; for there to be states *worse than non-existence*. This may seem uncontroversial to modern eyes, and indeed Hume presents it as an established truth, when in fact, in Hume's day, it was anything but. Consider Hume's response to the possible objection that the act of suicide suggests an ingratitude for life:

> Do you imagine that I repine at providence or curse my creation, because I go out of life, and put a period to a being, which, were it to continue, would render me miserable? Far be such sentiments from me. I am only convinced of *a matter of fact*, which you yourself acknowledge possible, *that human life may be unhappy, and that my existence, if farther prolonged, would become ineligible*. But I thank providence, both for the good which I have already enjoyed, and for the power, with which I am endowed, of escaping the ill that threatens me. To you it belongs to repine at providence, who foolishly imagine that you have no such power, and who must still prolong a hated being, tho' loaded with pain and sickness, with shame and poverty. (*EMPL*, 583–4; my emphasis)

This 'matter of fact' would have been disputed by optimists such as Leibniz and King, who believed that human life could indeed be unhappy, but could not become so miserable as to become *ineligible*; that is, no longer be worth living.[93] (Such ineligibility they fully concede to be a problem for divine benevolence.) Hume, however, sees this possibility of a life not worth living (rightly, I think) as a *matter of fact*, as Bayle did too. From

---

single text of scripture' (*EMPL*, 588). In contrast, Maupertuis discusses suicide only in a pagan context, from which he emphatically excludes Christianity; see chapter 4.

92. For an analysis of Hume's overall argument, see 'Holden, Religion and Moral Prohibition'; Lecaldano, 'Hume on Suicide'. I focus here on those parts relating to pessimism specifically.

93. The only possible exception involves the misery of the damned, with which Leibniz and King both struggle, but which Hume does not take into account: nowhere does the essay distinguish between death and annihilation or take into account the possibility of an afterlife.

this presupposition, which he does not prove but assumes to be a given, Hume moves to draw various conclusions. One is that we have no reason to believe that suicide is an act of rebellion against providence—far from it: 'whenever pain or sorrow so far overcome my patience as to make me tired of life, I may conclude, that I am recalled from my station, in the clearest and most express terms' (*EMPL*, 585). With regard to the duty we have to ourselves, Hume emphasises the same point made by Bayle and to some extent by Malebranche; that deep misery, of either the physical or the psychological kind, can render life worse than non-existence, *pire que le néant*:

> That Suicide may often be consistent with interest and with our duty to *ourselves*, no one can question, who allows that age, sickness, or misfortune, may render life a burthen, and make it *worse even than annihilation*. I believe that no man ever threw away life while it was worth keeping. (*EMPL*, 588; last emphasis mine)

This last sentence may give us some pause. Has no one ever committed suicide misguidedly? Cannot a person be mistaken, especially in a period of emotional upheaval, in judging their lives to be not worth living? Nowadays, we know this is only too common: many prospective suicides who have been unsuccessful, or have been dissuaded or prevented from even trying, later express their gratitude for this failure. It is both possible for a person to go through a *period* of their life being worse than non-existence; and to misevaluate their situation.[94] As, indeed, Madeleine de Puisieux had objected to Maupertuis: if someone tells you they want to die, this does not mean that 'life is an evil for them', merely that they are 'very unhappy with the current moment'.[95] In deepening our understanding of the psychology of suicide, Hume thus goes too far in the opposite direction, placing far too much weight on a person's self-evaluation and not enough on the possible factors complicating that self-evaluation.

94. Aaron Smuts gives the following example: 'For instance, after breaking up with her latest boyfriend of two weeks, a depressed adolescent might think that her life is not worth living' ('Five Tests', 443). Julian Savulescu, commenting on this phrase of Hume's, attributes to him a 'naïve optimism', which he rejects in the specific context of patients wanting to limit life-sustaining treatment: 'There are good reasons to believe that normal people, when evaluating whether it is worth living in a disabled state in the future, will undervalue that existence, even in terms of what they judge is best' ('Rational Desires', 665). Yandell (*Hume's 'Inexplicable Mystery'*, 295) calls this notion of Hume's 'a view which needs only to be stated clearly to be seen as false'.

95. Puisieux, *Caractères*, 177–8 (my translation): but note that according to her, the same qualification holds true for people who say they want to *live*.

This itself shows the limits of the Baylean–Humean approach to physical evil: if evil is purely defined as whatever is experienced as evil, this means that a person cannot be wrong about what constitutes an evil for them or even about the proportions of this evil. This is all the more so because neither author distinguishes short-term and long-term desires or interests.[96] Thus, if a certain event at a certain moment in time is experienced as something that makes life not worth living, then this is assumed to be the case; even if the person making the evaluation is in no fit state to do so, or would come to a different conclusion at a later time. This may suggest that Bayle and Hume are putting a very low price on life indeed, if it can be disposed of with so light a justification. But again, we should remember what both authors were up against. They were attacking the widespread notion that suicide is a form of cowardice and even a crime for which, in Hume's Scotland and elsewhere, not only the perpetrator (if unsuccessful in the act) but also the surviving relatives could be punished; not to mention the ostracisation that followed the body even into the ground, which could not be *holy* ground.[97] Thus, if both authors ended up going too far in trying to oppose the ruling set of cultural norms, they had good reason for doing so.[98]

At a closer look, furthermore, Hume's reason for making this claim (that 'no man ever threw away life while it was worth keeping') turns out to have less to do with a kind of 'naïve optimism' (Savulescu) and more with an appeal to charity and compassion in our interpretation of a suicide's motives. Considering the great obstacles that impede this act, such as the 'natural horror of death', we can safely assume 'that any one, who, without apparent reason, has had recourse to it, was curst with such an incurable depravity or gloominess of temper, as must poison all enjoyment, and render him equally miserable as if he had been loaded with the

96. At least, *not in this context*. As an anonymous reviewer pointed out, the distinction between short-term and long-term interests is central to Hume's argument on the need for government (*THN*, 3.2.7).

97. Lecaldano, 'Hume on Suicide', 662.

98. Hume gives an elaborate account in one of his letters of a personal experience with suicide. While stationed in Brittany, serving as secretary to General James St Clair, Hume found his friend Alexander Forbes near dead from suicide; having attempted to prevent his death, Hume was implored by Forbes to 'unloosen his Bandage & hasten his Death, as the last Act of Friendship I coud show him: But alas! we live not in Greek or Roman times.' Forbes died anyway; and Hume calls this 'one of the most tragical Stories ever I heard of, than which nothing ever gave me more Concern' (letter to John Home of Ninewells, 4 October 1746, in *Letters*, I, 97).

most grievous misfortunes' (*EMPL*, 588).[99] Here, far from neutralising suicide as one possible life decision among others, Hume draws us into the hidden tragic background of the phenomenon of suicide, thus deepening our reflection on not only the act itself but the circumstances that inspired it. In Hume as in Bayle, therefore, we may see the beginnings of, if not an outright sociology, then at least a psychology of suicide.

But problems remain, and Hume is perhaps at his most dubious when he discusses the question of suicide with regard to our duty to our neighbour and society at large. 'A man who retires from life, does no harm to society,' writes Hume: 'He only ceases to do good; which, if it be an injury, is of the lowest kind' (*EMPL*, 586).[100] Furthermore, he continues, it is likely that any person so miserable as to want to kill himself is already a 'burthen' to society, which would make the act not only 'innocent but laudable' (*EMPL*, 587). This is where we should become properly uncomfortable, since Hume's argument is beginning to sound less like a defence and more like a recommendation.[101] And this is, in fact, where the conclusion steers us:

> If Suicide be supposed a crime, 'tis only cowardice can impel us to it. If it be no crime, both prudence and courage should engage us *to rid ourselves at once of existence, when it becomes a burthen*. 'Tis the only way, that we can then be useful to society, by setting an example, which, if imitated, would preserve to every one his chance for happiness in life, and would effectually free him from all danger of misery. (*EMPL*, 588, my emphasis)

Thus, like Bayle, Hume emphasises both physical and psychological suffering as the hidden emotional background of suicide, which, like Bayle and Montaigne before him, he thinks should be associated with courage rather than with cowardice. But in trying to push back against the universal condemnation and ostracisation of suicide, Hume goes too far in the opposite direction, losing much of the caution, ambivalence, and subtlety that characterises his writings on pessimism and evil, and beginning to

99. This mention of a 'gloominess of temper' (which we should read as something like deep depression) is particularly significant, since it ascribes a central role to psychological suffering as a source of misery and suicide, equal to more blatant modes of (physical) suffering; see again chapter 1.

100. See also Voltaire's argument (against Pascal's objections to Montaigne's view of suicide): 'Philosophically speaking, what harm does a man do society by leaving it when he is of no further use to it?' (*Letters*, 136).

101. As Harris notes, Hume was read by some in 'precisely this way' (*Hume*, 548n., 366).

sound dangerously like those Stoic philosophers that he most condemned. Like Diogenes saying that we might as well throw his corpse into the fields, the voice speaking in 'Of Suicide' shows no appreciation of the many ways in which suicide deeply affects those who are left behind, such as friends and family or even children. We are left with a cold and hyper-rational argument that suicide may be laudable or even a duty in certain cases: few things could be further removed from Hume's reminder, in 'Of Moral Prejudices', that it is precisely within our human relations and the warm passions therein comprised that we find our humanity and, in the end, our consolation.

This makes me wonder how certain we are that the 'I' of this essay is entirely Hume's, and whether his attack on providence and defence of suicide might not go hand in hand with yet another satirical representation of those Stoic philosophers with whom he was so exasperated. Could not the cool-headed conclusion of the essay be meant as yet another example of philosophy and reason pushing beyond the bounds of our intuitions and moral sentiments? And could not an awareness of the dubious morality at play in the final pages of the essay be part of the reason why Hume in the end opted against publishing it?

Whatever the answer to such questions, one thing the essay certainly does is reinforce the link, hinted at in earlier chapters, between the philosophy of pessimism and the ethics of suicide. It is perhaps inherent to an entrenched sceptical pessimism, which sees no solution in religion or the afterlife, that something needs to be offered in response to the situation of the truly miserable, whose circumstances these authors have gone to such lengths to describe. What we begin to see here is not just an argument that suicide is not de facto immoral, but that it may in certain cases be the best or even the only response to some of life's darkest circumstances; that the prospect of this last 'refuge' may even function as a kind of consolation, a way out when all other remedies have failed.[102] Hence there may well be an inherent link between pessimism and the moral defence of suicide; a link that was subtle in Bayle and becomes outspoken in Hume. But the most valuable point made by Hume's 'Of Suicide', in my view, is one also made by pessimists from Bayle to Schopenhauer: that suicide is a reality that should invoke our compassion, and not our contempt.

102. It is, however, equally intriguing that later pessimists will seek precisely to weaken this link between pessimism and suicide; as we will see, Schopenhauer is deeply concerned to show that his pessimism is *not* an argument for suicide. This ambivalence is inherent to the gravity of the topic.

Humean Pessimism

As we have seen, Hume's presentation of the problem of evil is closely intertwined with the ongoing questions of pessimism: whether the evils of life outweigh the goods, and whether it can be the case for any creature that it would be better not to be.[103] With regard to the latter question, Hume does not even take into consideration the widespread optimist view that such a state of being does not actually exist: that it is impossible for there to be a creature (created under a good God) for whom it would be better not to be. He is most adamant on this point in the essay 'Of Suicide', where he presents it as an indisputable fact, a reality as clear as any, that there are some beings who would be better off by not existing; that there are states worse than non-existence. But this is perhaps one of the few questions in this context on which Hume articulates an unambiguous position. Indeed, one of the most striking aspects of his discussion of pessimism and the problem of evil is his refusal to come to fixed conclusions. To some extent, this may be because it is simply not necessary, especially in the *Dialogues*, where Hume, 'properly speaking, . . . had no position to advocate';[104] and where Philo, according to Peter Kivy, saw that it was neither possible nor necessary to logically refute the optimist: simply 'confounding' him was more than enough.[105] But we have also seen that Hume's refusal to pronounce judgement on the question of pessimism springs from a deep scepticism with regard to our capacity to weigh life's goods and evils in any objective way. As early as the 'Fragment on Evil', Hume saw that it was impossible to come to firm conclusions on this score, prejudiced as we all are by our own experiences and perspectives on the world. As such, he is epistemically much more cautious than Bayle ever was, which is just another way in which Hume out-Bayles his predecessor.

At the same time, the very scepticism that moderates Hume's pessimism is also what informs and strengthens it. His general reservations with regard to our cognitive abilities feed into a more particular scepticism about the extent to which we can exert power over ourselves or our emotional attitudes; over our very capacity for happiness. Far from our flourishing being mainly a matter of practice or learning, of willpower or reason or philosophy, Hume sees it as, for a large part, a matter of good

103. Again, Hume does not distinguish between *no longer existing* and *never having existed.*

104. Harris, *Hume*, 447 (see above, p. 195).

105. Kivy, 'Voltaire', 218: i.e. 'by bombarding [the optimist], so to speak, with the evil of the world'.

luck.[106] This idea, as we have seen, leads to a powerful anti-Stoic current throughout Hume's writings, where he again follows in Bayle's footsteps, and again outdoes him by so explicitly including our dispositions among the theodicean explananda, and formulating, for the first time in history, what I have called a dispositional problem of evil.[107]

It is this dispositional turn that is, to my mind, most interesting if read in the context of the wider theodicean debate. On the one hand, this move suggests yet another expansion of the category of physical evil, which is where Hume seems to place the passions and dispositions, traditionally associated rather with moral evil, on tacit Stoic assumptions. On the other, it also enforces the role played by psychological suffering, which is not only emphatically included in the broader category of physical or natural evil, but begins to rise in prominence over and against its bodily counterpart.[108] As Catherine Wilson notes, it is 'psychological misery' that begins to take over from bodily suffering, not just in Hume's *Dialogues*, but in the central concerns and preoccupations of theodicean thought:

> we may remark on the shift already emerging in the late books of Hume's *Dialogues*. Here it is no longer war, plague, and famine which the theist seeks to reconcile with his conception of God, but *psychological misery*—anxiety, terror, weakness, and distress. The problem of evil is no longer intimately linked with the central preoccupation of the late rationalist, the order and intelligibility of the physical world, and from this point forward Leibnizian optimism becomes increasingly vulnerable to the attacks of critics whose dominant concerns lie elsewhere.[109]

The specific inflections of Humean pessimism thus mirror the wider dynamics of the theodicean turn, in which the broader shift from moral to physical evil is followed up with a further shift, internal to physical evil,

106. Again, this is not to deny that habit as well as 'study and application' can have a positive effect on our happiness and dispositions: they can, but the extent to which they can depends on those very dispositions, and those are a matter rather of fortune (*EMPL*, 170–1). As a reviewer has pointed out, Hume does allow for a connection between virtue and happiness (see again *THN*, 3.3.3), though the Sceptic notes that these are not always well aligned (*EMPL*, 179).

107. On the ongoing influence of Stoicism on Hume's contemporaries, see Stewart, 'The Stoic Legacy'.

108. This shift is connected not only with a Baylean emphasis on experience in describing evils (sometimes associated with hedonism), but also with a more Epicurean/sceptical view of human nature, according to which our actions are driven by our passions rather than by reason, and with the inclusion of animal suffering into the notion of physical evil.

109. Wilson, 'Leibnizian Optimism', 783 (my emphasis).

from evils of the body to evils of the mind; from bodily to psychological suffering. This is not to say that it was Hume who effected this transition, which was surely sparked by Bayle and spurred on by a continued engagement with Baylean thought throughout the eighteenth century. But it is precisely through such avid readers of Bayle as Hume and Voltaire that something of a tradition begins to take shape; a tradition that receives its coherence as much from these pessimists as through the ongoing activity of their opponents: the *optimists*. It is no wonder that, a mere century later, the most famous of all philosophical pessimists would look back at the tradition of pessimism and see as one of his foremost forebears none other than David Hume, who explained 'with arguments very convincing yet quite different from mine, the miserable nature of this world and the untenableness of all optimism; here at the same time he attacks optimism at its source'.[110]

110. Schopenhauer, *WWR*.II.581–2, referring specifically to Hume's *Natural History of Religion*, and *Dialogues on Natural Religion*, parts X and XI.

CHAPTER SIX

The Art of Suffering

JEAN-JACQUES ROUSSEAU

Then I cried to them in a feeble voice which they could not hear, 'Madmen who ceaselessly complain of Nature, learn that all your misfortunes arise from yourselves!'

JEAN-JACQUES ROUSSEAU[1]

ROUSSEAU CAN BE CALLED an original thinker in more ways than one: not just in the sense of coming up with novel ideas, but in the sense of seeking for *origins*. If Rousseau's oeuvre shows one thing, it is his fascination with origins, be it the origins of language, of inequality, of morality, of society, or, yes, the origins of evil. For while Rousseau, in all of his work on origins, did not publish a treatise on *the origins of evil* as Leibniz and King did, the question of theodicy is nevertheless central to his thought, and as a consequence, so is the question of optimism versus pessimism. Of these terms, Rousseau only ever uses the former, but he does this in so straightforward and confident a manner that he may well be one of the first authors to use the term *optimism* positively and appreciatively, thus stripping it from its derogatory aura. Had he not done so, it is questionable how much currency and positive appeal the term would have even in our present day.

Considering Rousseau's explicit defence of optimism against Voltaire, it is interesting that Dienstag nevertheless classifies Rousseau as not just a pessimist, but *the* pessimist: a kind of 'patriarch of pessimism'.[2] As I have already suggested, the competing classifications of Rousseau as a pessimist

1. *Confessions*, VIII, 362.

2. Dienstag, *Pessimism*, 49, citing Walter Starkie; see chapter 2.

or optimist have to do primarily with the different possible conceptions of these terms, as future- or value-oriented. Where Dienstag, in ranking Rousseau (or at least the *early* Rousseau) among the pessimists, is speaking purely of future-oriented pessimism, my focus is on value-oriented optimism and pessimism instead, since these represent the core issues at stake in the debate on the problem of evil. In discussing Rousseau's theodicy, therefore, my principal concern is not whether Rousseau should be called an optimist or a pessimist, but the way in which he engages with aspects of both traditions and introduces new arguments into the theodicean debate. If I nevertheless classify Rousseau among the optimists, this is only in so far as he explicitly aligns himself with the optimists and against the pessimists—an alignment that itself is deeply telling of the opposing moral intuitions present in the background of this debate, in which consolation continues to play a central part.

As we will see, the question of the theodicy is urgent for Rousseau in a similar but converse way as it was urgent for Voltaire and Bayle. In his autobiographical writings, Rousseau speaks of a crisis of faith brought on by the *philosophes*, a crisis at the core of which seemed to be the question of misalignment and undeserved suffering.[3] If Rousseau was able to resolve these questions and anxieties to some extent, the problem of evil remained a delicate, even painful point for him, which seems to be why he reacted so strongly to Voltaire's Lisbon Poem.

There is, however, a difficulty in interpreting Rousseau's discussion of the problem of evil, and in an early article Susan Neiman aptly sums it up: 'where Rousseau seems to be addressing the traditional problem of evil, he is conventional, even reactionary; where his work is interesting, and revolutionary, he seems to be addressing different questions altogether'.[4] To some extent this is correct, and we will see how this is so. But it is not the whole story to be told about Rousseau's engagement with traditional theodicy—an engagement that might not be as revolutionary as one would expect of an author such as Rousseau, but is yet full of subtle innovations, of cunning twists and turns. Rousseau, like Kant after him, is an author who likes to take up old problems, tear up the traditional solutions, and start from scratch. This is not quite what he does with the problem of evil, but there is an element of starting from scratch even here, since Rousseau, throughout his engagement with the problems

3. See especially the third *Reverie*.
4. Neiman, 'Metaphysics', 140.

posed by the pessimists, refuses to play the game on the pessimists' terms. Here, as in so many other places, Rousseau makes his own rules.

In recent decades, there have been several attempts to interpret Rousseau's thought as delivering a kind of unconventional theodicy. The most important recent study is Frederick Neuhouser's book *Rousseau's Theodicy of Self-Love*, which offers an extensive discussion of Rousseau's central concepts *amour de soi*, and especially *amour propre*, in the context of Rousseau's explanation of evils.[5] However, in a recent article, Christophe Litwin has pointed out the limitations of any too straightforward application of *theodicy* to Rousseau's thought. Based on a reading of Rousseau against the background of Malebranche and Maupertuis, Litwin argues that while Rousseau does defend Leibniz's optimism against Voltaire, this defence is 'at odds with any kind of metaphysical or historical theodicy'.[6] This is an important caution: when Rousseau seems to arguing in favour of optimism, this does not necessarily mean that he is engaging in *theodicy*—a term that tends to be thrown around rather loosely in some of the literature, with hardly any link to either the wider theodicean tradition or theodicy's central concerns (especially that of *justification*). As we have seen in chapter 4, by the mid-eighteenth century the debate on optimism versus pessimism had already begun to part ways from the debate on theodicy, and there are good reasons for believing that Rousseau (like Maupertuis and La Mettrie before him) was more interested in the former than the latter. Nevertheless, as I will argue throughout this chapter, engaging in theodicy is exactly what Rousseau is doing, though he does it in his own incomparable Rousseauian way.

Here, I will focus primarily on three famous texts, in which Rousseau circles around the theme of theodicy, bringing to bear different aspects and considerations. These are the *Discourse on the Origins of Inequality*, the letter to Voltaire on providence, and *Emile*: texts, I need hardly point out, that have been discussed many times before. If I discuss them again, at length and in depth, this is because they are essential to the wider

5. Neuhouser, *Rousseau's Theodicy of Self-Love*; see also Neiman, 'Metaphysics, Philosophy: Rousseau on the Problem of Evil', and her *Evil in Modern Thought*, 36–57; Cassirer, *The Question of Jean-Jacques Rousseau*; Scott, 'The Theodicy of the *Second Discourse*'; Douglass, 'Free will and the problem of evil'; Gourevitch, 'Rousseau on Providence'; Lam, 'Rethinking the Source of Evil'; Cladis, 'Tragedy and Theodicy' (though the latter two studies focus specifically on moral evil).

6. Litwin, 'Rousseau and Leibniz', 85; see also his earlier articles 'Amour de soi et pensée du néant' and '"Le principe nécessaire de tous nos maux naturels"'.

context in which Rousseau needs to be inscribed: the dual traditions of pessimism and the problem of evil, the history of which cannot be complete without Rousseau.

Discourse on the Origin of Inequality

The circumstances for writing what is commonly referred to as Rousseau's 'Second Discourse' are well documented. Having won the Dijon Academy's essay prize in 1750 for his 'First Discourse' (*Discourse on the Sciences and Arts*), Rousseau entered into the same competition a few years later, this time with a *Discourse on the Origin and Foundations of Inequality Among Men*, to answer the Academy's question: 'What is the Origin of Inequality among Men, and is it Authorized by the Natural Law?'[7] As Jean Starobinski comments, if the first discourse contained 'a few couplets intended to impress the judges', the second discourse is 'harsh and uncompromising', as well as very, very long.[8] It is not a work designed for winning, and in fact it did not win, though it did make its author 'immortal'.[9]

In the *Second Discourse*, published in 1755, Rousseau famously turns the intuitive notion of progress on its head. Yes, he argues, mankind has developed itself prolifically in society. But this development is also the source of man's unhappiness; indeed, it is the single source of most moral and physical evils besetting mankind today. We cultured men, who look down upon the savages, would do better to look up to them, since in them a portion of the *original goodness* and happiness of mankind remains preserved.[10] To this effect, Rousseau offers his hypothetical reconstruction of the history of mankind—and of the origins of evil.

Now Rousseau could only make this argument by dismissing the Christian doctrine of original sin, or at least drastically remodelling it,[11] which Rousseau does, confidently and wholly unapologetically. According to him, man was not corrupted by the Fall: man was created good and happy and remained this way until he entered into societal relations with other

7. Cited in Gourevitch's Introduction to *Discourses*, xxi. On the conception of the *Second Discourse*, see *Confessions*, VIII, 361–3.

8. Starobinski, *Transparency and Obstruction*, 281.

9. Gourevitch, Introduction, *Discourses*, xv; see *Confessions*, VIII, 363.

10. On Rousseau's concept of man's original goodness, see Joshua Cohen, 'The Natural Goodness of Humanity'. Rousseau believes the 'Savage Peoples' represent the happiest stage in the development of mankind (*DOI*, 166–7).

11. Starobinski, *Transparency*, 290; Neiman, 'Metaphysics', 150.

men and began perfecting himself in order to stand out among all others. If there is a single root of all our evils, it is in the perception of inequality, from which originates that central societal vice: *amour propre* (as opposed to self-love, *amour de soi*).[12] The origins of evil, broadly construed, are therefore not to be sought in the fall of man as recounted in Genesis, but in man's desire to perfect himself upon entering society, where he becomes aware of inequality: 'The primary source of evil is inequality' (*OCR*.III.49; my translation).[13]

If this were true, it would mean that civilised humans are worse off than 'Savages', who are only a few steps removed from the state of natural man, as well as animals, who lack the freedom to perfect themselves. And Rousseau holds that experience tells us exactly that. If we compare savages with civilised men, he argues, we see that most evils plaguing the latter are absent in the former: savage man is much stronger, healthier, and better able to defend himself against other animals. As for 'the natural infirmities, childhood, old age, and illnesses of every kind': the first two are common to *all* animals, whereas the last belong mainly to man in society (*DOI*, 137). As for the progress made in the field of medicine, Rousseau is famously sceptical about its benefits, convinced as he is that 'we inflict upon ourselves more ills than Medicine can provide Remedies' (*DOI*, 137).[14] Such self-inflicted ills include 'extreme inequality in ways of life', the easy arousal of desire, the unhealthily exotic tastes of the rich contrasted with the bad food of the poor, and in general 'the innumerable sorrows [*chagrins*] and pains [*peines*] that are experienced in every station of life and that constantly gnaw away at men's souls'. He concludes:

> Such are the fatal proofs that most of our ills are of our own making, and that we would have avoided almost all of them if we had retained the simple, uniform and solitary way of life prescribed to us by Nature. If it destined us to be healthy then, I almost dare assert, the state of

12. For an elaborate study of these concepts, see Neuhouser, *Rousseau's Theodicy*, who argues that Rousseau's understanding of *amour propre* is not wholly negative, but features both a 'negative and positive potential' (ibid., 16); and his later book, *Rousseau's Critique of Inequality*.

13. As Robin Douglass notes, Rousseau's analysis of *amour propre* should be read against the backdrop of a long Augustinian tradition associating *amour propre* with the Fall, of which Rousseau's story is a secularised version; see Douglass, *Rousseau and Hobbes*, 152ff; and Brooke, 'Rousseau's Political Philosophy', 111–12.

14. This is a theme that runs through *Emile* as well as the autobiographical writings (*Confessions*, *Reveries*), where Rousseau presents his dismissal of medicine as based on personal experience.

> reflection is a state against Nature, and the man who meditates is a depraved animal.[15] (*DOI*, 137–8)

It's becoming clear where Rousseau is going with this: if most of man's evils are ultimately self-inflicted, then man has no business blaming God (or nature, or providence) for them. But we've been here before, and we can anticipate some of the more obvious objections, as Rousseau could too. For one thing, what about the suffering of animals? If animals suffer, how blessed a condition can that of original or natural man really be? The Leibnizian response would be to say that animals may feel pain but don't really suffer as such (that is, they cannot be *miserable*); and Rousseau seems to take roughly the same line. Natural man is indeed in a happy state, since 'his Desires do not exceed his Physical needs':

> The only goods he knows in the Universe are food, a female, and rest; the only evils he fears are pain, and hunger; I say pain, and not death; for an animal will never know what it is to die, and the knowledge of death, and of its terrors, is one of man's first acquisitions on moving away from the animal condition. (*DOI*, 142)[16]

According to Rousseau, therefore, the only original (and maybe 'real' or 'proper') physical evils are pain and hunger: all the others, it seems, are superimposed upon man's original condition.[17]

It is striking that while Rousseau acknowledges these 'original' evils, he makes no move to justify them; he does not seem to regard them as problematic in the way that Bayle does. In searching for the origins of evil, Rousseau seems to be thinking specifically of intense *human* suffering; the purely bodily pains of animals (or even of humans) do not qualify. Like Leibniz and King, Rousseau asks the question of what it really means to be miserable:

> I know that we are repeatedly told that nothing would have been as miserable as man in this [natural] state; and if it is true, as I believe I have proven, that he could have had the desire and the opportunity to

15. Gourevitch (*Discourses*, 357n.) notes that this last statement is 'rather guarded', while Cohen ('Natural Goodness', 117) goes so far as to claim that 'Rousseau does not make the daring assertion'. Fair enough, but he *almost* makes it.

16. Recall that this idea that an animal does not know the fear of death is commonplace: Bayle (and later Schopenhauer) are among the few who deny it.

17. Note that Rousseau feels no need whatsoever to justify pain and hunger here (which is in good Stoic fashion: see Rorty, 'The Two Faces of Stoicism', 343). He will, however, return to the question of bodily pain in *Emile* and offer a Kingian defence.

leave it only after many Centuries, then this would be an Indictment of Nature [*un procès à faire à la nature*], not of him whom nature had so constituted; but if I understand this term *miserable* correctly, it is a word either entirely devoid of sense, or which merely signifies a painful privation and suffering of Body or soul: Now, I should very much like to have it explained to me what kind of misery [*misère*] there can be for a free being, whose heart is at peace, and body in health. (*DOI*, 149–50)

This passage, in its mention of an 'Indictment of Nature', is especially telling for Rousseau's theodicean orientation, but it misses the mark in so far as Rousseau is trying to anticipate his critics' objections. After all, Rousseau had just specified that natural man is not free from pain or hunger: his body, at least, is not always 'in health'. So cannot natural man, like the animal, be miserable too? Again, the suggestion seems to be that although natural man *can* experience pain or hunger, he cannot properly be said to *suffer*, just as animals cannot. The missing element in the natural condition is that of reflection (as in Leibniz), coupled with freedom and perfectibility.[18] Societal man makes himself miserable by reflecting upon his condition (the perception of inequality) and by trying to perfect himself (the reaction to inequality). The most important point made in the previous passage, therefore, has to do not with the bodily but the mental or psychological aspects of natural man: a free being 'whose heart is at peace'.[19]

True misery, Rousseau continues, arises only in society, a fact he sees confirmed by the widespread phenomenon of suicide:

I ask, which of the two, Civil life or natural life, is more liable to become intolerable to those who enjoy it? Almost all the People we see around us complain of their existence, and some even deprive themselves of it as far as they are able, and the combination of divine and human Laws hardly suffices to stop this disorder: I ask whether anyone has ever heard tell that it so much occurred to a Savage, who is free, to complain of life

18. In the *Second Discourse* (*DOI*, 140–1), Rousseau identifies the faculties of freedom and perfectibility as the principal differences between man and animal (other differences being merely in degree); in *Emile* (IV, 270–1), he associates the 'distinctive faculty' rather with '*attention, meditation, reflection*'. On the role of free will in the *Second Discourse* as well as in the 'Profession of Faith of the Savoyard Vicar', see Douglass, 'Free Will'.

19. There are, however, some evils experienced by societal man that are not tied to inequality, such as the perception of death, which depends rather on the development of reflection and time-consciousness.

> and to kill himself? One ought, then, to judge with less pride on which side *genuine misery* [*la véritable misère*] lies.' (*DOI*, 150; my emphasis)[20]

Genuine misery: that is, the misery experienced as such by civilised man. It is important to note that, for Rousseau, the 'genuineness' here has to do rather with the *subjective experience* of misery than with the objectivity of the evil experienced. As Rousseau will argue in more detail in *Emile*, many evils that have the capacity to make man miserable are not evils in any objective sense: most of them are in fact imaginary, but this does not mean that they are not *real* evils, since they are experienced as such.[21]

Rousseau goes on to discuss the natural faculty of pity (*pitié*),[22] which becomes weaker in civilised man due to the development of reason and reflection; and, in the second part of the discourse, to reconstruct the development of mankind as it moves from a solitary existence to form families, groups, and finally societies. However, I here will discuss only one of the lengthy footnotes that Rousseau added to this work: one that, in good Baylean fashion, is almost an essay in itself.

THE NINTH NOTE: WHO IS 'ROUSSEAU'S PESSIMIST'?

The footnote in question is the well-known ninth note, which takes its cue from an unnamed 'famous Author':

> A famous Author, calculating [*calculant*] the goods and evils of human life and comparing the two sums, found the last greatly exceeded the first and that, all things considered, life was a rather poor gift for man. I am not at all surprised by his conclusion; he drew all his arguments from the constitution of Civil man: if he had gone back to Natural man, it is likely that he would have reached very different results, that he would have noticed that man suffers scarcely any evils but those

20. Note that Rousseau, in suggesting that suicide is a widespread phenomenon, is conceding an important point to the pessimists, and in fact offering more than they asked for: namely, that not just *some* but *many* people consider their lives not worth living. But Rousseau puts this to work for his own theory that the problem is not with life itself, but with *life in society*.

21. For this very Baylean point, see also Rousseau's letter to 'Philopolis' (*Discourses*, 226): 'None of this prevents a particular evil from being a real evil for the person who suffers it.'

22. As Rorty notes ('Rousseau's Therapeutic Experiments', 416n.) the English 'pity' does not quite capture all the layers of Rousseau's *pitié*; it is, however, not central to my argument here.

> he has brought on himself, and that Nature would have been justified [*justifiée*]. (*DOI*, 197)

In other words, Rousseau argues that it's completely understandable that this author concluded that life's evils outweigh its goods, since he was looking only at *civilised* man: it would have been a very different question if he had looked at natural man instead.[23] The rest of the note argues, essentially, that sociable man is responsible for all of his miseries, and explains why this is so.

Before we look more closely at Rousseau's argument, let's pause for a moment: Who is this 'famous Author' prefacing this discussion? Following Arthur O. Lovejoy, most editions identify 'Rousseau's Pessimism' as Maupertuis, who in his *Essai de philosophie morale* had indeed offered a calculation of the 'goods and evils of human life'.[24] While I think this is very plausible, it bears pointing out that that the unnamed author could with equal justification be identified as Bayle, by whose article *Xenophanes* Maupertuis was probably influenced. Both authors were famous; both had argued, albeit for different reasons, that the evils of life outweigh the goods. Of course, Maupertuis's essay, published only a few years before the *Second Discourse*, was the more timely one, and perhaps Rousseau was more likely to have left unnamed an author who was still alive.[25] Another reason in Maupertuis's favour is Rousseau's mention of the term *calculer*, which Maupertuis uses expressly throughout his essay and Bayle does not use at all.

However, Rousseau also says that his unnamed author concluded from this calculation that 'life was a rather poor gift for man', which Maupertuis does *not* argue, but Bayle does. Furthermore, while Maupertuis's essay did deliver a calculation of goods and evils, this calculation was in no way oriented towards the problem of evil: rather, it was intended to argue (against La Mettrie) that man's best chances of happiness lie in a virtuous life. In contrast, the pessimistic weighing of goods and evils in Bayle's *Xenophanes* was part of a wider argument against theodicy, and it is this theodicean context that provides the main reason for supposing

23. Or, presumably, at animals; Rousseau does not make this point explicitly, but I think he would agree with Buffon that in the case of animals 'there can be little doubt . . . that the sum of pleasure is greater than the sum of pain'. Buffon, *Œuvres complètes*, vol. 2, 332 (my translation). On Rousseau and Buffon, see Starobinski, *Transparency*, 323–32.

24. See Lovejoy, 'Rousseau's Pessimist'.

25. Note also that the Prussian Academy of Sciences, of which Maupertuis was president, had set as the topic of the 1755 prize competition a discussion of whether Pope's optimism was tenable; see Gourevitch, 'Rousseau on Providence', 568.

Bayle's article, not Maupertuis's essay, to form the background to Rousseau's ninth note. As we will see, this note carries powerful echoes of Bayle's *Xenophanes*; for instance, in the step-by-step discussion of moral and physical evils (which Maupertuis does not differentiate).

Let's now return to Rousseau's note to see how this is so. As Rousseau argues here, man has made himself miserable: 'man's blindness . . . causes him eagerly to run after all the miseries of which he is susceptible, and which beneficent Nature had taken care to keep from him' (*DOI*, 197). But hang on: Can it really be said that man is responsible for *all his miseries?* What of natural disasters; what of illness or bereavement? Rousseau bites the bullet: yes, man is in a way responsible for all of them, excepting maybe death, but here it is the fear and anticipation of death, brought about by reflection, that makes it into a source of misery. (Recall that for Rousseau, pain and hunger are indeed ills or evils, but not genuine *miseries*.)

Fully in the style of Bayle's *Xenophanes* and the Manichean articles, Rousseau then takes man's evils in turn, beginning with *moral evils*. In a passage echoing Bayle's renowned 'L'homme est méchant et malheureux' (*Manicheans*[1]*.D*), Rousseau argues instead that man is indeed *currently* wicked but *naturally* good:

> Men are wicked [*méchants*]; a sad and constant experience makes proof unnecessary; yet man is naturally good, I believe I have proved it; what, then, can have depraved him to this point, if not the changes that occurred in his constitution, the progress he has made, and the knowledge he has acquired? (*DOI*, 197)[26]

This initial assertion is followed by a long list of examples of how wicked man really is, rejoicing as he does at another's misfortunes, and finding advantage in another man's loss. In contrast: 'Savage man, once he has supped, is at peace with all of Nature and a friend to all of his kind' (*DOI*, 198). Besieged as he is by his passions, civil man will continue his search to satisfy them and 'end up by cutting every throat until he is sole master of the Universe. Such, in brief, is the moral picture [*le tableau moral*] if not of human life, at least of the secret aspirations of every Civilized man's heart' (*DOI*, 199).

Having thus listed the moral evils of civil man (as Bayle did in *Xenophanes* with man in general), Rousseau takes a breath and continues with physical evils. The list that follows is paradigmatic for a posteriori

26. At this point, Bayle would ask what the role of Providence is in this 'progress'; a question Rousseau does not consider in the *Second Discourse* (see below, pp. 245–46).

pessimists from Bayle to Schopenhauer and Benatar, and it is here that we find Rousseau at his most pessimistic:

> Compare without prejudices the state of Civil man with that of Savage man, and determine, if you can, how many new gates in addition to his wickedness, his needs, and his miseries, the first has opened to pain and to death. If you consider the mental pains that consume us, the violent passions that exhaust and waste us . . . ; if you take into account the fires and the earthquakes that consume or topple entire Cities, killing their inhabitants by the thousands; in a word, if you add up the dangers which all of these causes continually gather over our heads, you will sense how dearly Nature makes us pay for the contempt we have shown for its lessons. (*DOI*, 199)

The list continues for a few pages, moving from wars and shipwrecks to abortions, forced marriages, and unhealthy trades.[27] The point Rousseau is making is that all of these evils, which pessimists such as Bayle or Voltaire would trace back to God or providence, instead have their origins in man himself.

The links between *Xenophanes* and Rousseau's ninth note may be clear by now. Both in his reprise of the lists of moral and physical evils, which are now focused exclusively on civilised man, and in his resistance to any impious conclusion that might be drawn from this, Rousseau reveals himself to be operating in the same framework as set by Bayle. The context is indeed one of theodicy: of *justification* of the works of God. Consequently, if it was indeed Maupertuis that Rousseau had in mind in his prelude to the ninth note, this allusion is anecdotal rather than philosophically significant. But if it was Bayle, then this sheds an entirely different light on Rousseau's considerations in the ninth note as well as the *Discourse* as a whole: it suggests a deep and deliberate connection with a longer theodicean tradition, the history of which Rousseau was trying to rewrite.

I don't want to insist too much on this point, which arguably should itself be no more than a footnote to the story I am tracing here. But whatever the case for either Bayle or Maupertuis, what the mention of this unnamed pessimist indicates most clearly is the extent to which the

27. Bayle too mentions the evil of an unhappy marriage, especially for women (*DHC*: *Xenophanes*².H), as well as the tragic situation of unmarried women forced to commit abortions by the 'point of honour' (*DHC*: *Patin*); unlike Rousseau, however, Bayle does not seem to condemn the practice of abortion in itself; see Wootton, 'Pierre Bayle, Libertine?'

concerns raised so centrally in *Xenophanes* are at the forefront of Rousseau's mind. After all, even if Rousseau's pessimist *was* Maupertuis, it was most likely Maupertuis, reader of Bayle.

QUESTIONS

It is understandable that the *Second Discourse* would have left Rousseau's readers unsettled. This is not just because of the inversion of various cultural tropes, beliefs, and intuitions, not the least of which is Rousseau's understated dismissal of original sin, but because of its strongly *negative* character. Rousseau seems to be presenting the reader all of the problems without offering any solutions. In Susan Neiman's words: 'The second *Discourse* contains no prescriptions: it is a work of diagnosis or, as Rousseau suggested more darkly, even autopsy.'[28] This seems to have been Voltaire's sense, too, when he referred to the *Discourse* as 'your new book against mankind'.[29] To which Rousseau objected that, far from writing against mankind, he had 'pleaded the case of mankind against itself', and that his 'aim, in depicting human miseries, was excusable and, I believe, even praiseworthy; for I showed men how they bring their miseries upon themselves, and hence how they might avoid them' (*LV*, 233–4). Similarly, in his 'Preface to *Narcissus*', written just before the *Discourse*, Rousseau wrote: 'I point out something highly consoling and useful by showing that all these vices belong not so much to man, as to man badly governed' (*Discourses*, 101).[30] But, in fact, it remains unclear how this is *useful*, let alone *consoling*, since Rousseau tells us hardly anything in the *Discourse* about how these miseries can be avoided while still living in society.[31] His attempt to fill this hiatus will inform several of his later works, and especially *Emile*,

28. Neiman, 'Metaphysics', 153, referring to Rousseau's comment to a *First Discourse* critic that 'I am not unaware of the fact that once a man is dead one does not call the Doctor' (*Discourses*, 30).

29. Voltaire to Rousseau, 30 August 1755, cited in *Discourses*, 382n.

30. *Narcisse, ou L'amant de lui-même* is a play Rousseau wrote as a young man; it was eventually produced to little success in 1752, at which time Rousseau added the more philosophical preface, which he counted as 'one of my best pieces of writing' (*Confessions*, VIII, 361).

31. At the end of the ninth note, Rousseau points out that the conclusion is not that man should go back to live in forests: rather, man should continue to live in society and respect its laws and practise virtues while remaining 'contemptuous of a constitution . . . from which, in spite of all their cares, there always arise more real calamities than apparent advantages' (*DOI*, 204).

whose central issue is something of an open question: Can we preserve (or restore) some of man's original goodness and happiness while raising him for a life in society?

Furthermore, from a theodicean perspective, the *Discourse* leaves certain crucial questions open—questions that Bayle presumably would have been the first to raise, having to do with sadness, animals, and providence. First, we might ask, channelling Bayle, whether natural man does not experience psychological evils such as sadness and grief: after all, if he can love, surely he can grieve. But *can* he love? Or rather: Does he experience love in the same way as civilised man? It seems not, since Rousseau allows only for a very flimsy maternal love and fleeting sexual desire in the natural state (*DOI*, 145, 155, 161).[32] Consequently, as natural man does not form emotional alliances in the way that civilised man does, grief and sadness do not have the power to make him miserable. Hence, grief and sadness do not rank among the original physical evils afflicting natural man, such as pain and hunger, but among the self-inflicted miseries of societal man.

Second, we return to the perennial question of animal suffering, which Rousseau seems to discount on roughly Leibnizian grounds: by distinguishing pain from misery. Like Leibniz, Rousseau seems to hold that true misery requires an element of reflection, which crucially involves an awareness of time, and thereby introduces such temporal anxieties as hope and regret.[33] While animals and natural man do suffer in the sense that they experience hunger and pain (which are the only two *proper* or *original* physical evils), they do not suffer in the sense that they are *miserable*, for which reflection is needed, which includes an awareness of the element of time. As Rousseau will stress in *Emile*: 'Pain has little hold over someone who, having reflected little, possesses neither memory nor foresight' (*Emile*, 282).[34]

Hence, Rousseau is so far from acknowledging the problem of animal suffering that he initially sets up the example of animals as a kind of ideal condition to which we cannot return; having lost this simple wellness or

32. This is not to say that Rousseau values love *negatively*; on the contrary, he ranks 'conjugal love, and Paternal love' among 'the sweetest sentiments known to man' (*DOI*, 164). The point is that with such love come new evils such as grief. Compare Buffon, *Œuvres complètes*, vol. 2, 352: 'Only the physical aspect of this passion is good. . . . The moral is worthless, notwithstanding what people in love may say. What in fact is the moral aspect of love? Vanity' (cited in Starobinski, *Transparency*, 330).

33. See the 'Preface to *Narcissus*', *Discourses*, 102.

34. On this point, see Dienstag, *Pessimism*, chapter 2. It is unclear whether Rousseau also follows Leibniz in seeing reflection as essential to true *happiness* as well as true misery; my sense is that he does not.

wholeness, we can only go forward. While he recognises that there are some evils experienced by animals and original man, he does not feel the need to justify them, because they do not qualify as *misery*: they are not problematic in any deep or significant way. Since they were originally present, Rousseau takes them as inevitable (in much the same way as King does). This, again, is something that Bayle would dispute: surely nothing can properly be called *inevitable* from the perspective of an almighty creator. But Rousseau is willing to compromise some of God's power to save his goodness; and, as we will see, he has a notion of general providence that allows for the admission of particular evils.

In the *Discourse*, however, the role played by providence or the divine will remains entirely unclear, and this is the third theodicean question left unanswered in what is otherwise a strongly theodicean work. This is not to say that providence does not play an important part in the *Discourse*, but that this part is an underdeveloped one. Providence is what ensures the steady development of our faculties:

> Nothing . . . would have been as miserable as Savage man dazzled by enlightenment, tormented by Passions, and reasoning about a state different from his own. It was by a very wise Providence that the faculties he had in potentiality were to develop only with the opportunities to exercise them, so that they might not be superfluous and a burden to him before their time, nor belated and useless in time of need. (*DOI*, 150)

The question that remains unanswered is why providence did not prevent the downward spiral of man's perfectibility altogether; indeed, why would providence want man to develop these faculties at all, if they only bring him misery? This is not the whole story for Rousseau, who tells us in the final lines of the *Discourse* that the divine hand 'caused our happiness to be born from the very means that seemed bound to complete our misery' (*DOI*, 128). If our freedom and perfectibility and society itself are the principles of our deterioration and our misery, they are also the conditions of our potential happiness: they are what makes it possible for us to redeem ourselves.[35] But such partial restoration is only possible through

35. Though this possibility is by no means certain, least of all in political terms. As Rousseau writes to King Stanislaus I of Poland, it is inconceivable for 'a people, once corrupted to return to virtue': 'there is no longer any remedy' [*il n'y a plus de remède*], unless it be by some 'great revolution that is almost as much to be feared as the evil it pretends to cure' ('Observations', *OCR*.III.56; my translation). On the recurrent theme in Rousseau of the 'antidote in the poison', see Starobinski, *Blessings in Disguise*, chapter 5.

the kind of understanding of the human condition that Rousseau is aiming at, and which is summarised in the lines from the Roman poet Persius that bring the *Discourse* to a close: 'Learn what the god ordered you to be, / And what your place is in the human world' (*DOI*, 128). This, however, is not yet an explanation, nor a justification of providence as a Hume or a Bayle would demand to hear. Aware of this, Rousseau develops these themes in his letters and later works, where hope and consolation, which hardly feature in the *Discourse*, become increasingly important.

The Letter to Voltaire

The *Discourse* was published in 1755, the same year that saw the devastating Lisbon earthquake. In March of the following year, Voltaire published his virulent poem against providence; on 18 August, Rousseau wrote his letter to Voltaire, which was published without either's permission in October 1759.[36] In this famous letter, Rousseau steers between careful courtesy and outright criticism of Voltaire's pessimism, all the while articulating his own theodicean arguments in very telling ways.[37]

The central intuition behind Rousseau's letter to Voltaire is that pessimism, conceived as an extensive reflection on human weakness and misery, is morally compromised since it makes us downcast as well as passive or resigned; it takes away our hope as well as consolation.[38] This was an intuition Rousseau had formulated a few years earlier in his 'Preface to *Narcissus*':

> So many reflections on the weakness of our nature often do no more than divert us from generous enterprises. The more we think about the miseries of mankind, the more our imagination oppresses us with their weight, and too much forethought robs us of courage by robbing us of confidence. (*Discourses*, 99)

This, too, is Rousseau's main objection to Voltaire, which he wastes no time in pointing out to him:

36. *Confessions*, X, 498–501; Havens, 'Voltaire, Rousseau, and the "Lettre sur la Providence"', 119. Gourevitch, in an in-depth discussion of Rousseau's response to Voltaire, calls this letter 'Rousseau's most authoritative discussion of religious issues' ('Rousseau on Providence', 566).

37. While Rousseau does not use the term pessimism (only optimism), all the elements of pessimism are present in his portrayal and criticism of Voltaire's position.

38. It bears pointing out that Rousseau was aware of his own pessimistic tendencies, as he wrote in 1758 in a letter to his editor: 'I am well aware that my constant inclination is to put things in the worst possible light' (quoted in Starobinski, *Blessings in Disguise*, 147).

> You charge Pope and Leibniz with insulting our evils by maintaining that all is well [*tout est bien*], and you so greatly magnify the picture of our miseries that you heighten our sense of them; instead of the solace [*consolations*] I had hoped for, you only distress me. It is as if you feared that I might not see clearly enough how unhappy I am; and believed that you would greatly calm me by proving that all is bad. (*LV*, 232–3)

Here, we are already at the crux of the optimist/pessimist disagreement, which is an ethical one. Rousseau accuses Voltaire of a failure of consolation and perhaps compassion; which is just the thing of which Voltaire had accused the optimists. Rousseau continues in no uncertain terms, all the while calling optimism by its name, thus stripping it from its derogatory force and wearing it, perhaps for the first time in history, like a badge of honour:

> Make no mistake about it, Sir; the effect is the very opposite of what you intend. This *optimism* which you find so cruel yet consoles me amid the very pains which you depict as unbearable. Pope's poem allays my evils and inclines me to patience, yours embitters my suffering, incites me to grumble, and, by depriving me of everything but a shaken hope, reduces me to despair. (*LV*, 233; my emphasis)

Pope and Leibniz tell man to have patience; that his evils are 'a necessary effect of your nature and of the constitution of this universe'; that God chose the system that combined 'the least evil with the most good', and 'if he did not do better, it is that he could not do better'. As opposed to this:

> Now what does your poem tell me? 'Suffer forever, unhappy man. If there is a God who has created you, no doubt he is omnipotent; he could have prevented all your evils: hence do not hope that they will ever end; for there is no understanding why you exist, if not to suffer and to die.' I do not know what might be more consoling about such a doctrine than about optimism and even about fatalism. (*LV*, 233)[39]

As in the ninth note to the *Second Discourse*, Rousseau again moves to an evaluation of moral and physical evils. Both of these, he argues, are

39. It should be noted here that some pessimists, such as Schopenhauer in particular (of whose philosophy this passage is not a bad summary), do believe that pessimism and even fatalism can be consoling. In fact, Rousseau even shares this hunch in so far as he sees this-worldly hope as a source of anxiety and suffering; only when our hopes for improvement are lost can we begin to find peace (see *Reveries*, I, 29; and VIII, 128).

mostly of our own making. The exception now is not pain and hunger (the original and 'natural' evils of the *Second Discourse*), but only death, which is made an evil 'almost solely' by our anticipations of it:

> I do not see that one can seek the source of moral evil anywhere but in man, free, perfected, hence corrupted; and as for physical evils, if, as it seems to me, it is a contradiction for matter to be both sentient and insentient, they are inevitable in any system of which man is a part; and the question, then, is not why is man not perfectly happy, but *why does he exist*. Moreover, I believe I have shown that except for death, which is an evil almost solely because of the preparations made in anticipation of it, most of our physical evils are also of our own making. (*LV*, 234; my emphasis)

This passage tells us something the *Discourse* did not: for it now appears that Rousseau conceives of physical evils as intrinsic to sentience or consciousness, in much the same way as we have seen in King. We experience deprivation *because we experience*, period. And if suffering and limitation are intrinsic to experience, then pain and hunger are unavoidable in a sentient system of nature. The question then remains as to why such a suffering creature exists at all, a question to which Rousseau will tangentially return.

Meanwhile, we are back at the same counter-intuitive point made repeatedly in the *Discourse*: that most of our evils (and *all* of our miseries) are of our own making. But the context is now a concrete one: Rousseau feels called, by Voltaire's poem, to explain how the evils associated with the Lisbon earthquake also fit the category of self-infliction. Not an easy task: for how could a natural disaster possibly be of our own doing? According to Rousseau, while it is not the case that the earthquake itself was caused by humans, it was humans who turned it into a disaster. The results of the earthquake would not have been so devastating had humans not decided to build so many houses on the same spot, and had many of them not stayed behind with their belongings rather than fleeing at the first shock, as natural man surely would have done.[40] To the question of why providence had not occasioned the earthquake to happen in the wilderness, Rousseau responds that earthquakes certainly happen there too, only we

40. See also *Emile* (I, 59) on cities as 'the abyss of the human species'. Voltaire, in fact, makes a very similar point in, for example, his *Histoire de Jenni*, where he attempts 'to minimize the problem of physical evil by attributing the scope of its effects to human foolishness. As it might be, you cannot blame God if people persist in living on the San Andreas Fault' (Pearson, *Fables*, 113).

don't talk about them. Do we expect nature 'to be subjugated to our laws', so that 'all we need do in order to forbid it an earthquake in a given place is to build a City there?' (*LV*, 234).

He goes on to emphasise the importance of *perspective* in our evaluations of goods and evils: 'There are events that often strike us more or less depending on the angle from which we view them, and that lose much of the horror they inspire at first sight once we take the trouble to examine them more closely.' Thus there were surely some among the Lisbon dead who escaped 'greater misfortunes', since a quick death can be a relative good. 'As for me,' Rousseau continues, 'I see everywhere that the evils to which nature subjects us are much less cruel [*moins cruels*] than those which we add to them' (*LV*, 235). The ills or evils that remain once the superimposed miseries are stripped from them are mild in Rousseau's perspective; one wonders whether they ought to be called evils at all. All the cruelty of life stems from our own actions. Nevertheless, for all the evils we have added to our existence, we still prefer *to be* rather than *not to be*; we still consider life worth living:

> we have as yet not been able to perfect ourselves to the point of generally making life a burden to ourselves and preferring nothingness to our existence; otherwise discouragement and despair would soon have taken hold of most people, and mankind could not have long endured. Now, *if it is better for us to be than not to be*, this would be enough to justify our existence, even if we should have no compensation to expect for the evils we have to suffer, and even if these evils were as great as you depict them. (*LV*, 235; my emphasis)

Note in passing that Rousseau does not, in fact, concede either of the latter two conditional clauses: he believes that (1) there *will* be future compensation and (2) life's evils are certainly *not* so great as Voltaire depicted them.[41] As for that other conditional, 'if it is better for us to be than not to be', it bears pointing out that this, of course, is precisely what is in question; or would be, if Rousseau were as interested in justifying *creation* as he is in justifying *providence*. As we have seen, Bayle (followed in this by Hume and Voltaire) would deny that it is the case for all of us that it is better to be than not to be. So what, if anything, will Rousseau do with the

41. Note also the concern with justification, now made explicit, and the tacit point on suicide, which echoes the argument from suicide that King (and others) made against Bayle (see chapter 2). For more on Rousseau's views on suicide, and an interesting exploration of this passage, see Litwin, 'Amour de soi'.

residue of the truly miserable among us, for whom it would be better not to be? Let's keep this question in mind; we will return to it.

Rousseau now voices a familiar complaint: how difficult it is to argue objectively on the matter of weighing life's goods and evils, considering that most people, and especially philosophers, tend to exaggerate life's evils.

> But on this subject it is difficult to find good faith among men, and good computations [*de bons calculs*] among Philosophers; because in comparing goods and evils, the latter always forget the sweet sentiment of existence [*le doux sentiment de l'existence*], independent of any other sensation, and the vanity of scorning death prompts the former to malign life; rather like women who, given a stained dress and scissors, pretend to prefer holes to stains. (*LV*, 235)

The pessimists, of course, would turn this complaint around and argue instead that most people tend precisely to *overvalue* their lives out of fear of death, while optimist philosophers play down the terrible burdens of existence.[42] But the crucial concept here is Rousseau's notion of 'the sweet sentiment of existence, independent of any other sensation'. Rousseau's rather understated expressions here should not mislead us: this is, in fact, a highly original concept that is rightly introduced into the debate; Rousseau is correct in saying it isn't mentioned by the pessimists, but in fact it hasn't been mentioned by the optimists either.[43] The point is that we should not be restricting our inquiry to the weighing of goods and evils: according to Rousseau, the very experience of plain existence is a sweet one, when considered by itself. This is something the pessimists need not agree with (as Schopenhauer certainly will not), but it is a consideration that has its place in this debate: What, if anything, is pure existence *like*?[44]

However, if there is anything the optimists and pessimists can agree on, it is the difficulty of achieving any kind of objectivity when it comes to

42. This was Voltaire's objection to Leibniz and Pope, and Bayle's objection to an entire body of Christian apology; it will be David Benatar's objection to pro-natalists.

43. See *Reveries*, V, 89: 'The feeling of existence unmixed with any other emotion is in itself a precious feeling of peace and contentment.' This could be contrasted with Schopenhauer's contrary intuition that any state of being entirely free from longings or passions would itself be an unagreeable or even insufferable one; see chapter 8.

44. According to Litwin, the deeper point Rousseau is making here is that there is no symmetry between existence and non-existence: existence is not a good among other goods, and so there is something fundamentally misguided about the very exercise of weighing goods and evils. See Litwin, 'Rousseau and Leibniz' and 'Amour de soi'.

weighing life's goods against its evils. Bayle, upon reaching this difficulty in *Xenophanes*, brought in his thought experiment: *Would you want to live again if it meant reliving all your past sorrows as well as your past joys?* Voltaire, in a note to his poem, had reprised Bayle's conclusion: 'It is difficult to find anyone willing to live the same life over again, and experience again everything they experienced the first time' (*CRT*, 107/*OCV*.45a. 347). Rousseau now picks up on the same question:

> You think with Erasmus that few people would wish to be reborn in the same conditions in which they lived; but some peg their wares very high who would reduce them considerably if they saw any prospect of making a sale. (*LV*, 235)[45]

As in his criticism of the unnamed pessimist in the ninth note to the *Discourse*, Rousseau argues that it all depends on who you ask: rich people and men of letters will not want to relive their lives, miserable creatures as they are, but ask a peasant or 'honest burgher', and they will be more than happy to live again (*LV*, 236). In an important passage, it now becomes clear what Rousseau's assessment is of the truly miserable: those very few people for whom life is indeed 'a bad gift':

> These differences lead me to believe that it is often our abuse of life that makes it burdensome to us; and I have a far less favourable opinion of those who regret having lived, than of him who can say with Cato: 'I do not regret having lived, inasmuch as I have lived in a way that allows me to think I was not born in vain.' This is not to say that the wise man may not sometimes move on voluntarily without grumbling and despair, when nature or fortune distinctly conveys to him the order to depart. But in the ordinary course of things, human life is not, all in all, a bad gift [*un mauvais présent*], whatever may be the evils with which it is strewn; and while it is not always an evil to die, it is very seldom one to live. (*LV*, 236)

In other words, in the very rare event that our lives have become a burden to us and are no longer worth living, we usually have ourselves to blame. The truly miserable, then, do not pose a problem of evil in the way that Bayle believed they do.

45. See Erasmus, *Colloquies*, 'The Godly Feast', 192–3; where Erasmus in turn cites Cicero, *De Senectute*, 23.83–4. However, Voltaire did not mention Erasmus, and his source was most likely Bayle.

PROVIDENCE

To return now to the question of theodicy proper: How can an all-good, all-powerful, and all-knowing God allow the presence of evils in the world? As we know by now, there are many ways of approaching this question, and here we can distinguish two different (though ever connected) routes. It can be seen as a question of *providence*—How can God allow bad things to happen in the world?—or, rather, of *creation*—How can God have *made* a world so full of suffering in the first place, let alone a creature so capable of it? Rousseau, like Voltaire, is markedly less interested in the question of creation than in that of providence; indeed, as we have seen, he solves the former problem in little more than a sentence: 'if it is better for us to be than not to be, this would be enough to justify our existence' (*LV*, 235). He makes the same point on a wider scale, in the course of arguing that Voltaire failed to take into account the difference between particular and general evils:

> To come back, Sir, to the system you attack, I believe that one cannot examine it properly without carefully distinguishing between particular evil, whose existence no philosopher has ever denied, and general evil, which the optimist denies. The question is not whether each one of us suffers or not; but *whether it was good that the universe be*, and whether our evils were inevitable in the constitution of the universe. (*LV*, 240; my emphasis)

Hence, if it is good that there is something rather than nothing, then this is enough to justify creation, regardless of the evils it contains. This would be to set a very cheap price on the divine benevolence: it means that even a minimally tolerable creation, in which the worst sufferings are barely compensated by commensurate goods, would be acceptable to God.[46] But Rousseau, again, is not as concerned about creation as he is about providence, and he offers no further justification of the former.

But what, then, of providence? Even if we start off with a relatively good creation, how can we explain that providence allows for evils to obtain in human history? Why does God not prevent the suffering of his creatures? Moreover, why did he not prevent the entire tragedy of man's regression into society, which is apparently the source of all our troubles, in the first place? The answer, again, lies in the distinction between

46. A hard pessimist like Bayle or Benatar, furthermore, might deny the premise entirely: considering the world as it is, maybe it were indeed better there be nothing at all. See again Benatar, *Better Never to Have Been*.

particular and general evils; or rather, between the part and the whole. Instead of the Popean maxim *tout est bien*,[47] Rousseau argues that it would be better to say, *le tout est bien*; that is, 'The whole is good' or 'All is good for the whole' (*LV*, 240). He makes the same point in his 1755 letter to 'Philopolis' (Charles Bonnet), where he argues that neither Leibniz nor Pope denies that there are particular evils, only that there is *universal evil*; hence 'things may be good relative to the whole, though evil in themselves' (*Discourses*, 225).[48] So too: 'It was good *for the whole* that we be civilized since that is what we are, but it would certainly have been better *for us* if we were not so' (*Discourses*, 226; my emphasis). This, incidentally, is the very move essential to what I have called the optics of optimism, which prioritises the cosmic perspective over the creaturely.[49] What Rousseau shows here is not only his careful and considered reading of the optimists, but his deliberate alignment with their cause.

Returning to the letter to Voltaire, we witness a striking move, as Rousseau places his finger on the central problem of the theodicean debate, which is a problem not just of ethics or metaphysics, but of hermeneutics: How can we possibly draw any conclusion with regard to providence based on the phenomena we see around us? Any assessment of reality is always a matter of interpretation, and one that we have no way of testing against any other reality; a 'control group', as it were. After all, we don't know what a world *minus* providence looks like, nor do we know what a truly providential world looks like: the two might be identical, for all we know. Hence it is futile to reason on the basis of the goods and evils we think we see around us. This point of Rousseau's (which I have rather freely reconstructed) is aimed at the optimists as much as the pessimists, since optimism, if it obtains at all, can only ever be an a priori system: it can have nothing to do with what we see around us in the world. As Rousseau tells us:

> The true principles of optimism can be drawn neither from the properties of matter, nor from the mechanics of the universe, but only by

47. Recall that this rendition of Pope's 'Whatever is, is RIGHT' is not unproblematic; see chapter 3.

48. While this point is technically correct, both Leibniz and King see particular evils as purely negative entities, which is still a *kind* of denial: they are denying to evils (such as misery) the same kind of positive ontology that they admit to goods (such as happiness).

49. Here, I disagree with Litwin's argument ('Rousseau and Leibniz') that Rousseau's distinction of 'the good of the universe' and 'the good of mankind' sets him apart from Leibniz's theodicy, when in fact this is the very move made by Leibniz in the *Théodicée*, and by others after him (see chapter 2).

> inference from the perfections of God, who presides over all; so that one does not prove the existence of God by Pope's system, but Pope's system by the existence of God, and the question regarding the origin of evil is, without a doubt, derived from the question regarding Providence. (*LV*, 240)

In Rousseau's view, there is something ridiculous about reasoning from the phenomena, because everyone will interpret things to their own liking. The devout will explain all goods and evils as rewards or tests or punishments; *les Philosophes* will raise questions whatever happens. If a criminal was killed as a child, how could God let him die? If he wasn't and lives to commit atrocities, how could God let him live? 'Thus, regardless of the side which nature chose, Providence is always right among the devout, and always wrong among the Philosophers' (*LV*, 241).

Should we, then, reject *any* inductive argument about providence based on the phenomena, including any experience of misalignment (the suffering of the righteous; the flourishing of the wicked)?[50] Not quite. We can conclude from what we see in the world that providence most probably does not concern itself with 'particular events here below', but is 'exclusively universal', and restricts itself to 'presiding over the whole, without worrying about how each individual spends this short life' (*LV*, 241). This, then, is Rousseau's own conception of providence:

> the greatest idea of Providence I can conceive is that each material being be arranged in the best way possible in relation to the whole, and each intelligent and sentient being in the best way possible in relation to itself; which means, in other words, that for a being that senses its existence, *existing is preferable to not existing*. (*LV*, 241; my emphasis)[51]

Again, the sheer sentiment of being will settle the matter in favour of being, since Rousseau holds that it is generally a good feeling to sense that one exists. However, Rousseau recognises that there are times in most lives when existence seems rather more a burden than a boon, and he immediately qualifies his assertion that 'existing is preferable to not existing':

> But this rule has to be applied to each sentient being's total duration, and not to some particular instants of its duration, such as human life;

50. Note that Rousseau takes misalignment very seriously in *Emile* (see below, pp. 260ff). Compare Schopenhauer on poetic justice as a case of wrong perspective (*WWR*.I.254).

51. Again, this is not a particular providence, but a more general system of interlocking causes.

> which shows how closely related the question of Providence is to that of the immortality of the soul, which happily I believe, although I am not unaware that reason can doubt it, and to the question of eternal punishments, which neither you nor I, nor any man who thinks well of God, will ever believe. (*LV*, 242)

It should not be missed how incredibly Leibnizian Rousseau is being here. In order to see things from the perspective of the *whole*, we have to take into account not only the probable inhabitants of other worlds,[52] but also our own future lives: it is in the afterlife that any this-worldly misalignment will find its correction and compensation. However, while Leibniz wavers with regard to the misery of the damned, Rousseau firmly rejects eternal damnation, and thus steers clear of some of the more obvious objections raised against earlier optimists.[53]

In the end, the only question that matters is that of the existence and especially the *conception* we have of God:

> If I trace these various questions to their common principle, it seems to me that they all relate to the question of the existence of God. If God exists, he is perfect; if he is perfect, he is wise, powerful and just; if he is wise and powerful, all is well; if he is just and powerful, my soul is immortal; if my soul is immortal, thirty years of life are nothing to me, and they are perhaps necessary to the preservation of the universe. If I am granted the first proposition, the ones that follow will never be shaken; if it is denied, there is no use arguing about its consequences. (*LV*, 242)[54]

Whether or not this is convincing as a theodicean argument, one has to admire Rousseau's bravura in trying to unravel the age-old debate on the origins of evil in three sentences. Of course, it does nothing to explain or even elucidate any of God's considerations in mixing evils in with creation and failing to prevent them by his providence. But Rousseau's point is that we shouldn't even go there—and this, at least on the surface, was Bayle's point too: don't argue about something you know you cannot

52. Rousseau, like Leibniz, factors in the existence of intelligent (and presumably *happy*) aliens (*LV*, 240).

53. However, this wouldn't save him from a Bayle, who on various occasions asks why the system requires this-worldly misery in order to achieve other-worldly rewards, while questioning the ethics of creating a being destined for even non-eternal damnation.

54. That everything here depends not only on the existence but also the *conception* we have of God is a point made also by Schopenhauer (see chapter 8).

solve. Ultimately, then, we end up with a kind of fideism.[55] But in stark contrast to Bayle's tepid statements of faith, which have discredited their authenticity in the eyes of many readers, Rousseau's *credo* is marked by precisely that characteristic he himself values most highly: sincerity.[56] For while he fully grants that 'the objections, on either side, are always irrefutable, because they turn on things about which man has no genuine idea', nevertheless:

> I believe in God just as strongly as I believe any other truth, because to believe and not to believe are the things that least depend on me, because the state of doubt is too violent a state for my soul, because when my reason wavers, my faith cannot long remain in suspense, and decides without it; and finally because a thousand things I like better draw me toward the more *consoling* side and add the weight of *hope* to the equilibrium of reason. (*LV*, 242–3; my emphasis)

This, as Rousseau readily recognises, is only 'a proof of sentiment' and cannot be a demonstration for those Philosophers who 'do not grant the principle'; therefore, we should not argue with them. But nor should these philosophers argue with 'us' about these matters, not only because it is pointless to argue on the basis of different principles, but also for another reason: 'Namely that there is something inhumane about troubling peaceful souls, and distressing men to no purpose, when what one is trying to teach them is neither certain nor useful' (*LV*, 244).[57]

What it all boils down to, for Rousseau, is the right foundation of hope and consolation, and he does not hesitate to make this clear in his notorious *ad hominem* remark against Voltaire:

> I cannot help, Sir, noting in this connection a rather odd contrast between yourself and myself on the subject of this letter. Replete with glory, and with no illusions about vain grandeurs, you live free in the midst of abundance; assured of immortality, you philosophize serenely about the nature of the soul; and if the body or the heart suffers, you have Tronchin for physician and friend: yet you find only evil on earth. And I, obscure, poor, and racked by an incurable disease, I meditate

55. The same sentiment arises strongly in Rousseau's *Lettres morales*, echoes of which make it into the 'Profession of Faith of the Savoyard Vicar'; I thank Robin Douglass for pointing this out.

56. On which, see Trilling, *Sincerity and Authenticity*; Williams, *Truth and Truthfulness*, chapter 8.

57. Here, Rousseau also makes an argument for toleration.

> with pleasure in my retreat, and find that all is well. Where do these apparent contradictions come from? You yourself have given the explanation: you enjoy; but I hope, and hope embellishes everything. (*LV*, 246)

What are we to make of this paragraph? Mere rhetoric, meant to score points against the opponent? It does seem rather below the belt, even for the times; indeed, there is something almost funny about how performative this paragraph is, becoming a kind of contest about who is able to suffer most and complain the least.[58] But I think we would miss something important if we were to dismiss this passage as plain pathos with a sting to it.[59] It is rhetoric, yes, but at the same time it's more than that: Rousseau is pointing out that he, unlike Voltaire, is one *qui sait souffrir*, someone who knows to suffer well, a skill that, as he will later argue, Emile should also be taught. As such, it is telling both of the persona of the philosopher, who—even more than other people—should be able to rise above his suffering, and of the background dynamics of the debate in question. The issue of providence is one that *matters* to Rousseau in a way that he feels it doesn't matter to Voltaire, who he sees as merely playing intellectual games.[60] What Rousseau is trying to bring home to Voltaire is that he is also playing with people's hearts. It is revolting, he writes in the *Confessions*, how such a man 'living in the lap of luxury' dares to paint for his fellow men 'a frightening and cruel picture of all the calamities from which he is himself exempt'. Hence the need of a counterweight by someone like Rousseau, 'who had a better right to count up and weigh the evils of human life' (*Confessions*, IX, 399). The paragraph may indeed not be in good taste, but it may yet be sincere.[61]

Rousseau closes his letter by explaining again why he has argued at length about these matters:

58. See Starobinski (*Transparency*, 367–8) on the role played by 'the figure of the *suffering healer*' in 'the myth that grew up around Rousseau the man'.

59. See Neiman, 'Metaphysics', 146, who calls the conclusion of the letter 'if anything, merely pathetic'.

60. I don't think Rousseau's objection is fair in so far as it applies to the Lisbon Poem, where Voltaire's indignation is real enough, but it might not be entirely unfair if applied to *Candide* (see chapter 3).

61. At least in so far as it expresses his outright dislike of Voltaire, as indeed he expressed it elsewhere: 'I do not like you, sir' (*Confessions*, X, 500; see also VIII, 370). As for Rousseau's representation of his own misery, some questions might be raised as to how poor and obscure he really was at the time of writing the letter, when Rousseau was at the height of success, well before his disgrace by *Emile*.

> what is at stake is the cause of Providence from which I expect everything. After having so long derived solace [*consolations*] and courage from your lessons, it is hard on me that you now deprive me of all this, to offer me no more than an uncertain and vague hope, rather as a present palliative than as a future reward. No: I have suffered too much in this life not to expect another. All the subtleties of Metaphysics will not make me doubt for one moment the immortality of the soul and a beneficent Providence. I sense it, I want it, I hope for it, I shall defend it to my last breath; and of all disputations I will have engaged in, it will be the only one in which my own interest will not have been forgotten. (*LV*, 246)

Thus the letter to Voltaire does many things: it tells us more about Rousseau's conception of providence and suffering, and how most of the evils we experience are indeed of our own making. But above all, what the letter makes clear is what is really at stake in this debate: not just the credibility of providence, but the grounding of hope and consolation within this 'great and consoling dogma' (*LV*, 241). Hope and consolation are the reasons for Rousseau's opting for optimism (albeit a 'sober, somber optimism'),[62] faith, providence, and immortality; these, for him, form the central battleground and the point of contention of the entire theodicean debate. Rousseau may not be the first to be concerned with these questions, but he is the first to be quite so clear about what is at stake in the debate on theodicy; the moral dimensions of the problem of evil.

It is striking, then, that while Rousseau is deeply aware of how much hope and especially consolation matter in this debate, he is completely oblivious to the fact that these are also a concern of his opponent, Voltaire. Throughout the letter, Rousseau scores some good points against Voltaire, whose exemplification of the Lisbon earthquake as a prima-facie argument against providence is perhaps more poetically than philosophically convincing. But if it is the case that Voltaire's point was not so much to refute providence as it was to chide optimism for its failure in consolation, then Rousseau's critique misses the mark.[63] For if theodicy is really a question of ethics as well as metaphysics, then its central question is not just whether evils can be justified, but which theory offers most in the way of

62. Gourevitch, 'Rousseau on Providence', 604.

63. See chapter 3. Rousseau believed that Voltaire replied to his letter with 'nothing less than his novel *Candide*, of which I cannot speak because I have not read it' (*Confessions*, IX, 400).

consolation: How can we speak to human suffering in the most consoling and compassionate way?[64] The same considerations, as we have seen in Bayle and Voltaire, could equally lead to pessimism—but Rousseau fails to see the ethical drive active in pessimism, just as the pessimists fail to see it in the optimists.

But Rousseau's argument is not just about the ethical question: he is also trying to strike some theoretical points against the challengers of theodicy. What is most powerful about his argument is the way in which he refuses to let the pessimists set the terms of the debate. Rousseau does not make any of the concessions that got Leibniz and King into so much trouble. He does not accept that the existence of a truly miserable being, or even of many miserable beings, is a problem of evil; in fact, he does not accept that *any* argument based on the evils we see in the world can pose an objection to providence. Furthermore, he does not accept that having to compromise some of God's power to save his goodness is a weakness or even an impiety. As for the very dilemma that must have caused centuries of thinkers sleepless nights, Rousseau considers it no more than a little puzzle, easily solved: if we have to choose between God's goodness and omnipotence, so much for his omnipotence.[65] Rousseau isn't at all concerned about keeping all three omni's perfectly intact at any cost, and while this for a metaphysician such as Leibniz might indeed be a weakness, for someone entering the theodicean debate on primarily *ethical* terms, it is rather a strength. The fragility of Rousseau's approach is such that it also touches his conception of God.

Thus Rousseau shows a subtle understanding of the dynamics and pitfalls of the debate on evil; a debate into which he introduces himself by answering different sets of questions. Instead of asking why there are evils at all, Rousseau asks why there are so many evils in human existence that are not strictly necessary; that could have been avoided. When he goes on to answer these questions himself, this is not out of a purely theoretical interest, but because he believes them to have practical import: understanding them will help us reframe society and individual life in such a way that most evils can again become preventable. This is why education is so important, and why *Emile* is so crucial for understanding Rousseau's entire theodicean project.

64. In Neiman's view ('Metaphysics', 146), it is Voltaire who here 'appears not only the more serious but the more compassionate thinker'.

65. See *Emile*, I, 67: 'Of all the attributes of the all-powerful divinity, goodness is the one without which one can least conceive it.'

Emile

Emile, or On Education cost Rousseau 'twenty years of meditation, and three years to write' (*Confessions*, VIII, 360). Its famous opening lines summarise the essence of the *Second Discourse* in particular, from the conclusions of which *Emile* takes its cue: 'Everything is good as it leaves the hands of the Author of things; everything degenerates in the hands of man' (*Emile*, I, 37). Again, we are back to the theme of origins, but this time the origins in question are those of an individual human life, and the aim is not simply descriptive. Rather, the aim is to offer guidance, not to society at large, but to the individual *before* he enters society: before society has had a chance to corrupt him. Having offered little in the way of solutions in the *Discourse*, Rousseau now changes tack, for *Emile* is all about solutions.[66] What would it be like, Rousseau asks, to raise, not a citizen, but a *man*, and to raise him according to nature, as uncorrupted as possible by society, while yet preparing him for a life in that society?[67] He takes under his charge a fictional ward, and that ward is Emile.

I will here not discuss the arduous educational trajectory plotted by Rousseau, but focus purely on the way in which *Emile* continues certain earlier theodicean themes, and develops them in important ways. *Emile* may not seem an obvious candidate for a theodicean work, and it is not usually read as one. I do not mean to argue here that the work is itself a kind of 'theodicy', but only that there's no going around *Emile* when it comes to discovering Rousseau's theodicean thought. Furthermore, if *Emile* shows anything, it is that Rousseau continued to toil at the question of the problem of evil, to which neither the *Second Discourse* nor the letter to Voltaire presented his final statement. More than in these earlier writings, he now focuses more closely (though ever confusingly) on the typology and genealogy of different sets of evils, and points the discussion towards a theme that has quietly been present all along: the art of suffering, *savoir souffrir*.

66. The other search of solutions occurs, of course, in the *Social Contract*, which is often read side by side with *Emile*; a tendency criticised by Douglass, 'The Moral Psychology of The Social Contract'. I here focus on *Emile* as a work explicitly and directly concerned with theodicy.

67. Neuhouser (*Rousseau's Theodicy*, 20–1) interprets Rousseau as wanting to educate both a man *and* a citizen in *Emile*; against this, see Douglass, 'Moral Psychology'; and O'Hagan's review of Neuhouser, 221ff.

EVILS

Let's begin with the typology or characterisation of evils: the question of what kinds of evils there are and how to evaluate them. These are familiar questions, not just from the history of theodicy, but also from Rousseau's earlier writings, where we have seen him use the terms *moral* and *physical evils* and distinguish original or 'natural' evils (those that are innate to man's nature) from unnatural or self-inflicted evils (which are our own doing).[68] However, how exactly the moral/physical distinction related to the original/unnatural distinction was not clearly articulated, and possibly Rousseau was aware of this under-articulation, for he returns to the matter in *Emile*, where he clarifies some things only, it seems, to complicate them further.

Now the concepts of *moral evil* and *physical evil* may seem perfectly straightforward to us, having seen them used easily and confidently by Bayle, Leibniz, Hume, and Voltaire.[69] We have learned that, from Bayle onwards, moral evil is sin or crime, whereas physical evil is suffering, broadly construed. We have also seen—in Bayle, for instance—that physical evils (i.e. suffering) can in turn be divided into *bodily* physical evils, such as pain and illness, and *psychological* physical evils, such as sadness and grief. In other words, we suffer evils of the body, but we also suffer evils of the mind or soul. In Bayle, again, the wider category of physical evil included *any kind of suffering*, whether bodily or psychological, deserved or undeserved. This is also how Rousseau used the concepts of moral and physical evil in his earlier writings. In *Emile*, however, he seems to collapse the body/soul categories into the moral/physical categories: he now begins to equate *physical evils* with evils of the body and *moral evils* with evils of the soul.

Consider this passage, which occurs early on in book I:

> The fate of man is to suffer at all times. The very care of his preservation is connected with pain. Lucky to know only *physical ills* in his

68. Note that while in most of this book I treat the terms 'natural evil' and 'physical evil' as roughly equivalent, I make an exception for Rousseau: in this chapter, 'natural evil' is an evil that comes from nature ('original' or 'necessary') and to some extent distinct from 'physical evil', as this section explains.

69. Litwin ("Le principe nécessaire") offers an interesting argument on why 'metaphysical evil' is absent in Rousseau's philosophy—but as we have seen the concept was already obsolete in many early eighteenth-century theodicies (such as those discussed in chapter 3), as Leibniz's three-part division of evils, with its scholastic residue of metaphysical evil, made a quiet exit. In using only the stripped-down Baylean categories of moral and physical evil, Rousseau was not unconventional.

> childhood—ills far less cruel, far less painful than are the other kinds of ills and which far more rarely make us renounce life than do the others! One does not kill oneself for the pains of gout. There are hardly any but *those of the soul* which produce despair. We pity the lot of childhood, and it is our own that should be pitied. Our *greatest ills* come to us from ourselves. (*Emile*, I, 48; my emphasis)

Thus Rousseau feels, like Bayle, that evils of the soul are much worse than those of the body: that these are the evils most likely to drive us to despair. Like Bayle, furthermore, he places the source of our unhappiness in our experience rather than in some kind of objective grounding of our experience: 'unhappiness consists not in the privation of things but in the need that is felt for them' (*Emile*, II, 81).[70] But unlike Bayle, Rousseau concludes from this that most of our evils are of own making, *especially the evils of the soul*, since it is not reality that forces them on us, but our imagination or opinion:

> The real world has its limits; the imaginary world is infinite. Unable to enlarge the one, let us restrict the other, for it is from the difference between the two alone that are born all the pains which make us truly unhappy. Take away strength, health, and good witness of oneself, all the goods of this life are in opinion; take away the pains of the body and the remorse of conscience, all our ills are imaginary. (*Emile*, II, 81)

Here, then, is a third division of goods and evils into two categories: that of *real* or *true* or *proper* goods and evils, which do not depend on our imagination, and *imaginary* goods and evils, which do depend on our imagination and for which, therefore, we are wholly responsible. Under real or proper evils are included only pains of the body (physical evils) and 'remorse of conscience' (a moral evil); while under real or proper goods are included only strength and health (physical goods) and 'good witness of oneself' (a moral good). All the rest are imaginary or 'matters of opinion':

> Our moral ills [*maux moraux*] are all matters of opinion, except for a single one—crime; and this ill depends on us. Our physical ills [*maux*

70. Rousseau offers a negative conception of both happiness and unhappiness in *Emile* (II, 80): 'We do not know what absolute happiness or unhappiness is. . . . The happiest is he who suffers the least pain; the unhappiest is he who feels the least pleasure. . . . Man's felicity on earth is, hence, only a negative condition; the smallest number of ills he can suffer ought to constitute its measure.'

> *physiques*] are themselves destroyed or destroy us. Time or death is our remedy. (*Emile*, II, 82)[71]

However, as I have suggested above, here the category of moral evils is not restricted to crimes or sins. Unlike Bayle and others after him, Rousseau places evils of the soul, such as 'inner pains, affliction, languor, and sadness', under 'moral suffering', *des peines morales* (*Emile*, IV, 227).

Recall that sadness (*tristesse*) was a question left over from the *Second Discourse* and hardly discussed in the letter to Voltaire: Are grief and sadness really things that depend on us? Does natural man not suffer bereavement? Rousseau's answer seems to be that sadness and even grief are indeed afflictions of societal man alone; that they are things that depend on our imagination. This also seems to be the reason why he considers sadness a *moral* rather than a *physical* evil: Rousseau assumes that evils of the soul are more strongly rooted in our imagination than evils of the body, and more likely to be self-inflicted.[72] Another reason may be that evils of the soul are more likely to depend on our perceptions of and inclinations towards other people: thus grief depends crucially on our love of others.[73] This question, to which I will return, plays a crucial part throughout *Emile*.

The more important distinction, however, seems to have to do rather with 'natural' (or necessary) and 'unnatural' (or unnecessary) passions. According to Rousseau, while our natural passions (shared with natural man) tend to our preservation, all the others tend to our subjection or destruction:

> Our natural passions are very limited. They are the instruments of our freedom; they tend to preserve us. All those which subject us and destroy us come from elsewhere. Nature does not give them to us. We appropriate them to the detriment of nature. (*Emile*, IV, 212)

Following this distinction between the passions, we can likewise distinguish between natural evils, which nature imposes on us, and unnatural evils, which come from ourselves:

71. Note that in these two passages, crime and remorse of conscience are considered two sides of same coin, as action and effect: remorse is the evil we suffer as a result of the evil we have done; hence 'this ill depends on us', and both belong to the category of moral evils.

72. In this, he follows a long tradition; see chapter 1 on the derivative nature of sadness in early modern philosophy.

73. That is, this is the point at which we enter the moral order and become concerned with others, not just ourselves; the point at which *amour de soi* turns into *amour propre* (*Emile*, IV, 235).

> nature delivers us from the ills it imposes on us, or it teaches us to bear them. But nature says nothing to us about those which come from ourselves. It abandons us to ourselves. It lets us, as victims of our own passions, succumb to our vain sorrows and then glorify ourselves for the tears at which we should have blushed. (*Emile*, V, 445)

There is nothing problematic, then, about *natural* evils, since nature helps us to bear them: it is only our *unnatural* evils, rooted in our imagination, that require justification and immediately receive it by way of this very rootedness. If our evils are self-inflicted, according to Rousseau, then nature is not to blame.

Hence, throughout all these distinctions, the only thing that really matters is the extent to which our evils are due to us: this is the question to which we can reduce all others, and that drives the moral/physical distinction. Since imagination is so crucial, some evils that Bayle and Leibniz (and philosophers now) would have called *physical* instead shift category to the *moral*—such as grief and sadness, but also death and certain kinds of physical suffering, which according to Rousseau are evils only because *we add something to them*. Again, Rousseau's aim in *Emile* is not simply to diagnose but to cure, and in order to equip us for coming to terms with physical as well as moral evils, we need to understand how they come into being, and to what extent they are or are not avoidable. These are themes explored at length in the later books of *Emile*, and especially in the 'Profession of Faith of the Savoyard Vicar'.

'PROFESSION DE FOI DU VICAIRE SAVOYARD'

This is the notorious section, introduced midway in book IV of *Emile*, where a hypothetical Savoyard vicar sets out his rather minimalist articles of faith (*Emile*, IV, 266–313). As Rousseau was later to confess, the vicar's profession is 'more or less' representative of his own position: in fact, it is the resolution of Rousseau's crisis of faith brought on by *les philosophes*; a crisis in which the problem of evil featured prominently.[74] No one really bought into the thin guise of the Savoyard vicar, and so the 'Profession' ended up getting Rousseau into a lot of problems, while being so successful that it was often published separately in years to come. It was, not

74. *Reveries*, III, 55; see also Rousseau's 'Letter to Beaumont' (1763) (*CWR*.IX.19–101, esp. 46–47). An earlier, less technical version of the 'Profession', however, appears to have 'corresponded more closely to Jean-Jacques' deepest feelings' (Pierre Maurice Masson, cited in O'Hagan, *Rousseau*, 237).

coincidentally, the only part of *Emile* that Voltaire approved of, calling it 'forty of the boldest pages ever written against Christianity'.[75]

While the 'Profession' was thus read as highly subversive, it should be noted that none of its subversive or even innovative force resides in its theodicean aspects, which continue to run roughly along Leibnizian lines.[76] Not much is added here that we have not encountered already in Rousseau's earlier writings: nevertheless, the 'Profession' is important for understanding Rousseau's theodicean exercise, and this is so for three reasons. First, it develops some central themes; second, it elucidates the genesis of Rousseau's theodicean considerations (what he does and does not consider problematic, in the sense of a *problem* of evil); third, it represents Rousseau's definitive statement on the problem of evil as well as the entire question of faith.[77]

The 'Profession' as a whole is a loosely Cartesian exercise of trying to find certain basic truths by a method of doubt, but without any pretension of arriving at any absolute certainty. What the Savoyard vicar arrives at is a deistic minimal conception of God as 'a single intelligence' who governs all things (*Emile*, IV, 276–7). Everything seems to be going smoothly, until the searching soul, having contemplated the earth and the beasts, looks at man instead, and is confronted with the existence of evil in the world:

> What a spectacle! Where is the order I had observed? . . . Concert reigns among the elements, and men are in chaos! The animals are happy; their king alone is miserable! O wisdom, where are your laws? O providence, is it thus that you rule the world? Beneficient Being, what has become of your power? I see evil on earth. (*Emile*, IV, 278)[78]

Je vois le mal sur la terre: only Jean-Jacques could represent the problem of evil so pithily. Hardly less plucky is his solution:

> If man is active and free, he acts on his own. All that he does freely does not enter into the ordered system of providence and cannot be imputed to it. Providence does not will the evil a man does in

75. Voltaire to Damilaville, 14 June 1762 (*D*10507; cited in English in Pearson, *Voltaire Almighty*, 295). Joshua Cohen ('Natural Goodness', 139) interprets the Profession 'as anticipating Kant's conception of reasonable faith'.

76. On Rousseau's reading of Leibniz, see Litwin, 'Rousseau and Leibniz', 77–8; I am, however, not in agreement with Litwin's attempt to place Rousseau's philosophy 'at odds with any kind of theodicy' (77).

77. Douglass ('Free Will', 648–9) rightly points out the different orientation of the *Second Discourse* and the 'Profession', the former being more concerned with tracing the development of evil, the latter with responsibility for evil (i.e. justification).

78. Note again that the problem of evil does *not* arise for Rousseau at the level of animals.

> abusing the freedom it gives him; but it does not prevent him from doing it. . . . It has made him free in order that by choice he do not evil but good. . . . To complain about God's not preventing man from doing evil is to complain about His having given him an excellent nature . . . (*Emile*, IV, 281)

This is in essence the classic free-will response to the problem of evil, which Bayle rejected on the basis that freedom was surely a poor gift if it came at the price of the overwhelming suffering of mankind (of which God was necessarily aware). According to Rousseau, of course, it did *not* come at this price: man did not and does not need to be so miserable. We are wicked and unhappy due to the abuse of our faculties; all moral and physical evils fall back onto us:

> It is the abuse of our faculties which makes us unhappy and wicked. Our sorrows, our cares, and our sufferings come to us from ourselves. Moral evil is incontestably our own work, and physical evil would be nothing without our vices, which have made us sense it. (*Emile*, IV, 281)

As for natural or unavoidable evils such as pain (which also occurs in animals and in natural man), Rousseau takes the Kingian or roughly deist line, arguing that such evils are useful to the creature:

> Is it not for preserving ourselves that nature makes us sense our needs? Is not the pain of the body a sign that the machine is out of order and a warning to look after it? (*Emile*, IV, 281)[79]

Death, furthermore, cannot properly be called an evil, since it is designed to put an end to our miseries, and without the element of *foresight* would not even be experienced as an evil:

> Death . . . Do not the wicked poison their lives and ours? Who would want to live always? Death is the remedy for the evils you do to yourselves; nature did not want you to suffer forever. How few ills there are to which the man living in primitive simplicity is subject! He lives

79. See also *Emile*, II, 87, where Rousseau argues that pain also has a moral function, since man needs to know 'the little ills' in order to experience 'the great goods': 'Such is his nature. If the physical prospers, the moral is corrupted. The man who did not know pain would know neither the tenderness of humanity nor the sweetness of commiseration. His heart would be moved by nothing. He would not be sociable; he would be a monster among his kind.' A similar point is made by Lactantius, *De ira dei*, XIII.

> almost without diseases as well as passions and neither foresees nor senses death. When he senses it, his miseries make it desirable to him; from then on it is no longer an evil for him. (*Emile*, IV, 281)[80]

The central problem is in this added element of foresight or reflection, which civilised man adds to innocuous physical evils, making them a source of misery: 'To the evil he senses, he adds the evil he fears. Foresight of death makes it horrible and accelerates it' (*Emile*, IV, 282).

The quest for the origins of evil can now be concluded:

> Man, seek the author of evil no longer. It is yourself. No evil exists other than that which you do or suffer, and both come to you from yourself. General evil can exist only in disorder, and I see in the system of the world an unfailing order. Particular evil exists only in the sentiment of the suffering being, and man did not receive this sentiment from nature: he gave it to himself. Pain has little hold over someone who, having reflected little, possesses neither memory nor foresight. Take away our fatal progress, take away our errors and our vices, take away the work of man, and everything is good. (*Emile*, IV, 282)

It is worth pausing here to note how completely unconvincing this paragraph would be to an author like Bayle. While he would agree that particular evils exist 'only in the sentiment of the suffering being', Bayle would dismiss the general/particular distinction and argue that this applies to *all* evils: we have no concept of an evil outside our sentiment—that is, our experience. Furthermore, Bayle might argue that to deny providence any say in the development of human history and our corruption of ourselves is to leave providence no meaningful role whatsoever. What can we expect of a God who absents himself from his creation to such a terrible extent; how does this offer hope or consolation? The answer, for Rousseau, lies in the afterlife.

He arrives there through the familiar question of misalignment: How is it that 'the wicked man prospers, and the just man remains oppressed' (*Emile*, IV, 282)? This is far from a neutral question for Rousseau: as he would later write in his third *Reverie*, the question of misalignment is one he took very seriously and applied to his own situation—for Rousseau did not understand why he in his innocence suffered as he did

80. This echoes King's notion that at the very moment when our miseries become intolerable, nature takes them away together with our lives (see chapter 2).

(*Reveries*, III, 59).[81] Hence, if his answer seems somewhat nonchalant, the road to this answer was anything but so.

Like Leibniz and Wollaston before him, Rousseau's vicar holds that the justification for any this-worldly misalignment lies in the afterlife, which is where God will keep the promise he has made to mankind: that if we are just, we will be happy.[82] The ultimate justification can only reside in immortality: 'If the soul is immaterial, it can survive the body; and if it survives the body, providence is justified' (*Emile*, IV,283). God cannot have created humans for the purpose of suffering; that is how we can be confident that there will be otherworldly compensation:

> [God], having created them as sensitive beings did not create them to suffer; and since they did not abuse their freedom on earth, they did not fail to attain their destiny due to their own fault. Nevertheless they suffered in this life; therefore they will be compensated in another. (*Emile*, IV, 284)

As in the letter to Voltaire, it is acknowledged here that this is not something that admits of any hard proof or conclusive demonstrations: rather, the justification is a *moral* one. We are justified to believe in the immortality of the soul because it is the doctrine that offers most hope and consolation.[83] This, again, is of personal importance to Rousseau, who in the midst of his anxieties needs to believe that 'this life [is] merely a testing time', and that his torments would find 'a glorious recompense' (*Reveries*, III, 57).

Thus the 'Profession' operates roughly along the same lines as the *Discourse* and the letter to Voltaire, mostly following earlier accounts such as those by Leibniz and King, but also introducing a historical element to the question after the origins of evil while excising the role played by original sin.[84] Its main difference from the earlier texts lies in the way it

81. See also *Reveries*, II, 45: 'God is just; his will is that I should suffer, and he knows my innocence. That is what gives me confidence. My heart and my reason cry out that I shall not be disappointed. Let men and fate do their worst, we must learn to suffer in silence, everything will find its proper place in the end and sooner or later my turn will come.'

82. This would seem to counter Neiman's point that Rousseau's account of evil features only *this-worldly* alignment; that '[t]he result of evil is immediate misery—not in the world to come, but in our own' ('Metaphysics', 152).

83. See also *Emile*, II, 82: If we were physically immortal, then 'we would be most unhappy beings', for 'what hope, what consolation would remain to us'?

84. Which was probably the aspect most responsible for Rousseau's condemnation. As Cassirer notes (*The Question of Jean-Jacques Rousseau*, 74): 'The mandate in which

gives much more weight to the question of misalignment and undeserved suffering, and emphasises to a greater extent the necessity of an afterlife. This might give us some pause. Rousseau's assertion that God cannot have created man to suffer, and therefore our suffering will necessarily be compensated, sits rather uncomfortably with his earlier suggestion that all our true miseries are of our own making. The earlier point had been that such suffering is therefore not problematic in any deep way, but now Rousseau concedes that there *is* a kind of undeserved suffering that forms a problem of evil, and can only be explained by positing an afterlife.

I'm not sure whether Rousseau is strengthening or weakening his case by this concession that there is something fundamentally *problematic* about misalignment, instead of just dismissing this as a case of mistaken perspective: something strictly irrelevant to the system as a whole. Isn't this to give back to the pessimists an initial advantage he had originally retained? But perhaps there's more at stake here than simply winning the argument. If it is indeed the case that the 'Profession' was the outcome of a personal struggle, a crisis of faith, then what this move suggests is that Rousseau, more than in his earlier writings, was now experiencing undeserved suffering as a real and personal problem; moreover, that *misalignment* is the only real problem of evil he concedes. It is striking, again, that Rousseau's vicar does not attempt to justify creation itself, or to provide any deep theory of providence: the central concern seems to be less with justifying God or even providence than with explaining personal suffering and grounding the belief in an afterlife. As such, the 'Profession of Faith of the Savoyard Vicar' represents less a theodicean argument than a personal exercise in hope and consolation; a profession, indeed.

But if the discussion thus far clarifies some of the conceptual underpinning of Rousseau's theodicy, as well as the considerations at play in the background, it seems to offer little in the way of consolation *here and now*. After all, we're told that moral evils are imaginary, while physical evils are remedied either by time or by death. Most of the time, we have only ourselves to blame. But even if our sufferings are ultimately compensated in an afterlife, how is this at all helpful to the person suffering from deep grief or chronic pain *right now*? Wasn't Rousseau aiming to help us remedy our miseries in *this life*, considering that our sorry predicament as humans in society cannot be undone? The answer is yes, for aside from the consolation of an afterlife, there is another consolation Rousseau is aiming

---

Christophe de Beaumont, archbishop of Paris, condemned *Emile*, laid the chief emphasis on Rousseau's denial of original sin.'

at, which is that if we learn to understand these evils better, we can learn to cope with them: we can learn how to *suffer well*.

SAVOIR SOUFFRIR

This is a skill that is native to man in his natural state, as it is to animals: 'Naturally man knows how to suffer with constancy and dies in peace' (*Emile*, I, 54). Not only are animals and natural man subject to fewer ills (only the bodily ones such as pain and sickness, hunger and death), but they are also better able to bear these; for instance, showing more resignation in the face of death:

> Naturally man worries about his preservation only insofar as the means to it are in his power. As soon as these means escape him, he becomes calm and dies without tormenting himself uselessly. The first law of resignation comes to us from nature. Savages as well as beasts struggle very little against death and endure it almost without complaint. (*Emile*, II, 82)[85]

This is also what Rousseau wants for Emile: 'To suffer is the first thing he ought to learn and the thing he will most need to know' (*Emile*, II, 78). Knowing how to suffer is at the centre of Emile's education: like the Savoyard vicar, Rousseau the instructor wishes to teach his ward 'the difficult art of patiently bearing adversity' (*l'art difficile de supporter patiemment l'adversité*) (*Emile*, IV, 262). This art of suffering is something that pertains to the body as well as to the soul. Physical suffering is to some extent unavoidable, and the remedies of medicine tend only to make matters worse: 'we suffer more the less we know how to suffer; and we give ourselves more torment in curing our maladies than we would have in enduring them' (*Emile*, II, 82). Hence, though we cannot prevent physical evils from happening, we can train ourselves to bear them better:

> What does not admit of exceptions . . . is man's subjection to pain, to the ills of his species, to the accidents, to the dangers of life, finally to death. The more he is familiarized with all these ideas, the more he will be cured of the importunate sensitivity which only adds to the ill itself the impatience to undergo it. The more he gets used to the sufferings which can strike him, the more, as Montaigne would say, the sting of

85. Contrast Bayle's passage on the frightened hare (chapter 2).

> strangeness is taken from them, and also the more his soul is made invulnerable and hard. (*Emile*, II, 131)

The problem is that, instead of acclimatising himself to physical evils and thus suffering only what is unavoidable, man increases his own suffering by extending his desires over many times, places, persons, and things, so that 'our ills are multiplied by all the points where we can be wounded' (*Emile*, II, 83; see *Emile and Sophie*, 694). This may seem a standard Stoic point, and to some extent it is, but while for the Stoics reason and reflection are part of the solution, for Rousseau they are rather part of the problem.[86] The true source of all our miseries is not in the thing itself, but in what we add to it:

> Foresight! Foresight, which takes us ceaselessly beyond ourselves and often places us where we shall never arrive. This is the true source of all our miseries. (*Emile*, II, 82)[87]

What Emile, therefore, should learn above all is how to distinguish the avoidable from the unavoidable evils, and to arrange his attitudes accordingly:

> Men are not naturally kings, or lords, or courtiers, or rich men. All are born naked and poor; all are subject to the miseries of life, to sorrows [*chagrins*], ills, needs, and pains of every kind. Finally, all are condemned to death. This is what truly belongs to man. This is what no mortal is exempt from. Begin, therefore, by studying in human nature what is most inseparable from it, what best characterizes humanity. (*Emile*, IV, 222)[88]

This passage may seem confusing, since we've been told throughout that while some evils are necessary, most of our miseries are of our own doing, especially the evils of the soul. But Rousseau's terminology is less than rigorous: the point is that no one is immune from suffering entirely, but we should distinguish the unavoidable kinds of suffering from the avoidable kinds.

86. Which is not to say that they are not part of the solution, too. See Starobinski, *Blessings in Disguise*, 127: 'The development that has made us unhappy must be carried even further: reflection must be perfected, amour-propre put to work, the imagination channelled. Alienation must be made reciprocal and complete.'

87. See also *Emile*, III, 177, and the first *Reverie*.

88. I'm not certain that *sorrow* is the proper translation here for *chagrin*, which can also designate a physical discomfort.

This brings us, at long last, to that question left over from the *Second Discourse*: What to make of spiritual or psychological suffering, of grief and sadness? These, we have seen, are generally discounted. Rousseau does not rank either grief or sadness among the natural or necessary evils; he does not believe that animals and natural man are afflicted by them. With the exception of remorse of conscience, psychological evils are considered imaginary and unnecessary. This is not to say that they are not *real* evils for us: we know from his personal writings that Rousseau is neither unaware nor dismissive of evils such as grief and sadness. On the contrary: it is precisely because he believes that evils of the soul are the only ones that lead to real despair that he is so adamant about finding a solution to the problem of psychological suffering.

A crucial episode in this context is that of the fateful letter: the arrival of bad news. This episode contains two parts and as such represents one of Rousseau's most carefully orchestrated dramatic feats: first announced and prepared in book II, it comes to its dramatic conclusion only towards the end of book V (which is the last book of *Emile* itself). Early on in book II, Rousseau introduces the example of a man at the height of his happiness, who suddenly becomes extremely distraught ('he weeps, writhes, moans, tears his hair'), for no other reason than that he received a letter in the post. Rousseau asks him:

> Senseless man, what ill has this piece of paper done to you then? Of what limb has it deprived you? What crime has it made you commit? Altogether, what has it changed in you yourself to put you in the state in which I see you? (*Emile*, II, 83)

How can a single letter, which speaks only to our imagination, make such a difference to our evaluation of our lives? Whatever the cause of this man's unhappiness, it is not there before him: had the letter never arrived, he would have continued at the height of happiness. How then, can his unhappiness be real?

> If the letter had gone astray, if a charitable hand had thrown it into the fire, the fate of this mortal, happy and unhappy at once, would have been, it seems to me, a strange problem. His unhappiness, you will say, was real. Very well, but he did not feel it; where was it then? His happiness was imaginary. I understand. Health, gaiety, well-being, contentment of mind are no longer anything but visions. We no longer exist where we are; we only exist where we are not. Is it worth the effort to have so great a fear of death if what we live off of [*ce en quoi nous vivons*] remains? (*Emile*, II, 83)

We are reminded here of what Rousseau considers to be true or necessary goods and evils, and merely imaginary ones. Grief, it seems, is marked for the latter, for if the message contained anything, it was presumably the news of the death of a loved one.[89]

To make sense of this passage, let's bring in Bayle again. Presumably, Bayle would have agreed with Rousseau that the man's happiness would have been real enough if he had not received the letter, since happiness is a matter of our experience. However, he would have denied that this means that the man's *unhappiness* upon receiving the letter is any less real. To be bereaved is a real evil, for Bayle; it may even be the most powerful of all our evils, since it is experienced as such. This, after all, was part of the message of *Xenophanes* and other articles, and of the grieving fathers featured therein. Furthermore, grief, for Bayle as for Hume, is an evil against which philosophy is powerless. *There is no such thing as the consolation of philosophy*: all we can do is speak of grief with sympathy, and try not to make matters worse.

Rousseau does not share this assumption. He counts grief as a moral and therefore an imaginary evil—which again is not to say it is not a *real* evil for those who experience it as such, but that it is an *unnecessary* one, depending as it does on our imagination. But if it is indeed unnecessary, then it can be remedied: and this, *this* is where consolation is to be found. As Rousseau closes the first part of this episode: 'O man, draw your existence up within yourself, and you will no longer be miserable' (*Emile*, II, 83).

But this is not the only ill-fated letter we see arriving in *Emile*. The same thing happens in book V, when Emile is a young man deeply in love with Sophie, who has finally consented to marry him. This time, the recipient of the unwelcome news is Emile himself, for Rousseau the educator decides to put him to the test. He enters Emile's room with a letter in his hand: 'staring fixedly at him, I say, "What would you do if you were informed that Sophie is dead?"' (*Emile*, V, 442). This, arguably, is the dramatic climax of *Emile* itself: just when happiness is within reach, everything is suspended, and we are brought face to face with the fragility of life and happiness. For we, the readers, don't know that the educator is bluffing; like Emile, we are meant to believe, for a moment, that all is lost—that Sophie is dead.

89. As the second part of this episode will confirm. Note that Emile, in his misery, will later remember this advice, only to find it makes no difference to his current sufferings (*Emile and Sophie*, 694).

Rousseau keeps the desperate Emile (and us) in suspense for only a few moments and a single paragraph; then he smiles and reassures him. Sophie is alive and well, but it is time for Emile and him to have a chat about life and happiness. He now warns Emile that he has gained a new enemy: himself. For by loving Sophie he opens himself to a number of evils from which he has so far been immune, as the episode with the letter proved to him:

> Nature and fortune had left you free. You could endure poverty; you could tolerate the pains of the body; those of the soul were unknown to you. . . . In learning to desire, you have made yourself the slave of your desires. Without anything changing in you, without anything offending you, without anything touching your being, how many pains can now attack your soul! How many ills you can feel without being sick! How many deaths you can suffer without dying! A lie, a mistake, or a doubt can put you in despair. (*Emile*, V, 443)

Emile must learn that 'Everything on earth is only transitory', and that Sophie too will die one day. Henceforth he must learn to control his heart and 'conquer his affections' (*Emile*, V, 444). He is still to love, but to love in the awareness that Sophie's presence in the world is transitory; he is to bulwark himself against the onslaught of fate: 'All passions are good when one remains their master; all are bad when one lets oneself be subjected to them' (*Emile*, V, 445).

Such Stoic-sounding passages stand in stark contrast to Hume's notion that the deepest expressions of grief are a sign of moral merit, not of weakness.[90] For Rousseau, love can be good only so long as it is a measured, well-proportioned sort of love, where the lover remains in control of (and perhaps at some distance from) his affection.[91] But grief is ever bad, because it is a sign of the passions getting the better of us; like pain or poison, it 'o'ercrows my spirit'.[92] Rousseau, like many of his age who had inherited, perhaps reluctantly, a dogged Stoicism, did not see grief as a valuable affect. Nevertheless, there are reasons not to overstress

90. Hume, *THN*, 3.3.3.6 (see chapter 5).

91. Amélie Oksenberg Rorty points out that Rousseau's distinction between 'harmful passion erroneous passions' (the wrong kind of love) and the 'benign and rational sentiments' of friendship and familial affection (the right kind of love) tracks the Stoic contrast between *pathē* and *eupathē* (Rorty, 'The Two Faces of Stoicism', 349; 'Rousseau's Therapeutic Experiments', 425).

92. Shakespeare, *Hamlet*, act 5, scene 2; cited by C.S. Lewis, *The Problem of Pain*, 105.

Rousseau's debt to the Stoics, of whom Rousseau was often highly critical.[93] There are indeed strong Stoic tenets in the idea that we are able to control our passions to such an extent as to temper our loves and even our grief, and that such control would be a sign of strength: 'It is not within our control to have or not to have passions. But it is within our control to reign over them' (*Emile*, V, 445; see also *Emile and Sophie*, 686). But belying the confidence of such impressions is the fact that Rousseau, in many instances, was very pessimistic about the extent to which such control is actually possible.[94]

The episode with the letter may strike us as pointless, or callous, or even cruel. Who would even consider putting Emile to the test like that, merely for the purpose of teaching him a lesson? But there may be something deeper at play here. It is sometimes forgotten that in the same year that *Emile* was published, Rousseau, exiled and unhappy, started writing a sequel entitled *Emile and Sophie, or, The Solitaries*, which continues the story through letters written by Emile to his tutor. Even the opening lines ('I was free, I was happy, oh my master!'—*Emile and Sophie*, 685) make it clear that here there is no need for false alarms: disaster strikes for real. In the first two letters, we learn that the lovers have lost a daughter and Sophie has lost her parents. Neglected by Emile, she becomes pregnant by another man. Emile leaves her and his son, is captured by pirates and enslaved, but manages to become a slave overseer himself. This is where the novel breaks off, since Rousseau never finished it, but we know from his notes and letters the tragic course it was supposed to take. The idea was for Emile to retire to a remote island, where he would meet another woman, before finally being reunited with Sophie (their son also having died). Only after Sophie's death does he learn that the event which he had read as infidelity was actually involuntary: Sophie had been innocent all along.[95]

In a way, then, this is Rousseau's *Candide*—a novel of disaster, but one in which the central question is not *Why does disaster strike at all?* but, rather: *How are we to bear it when it does?* As Emile writes to his tutor:

93. See, e.g., Joshua Cohen, 'Natural Goodness', 137–8, who argues that Rousseau's association with Stoicism has been 'very much exaggerated', since 'Emile's teacher rejects the Stoic ideal of extirpating the passions'.

94. Excellent on the ambiguities of Rousseau's Stoicism is Rorty, 'Rousseau's Therapeutic Experiments' and 'The Two Faces of Stoicism'; see also Starobinski, *Transparency*; Brooke, 'Rousseau's Political Philosophy'.

95. It turns out that Sophie's seduction was a violation, involving undefined aphrodisiac substances; see Wirz, 'Note sur *Émile et Sophie*', 296–7.

> Never have I known the value of your efforts better than after harsh necessity made me feel its blows so cruelly and deprived me of everything except myself. I am alone, I have lost everything, but I have myself left, and despair has not annihilated me. (*Emile and Sophie*, 685)

Thus I wonder whether Rousseau, in the ominous episode of the letter in *Emile*, is not consciously preparing Emile for something. As Emile's educator, he does not know anything except the general vicissitudes of living, but as the author of *Emile*, perhaps he knows that life has real evils in store for him. This is why he has Emile's teacher trying to prepare him for them; like Rousseau, on another level, seems to be preparing himself.[96] For again, if the episode with the letter seems cruel to us, it is because the educator is wilfully *subjecting another person* (Emile) to such a test. But what if we read it rather as Rousseau testing himself, and preparing *himself* for what life may yet have in store for him? As he writes in the Third Reverie: 'For my part, when I have set out to learn something, my aim has been to gain knowledge for myself and not to be a teacher' (*Reveries*, III, 49). The message the educator is trying to impress on Emile turns out to be the same that Rousseau is trying to impress upon himself: 'that the source of true happiness is within us, and that it is not in the power of men to make anyone truly miserable who is determined to be happy' (*Reveries*, II, 36).[97]

To such expressions, we know that Bayle would urgently (and, I think, *rightly*) object, arguing that true misery is not so easily defeated; that it is indeed possible to make someone truly miserable without that person being able to do anything against it (which is what Louis XIV did to him by imprisoning his brother). Furthermore, to make us so entirely responsible for our own happiness as well as our misery is only to make things worse by overburdening our will: aside from our suffering, we now have to bear the *guilt* for that suffering. Be that as it may: it is in this sense of agency and self-determination that Jean-Jacques looks to find hope as well as consolation. This realisation is a red thread through Rousseau's

96. His training, however, turns out to be ineffective: without the guiding presence of the tutor, Emile quickly falls apart—which, as Nancy Senior argues ('Les Solitaires as a Test for Emile and Sophie', 534–5), shows the failure of Emile's education, rather than Sophie's.

97. On the art of suffering see also the eighth *Reverie*. Rousseau himself gladly took on a therapeutic role for some people who wrote to him for advice in their sufferings; see Starobinski, *Blessings*, 134–44.

oeuvre, going back at least to the *Second Discourse*.[98] And so, while the alternative title of *Emile* is *On Education*, it could equally have been *the Art of Suffering*.

Rousseau versus the Pessimists

Thus we have followed Rousseau in his quest for origins—but how original is his theodicy? As we have seen, the main *theoretical* innovation resides in Rousseau's introduction of a historical element into the question of the origins of evil.[99] While he fully acknowledges the evils of human life, Rousseau denies that these are essential to the human condition, which is originally one of *goodness*. Somewhere along the way, something went wrong, but instead of the Fall and original sin, Rousseau posits human overdevelopment: the notion that perfectibility is always at the same time corruptibility. Far from being a tragic point, however, this is meant to be a consoling one, since the principle of our corruption—be it freedom, subjectivity, society, or even *amour propre*—is also the principle of our redemption: corruptibility is at the same time perfectibility.[100] This is not yet a 'secular theodicy',[101] since it aims at the defence of providence and depends crucially on the conception of an afterlife, but it is edging in that direction. What are the causes of our evils; how can we alleviate them? Unlike other optimists, Rousseau is not just focused on justification, but on amelioration, even though he is sceptical, at times even pessimistic, about our chances on this score.[102]

98. As Rousseau writes to Malesherbes, after he had discovered the source of human wickedness and misery 'in the false opinions of men, I felt that it was only these very opinions that had made me unhappy myself' (*CWR*.V.576).

99. Other innovations are subtler and more methodological, such as his repeated disturbance of common theodicean patterns, but also the 'hermeneutical' point made against Voltaire.

100. On the ambiguous corruptive–redemptive force of *amour propre*, see Neuhouser, *Rousseau's Theodicy*; Starobinski, *Blessings in Disguise*, 118–50; Cassirer, *Question*, 76–8.

101. Neuhouser, *Rousseau's Theodicy*, 4.

102. As *Emile and Sophie* seems to suggest. The tragic tones of this sequel, and Emile's failure to live up to his education, should moderate interpretations of *Emile* as an almost redemptive work by which 'something like salvation is conceivable' (Neiman, 'Metaphysics', 153). On the pessimistic strains in Rousseau's thought, see again Dienstag, *Pessimism*, chapter 2; and Cladis, 'Tragedy and Theodicy'; also the final pages of Rorty, 'Rousseau's Therapeutic Experiments'. The *Social Contract* and later political writings provide the political continuation of this principle of amelioration.

To my mind, Rousseau's theodicy is particularly interesting for the subtle, perceptive way in which he reads the pessimists as well as the optimists, whose background intuitions and considerations he teases out into the fore. Instead of summarising his overall argument, therefore, it may be more productive to reconstruct it as a kind of dialogue between himself and the pessimists (especially Bayle, but also Hume and Voltaire). Such a conversation might run roughly as follows:

ROUSSEAU: Nature created man good and happy. Man is responsible for all man's miseries.

PESSIMISTS: What about earthquakes and natural disasters?

ROUSSEAU: Earthquakes would not be a problem if man had not built cities on the spot.

PESSIMISTS: What about migraines, or toothache? Surely we don't *choose* to have those?

ROUSSEAU: No, some of these are unavoidable, but we make matters worse by seeking out doctors and because we don't know how to suffer well. In the natural state, man was physically healthier, but also better able to cope with pain.

PESSIMISTS: What about animals? If animals suffer, so does natural man.

ROUSSEAU: I agree with Leibniz that animals don't suffer in any meaningful way. They experience some pain, but not real misery; they lack anxiety, and the fear of death.

PESSIMISTS: What about grief, sadness, melancholy? These aren't avoidable.

ROUSSEAU: But they are. In the natural state, where there is no love as we have it now, grief is not such a problem. We can all learn to suffer less.

PESSIMISTS: Hang on. Even if only civilised man is truly miserable, how could God have constituted him so fallible and corruptible? If man is so avowedly unhappy, why create man at all, why not a different creature instead?

ROUSSEAU: The constitution of man is as good as it could be while preserving the faculty of freedom, by which man has the power to achieve true happiness. The only real question is whether it is better for man to exist under these circumstances than not to exist at all. Do not forget the sweet sentiment of existence.

PESSIMISTS: Do not forget the burdens and miseries of existence either. But what of providence? Why didn't God guide man providentially so he did not end up making himself miserable?

ROUSSEAU: You have a mistaken conception of providence, which concerns itself only with the general good: the good of the whole. *Le tout est bien.*

PESSIMISTS: Why then do the righteous suffer?

ROUSSEAU: They will be rewarded in the afterlife.

PESSIMISTS: How do you know this for certain?

ROUSSEAU: I don't. But it is the most hopeful, the most consoling thing to believe.

At which point the debate reaches a stalemate, and becomes instead a question of ethics: Which view of humanity is more consoling? Whereas Bayle argued that suggesting we are the cause of our own suffering only makes our suffering worse, Rousseau believes it is precisely in such an experience of agency that we find our greatest consolation. This gives us yet another way to frame the debate between optimists and pessimists, the former tending to emphasise our *capacity*, the latter our *fragility*. The real question at stake here, then, is not just a metaphysical but also an ethical one: Which philosophy serves us best in terms of compassion and consolation—as well as, perhaps, hope? At the same time, neither Voltaire nor Rousseau, nor any of the optimists and pessimists before or after them, seem to be aware that what is at stake for them is equally at stake for the opposing side. Rousseau may have been the first to acknowledge so explicitly that hope and consolation are at the centre of the optimist/pessimist divide, but in doing so he was continuing the musings of those very optimists and pessimists who came before him—especially Voltaire.

In order to evaluate Rousseau on his own terms, then, the main question to be asked here is whether his theodicy does a better job at consolation than the Baylean-Voltairean intuition that all we can do is speak honestly about the evils that befall us. What is troubling to me is that Rousseau sees most forms of human suffering as unnecessary and exaggerated, including grief, as we have seen in *Emile*. This is precisely the kind of optimism Bayle and Voltaire were objecting against, and the reason why it is especially troubling is that Rousseau believes that pity is not due when our ills are of own making (that is, most of the time). Were a rich man unhappier than a poor man, says Rousseau, then 'he would not be pitiable, because his ills are all his own doing, and whether he is happy depends only on himself'. A poor man cannot avoid 'the physical sentiments of fatigue, exhaustion, and hunger'; but for a rich man to be unhappy, he can have only himself to blame (*Emile*, IV, 225).

What is missing from Rousseau's theodicean thought is an awareness of the crucial point made by Hume (and hinted at by Bayle): that our very *dispositions* make up an at least equally problematic part of the physical evils to be explained by any successful theodicy. Rousseau's view on the art of suffering may draw on deep Stoic sources, but it is flattened out in the idea that barring only extreme poverty, our happiness depends wholly on ourselves: a notion that foreshadows the shallow modern mantra that 'you're responsible for your own happiness', which does so little to acknowledge the real fragilities of life, the good, and happiness itself. To my mind, this is a real weakness in Rousseau, however well-intended; and I recognise the Baylean point that this could be seen as a failure in consolation. What saves Rousseau is the avowedly personal dimension, the sense of urgency behind his more overt theodicean statements.[103] Rousseau saw himself, and, more importantly, *presented* himself as a suffering soul who struggled to interpret the meaning behind his sufferings.[104] As such, he perceived Voltaire's pessimistic musings not simply as philosophically suspect but as a personal affront against one whose very 'birth was the first of my misfortunes' (*Confessions*, I, 19). Rousseau feels personally offended by Voltaire's pessimism: Who are *you*, he asks Voltaire, to tell *me* that life is not worth living? At heart, this is the same visceral emotional–ethical objection that Voltaire had made against the optimists: *you have no right to speak of suffering in the way that you do.*

But if Rousseau and Voltaire disagreed on the matter of consolation, they equally disagreed on the question of hope. For while Rousseau is often pessimistic about *this-worldly* hope, which keeps awake our expectations and produces anxiety, he puts great stock in *other-worldly hope*: that is, hope for a life to come. This hope is wholly reliant on our conception of God's goodness and justice; and this is why pessimists, in destroying this conception, take away hope as well as consolation. Voltaire, at the end of the Lisbon Poem, cautiously moved towards this-worldly hope instead, but this, for Rousseau (showing himself a true pessimist in *some* respects), is in some ways a contradiction in terms. It may indeed be possible for our situation to improve, and it is our duty, as individuals and as a society, to aim our efforts at such improvement. But while this is indeed the right end of our earthly efforts, it is *not* the proper object of our hope. Rather, if this-worldly hope is *all* we have, then we have no hope at

103. Which I take to include the Savoyard 'Profession' and the letter to Voltaire as well as the *Reveries* and *Confessions*.

104. On Rousseau's experience of suffering and persecution, see Starobinski, *Transparency*, chapter 9.

all.[105] As Starobinski writes: 'The crucial thing is the will to consolation: it demands an afterlife.'[106]

We can see now why Dienstag emphasised Rousseau's pessimism as he did. If we take a future-oriented conception of pessimism as our guiding thread, then there are indeed good reasons to rank Rousseau among the pessimists. However, in so far as we are looking at optimism and pessimism as the central battleground in the debate on evil, it is to their *value-oriented* conceptions that we must turn. There can be no doubt that in the matter of theodicy and the evaluation of existence, Rousseau should be ranked—indeed, *ranks himself*—among the optimists.

I close with a brief note on three ways in which Rousseau's theodicy is indicative of wider shifts in the debate on the problem of evil. First, Rousseau's decisive excision of the doctrine of original sin is not incidental: it signals a deeper cultural concession that this doctrine creates as many problems as it solves; a gradual edging away from a strict Augustinian interpretation that we are all guilty through our birth. This development was not simply a function of the charges laid against Christianity by the deists and *philosophes*: it had been prepared in Rousseau's Geneva itself by ethically oriented Calvinists such as Jean La Placette, Jacques Abbadie, and especially Jean-Alphonse Turretini, under whose guidance the doctrine of original sin was formally moderated.[107] But it was Christianity's challengers who were to drive the point home, drawing heavily on Bayle, who had argued *ad nauseam* that the doctrine of original sin, like those of eternal damnation and predestination, was rationally and ethically untenable.

Second, and connectedly, Rousseau and Voltaire reveal a silent affinity in that they both interpret theodicy as primarily a matter of providence, rather than of creation. Voltaire, for all his Baylean musings, is less

105. This point, I feel, is missed by various critics, including Neiman ('Metaphysics', 162) and Neuhouser (*Rousseau's Theodicy*, 5–8), who both fail to acknowledge Rousseau's theodicean reliance on *other-worldly* redemption. While it is true that 'Rousseau allows for at least the possibility of a this-worldly remedy for human corruption' (Neuhouser, ibid., 5), throughout his theodicy he repeatedly conceives of hope and redemption in traditional Christian terms, which is why we cannot speak unproblematically of a 'secular theodicy'. Furthermore, while Rousseau's *explanation* of evil can indeed be called 'naturalistic' (as in Neiman, 'Metaphysics', 150), his *justification* (the proper domain of *theodicy*) still depends crucially on a providential framework.

106. Starobinski, *Blessings in Disguise*, 134.

107. See Rosenblatt, *Rousseau and Geneva*, 11–17, and Pitassi, *De l'orthodoxie aux lumières*, for a wider analysis of the doctrinal changes in Genevan Calvinism.

interested in the creation of a miserable creature than in the role providence played (or failed to play) in its misery. Rousseau, in turn, has the Savoyard vicar say a great deal about providence, whereas of creation he says only this:

> The idea of creation confuses me and is out of my reach. I believe it insofar as I can conceive it. But I do know that He formed the universe and all that exists, that He made everything, ordered everything. (*Emile*, IV, 285)

This is not to say that creation does not feature either in Rousseau or Voltaire; merely that it does not feature as centrally as it does in Leibniz and especially Bayle: it is no longer the primary concern in the debate. It is yet another sign of Kant's philosophical acuity that, for all his interest in Rousseau, he steers his discussion of theodicy firmly back to the question of creation, as it had been framed by Bayle.

Third and finally, we see a kind of inversion of the question of theodicy, the focus of which no longer lies primarily on God but on humanity and on society. As Cassirer notes, Rousseau carried the problem of evil 'beyond the realm of metaphysics and placed it in the center of ethics and politics', thus emphasising the responsibility *of* society in healing the wounds inflicted *by* society.[108] As D'Alembert wrote in his critique of *Emile*, instead of railing at evils, it is the task of the philosopher to ask what can we do to improve our condition, whether by remedies or palliatives.[109] These words were meant as a criticism of Rousseau, but Rousseau would most probably have agreed that this is the proper task of any useful philosophy, the task he himself was trying to perform. This is certainly how the early Kant read Rousseau, believing as he did that, just as Newton had proved the cosmic order and regularity of the universe, Rousseau had 'discovered for the very first time beneath the manifold of forms adopted by the human being the deeply hidden nature of the same and the hidden law, according to which providence is justified by his observations'. Before these authors, the objection of King Alfonso X of Castile, who thought he could have offered God some good advice when he created the world, and the objection of Manes, who believed there was an evil as well as a good god, still held. But no longer: 'After Newton and Rousseau, God is justified, and henceforth Pope's theorem is true.'[110]

108. Cassirer, *Question*, 76.

109. Jean d'Alembert, 'Jugement sur *Emile*', 299.

110. Kant, *Observations on the Feeling of the Beautiful and the Sublime*, 105 (20:58–9); this is a fragment from the *Nachlass* written between 1764 and 1768. For discussion of this

Has theodicy been solved, then? Kant here seems to suggest that all is well now in the world. But, as we know, the story does not end here. Kant himself will reopen the case of theodicy once more in the hope of closing it (though not solving it) once and for all. To do so, he will take us back to the origins, not of evil, but of theodicy itself: he takes us to the Book of Job.

---

passage, see Neiman, 'Metaphysics'. On the anecdote regarding Alfonso, see Leibniz, *EdT*, 193.247–8/*G*.VI.231. Rousseau mentions Alfonso's 'blasphemy' in a reply to his critics after the *First Discourse* (*Discourses*, 37).

CHAPTER SEVEN

The Failure of Theodicy

IMMANUEL KANT

For God deigned to lay before Job's eyes the wisdom of his creation, especially its inscrutability. He allowed him glimpses into the beautiful side of creation, . . . but also, by contrast, into the horrible side, by calling out to him the products of his might, among which also harmful and fearsome things . . .

IMMANUEL KANT[1]

ONE OF THE MOST FAMOUS texts in the history of theodicy is certainly Kant's essay, boldly titled 'On the Failure of All Philosophical Trials in Theodicy',[2] and first published on the heels of his 'critical' decade, in 1791.[3] The essay is sometimes presented as a negative counterpart to Leibniz's *Essais de Théodicée*, the idea being that what Leibniz had started, Kant brought to a close; that 'with the diagnosis of the failure of all philosophical

1. Kant, 'Theodicy', 8:266.

2. For the theodicy essay (hereafter: 'Theodicy' or 'the Essay'), I have used the translation by George Di Giovanni (in *RRT*, 19–38; revised edition in *RBMR*, 17–35): however, I see no need whatsoever to translate *Mißlingen* as 'miscarriage' instead of the less charged 'failure' and so have adapted this throughout. All Kant references are to the Prussian Academy Edition unless otherwise stated: most modern editions and translations of Kant refer to this edition as well, but where they do not, I include pagination of the respective edition.

3. So named after Kant's three *Critiques*: the *Critique of Pure Reason* (1781, second version in 1787; hereafter *KrV*), the *Critique of Practical Reason* (1788; hereafter *KpV*), and the *Critique of the Power of Judgment* (1790; hereafter *KU*). I cite the Cambridge translations; see the bibliography.

theodicy Kant also ended the "century of theodicy".[4] This also seems to be more or less what Kant had in mind when writing the essay. We know how much he liked to close the book on the big philosophical questions of the past and to present himself as starting anew, in subtle or not-so-subtle ways. Kant was never shy about this ambition, famously claiming a Copernican turn in philosophy with his first *Critique*,[5] and in later years arguing that the only progress that had been made by metaphysics since Leibniz and Wolff was his own philosophy.[6] Some of the same spirit reigns in the essay, where Kant argues not only that all previous philosophical theodicies have failed, but that all future ones *must also fail*, thus seeming to close the book, not just on a topic, but on an entire philosophical genre.

But is this what is happening? There are a few curious things about Kant's theodicy essay, in the context of his wider oeuvre. For one thing, it seems a marked departure from his earlier works, which included an essay in emphatic defence of Leibnizian and even Popean optimism. This in itself need not be surprising: after all, Kant changed his mind on many things, especially during his critical turn, and for this reason the most obvious way to read the theodicy essay would be to fit it into the pre-/post-critical divide.[7] The idea is that Kant, having circumscribed the limits of reason, recognised that theodicy, in its attempt to make claims about the supersensible world, was an instance of reason surpassing its boundaries; and so 'the whole enterprise of theodicy is one more victim of the critical turn'.[8]

There is much to be said for this explanation, were it not for a significant problem that scholars have increasingly recognised: the chronology is all wrong.[9] Kant was still seriously attempting a theodicy of his own as late as 1783–1784, in his *Lectures on the Philosophical Doctrine of Religion*

4. Schulte, 'Zweckwidriges in der Erfahrung', 371, quoting C.-F. Geyer for the term *Jahrhundert der Theodizee*. My translation.

5. *KrV*, 3: Bxvi–xviii.

6. Kuehn, *Kant: A Biography*, 376–8: Kant was working on an essay making this claim in 1793, though he never published it.

7. For examples, see Schulte, 'Zweckwidriges', 372. Note, however, that Kant didn't always like to admit or explain that he changed his mind, which is why his views during the critical period are often seen as stable: see, for instance, Kleingeld's argument that Kant 'radically revised his views on race during the 1790s' ('Kant's Second Thoughts on Race', 586, 575). I thank Jens Timmermann for pointing this out.

8. Duncan, 'Moral Evil, Freedom and the Goodness of God', 973 (this is not his own opinion).

9. See, e.g., Schulte, 'Zweckwidriges'; Brachtendorf, 'Kants Theodizee-Aufsatz'; Duncan, 'Moral Evil'.

and several other essays, 'all of which postdate the first *Critique*'.[10] These lectures, furthermore, are not an aberration, showing much continuity with the last two *Critiques* in particular, with the post-critical writings on religion, and with the theodicy essay itself, written only seven years later. It would seem, then, that there are at least three stages in Kant's theodicean thought: an early 'optimistic' stage, under the influence of Leibniz and Wolff, but also Pope, in the 1750s (pre-critical); a last attempt at theodicy in the mid-1780s (in the heart of the critical period); and finally, the rejection of all philosophical theodicy in the 1790s (post-critical).

What to make of this? Did something happen between 1784 and 1791 that forced Kant to change his mind? Should the *Lectures* be taken out of the equation after all or counted as more provisional than Kant's other works? Or is the common interpretation of the theodicy essay mistaken, and is the essay, in fact, not a rejection but a *refoundation* of theodicy as a philosophical project?[11] I am no Kant scholar, and I do not claim to be able to solve this puzzle once and for all. But as a scholar of theodicy, I will examine this question, and especially Kant's essay, as a fascinating and defining moment in the intellectual history of the problem of evil, and indeed of pessimism, with which it is closely intertwined. By doing so, I inevitably will also have some things to say about Kant, and I will offer my own tentative suggestions about what might be going on in the essay on theodicy, which I read as one of philosophy's most striking exercises in auto-refutation: in self-critique. But I will also pause to consider a sad and strange correspondence between Kant and a young disciple, Maria von Herbert, who ran up against the limits of Kantian philosophy, and in whose single-minded cry for help we may learn more about the dangers of theodicy than in all these pages combined.

'Heil uns, wir sind!': The Optimistic Kant

First, let's take a look at the early 'optimistic' Kant. Midway through the 1750s, in the very years during which Voltaire, Rousseau, and Hume were writing about evil, Kant too was giving the question of theodicy careful thought. When the Prussian Royal Academy set the question of Pope's optimism for the 1755 prize-essay competition, Kant drafted several reflections on the topic, and while he did not compete in the end, his manuscript

10. Duncan, 'Moral Evil', 974, who also mentions Kant's essays 'Conjectures on the Beginning of Human History' (1786) and 'Idea for a Universal History with a Cosmopolitan Purpose' (1784).

11. The first of these views is Duncan's; the last is Brachtendorf's.

notes give us some insight into his line of thought.[12] Here, he associates optimism with Leibniz specifically, defining it as 'the doctrine which justifies the existence of evil in the world by assuming that there is an infinitely perfect, benevolent and omnipotent original Being' (17:230–1). Adopting Leibniz's threefold classification of evils, Kant thinks that considering this distinction is enough 'to be persuaded of the truth of our account' (17:231). He follows Leibniz in claiming that the defects of the parts are justified by the good of the whole, and moral evils are justified as a necessary consequence of human freedom. There was no way in which God could have created a good world without admitting such evils: 'In a word: nothing else was possible; evil had to be' (17:232).[13] However, his acceptance of Leibniz is not unconditional, for his notes also include a 'Comparison of Pope's system with [Leibniz's] optimism' in which Kant defends the 'superiority of [the] former' (17:233).[14]

Here, he takes issue with Leibniz's acknowledgement of evils in existence: 'Leibniz admitted that the irregularities and imperfections, which upset those who are of good disposition as if they were true ills [*Übel*], were indeed true ills' (17:233).[15] This is, in fact, Leibniz's Baylean inheritance with regard to physical evil, according to which whatever is experienced as an ill or evil *is* an evil. In my view, this is to Leibniz's credit, and makes his account more sophisticated than that of any theodicist who tries to explain away evils entirely.[16] Kant, at this stage at least, disagrees, and feels this is precisely the weakness of Leibniz's account. By giving undue weight to the 'absurdities and abhorrent irregularities' in the world, Leibniz effectively blocks any demonstration of God's existence from our 'contemplating the excellent arrangements which the world everywhere displays' (17:238). Instead of Leibniz's a priori optimism, which hinges on the assumption that God exists, Kant prefers Pope's a posteriori argument, which emphasises the goodness of creation and allows us to infer God's existence from it: 'Pope subjects the creation to detailed scrutiny,

12. All citations to Kant's three-manuscript 'Reflections' on optimism are to the English edition of Kant's *Theoretical Philosophy*, translated by David Walford and Ralf Meerbote (*TP*:77–83/17:229–39).

13. 'Kurtz. Es war nicht anders moglich, es musste Böses sein.' See below, *Objection ZW.1.b*, where Kant refutes this claim.

14. Note that Kant associates the term 'optimism' (*optimismus*) with Leibniz, not Pope.

15. I have adapted the translation and substituted 'ills' for 'imperfections', which is a better rendition for the German *Übel*, also considering Kant's other uses of this term. In general, Kant uses *Böse* for moral evils; *Übel* for physical evils (see below, n. 35).

16. Though recall that Leibniz, unlike Malebranche, refuses a positive ontology for evils: see chapter 1.

particularly where it most seems to lack harmony; and yet he shows that each thing, which we might wish to see removed from the scheme of greatest perfection, is also, when considered in itself, good.' Kant's approval is not muted: of all possible paths of 'rendering the beautiful proof of God's existence accessible to everyone', the one chosen by Pope is best, and this path constitutes 'the perfection of his system' (17:234). Taking the deist chain-of-being route means, furthermore, that no creature, no matter how miserable, has any ground for complaint, for existence justifies itself: to wish for a different or better nature (say, with better faculties of understanding or better inclinations) would be to wish not to exist at all, which no one could want. Therefore, 'let us listen with contempt [*mit Verachtung*] to the lamentations of those to whom, so they think, heaven has not granted a satisfactory share of perfections' (17:235–6).

It should be noted that these fragments were left unfinished and unpublished, and Kant would soon change his mind on this kind of demonstration of God's existence:[17] we should not, therefore, see these notes as Kant's considered view even at the time of writing. But a few years later, Kant did publish an essay titled 'An Attempt at Some Reflections on Optimism' (1759), in response to Daniel Weymann, one of his enemies at the University of Königsberg, who had argued against Leibniz's claim that there is a best of all possible worlds and this is our world. A mere day after Weymann defended his dissertation 'de mundo non optimo', Kant published his essay on optimism, in which he defended the notion that there must be one world more perfect than all the others, from which it follows naturally that this world is our world (since the notion that God would prefer a less perfect world to a more perfect one is nonsensical).[18] But the most striking feature of the essay is how adamantly Kant expresses his conviction that optimism is right:

> I am, accordingly, convinced, and perhaps some of my readers are convinced too. I am also happy to find myself a citizen of a world which could not possibly have been better than it is. Unworthy in myself but chosen for the sake of the whole by the best of all beings to be a humble member of the most perfect of all possible plans, I esteem my own existence the more highly, since I was elected to occupy a position in the best of schemes. To all creatures, who do not make themselves

17. Kant rejects the 'physico-theological' argument for God's existence (based on the perception of beauty and order in creation) in *The Only Possible Argument in Support of a Demonstration of God's Existence* (1763), and more definitively in the first *Critique*.

18. Kant published this essay as part of an advertisement of his upcoming lectures on 7 October 1759 (Kuehn, *Kant*, 122–4).

> unworthy of that name, I cry: 'Happy are we—we exist!' And the Creator is well pleased with us. (2:34–5)

Heil uns, wir sind!—if there is a pathos of optimism, it is this cheer of existence, this exultation in the sheer sentiment of being (as we have encountered in Rousseau). Optimism emerges here as the theory that rises up to meet us halfway: while it works theoretically, it is also right experientially, as it does justice to our experience of life. The sentiment is repeated in Kant's closing statement, a bold declaration for the optics of optimism:

> Measureless spaces and eternities will probably only disclose the wealth of the creation in all its extent to the eye of the Omniscient Being alone. I, however, from my viewpoint and armed with the insight which has been conferred upon my puny understanding, shall gaze around me as far as my eye can reach, ever more learning to understand that *the whole is the best, and everything is good for the sake of the whole.* (2:35; Kant's emphasis)

To take the cosmic perspective over the creaturely: we have heard such things before. The mood of the essay is very Popean, giving no weight or even thought to the miseries of existence, the experiential reality of which Leibniz at least was concerned to acknowledge. Like those optimists before him, Kant, at this point, does not allow for a negative value to existence or believe that non-existence can be preferable—hence the creature can have no complaint. Moreover, it does not sound as though the problem of evil and suffering is really a *problem* for Kant: convinced by the claims of optimism, he is mostly concerned to get the details right and position himself somewhere along the Leibnizian–Popean spectrum. Fair enough—but is that really *theodicy*?

The 1760s see Kant turning more attentively to the problem of evil, without it becoming a matter of deep concern for him. Ernst Cassirer and Susan Neiman have made much of Kant's comments on Newton and Rousseau, who together he appears to have credited with solving the problem of evil. The idea is that just as Newton's laws had explained physical evils (an effort Kant himself continued in his three essays on earthquakes, written shortly after Lisbon), Rousseau had explained moral evils by laying bare man's inner drives and untangling the origins of evil.[19] But while

19. See the end of chapter 6; for discussion, see Neiman's article 'Metaphysics, Philosophy'; Cassirer, *Rousseau*, 72. Kant's three essays on earthquakes (1:419–72) were published in 1756 and are mostly scientific in character.

Kant's fascination with Rousseau in particular is enduring, his optimism about the ability of human reason to solve the problem of evil is not so robust, and as we will see, the later Kant is both more equivocal about the quandaries of theodicy and more sensitive to the realities of evil.

Should there be any doubt that Kant changed his mind on optimism, we have the following testimony to enlighten us. Having asked Kant about the essay on optimism, Borowski (one of Kant's friends and earliest biographers) reports the following: 'Kant, with genuinely solemn seriousness bade me think no more of this work on optimism, urging me, should I ever come across it anywhere, not to let anyone have a copy but to withdraw it from circulation immediately'.[20] Could it be that part of Kant's embarrassment stems from the fact that he had published his essay on optimism in the very same year as Voltaire published *Candide*, which challenges precisely the kind of narrative Kant was offering there? Kant admired *Candide*, to such an extent that he closed his 1766 examination of Swedenborg's visions with 'the advice which *Voltaire* gave to his honest *Candide* after so many futile scholastic disputes: *Let us attend to our happiness, and go into the garden and work!*' (2:373; Kant's emphasis).[21] But Kant did not simply lose interest in optimism, or dismiss it as just another vain dispute. He returned to optimism, and to Leibniz, in the next phase of his engagement with theodicy, which takes us to the heart of the critical period.

A Last Attempt at Theodicy?

By the mid-1780s, Kant was thinking about evil again, in a variety of contexts. He had just published his first *Critique* (1781), and had turned his mind to ethics: at the same time, he was lecturing extensively at the University of Königsberg.[22] The central text in which he picks up the question of theodicy is one of his lectures on moral theology (hereafter 'the Lecture'), which he first gave in 1783–1784 and repeated several times in the

20. Translation cited from *TP*, lvi–lvii. See Borowski, *Darstellung des lebens und charakters Immanuel Kant's*, I, 58–9n. Borowski wrote this section in 1792 (Kuehn, *Kant*, 10) and in this footnote suggests this happened 'a few years ago'.

21. Kant, *Dreams of a Spirit-Seer Elucidated by Dreams of Metaphysics* (1766), in *TP* 301–60. This is not a direct quote from Voltaire's *Candide*, but rather a mixture of 'the sentiments of the Turk and of the philosopher *Martin*' (editorial footnote, *TP* 456n.).

22. In 1785, Kant published his *Groundwork of the Metaphysics of Morals*, followed in 1788 by the second *Critique*.

years that followed.[23] This text, however, is very close in orientation to the dialectic of the *Critique of Practical Reason* of 1788 (hereafter 'the Dialectic'), to such an extent that the two texts can and perhaps should be read side by side. In both works, Kant grounds the concept of God as a moral concept, one that is practically necessary. The basic idea is that while we are not justified in inferring the existence of God from our *experience* (an idea that Kant had long rejected), we *are* justified in assenting to the existence of God, complete with his moral attributes, for reasons of *morality*. The same applies to the doctrine of the immortality of the soul. Both doctrines feature as the *postulates of pure practical reason*, without which we would lack the incentive to act in accordance with the moral law.[24]

Why is this so? As Kant argues in the Lecture, the answer has everything to do with *misalignment*. Since in the present course of things, virtue or morality is not always connected with happiness, we would have no reason to make ourselves 'worthy of happiness through morality' unless there were a being that could ensure this happiness in a future state: 'there would be no incentives to act in accord with these duties as a rational human being if there were no God and no future world' (28:1073). The point is *not* that we need selfish reasons for moral actions, but that unless there were some deeper connection between happiness and virtue (the worthiness of happiness), the moral law itself would become a kind of lie. As Kant argues in the Dialectic, the highest good resides in this alignment between happiness and virtue: 'virtue and happiness together constitute possession of the highest good in a person, and happiness distributed in exact proportion to morality . . . constitutes the *highest good* of a possible world' (5:110–11; Kant's emphasis). But since this alignment is sorely lacking in the world we experience around us, it leads to a problem: the highest good appears to be practically impossible, and if this is so, then the moral law itself 'must be fantastic and directed to empty imaginary ends and must therefore in itself be false' (5:114). This apparent contradiction is what Kant calls the *antinomy of practical reason*.[25]

23. The text we have is a transcription (28:989–1126); published in English as *Lectures on the Philosophical Doctrine of Religion* (*RRT*, 338–451); I cite this translation.

24. Kant defines a postulate as 'a *theoretical* proposition, though one not demonstrable as such, insofar as it is attached inseparably to an a priori unconditionally valid *practical* law' (5:122). While the first element of the highest good (morality) leads to the postulate of immortality, the second element of the highest good (happiness proportioned to morality) leads to the postulate of the existence of God (5:124). Here, I focus on the doctrine of the existence of God.

25. Kant famously resolves the antinomy by distinguishing appearance from noumenon, similar to his resolution of the free-will problem.

The problem, in other words, is that while the moral law itself does not give 'the least ground' for a necessary connection between morality and happiness, we nevertheless require such a connection in our practical strivings: 'we *ought* to strive to promote the highest good (which must therefore be possible)'. But the highest good in the world, in which morality and happiness are aligned, is possible only on the assumption of a moral author of the world.[26] Hence 'it is morally necessary to assume the existence of God', though this moral necessity is strictly subjective: it is a need or requirement, *not* a duty (5:125). We require the concept of God as the author of a world possessed of the highest perfection ('the best world') in order to fulfil the tasks posed by our practical reason: 'He must be *omniscient* in order to cognize my conduct even to my inmost disposition in all possible cases and throughout the future, *omnipotent* in order to bestow results appropriate to it, and so too *omnipresent, eternal*, and so forth' (5:140).[27] The concept of God, therefore, belongs not to physics but to *morals* (5:138–40).[28]

Roughly the same point is made in the Lecture, but here Kant focuses rather on God's *moral* attributes:

> A being who is to give objective reality to moral duties must possess without limit the moral perfections of *holiness, benevolence and justice. These attributes constitute the entire moral concept of God.* They belong *together* in God, but of course *according to our representations* they have to be *separated from one another*. Thus through morality we recognise God as a *holy lawgiver*, a *benevolent sustainer of the world*, and a *just judge*. (28:1073; Kant's emphasis)

These three moral perfections (*holiness, benevolence, justice*) are only mentioned marginally in a footnote in the Dialectic (5:131n.), and yet they have a central role to play in both the Lecture and the theodicy essay (hereafter the Essay), to such an extent that Christoph Schulte suspects 'the manuscript of the lecture to have served Kant as a template for the

26. 'Consequently, the postulate of the possibility of the *highest derived good* (the best world) is likewise the postulate of the reality of a *highest original good*, namely of the existence of God' (5:125). On 'the best world', see also the Lecture (28:1098–9).

27. Note that here Kant uses the three traditional divine attributes (the three 'omni's') central to theodicy, whereas later he will focus purely on three of God's *moral* attributes. I will return to this below (pp. 295–97).

28. In contrast to his earlier reflections on Pope, Kant now rejects any inference of God's infinite perfections from what we know of the world, though he allows for the inference of an (imperfectly) wise, beneficent, powerful creator (5:139).

essay'.[29] Considering the tight conceptual continuity of both texts, it seems only likely that Kant had the former on his table while writing the latter. Most strikingly, both texts use the triad of God's moral attributes to present a triad of objections to theodicy, which in the Lecture, Kant still tries to resolve: 'Let us now look carefully at these objections ourselves and test our powers on them' (28:1077).

I will return to the Lecture's specific arguments when discussing the Essay below. For now, let me note a curious feature of these three texts (the Lecture, the Dialectic, and the Essay), which are deeply continuous in some ways, yet strangely disjointed in others. As such, we might see these three texts as tectonic plates, which partly overlap or converge but are also pressing against each other, causing tears, ruptures, and fault lines, with the result that the texts agree in some points and disagree in others, but don't always do so consistently. For instance, while all three texts have to do in some way with misalignment or disproportion, this is conceived in different ways: the Lecture and Dialectic focus on the misalignment between *virtue and happiness*, while the Essay focuses rather on the misalignment between *crime and punishment*. These two kinds of misalignment are often regarded by scholars as two sides of the same coin, a positive and negative side perhaps, but ultimately symmetrical. This may have been Kant's opinion in the Lecture, but it was no longer in the Essay, where Kant categorises both kinds of misalignment as a different class of evil.

Nor is the Essay always the odd one out. As mentioned above, the Dialectic pays little attention to the concept of God's justice (or any of the moral attributes), which is so crucial to both the Lecture and the Essay.[30] But the most remarkable contrast that emerges from these three texts is that the Lecture, for all its continuity with the others, still espouses Kant's earlier arguments for optimism, which the Dialectic, and especially the Essay, seem to reject entirely.[31] Indeed, in the Lecture, Kant seems to use the very same conceptual structure to defend his own theodicy as he uses in the Essay to prove the failure of *any* philosophical theodicy, whether past, present, or future.

29. Schulte, 'Zweckwidriges', 382 (my translation).

30. The Lecture does focus on God's justice, but with different questions in mind (in particular, a different kind of misalignment).

31. Its confidence, too, is marked: 'How happy we are that neither moral nor physical evil can shake our faith in one God who governs the world in accord with moral laws!' (28:1126).

The Essay on Theodicy

But how does one prove such a thing? According to Schulte, Kant sets up all the elements for his judgement on theodicy in the opening 'definition sentence' (*Definitionssatz*) of the Essay: 'By "theodicy" we understand the defense of the *highest wisdom* of the *creator* against the charge which *reason* brings against it for whatever is *counterpurposive* in the world' (8:255).[32] One term stands out, and not just for its awkwardness in English: throughout the essay, Kant contrasts that which is *counterpurposive* (*zweckwidrig*) with that which is *purposive* (*zweckmäßig*) in our experience of the world.[33] These, for Kant, are the umbrella terms for what earlier thinkers would have called the goods and ills of existence; and, in fact, he did not use the term *counterpurposive* in any substantial way before this time.[34]

Nor is this conceptual innovation a casual one. The Essay goes on to define three distinct kinds of counterpurposiveness (*Zweckwidrigkeit*), of which the first two kinds should not surprise us: they are moral evil (*Böse*) and physical evil (*Übel*),[35] or, in Kant's new framework, the 'absolutely' and 'conditionally counterpurposive' (8:256–7). According to Kant, moral evils can never be 'condoned or desired' by the divine wisdom 'either as end or means', while physical evils can coexist with the divine wisdom as means, though never as an end (8:256). This makes it sound as though Kant were still following the deists in conceiving physical evils as ineliminable aspects of the physical world, but he will later turn against this line of argument in so far as *the rational creature* is concerned: in other words, physical evil is unproblematic for Kant only in so far as it applies to *non-human suffering*. But if we were expecting Kant to deliver the Leibnizian triad of moral, physical, and *metaphysical evil*, this is not quite what we

32. Emphasis added based on what Schulte believes are the crucial elements of Kant's argument: Schulte, 'Zweckwidriges', 371.

33. I will use the English terms, while noting that *zweckwidrig* is not as awkward a term in German as 'counterpurposive' is in English.

34. Note that Kant does not use these terms in the Lecture. In the *Groundwork* and second *Critique* (*KpV*), Kant does begin to speak of what is *purposive* (*zweckmäßig*), but does not contrast this with counterpurposiveness. *Zweckwidrigkeit* thus seems to be a late arrival in Kant's conceptual framework: the first significant appearance I have found is in the third *Critique*, where Kant contrasts the purposive and counterpurposive (*KU*, 5:439).

35. See *KpV* 5:59–60, where Kant emphasises the usefulness of these German terms, in contrast to the ambiguous Latin *malum* (and *bonum*); and the 'Danzig' lecture, where Kant calls *Übel* 'the cause of physical repugnance', *Böse* 'the cause of moral repugnance' ('Danzig', 28:1286; my translation).

receive.[36] Kant does introduce a third kind of counterpurposiveness, but this is *not* Leibniz's metaphysical evil (the evil of limitation): rather, it has to do with a particular tension between the first two kinds of evils. If moral evils were crucially linked to physical evils as crime is linked to punishment, then this would still be a kind of 'purposiveness', and yet experience tells us this is not the case. Hence, the third kind of counterpurposiveness arises from 'the disproportion between crimes and penalties in the world': 'It is of this purposiveness in the world that one asks whether, in this respect, everyone in the world gets his due' (8:257). This is the disproportion I have designated throughout this book as *misalignment*—the suffering of the righteous as contrasted with the prosperity of the wicked—though as we will see, Kant here appears to be concerned mainly with the second kind.[37]

This new conceptual framework allows Kant to take a different approach to the question of theodicy, which he now formalises using two sets of categories: on the one hand, the three kinds of counterpurposiveness or *Zweckwidrigkeit* (hereafter *ZW.1*, *ZW.2*, and *ZW.3*); on the other, the three moral attributes of God: holiness, goodness (or benevolence), and justice. The originality of this, from the viewpoint of the wider history of theodicy, is striking. As in the Lecture, Kant chooses to rethink the problem of evil as a conflict *not* with the three 'omni's' (omnibenevolence, omniscience, and omnipotence), but with God's moral attributes alone, which Kant, in another departure from tradition, redefines as holiness, goodness, and justice.[38] There is no precedent for this: while Kant had drawn the definitions of holiness, goodness, and justice from Alexander Baumgarten's *Metaphysics*, these were only a few of the many perfections Baumgarten had attributed to God.[39] Kant, in contrast, insists on the coherence of the triad, arguing that the three moral attributes cannot be conceived in any other way, cannot be reduced to each other, and cannot even be reordered.[40] Thus he 'seems to be following his practice in the table of categories, which are arranged in triads, with the third member

36. Nor does the Lecture make use of metaphysical evil, though Alexander Baumgarten's *Metaphysics*, on which Kant drew heavily for his lectures, does.

37. This is not to say that the problem of misalignment is a new problem in the history of theodicy: far from it, but Kant seems to be the first to admit it into the central taxonomy of problems of evil.

38. Thus it appears that Kant unfolds the moral attribute of omnibenevolence (or perfect goodness) into three distinct attributes.

39. Baumgarten, *Metaphysics*, 300–9; the list includes attributes such as faithfulness, forbearance, sincerity, etc.; while holiness is discussed separately, at 286.

40. See also Kant's footnote in *KpV* 5:131n.

consisting in some sort of combination of the first two'.[41] The same seems to apply to the triad of counterpurposiveness.

The reason for this organisation becomes clear in what follows. In both the Lecture and the Essay, Kant opposes each kind of evil or counterpurposiveness to one of God's moral attributes (which in the Essay he relates in turn to God's distinct roles as creator, ruler, and judge).[42] Thus, to moral evils, he opposes God's *holiness* (*Heiligkeit*) in his capacity as law-giver and creator. To physical evils, he opposes God's *goodness* (*Gütigkeit*) in his capacity as ruler and preserver.[43] Finally, to misalignment, Kant opposes God's *justice* (*Gerechtigkeit*) in his capacity as judge (8:257; 28:1076–7).

In the latter contrast, there is an important difference between the two texts. In the Lecture, Kant conceives misalignment broadly as 'the unequal apportionment of good and evil in the world, standing in no community with morality' (28:1076–7), which applies both to the suffering (or lack of reward) of the righteous and the prosperity (or lack of punishment) of the wicked.[44] In the Essay, Kant narrows this down to a specific form of misalignment: namely, the disproportion between the deeds of the wicked and the punishment that befalls them. Only the prosperity of the wicked poses a problem for God's justice. In a footnote, often overlooked, he explains why this is so. The '*well-being* which does not befall the good' is not a problem for God's justice, since we have no right to expect rewards from God: 'one who only does what he owes can have no rightful claim on God's benevolence' (8:257n.).[45] The suffering of the righteous is then problematic only in so far as *any* suffering or physical evil experienced by a rational being is problematic, and so it falls squarely under the *second* kind of counterpurposiveness, posing an objection to God's *goodness*, but not to his justice.[46]

41. Wood and Di Giovanni, editorial footnote, *RRT*, 479n.

42. Again, see *KpV* 5:131n.

43. Again, Kant considers physical evil a problem only with regard to rational beings: he does not consider animal suffering (though he mentions it briefly in a footnote in *Religion*, 6:73n.).

44. And, in fact, Kant goes on to discuss both cases of misalignment: 28:1081.

45. In the Lecture, Kant defines justice as the '*limitation of benevolence by holiness*' (28:1074; his emphasis); see also *KpV* 5:131. That the prosperity of the wicked is very much at the forefront of Kant's mind in this period is underlined by his discussion of it on the first page of the *Groundwork* (4:393).

46. This point—that the two kinds of disproportions fall under different kinds of counterpurposiveness—is often neglected in the literature, which tends to treat both kinds as symmetrical (e.g. Schulte, 'Zweckwidriges', 382, 389; Brachtendorf 'Kants Theodizee-Aufsatz', 66; Neiman, 'Metaphysics', 158). This is not to say that the suffering of the

The threefold distinction of God's moral attributes allows Kant to organise the various avenues of theodicy under three heads, and three sets of tensions: between an aspect of experience and an aspect of God. Each tension gives way to a particular problem of evil, a fundamental objection to theodicy, which in turn is answered with three kinds of solution, each of which Kant either refutes or dismisses out of hand. I will go into these objections and Kant's discussion of them in some detail, to connect these with the wider theodicean tradition, but also to compare them to Kant's own earlier arguments. Reading Kant's essay on the failure of theodicy, in view of his earlier work, it is hard to escape the impression that his thoughts are folding in on themselves: that Kant is arguing with himself as much as, or more than, the wider tradition of theodicy. In what follows, therefore, I will discuss Kant's objections to past theodicies side by side with Kant's own theodicean efforts, until a picture emerges not only of the 'all-crushing' critic of metaphysics, but of a philosopher critiquing himself.[47]

ZWECKWIDRIGKEIT 1 (ZW.1): THE PROBLEM OF MORAL EVIL

The first objection to theodicy contrasts moral evil with God's holiness. Three traditional counter-arguments are considered, and rejected, by Kant.

ZW.1.a *We should not judge God's wisdom according to our own*

In a bold opening move, one of the most common lines of theodicean justification (and central to the Lutheran tradition) is dismissed out of hand. This is the argument that God's ways are not our ways; we cannot see into the divine wisdom, which operates according to 'totally different rules, incomprehensible to us'; things that may seem counterpurposive 'to our view of things' may yet be purposive 'when considered from the highest'.[48] Kant will have none of this: 'This apology, in which the vin-

righteous is not a serious problem of evil for Kant: it is (witness the discussion of Job that follows), but it is so for different reasons than apply to the prosperity (or lack of suffering) of the wicked.

47. Mendelssohn famously spoke of 'the all-crushing Kant'; see Kuehn, *Kant*, 251.

48. This view is central to not just the Lutheran tradition, but also the more Augustinian strands of Calvinism and the theologians of Port-Royal; in both cases, it is generally combined with an appeal to God's power (prioritised over his goodness or wisdom).

dication is worse than the complaint, needs no refutation; surely it can be freely given over to the detestation of every human being who has the least feeling for morality' (8:258).

Kant is not refuting himself here. It is true that the early essay on optimism had argued that theodicy requires a shift of perspective, and that things that seem bad to us may serve a greater or higher good, which is a central part of the optics of optimism. It is also true that the Lecture, which itself refers approvingly to the essay on optimism,[49] makes a clear-cut distinction between human and divine wisdom: 'the divine wisdom is distinguished from human wisdom not only in quantity but also in quality' (Lecture, 28:1058). But Kant's dismissal here, which is based on moral rather than theoretical grounds, only touches on the differentiation between two moral standards, not the notion of God's wisdom surpassing that of man (to which Kant will return in the course of the Essay). His indignation is aimed at the notion that God operates according to different *moral standards* than man. This can certainly not be the case: indeed, it is precisely on our morality that we must base our notion of the divine. The tradition rejected here is primarily that of his Lutheran contemporaries, and once this is out the way, the road is clear for Kant to tackle what he considers to be more interesting arguments: his own.

ZW.1.b *Moral evil could not be prevented because it is 'founded upon the limitations of the nature of human beings, as finite' (8:258–9)*

The second argument is central to the philosophical tradition of theodicy: we have encountered it in Leibniz but also in King, who was in turn channelled by the deists and especially Pope, who the early Kant so admired. Nor was this legacy long behind him, for Kant had himself made this argument in the Lecture: 'Evil is also *not a means to good*, but rather arises as a *by-product*, since the human being has to struggle with his own limits, with his animal instincts' (28:1078; his emphasis). And more elaborately:

> The possibility of deviating from the moral law must adhere to every creature. For it is unthinkable that any creature could be without needs and limits. God alone is without limitations. . . . If the human being is

49. In the context of the argument that 'the world created by God is the *best* of all possible worlds' (28:1097; Kant's emphasis).

> to be a free creature and responsible for the development and cultivation of his abilities and predispositions, then it must also be within his power to follow or shun the laws of morality. (28:1113)

Kant's rejection of this argument in the Essay is curt, but poignant: if evil were an inevitable side effect of our constitution, then 'the evil would thereby be justified, and, since it could not be attributed to human beings as something for which they are to be blamed, we would have to cease calling it "a moral evil."' (8:259). The point is casually made, but Kant here puts his finger on one of the central dilemmas of theodicy: How to harmonise God with evil, while ensuring that God is still God, and evil is still evil?

ZW.1.c *God does not cause but only permits evil as a human deed of freedom*

The same problem arises in the next theodicean strategy, closely related to the previous. Again, Kant himself had made this claim in the Lecture, and in fact he had done so at the end of the passage quoted above (*ZW.1.b*), suggesting again that Kant had the text of the Lecture in mind, or even before him on the table, while writing the Essay. In the Lecture, he explicitly argues that 'if God does not prevent evil in the world, this never sanctions evil; it only permits it' (28:1113). In the Essay, he rejects this argument for the same reason as the previous one: if even God is unable to prevent moral evil, this would mean that evil is not an evil at all, but merely an 'ill' rising from the 'necessary limitations of humanity as a finite nature', for which humanity cannot be blamed (8:259). These two refutations are as closely linked in the Essay as Kant's original arguments were in the Lecture.

His discussion of moral evil ends here, and what is perhaps most striking is not just that Kant's dismissal touches upon at least some of his earlier arguments (even some that he had proposed very recently), but that Kant does not seem very concerned with the problem of *moral evil*, dismissing the arguments in an effective but also off-the-cuff way. This is curious, considering not only that it may well have been moral evil that turned Kant's attention back to theodicy, but also that Kant would go on to write elaborately on moral evil in his later works.[50] In the Essay, however, Kant's

50. See below, pp. 317–18, for Sam Duncan's argument on Kant and Schmid.

philosophical engagement intensifies as he moves to the other kinds of counterpurposiveness, though his refutations remain uncommonly terse. The reason is that these are but the preliminaries to Kant's real argument, which seeks to close the book on theodicy as a whole, rather than get down into its finer details. Nevertheless, his refutations provide a fascinating cross-section of the state of theodicy at the end of the eighteenth century, not to mention of Kant's own philosophical state of mind. Next up is the problem of physical evil, where the central question is also that of pessimism: Is it true that evils outweigh the good of life? And if so, what to make of human suffering?

ZWECKWIDRIGKEIT 2 (*ZW.2*): THE PROBLEM OF PHYSICAL EVIL

This second objection to theodicy contrasts physical evil with God's goodness. By physical evil, Kant means *this-worldly* ills suffered by *rational* beings: the question of animal suffering does not arise for him, nor does the misery of the damned.[51] Instead, the first theodicean strategy that Kant tackles is the argument from suicide.

ZW.2.a *The goods of life outweigh the evils; if not, more would commit suicide*

According to this argument, which we have encountered in King and others,[52] it cannot be the case that ills preponderate in human life, since most people want to remain in existence, and there are only a few who are 'insane enough' to commit suicide; to which Kant adds that even those who do so 'simply pass over into the state of insensibility where pain as well cannot be felt' (8:259).[53] Kant had (to my knowledge) never himself made the argument from suicide, but in his early reflections on optimism

51. In the 1794 essay 'The End of All Things', Kant holds that we cannot judge the question of eternal damnation on theoretical grounds: however, he notes that if the damnation of even one person is accepted, this immediately constitutes a problem of evil: 'for why, one could ask, were even a few created—Why even a single individual?—if he is supposed to exist only to be rejected for eternity? For that is worse than never having been at all' (8:329). This is exactly Bayle's point against most of the Protestant tradition.

52. See especially chapter 2 for King's argument from suicide. I am uncertain as to Kant's source for this argument, which Leibniz himself does not mention.

53. Kant seems to take the traditional line in seeing suicide as a form of insanity: see his letter 'On the power of the mind to master its morbid feelings by sheer resolution' (1798, in *RRT*, 7:99).

he had upheld the prima-facie goodness of life ('Happy are we—we exist!'), and had preferred Pope over Leibniz precisely because the latter, even in his optimism, still gave too much weight to the evils of existence. By contrast, the Lecture is markedly more pessimistic. Just as Leibniz had made recourse to the possibility of angels and aliens on other globes, so too Kant argues that *the whole* of the world must encompass more than just this earth, where after all, the goods and evils seem to balance each other:

> For surely if our terrestrial globe were the whole world, it would be difficult to know it to be the best and to hold by this with conviction; for, to speak with sincerity, on this earth the sum of pain and the sum of good might just about *balance each other*. (28:1097; Kant's emphasis)[54]

The Essay goes one step further, repeating a point Kant had already made in the third *Critique* of 1790, that no one of sound mind would want to live again, even if they could choose the circumstances:

> But surely the reply to this sophistry [i.e. the argument from suicide] may be left to the sentence of every human being of sound mind who has lived and pondered over the value of life long enough to pass judgment, when asked, on whether he had any inclination to play the game of life once more, I do not say in the same circumstances but *in any other he pleases* (provided they are not of a fairy world but of this earthly world of ours). (8:259; my emphasis)[55]

Thus Kant replies to the argument from suicide by arguing that it is *completely self-evident* that life's evils outweigh the goods, and uses an extreme version of the Baylean thought experiment to back this up, apparently unaware of how counter-intuitive his conclusion was.[56]

Such ultra-Baylean bleakness would seem to bolster one scholar's reading of a deeply 'pessimistic' Kant,[57] but it should be recalled that, as Kant

54. But in the Lecture, Kant holds that physical evils such as pain are useful since they lead us to happiness, and that we are capable of making most ills 'harmless to ourselves' (28:1080–1). See again his letter 'On the power of the mind' on our ability to conquer depressive modes of being. Kant makes similar suggestions on the whole of the world in another lecture of 1784 ('Danzig', 28:1287).

55. For the same point in the *KU*, see 5:434 (discussed below, p. 327).

56. Schulte ('Zweckwidriges', 393) notes that this point was one of the first to be criticised by Kant's contemporaries.

57. Though Vanden Auweele in his *Pessimism in Kant's Ethics and Rational Religion* defines pessimism very narrowly, as having to do with 'one's given capacities and how these can navigate toward a desired end' (20). This is not quite the broader existential pessimism under discussion in this chapter.

makes clear in the *Critique*, this experiential pessimism is just the flipside of the deeper point that we should *not* measure the value of life by what we enjoy or suffer but by the worth of our actions. This, to some extent, is on a par with the existentialist response to Schopenhauer's pessimism, but it is not the point Kant is making in the Essay. Here, he is content to point out that the preponderance of evils is self-evident and completely intuitive: in so far as our *experience* goes, the pessimists are right.

ZW.2.b *The preponderance of evils stems from the nature of the animal creature*

The next strategy is another version of the limitation argument mentioned above (*ZW.1.b*), though here it is applied to *physical evils*. According to this line of argument, which is especially pronounced in the chain-of-being theodicies of King and Pope, 'the preponderance of painful feelings over pleasant ones cannot be separated from the nature of an animal creature such as the human being'[58] (8:260). Physical evils, in other words, are simply unavoidable, unless God had chosen to create a different being instead. Kant himself had argued along this line in his early essay and notes on optimism, and again in the Lecture, where he again rejected any kind of creaturely complaint:

> If one went so far as to ask why God created me, or humanity in general, this would certainly be *presumptuousness*, for it would be as much as to ask why God completed and joined together the great chain of natural things through the existence of a creature like the human being. Why did he not instead leave a *gap*? Why didn't God make the human being into an angel instead? But then would he have still been human? (28:1079)[59]

To wish to be relieved of moral and physical evils is to wish to be a different creature entirely, and this, to the Kant before the Essay, is something no one could want.

58. Here, Kant refers to Pietro Verri's 'book on the nature of pleasure', i.e. his *Sull'indole del piacere* of 1773.

59. Here, Kant is speaking of moral evils, but the argument applies to physical evils as well. In Kant's fragments on optimism, he explicitly espouses the idea of 'the chain of beings' (*die Kette der Wesen*); and argues that 'there is nothing at all which constitutes a greater defect for the world in general than for there to be a nothingness in some part or other of it' (17:235).

Now, Kant had rejected the *moral* limitation argument because it would remove human responsibility to the extent that evils would stop being evils (*ZW.1.b*). This does not apply for the *physical* limitation argument: ills are still ills even if they are unavoidable. It could of course be argued, as the early Kant had done in objection to Leibniz, that certain ills are only *apparent* ills, not *real* ills.[60] But the Kant of the Essay no longer wants to deny the reality of evils *or* the status of experience, which determines our estimate of them. In taking the problem of evil as seriously as he does, Kant is acknowledging that there is indeed something that experience tells us about the world that poses an objection to religion, to a moral vision of the world and its creator.[61] And the question Kant opposes to the physical limitation argument, here at the midway point of his discussion of theodicean strategy, is also the crucial question, underlying the entire discussion and each of the facets of theodicy: 'why the creator of our existence called us into life when the latter, *in our correct estimate*, is not desirable to us' (8:260; my emphasis).

It is the question Bayle too had asked: Why did God create us at all if the costs are so high to the creature?—How could God create even a single being whose life is not worth living? The answer that 'If God had created us differently, he would have created a different creature' is utterly worthless to a Baylean interlocutor (or, indeed, any entrenched pessimist), who would happily accept this consequence if it meant changing even slightly the horrific preponderance of moral *and* physical evils in the world.[62] In the very phrasing of this question, Kant again seems to come down on the side of the pessimists: not only does experience tell us that evils outweigh the goods, but this 'estimate' is also 'correct' (*nach unserm richtigen Überschlage*).[63] It should be noted, moreover, that while Kant's original framing of the problem of physical evil (*ZW.2*) suggested that this is a

60. See also 17:233, 17:238.

61. See Schulte, 'Zweckwidriges', 388–91, who points out the large role accorded to experience throughout the Essay.

62. In fact, later pessimists such as Cioran will speak with envy of what they perceive to be the better condition of animals; why could not man have been created thus? Dienstag (*Pessimism*, esp. chs. 4 and 8) appears to agree with this view, giving little weight on the many evils of animal existence.

63. Kant would have been familiar with the Baylean strand of pessimism through Leibniz's refutation, but also through Hume's *Dialogues* and Voltaire's *Candide*. But did Kant read Bayle? Probably yes, though the extent of his reading and processing of Bayle's thought remains unclear. For a few cursory discussions, see Rees, 'Kant, Bayle, and Indifferentism'; Boehm, *Kant's Critique of Spinoza*, 12; Ferrari, *Les sources françaises de la philosophie de Kant*, 91–9, 267–70.

problem of *providence*, in that it applies to God as ruler/preserver, it now appears that the problem of physical evil is, like that of moral evil, a problem of *creation*: the crucial question is how God was justified in *creating* us under these conditions in the first place.

ZW.2.c *We suffer now in preparation of future happiness, of which we become worthy through adversity*

The third justification has to do with the idea of otherworldly reward: we suffer now in preparation of future happiness, and 'we are to become worthy of that future glory precisely through our struggle with adversities' (8:260). While this argument is central to the Christian tradition, we have learned that it is not without costs: the risk of lending too much importance to heaven and salvation in establishing a theodicy is that it automatically raises questions with regard to hell and damnation—specifically, the misery of the damned.[64] This is a problem of which Kant is aware: thus the Lecture argues against the doctrine of predestination, which presupposes 'an *immoral* order of nature', according to which certain beings would be necessarily unworthy of blessedness: 'these unfortunates would be *sacrifices* to *misery*' (28:1116; his emphasis). A similar sentiment arises in the Essay, where Kant objects to the notion that every single being must *necessarily* suffer in order to be worthy of happiness:

> But, that before the highest wisdom this time of trial (to which most succumb, and in which even the best is not happy about his life) must without exception be the condition of the joy eventually to be savored by us, and that it was not possible to let the creature be satisfied with every stage of his life—this can indeed be pretended but in no way can there be insight into it; in this way one can indeed cut the knot loose through an appeal to the highest wisdom which willed it, but one cannot untie the knot, which is what theodicy claims to be capable of accomplishing. (8:260)

Two things are curious about this dismissal. First, Kant is explicitly rejecting only a very specific version of the adversity argument: namely, the idea that every creature, *without exception*, must suffer as a condition of its eventual joy. Second, Kant seems to be dismissing the argument mainly on procedural grounds: that is, he dismisses the argument as

64. This is why King and Leibniz are so ambivalent about eternal damnation; see chapter 2.

not really an argument, as a way of cutting the knot rather than untying it, when it is precisely this untying that 'theodicy claims to be capable of accomplishing'.[65]

But it could be asked in response whether 'cutting a knot' is not precisely what Kant's own postulates of practical reason are meant to accomplish. These postulates, after all, do not *prove* the existence of God or the immortality of the soul, but they do *justify* our belief in these doctrines on moral grounds, which are also rational grounds. So perhaps Kant's objection is directed not so much at the content of the argument as at the claim underlying it: *the claim that this argument could untie the theodicean knot*. The view that adversity makes us worthy of happiness may not be entirely mistaken, but the point is that it's not really a *theodicy*, or at least not a philosophical or doctrinal one: it does not prove anything about the connection between the highest wisdom and the evils of existence; it does not give us insight—it cuts the knot rather than untying it. Then again, perhaps cutting the knot is precisely what we should be after, as long as we do so in the right way, without exceeding our epistemic boundaries. The question remains, then, whether Kant is closing the door firmly on this line of argument, or whether he is leaving it ever so slightly ajar. I will return to this question shortly: first, we must turn to the third kind of counterpurposiveness, and the problem of misalignment.

ZWECKWIDRIGKEIT 3 (*ZW.3*): THE PROBLEM OF MISALIGNMENT

The third objection to theodicy contrasts misalignment with God's justice. In a footnote, Kant comments that this is the theodicean problem that 'imposes itself on the mind' most powerfully, which is why, on the rare occasion that 'an unjust, especially violent, villain does not escape unpunished from the world, then the impartial spectator rejoices, now reconciled with heaven'. Why should these rare instances of poetic justice evoke such strong feelings in us, and 'make us detect God's hand' in the dealings of life? 'Because nature is here moral, uniquely in a way that we can hope but rarely to perceive in the world' (8:260). But just as the experience of alignment reconciles us with God, so too the experience of misalignment

65. Bayle (who uses the metaphor of the Gordian knot in *Paulicians*[2]*.M*) would go further and argue that the argument runs up against God's omnipotence: if God wanted humanity to be saved, he (being omnipotent) could have brought us to that state from the beginning. But Kant is not as concerned with omnipotence as earlier thinkers: he frames the problem of evil in terms of God's *moral* attributes alone.

confronts us most forcefully with the counterpurposiveness of things.[66] Again, three justifications of such misalignment are considered.

ZW.3.a *The depraved are punished even in this world by reproach of conscience*

The first response to the problem of misalignment denies the premise: 'The pretension that the depraved go unpunished in the world is ungrounded, for by its nature every crime already carries with it its due punishment, inasmuch as the inner reproach of conscience torments the depraved even more harshly than the Furies' (8:261). This is perhaps the clearest instance of Kant refuting his own arguments, since this is the very point Kant had made in the Lecture (when discussing misalignment as an objection to God's justice). There, Kant had argued that, 'If we investigate this closely we find that the disproportion between [good conduct and well-being] is not really so large'. On the outside, it may indeed seem that the wicked prosper, but if we were to look within we would see that they were torn apart by their conscience: 'The restlessness of his conscience torments him constantly, agonizing reproaches torture him continually, and all his apparent good fortune is really only self-deceit and deception' (28:1081). In the Essay, Kant objects to this argument as resting on a faulty psychology, in which the virtuous project their own experience of conscience onto the wicked: 'here the virtuous man lends to the depraved the characteristic of his own constitution'. In reality, such pangs of conscience may be wholly or mostly absent from the mind of the truly depraved, or compensated 'abundantly' by the sensual pleasures afforded by the crime (8:261).[67] The supposed torments of conscience, then, can offer no solution to the problem of misalignment.

ZW.3.b *Sufferings enhance the value of virtue*

If we do accept what experience tells us about the misalignment 'between guilt and punishment in this world', we might yet reply with a version of the adversity argument mentioned above (*ZW.2.c*), and argue that 'it is a property of virtue that it should wrestle with adversities', 'among which is the pain that the virtuous must suffer through comparison of his own

66. Kant's 'Danzig' lecture of 1784 calls this the 'most popular' objection against God's moral attributes (28:1287; my translation). See chapter 8 for Schopenhauer's comments on poetic (in)justice.

67. See chapter 4 for La Mettrie's view on regret and conscience.

unhappiness with the happiness of the depraved' (8:261).[68] According to this line of thought, central to the Christian interpretation of the Book of Job, 'sufferings only serve to enhance the value of virtue', so that 'this dissonance of undeserved ills resolves itself before reason into a glorious moral melody' (8:261). Such a moral melody was precisely what the Lecture had been trying to achieve. Having used the 'bad conscience' argument on the wicked, in the Lecture Kant suggests that the suffering of the righteous provides them with the occasion to exercise their virtue, for if all good conduct were rewarded by this-worldly happiness, then we would be motivated solely by self-interest: 'If there were no disproportion at all between morality and well-being here in this world, there would be no opportunity for us to be truly virtuous' (28:1081). Again, the textual closeness of the Essay and the Lecture is striking, with the former refuting the very arguments that had been made side by side in the latter (*ZW.3.a* and *ZW.3.b*).

To his earlier argument, Kant now raises the following objection. The justification by virtue would only work *if* at the end of life, virtues were indeed rewarded and crimes punished, for otherwise 'the suffering seems to have occurred to the virtuous, not *so that* his virtue should be pure, but *because* it was pure', which is 'the very opposite of the justice of which the human being can form a concept for himself' (8:261–2). This point is similar to Kant's response to the adversity argument (*ZW.2.c*): to justify evils by this road would create a necessary connection between virtue and suffering, and that is indeed the 'opposite' of justice. But if experience tells us (as Kant affirms) that we cannot expect to be rewarded for our efforts at the end of *this* life, what about the possibility of a *future* life? Kant dismisses this line of argument in the same way as he had done before (*ZW.2.c*): 'such a possibility cannot count as *vindication* of providence; rather, it is merely a decree of morally believing reason which directs the doubter to patience but does not satisfy him' (8:262). Again, to refer to a future life does not untie the theodicean knot, it merely cuts it through, and as such is not properly a *theodicy* at all, or at least not a *doctrinal* one.[69] And again, it seems that Kant, in closing this road, is not blocking it altogether. After all, he had suggested that *if* we can be somehow justified in believing that virtue is indeed rewarded in the end, then our

68. Note that here Kant does include the suffering of the righteous as a problem of the third kind of counterpurposiveness (*ZW.3*), where earlier he placed it under the second kind (*ZW.2*); the reason may well be that he is following the Lecture here, in which the two kinds are symmetrical.

69. On this distinction between doctrinal and authentic theodicy, see below, pp. 310–11.

sufferings might after all carry a deeper meaning, which may reconcile us to the divine wisdom. It is true that such a belief, in so far as it incorporates a future life, can only be a 'decree of morally believing reason'—but what if this kind of decree is exactly what we should be aiming for in dismantling philosophical theodicy?

ZW.3.c *In a future world, a different order of things will obtain*

Kant's final objection to theodicy focuses specifically on the claim that misalignment in this world will be compensated in the next: 'in a future world a different order of things will obtain instead, and each will receive that which his deeds here below are worthy of according to moral judgment' (8:262). This is a view as crucial to Leibniz, with his notion of a *City of God*, as it had been to most of the Christian tradition—but less so to the deists, who staked everything on proving *this-worldly* alignment. Kant himself, in the Lecture, had argued that we should conceive of divine justice as justice *within* the order of nature, since there is already alignment within creation:

> This justice within the order of nature consists in the fact that God has already laid down in the course of things and in his plan for the world, the way in which a human being's state will be proportioned to the degree of morality he has attained. *Well-being is inseparably combined with good conduct, just as punishment is combined with moral corruption.* Moral perfection in this life will be followed by moral growth in the next, just as moral deterioration in this life will bring a still greater decline of morality in that life. (28:1084–5; my emphasis)[70]

In the Essay, Kant rejects any claim to other-worldly realignment on roughly the same grounds as he did the adversity argument (*ZW.2.c*) and the justification by virtue (*ZW.3.b*): as 'arbitrary'. Here, however, he goes into more detail:

> unless reason, as a faculty of *moral legislation*, is pronouncing a decree in accordance with this legislative interest, it must find it probable, according to the mere laws of *theoretical cognition*, that the way of the world determines our fates in the future just as it does here, according

70. I think it likely that the later Kant would be uncomfortable with his own language here, since according to his own principles, he should limit himself to justifying assent on practical grounds rather than stating these beliefs outright.

> to the order of nature. For what else does reason have as a guide for its *theoretical conjecture* except natural law? (8:262; my emphasis)

Here, Kant is drawing a contrast, well known from the *Critiques*, between two functions or faculties of reason: *moral-practical* and *theoretical-speculative*. In so far as theodicy is making *theoretical* claims, it must also adhere to the dictates of theoretical reason, and this does not allow us to make wild conjectures about the state of a future world. Even if we are permitted the hope of a future life, we have to found our rational expectations on what we know in *this world*: we have no reason to expect that in a future order different laws will obtain, or that there will be better alignment in the unknown world when there is none in the world we know. Such alignment, in other words, 'is just as little to be expected there as here' (8:262).

But again, there is something equivocal about Kant's rejection, as though one hand was closing the door that the other hand was inching open. Note, for instance, the caveat in the passage just quoted: '*unless reason*, as a faculty of moral legislation, is pronouncing a decree in accordance with this legislative interest' (my emphasis). As before, Kant seems to be hinting at a moral decree that might yet apply at the very point at which theoretical reason runs up against its limits. In the Dialectic and elsewhere, Kant allows the belief in a future order on moral-practical grounds, but not on speculative-theoretical ones (5:122–4). The question is: Could the same be true for the belief in eventual *alignment*?

FAILING AT THEODICY

Kant's discussion of traditional theodicy ends here, but not before Kant delivers what Schulte calls the *Resultatssatz*, or 'result sentence', of the proceedings:

> Every previous theodicy has not performed what it promised, namely the vindication of the moral wisdom of the world-government against the doubts raised against it on the basis of what the experience of this world teaches—although, to be sure . . . neither can these doubts prove the contrary. (8:263)[71]

But although Kant believes to have shown that all *previous* theodicies have failed, it might still be the case that *future* theodicies will do better.

71. See Schulte, 'Zweckwidriges', 381; and see *KpV* 5:143: the postulates cannot be *proven* by speculative reason, but nor can they be *refuted*.

The final step Kant now wants to take is to close the book on not only past theodicies, but on any future attempt. This can only be done by proving 'that our reason is absolutely incapable of insight' into the relationship between the experiential world and the divine wisdom: by demonstrating 'the necessary limitation of what we may presume with respect to that which is too high for us' (8:263). Briefly, Kant argues that from observing the arrangement of things in the sensible world, we have the concept of an 'artistic wisdom', and from observing our own moral faculty, we have the concept of a 'moral wisdom', both of which point to the possibility of a perfect creator of the world: 'But of the *unity in the agreement* in a sensible world between that artistic and moral wisdom we have no concept; nor can we ever hope to attain one' (8:263; Kant's emphasis). There is no way for reason to establish that God is morally active in the sensible world: this is 'an insight to which no mortal can attain'. Hence even all *future* philosophical trials in theodicy are doomed to fail (8:264).

The argument is shrewd, but its placement is peculiar. For one thing, the argument, if successful, makes all of the previous discussion redundant: if every attempt at theodicy is doomed to fail, then by definition this applies to past theodicies as well. For another, the argument reads like a closing statement: everything seems to come to a halt once these final words are spoken. After all, Kant has already developed his case for the failure of all rational theodicy: he has made his argument; he has proven his point—he could just have ended there. In many ways, it would have been the most natural way to end the Essay. Instead, after what seems like a full stop, the Essay reopens and veers off into a different direction, almost as though it were written not from beginning to end, but from two directions, from the beginning and from the ending, like two separate essays meeting in a curious gap in the middle. I don't mean to say that the two parts aren't related—they are—but that they also seem to be doing something quite different. For the first part closes the book on philosophical theodicy, whereas the second part continues at some length to explore one last theodicean route: that of authentic theodicy and the Book of Job.

JOB'S AUTHENTIC THEODICY

In the second part of the essay, Kant introduces a distinction between two kinds of theodicy, one doctrinal and one authentic (where the term *authentic* relates to originality, similar to an authentic legal document as opposed to a mere copy).[72] Doctrinal theodicy is when we see the world as a publication of God's purposes and we try to infer God's will from his work. Authentic theodicy is when God 'becomes himself the interpreter of his will' *through our reason*, by which we form our concept of God as a moral and wise being (8:264). This is the kind of theodicy that Kant reads (allegorically) in the Book of Job.

In itself, the appearance of Job in an essay on theodicy is nothing surprising: the Book of Job has echoed down the centuries as one of the most powerful narratives of suffering, and as one of the templates for framing the problem that it poses. After a temporary lull in theodicean interpretations of Job in the seventeenth century, the eighteenth century turns back to Job with a vengeance. Various scholars have remarked upon the 'Job revival' of the eighteenth century: a powerful shift in intensity and scope, spurring new publications, translations, and paraphrases, especially in Germany and England.[73] One might add to this a shift of orientation: a Job 'reinvention', so to speak. I have to be tentative, but I believe it could be argued that there is a kind of thematic turn, from *repentance* to *perseverance*, in the Enlightenment's interpretations of the Book of Job. What I mean is that earlier interpretations emphasised the theme of Job as, somewhat paradoxically, both patient *and* repentant: Job's virtue is proven by his repentance combined with his restoration, which ensures that both God and Job (and perhaps even his friends, for Job did in the end have something to repent of) are ultimately justified.[74] As opposed to this, the eighteenth century invents a heroic or tragic Job who stays true and stands tall, over and against the hypocrisy of his friends. As Job's restoration sheds its importance,[75] a change of emphasis occurs: refracted

72. Shell, 'Kant's Secular Religion', 26. Kant uses the term 'authentic' in other writings of the period, always in contrast to 'doctrinal' and always in reference to the interpretation of Scripture: see *The Conflict of the Faculties* (1798), 7:48, 7:66–7; and *Religion*, 6:114.

73. See Sheehan, *The Enlightenment Bible*, 160–76, and 'The Poetics and Politics of Theodicy'; Lamb, *The Rhetoric of Suffering*; Neiman, *Evil in Modern Thought*, 17–19. A similar development cannot, it seems, be claimed for France; thus Schwarzbach ('The Eighteenth Century Confronts Job', 142) remarks upon 'the rather limited appreciation of the book of Job' among French Enlightenment figures.

74. For one example, see William Sherlock's *A Discourse Concerning the Divine Providence* of 1694, who quells providential objections regarding Job's afflictions by pointing to his rewards and restoration.

75. A shift perhaps connected with developments in biblical criticism: in 1737, Albert Schultens (*Liber Jobi*) suggested that both prose parts of Job are later additions: not only the Prologue (as had been argued before by Richard Simon in his *Histoire Critique* of 1678), but also the Epilogue, which includes Job's restoration. The same idea is floated

through the myriad pages written on Job are no longer his patience or his repentance so much as his indignation, his integrity, and his pious perseverance, even in the face of his creator.[76] It is the 'rhetoric of suffering' (Lamb) or 'poetics of theodicy' (Sheehan) that command the imagination now: the grit and fervour of Job's authentic crying out to God.[77]

But however prominent the question of Job was in the eighteenth century, Kant himself had not offered any significant discussion of Job in his philosophical writings before the Essay. And yet the story of Job seems to have held an attraction to him for some years. The first real sign of this fascination appears in a letter from 1775, where Kant, in response to a query by Johann Casper Lavater, explicitly identifies himself with Job:

> You ask for my opinion of your discussion of faith and prayer. Do you realize whom you are asking? A man who believes that, in the final moment, only the purest candor [*die reineste Aufrichtigkeit*] concerning our most hidden inner convictions can stand the test and who, like Job, takes it to be a crime to flatter God [*Gott zu schmeichlen*] and make inner confessions, perhaps forced out by fear, that fail to agree with what we freely believe. (10:175–6)[78]

Furthermore, while the Lecture discussed throughout this chapter does not mention Job, another lecture of 1784 does. Having again formalised the problem of evil according to the threefold schema of moral evil, physical evil, and misalignment, here Kant writes that the Book of Job, 'the most philosophical book in the Old Testament', aims at the same goal as Leibniz's *Theodicy*: to refute objections relating to God's holiness, goodness or justice ('Danzig', 28:1287; my translation).

The two key elements of Kant's interest in Job thus seem to be *sincerity* (as the opposite of hypocrisy) and *the problem of evil*—and both elements are combined in a remarkable fragment, little noted in the literature, from Kant's manuscript *Nachlass*. In this fragment, written around 1783–1784,

---

in 1695 by John Toland in a letter sent to unnamed 'Reverend' (in *A Collection of Several Pieces*, II, 315–6).

76. See Lamb, *Rhetoric*, 117–18. See also Neiman (*Evil*, 17), who overstates the point somewhat: 'Sometime during the Enlightenment, commentators stopped looking for ways in which Job's torments could be justified. . . . Earlier writers identified with Job's friends, the theodicy-makers who found justification. Later ones identified with Job, who found none.'

77. Lamb, *The Rhetoric of Suffering*; Sheehan, 'The Poetics and Politics of Theodicy'.

78. All letters cited from Arnulf Zweig's translation (*Correspondence*) unless otherwise stated.

Kant expresses both apprehension and admiration for the kind of spirit exemplified by Hume (presumably in the *Dialogues*) and Job:

> The reader feels a certain timid apprehension about getting involved with Hume's considerations and objections, which seem to express presumptuousness. At the same time there is something noble, sincere and unhypocritical [*etwas edles, aufrichtiges und ungeheucheltes*] which shines forth from the effort to undertake judgment without slavish fearfulness, like Job. Not in order to condemn God's ways, but in order to confess one's qualms to oneself undisguisedly, without allowing oneself to be seduced into suppressing these and uttering flattering praises instead, out of the fear of becoming disrespectful, as was the case with Job's friends. (18:445–6; my translation)

The same elements are crucial for understanding the second part of Kant's Essay, which develops these thoughts in greater depth.

Like Voltaire's *Candide*, which Frederick the Great would call 'Job in modern dress' (*Job habillé à la moderne*),[79] Job's tale is one of the highest happiness followed by the deepest misery—or perhaps not *quite* the deepest. Kant underlines Job's many blessings, all but one of which are taken away from him:

> He was healthy, well-to-do, free, master over others whom he can make happy, surrounded by a happy family, among beloved friends—and on top of all of this (what is most important) *at peace with himself in a good conscience.* A harsh fate imposed in order to test him suddenly snatched from him all these blessings, *except the last.* (8:265; my emphasis)

All that is left to Job is his good conscience. And yet, besieged as he is by God, Job is pressured by his friends to declare his guilt and to confess that he must have a bad conscience: after all, had he truly been innocent, why would God strike him down? Thus 'Job's friends declare themselves for that system which explains all ills in the world from God's *justice*, as so many punishments for crimes committed' (8:265; Kant's emphasis). By contrast, Job himself stands by his innocence, and 'declares himself for the system of *unconditional divine decision*': God does as he wills (8:265; Kant's emphasis).[80] But the importance, for Kant, lies not so much in the

79. Frederick II to Voltaire, 28 April 1759, *D*7554.
80. See Job 23:13.

divergence of opinions between Job and his friends as it does in the 'spirit' or character [*der Character*] of the two sides of the debate:

> Job speaks as he thinks, and with the courage with which he, as well as every human being in his position, can well afford; his friends, on the contrary, speak as if they were being secretly listened to by the mighty one, over whose cause they are passing judgment, and as if gaining his favour through their judgment were closer to their heart than the truth. (8:265)

Kant thus contrasts the 'malice' (*Tücke*) of the friends with Job's 'frankness' (*Freimütigkeit*), which is 'so far removed from false flattery as to border almost on impudence' (8:265–6). As a result, Job has all the appearances against him, his friends seeming to project 'greater speculative reason and pious humility', so that any dogmatic institution (such as a synod or inquisition) would surely have found against him (8:267).[81] Nevertheless, God ultimately finds in favour of Job and against his friends, *not* because one side is more in the right doctrinally—Kant notes that Job too 'admits having hastily spoken about things which are too high for him'—but because Job's position is the more *conscientious* one: 'God finds against his friends, for (as conscientiousness goes) they have not spoken as well of God as God's servant Job' (8:267). From this, we can conclude that

> only sincerity of heart [*Aufrichtigkeit des Herzens*] and not distinction of insight; honesty [*Redlichkeit*] in openly admitting one's doubts; repugnance to pretending conviction where one feels none, especially before God (where this trick is pointless enough)—these are the attributes which, in the person of Job, have decided the pre-eminence of the honest man [*des redlichen Mannes*] over the religious flatterer in the divine verdict. (8:267)

Hence, Job is represented as full of doubts, but as fully sincere of heart, since he refuses to 'pretend conviction where he feels none', and since he openly admits his doubts. He may well be wrong, and his friends, who hold the more convincing *theoretical* position (at least superficially so), may be right, but God prefers Job for the purity of his intentions, his resistance to hypocrisy.[82] The crucial verse, for Kant, is Job 27:5, where Job

81. The allusion to contemporary religious institutions, which were becoming increasingly stringent in imposing censorship, would not have gone unnoticed by Kant's readers.

82. The Lecture also rejects flattery (*Schmeichelei*): 28:1117.

'in the midst of his strongest doubts, could yet say': 'Till I die I will not remove mine integrity from me' (8:267).

Kant's reprise of Job's trials constitutes more than an evaluation of Job: it is a challenge to the deeply rooted ethic that is implicit in much of traditional theodicy. After all, a long line of theodicean thought had dismissed as presumptuous or ungrateful any challenges or doubts or complaints with regard to God's responsibility for evils: from Job's friends accusing Job of presumption, to King and Leibniz reproving authors such as Bayle for ingratitude, to the early Kant himself suggesting that we 'listen with contempt' to lamentations where gratitude is due.[83] Kant now turns this around and comes instead with a radically different valuation of the Baylean complaint. Doubt is not the problem, says Kant: we should be infinitely more concerned about religious falseness, flattery, and hypocrisy, which constitute a danger to faith as much as they do to character, to integrity and personhood, to the very morality of a nation. If religious professions are extorted from people, as by requiring theology students to profess their faith by formal oaths,[84] this will serve only to create a nation of flatterers and hypocrites—the antidote for which lies in religious toleration, but also in an ethic that values sincerity and integrity over the ownership of objective truth, especially when such ownership cannot be rationally defended.

Those who dare lay bare their doubts towards God—a Bayle, a Hume, a Job—should therefore not be detested but *admired* for their integrity in not speaking according to their interests, no matter how uncomfortable this integrity may make us. The example of Job proves that a 'trial' against God, in which objections are brought forward against his goodness or wisdom, need not be 'presumptuous or sacrilegious', but can be carried out with 'with a sincere attitude' (23:85). To stand by such integrity, even in the shadow of doubt, is better than hypocritically praising God when the heart says otherwise.[85] Doubt, even religious doubt,

83. See again 17:235–6. At the end of 'Conjectures' (1786), Kant does criticise those who express discontent with providence, not because this is ungrateful but because it discourages us from trying to improve ourselves (8:120–23/*PW*, 231–4). In the Essay, then, Kant is not saying he approves of discontent *qua* discontent, but as the sincere expression of the creaturely complaint.

84. This was only one of the new strictures imposed by the new regime of Frederick William II; Kant was deeply opposed to any such 'spiritual torture' (8:268–9n.), a concern that echoes throughout the Essay. On the historical background, see Wood's introduction (*RRT*, xv–xxii); Shell, *Kant and the Limits of Autonomy*, 187–8; Kuehn, *Kant*, chapter 8.

85. Kant makes this point in his first sketches of the theodicy essay: see the 'Vorarbeit' from the *Nachlass* (23:83–5), written ca. 1790–1791.

is for Kant not a negative thing, as long as it is authentically held and sincerely expressed.[86] Nor does it preclude real moral faith: rather, it's insincerity and dogmatism that are the true enemies of religion.[87] Just as our actions have moral worth only when they are done from duty,[88] so too religious belief has moral worth only if it is sincerely held. Sincerity, in other words, is what gives faith its value. This is why Kant objected to religious oaths as well as to prayer, holding firm to his position that expressions of faith or devotion are meaningless if they are obtained by extortion or expressed with some ulterior motive in mind.[89] In a lengthy 'Concluding Remark', Kant develops these questions further (in particular, in relation to oath-taking), so that what has begun as an essay on theodicy ends as an essay on sincerity. The crucial virtues, in matters of faith, are those of *sincerity* and *honesty* (*Aufrichtigkeit* and *Redlichkeit*): 'sincerity in taking notice of the impotence of our reason', and 'honesty in not distorting our thoughts in what we say, however pious our intention' (8:267). It is better to doubt sincerely than to express a truth half-heartedly.[90]

BUT IS IT THEODICY?

We seem to have come a long way from the problem of evil, and indeed towards the end of the Essay, when Kant starts talking at length about lies and self-deception, we may wonder whether this is at all pertinent to the question of *theodicy*. This seems to be the reason why much of the scholarship focuses on the first part of the essay, which closes the book on theodicy, rather than the second part, with its strange foray into questions of

86. See also *KU* 5:472–3 on the contrast between unbelief (*Unglaube*) and dubiety (*Zweifelglaube*); the latter, according to Brachtendorf ('Kants Theodizee-Aufsatz', 82) is Job's kind of faith.

87. See Kant's letter to Johann Gottlieb Fichte, 2 February 1792 (11:321–3), where Kant contrasts dogmatic faith with moral faith, which does not preclude doubt (11:322).

88. Kant, *Groundwork*, 4:393–405.

89. See the fragment from the *Nachlass* cited above (p. 313), as well as Kant's letter to Lavater, both of which mention Job, as well as the 'Vorarbeit', which notes that Job 'made the most conscientious honesty [*die gewissenhafteste Redlichkeit*] the principle of all his expressions of faith' (23:85).

90. This again is a very Baylean point: see my article 'The Left Hand of the Enlightenment', which compares themes of error and sincerity in Kant and Bayle. In his final years, Kant seems to have been obsessed with questions of truth, truthfulness, sincerity, and (self-)deception; this new fascination forms a crucial background to his reply to Maria von Herbert's letter.

truth and truthfulness, and its idiosyncratic use of the Book of Job.[91] And yet Kant himself thought these topics (and the two parts of essay) crucially related, by the concepts of doctrinal and authentic theodicy. After all, the key elements of Job's significance for Kant—*theodicy* and *sincerity*—are also the key themes of the Essay, with Job the hinge between the two. This linkage does not strike me as an accidental one. It suggests that the problem of evil can add to our understanding of religious sincerity—but also that the topic of sincerity can add to our understanding of the problem of evil. It is now time to gather all these elements, and turn back to the puzzle set in this chapter: what to make of Kant's argument about the impossibility of theodicy, and more specifically, of the strange mixture of continuities and discontinuities between the Essay and the Lecture, written only seven years earlier? Here are a few possibilities.

According to Schulte and others, it is clear that Kant changed his mind between the Lecture and the Essay.[92] While Kant still defended a doctrinal theodicy in the Lecture and other writings, he rejects *any* kind of philosophical theodicy in the Essay, leaving only the option of fideism, which is the point of bringing in the Book of Job—to show that any answer to the problem of evil can only be a fideistic one: 'All that remains is the wager of faith.'[93] In other words, when Kant speaks of *authentic* theodicy, this is not *really* theodicy at all, at least not of the *philosophical* kind.[94] As for *why* Kant changed his mind so radically, Sam Duncan has recently argued that this has to do with the publication in 1790 of a treatise by Carl Christian Eberhard Schmid, 'an early expositor and popularizer of Kant's work', who (unintentionally) offered a kind of *reductio ad absurdum* of Kant's argument on moral evil.[95] Following Kant's arguments to what he believed was their logical conclusion, Schmid ended up over-explaining moral evil, to such an extent that humanity would no longer be responsible

91. But see Pihlström and Kivistö, *Kantian Antitheodicy*, for an emphatic exposition of precisely the Joban part.

92. See especially Schulte, 'Zweckwidriges', and Duncan, 'Moral Evil', but note that both offer different explanations for this change.

93. Cavallar, 'Kants Weg von der Theodizee zur Anthropodizee und retour', 102; Schulte, 'Zweckwidriges', 392—both are criticised by Brachtendorf, 'Kants Theodizee-Aufsatz', 65.

94. In fact, according to Pihlström and Kivistö (*Kantian Antitheodicy*, 48), Kant's 'authentic theodicy' would more rightly be termed an 'antitheodicy'. While I am sympathetic to their argument, I cannot quite agree in their pitching Kant against theodicy *tout court*; for reasons that will become clear towards the end of this chapter.

95. Duncan, 'Moral Evil', 974, discussing Schmid, *Versuch einer Moralphilosophie* (1790).

for evil, so that evil would stop being just that—*evil.* This is exactly the kind of argument that Kant opposes, *twice*, in his discussion of the problem of moral evil (see *ZW.1.b* and *ZW.1.c*). Duncan's suggestion fits the chronology perfectly: Schmid's treatise was published in 1790, following which Kant not only published the Essay, but spent most of his remaining years working on precisely the question of moral evil (in his famous and controversial arguments on radical evil).

This is a very persuasive argument. If I remain hesitant, it is for the simple reason that moral evil has a very small part to play in the Essay: the emphasis lies rather on the other kinds of counterpurposiveness, physical evil and especially misalignment. As Duncan acknowledges, Kant seems 'more cognizant of the problem posed by natural evil' in the Essay than in the earlier works: nevertheless, 'the most natural reading is that the impossibility of explaining moral evil is the decisive factor'.[96] I'm not convinced. The Schmid treatise may very well have provided the *occasion* for Kant to have re-examined his earlier theodicy arguments (and the Lecture in particular), but the Essay itself manifests markedly different preoccupations, and any successful explanation of Kant's change of heart needs to take this into account.

But was this change of heart really as drastic as is often considered? Johannes Brachtendorf thinks not. Another explanation for the striking continuity between the Lecture and the Essay could be that there *is*, in fact, more continuity than departure. According to Brachtendorf, Kant was not refuting his earlier arguments at all: the Essay constitutes not a rejection but a *refoundation* of theodicy, with all the help and tools of critical philosophy.[97] Kant is opposing the kind of theodicy that wants to defend God's moral wisdom without having at its disposal 'the concepts that can only be won on the way of practical philosophy, namely "freedom", "highest good" and "immortality"'.[98] That is, Kant is rejecting a theodicy built on *theoretical–speculative* grounds, but he leaves open the possibility of an entirely different kind of theodicy built on *moral–practical* ones. Far from amounting to fideism, such an *authentic* theodicy is based firmly on our practical reason, and as such is not unphilosophical: it is a form of religion kept within the boundaries of mere reason. Furthermore, Brachtendorf points out that far from turning his back on the theodicean tradition, many of Kant's points in the Essay are firmly rooted in the arguments of

96. Ibid., 987.
97. Brachtendorf, 'Kants Theodizee-Aufsatz', 74.
98. Ibid., 73 (my translation).

Leibniz and other thinkers of theodicy. Kant, on this view, is not crushing the field of theodicy so much as he is purifying it.

It is along these interpretative avenues that I will place my own suggestions. Based on the discussion thus far, there are a few elements that I think are crucial for any credible interpretation of Kant's essay on theodicy. First, it seems clear to me that Kant does see himself as closing the door on past theodicy, as ushering in yet another clean break from a fossilised tradition, and as extending this break into the future. Second, it also seems clear that Kant leaves this door ajar at several points.[99] Third, there is no denying the contrast between the Essay and the Lecture: most of the arguments Kant is refuting are ones he had made himself, if not in the Lecture then in the early writings on optimism.[100] Fourth, the question of sincerity and of the Book of Job should not be dismissed as accidental additions to Kant's argument: to do justice to the Essay, we have to take it as a whole—all the more so since, while the first part takes the Lecture as its template, the second part, and especially the section on Job, is all new.

THE KANTIAN KNOT

If we do want to stay true to the mood of the Essay as a whole, it seems untenable to hold that Kant's rejection of theodicy is absolute, and all that remains is a version of fideism.[101] This does not do justice to the careful considerations of the second part of the Essay, or to Kant's suggestion throughout that something new is happening here. If all we're left with is fideism, then there is nothing new under the sun: this is *exactly* the position of Bayle and other fideists, according to whom all rational theodicies are dead ends, and the only way out is to 'captivate the understanding under the obedience of faith'.[102] Furthermore, considering Kant's lifelong resistance to any kind of fideism, it seems unlikely that he would plead for it here.[103]

If this is indeed what Kant ends up doing, it's surely not what he is *trying* to do, what he *sees himself as doing*. Kant does leave open the

99. See above, especially *ZW.2.c*, *ZW.3.b*, and *ZW.3.c*.

100. See Duncan, 'Moral Evil', 987n.: 'In the theodicy essay, Kant denies that theodicies have met any of these charges, while in the *Lectures* he lists the same charges and believes that he can meet them himself.'

101. Cavallar, 'Kants Weg', 102; Schulte, 'Zweckwidriges', 392.

102. A recurrent phrase in Bayle, who is possibly parodying other fideists such as his enemy Pierre Jurieu; see my *Bayle, Jurieu*, chapter 4.

103. Hence Kant's criticism of Jacobi and Mendelssohn: see Kuehn, *Kant*, 306–11.

possibility of authentic theodicy. But the term 'authentic' can be misleading here, especially as it is opposed to the serious-sounding 'doctrinal'. While the idea of an authentic theodicy is crucially related to that of sincerity, it does *not* mean throwing reason overboard and believing whatever feels right to us, let alone sacrificing reason on the altar of faith. In the Concluding Remark, Kant connects the themes of authenticity and sincerity with those of conscience and conscientiousness, which are as central to religious as to moral belief: our integrity depends entirely on the care we have taken in making sure that our beliefs and judgements are well grounded, and that our level of conviction is high enough for us to profess them or act on them.[104] Integrity is no easy thing, and neither is authentic theodicy, which has everything to do with morality, with practical reason, with the mature religion of reason that Kant is trying to establish.[105] To leave such considerations to one side is to leave behind the second half of the Essay, which to all appearances matters just as much to Kant as the first half, *if not more so*.

Recall that the crucial verse, for Kant, is Job 27:5: 'Till I die I will not remove mine integrity from me'.[106] It is followed by what may well be the key sentence in Kant's Essay, its real *Resultatssatz*:

> For with this disposition [Job] proved that he did not found his morality on faith, but his faith on morality: in such a case, however weak this faith might be, yet it alone is of a pure and true kind, i.e. the kind of faith that founds not a religion of supplication, but a religion of good life conduct. (8:267)[107]

This is the final sentence before the Concluding Remark, and so to all purposes the closing statement of the Essay itself. The problem of theodicy, for Kant, dissolves entirely into the question of morality and sincerity. It's not that the questions posed by theodicy are themselves 'childish', as are those concerning eternal damnation: Kant shows throughout his works

104. These themes are central to *Religion within the Boundaries of Mere Reason*; see my article 'The Left Hand'; and see also Kant's letter to Friedrich Wilhelm II: 'anyone who confesses a revealed faith must be conscientious, viz., he must assert no more than he really knows, and he must urge others to believe only in that of which he himself is fully certain' (11:529).

105. Again, the Essay is closely aligned in this with *Religion*, both of which seem to result from a similar shift in Kant's thinking, as Duncan points out ('Moral Evil', 989).

106. Job 27:5 (KJV). In the German version used by Kant: 'Bis daß mein Ende kommt, will ich nicht weichen von meiner Frömmigkeit'.

107. For Schulte's *Resultatssatz*, see above, p. 309.

that he takes the problem of evil very seriously indeed.[108] As he writes in the *Critique of Practical Reason*, the reason why the Greek philosophers before Anaxagoras did not attain the concept of a single rational cause of the world was not that they lacked insight but that 'the ills in the world seemed to them to be much too important objections to consider themselves justified in such a hypothesis'. In this, says Kant, 'they showed understanding and insight': the problem of evil is not one to be quickly brushed aside (5:140). But nor should it be answered too casually, or too confidently. Job is exemplary because his heart is in the right place, but also because his *orientation* is: his primary concern remains that of integrity and sincerity, not of doctrinal truth.

The only submission Kant concedes for Job is that Job admits to having spoken 'hastily', and indeed 'unwisely', about 'things which are too high for him' (8:266). Then again, so had Kant. In his earlier writings on optimism, and again in the theodicy of the Lecture, Kant had gone beyond what critical philosophy permitted him: he had spoken of things that were too high for human reason; he had declared himself for a system rather than accepting that theoretical–speculative reason could not go so far; *he had engaged in doctrinal theodicy*.[109]

Considering Kant's identification with Job in other respects, would it be going too far to see it here too? If it is right to read the first part of the Essay as a striking exercise in auto-refutation, almost every argument refuted there having been contended by Kant himself, the turn to Job gains a different shading. Kant certainly does not believe himself to be guilty of the kind of flattery for which he condemns Job's friends,[110] but he does perhaps share with Job that initial transgression of having spoken of things too high for him. If this is so, then Kant's submission mirrors Job's own, and so too his justification. As Kant wrote to a distressed young woman in the same year as the Essay was published, a sermon is customarily divided into three parts, 'doctrine, discipline, and solace', and if the first two are attended to, the third will naturally follow (11:334). Could something similar be taking place in the Essay? A 'doctrine' that refutes

108. In *Religion* (6:70n.), Kant dismisses debates on whether 'the punishment of hell [will] be finite or everlasting' as '*childish questions*' (his emphasis).

109. For instance, in the passage from the Lecture quoted above (p. 308): 'Moral perfection in this life will be followed by moral growth in the next, just as moral deterioration in this life will bring a still greater decline of morality in that life' (28:1084–5). Kant's language here seems much too resolute, according to his own principles.

110. With the exception perhaps of the early optimism essay that so embarrassed him in his later years.

Kant's earlier arguments on theoretical grounds; a 'discipline' where Kant sanctions himself in sanctioning Job (and Job's friends); after which the 'solace' will surely follow—the solace of knowing that his integrity has not, and never will be, removed from him. Could the Essay, aside from being a declaration on the fate of theodicy, also be an exercise in self-sanctioning and in sincerity—in the very character and conscientiousness that Kant is exploring in the final lines?

This is all conjecture, of course, and I want to be cautious. But the fact remains that Kant is spending a lot of ink refuting his earlier arguments, and this seems enough to undermine Brachtendorf's provocative suggestion that the Essay amounts to a *refoundation* of theodicy. Such a possibility is belied by the very title of the Essay, and by Kant's sweeping statements that *all* 'philosophical trials in theodicy', *past, present, and future*, are doomed to fail. There's a hard balance to be kept in trying to preserve both Kant's innovative force *and* his inheritance from past authors, and Brachtendorf rightly stresses the ways in which Kant is in dialogue with the wider theodicean tradition, and especially with Leibniz.[111] It seems mistaken, however, to classify this relation as mainly one of continuity and inheritance: Kant is refuting Leibniz and the Wolffians almost as much as he is refuting himself. Whatever else Kant is doing, he is definitely taking a stance against theodicy as we know it.

But if it goes too far to inscribe Kant into the theodicean tradition, the very cord to which Kant is trying to break, Brachtendorf is surely right in suggesting that Kant's considered view on theodicy is in close alignment to the postulates of practical reason. There are strong resonances between Job's bid for integrity and Kant's remarks on assent in the Dialectic, where he argues that since the three postulates (God, freedom, and immortality) are grounded in the needs of pure practical reason, we are justified in giving our assent to them, in order to do our duty. For this reason:

> the upright man [*der Rechtschaffene*] may well say: I *will* that there be a God, that my existence in this world be also an existence in a pure world of the understanding beyond natural connections, and finally that my duration be endless; I stand by this, without paying attention to rationalizations, however little I may be able to answer them or to oppose them with others more plausible, and I will not let this belief be taken from me; for this is the only case in which my interest, because

111. Brachtendorf, 'Kants Theodizee-Aufsatz', *passim*.

> I *may* not give up anything of it, unavoidably determines my judgment. (*KpV* 5:143; Kant's emphasis)[112]

As Job stands by his integrity, so too the upright man is justified in holding to his belief in the existence of God and the immortality of the soul, and in saying, in the face of all 'rationalizations': 'I will not let this belief be taken from me'.[113] It is this kind of justification that the Essay too is aiming at: to be engaged in an authentic theodicy is to be justified in giving one's assent from a moral and first-person point of view.[114]

But assent to *what*, exactly? While the *Critiques* justify the belief in God, freedom, and immortality, the second part of the Essay seeks to justify the belief that even though our reason reveals no connection between the moral and natural orders of creation, between God's moral and artistic wisdom, nevertheless there is such a connection: *we may believe in a moral world*. Thus Job, following his submission, is rewarded with a divine vision, in which God allows him 'glimpses into the beautiful side of creation' as well as 'into the horrible side', which is full of counterpurposiveness—the dark matters of existence: 'And yet God thereby demonstrates an order and a maintenance of the whole which proclaim a wise creator, even though his ways, inscrutable to us, must at the same time remain hidden' (8:266).

This belief in a moral world is not itself a postulate—or is it? In the Lecture, Kant suggests that it might be. There, instead of naming as the three postulates God, freedom, and immortality, as he does consistently in the *Critiques*, Kant presents us with a slightly different list:

> the three articles of moral faith, *God, freedom of the human will*, and *a moral world*, are the only articles in which it is permissible for us to transport ourselves in thought beyond all possible experience and out of the sensible world; only here may we assume and believe something from a practical point of view for which we otherwise have no adequate speculative grounds. (28:1091; Kant's emphasis)[115]

112. This passage gives force to Neiman's suggestion that Job's 'fate might be said to form the focus of discussion of the "Dialectic" of the second Critique' ('Metaphysics, Philosophy', 149). See also *KU*, section 91.

113. '. . . ich beharre darauf und lasse mir diesen Glauben nicht nehmen' (5:143).

114. Justified—but never *required*, not in the sense of having a *duty* to believe.

115. In a fragment dated between 1785 and 1788, Kant describes the belief or faith in a 'future life' as a faith 'of the second rank' ('ein Glaube vom zweyten Rang'): 'For it is not necessary that we exist or exist eternally, but it is necessary that, as long as we live, we behave ourselves in a way worthy of life' (Reflection 8101, 19:644; my translation). See the editorial footnote in *RRT*, 480n.

It seems, then, that in the Lecture, Kant is trying to justify, *on practical grounds*, our belief in a moral world, a world in which there is alignment between virtue and happiness as there is between crime and punishment. This is one effort that the Essay does not refute: in fact, in his later works, Kant will continue his attempt to conceptualise a kind of *this-worldly alignment*, especially in his writings on religion.[116] It is also why the problem of evil is truly a problem for Kant, not so much from a theoretical as from moral point of view. Evil, or counterpurposiveness, is the ongoing element of resistance to Kant's 'optimism': it is the stubborn residue of existence that stands in the way of our assent to a moral world and threatens to make us dissatisfied with providence and the natural order of things.[117]

On this point, at least, the Essay is not in disagreement: the difference with the Lecture lies rather in *the way in which* the problem is to be responded to. While the Lecture still tries to untie the theodicean knot, by answering the objections to theodicy one by one, the Essay recognises that the Lecture went too far: that its author did not remain within the boundaries of pure reason. By contrast, the Essay does not seek to refute *any* of these objections, but fully admits that the knot cannot be rationally untied: in fact, Kant does all he can to tighten it in places where it might seem to be coming loose. At the same time, he also suggests that the knot may yet be severed. If, like Job, we base our faith on morality, rather than our morality on faith, we are justified in giving our assent to a moral world, *purely* on moral–practical grounds. Hence the hints of a 'moral decree' and reason as a 'faculty of moral legislation' (*ZW.3.b* and *ZW.3.c*); hence the many moments where Kant seems to be creating openings as well as closures. Like the belief in God's existence or the soul's immortality, the belief in a moral world can be assented to as an exception to the rule, the shadow postulate of practical reason. If Kant does not end up promoting this belief to the level of a postulate, this is because he does not have to: the postulates of God's existence and the soul's immortality are enough, in that the belief in eventual alignment is implied in both. In so far as we are justified in giving our assent to the existence of God, adorned with the moral attributes, we are also justified in assenting to a moral world, a vision of existence in which nature is ultimately moral.

What we are left with after the wreckage of doctrinal theodicy, therefore, is not a budding genre or philosophical discipline, but a radically

116. E.g. *Religion*, 6:61: since the human being is never free of guilt, he 'can regard himself as responsible for the sufferings that come his way, whatever the road'.

117. On this dissatisfaction, see 'Conjectures' (8:120–3/*PW*, 231–4).

individual and even personal exercise, which hearkens to the bounds of theoretical reason, while fulfilling the ends of practical reason: it is rational only in this sense. Only in so far as this belief in a moral world is required by our practical reason, and only in so far as it is fully sincere, can we claim to be engaged in a truly *authentic* theodicy—one that cuts the knot indeed, but does so for the right reasons. When Kant closes a door, he opens a window.

The Clear Eyes of Maria von Herbert

In the early 1790s Kant, now in his late sixties, received several letters from troubled youngsters struggling with a reluctance for life and a desire for death. One was Maria von Herbert, a young woman of about twenty-one, who had immersed herself in Kant's philosophy and wrote to him, 'Great Kant,' in a desperate *cri de cœur*: 'As a believer calls to his God, I call upon you for help, for solace, or for counsel to prepare me for death.'[118] Her first letter speaks of a heart that has split 'into a thousand pieces': she has lost the love and friendship of a man to whom she had confessed 'a protracted lie', and she would have killed herself had she not read Kant's works, which tell her 'it is wrong for me to die because my life is tormented, and I am instead supposed to live because of my being'. The problem is that while Kant has convinced her of a future existence, 'I found nothing, nothing at all for this life': no reason for continuing to live in the absence of that friendship that meant the world to her. She implores Kant to come to her aid: 'put yourself in my place and either damn me or give me solace' (11:273–4).

Her second letter, written more than a year later, is something darker still.[119] She has regained the friendship that meant so much to her and yet she is 'dissatisfied': for the friendship, while it gives her enjoyment, is 'pointless', and she feels reproached for this by her 'clear vision', or rather, her 'clear eyes' (*meine hellen Augen*). More than this: 'I get an empty feeling that extends inside me and all around me, so that I am almost superfluous to myself' (11:401). There is no purpose to her life, and nothing seems worth doing; everything good seems shadowed by 'sordidness', and she is tormented by a 'boredom', a sense of pointlessness, 'that makes my life unbearable'. What should she strive for? 'Don't think me arrogant for

118. Maria von Herbert to Kant, [August?] 1791 (11:273–4). Here and there, I have slightly modified Zweig's translation (*Correspondence*). On the disjunction contained in this plea, see Ritter, 'Solace or Counsel for Death'.

119. Herbert to Kant, January 1793 (11:401–3).

saying this, but the commandments of morality are too trifling for me.' Having fulfilled the commands of the categorical imperative, she still finds herself locked in a life of 'empty vegetating', an 'unbearable emptiness of soul' (11:401–2). Meanwhile, her despair is deepened by the contrast with what she sees around her: 'Experience wants to take me to task for this bad temper I have against life by showing me that almost everyone finds his life ending too soon and everyone is so glad to be alive.' There is only one thing she desires now: 'to shorten this so useless life of mine'; 'each day interests me only to the extent that it brings me closer to death'. Again she asks Kant for his opinion, for her own 'concept of morality is silent on this point, whereas it speaks very decisively on all other issues' (11:402).[120]

Her third letter, again sent a year onward, gives us a final view of her 'spiritual progress' and 'frame of mind'.[121] She tells Kant that for a long time she struggled to harmonise her innocent suffering with the concept of a just God:

> For a long time I tortured myself and couldn't make sense of many things; for I confused God's arrangement with the contingencies of fate, and I failed to be satisfied with just the feeling of being [*mit dem Gefühl von Dasein*]. There you can see immediately how things stood with me, for I wanted too much, I regarded the coincidental misfortunes of life as sent to me by God, and I bristled at the injustice, for my conscience was free of guilt. (11:485)

Such thoughts might well have led her to kill herself, had it not been the case that 'from an entirely different quarter a moral feeling awoke in me': the adversities continued and yet she was able to achieve 'an imperturbable peace of mind'. She has not lost her desire for death, but she has understood it better, her 'view has changed':

> I think that death, from an egoistic point of view, must be the most pleasant thing for every true human being, and only if people take morality and friends [*Moralität und Freunde*] into account can they with the greatest desire to die still wish for life and try to preserve it no matter what. (11:486)

120. See Langton, 'Duty and Desolation', 484, who notes that 'Kant's conviction that suicide is incompatible with the moral law is not nearly as well founded as he liked to think'; and Ritter, 'Solace', section ii, who suggests that Herbert is asking Kant to do one of two things: 'Concede that a voluntary death is morally permissible or give me something that may help me to find a new purpose in life.'

121. Herbert to Kant, early 1794, 11:485–6.

Ten years later, she had killed herself.[122]

Kant's other troubled correspondent was Johann Benjamin Erhard, a young man of twenty-six and a student of Kant's, who did not hesitate to lay bare his soul to his teacher. 'Your letter,' he writes to Kant of an earlier missive, 'was a source of consolation to me. It caught me in a melancholy state from which I often suffer'.[123] He speaks openly of the 'spiritual malaise', the 'moral fever' that has afflicted him since his youth, and that is marked by the 'ebb and flow of my self-respect and of my faith in other people'. He finds it hard to refrain from seeking his good fortune in the world through the weakness of others, and he wonders whether Kant finds it equally hard to devote his talents 'entirely to the world', and not to himself. He speaks, too, of his longing for death, which even in his 'most cheerful hours' he sees as 'something desirable', and of his belief that once he has accomplished all that he is capable of in the world, it would not be wrong to ask 'to be allowed to leave the scene'. This longing, this '*moral* yearning for death', is not the same thing as 'the desire to commit suicide, which I have often felt' (11:406–7). It is rather a veridical response to the ills of existence, something Erhard feels only few contemporary authors have discussed. One exception is Jonathan Swift, who held, with Bayle, that given the chance, no one would honestly want to 'repeat his role on earth'. Another is Kant himself.

Kant, after all, had, in a much-cited footnote to the *Critique of Judgment* (1790), written that if we assess life merely by what we enjoy, then its value would be 'Less than zero: for who would start life anew under the same conditions, or even according to a new and self-designed plan (but one still in accord with the course of nature)'? (5:434).[124] Similarly, in his 'Conjectures on the Beginning of Human History' (1786), he writes that 'anyone who continues to wish that life might last longer than it actually does must have little appreciation of its value, for to prolong it would merely add to the length of a drama made up of endless struggles with adversity' (8:122). Kant, it seems, was no stranger to the ills of life, at least not in his later years, when his writings were uncommonly outspoken about the negative value of life if it is measured purely experientially; that is, in terms of *enjoyment* (which, according to the pessimists, is the only

122. Herbert disappeared in 1803, when she was 33; her body was never found but her brother Franz Paul tells us that she killed herself, and, while heartbroken, defends her decision as one of 'courage' rather than 'faint-heartedness' (cited in Ritter, 'Solace', section i).

123. Johann Benjamin Erhard to Kant, 17 January 1793, 11:406–7.

124. Compare his similar comment in the Essay (8:259): see above, p. 301.

way we have of measuring it).[125] But Kant was no pessimist, at least not of the Baylean strain: his point was that we must measure life by the worth of our actions, by 'the value that we ourselves give to our lives', by aiming for higher purposes and living in accordance 'with the end that nature has set for us' (5:434; 5:442). His point was also that we must recognise our own responsibility for the evils in the world instead of blaming providence, not only so that we do not become disheartened, but also so that we do not lose any opportunity for self-improvement.[126]

This applies to the progress both of humanity and of the suffering individual, even in the most concrete practical terms, as is suggested by the older Kant's comments 'On the power of the mind to master its morbid feelings by sheer resolution.'[127] The opposite of the mind's power of self-mastery is hypochondria, or 'the weakness of abandoning oneself despondently to general morbid feelings that have no definite object', a 'fainthearted brooding about the ills that could befall one'. Kant calls it a kind of 'insanity', since once in this state the 'self-tormentor' is unable to master his melancholia, and yet he is the only one who can: 'A reasonable human being does not permit himself any such hypochondria', but recognising that his anxiety has no object would turn his attention 'to the business at hand'. Kant then writes: 'I myself have a natural disposition to hypochondria because of my flat and narrow chest, which leaves little room for the movement of the heart and lungs; and in my earlier years this disposition made me almost weary of life.' But seeing that the cause was 'purely mechanical' and 'nothing could be done about it', he learned to master 'its influence on my thoughts and actions by diverting my attention from this feeling, as if it had nothing to do with me'. This, for Kant, was enough: our lives become 'cheerful more through what we freely *do* with life than through what we *enjoy* as a gift from it' (7:103–4; his emphasis).[128]

But if it was enough for Kant, was it enough for his youthful sufferers? It does not sound like the most useful advice, let alone an effective consolation, to be told that our melancholia or depression or 'hypochondria' is

125. Here, I take Kant's 'enjoyment' as meaning: subjective experience. Kant makes the same point in his letter to Herbert: 'the value of life, insofar as it consists of the enjoyment we can get out of people, is generally overestimated' (11:334).

126. See again 'Conjectures' (8:120–23/*PW*, 231–4).

127. This essay is written in the form of a letter to C.F. Hufeland, in January 1798 (7:97–116; in *RRT*, 313–27).

128. Though other letters suggest that Kant was not always in such complete control, e.g. Kant to Karl Leonhard Reinhold, 21 September 1791: 'I have to look forward impatiently to a good mood without getting into one, being unable to exercise any control over my own mind' (11:288).

of our own making, but at the same time, once it has truly taken hold of us, that there is nothing we can do.[129] Similarly, to be told to find satisfaction in life, not through what we enjoy or suffer, but through our deeds, may inspire the already heartened, but cannot fail to ring hollow with the truly torn. For Erhard, who is male and in control of his destiny, who is seeking consolation but not crying out for help, it is enough: if we do what we can in life, then death can be a friend to be welcomed at the end. For Herbert, who is stuck in a life the pointlessness of which her eyes make devastatingly clear to her, the words are meaningless, or worse. While she mentions to Kant her 'chronic poor health', which 'sometimes causes a frenzy of mind that reason alone cannot cure', on the whole it seems that her affliction lies elsewhere, and is a thing darker and deeper than Kant's mild hypochondria (11:402).

Failing to see this, Kant fails to understand the nature of her cry for help. He does reply to her first letter: indeed, she had forced his hand by threatening that if he were not to reply to her, he would not be acting according to his categorical imperative (11:274). But he seems genuinely engaged, remarking to a friend that her letter 'interested him far more than others because "it spoke of truth and trust"',[130] and mulling over her question before carefully drafting his reply. Kant clearly believes he is doing his duty by her, but he seems mistaken about what this duty is.[131] Instead of answering Herbert's tormented question about suicide and finding purpose in life, Kant focuses instead on questions of truth and deception, which were topics close to his own heart at the time.[132] What was the nature of the truth that Herbert had concealed from her friend?

129. While Kant's 'hypochondria' does at times sound like depression, it goes too far to say, with Eugene Thacker, 'that Kant suffered from depression'; Kant's point is precisely that he did not, and for two reasons: first, that the affliction itself was physical or 'mechanical' in nature; second, that he was able to master his psychological responses to it. See Thacker, *Starry Speculative Corpse*, 4–8.

130. Borowski, cited in Kant's *Correspondence*, 380.

131. Perhaps Kant cannot be blamed for this; in an accompanying letter to Kant's reply to Herbert (sent to her brother Paul), Erhard stresses twice the 'indeterminacy' of her query: 'I do not know whether the answer will be effective enough, but the demand was very indeterminate and Kant consulted extensively with me about what might be the cause, which was indicated only very indeterminately.' Cited in Ritter, 'Solace', section ii.

132. Kant's letter to Herbert (11:331–4) is preserved as a draft and not dated, but recent scholars have suggested that he probably sent it as early as September 1791, which suggests that 'Kant responded immediately' (Ritter, 'Solace', section ii, after Baum, *Weimar—Jena—Klagenfurt*, 185n.; Bol, 'Themes in von Herbert's Letters to Kant', 11). On sincerity, see above, pp. 310ff. For discussion of Kant's arguments on deception in reply to Herbert, see Langton, 'Duty'; Mahon, 'Kant and Maria von Herbert'; Bol, 'Themes', chapter 2.

Did she regret deceiving him—or did she regret confessing her deception? Only the former kind had moral worth—and if the friendship was as real as her regret was sincere, then her friend would forgive her in the end.[133] But the matter of deception was only the occasion for Herbert's despair, not its deeper ground. Her struggle was with what she perceived to be the uselessness of her life, and if Kant could be excused for missing this in her first letter, the point was made with devastating clarity in the second and third. Twice she has asked Kant for his opinion on suicide and finding meaning in life beyond mere completion of the moral imperative; the third time she writes only to communicate her own conclusions, based on her acquaintance with his works.

By this time, however, Kant has turned away from her, aided in this by none other than his other young correspondent, Erhard, who had himself been friends with Herbert. After replying to her, Kant wrote to Erhard to ask 'whether Fräulein Herbert was encouraged by my letter' (11:399).[134] But Erhard, in the very same letter in which he speaks of his own 'moral fever' and death wish, describes Herbert as someone who has 'capsized on the reef of romantic love', someone whose 'moral feeling is totally severed from prudence and is therefore coupled with fantasy'; and in doing so dismisses her spiritual turmoil as a form of hysteria (11:407).[135] Shortly after receiving this letter, Kant sends on Herbert's letters to another female correspondent, as 'an example of warning, to guard you against the aberrations of a sublimated fantasy'; referring to Herbert as *die kleine Schwärmerin*, the 'ecstatical young lady'.[136] Kant and Erhard, neither a stranger to the shadow side of life, both seem to have turned against her. It is hard not to read in their expressions a failure of some kind.

133. Ritter ('Solace', section iii) is 'in qualified disagreement with several commentators who think that Kant does poorly as an advisor and comforter'; he rightly points out that Kant is very concerned to help Herbert stop blaming herself, and that Herbert herself (in her second letter) felt that Kant had understood her. But as Ritter also notes, Herbert does insist on the deeper question on suicide and purpose in life, the one that Kant had not yet answered.

134. Kant to Erhard, 21 December 1792, 11:398–9. As Ritter notes, another letter to Reinhold suggests that Kant did intend to write to Herbert again, but if there was a second letter, Herbert never received it (Ritter, 12; Bol, 'Themes', 11).

135. Ritter notes that 'Erhard was singularly prejudiced towards women' ('Solace', section ii).

136. Langton ('Duty and Desolation', 499–505) argues that in forwarding Herbert's letters, Kant 'is doing something with her as one does something with a tool'; Herbert is no longer considered a moral agent or even a 'co-author' but a mere object of pity, who can be made an example of.

The reason why I close this chapter with what is only a footnote in Kant scholarship is not to make a point of criticising past philosophers' attitudes towards women (if it were, chapter 8 would be even bleaker than it already is). Nor is it simply to acknowledge the uncomfortable truth that almost all philosophers featured in this book are men.[137] Rather, the reason is that Herbert asks a question worth asking: What can philosophy offer us when the resources of life have run out; when we have fallen hard on the rock bottom of existence; when we could say with Herbert that we struggle with an 'unbearable emptiness of soul', or with Tolstoy that 'there was no life in me because I had no desires whose gratification I would have deemed it reasonable to fulfil'?[138] Herbert's predicament is not unlike the crisis undergone by Emily Wharton's tragic heroine Lily Bart, of whom Danuta Reah writes: 'Her only hope of real freedom is to undergo a complete change in her understanding of value and worth, and this she cannot do.'[139] And it is worth considering how else Kant might have answered Herbert's plea for help: Is there anything he could have said that would have made a difference to her life?

The sad truth is that Kant could not have helped Maria von Herbert, even if he wanted to: the tools of critical philosophy may serve to scrutinise the morality of one's actions (and this is what Kant's letter duly offers her), but they fall short when it comes to justifying an existence that is itself empty of use or meaning—or at least (which is terrible enough) experienced as such. In so far as Kant recognises the experiential claims of pessimism, the badness of existence if it is measured only by enjoyment, he should recognise this too. 'Where there is life there is faith,' writes Tolstoy, and elsewhere: 'As long as there is life, there is happiness.'[140] But where there is no sense of meaning, Herbert asks us, *can there be life?*[141]

I do not think Kant can be blamed for being unable (for let us assume he is not *unwilling*) to provide Herbert with a reason for living, which goes far beyond the bounds of what any person can do for another. But

137. With the exception of Emilie du Châtelet and Madeleine du Puisieux (albeit very briefly discussed). For an important recent study of theodicy as discussed by early modern female philosophers, see Hernandez, *Early Modern Women and the Problem of Evil.*

138. Tolstoy, *A Confession*, 18.

139. Reah, Introduction to Wharton, *The House of Mirth*, xi.

140. Tolstoy, *Confession*, 58; *War and Peace*, 1053 (see chapter 9).

141. Note also that Herbert's rejection of the sheer 'feeling of being' as a sufficient ground for wanting to live poses an important objection to Rousseau's comments on the 'sweet sentiment of being' (*LV*, 235): for there is no prima-facie reason for thinking, as Rousseau does, that this sentiment of being is necessarily a positive experience. See Schopenhauer on boredom.

if this is not a problem for Kant, it is a problem for his philosophy, and there are several objections to his ethics that arise at this point.[142] One is that 'in Kant, there is no space for meaning as something distinct from morality'.[143] Herbert's letters suggest that it is not enough to define the highest good in terms of morality and happiness alone; a third element is needed, namely that of *meaning* or *purpose*, distinct from both: this is what Herbert is asking Kant, and this is what he cannot give her.[144] And in the wake of this problem arises another, which is that not only is Kant unable to offer meaning to Herbert, but he cannot even offer *consolation*. Kant never quite escapes the Stoic temptation of believing that our mental states are ultimately in our hands, and so too is our (psychological, if not our physical) suffering.[145] We must measure the worth of life by our actions; to this extent, we are in control of our destinies. It is a well-known feature of Kant's ethics that it is built on duty and reason, which is why he excludes animals from moral consideration, and sidelines sympathy in the moral realm. But a different ground for ethics can be imagined, such as *compassion*, and if there is one virtue central to the philosophy of pessimism, it is this.[146]

The philosopher discussed in chapter 8 would not, in all likelihood, have given a better answer to Herbert: even barring his misogyny, it is unlikely that a philosopher of the darkest pessimism would have been able to give her the kind of meaning she found lacking in life. But he could perhaps have offered her more in the way of consolation, however bleak—by reassuring her, for instance, that she was not to blame for seeing what she

142. For some philosophical literature on Herbert's exchange with Kant, see Langton, 'Duty and Desolation'; Ritter, 'Solace or Counsel for Death'; Mahon, 'Kant and Maria von Herbert'; and, most recently, the excellent master's thesis by Geertje Bol ('Themes'), to whom I owe my own introduction to Maria von Herbert.

143. Bol, 'Themes', 128.

144. Bol argues that Herbert's letters 'constitute an early critique of Kant's moral philosophy'. They suggest that 'besides happiness and morality—the dichotomy Kant upholds—we need a third good, namely, that of meaning'; and that 'philosophy does not have room for the significance of this third good'. Bol, 'Themes', 6–7; see also her chapters 3 and 4, and Wolf, 'Happiness and Meaning'.

145. However, note that Kant believes happiness to be mostly a matter of luck or fortune; see Bol, 'Themes', 68–9, referring to *Groundwork* 4:393 and *MS* 4:482. But it seems to me that these '*gifts of fortune*' (4:393; Kant's emphasis) apply rather to external (physical) than internal (psychological) circumstances; e.g. *MS* 4:483: 'none of the pains, hardships, and sufferings of life . . . can rob him of consciousness of being their master and superior to them all'. Thus Kant does not make room for a *dispositional problem of evil*, as Hume does.

146. See Schopenhauer, *The Two Fundamental Problems of Ethics*, 219–21, where he juxtaposes various foundations of morality, by Kant and others, and as his own mentions compassion.

did in her desolation; that there might be something valuable and veridical in the dark matters she perceived with her clear eyes. As Thomas De Quincey writes of 'Our Lady of Darkness', one of his mythologised *ministers of suffering*, the 'defier of God', 'mother of lunacies', and 'suggestress of suicides':

> Deep lie the roots of her power; but narrow is the nation that she rules. For she can approach only those in whom a profound nature has been upheaved by central convulsions; in whom the heart trembles and the brain rocks under conspiracies of tempest from without and tempest from within.[147]

But those unlucky enough to be visited by her are darkly rewarded, not with moral growth or eventual happiness, but with a depth of vision terrible in its clarity:

> So shall he be accomplished in the furnace—so shall he see the things that ought *not* to be seen—sights that are abominable, and secrets that are unutterable. So shall he read elder truths, sad truths, grand truths, fearful truths. So shall he rise again *before* he dies.[148]

A different way of responding to Herbert might have been simply to acknowledge the reality of her unhappiness, to remind her that she was not to blame for feeling as she did, and to suggest perhaps that such misery may yet allow for a depth of feeling, an expansion of sympathy, a 'sharpening of the moral vision which makes all human suffering so near and insistent that the other aspects of life fade into remoteness'.[149]

There is something in this that is also the value of pessimism. To stake consolation over judgement; to do justice to the suffering of others; to remind each other with kindness and compassion that we are not ultimately responsible for our miseries—these are no little boons. For the real failure of theodicy, and of most other philosophies of optimism to this day, comes when they fail to take suffering seriously—and this is something even Kant had failed to see.

147. Thomas De Quincey, *Suspiria de Profundis* (first published in fragments in 1845; final version published posthumously in 1891), 152. *Our Ladies of Sorrow* are threefold: 'Our Lady of Tears', 'Our Lady of Sighs', 'Our Lady of Darkness'. De Quincey: 'I know them thoroughly, and have walked in all their kingdoms' (*Suspiria*, 148).

148. De Quincey, *Suspiria*, 152; his emphasis.

149. Wharton, *House of Mirth*, 203.

CHAPTER EIGHT

The Flute-Playing Pessimist

ARTHUR SCHOPENHAUER

> . . . *Schopenhauer, pessimism notwithstanding,* actually*—played the flute . . . every day, after dinner. You can read it in his biography. And just out of curiosity: a pessimist who negates both God and world but* stops *before morality,—who affirms morality and plays his flute, affirms* laede neminem *morality: excuse me? is this really—a pessimist?*
>
> FRIEDRICH NIETZSCHE[1]

CAN A PESSIMIST PLAY THE FLUTE? Can a philosopher who holds that we should deny the world as well as the will itself yet continue to affirm morality and sound his flute? Is this really pessimism—and if so, is Schopenhauer really a pessimist?

Born in Danzig in 1788, the first child of an already unhappy marriage, Schopenhauer did not have the easiest start in life.[2] Following the suspected suicide of his father in 1805, Schopenhauer spent a few years working as a merchant out of a sense of guilt, then moved to Göttingen and later Berlin to study, first medicine and then philosophy. Schopenhauer

1. Nietzsche, *Beyond Good and Evil*, section 186 (his emphasis). A similar criticism came from Kierkegaard; see Cartwright, 'Schoperhauerian Optimism', 153–7. '*Laedeneminem* morality' refers to the ethical principle 'Neminem laede, imo omnes, quantum potes, jura' ('Harm no one; rather, help everyone to the extent that you can'): Schopenhauer, *The Two Fundamental Problems*, 158–9.

2. On Schopenhauer's confused childhood and the conflicted relationship between his parents, see Safranski, *Schopenhauer*, chapters 1–4; also Magee, *The Philosophy of Schopenhauer*, 10–14, who offers a reductive reading of Schopenhauer's pessimism as basically pathological and therefore of little philosophical import (for criticism, see Young, *Willing and Unwilling*, 136; Dienstag, *Pessimism*, 85).

was still a young man when, in 1819, he published his *magnum opus*, ambitiously titled *The World as Will and Representation* (*WWR*.I),[3] but he would never in his later life look back on this as merely the work of his youth. On the contrary, with a remarkable consistency, Schopenhauer would stay true to his ideas as he first articulated them, and his next major publication comprised a sequel to this first work, published a full twenty-five years later, in 1844. This second volume (*WWR*.II) remains fully in agreement with his earlier views, which he nevertheless saw fit to nuance and develop as his thought matured. In a way, it could be said that Schopenhauer wrote the same book twice. He continued to work on the same topics up to his death in 1860, publishing a two-volume work of essays and aphorisms in 1851, entitled *Parerga and Paralipomena* (*PP*), a third revised edition of *The World as Will* in 1859, and leaving behind various manuscript notebooks, ever elaborating on questions of ethics, metaphysics, and, of course, pessimism. He also continued to play the flute.

There is perhaps no philosopher whose name is more intimately connected with pessimism than Schopenhauer—and there is perhaps no pessimist whose philosophy has been so widely misunderstood. In this chapter, I aim to do a simple and yet not so simple thing: I mean to discuss Schopenhauer's pessimism in such a way *that does it justice*.[4] My reason for this is twofold. First, since Schopenhauer is undoubtedly a key figure in pessimism, and arguably the thinker who turns pessimism into a coherent philosophical tradition for the first time, it seems to follow that if we fail to understand Schopenhauer's pessimism, we fail to understand pessimism at all. Second, it is my concern that if we focus only on the more technical parts of Schopenhauer's argument, we miss out on its rich and complicated understory, which branches back into questions posed by earlier pessimists and forwards into those posed by later ones.[5]

In what follows, I will not attempt to present any definitive reading of Schopenhauer, but I will try to shed new light on some of these

3. *Die Welt als Wille und Vorstellung* went through three editions in Schopenhauer's lifetime: the first edition of 1819, the second edition (with added second volume and additions to the first) of 1844, and the third edition of 1859 (again revised by Schopenhauer). Quotations are from E.F.J. Payne's classic translation (*WWR*), with minor adjustments adapted from the new Cambridge translation by Norman, Welchman, and Janaway (*WWR*.Cam.).

4. Which is not to say that earlier accounts have not done so. There are several important treatments of Schopenhauer's pessimism—for example, by Young, Janaway, Dienstag, Cartwright, and Woods—and I draw from these in many instances; the main difference in my treatment is its orientation on the wider pessimist and theodicean tradition.

5. Such as Bayle (before) and Benatar (after).

considerations by showing how they are connected with the wider debates on pessimism and the problem of evil. By first setting out Schopenhauer's *case* for pessimism, then his deeper *reasons* for pessimism, and finally the resulting *problems* for pessimism, I will evaluate some of the subtler points of Schopenhauer's pessimism *according to the principles of that pessimism itself*, which shares a deep affinity with the wider pessimist tradition. I will try to show how Schopenhauer's morally motivated and 'flute-playing' pessimism is, as Nietzsche rightly saw, not entirely negative in character—but I will also argue that, far from being a weakness for his pessimism, this is precisely its strength; and that this is so precisely according to the deeper ethical drive present in the entire pessimist tradition, oriented as it is on compassion and consolation, as well as, more problematically, hope. What this means in practice is that I will focus primarily on those parts of Schopenhauer's writings that deal with pessimism, which I will roughly distinguish into three statements or 'Rounds': Round One (*WWR*.I), Round Two (*WWR*.II), and Round Three (*PP*).[6] This approach may risk some selectivity—and yet I believe it is appropriate for reading Schopenhauer as he deserves (and intended) to be read.

There is, for Schopenhauer, something very essential or even *original* (in the sense of pertaining to *origins*) about pessimism. Especially in his later works, where he reconsiders the pessimist tenets of his philosophy and styles it, for the first time, *pessimism*, Schopenhauer recognises pessimism as central to philosophy proper.[7] For Schopenhauer, there is a non-contingent relationship between pessimism and philosophy—and possibly, as I will suggest in the course of this chapter, between philosophy and the problem of evil. Hence, if we look back to Camus's question of what is the *fundamental question of philosophy*, for Schopenhauer this is undoubtedly the question of pessimism, which arises even before the

6. This distinction is meant mostly as an analytical tool and should not be overinterpreted; the point is simply to introduce a layer of subtlety into the discussion and watch for shifting themes in Schopenhauer's oeuvre. (I have employed a similar but much more emphatic distinction in my work on Bayle; see my *Bayle*, chapter 5). Pessimism also arises in passing in some of Schopenhauer's other works, e.g. *On the Basis of Morality* (1840).

7. See, e.g., *WWR*.II.170–2 (on which more below). Schopenhauer speaks of *Optimismus* many times in vol. I, but he uses the term *Pessimismus* for the first time in vol. II, at which point he characterises his own philosophy as one of pessimism. I agree with Janaway ('Schopenhauer's Pessimism', 323) and others that Schopenhauer's pessimism *does* have a 'close link with his central metaphysics'—versus Magee (*Philosophy*, 14), who argues that while Schopenhauer's 'whole philosophy is expressed in a vocabulary of pessimism', almost all of it 'could be formulated with equal accuracy in a vocabulary of optimism, or in a vocabulary agnostic as between the two'.

question of idealism does. What this suggests is that pessimism, for Schopenhauer, is not some separate branch of his system that can be separated from the whole: it is at the core, the stem, the beating heart of his philosophy, as well as of *any* philosophy that deserves the name. It is pessimism that drives us to philosophise: 'philosophical astonishment is at bottom one that is dismayed and distressed; philosophy, like the overture to *Don Juan*, starts with a minor chord' (*WWR*.II.171).

WILL AND REPRESENTATION

But if pessimism is the point at which philosophy begins, it is not the starting point of *The World as Will and Representation*.[8] In order to make the case for pessimism and, in connection with this, for redemptive resignation, Schopenhauer must first set out the metaphysical groundwork of his philosophy, and we must follow him there. The first two books of the first volume of *The World* take their cue from the Kantian principle that our experience gives us entry only into the phenomena, behind which the *thing-in-itself* must necessarily remain hidden: we have no access to it except through our experience.[9]

This remains a central point throughout Schopenhauer's philosophy, which nevertheless diverges from the Kantian principle in a subtle but highly controversial way. For as Schopenhauer goes on to argue, the world reveals itself to us both as will *and* as representation, as *Wille* as well as *Vorstellung*. As living beings that are capable of reflection, we are aware of that force of life known as the *will* within ourselves, and to this inner will we each have privileged access, as observers of ourselves.[10] Starting from this experience of will within ourselves, we can understand that the same will is at work in all of nature; that there is no other way by which to make

8. Pessimism is discussed first in book IV of *WWR*.I, then again in the latter part of *WWR*.II, and in several essays of the *PP* (as well as in the notebooks).

9. The structure of volume I is as follows: books I and II set out the (Kantian) groundwork, book III covers aesthetics, and book IV focuses on the human condition: items regarding experience, morality and salvation—which is where Schopenhauer first lays out the philosophical case for pessimism.

10. The concept of *will* in Schopenhauer is notoriously confusing. As Janaway notes, this will is 'not essentially rational or conscious', but rather a kind of organizing principle behind all living beings ('Schopenhauer's Pessimism', 325–6); Magee (*Philosophy*, 444) extends it further to everything that is in existence: 'The will as such has nothing, I repeat nothing, to do with human agency or conscious experience of any kind. . . . The will is in us only because it is in everything. It *constitutes* us as it constitutes everything.' Magee (ibid., 446) also points out that Schopenhauer's original term for what would become *Wille* was *Kraft* ('force').

sense of the inner being of the world. From this, we can conclude that the inner nature of things, the 'sole kernel of every phenomenon' is the *will*; and that we do have a certain privileged access to this will that goes beyond our knowledge of mere phenomena or representations (*WWR*.I.118).

At this point, the question arises of whether Schopenhauer, in this positing of the world as representation *and also* as will, is being true to his own Kantian principles: Doesn't his thesis of world as *will* suggest that this is something entirely other than world as representation? Isn't Schopenhauer claiming that most un-Kantian of all things: that he has found access to the thing-in-itself (*Ding an sich*)? While Schopenhauer is often read this way, and himself gives ample reason for coming to such a conclusion (for instance, by suggesting, at various points, that the will *is* the thing-in-itself),[11] there is also another way of reading him. On Julian Young's interpretation, for instance, Schopenhauer's 'will' is not identical with the thing-in-itself but is rather a different *kind* of representation. Young posits a trichotomy, in which the world-as-will stands between the world-as-representation and the thing-in-itself as a sort of final barrier, a place where the phenomenal veil runs thin but is still present. As Young and Magee rightly point out, Schopenhauer himself is concerned to nuance those of his statements that would seem to equate will with thing-in-itself.[12] For instance, while speaking of the 'kernel of the phenomenon' in the second volume, Schopenhauer emphasises that 'this kernel can never be entirely separated from the phenomenon,' but 'is known always only in its relations and references to the phenomenon itself' (*WWR*.II.183).

Hence, this inner kernel, the act of willing we experience within ourselves, is 'only the nearest and clearest *phenomenon* of the thing-in-itself'; it is where the veil between phenomenon and thing-in-itself runs thinnest. The will we experience within ourselves, therefore, is *not* the thing-in-itself, since it is still structured through our experience, especially through the form of *time*.[13] But it is the closest thing we have, and by virtue of this *relative* 'immediateness', it functions as a sort of 'representative' for us; a representative, that is, of the thing-in-itself: 'Accordingly we have

11. Thus Schopenhauer defines the *will* as 'the kernel and in-itself of everything' (*WWR*.I.309), and as 'the being-in-itself of every thing in the world' (*WWR*.I.118).

12. Young, *Willing*, 27–35; likewise Magee (*Philosophy*, 443–5) argues that the will is not the noumenon, and Schopenhauer did *not* teach that we can have 'direct knowledge of the noumenon'.

13. Though not by space or causality, which structure our sensory perception; see *WWR*.II.197.

to refer the whole world of phenomena to that one in which the thing-in-itself is manifested under the lightest of all veils' (*WWR*.II.197). When speaking of will as thing-in-itself, therefore, this is a manner of speech that is warranted by the *proximity* of the will to the thing-in-itself: '*in this sense* I teach that the inner nature of every thing is *will*, and I call the will the thing-in-itself' (*WWR*.II.197; my emphasis). Thus Schopenhauer's approach seems more gradualist than dualist: if the thing-in-itself is the core of the world, the will is the very first layer of experience, the innermost shell around that core; it's the closest we can get. Schopenhauer's intuition is that we can draw inferences from this first layer; that all things being equal, the most thinly veiled information is more likely to be the truest.[14]

While I will leave this question open here, throughout the following discussion I will myself assume that Schopenhauer is operating consistently on the level of experience or the phenomenon, and that his exercise is one of approximating the thing-in-itself solely *through the relation of that thing to our experience*. This assumption seems to match what Schopenhauer says about salvation, for when he does speak of the *beyond* of our experience, he speaks of something that we truly cannot reach. To my mind, Schopenhauer refers directly to the thing-in-itself only when he refers to *nothing* (on which, more below). Bearing this in mind, I will move directly to those parts of his works in which Schopenhauer develops his case for philosophical pessimism.

The Case for Pessimism

In tracing the pessimist tradition thus far, we have seen the case for pessimism made in terms that could be described as *passionately a posteriori*: it is precisely in the experiential or phenomenological aspect of these arguments that their intuitive force is supposed to reside. This is what powers Bayle's project, built entirely and explicitly on a posteriori foundations, and Voltaire's even more so. After all, Voltaire's exercise in pessimism was propelled and perhaps made credible primarily by the Lisbon earthquake; and it is in this sense that I have asked how well it would have worked had Lisbon never occurred.

One thing that sets Schopenhauer apart from previous pessimists, therefore, is his explicit ambition to make an *a priori case* for philosophical pessimism: that is, a 'perfectly cold and philosophical demonstration of

14. For criticism of this assumption, see Young, *Willing*, 30.

the inevitable suffering at the very foundation of the nature of life', which 'starts from the universal and is conducted *a priori*' (*WWR*.I.323–4). In the words of Young, 'On Schopenhauer's approach, suffering is to be connected, non-inductively, with the *human* condition as such.'[15] The question is how this can be done convincingly: Is it even possible to make an a priori or non-inductive argument for pessimism, if all pessimist arguments thus far have leaned so strongly on experience?

Young,[16] in his discussion of Schopenhauer's pessimism, identifies four distinct though closely connected a priori arguments, having to do with the following:

1. The *negativity* of happiness.
2. The human propensity for *boredom*, as the state into which we necessarily lapse when all our other desires have been achieved.
3. The human situatedness in *time*.
4. The effect of *egoism* in human affairs—which, after Benatar, might also be called the 'misanthropic argument': that is, the idea that 'The chief source of the most serious evils affecting man is man himself; *homo homini lupus*'[17] (*WWR*.II.577).

In my interpretation, the first of these arguments is by far the most important foundation of Schopenhauer's pessimism: namely, the positivity of pain, misery, and evils in general versus the negativity of pleasure, happiness, and goods in general. Correspondingly, I take Schopenhauer's to be primarily a *value-oriented pessimism*.[18]

This argument, on the negativity of happiness, should not strike us as entirely novel: the first blow to optimism in this context had already been delivered by Malebranche and especially Bayle, who argued for the positivity of pain and evils *next to*, if not quite opposed to, the positivity of the

15. Ibid., 137 (his emphasis).

16. Ibid., 137–45; see also David Woods's list of Schopenhauer's pessimist claims ('Schopenhauer's Pessimism', 31).

17. See Benatar, 'Anti-Natalism', 78–121. Schopenhauer's examples of man's cruelty to man include 'Negro slavery', as well as child labour and heavy factory work, which entails having to perform the same monotonous tasks for ten to fourteen hours a day from childhood to death, which 'is the fate of millions' (*WWR*.II.578).

18. Here, my interpretation differs from Dienstag's, who suggests this is a derivative point, not as central to Schopenhauer's philosophy as is 'the centrality of the problem of time' (*Pessimism*, 85n.). In my view, this should be the other way around: future-oriented pessimism, for Schopenhauer, is the derivative of his much deeper, much wider value-oriented pessimism, which is precisely what connects him with an earlier pessimist tradition.

good. In fact, as we have seen in the discussion of *Xenophanes*, there are times when Bayle gives the impression that pain has *more* reality or more positivity, more phenomenal force, than pleasure does; that, all things being equal, evils have the intrinsic quality of weighing more heavily than goods. Yet neither Bayle nor Malebranche goes so far as to make the further claim that happiness or pleasure is purely negative; nor would Voltaire or Hume suggest this in their wake. And it is, of course, precisely these thinkers' a posteriori approach that prevents them from denying the positivity of pleasure, which to them would surely seem just as counterintuitive as to deny the positivity of pain. How, then, does Schopenhauer make this claim?

Round One: 'The Dark Abodes of Misery'

Let's begin by looking at Schopenhauer's first statement of pessimism, in vol. I of *The World*, which I will designate as 'Round One'. Early on in book IV, Schopenhauer defines *suffering* as the 'hindrance [of the will] through an obstacle placed between it and its temporary goal', and '*satisfaction*, well-being-happiness' as the will's 'attainment of the goal'. In Schopenhauer's conception, what this means is that we experience and see around us constant suffering without lasting happiness, since satisfaction is only fleeting or momentary: it is never other than the starting point of a new striving.[19] We see this clearly, says Schopenhauer, in all of conscious life: not only in human life, but also 'in the life of the animal kingdom, the constant suffering whereof is easily demonstrable'. Consequently, everyone can 'sufficiently convince himself in the suffering animal world how essentially *all life is suffering*' (*WWR*.I.309–10).

There are two important initial points to be made here. First, it is questionable whether this can properly be called an a priori argument, since it leans heavily on confirmation by experience: in fact, it can be argued that the most *convincing* elements of Schopenhauer's argument are those that excel in phenomenological force and seem to rely on a posteriori intuitions (such as the famous example of the experience of an animal eating another versus that of the animal being eaten: *PP*.II.263). Furthermore, even if the argument is basically a priori, it hinges even more crucially on the definitions of suffering and satisfaction, which don't receive any justification other than what experience can give us. To this,

19. As Woods argues, this does not mean that satisfaction is not real, just that it 'never lasts' ('Schopenhauer's Pessimism', 51).

any Baylean pessimist *or* experience-minded optimist might object that these definitions miss the mark, since evils are only evils if experienced as such, and we don't always suffer if we don't get what we want immediately; conversely, happiness doesn't always reside in the attainment of some goal but can be a more basic underlying state of being (such as, simply, a happy temperament).[20]

The second point to be made is not critical but descriptive: it is to note the inclusion of animals in the pessimist condition. This is a point to which I will return (as Schopenhauer often does), since his pessimism has sometimes been misrepresented as focusing purely on the human condition,[21] when in fact Schopenhauer suggests even here, at the very opening of his argument for pessimism, that it is intrinsic to the animal condition: that is, to any being burdened with consciousness.[22] While it is indeed true for Schopenhauer that humans, at least in some ways, suffer *more* or at least *differently*, it is even more profoundly true for him that theirs is not the only tragic state of being. I will return to this below.

Having made these two initial points, let's go back to Schopenhauer's discussion, which now moves to develop the case for pessimism by the crucial concept of *boredom*. According to Schopenhauer, the basis of all willing is need, lack, and therefore pain (which accompanies our experience of need or lack); hence the will is destined to lead to pain: we experience pain whenever we strive for something we desire or lack, which is most of the time. (*WWR*.I.312). So far so good: even if we concede that this is our most common state of being, this still leaves room for a happier state that takes place whenever that which we desire has been achieved or attained—what Schopenhauer describes as *satisfaction*. But satisfaction, for Schopenhauer, is itself a problematic thing. Either it is completely momentary, since any desired object loses its attraction as soon as it has been attained, so that the will immediately fixes itself to some other as yet unattained (or even unattainable) thing—or, if it is *not* momentary, it gives

20. Or in the *prospect* of attainment of one's goal: see Simmel, *Schopenhauer and Nietzsche*, 30; Janaway, 'Schopenhauer's Pessimism', 333–4.

21. E.g. Dienstag, *Pessimism*, especially 86–8; Young, *Willing*, 144.

22. There is a connection with certain strains in the utilitarian tradition here, which is equally oriented on experience: recall Jeremy Bentham's famous intuition according to which, when considering the moral status of animals, 'the question is not, Can they *reason*? nor, Can they *talk*? but, Can they suffer?' (Bentham, *An Introduction to the Principles of Morals and Legislation*, 283n.; his emphasis). See Young (*Willing*, 159n.), who thinks Schopenhauer is implicitly espousing a kind of act-utilitarianism.

way to something at least as bad as the suffering of striving: the state of being known as *boredom*.[23]

According to Schopenhauer, whenever we are deprived of objects of willing, 'a fearful emptiness and boredom' come over us, so that existence itself becomes a burden to us: 'Hence . . . life swings like a pendulum to and fro between pain and boredom, and these two are in fact its ultimate constituents' (*WWR*.I.312).[24] Existence thus reveals itself to be a constant and ultimately pointless struggle to maintain that existence: pointless because this struggle is accompanied by the certain knowledge that, even if we are very successful in our striving to keep existing, death will get us in the end. Life, for Schopenhauer, fluctuates continually between the states of willing (or suffering) and attainment (or satisfaction): but once we come to possess some desired thing, that very fact of 'possession takes away its charm' (*WWR*.I.314). What happens then is one of two equally painful courses: either the wish or need or lack appears again, now fixed on some other object, or sheer boredom takes its place.

This pivotal part of Schopenhauer's argument, which sees existence as continually divided between 'the Scylla of want and the Charybdis of boredom',[25] is also one of the most heavily criticised. The most basic point to be made against this a priori argument for pessimism is that it seems exaggerated and counter-intuitive: most of us simply do not experience life as a pendulum swinging between pain and boredom; nor need anyone agree with Schopenhauer's general statement that the attainment of any goal always takes away its charm. What's more, Schopenhauer's equation of striving or desiring with suffering seems to beg the question in more ways than one. Not only could we simply disagree, on introspective grounds, with this equation, but the very definition of striving-as-suffering seems to play down the meaning and reality of suffering to an even greater extent than we have seen in 'optimistic' attempts to explain suffering away.[26] Suffering, conceived as day-to-day striving to attain *any* goal whatsoever, is so broad and general a term as to become almost trivial or meaningless. This is all the more striking since it is precisely Schopenhauer's powerful

23. On striving and satisfaction, see, e.g., Janaway, 'Schopenhauer's Pessimism', Woods, 'Schopenhauer's Pessimism', chapter 2.

24. A similar point on life going back and forth between striving and boredom is made by Pascal, *Pensées*, fragments L622/B131 and L136/B139; and in Voltaire's *Candide* (77/ *OCV*.48.256) by Martin the Manichean, who 'concluded that human beings are born to live either in convulsions of restlessness or in the lethargy of boredom'.

25. Young, *Schopenhauer*, 213.

26. I return to this briefly in chapter 9.

descriptions of true, deep suffering (that is, the a posteriori part of his argument) that continue to move readers to this day.[27]

Nevertheless, if Schopenhauer's overall argument is overstated, there seems to be a valuable intuition here, having to do with the Schopenhauerian concept of boredom in particular. Language may be deceptive here: as Young points out, the English term 'boredom' seems too trivial a term to cover the meaning of the German *Langeweile*, which really designates a 'complex existential malaise', something akin to depression.[28] *Langeweile* is not at all a negative or privative state of inaction: it is rather a positive and ambiguous state of suffering, in the more emphatic meaning of the term. Schopenhauer himself hastens to make this point: 'Boredom is anything but an evil to be thought of lightly; ultimately it depicts on the countenance real despair.' Once we are free from want or cares, then boredom assails us, and humans become 'a burden to themselves'. It is at this point that death becomes a desirable prospect, 'and a man voluntarily hastens to it'. Thus boredom, according to Schopenhauer, is a common cause of suicide among convicts (*WWR*.I.313).[29] If this is so, then *Langeweile* can be recognised by its effects and attributes as something akin to Baylean *chagrin*: a psychologically oppressive 'deadening' state 'that makes existence a burden to us' (*WWR*.I.319); something as apt as intense physical suffering to drive us to desire death. This is indeed an experience to be accounted for in any description of individual or even societal suffering—indeed, it is strongly reminiscent of Maria von Herbert's testimony to Kant regarding the unbearable emptiness of her existence.[30] Where Schopenhauer goes too far is in his insistence that *Langeweile* is an intrinsic part of *any* human life.

27. As Cartwright rightly notes ('Schopenhauer on Suffering', 59), the a priori arguments are 'the least persuasive elements in Schopenhauer's pessimistic arsenal. Rather, it is his graphic accounts of human stupidity, cruelty, and folly, of the cruelty of nature, and of the all-pervasive presence of misery and want, suffering and pain, that cast his thick fog of gloom over existence.'

28. Young, *Willing*, 141, and *Schopenhauer*, 210; see Woods, 'Seriously Bored', 964–7. See also Prins's description of boredom as carrying within it 'a nameless suffering, a suffering without apparent cause' (*Uit Verveling*, 28–9; my translation); and Bol, 'Themes', chapter 4, for a discussion of 'profound boredom'.

29. On Schopenhauer's views of penitentiary methods and especially solitary confinement, see Woods, 'Seriously Bored'.

30. See chapter 7. Young (*Willing*, 142–3), writing in the 1980s, relates Schopenhauer's concept of boredom both to the modern concept of depression and to the condition of contemporary Western society at large; the latter suggestion would receive all the more force when applied to the present-day 'age of distraction'. For an interpretation of boredom as the fundamental mood [*Grundstimmung*] of modern society, see Prins, *Uit Verveling*.

Following his discussion of the negativity of happiness combined with the conception of existence as an ebb and flow between suffering and boredom, Schopenhauer pauses, as though to catch his breath. So far, he tells us, he has demonstrated a priori that human life is not capable of true happiness but is intrinsically a tragic state, its modes of being mere variations on a wider theme, which is suffering. From here, he could go on to deliver an a posteriori argument in the style of Bayle or Voltaire, but this exercise, in Schopenhauer's view, would be without end, and would take us away from 'the standpoint of universality which is essential to philosophy' (*WWR*.I.323). Furthermore, such an a posteriori demonstration would be open to the charge of one-sidedness, since it would necessarily start from particular facts. Nevertheless, Schopenhauer sees fit to mention that such a posteriori confirmation is easily available everywhere in the world (*WWR*.I.324), and he continues very much in the spirit of Bayle's *Xenophanes* (which is, of course, also the spirit of Voltaire's *Candide*), pointing out that what our own experience tells us, and what history and the great poets teach us, is that the human world is a 'kingdom of chance and error', a world in which evils and sufferings prevail while 'everything excellent or admirable is always only an exception, one case in millions' (*WWR*.I.324).

On an individual level, we know from our own lives that 'every life-history is a history of suffering'. The reason why we often conceal our own unhappiness from others is that we are concerned to prevent their *schadenfreude*, which in Schopenhauer's world-view is the king of vices:

> as a rule, every life is a continual series of mishaps great and small, concealed as much as possible by everyone, because he knows that others are almost always bound to feel satisfaction at the spectacle of annoyances from which they are for the moment exempt; rarely will they feel sympathy or compassion. (*WWR*.I.324)

From this continual misrepresentation of our own states of being to each other arises the skewed view that many of us have of the human predicament.[31]

It is at this point, where Schopenhauer is at his most Baylean, that he repeats the Ciceronian thought experiment we have encountered in Bayle

31. This idea of a structurally warped evaluation of our own and others' lives is something that later pessimists such as Benatar, armed with scientific research, will refer to psychological mechanisms such as Pollyannaism (Benatar, *Better Never to Have Been*, 64–9). Schopenhauer's mechanism of concealment is reminiscent of practices in social media, where users feel communally pressured to show only their happiest pictures and updates to their peers (Freitas, *The Happiness Effect*).

and seen echoed throughout the pages of later writers: the question of whether having lived once, we would want to go through life again. Schopenhauer's reply, by this stage, should not be surprising:

> But perhaps at the end of his life, no man, if he be sincere and at the same time in possession of his faculties, will ever wish to go through it again. Rather than this, he will much prefer to choose complete non-existence. The essential purport of the world-famous monologue in *Hamlet* is, in condensed form, that our state is so wretched that complete non-existence would be decidedly preferable to it. (*WWR*.I.324)[32]

Since, in Schopenhauer's conception, it is preferable either no longer to exist or even never to have existed in the first place (he is ambiguous about what he means by non-existence), death should not strike us as such a disaster: 'the shortness of life, so often lamented, may perhaps be the very best thing about it' (*WWR*.I.325). He approvingly cites Herodotus's observation that by the end of life, everyone will have wished more than once that they don't have to live through the next day (*WWR*.I.324–5). Hence, if suicide were strictly a question of 'to be or not to be', then we could choose the lesser evil (not to be) unproblematically; the reason we resist this option is that we have a sense that death is not 'an absolute annihilation' (*WWR*.I.324).

In other words, Schopenhauer is in firm agreement with that darkly expressed Baylean intuition that for some, many, or all conscious creatures it would be better not to be. Furthermore, again in a very Baylean vein, Schopenhauer launches a sweeping attack on Leibnizian–Popean optimism, charged with the same kind of moral indignation we have seen in Bayle and Voltaire alike:

> If, finally, we were to bring to the sight of everyone the terrible sufferings and afflictions to which his life is constantly exposed, he would be seized with horror. If we were to conduct the most hardened and callous optimist through hospitals, infirmaries, operating theatres, through prisons, torture-chambers, and slave-hovels, over battlefields and to places of execution; if we were to open to him all the dark abodes of misery, where it shuns the gaze of cold curiosity, and finally were to allow him to glance into the dungeon of Ugolino where prisoners

32. Note that Schopenhauer's thought experiment is even less well defined than Bayle's: would the offer of reliving mean living *the same life* again—or would it mean being reborn as someone else? Either way, the point is that, on Schopenhauer's view as on Bayle's, it would be rational to say no to such an offer of re-living, and irrational to say yes.

> starved to death, he too would certainly see in the end what kind of a world is this *meilleur des mondes possibles*. (*WWR*.1.325)[33]

The strong ethical drive behind this statement aligns Schopenhauer with earlier pessimists, with whom he shares the intuition that optimism neglects or even makes a mockery of the reality of suffering and is therefore morally as well as theoretically in the wrong. Indeed, in the following passage, Schopenhauer makes it explicit that the objection against optimism is at least partly a *moral* one:

> For the rest, I cannot here withhold the statement that *optimism*, where it is not merely the thoughtless talk of those who harbour nothing but words under their shallow foreheads, seems to me to be not merely an absurd, but also a really *wicked*, way of thinking, a bitter mockery of the unspeakable sufferings of mankind (*WWR*.I.326; his emphasis)

Thus, despite the methodological divergence of Schopenhauer's particular brand of philosophical pessimism (which does not yet bear the name), he nevertheless reveals himself to be closely associated with earlier a posteriori pessimists, into whose ranks he will eventually inscribe himself.

Round Two: Theodicy Revisited

Schopenhauer's first statement of pessimism ends here. For his second statement—'Round Two'—we need to fast-forward twenty-five years to the sequel of *The World as Will and Representation*, where we find that Schopenhauer's ink-black pessimism was not a dalliance of youth. Although many have objected to the 'melancholy and cheerless nature of my philosophy' (*WWR*.II.581–2), he has not changed his mind: on the contrary, he now explicitly associates his philosophy with pessimism, which he restates in even more emphatic terms.

For instance, even more stress is placed on the pivotal pessimist premise, here carried to its strongest version yet: not only can non-existence be better than existence, but it would be better for all creatures never to have been. According to Schopenhauer, since 'our existence is happiest when we perceive it least'—for instance, when we are free from pain or other troubles—it follows that 'it would be better not to have it' (*WWR*.II.575). We find traces of this tragic condition of ours, in which we are bound to

33. Recall Bayle's refrain, repeated by Leibniz, on the misery of the world demonstrated by hospitals, prisons, gallows, and beggars (*DHC*: *Manicheans*[1]*.D*).

pursue an existence without which we would nevertheless have been better off, in all corners of human life: 'since our state or condition is rather something that it were better should not be, everything that surrounds us bears the traces of this—just as in hell everything smells of sulphur' (*WWR*.II.577). Goethe's Mephistopheles (from *Faust*) is enthusiastically quoted to the effect that it would have been better if nothing had been created:

> And rightly so, for all things that exist
> Deserve to perish, and would not be missed—
> Much better it would be if nothing were
> Brought into being.[34]

Furthermore, similarly to Bayle's balances in *Xenophanes*, in his later writings Schopenhauer includes a more thorough attempt to weigh life's evils against its goods. Thus he suggests that we calmly compare the sum of life's possible pleasures with life's possible pains: 'I do not think it will be difficult to strike the balance.' However, this exercise is unnecessary:

> it is quite superfluous to dispute whether there is more good or evil in the world; for *the mere existence of evil* decides the matter, since evil can never be wiped off, and consequently can never be balanced, by the good that exists along with or after it. (*WWR*.II.576; my emphasis)

He cites Petrarch's heartbroken expression that 'a thousand joys aren't worth a single sorrow': *Mille piacer non vaglion un tormento*.[35]

Such statements, even more than Schopenhauer's a priori argument in Round One, seem to beg the question, relying as they do on an extremely counter-intuitive stipulation: that even the faintest amount or briefest moment of discomfort would be enough to make life not worth living; that 'any suffering at all invalidates the whole world'.[36] This does seem to be what Schopenhauer is suggesting—but I think the deeper point he is trying to make has to do rather with *justification*: the point is that even if the goods of life vastly outweigh the evils, even so, this does nothing to *justify* existence. As long as a single grain of evil subsists, existence cannot be said to be preferable over non-existence, in which no evils subsist. This, within a philosophical framework that posits evils as positive and goods

34. Goethe, *Faust: Part One*, v. 1339–42; quoted by Schopenhauer in *WWR*.II.574.

35. Petrarch, *Canzoniere*, no. 231, v. 4, here in translation by Mark Musa; quoted by Schopenhauer in *WWR*.II.576.

36. Janaway, 'Schopenhauer's Pessimism', 332.

as negative, seems only consistent. 'The mere existence of evil decides the matter'—the 'matter' in question being that it would still be better not to exist at all.[37]

According to Schopenhauer, therefore, the real point of pessimism over optimism is not so much that the evils of life outweigh the goods (although he certainly believes this to be true)—but that the appearance of *any* evils whatsoever presents a prima-facie proof against the goodness of existence. Thus, just as a single torment, a single grain of suffering is enough to pose a challenge to any optimistic justification of existence (and, therefore, creation), so too a single suffering life should be enough to make us feel sorry about the creation of the world entire:

> For that thousands had lived in happiness and joy would never do away with the anguish and death-agony of one individual; and just as little does my present well-being undo my previous sufferings. Therefore, were the evil in the world even a hundred times less than it is, its mere existence would still be sufficient to establish a truth that may be expressed in various ways, although always only somewhat indirectly, namely that we have not to be pleased but rather sorry about the existence of the world; that its non-existence would be preferable to its existence; that it is something which at bottom ought not to be, and so on. (*WWR*.II.576)[38]

What Schopenhauer is affirming here is what I have called the stronger version of the pessimistic premise, according to which a single item of suffering (be it an individual life or a simple 'grain' of suffering) is enough to pose a challenge to optimism and to any theodicean justification of existence. Such passages suggest that Schopenhauer, while not addressing theodicy explicitly, is nevertheless operating within a theodicean context: even more so than in Round One, his concern is with justification as much as it is with theodicean optimism, and especially with the optimist view that life is intrinsically a gift, something about which we should be 'pleased' and grateful. Against this optimist view, Schopenhauer will counterpose the neo-pagan or tragic view that life is instead a kind of debt, and he will cross this view with Christian categories to arrive at a curious notion of original sin. To understand this argument, and the way in which

37. This is, in essence, the same argument as developed more fully by David Benatar in the context of anti-natalism.

38. This passage is followed by a quotation from Byron's *Childe Harold* (IV, stanza 126) on the seen and unseen woes of man ('Disease, death, bondage'), which tell us that 'Our life is a false nature'.

Schopenhauer's pessimism is still crucially connected with the problem of evil, we need first to take a closer look at his treatment of theodicy in Round Two.

THEODICY AND THE PESSIMIST TRADITION

After Schopenhauer has developed his version of the pessimist premise, arguing that existence, if it includes any evils whatsoever, is worse than non-existence, he pauses at length to discuss the competing philosophical traditions of optimism and pessimism (*WWR*.II.581–88). This historical overview is at the same time a critical reflection on the themes at hand *and* an attempt to situate Schopenhauer's own philosophy into a previous pessimist tradition, which is being created by this very exercise. While this discussion is often mentioned by scholars only briefly and in passing, if at all,[39] it is in fact highly telling of the shifting orientations of Schopenhauer's pessimism—which only now receives this name.

For one thing, while in Round One Schopenhauer's mentions of optimism are sporadic and haphazard, appearing most commonly as an off-the-cuff jibe at any life-affirming religious or philosophical mindset (such as, it appears, the entire Old Testament),[40] in Round Two he explicitly discusses optimism as a systematic philosophical tradition crucially oriented towards theodicy. Thus he associates 'the system of *optimism*' with the view that this world 'is the best of all possible worlds', and places Leibniz, as 'the founder of systematic *optimism*', as the main target of the pessimist tradition. The only virtue of the *Theodicy*, says Schopenhauer, is that it 'later gave rise to the immortal *Candide* of the great Voltaire', thus ironically proving Leibniz's point that some evils do produce a greater good. (*WWR*.II.581–3; his emphasis).[41]

39. E.g. Dienstag, *Pessimism*, 84n. A recent exception is Woods's dissertation ('Schopenhauer's Pessimism'), which duly calls attention to Schopenhauer's embeddedness in the theodicean debate (especially via Leibniz and Rousseau).

40. See, e.g., *WWR*.II.580, 621, 624. The condemnation of the Old Testament has to do with the affirmation in Genesis 1:31, abhorrent to Schopenhauer, that all was 'very good'; he mentions the myth of the fall of man as the only thing 'that reconciles me to the Old Testament' (*WWR*.II.580). The Book of Job is mentioned only once, in the context of Swift reportedly celebrating his birthday by reading the Bible passage in which Job curses the day he was born (*WWR*.II.586).

41. On young Schopenhauer's reading of Voltaire and his ensuing concern with theodicy, see Safranski, *Schopenhauer*, chapter 4. Schopenhauer does not give a very fair or in-depth treatment of either optimism in general or particular optimists; thus he makes the common mistake of equating Leibniz with Pope.

But what exactly is Schopenhauer's problem with theodicean optimism? As his many references to Voltaire (as well as Hume) suggest, Schopenhauer's main objection is that such optimism contradicts our experience of a suffering creation: 'the optimism of Leibniz conflicts with the obvious misery of existence' (*WWR*.II.184).[42] Against the optics of optimism, Schopenhauer raises the following objection:

> an optimist tells me to open my eyes and look at the world and see how beautiful it is in the sunshine, with its mountains, valleys, rivers, plants, animals, and so on. But is the world, then, a peep-show? These things are certainly beautiful to *behold*, but to *be* them is something quite different. (*WWR*.II.581)[43]

As we know by now, this is not a very fair representation of Leibniz's optimism, any more than Voltaire's was: Leibniz, as we have seen, did not hold that *all* is good or beautiful; that is *not* the point of his cosmic perspective.[44] But the point in Schopenhauer's last sentence is well taken: this is none other than the reassertion of the creaturely perspective against the cosmic; the Baylean–Voltairean opposition of embodied experience over and against abstracted and disembodied theological vision.

Against Leibniz and theodicean optimism in general, with which he also associates Shaftesbury, Bolingbroke, Pope, and Rousseau,[45] Schopenhauer instead sides with their pessimist detractors, thus supplying us with a brief bibliography of modern pessimism to date—or at least of those pessimists with whom he was familiar. Favourite among Schopenhauer's pessimists are Hume and Voltaire, the former of whom 'explains without reserve in the tenth and eleventh books of his *Dialogues on Natural Religion*, with arguments very convincing yet quite different from mine, the

42. Against Leibniz's view that this world is the *best* of all possible worlds, Schopenhauer believes (not in his finest hour) that he could prove it is the *worst* (*WWR*.II.583–4). I feel that much of the literature has tended to give far too much weight to this very weak argument, the purpose of which seems to be mainly provocative: Schopenhauer does not develop it in great detail; nor does he return to it, as he does to his other core arguments. My sense is that it should be passed over lightly.

43. See *PP*.I.421: 'All things are delightful to *see*, but terrible to *be*' (his emphasis).

44. Such passages are more fitting of Pope's poetic optimism: that Schopenhauer is nevertheless thinking of Leibniz appears from his recurrent mention of the doctrine of the best of possible worlds. On Schopenhauer's reading of Leibniz, see Woods, 'Schopenhauer's Pessimism', chapter 3.

45. *WWR*.II.584: 'Therefore, when Leibniz, Shaftesbury, Bolingbroke, and Pope appeared with optimism, the general offence caused by it was due mainly to the fact that optimism is irreconcilable with Christianity.' *WWR*.II.585 mentions Rousseau's 'optimism and humanism'.

miserable nature of this world and the untenableness of all optimism; here at the same time he attacks optimism at its source' (*WWR*.II.581–2).[46] The distinctness of Hume's arguments from Schopenhauer's has to do, of course, with their principally a posteriori nature, but this difference seems to be purely methodological: Schopenhauer considers his own work in full alignment with the earlier pessimist tradition.

This alignment appears also by the praise Schopenhauer repeatedly bestows on Voltaire's 'Lisbon' writings, especially *Candide*. Intriguingly, the morally charged terms Schopenhauer uses to describe *Candide* are strongly reminiscent of Kant's essay on theodicy, opposing sincerity (associated with pessimism) to 'hypocritical flattery' (associated with optimism):

> Even by the name of his hero, Voltaire indicated that it needed only sincerity to recognize the opposite of optimism. Actually optimism cuts so strange a figure on this scene of sin, suffering, and death, that we should be forced to regard it as irony if we did not have an adequate explanation of its origin in its secret source (namely hypocritical flattery with an offensive confidence in its success), a source so delightfully disclosed by Hume [in his *Natural History of Religion*], as previously mentioned. (*WWR*.II.583)

Turning his gaze to Voltaire's poem on the Lisbon earthquake, 'which also is expressly directed against optimism' (*WWR*.II.584), Schopenhauer briefly reconstructs the confrontation between Voltaire and Rousseau, siding firmly with the former as the place-holder of pessimism. He offers several reasons why Voltaire is 'placed decidedly higher than Rousseau', the most important one being Voltaire's 'insight into the preponderating magnitude of the evil and misery of existence with which he is deeply penetrated' (*WWR*.II.584–5). In contrast, Rousseau showed himself to be acting 'in the interests of optimism' by disputing this preponderance of evil in his 'Profession de foi du vicaire Savoyard', while attacking Voltaire's 'fine poem' in his letter of 18 August 1756. The main problem with Rousseau's philosophy, Schopenhauer argues, is as follows:

> the fundamental characteristic and πρῶτον ψεῦδος [first false step] of Rousseau's whole philosophy is that he puts in the place of the Christian doctrine of original sin and of the original depravity of the human

46. See also *WWR*.II.591: 'The evil and misery of the world, however, are not in accord even with *theism*; and so it tried to help itself by all kinds of shifts, evasions, and theodicies which nevertheless succumbed irretrievably to the arguments of Hume and Voltaire.'

> race an original goodness and unlimited perfectibility thereof, which had been led astray merely by civilization and its consequences; and on this he then establishes his optimism and humanism. (*WWR*.II.585)

The first two pillars of the modern pessimist tradition, therefore, are Voltaire and Hume, with whom Schopenhauer considers his own philosophy essentially, if not methodologically, aligned. But he goes on to mention a third modern predecessor, Lord Byron, and specifically his poem *Cain*:

> Just as in *Candide* Voltaire in his facetious manner wages war on optimism, so has Byron done the same, in his serious and tragic way, in his immortal masterpiece *Cain*, and for this reason he too has been glorified by the invectives of the obscurantist Friedrich Schlegel. (*WWR*.II.585)[47]

Following this discussion of the early Enlightenment confrontation between optimism and pessimism, Schopenhauer adds that he could go on to list countless sayings of 'great minds of all ages', but 'there would be no end to the citations'—and so he limits himself to just a few. Here (*WWR*.II.585–8), he presents a brief selection of classic pessimistic literature, from the ancients (Plutarch, Heraclitus, Theognis, Sophocles, Euripides, Homer, and Pliny, several of whom offer a variety of the 'wisdom of Silenus': that the best thing in life is not to be born, the second best to die as quickly as possible) to the moderns (Shakespeare, Byron, Gracián). He ends the chapter with a glowing gesture towards Leopardi, who presents the wretchedness of existence 'on every page of his works', but in such a way 'that he never wearies us, but, on the contrary, has a diverting and stimulating effect' (*WWR*.II.588). Pessimism, as readers of Schopenhauer themselves will know, need not be dull and dreary.

It may be clear by now why I have paused at length on this nineteenth-century discussion of earlier pessimists. When Schopenhauer attempts to inscribe himself into a previous pessimist tradition, his three primary quoted modern predecessors (Hume, Voltaire, Byron) are each quoted *exactly* in the parts of their works that are directly and deeply influenced by Bayle: this is as true for Hume's tenth and eleventh *Dialogues* as it is for Voltaire's 'Lisbon' writings and for Byron's tormented poem *Cain*, which is full of Baylean musings on both the problem of evil and the ethics of creation.[48] What these writings make up is precisely the Baylean

47. On Schlegel's criticism of Voltaire, see chapter 3, at p. 140.

48. Byron's *Cain* is especially noteworthy because it unites the questions posed by Bayle and Benatar: (1) Is God justified in creating humans, considering the suffering that would befall them? And (2) are *humans* justified in creating new humans, considering the evils

legacy: whether or not Schopenhauer mentions him, the tradition into which Schopenhauer is inscribing himself is a Baylean one. It would be mistaken to see this as a trivial point, a mere way to buffer the case for Bayle as 'arch-pessimist' or 'patriarch of pessimism', in lieu of Dienstag's Rousseau. The point is rather to highlight the central place of the problem of evil and theodicean thought in the modern pessimist debate, which by the time of Schopenhauer's writing does seem to have taken on the coherence and consistency of a *tradition*.

The fact that Schopenhauer in his later writings has become increasingly aware of the thematic of theodicy becomes even clearer if we look at the third edition of *The World*, published in 1859, where he adds a long footnote on the theodicean debate in the *first volume* of the work. Here, he mentions that the perceived contradiction between the goodness of God and the misery of the world has become the 'inexhaustible theme of a controversy, lasting nearly a hundred years, between the Cartesians, Malebranche, Leibniz, Bayle, Clarke, Arnauld, and many others'. The one fixed dogma for these authors, Schopenhauer argues, is the existence of God together with God's three essential attributes, which is why these authors keep going in circles, when the source of the dilemma lies in precisely this 'fundamental assumption' (the existence of God with his three attributes). He concludes: 'Bayle alone shows that he notices this' (*WWR*.I.406–7).[49] Hence, while Schopenhauer is not explicitly reacting to theodicy in the way that Bayle and Voltaire are, he is (at least by Round Two) acutely aware of anti-theodicean pessimism, and agrees with it. In Schopenhauer's view, the pessimists were right; the pessimists won. And yet his sentiment also seems to be that while this was a battle well fought, it is not his *own* battle. He represents the theodicean controversy as a closed case, a thing of the past, a debate that lasted around a hundred years and in which the pessimists emerged victorious. This would seem to fit the chronology of what I have tentatively called 'the theodicean turn', beginning roughly with Bayle and Malebranche and culminating with Kant (whose essay on theodicy is nevertheless not mentioned).

Hence, while his pessimism is built on different principles, what Schopenhauer reveals throughout his writings, and *especially* in Round Two,

of existence? On Bayle's influence on Byron's works, see Aycock, 'Lord Byron and Bayle's "Dictionary"'.

49. Schopenhauer cites Bayle a few times, especially in his later works (e.g. *PP*.II.329, citing *Origen*[1].*B*), but does not show signs of having engaged with him in any depth.

is that he recognises experience, or the creaturely perspective, as a crucial element of pessimism, and as something that correctly refutes theodicean optimism. In inscribing himself into a previous pessimist tradition, and presenting that tradition as diametrically opposed to specifically *theodicean* optimism, and commending his predecessors as he does, Schopenhauer shows himself to be affirming what is ultimately a very Baylean pessimism. At the same time, as we will see, his argument will lead to a very un-Baylean moment.

Round Three: Parerga and Paralipomena

Before we go there, a few comments are in order on Schopenhauer's third statement of pessimism, in several sections of the two-volume collection *Parerga and Paralipomena*, published in 1851.[50] This work, while comprising the least systematic presentation of Schopenhauer's pessimism, is arguably also the most accessible and, therefore, the most commonly read; the sections dealing with pessimism are often even published separately.[51] And yet it is questionable whether Schopenhauer did himself any favours here. It is true that these essays make his philosophy very accessible, but they also flatten some of his key concerns: there is no room for the same kind of depth or nuance that marks those parts of his earlier works where Schopenhauer is at his best. Nevertheless, these essays are again indicative of the wider development of Schopenhauer's thought, and the sharpened focus he bestows on several central themes.

The most important essay for our current purposes is titled 'Additional remarks on the doctrine of the suffering of the world' (*PP*.II.262–75). What is especially striking about this retelling of his pessimist argument is that it is framed almost entirely in a posteriori terms. After presenting his initial supposition (that suffering is the end of life), and reasserting the central point of the 'negativity of well-being and happiness' versus 'the positivity of pain' (*PP*.II.262), Schopenhauer bolsters his argument primarily with reference to our internal and external experiences: that is, our experience of ourselves and our experience of the world. Hence the famous passage:

50. It is perhaps not entirely appropriate to speak of 'Round Three', coming as it does on the heels of Round Two; recall that I employ this distinction wholly for analytical purposes. Magee (*Philosophy*, 245) offers an 'idiomatic' translation of *Parerga and Paralipomena* as 'Additions and Omissions'.

51. Such as in the Penguin edition *On the Suffering of the World*.

> Whoever would like to briefly test the assertion that pleasure outweighs pain in the world, or that they are at least in equilibrium, should compare the feelings of the animal that devours another with those of the one being devoured. (*PP*.II.263)[52]

Here, we also find the same historical argument that Bayle opposed to Maimonides: 'History shows us the life of peoples and finds nothing to report but wars and uprisings; the peaceful years appear only as brief pauses, interludes occurring now and then' (*PP*.II.263). Some themes, such as the burden of time and the oppression of boredom, are given a more central place in the essays than in his earlier works—but, nevertheless, it is still a mostly value-oriented pessimism that Schopenhauer displays in this 'Round Three'. Perhaps the most striking innovation in this round, and in Schopenhauer's later writings in general, is his increasingly emphatic consideration of the condition of animals as suffering beings deserving of our sympathy. This is tied in with yet another of Schopenhauer's central themes that has sometimes been misrepresented: the distinction between animals and humans.

ANIMAL SUFFERING

The common misperception has to do not so much with the distinction between humans and animals itself, which certainly is important for Schopenhauer, but rather with the precise nature of this distinction and with the consequences it has for his pessimism. While it is true that many passages seem to confirm the common view that Schopenhauer sharply distinguishes the human condition from that of the animal, and that he posits pessimism as a uniquely human question and predicament,[53] I nevertheless believe this view to be mistaken: not only is Schopenhauer's distinction much more gradual than often supposed, but this very gradualness means that animals are included in the tragic condition that pessimism describes.

One of the central ideas raised in both volumes of *The World* is that a creature's capacity for pain and suffering increases in proportion to its level of consciousness: therefore, the more developed animals have a higher capacity for suffering, and humans the highest of all (*WWR*.I.310).[54] This

52. This passage will be quoted by Benatar, who makes a similar point ('Anti-Natalism', 49).

53. See Dienstag, *Pessimism*; Young, *Willing and Unwilling*.

54. Correspondingly, within the category of mankind it is that exceptional individual known as the *genius* who suffers beyond all others.

notion receives further treatment in the *Parerga*, where Schopenhauer explains man's increased capacity for pain as well as pleasure in terms of man's understanding of 'the absent and the future, whereby care, fear and hope appear in existence for the first time' (*PP*.II.264). The dividing capacity is that of *reflection*, which exists in humans but not in animals, and is what makes the animal condition, *in some ways*, an enviable one:

> For along with reflection the animal lacks the condenser of joys and sufferings, which therefore cannot pile up as this occurs in humans by means of recollection and foresight. Instead, in animals the suffering of the present always remains, just as it is the first time, the suffering of the present, even if it recurs innumerable times in succession, and it cannot be added up. Hence the enviable carelessness and peace of mind of animals. (*PP*.II.265)

This view of animals as the 'embodied present' (*PP*.II.267) is essentially the same view we have encountered in Leibniz, where the capacity of *reflection* means that humans are capable of experiencing *misery* instead of mere *pain*, which is what animals feel, bound as they are to the present. Misery, on this view, is pain combined with reflection; just as happiness is pleasure combined with reflection: therefore, animals, in so far as they lack reflection, are capable of superficial pains and pleasures, but not of deeper misery or happiness.

However, as Nicholas Jolley mentions in discussing Leibniz,[55] this capacity is a two-edged sword, and Schopenhauer shows that he recognises this. After all, if animals lack anxiety and accumulative suffering or the kind of despair that leads to suicide, they also lack the kind of reflection that can attenuate current misery, such as hope, or the anticipation of a better condition, or the simple awareness that our pains will end at some point:

> Accordingly the life of an animal contains less suffering, but also less joy, than a human's. This is based chiefly on the fact that, on the one hand it remains free of *care and anxiety* and their attending agony, and on the other hand it lacks real *hope*, and therefore does not share in that anticipation of a joyful future through thinking. . . . As a result it is in this sense hopeless. (*PP*.II.266; his emphasis)

Then again, in good neo-pagan style, hope for Schopenhauer is not an unmixed blessing but part of what makes the human condition so

55. Jolley, 'Is Leibniz's Theodicy a Variation?', 67n.

unfortunate: since whatever hope adds to our pleasure in terms of anticipation, it 'afterwards detracts from the actual enjoyment of it, inasmuch as the thing itself then satisfies that much less'. And so the animal condition would again seem enviable, since an animal 'enjoys, entirely and undiminished, what is actually present and real': 'evils press on an animal merely with their actual and own weight, whereas for us fear and foresight, the dread of evil, are often multiplied tenfold' (*PP*.II.267).

While it is certainly the case that the distinction between humans and animals is a central concern of Schopenhauer's, and that he believes humans to have a special capacity for suffering that animals lack, this is only part of the story he is trying to tell. Elsewhere, he seems equally concerned to close or narrow the gap between the human and the animal condition, at least in terms of their existence as suffering creatures. Recall that even in the opening lines of his first statement of pessimism, Schopenhauer asks us to consider 'the suffering animal world' in order to convince ourselves that '*all life is suffering*' (*WWR*.I.310; his emphasis). From the start, suffering is thus presented as the prerogative of all *conscious* creatures, not only of self-conscious creatures. The noble man, whose eyes are fully opened, will not limit his gaze to the suffering of humankind: 'Wherever he looks, he sees suffering humanity and the suffering animal world, and a world that passes away' (*WWR*.I.379). And in the *Parerga*, as we have seen, Schopenhauer raises the example of animals devouring each other in order to evoke our sense of the suffering of life (*PP*.II.263).

It is important to note, to this effect, Schopenhauer's strongly gradualist approach whenever he speaks of the distinction between humans and animals, especially in his later writings.[56] Man is not radically different from other beings in nature, he writes in Round Two, but 'different only in degree' (*WWR*.II.174). While philosophers throughout history have tried to make humans maximally different from animals by making intellect the essence of man, Schopenhauer believes this is deeply mistaken: 'man's real inner nature' should be placed 'not in consciousness, but in the will', which is precisely what man shares with all animals (*WWR*.II.198). Other passages too suggest that humans and animals are more alike than different; this is why we intuitively understand animals as similar to us in many ways, and are able to sympathise with them:

56. Thus John Gray (*Straw Dogs*, 41) seems right in suggesting that 'for Schopenhauer we are at one with other animals in our innermost essence. . . . Like other animals, we are embodiments of universal Will, the struggling, suffering energy that animates everything in the world.'

> Directly from our own nature we understand all the actions and attitudes of animals that express stirrings and agitations of the will; and so to this extent we sympathize with them in many different ways. (*WWR*.II.204)

Therefore, while the distinction between humans and animals is indeed a principal concern for Schopenhauer, it should not be overstated: 'The gulf between a very intelligent animal and a man of very limited capacity is possibly not much greater than that between a blockhead and a genius' (*WWR*.II.204). Furthermore, if we take a look at what Schopenhauer says of animal suffering *in its own regard*, then it does not seem right to present the animal condition as a blessed state to which we cannot return. If animals are better off in some ways, they are worse off in others; for instance, with respect to freedom, 'man's greatest prerogative, which is for ever wanting in the animal' (*WWR*.I.404). Hence, while Schopenhauer is not suggesting that the animal condition is more tragic than the human, he does seem to argue that it is tragic nonetheless. And this seems to inform his awareness, which is stronger than that of most philosophers in his day, that humans do not have unlimited rights over animals.

This point, tacit in much of Schopenhauer's writings, becomes explicit in an important footnote in the first edition, where he offers a kind of utilitarian reflection on the extent of man's right to make use of animals (*WWR*.I.372–3). This right, says Schopenhauer, rests on the fact that the pain that an animal suffers through death or work is still not as great as what man would suffer by being deprived of the animal's flesh or strength:

> Therefore in the affirmation of his own existence, man can go so far as to deny the existence of the animal. In this way, the will-to-live as a whole endures less suffering than if the opposite course were adopted. At the same time, this determines the extent to which man may, without wrong, make use of the powers of animals. This limit, however, is often exceeded, especially in the case of beasts of burden, and of hounds used in hunting. (*WWR*.I.372)

In the second edition he adds that, in his opinion, 'that right does not extend to vivisection, particularly of the higher animals', which some Cartesians famously condoned:[57] 'On the other hand, the insect does not suffer through its death as much as man suffers through its sting. The Hindus

57. On vivisection, and on the moral requirement to chloroform animals before killing them, see *PP*.II.336–9.

do not see this' (*WWR*.I.373). Nevertheless, Schopenhauer is highly appreciative of the Hindu abstinence from animal food (*WWR*.I.388), in which he seems to recognise not only a personal exercise of inhibition but a *moral* achievement, something closely connected with Schopenhauer's ethical ideal of sympathy. According to Schopenhauer's ethics, if this ideal is rightly exercised, then it will also be extended to animals. Not only will the noble man refrain from causing suffering in humans, but he will 'not cause suffering even to an animal' (*WWR*.I.372). Thus it is in part Spinoza's 'contempt for animals' as 'mere things for our use' that condemns his ethics in Schopenhauer's eyes (*WWR*.II.645; *PP*.I.69).

The same theme returns to the fore in the second volume, where Schopenhauer repeatedly commends the love for animals as well as abstinence from eating them, praising St Francis for loving his animals as sisters and brothers, while mentioning early religious groups such as the Marcionites and Nazarenes for their vegetarianism (*WWR*.II.614, 621–3). This concern for the suffering of animals becomes even more prominent in the *Parerga*—and especially in Schopenhauer's handwritten additions to this work, written in the last years of his life.[58] For instance, the advantage initially given to animals in so far as they are the 'embodied present' is withdrawn in the following addition to that passage:

> this aforementioned quality of animals to be satisfied by mere existence more than we are, is abused by egoistic and heartless human beings and often exploited to such a great extent that we allow them nothing, but nothing at all besides mere bare existence. (*PP*.II.267)

The examples he gives are of birds confined to small cages and dogs kept on a chain. To which he adds, in a passage that brings to mind the famous myth of Nietzsche embracing a beaten horse: 'I can never look at such a dog without heartfelt compassion for it and deep indignation for its master' (ibid.; see *PP*.II.339).[59] If we compare such personal expressions to Schopenhauer's more abstract passages on the noble man seeing the connectedness of suffering in all beings and therefore feeling sympathy for all of them, the suggestion seems to be that this was the state in which

58. The Cambridge edition of Schopenhauer's works is excellent in distinguishing the various layers to the *Parerga* as well as *The World*.

59. There is little evidence that Nietzsche's incident with the horse actually took place: it is possibly based on a passage in Dostoevsky's *Crime and Punishment*. See Townsend, 'Nietzsche's Horse'.

Schopenhauer found himself.[60] Whoever is able to see the same will in *all creatures*, he writes, 'is certain of all virtue and bliss, and is on the direct path to salvation' (*WWR*.I.374). It is the will that is the foremost principle of suffering; and it is the will that is present in animals as much as it is in man.[61]

Hence, considering the gradualist distinction between humans and animals combined with Schopenhauer's intense concern for animal suffering, I think it is right to say that pessimism, for Schopenhauer, does extend to the condition of animals—even though it becomes more emphatic in that of humans—and where pessimism extends, so too should our sympathy. This, to my mind, is a credit to Schopenhauer's philosophy—but it may also pose a problem for him, as we will shortly see.

The Reasons for Pessimism

So much for the technical basis of Schopenhauer's case for pessimism. A different way of approaching this part of his philosophy is to ask why pessimism matters so much to Schopenhauer. After all, while he is acutely aware of earlier pessimists, Schopenhauer is not reacting explicitly to theodicy as Bayle and Voltaire were, and he believes theodicean optimism to have been well refuted by thinkers such as Voltaire and Hume. Why, then, is pessimism so crucial for Schopenhauer? Why is it pessimism that is presented as a kind of climax to his entire system? In other words: Why pessimism at all?

In my view, there are three main reasons behind Schopenhauer's pessimism. The first may seem all too obvious: *Schopenhauer believes pessimism to be true*. When he cites the tragic poets, it is because he believes they were right in describing a world of suffering. Hume and Voltaire are seen to win out over Leibniz and Rousseau not because their arguments were cleverer, but because of the overwhelming descriptive and explanatory power of pessimism over optimism. If, unlike these earlier thinkers,

60. See also *PP*.II.199: 'The readers of my *Ethics* know that for me the foundation of morality ultimately rests on that truth which has its expression in the *Veda* and *Vedanta* in the enduring mystical formula *tat tvam asi* [you are that], which is uttered with respect to each living thing, be it human or animal.'

61. In another handwritten addition, Schopenhauer considers it an 'obvious simple truth' that 'an animal is essentially the same as a human being': this is why we owe animals, not mercy (which is what we extend to sinners, when animals are 'innocent'), but *justice* (*PP*.II.335).

Schopenhauer tries to make the a priori case for pessimism, it is in order to remove from pessimism its last weakness (as an a posteriori argument) and build from it a systematic philosophy that is internally consistent as well as factually true. Again, it is no accident that pessimism forms the pinnacle of Schopenhauer's philosophy, since for him it is intrinsic to the very nature of philosophy that it begins with a 'minor chord'. As Schopenhauer continues that passage:

> It follows from this that philosophy cannot be either Spinozism or optimism. The more specific character, just mentioned, of the astonishment that urges us to philosophize, obviously springs from the sight *of the ill and evil* [*des Übels und des Bösen*] in the world. Even if these were in the most equal ratio to each other, and were also far outweighed by the good, yet they are something that absolutely and in general ought not to be. (*WWR*.II.171–2; Schopenhauer's emphasis)[62]

Here, Schopenhauer links the very origins of the philosophical exercise to pessimism, which therefore is central not only to Schopenhauer's philosophy but to *philosophy in general* (that is, philosophy *proper*). There is, then, a non-contingent relationship between philosophy and pessimism—and also, it seems, between philosophy and the problem of evil. Schopenhauer's words suggest that evil and suffering are a problem even *prior to* and *independently from* the postulate of a creator: they form an immediate problem that opens up the kind of wonder or astonishment that is properly the sphere of philosophical thought.[63] (To which the optimist could rightly pose the question of whether an encounter with the *good*, or a sheer astonishment at the beauty of the world, might not achieve the same.)

A second, less obvious reason behind Schopenhauer's pessimism has to do with a moral drive that, while less evident in Schopenhauer than in other pessimists, is present nonetheless. This is yet another point on which Schopenhauer has often been misunderstood: for Schopenhauer is not a nihilist or a fatalist, and his pessimism is not born from a Nietzschean

62. Here, I have adapted Payne's translation from the Cambridge edition (*WWR*.Cam. II.181), since Payne translates *Übel* and *Böse* as 'evil' and 'wickedness', whereas Schopenhauer is here properly speaking of 'ill' and 'evil'; that is, of physical and moral evil, respectively (for which he also uses the terms *Schlechtigkeit* and *Jammer*, e.g. *PP*.II.198).

63. On wonder (θαυμάζειν, *thaumazein*) as the beginning of philosophy, see Plato, *Theaetetus*, 155d. and Aristotle, *Metaphysics*, 982b. Note in this context the young Schopenhauer's remark to the elderly poet Christoph Martin Wieland: 'Life is an unpleasant business; I have resolved to spend it reflecting upon it' (cited in Safranski, *Schopenhauer*, 105).

impulse to do away with morality, or sympathy, or truth. Schopenhauer believes that there is a deeply redemptive as well as didactic value to pessimism: that this philosophy is able to offer, on the individual level, a prospect of consolation or even *redemption*, and, on the social level, a powerful motivation for moral improvement. Schopenhauer's pessimism, therefore, cannot rightly be understood without also understanding its connection with consolation and redemption on the individual level, and to ethics on the social.

A third, even less obvious reason, has to do with what Schopenhauer calls *eternal justice*. Deep within the heart of Schopenhauer's anti-theodicean enterprise there occurs what seems to be a theodicean moment: an almost Augustinian-sounding justification of suffering by way of guilt, which for Schopenhauer is crucial to the very project of pessimism. This justification, which draws equally from Christian and pagan sources, is perhaps one of the most curious aspects of Schopenhauer's philosophy—and this too is essential for understanding the deeper mechanics of his philosophical project. Before moving on to ethics, consolation, and redemption, therefore, let us see what can be made of this 'eternal justice'.

Schopenhauer's Scales: Eternal Justice

Eternal justice, which is discussed in book IV of the first volume of *The World*, has to do with the idea of an intrinsic *alignment* of sin or guilt with suffering.[64] This is a notion with a long lineage in the Christian tradition, from the Augustinian view of creation itself, where no one suffers undeservedly, to Leibniz's view of the afterlife: the City of God, where moral evils and physical evils are perfectly aligned. In these views, however, the alignment is a causal one: suffering is caused by a previous sin. This is not Schopenhauer's view. Eternal justice, for him, cannot be retributive, since it is eternal: it is not bound to time. In eternal justice, which according to Schopenhauer is *actually found* in the inner nature of the world, 'the punishment must be so linked with the offence that the two are one' (*WWR*.I.351). The resulting alignment is one by which the world itself bears responsibility for its existence:

> In this sense we can say that the world itself is the tribunal of the world. If we could lay all the misery [*Jammer*] of the world in one pan of the

64. For an excellent and extensive discussion of eternal justice in Schopenhauer, with which I am broadly in agreement, see Woods, 'Schopenhauer's Pessimism', chapter 5.

scales, and all its guilt [*Schuld*] in the other, the pointer would certainly show them to be in equilibrium. (*WWR*.I.352)

What to make of this idea of a perfect balance between guilt and suffering in Schopenhauer's scales? In the context of theodicy proper, as we have seen, Schopenhauer takes the pessimist line, firmly opposing the Judaeo-Christian idea of existence as intrinsically justified as well as the words from Genesis, repeatedly singled out for criticism, that 'all was very good' (II.623–4). But unlike the earlier pessimists, who believe the question of misalignment is well placed—that it is right to wonder, with Job, why the righteous suffer and the wicked prosper—Schopenhauer believes this question to be deeply misguided. It is true that we perceive the misalignment between guilt and suffering from an *individual* perspective—but this is *not* the perspective from which we should be looking for eternal justice, which is a deeper state of being of the world and can only be gleaned by deeper philosophical reflection. The individual perspective, stuck as it is on the level of individual perceptions, will represent the phenomena of the will as separate and opposed, and this results in the confused idea of misalignment:

> For pleasure appears to [the individual] as one thing, and pain as quite another; one man as tormentor and murderer, another as martyr and victim; wickedness as one thing, evil as another. He sees one person living in pleasure, abundance, and delights, and at the same time another dying in agony of want and cold at the former's very door. He then asks where retribution is to be found. (*WWR*.I.352)

The problem is that the individual, in embracing the pleasures of life, doesn't know that by this very act of will 'he seizes and hugs all the pains and miseries of life, at the sight of which he shudders'.[65] What the individual fails to see is that pains and pleasures, goods and evils are just different aspects of 'the phenomenon of the one will-to-live' (ibid.). Thus the problem posed by misalignment is essentially a problem of perception, which confronts us with the two moral outrages of theodicy, the wicked prospering and the righteous suffering:

> [Such a view] sees the wicked man, after misdeeds and cruelties of every kind, live a life of pleasure, and quit the world undisturbed. It

65. While this idea (that by indulging our pleasures we also strengthen our pains) is essentially a Stoic point, Schopenhauer is deeply critical of Stoic 'eudaemonology' in general: see below, p. 378.

> sees the oppressed person drag out to the end a life full of suffering without the appearance of an avenger or vindicator. (*WWR*.I.353)[66]

But when we begin to understand that such a view is limited to our knowledge of the phenomena, then we will understand that, on a deeper level, *there is no misalignment*, since all the individual sufferings of the world 'always concern the one and the same inner being':

> Tormentor and tormented are one. The former is mistaken in thinking he does not share the torment, the latter in thinking he does not share the guilt. If the eyes of both were opened, the inflicter of the suffering would recognize that he lives in everything that suffers pain in the whole wide world, and, if endowed with the faculty of reason, ponders in vain over why it was called into existence for such great suffering, whose cause and guilt it does not perceive. On the other hand, the tormented person would see that all the wickedness that is or ever was perpetrated in the world proceeds from that will which constitutes also *his* own inner being, and appears also in *him*. He would see that, through this phenomenon and its affirmation, he has taken upon himself all the sufferings resulting from such a will, and rightly endures them so long as he is this will. (*WWR*.I.354; his emphasis)

I cite this passage at length, since it speaks to the very core of Schopenhauer's philosophical enterprise: here, we begin to see that the conception of world as will and representation has deep significance for the way we exist in the world and for our conduct, both on an individual and an interpersonal level. On an individual level, this conception tells us that we are each responsible for our suffering in so far as we choose to continue to affirm our wills; and that we must engage less in our pleasures in order to engage less in our pains. On the social or interpersonal level, the conception of a shared will behind the illusion of individuality teaches us that to inflict suffering on another is to inflict suffering on ourselves.

But there is yet another element at play here, one that is equally crucial to Schopenhauer's vision of pessimism, and this is the idea of *guilt* [*Schuld*]—which Schopenhauer, on more than one occasion, develops in explicitly Augustinian terms. Thus he describes eternal justice as 'the balance inseparably uniting the *malum culpae* with the *malum poenae*'

66. Note that Schopenhauer's argument here resembles the 'optics of optimism', which similarly eliminated the prima-facie injustice of misalignment (and of suffering in general) by referring to it as a case of wrong or limited perception.

(*WWR*.I.355): it is by virtue of eternal justice that 'the evil of punishment is reconciled with the evil of guilt' (*PP*.II.198).[67] This reconciliation of sin and suffering, on Schopenhauer's view, is neither causal nor retributive: what eternal justice teaches us is that sin and suffering are ultimately the same thing. Nevertheless, there is a deeper kind of guilt underlying all our particular sins and sufferings, and it is this kind of guilt that Schopenhauer connects with the Christian idea of *original sin*, which, according to Augustine, is 'sin and punishment at the same time' (*WWR*.I.405).[68] Of course Schopenhauer, in speaking of original sin, is not referring to the Adamic fall of man, but to a more abstract notion: the idea that all of our actual guilt springs from a common root, which is our *essentia et existentia*: 'Accordingly, original sin is really our only true sin' (*WWR*.II.604).

But what exactly *is* this original sin, which is the 'root' of all our guilt? The problem is that Schopenhauer is confusing matters by using Christian terms such as guilt and original sin and *malum culpae*, when in fact he is making a neo-pagan point: he is not speaking of moral guilt as conventionally understood, but rather of a kind of *natural guilt*, drawn deeply from the tragic tradition. We are guilty, in a tragic sense, not because of any action we have done: we are guilty *because we exist*.[69] Thus, in his chapter on tragedy, Schopenhauer opposes to *poetic justice*, which rewards the righteous and punishes the wicked, a tragic concept of *eternal justice*, according to which man is guilty for being born:

> only a dull, insipid, optimistic, Protestant-rationalistic, or really Jewish view of the world will make the demand for poetic justice, and find its own satisfaction in that of the demand. The true sense of the tragedy is the deeper insight that what the hero atones for is not his own particular sins, but original sin, in other words, the guilt of existence itself:

67. This sentence is drawn from Schopenhauer's handwritten additions to the first edition of the *Parerga*; see *PP*.II.600, n.16.

68. Schopenhauer refers to Augustine's *Contra secundam iuliani responsionem imperfectum opus*, I, 47.

69. While many commentators have (duly) criticised this part of Schopenhauer's argument, they fail to note how deeply this is rooted in the tragic tradition: e.g. Cartwright, 'Schopenhauer on Suffering', 52–3; Fox, 'Schopenhauer on Death', 161–2. This influence does not change the fact that Schopenhauer's arguments are shaky on this point, but it may elucidate the background intuition at work here, as well as the fact that Schopenhauer is not so much speaking of *moral guilt*, personally deserved, than of a kind of natural guilt or intrinsic debt or indebtedness—in Ricoeur's words, 'the guiltiness of being' (*The Symbolism of Evil*, 220). Compare Cioran, *The Trouble with Being Born*, 15: 'I do not forgive myself for being born.'

> *Pues el delito mayor / Del hombre es haber nacido* [*For man's greatest offence / Is that he has been born*]. (*WWR*.I.254)[70]

The latter words, drawn from Calderón, are cited twice in Round One and a third time in Round Two, where Schopenhauer seems increasingly concerned with questions of *justification*.[71] Since existence is not a *good*, the world is not intrinsically justified: if anyone were to ask 'why there is not nothing at all rather than this world, then the world cannot be justified from itself' (*WWR*.II.579). Against the optimist view that life is 'given out as a gift, whereas it is evident that anyone would have declined it with thanks, had he looked at it and tested it beforehand', Schopenhauer affirms the neo-pagan view of life as *debt*:

> Far from bearing the character of a *gift*, human existence has entirely the character of a contracted *debt*. The calling in of this debt appears in the shape of the urgent needs, tormenting desires, and endless misery brought about through that existence. As a rule, the whole lifetime is used for paying off this debt, yet in this way only the interest is cleared off. Repayment of the capital takes place through death. And when was this debt contracted? At the begetting. (*WWR*.II.580)[72]

For Schopenhauer, the fundamental difference between all religions (and, perhaps, all philosophies) lies in whether they are *optimistic* or *pessimistic*: that is, 'whether they present the existence of this world as *justified by itself*, and consequently praise and commend it, or consider it as something that can be conceived only as *the consequence of our guilt*' (my emphasis; *WWR*.II.170). In so far as Christianity presents the human condition as 'both exceedingly sorrowful and sinful', it is ranked among the pessimistic religions (ibid.), and placed into near-perfect alignment with Schopenhauer's philosophy—as well as with the tragic poets. According to Schopenhauer, both traditions *rightly* connect our suffering and our guilt:

> If we wish to measure the degree of guilt with which our existence itself is burdened, let us look at the suffering connected with it. Every great

70. Note that Schopenhauer regards tragedy as 'the summit of poetic art' since it describes 'the terrible side of life' (*WWR*.I.252). The last words are drawn from the play *La Vida es Sueño* (*Life is a Dream*) by the Spanish poet and playwright Pedro Calderón de la Barca (1600–1681).

71. *WWR*.I.254, *WWR*.I.355, *WWR*.II.603. Schopenhauer himself translates *delito* with *Schuld* (guilt).

72. As Cartwright notes ('Schopenhauer on Suffering', 55), Schopenhauer is here playing 'on the ambiguity of the German noun *Schuld*, which can mean either "debt" or "guilt"'.

> pain, whether bodily or mental, states what we deserve; for it could not come to us if we did not deserve it. (*WWR*.II.580)[73]

A PESSIMIST THEODICY?

This is where we might begin to grow uncomfortable with Schopenhauer's notion of 'eternal justice', which now turns out to rest on a considerable assumption: that there is no suffering unless deserved. This is essentially the *nisi mereatur* of Augustine, but it seems strangely placed within the context of a cosmos stripped of an Augustinian creator. How can Schopenhauer suppose that his notion of natural guilt makes the fabric of the world ultimately *just* or *justified* in any meaningful way? It is one thing to speak of debt or guilt—it is quite another to speak of *justice*, let alone of *justification*, as he does in this passage:

> The justification [*Rechtfertigung*] for suffering is the fact that the will affirms itself even in this phenomenon; and this affirmation is justified and balanced by the fact that the will bears the suffering. (*WWR*.I.331)[74]

Original sin, then, is nothing other than the *affirmation of the will-to-live*, which is the deeper cause of all our sufferings: it is by affirming our will-to-live that we are capable of suffering at all.[75]

A further reason for discomfort might be that Schopenhauer is constantly slipping back to the individual level he was so eager to avoid. We might be willing to concede that the *overall* amount of suffering in the world is in perfect proportion to the *overall* amount of guilt—but there are times when Schopenhauer seems to suggest that this proportion or balance also exists in every individual.[76] Since by continuing to affirm our

73. Schopenhauer also sees the mechanism of conscience as an expression of our 'consciousness of eternal justice': we sense on some level that 'the offender and the offended are in themselves one, and that it is the same inner nature which . . . bears both the pain and the guilt' (*WWR*.I.357; *WWR*.I.365–5).

74. Schopenhauer's choice of the term eternal justice has been explained (and criticised) in different ways (see Woods, 'Schopenhauer's Pessimism', 148–51); I here note only that the term 'justice' [*Gerechtigkeit*] tends to go hand with 'justification' [*Rechtfertigung*].

75. See *WWR*.I.405 and *WWR*.II.608, where Schopenhauer aligns the Christian doctrines of original sin and salvation with *affirmation* and *denial* of the will-to-live, respectively. See *PP*.I.60–1: the author of the guilt of sin and ill (*Übel*) is the will itself. Note that in Schopenhauer's version, original sin is not *posterior* to creation but intrinsic to it.

76. Several critics have raised questions at this point; for discussion, see Woods, 'Schopenhauer's Pessimism', 152–6.

will we continue our suffering, we each bear an element of responsibility for our present misery. And since each individual, simply by existing, participates in the will, accordingly 'in all that happens or indeed can happen to the individual, justice is always done to it' (*WWR*.I.351).[77]

There are other problems. First, with regard to the matter of an ultimate balance between guilt and suffering, the question begged is how we could possibly know this a priori. As Young points out, it is striking that Schopenhauer makes no 'attempt whatsoever to confront the sceptic about the ultimate justice of the world. It is just assumed that there *must* somehow be a just order to the world.'[78] For this reason, Young sees this point as a kind of necessary assumption to ground our moral demands: rather than justifying this claim, Schopenhauer is concerned with explaining morality itself. However, it seems to me that Schopenhauer's concern is mainly justificatory in nature: a justification not of morality but of the reality of suffering. Somehow, Schopenhauer does want to prove that the world is, on the level of the thing-in-itself, ultimately just—and he wants to prove this from the fact of existence itself. This is also where his exercise sits so oddly with the pagan idea of natural guilt, since the tragic poets were not concerned with *justifying* existence in this way.

Second, an objection might be raised similar to the kind that earlier pessimists opposed to optimists such as Leibniz: that to add guilt to suffering is simply to make our suffering worse. How does this offer consolation? More importantly, how is it any better than an optimist discourse that reduces all our sufferings to sin and makes us ultimately responsible for all our suffering? It could be argued, of course, that consolation is simply not what Schopenhauer is after.[79] But several of his remarks in the *Parerga* in particular suggest otherwise, and it seems only right to evaluate Schopenhauer on his own terms. The question then remains what these terms are exactly, for Schopenhauer's intuition seems to be that to add guilt to suffering is not to make suffering worse, but *less*. (I will return to the question of consolation below.)

77. Woods believes this passage has nothing to do with individual fairness but simply with the essential point that 'the illusory individual is ultimately identifiable [with] the will-to-life' ('Schopenhauer's Pessimism', 155). This is a fair point, but it does not take into account Schopenhauer's stress on individual responsibility for suffering to the extent that we choose to affirm the will-to-live.

78. Young, *Willing*, 120–1; his emphasis. See also Cartwright's criticism of Schopenhauer's non sequitur ('Schopenhauer on Suffering', 54).

79. As argued by Hamlyn ('Eternal Justice', 288); see Woods, 'Schopenhauer's Pessimism', 164–7.

Third, from a Baylean perspective, we might wonder whether it is correct to excise the tension posed by misalignment and by the brute fact of suffering in the world. Is Schopenhauer's notion of eternal justice not just another theodicy, albeit a secular one? Is this not just another attempt, we might ask, channelling Bayle, to explain away suffering by some vague notion of natural guilt? And *why attempt justification at all?* Is this not an optimist intuition, and ultimately a theodicean exercise?

That Schopenhauer is the bearer of theodicean instincts is suggested by several passages on the suffering of animals, which poses a problem for his notion of eternal justice as it did for Augustine's *nisi mereatur*—since animals are innocent of their existence in ways that humans are not; they have committed no offence and can expect no redemption (since they lack freedom: *WWR*.I.404). Schopenhauer recognises this problem at several points in the *Parerga* in particular, where he asks: 'To what end this tormented, fearful will in thousands of forms without the freedom to redemption which is conditioned by soundness of mind?' Schopenhauer's answer is uncharacteristically hesitant: 'the will to life must *devour its own flesh* . . . , and it is a hungry will'; furthermore, 'the capacity for suffering in animals is much smaller than in mankind' (*PP*.II.290–1; his emphasis).[80] Thus Schopenhauer, in resisting theodicean optimism, ends up following precisely the argumentative structure of traditional theodicy. In order to justify both human and animal suffering, he emphasises, à la Leibniz, the greater capacity of humans for suffering, as well as, à la King, *a way out of suffering*, without which this capacity would be a 'pointless cruelty':

> the capacity for pain would have to reach its zenith only where the possibility for negation of the will is present, by virtue of reason and its soundness of mind. For without this, the capacity for pain would be nothing but a *pointless cruelty*. (*PP*.II.268–9; my emphasis)

Schopenhauer's theodicean instinct arises exactly at this point: life is suffering, but this suffering is neither pointless nor cruel, since there is a way out.[81] Ultimately, therefore, the creature has no just complaint. To

80. For the rest, any explanation would be 'hypothetical' or even 'mystical', and so Schopenhauer lets the question lie (*PP*.II.290–1). See also *WWR*.II.354 (in the context of generations of turtles being born only to be eaten alive by dogs): 'For what offence [*Verschuldung*] must they suffer this agony? . . . The only answer is that the *will-to-live* thus objectifies itself.'

81. See also the opening lines of the same essay, which deliver a kind of converse theodicy: 'If suffering is not the closest and most immediate goal of our life, then our existence is the most inexpedient thing in the world. For it is absurd to assume that endless pain,

which a Bayle or a Hume might object: Why could it *not* be a 'pointless cruelty' that we suffer as we do? Is it not precisely the case that we often suffer, and suffer undeservedly, without a way out of suffering? Is this not precisely what decides the *tragic nature* of our existence?

We seem to be back where we started, with Bayle and Leibniz, King and Voltaire. Without awareness of the fact, pessimism has looped back to the problem of evil and created a paradoxical thing: a pessimist theodicy.[82]

ETHICS

Another problem shadowing Schopenhauer's system of eternal justice has to do with the question of moral motivation. If suffering is all there is, the objection might be raised, why should we care about our fellow creatures? If suffering is the purpose of life; if we are each, by the very fact of our existence, inherently responsible for our own sufferings; if guilt and misery are perfectly balanced in the very nature of things—why should we be concerned with morality at all? More concretely: Why should we try to make *others'* suffering less, rather than simply focusing on alleviating our own? We are beginning to understand why Schopenhauer opts for pessimism—but if pessimism, why morality? *Why bother?*

Schopenhauer does not recognise or even address this concern, which seems to arise naturally whenever he discusses the many varieties of human cruelty, from bloodthirst to slavery (e.g. *WWR*.II.578). The reason is that Schopenhauer thinks the truth is rather the other way around: a recognition of pessimism will make us *more* and *better* morally motivated, not less so. This intuition goes to the heart of Schopenhauer's ethical orientation—of which I will say only a few things, as it relates to his pessimism.[83]

One of the passages where Schopenhauer's belief in the *moral competency of pessimism* appears most clearly occurs in the *Parerga*. Here, Schopenhauer proposes an alternative to Kant's categorical imperative,

---

which springs from the essential to life and of which the world is everywhere full, should be pointless and purely accidental' (*PP*.II.262).

82. Here, I part ways with Woods ('Schopenhauer's Pessimism', 159–68) and align Schopenhauer with the theodicean thinkers *in so far as* he parts ways with those pessimists who argued that suffering can and ought have no justification.

83. While Schopenhauer himself suggests that his 'ethical book' (i.e. book IV, on the conduct of man) is nowhere prescriptive, since philosophy cannot have an effect on actions (*WWR*.271–2), this seems to belie both the nature of his exercise and the moral force of (some of) his arguments as well as the impact it has had on his readers, as Young rightly points out (*Willing*, 103–4).

according to which our actions towards others should always be accompanied by respect for their intrinsic dignity. This lofty Kantian concept of human dignity is deeply problematic for Schopenhauer, considering 'a creature as sinful in willing, as limited in intellect, and as vulnerable and frail in body as the human being'. According to Schopenhauer, it would be a mistake to let our actions be guided by an objective evaluation of other humans 'according to value and dignity', since such an objective view would only highlight humanity's imperfections, and lead us to hatred and contempt rather than compassion. Our moral gaze should be otherwise directed:

> Instead, focus alone on his suffering, his distress, his fear, his pain—then you will always feel kinship with him, sympathize with him and instead of hatred or contempt sense that compassion for him which alone is *agape*, and to which we are exhorted by the gospels. (*PP*.II.184)

The crucial concept in morality, for Schopenhauer, is *Mitleid*: pity, sympathy, compassion. This can be understood cognitively in terms of the idea that individuation is merely a form of the phenomenal world, and that our individuality does not apply to the thing-in-itself: 'According to the true nature of things, everyone has all the sufferings of the world as his own' (*WWR*.I.353). But it is more directly experienced as the intensely moral feeling that *my* suffering is *your* suffering: 'Tormentor and tormented are one' (*WWR*.I.354). Compassion is what opens up the moral dimension within us: whereas envy 'builds the wall between You and I more firmly; for compassion it becomes thin and transparent' or is even torn down completely, to the point that 'the difference between I and not-I disappears' (*PP*.II.186). The more emphatically we draw the distinction between ourselves and others, the less likely we will be to act morally (that is, compassionately) towards them, and the more likely we will be to use the suffering of others to alleviate our own, either physically (by pursuing our goals to expense of theirs) or emotionally (by rejoicing at others' suffering—the supreme vice of *schadenfreude*).[84]

This is why pessimism is especially powerful as a moral motivator, in Schopenhauer's eyes: it fosters a sense of solidarity as fellow sufferers, of suffering *with* each other, which is the literal meaning of *compassion* or

84. See *PP*.II.263: 'The most effective consolation [*Trost*] in any misfortune, in any suffering, is to look over at the others who are even less fortunate than us, and this anyone can do.' Throughout *WWR*, Schopenhauer is concerned to dismiss *schadenfreude* as a *wrong* form of consolation (as well as the ultimate source of cruelty: *WWR*.I.363–4); just as moral egoism is the wrong basis for morality.

Mitleid. If we begin to 'conceive of the world as the work of our own guilt, therefore as something that it were better did not exist' (*PP*.II.271), then we can accustom ourselves to 'regarding this world as a place of penance, hence as a prison, a penal colony as it were, a labour camp' (*PP*.II.272). The result of such a perception would not be despair or immorality, but rather an attitude of deep sympathy and compassion for our 'fellow-sufferer[s]':

> In fact, the conviction that the world and therefore also mankind is something that actually should not be, is designed to fill us with forbearance towards one another, for what can be expected of beings in such a predicament? Indeed, from this point of view one could arrive at the notion that the really proper mode of address between human beings, instead of *Monsieur, Sir*, etc. would be *Leidensgefährte, Socî malorum, compagnon de misères, my fellow-sufferer*. (*PP*.II.273; his emphasis)

Seeing each other in this light, Schopenhauer argues, will remind us of most essential things of life: 'of tolerance, patience, forbearance and love of one's neighbour, which everyone needs and therefore everyone owes as well' (*PP*.II.273). It is thus a misanthropic and deeply pessimistic view of the world that is a foundation for what can only be described as a *pessimist ethics*.[85] Hence, if human egoism, the principle of *homo homini lupus*, is part of the reason behind the tragic condition of man, it is precisely an awareness of this tragic condition that helps us overcome egoism and see each other not as wolves, but as companions in misery, partners in suffering. If pessimism is the problem, it is also part of the solution.

CONSOLATION

This is true not only for ethics and our interpersonal relationships, but also for our personal experience. As I have said above, Schopenhauer also feels that pessimism has value for the *individual* human sufferer. There are two parts to this value, one more easily attainable than the other: pessimism can offer us *consolation*, or it can lead us down the difficult path of *resignation*, which is also the path of redemption or salvation. The former is understated and easily missed: while Schopenhauer's philosophical system is threaded with consolation, it doesn't receive a central treatment on its own account, as resignation and redemption do. Nevertheless, it is

85. This again reinforces Dienstag's important point that pessimism need not be fatalist or nihilist, but can be a drive to (in this case) *sympathetic* action.

my sense that something very important is missed if we fail to take into account Schopenhauer's concern with consolation in general, and especially the consolation of (pessimist) philosophy.

That Schopenhauer is aware of the importance of consolation in human life appears from his discussion of 'man's need for metaphysics'—a need that he associates partly with practical purposes (the need of a system to govern our actions), and partly with 'the *indispensable consolation* in the deep sorrows of life' (*WWR*.II.167, my emphasis; *PP*.II.305). This need is mostly satisfied by religions rather than by true philosophy, but these religions often provide the wrong kind of consolation, by offering false hope. For Schopenhauer, the grounding of consolation lies elsewhere, not in the hope that suffering may be avoided or even compensated in a future life, but precisely in the awareness of the *inevitability* of suffering.

In Schopenhauer's eyes, nothing is more effective for consolation than fatalism, or an awareness of the necessity of all things (*WWR*.I.306).[86] The Sisyphean character of Schopenhauer's pessimism is that whenever we drive out one form of suffering, another takes its place; and even at the zero point of suffering we are left with 'the pain of boredom as the sensation of the emptiness of existence'.[87] This sounds like a source of despair, but Schopenhauer presents it as a possible source of consolation (*Trost*). In general, it is the seemingly *accidental* nature of our suffering that gives it its sting. We aren't distressed as much by inescapable evils, such as old age and death. But Schopenhauer argues that all pain, all suffering, is inevitable and essential to life; only its specific *form* is accidental. If we reflect on this, we might learn to feel a kind of 'stoical indifference' and be less concerned by own welfare (*WWR*.I.315). Despite this reference to Stoicism, the deeper intuition here is one shared with Bayle: to be told that our suffering is our own fault and could have been avoided only makes our suffering worse.

At the same time, as we have also seen, Schopenhauer does believe we are each responsible for our suffering; that we are darkly guilty in some deeper existential way. But this guilt, too, is strangely linked to consolation. Part of the point behind the entire exercise on eternal justice seems to be precisely that it offers consolation: we do not suffer undeservedly, and so we do not suffer pointlessly. In so far as suffering is the end of life, we are *supposed* to suffer; and in so far as we each participate in the will,

86. See also Cioran, *The Trouble with Being Born*, 173: 'There is something enveloping and voluptuous about the notion of fatality: it keeps you warm.'

87. Woods, 'Seriously Bored', 967.

we are each the cause and affirmers of our own suffering. The idea in the background seems to be that the worst kind of suffering would be to suffer without cause; to be afflicted by truly *meaningless* suffering; to be caught within the trappings of a truly *cruel* creation.[88]

Thus, on the one hand, we are responsible for our suffering, but on the other, suffering is unavoidable. We suffer because we exist; we are guilty because we exist. Paradoxically, therefore, we may feel guilty *at the same time as consoled*, since our guilt, like our suffering, was unavoidable, and is shared by all human beings.[89] Consolation thus arises, too, from a sense of *connectedness* through suffering. Not only are we bound by guilt and sympathy to other sufferers as *compagnons de misère*, but we are bound to the world itself, which suffers with us and through us. It is primarily through an understanding of ourselves and of the *moral side* of the world that consolation can be found.[90] The question then remains whether this *works* as consolation, and if it does, whether it works better than that offered by traditional religions and philosophies—a question to which I will return below.

REDEMPTION

There is another way in which pessimism can have value to the individual sufferer, offering not just consolation, but full-fledged *redemption* (*Erlösung*). We come now to one of the most controversial parts of Schopenhauer's philosophy, which may itself be responsible for the longstanding association of pessimism with passivity and resignation—an association that seems at least partly warranted.

The problem many readers from Nietzsche onwards have had with Schopenhauer's pessimism lies not so much in this pessimism itself as in his suggestion of a *response*. If, following so many bleak pages describing the human condition, Schopenhauer had ended with some kind of

88. Compare to this effect Schopenhauer's comments on 'pointless cruelty' in, e.g., *PP*.II.269.

89. The will itself shares in our suffering and possibly even in our guilt, as Schopenhauer suggests in this enigmatic passage: 'With me, on the other hand, the will, or the inner nature of the world, is by no means Jehovah; on the contrary, it is, so to speak, the crucified Saviour, or else the crucified thief, according as it is decided' (*WWR*.II.645).

90. See *WWR*.II.589: the world can be considered from its physical or from moral side, but 'only on the moral side is consolation to be found', since here our inner nature is revealed to us. Note that Schopenhauer himself found consolation in the reading of the *Upanishads*: 'it has been the consolation of my life and it will be that of my dying' (*PP*. I.357).

heroic affirmation or Nietzschean *amor fati*, some proposal to make the most of life against all odds, this would have made his pessimism more palatable.[91] Instead, he does the opposite. The only proper response to pessimism, for Schopenhauer, is not to affirm the will-to-live (which affirmation is our 'original sin') but, famously, to *negate* or deny it: it is the *negation of the will* (*die Verneinung des Willens*) that Schopenhauer calls 'redemption'.[92] As long as we continue to affirm our existence, we continue to suffer: the pleasures we experience will continue to be vastly outweighed by our pains. The only way out of the cycle of suffering is by negating the will-to-live.

There are two paths towards this negation or denial, one more difficult than the other (*WWR*.I.392; *WWR*.II.630). The more difficult path is through knowledge alone. This path is open to only a few people, since it requires a deep inner grasp of Schopenhauer's theoretical principles, and the application of these to one's own situation. The noble man who treads this path manages to see through the 'veil of Maya' or principle of individuation, to such an extent that he no longer makes the distinction between self and others: 'everything lies equally near to him' (*WWR*.I.378–9).[93]

The second, more accessible path is by an experience of intense suffering: that is, of 'suffering personally felt, not the suffering merely known' (*WWR*.I.392). This is a kind of 'purification through suffering' (*WWR*.I.394),[94] which tends to occur only at the approach of death; for instance, in martyrs awaiting execution. To achieve resignation by way of experience, not knowledge, the will must be broken by 'the greatest personal suffering', at which point the individual is ready to renounce the world and welcome death: 'for him who ends thus, the world has at the same time ended' (*WWR*.I.382). As examples, Schopenhauer mentions convicts repenting and resigning themselves to their fates prior to

91. See Young (*Willing*, 109), who mentions 'the acceptance of pessimism but the insistence that heroism or simply living itself has a higher value than happiness' as 'the response to the Schopenhauerian argument that runs through much existentialist philosophy'. This is the kind of 'heroic pessimism' rejected by Ligotti, who associates it with, e.g., Dienstag, Unamono, and Camus (Ligotti, *Conspiracy*, 30–3). For Nietzsche's concept of *amor fati*, see *The Gay Science*, section 276.

92. Payne uses the terms salvation and denial for *Erlösung* and *Verneinung*, where the Cambridge translators opt rather for redemption and negation; I mainly follow the latter.

93. It is unlikely that Schopenhauer saw this path as open to women, though they are not excluded in principle; note to this effect Janaway's comment on Schopenhauer's appreciation for female mystics ('Schopenhauer's Pessimism', 343n.).

94. See *WWR*.II.639: 'Life then presents itself as a process of purification, the purifying lye of which is pain.'

execution, as well as the tragic sufferings of Gretchen in Goethe's *Faust*. It is at this point, once a person has drunk 'to the dregs the greatest measure of suffering' (*WWR*.I.393), that the 'last secret of life' reveals itself:

> The last secret of life has revealed itself to them in the excess of pain, the secret, namely, that ill and evil [*das Übel und das Böse*], suffering and hatred, the tormented and the tormentor, different as they may appear to knowledge that follows the principle of sufficient reason, are in themselves one. (*WWR*.I.394)[95]

But one need not be on death row in order to embark upon the path to enlightenment: one can achieve the same by combining a thoroughly Christian ethic of extreme charity and compassion with a personal policy of detaching oneself from the world and from all acts of willing (*WWR*.I.382, 386). If this sounds like asceticism, that's because it is (*WWR*.I.392). In the first volume in particular, Schopenhauer's asceticism is strong, going so far as to recommend self-castigation and mortification of the flesh, and commending the examples of Christian as well as Eastern ascetics. However, as Young points out,[96] this motif is toned down in the second volume, where Schopenhauer suggests that ethics, if consistently and rigorously put into practice, is enough to put us on the path to resignation, rendering '*asceticism* in the narrowest sense' superfluous: 'Justice itself is the hair shirt that causes its owner constant hardship, and philanthropy that gives away what is necessary provides us with constant fasting' (*WWR*.II.607).[97]

But not all is sore and gloomy in Schopenhauer's secularised asceticism. Belying some of these darker ascetic passages are those that speak rather of a *cheerful* abandonment of the world: thus the man who embarks upon the path to resignation 'is full of inner cheerfulness and true heavenly peace', 'a deep calm and inward serenity' (*WWR*.I.390). It is this cheerful mode that is part of what distinguishes the Stoic equanimity of ancient tragic heroes from Christian resignation and the spirit of 'Christian tragedy':

> the tragic heroes of the ancients show resolute and stoical subjection under the unavoidable blows of fate; the Christian tragedy, on the other hand, shows the giving up of the whole will-to-live, cheerful

95. I again adapt Payne's translation and translate *Übel* and *Böse* rather as 'ill' and 'evil' to match the earlier passage *WWR*.II.171–2.

96. Young, *Willing*, 125.

97. I have substituted the phrase 'hair shirt' for Payne's 'hairy garment', as suggested by an anonymous reviewer.

> abandonment of the world in the consciousness of its worthlessness and nothingness [*Nichtigkeit*].[98] (*WWR*.II.434)

This passage also begins to suggest why Schopenhauer's concept of abandonment, though it overlaps with the Stoic concept of *ataraxia*, is not the same thing. For while both concepts demand that we free ourselves from our pleasures as well as pains in order to achieve a state of serenity, and Schopenhauer himself praises the value of Stoicism as 'a spiritual dietetics' (*WWR*.II.159), he also repeatedly and explicitly criticises Stoicism for its *this-worldly* orientation. The great mistake of Stoicism, according to Schopenhauer, is to suggest that there can be a life without suffering in this world (*WWR*.I.90).[99] This means that Stoic ethics is just another way of trying to achieve a life as painless and therefore as happy as possible: it is just another species of *eudaemonism* or *eudaemonology* (and these, flowing from Schopenhauer's pen, are not positive terms).[100] The problem with Stoicism is that it 'has not, like Indian, Christian, and even Platonic ethics, a metaphysical tendency, a transcendent end, but an end that is wholly immanent and attainable in this life' (*WWR*.II.159). So too the Stoic sage is just 'a wooden, stiff lay-figure with whom one can do nothing' (*WWR*.I.91): the Stoic sage is not alive or interesting in the way that Christian or Eastern mystics are; it is not a hot-blooded, high-spirited ideal.

Thus, while it is true that Schopenhauer's philosophy displays strong Stoic elements, the overall project of Stoicism, in his view, is a misguided one: it is the mistake of those 'who were still entirely absorbed in life, and did not seriously look beyond this' (*WWR*.II.628). It is not Schopenhauer's aim to make our *this*-worldly existence acceptable to us, or to make life worth living: he wants to provide an *alternative*, which can only be achieved by negating the will. It is in this sense that he speaks specifically of redemption. The problem that then remains is that Schopenhauer, in giving us redemption as the only alternative to suffering, doesn't seem to

98. Payne translates *Nichtigkeit* as *vanity*, but I agree with Janaway ('Schopenhauer's Pessimism', 318) that this 'loses much of its power', and have followed him in using the term *nothingness* instead. This, however, should not be taken to mean non-existence, but rather, a form of profound worthlessness. On nothingness, see also *PP*.II.255–61.

99. See Young, *Willing*, 130–1.

100. Eudaemonism [*Eudämonismus*]: *WWR*.II.159; eudaemonology [*Eudämonologie*]: *PP*.I.273. While Dienstag (*Pessimism*, 107, 111) is right to point out that Schopenhauer does develop a kind of eudaemonology in the *Parerga* as a way of living tolerably or at least 'less unhappily' (*PP*.I.356), this misses Schopenhauer's deeper objections to Stoicism's this-worldly striving.

be giving us very much—for it remains unclear, down to the final pages, what exactly Schopenhauerian salvation *means*. Is it a purely negative concept, denoting solely the purely negative activity of denying the will, of 'overcoming and annihilating the world' (*WWR*.I.330)? If so—if it is *purely* negative—can it be a real alternative?

One way of answering this question would be to infer that negation *does* have a concrete, practical meaning: that in a secular cosmos, it could only ever mean one thing. After all, if life is so universally bad and affirming life just makes things worse—what is the alternative? If death, to the suffering individual, becomes 'most welcome, and is cheerfully accepted as a longed-for deliverance' (*WWR*.I.382)—then why would we not precipitate it? In other words: Isn't this just an argument for suicide?

SUICIDE

Schopenhauer anticipates this possible inference, which he is very concerned to refute: in the first volume of *The World*, the chapter on suicide (ch. 69) follows on the heels of the chapter on negation (ch. 68), and he returns to the question in his later writings, especially the famous essay 'On Suicide' in the *Parerga*.[101] His treatment of the question, complicated and ambiguous as it is, comprises perhaps the most misunderstood part of his philosophy. One of the first associations many people have with Schopenhauer is that he condones suicide—or even recommends it.

It is true that Schopenhauer, and especially the *later* Schopenhauer, believes that all of the common moral, theological, and legal arguments against suicide fail miserably. In his essay on suicide, he writes, echoing Hume, that 'quite obviously there is nothing in the world to which everyone has such an indisputable *right* as his own person and life' (*PP*.II.276; his emphasis). This 'obvious' point is confirmed, according to Schopenhauer, by our moral sentiments: we feel indignation or resentment when we hear about murder or theft, but only 'sorrow and compassion' when we hear about suicide. But if this is so, what is the deeper reason behind the universal condemnation of suicide by the monotheistic religions and by most European philosophers?

> Could it not be this, that the voluntary giving up of life is a poor compliment to the one who said 'everything was very good'? Then once again

101. Schopenhauer's interest in suicide has been connected with the suspected suicide of his father; see Magee, *Philosophy*, 4.

> it would be the obligatory optimism of these religions which denounces the killing of oneself in order not to be denounced by it. (*PP*.II.279)[102]

Suicide is thus not a sign of crime or madness, but a tragic fact of suffering existence, something to be pitied and mourned but not condemned—something that may even offer to the desperately depressed something in the way of consolation: 'Indeed, we even find a certain consolation in the fact that, in the worst cases, this way out is actually open to us' (*WWR*.II.240). This idea, of the *consolation of the idea of suicide*, would be repeated and made famous by Nietzsche; it continues to be affirmed by some who suffer or have suffered depression.[103]

Thus it would seem that Schopenhauer propounds a *pro-suicide* philosophy—were it not for the fact that, in both volumes of *The World* as well as the *Parerga*, he formulates an emphatic argument *against* suicide. Choosing to end one's own life prematurely, according to Schopenhauer, is not at all an answer to the problem posed by the affirmation of the will-to-live:

> Far from being denial of the will, suicide is a phenomenon of the will's strong affirmation. For denial has its essential nature in the fact that the pleasures of life, not its sorrows, are shunned. The suicide wills life, and is dissatisfied merely with the conditions on which it has come to him. Therefore he gives up by no means the will-to-live, but merely life, since he destroys the individual phenomenon. (*WWR*.I.398)

Not only is suicide, therefore, a false alternative—a kind of cunning of reason that reaffirms the individual's will-to-live by the very act of supposedly denying it—but it is, in fact, doubly tragic, since it does away with existence at the precise point that existence might become redemptive. The very suffering that drives some people to suicide could have led them instead to 'true redemption':

> the only relevant moral reason against suicide . . . lies in the fact that suicide is counter to achieving the highest moral goal insofar as it substitutes a merely illusory redemption from this world of misery for the real one. (*PP*.II.279)

102. But compare *WWR*.I.399, where Schopenhauer suggested that this condemnation springs from the intuition that suicide is actually an affirmation, not a negation, of the will.

103. See Nietzsche, *Beyond Good and Evil*, section 157; Zwagerman (interviewing Andrew Solomon), *Door eigen hand*, 55–7.

Hence, if ever a man were dissuaded from suicide by a *moral* incentive, his rationale would be as follows:

> 'I do not want to avoid suffering, because it can help to put an end to the will-to-live, whose phenomenon is so full of misery, by so strengthening the knowledge of the real nature of the world now already dawning on me, that such knowledge may become the final quieter of the will, and release me for ever.' (*WWR*.I.400)

The question then remains whether this works at all: whether this is a sufficiently strong argument against suicide as a way of escaping the human predicament of suffering.[104] There are obvious problems here. For one thing, if suffering is what impels the individual to negate the will, why cannot suffering impel to suicide—with equal justification? Surely a suicidal person doesn't care about the great Schopenhauerian will or that the phenomenon is an illusion: after all, from the suicide's point of view, it's the *phenomenon* that suffers. It would seem only rational to do away with the individual phenomenon, for with the illusion of individuality perishes the individual experience of suffering. The will-to-live may not be defeated—but at least it will no longer be *this person's* will. Schopenhauer may compare the suicide to a sick man who prefers to retain his illness rather than allow a painful cure to be completed (*WWR*.I.399), but this comparison doesn't make sense, since the individual ceases to be: if the illness remains, there is no one who suffers from it.

Another concern might stem from Schopenhauer's confirmation of the suicide's desperate perspective as a proportionate one: rather than trying to convince prospective suicides that their perceptions of the world are skewed or distorted, Schopenhauer suggests that they are only justified. Suicide, for Schopenhauer as for Bayle, is not a sign of a warped or wicked mind, but of a damaged and suffering creation, which it is only natural to want to flee. Both thinkers associate suicide especially with mental or spiritual rather than physical suffering; both thinkers, furthermore, treat

104. A related question arises in the context of procreation, where Schopenhauer argues roughly that the fundamental badness, even *wrongness*, of existence (it ought not be), does *not* mean we should not bring more humans into existence; though elsewhere he praises gnostics and saints for not reproducing. The fact that Schopenhauer does not discuss this question in any depth (in contrast to that of suicide) shows again the extent to which the ethics of procreation remains a blind spot for philosophers until the twentieth century. An exception, again, is Byron's *Cain*, which muses on this question insistently, e.g. in this passage: 'Here let me die: for to give birth to those / Who can but suffer many years, and die, / Methinks is merely propagating death, / And multiplying murder' (*Cain*, act II, v. 67–70).

suicide primarily as a phenomenal fact and only secondarily as a moral problem.[105] As such, the fact of suicide poses a prima-facie problem for optimism of any kind—whereas optimism itself poses only the feeblest response to any person on the edge of suicide.[106]

Is this a cruel and unfeeling treatment of the phenomenon of suicide—or is it rather a deeply compassionate one? Is it an empty and callous argument against suicide, or is it rather an especially rich and thoughtful one, in that it takes seriously the existential experience of the truly desperate person? I lean towards the latter interpretation. Instead of offering a moralistic or legalistic argument against or indeed *for* suicide,[107] one that remains coldly on the outside of the experience that informs the act, Schopenhauer offers a *psychologically sensitive* treatment of suicide, formulated from the inside of this experience, rather than from the outside, looking in. As Dienstag notes, 'What distinguishes pessimists from optimists here is their willingness to take the rationale for suicide *seriously* and to admit that it is sometimes difficult to make a case for remaining a part of this world.'[108] Hence, Schopenhauer's attempt to travel a long way *with* prospective suicides, to take their experience as seriously as he does, may be a weakness—it may also be strength.

Perhaps there is something valuable, too, in Schopenhauer's attempt to present a different perspective to the experience of deep and dreadful suffering, as a crack in the foundations of the self through which may grow the seed of transformation; the utterly fragile point at which another reality may begin to open up to us. It is again questionable if such a view of suffering as a kind of state of grace could be at all convincing to the individual sufferer, any more than *any* arguments could be. But the moral strength in Schopenhauer's approach, as in that of other pessimists, is in his unflinching acknowledgement of the bare reality of suffering; in his refusal to suggest that suffering is wrong, or that the desire to end one's life is wrong; and in his attempt to dissuade prospective suicides *even though they are*

105. See *WWR*.I.299: 'Just because mental pain, being much greater, makes one insensible to physical pain, suicide becomes very easy for the person in despair or consumed by morbid depression [*krankhaftem Unmut*].'

106. Zwagerman (interviewing Solomon), *Door eigen hand*, 59–60.

107. As in Hume's 'Of Suicide', to which Schopenhauer approvingly refers while emphasising it is based on 'cold reason' [*mit kalter Vernunft*] (*PP*.II.278–9).

108. Dienstag, *Pessimism*, 103; his emphasis. This crucial point is missed by Young (*Willing*, 128), who reads Schopenhauer as objecting to the suicide's experience as one of 'facile optimism'.

not in the wrong.[109] Whether this argument *works* is another question: my point is merely that the *structure* of Schopenhauer's response seems to get something right in its attempt to give due weight to the experience of people desperate enough to want to kill themselves. Hence, whether or not we find his arguments consistent or convincing, we should at least take Schopenhauer's word for it that suicide is *not* what he has in mind when speaking of negation and resignation. But if not suicide—what then?

NOTHING

We come now to the crux, the great *dénouement* of Schopenhauer's philosophy—and what an anti-climactic one it is. After everything that is demanded of those wanting to embark upon the path of Schopenhauerian redemption, what the long-awaited compensation comes down to is—literally—*nothing*. If Voltaire's last word in *Candide* was *espérance*, Schopenhauer's last word in the first volume of *WWR* is, just as tellingly, *Nichts*:

> we freely acknowledge that what remains after the complete abolition of the will is, for all who are still full of the will, assuredly nothing. But also conversely, to those in whom the will has turned and denied itself, this very real world of ours with all its suns and galaxies, is—nothing. (*WWR*.I.411–2)

The prospect of Schopenhauerian salvation thus reveals itself to be one long road to *nothing*, which is achieved only at the moment we ourselves, in our individuality, also cease to be. Delivered from ourselves, we are delivered instead to nothingness. And so Schopenhauer's system might well be served by the words that Dante placed on hell itself: '*All hope abandon, ye who enter here*.'[110]

But why should we be persuaded by the idea of negation of the will-to-live, if the only alternative that is offered us is this obscure cessation of ourselves? And even if we are persuaded—why should it *inspire* us to embark upon the difficult path Schopenhauer has in mind for us? If this is redemption—does it deserve the name?

The problem is that Schopenhauer runs up against the limitations posed by his own philosophy, limitations that would be echoed by

109. This latter part (the attempt at dissuading) is absent in Hume (as in Bayle), who does not appear at all concerned with the idea of people taking his words as incentive; Schopenhauer seems aware of his responsibility here. On this concern see the Introduction.

110. Dante, *Inferno*, Canto III.

Wittgenstein in the famous last words of his *Tractatus*: 'Whereof one cannot speak, thereof one must be silent.'[111] Philosophy, for Schopenhauer as for Wittgenstein, must be communicable; philosophy is *cosmology* and cannot become *theology*; philosophy must restrict itself to the world. As Schopenhauer writes in the second volume, commenting on the ending of the first: 'it is in keeping with this that, when my teaching reaches its highest point, it assumes a *negative* character, and so ends with a negation'. But Schopenhauer's point is that this is a *relative* nothing, not an *absolute* nothing: it is a nothing that might yet be *something*, if seen from a different perspective: 'Now it is precisely here that the mystic proceeds positively, and therefore, from this point, nothing is left but mysticism' (*WWR*.II.612).

Mysticism: the knowledge of the incommunicable; the great foe of Enlightenment philosophers from Bayle to Kant. Surely, if mysticism begins where philosophy ends, Schopenhauer's point must be: so much the worse for mysticism. But while it is true that Schopenhauer sees mysticism and philosophy as incommensurable in principle, nevertheless, as Young points out, Schopenhauer evaluates mysticism positively.[112] Not only do the last words of the first volume leave open a space for mystical knowledge by the *relativity of nothingness*—but in the second volume, Schopenhauer also points to the wide agreement of mystical experience across different cultures and traditions (*WWR*.II.613).[113] Hence, against the common interpretations of Schopenhauer as a nihilist or 'absolute pessimist', Young argues that such readings are 'insensitive to the intense theological preoccupation that permeates, particularly, Book IV [of *WWR*]'. According to Young, Schopenhauer's concept of resignation is not purely negative, but also oriented towards some darkly intuited positive element: an existence of another kind. When Schopenhauer says that the saintly ascetic achieves redemption, he is speaking of an *otherworldly* state, and this is why he opposes Stoic *ataraxia*, which, being a this-worldly solution, leads *away* from salvation, rather than towards it.[114] In Young's view, therefore, not only does Schopenhauer accept a 'field of illuminism' or mysticism (*PP*.II.14)—but 'it is upon the veridicality of mystical insight into another, ecstatic, world, a world relative to which this one

111. Wittgenstein, *Tractatus Logico-Philosophicus*, no. 7.

112. Young, *Willing*, 132; as Young also points out, Schopenhauer's problem with Fichte and others is that they carry mysticism or illuminism *into philosophy* (ibid., 34).

113. Ibid., 132.

114. Ibid., 130.

is a mere "dream", that, for Schopenhauer, our only chance of "salvation" depends'.[115]

If this interpretation is right, as I think it might well be, it still leaves unanswered the question what this positive element of redemption entails: in Kantian terms, what it is that we may hope for. This, again, is where mysticism may (and perhaps *should*) continue where philosophy cannot:

> Accordingly at the end of my own philosophy I have, to be sure, alluded to the field of illuminism as something that exists, but I guarded against taking even a single step into it. . . . I have allowed illuminism to have its free space, where in its own way it might arrive at the solution to all riddles. (*PP*.II.14)

True to his word, Schopenhauer does not venture a step out of philosophy—and yet there are moments when he seems to be probing around the edges of the inexpressible. Thus he writes that something happens to us in the aesthetic experience of *tragedy*, which presents to us not only 'the terrible side of life', but something on the other side of life itself:

> we become aware that there is still left in us something different that we cannot possibly know positively, but only negatively, as that which does *not* will life. Just as the chord of the seventh demands the fundamental chord; just as a red colour demands green, and even produces it in the eye; so every tragedy demands an existence of an entirely different kind, a different world, the knowledge of which can always be given to us only indirectly, as here by such a demand. At the moment of the tragic catastrophe, we become convinced more clearly than ever that life is a bad dream from which we have to awake. (*WWR*.II.433)

This is a different tone from those passages where Schopenhauer speaks only negatively of resignation. Here and in other passages, Schopenhauer seems to be tentatively feeling around the edges of where his philosophy can bring him, and hinting at what lies beyond—another world, a different range of experience—without actually going there. It is suggested that our aesthetic experience itself intimates such a beyond, which Schopenhauer, bound as he is by the limits of his own philosophy,

115. Ibid., 34. See also Magee (*Philosophy*, 451), who emphasises the often neglected 'mystical side' of Schopenhauer as 'basic to the whole thrust and tenor of his philosophy'. Illuminism for Schopenhauer has to do with a 'subjective source of cognition' and is thus opposed to rationalism; but only when it 'takes religion as its basis' does it become mysticism (*PP*.II.12–14).

is unable to describe. But the fact that philosophy cannot *say* more than this doesn't mean there is nothing more to be discovered. We know that Schopenhauer was fascinated with mystics such as Jacob Böhme, who formed the topic of his last recorded conversation, just a few days before his death.[116]

This vagueness, at the very edges of Schopenhauer's system: this is where philosophy meets mysticism. The philosopher Schopenhauer does not go down this path, but nor does he close it off. His 'nothing' represents not a period so much as a comma or a question mark: an openness that is itself the character of mysticism; an emptiness that may yet be a fullness; a nothing that may yet be a something. This is a very thin kind of hope—and yet it is a kind of hope. Or is it?

The Problems of Pessimism

Thus far, I have discussed Schopenhauer's case for pessimism as well as his deeper reasons for pessimism, which reveal his concerns with justification as well as with the human constitution—with ethics, consolation, redemption, and suicide. Of course, there is much more that can be said about Schopenhauer's philosophy: I have chosen to focus on those questions relating directly to pessimism and theodicy, such as the central question of how to do justice to the reality of suffering without, by this very reflection, making suffering worse than it already is. Throughout, I have tried to critique Schopenhauer according to the concerns and principles of pessimism itself—that is, according to those concerns and principles that Schopenhauer shares. It is in this respect, and from the perspective of pessimism itself—which does *not* want to be (I argue throughout) a philosophy of despair—that three central problems remain, having to do with method, with nihilism, and, finally, with hope and consolation.

METHOD

If we look back at most pessimists discussed so far, one of the things they have in common is the highly unsystematic nature of their pessimism. This may seem an accidental correlation, but I don't think it is: considering that early pessimism is drenched in a profound awareness of the limitations of our abilities, it seems appropriate for a certain sceptical or

116. Safranski, *Schopenhauer*, 348.

fragmentary quality to cling to the exercise of pessimist philosophy.[117] In other words, pessimists don't build systems. But Schopenhauer does. And so we might ask, from the viewpoint of the wider pessimist tradition, whether the *systematic* nature of Schopenhauer's pessimism poses a problem for that pessimism itself.

But how systematic, really, is Schopenhauer's pessimism—or rather, how *necessary* is it that it is so? If we look at the great system builders—Spinoza, Kant, Hegel—there seems to be a necessary quality to the systematic nature of their philosophy: it *has* to be a system. But Schopenhauer suggests, at one point at least, that this is not the case for his:

> I regard it as a great merit of my philosophy that all its truths have been found independently of one another, through a consideration of the real world; but their unity and agreement, about which I did not concern myself, have always appeared subsequently of themselves. (*WWR*.II.185)

Thus Schopenhauer seems to represent the coherent and consistent quality of his philosophy as a contingent thing, a happy coincidence rather than the outcome of a rigorous systematism. Maybe, then, it is something of a misrepresentation to designate Schopenhauer's philosophy as a system at all.

But even if this is the case, a deeper problem with Schopenhauer's systematic tendency remains, and that is his attempt to construe an *objective* or a priori pessimism—something that he believes to be a strength, but may also be a weakness. In a way, by positing a metaphysical pessimism, and suggesting that pessimism is true for all creatures *whether or not they believe it to be*, Schopenhauer ends by opting for a cosmic rather than a creaturely perspective. Crucial to the cosmic perspective is the idea that we can somehow go beyond the individual creaturely experience, which is exactly the point beyond which earlier pessimists argued that *we cannot go*. In suggesting that there is an a priori way to describe our experience objectively, Schopenhauer is untrue to one of the central tenets of earlier pessimism: that the buck stops here; there is no going past the creaturely perspective into the cosmic.

Maybe this is an unfair point to make. For it is also true that pessimists such as Bayle were aiming, through the use of thought experiment and introspection as well as observation, precisely at a kind of objectivity—an

117. See also Dienstag, *Pessimism*, chapter 7, on the fragmentary or aphoristic tendencies of pessimism.

aim in which contemporary pessimists such as David Benatar are also united.[118] There is a common and perhaps lamentable temptation in pessimists to want to speak not only of the experience of individual sufferers, but to over-interpret *all experience* as so many modes of suffering. This is open to the same objection as theodicean optimism, which tended to explain away suffering or play it down. The pessimists are surely right to object that it is callous to dismiss the suffering of others as a sign of weakness or even sin. But is it any better to tell people that they are deluded if they think they are *not* suffering, since deep down they must be (and if only they were philosophers, surely they would see this)? There is an element of arrogance here that clings to pessimism as it does to optimism—and especially in those pessimists who begin to slip from the particular to the universal, from the subjective to the objective. This is, of course, precisely what Schopenhauer is doing—and yet it could be argued that Schopenhauer is *less* guilty than others of over-interpreting our experience. After all, Schopenhauer honestly believes his to be an a priori argument: he is emphatically not arguing *from* experience but *towards* experience; experience is to confirm his theory, not to ground it.

But does experience actually confirm his theory? Many would deny that it does. To many and perhaps most of us, a large portion of Schopenhauer's descriptions of what life is will seem wildly exaggerated and counter-intuitive, and this is a problem that will haunt his philosophy as long as it continues to be read. However, if Schopenhauer is guilty of exaggeration, so too are many of his readers and commentators, not all of whom have represented him with sufficient nuance, subtlety, and distance. It is easy to exaggerate Schopenhauer; it is not so easy to do him justice. But it is by trying to do him justice that the richness and moral depth of his strange system reveal themselves. We fail to do so at our cost.

NIHILISM

It is precisely this richness, this moral depth, that may succeed in countering a more serious objection often raised against Schopenhauer's philosophy and against pessimism in general. This is the objection, mentioned briefly above, that the outcome of Schopenhauer's pessimism—his grand and final 'nothing'—sounds literally like nihilism. Surely we are right to

118. However, Bayle, through his thought experiment, is still speaking to the individual experience; he believes precisely that he can draw the universal from the particular (see chapter 1).

criticise Schopenhauer for his characterisation of life as essentially bad, for his opposition to affirmation and to any attempt to find meaning or happiness in life. What could such assumptions lead to if not to moral lethargy and political passivity? As Schopenhauer himself suggests, even if the state were to achieve its ends completely and something like a utopia were realised on earth, then the evils essential to life would still maintain human suffering; and even if these evils were removed, boredom would step in (*WWR*.I.350). Why, then, should we try anything at all, whether for our own betterment or for that of others? What does this sound like, if not the end of ethics, the end of hope?

Such points are well taken—and yet it is not fair to reduce Schopenhauer entirely to them. Four central tenets of his philosophy resist the interpretation of Schopenhauer's pessimism as sheer nihilism, three of which have been discussed already. These are, first, Schopenhauer's deep concern to offer something in the way of consolation to the individual sufferer, to whose suffering he gives a different kind of meaning. It is not wrong or weak or even unnecessary to suffer: suffering is our lot as feeling creatures, and it is in the awareness of this lot that we can find our consolation. In fact, it is through suffering, even extreme suffering, that the possibility of 'grace' (*Gnade*) opens up for us, and we may be lifted into a different kind of being.[119] This leads to the second point: redemption, of which, as a philosopher, Schopenhauer can speak only in negative terms—but if Julian Young is right, we can catch Schopenhauer in this tentative probing of his, a probing for glimpses of the beyond that he nevertheless resists putting into words.[120]

The third point has to do with ethics. Ethically, Schopenhauer is excellent. From his treatment of sympathy as the foundation of morality to his discussion of *schadenfreude* and egoism, we find a thinker imbued throughout with the highest moral awareness–even if he did not always follow through on his own principles. As Max Horkheimer wrote appreciatively, Schopenhauer's philosophy 'removes from the world the treacherous gold foil which the old metaphysics had given it . . . , thus exposing the

119. Schopenhauer speaks of 'grace' especially in chapter 70 of *WWR*.I.

120. But note that for philosopher A. Phillips Griffiths, the salvation aspect of Schopenhauer's philosophy is precisely what condemns it: 'I cannot stomach his hideous optimism. He said there was "a road to salvation"; and he was not being ironical' (Griffiths, 'Wittgenstein and the Four-Fold Root of the Principle of Sufficient Reason', 3; see Cartwright, 'Schoperhauerian Optimism').

motive for solidarity shared by men and all beings: their abandonment'.[121] To embark upon the moral path, for Schopenhauer, is itself to find oneself consoled: just as the egoist lives in a world of 'strange and hostile phenomena', so too '[t]he good person lives in a world of friendly phenomena; the well-being of any of these is his own well-being' (*WWR*.I.374).[122] This is not nihilism in any conventional meaning of the term—unless there can be a nihilism that is at the same time moral, redemptive, and consolatory.

For the fourth and final point, not discussed so far, we must return for a moment to another common critique of Schopenhauer's pessimism: that it is so exaggerated as to be not worth taking seriously anymore, becoming almost funny or silly and lending itself to parody. As I have argued, we lose something crucial if we read Schopenhauer in this way. It is useful in this context to recall those earlier pessimists so far discussed, and especially what they were responding to. Bayle's pessimistic musings did not come out of nowhere, but were a response to rational theodicies that tended to explain away the evils and sufferings of life; likewise, Voltaire's *Candide* was in acute opposition to those 'optimisms' he associated with Leibniz and King. These responses, we have seen, were ethically motived, and they retain their principal value precisely in this motivation. Throughout this chapter, I have tried to show that Schopenhauer too is arguing *against* something, and doing so *at least in part* for moral reasons. His pessimism becomes the more understandable when it is considered as a *counterpoint* or *counterweight* to the two specific optimisms of his time: first, the ongoing theodicean depictions of the goodness of life and of the world itself; and, second, the achievability of human happiness.[123] Schopenhauer's quarrel with many ancient philosophies or *eudaemonologies* is not only that they grossly misrepresent this achievability of happiness, but that their representation fails to do justice to the intrinsic tornness and fragility of the human condition. It is partly in counterpoint to this overestimation of our capacity for happiness that Schopenhauer seeks to draw light on 'the terrible side of life'.[124] In so far as he is, I believe this exercise to be justified, and important.

121. Horkheimer, 'Schopenhauer Today', 81–2; see Young, *Willing*, 104. The phrase 'by men and all beings' may draw our attention to what is perhaps the greatest objection to Schopenhauer's ethics: his failure to extend the principle of sympathy to women.

122. A point echoed by Wittgenstein, *Tractatus*, no. 6.43: 'The world of the happy is quite another than that of the unhappy' (though here the point is happiness, not virtue).

123. See chapter 9. Consider, in this context, Woods's cautious remark ('Schopenhauer's Pessimism', 34): 'One might even suggest that his pessimism is inherently oppositional in essence; it always has in mind some kind of optimism as a target.'

124. '[D]ie schreckliche Seite des Lebens' (*WWR*.I.252; *WWR*.II.433, 435; *PP*.I.421).

Of course, this is not enough to waylay the objection that Schopenhauer's pessimistic view of life is itself exaggerated and coarsely one-sided—an objection I consider to be a valid one. But, in the ongoing effort to do justice to Schopenhauer, I would also point out that his philosophy is not always uttered in this minor chord. There is neither time nor space here to discuss Schopenhauer's glowing theories on the aesthetic experience—but there is one passage in his chapter on music that may be significant here. In a curious inversion of the aesthetic strategy in theodicy—which compares existence to a piece of art of music, where the minor discords or imperfections are resolved in a greater harmony—Schopenhauer instead compares music to existence. Just as our existence is a pendulum between suffering and boredom, so too in music the melody always ends up returning to the keynote or tonic (*WWR*.I.260). But there are things that have happened in between. Certain quick harmonious melodies, for Schopenhauer, correspond to a state of 'happiness and well-being', whereas slow discordant melodies correspond to 'delayed and hard-won satisfaction', and a sustained keynote to languor itself. Short phrases of 'rapid dance music' represent ordinary and easily attainable happiness—but an *allegro maestoso* signifies 'a greater, nobler effort towards a distant goal', and an *adagio* the suffering of such a noble endeavour, whose pain is keenest if represented in the minor key. Finally, in a transition from one key into another, Schopenhauer compares to death itself (*WWR*.I.260–1).

This analogy, to my mind, is especially interesting since it seems to work in two directions: it says something about *music*, but it also says something about *existence*. It suggests to me that when Schopenhauer is speaking of suffering, he is not necessarily always speaking of something that is *purely* bad or horrible. It is, after all, in our suffering that we begin to know ourselves and the world and are able to be drawn into some other reality, whether by aesthetic experience or by a quieting of the will.[125] Just as in music a melody may stray painfully far from the keynote, passing from one discord to another, and hurt us in its minor key, yet the overall experience may be one of an astounding beauty, a sublimity that is transmitted precisely through suffering. This is the kind of profundity that De Quincey associates with *rapture*, and I will call it by that name.[126] The question is whether suffering, for Schopenhauer, does not play something

125. Aesthetic experience itself has the power to temporarily negate the will; so too art can offer momentary consolation: 'The pleasure of everything beautiful, the consolation afforded by art, the enthusiasm of the artist which enables him to forget the cares of life' (*WWR*.I.267).

126. De Quincey, *Suspiria de Profundis*, 160–1.

of the same role in his pessimism as rapture does in his theory of music. Suffering may be the tonic or keynote of human existence, but this does not mean that existence is restricted to suffering alone. Suffering, while always painful, need not be *solely* so: it can also be potentiality, an opening of things—and this, again, is why Schopenhauer is so deeply concerned to argue against suicide, which closes off the possibility of transformation at the moment of its opening. The keynote of life, like that of music and of philosophy, may well reside in that dark minor chord—but that does not mean that other notes may not be born from it as well. Hence, when Nietzsche mockingly calls Schopenhauer a 'flute-playing pessimist', from Schopenhauer's view, this could as easily be a compliment.[127]

These comments are all tentative: I recognise the importance of not carrying them too far. Schopenhauer does emphasise, again and again, 'the wretched nature of the world' (*WWR*.II.621), 'the dark abodes of misery' (*WWR*.1.325); and he does believe that the world is something that it would be better had not been. My point is merely that Schopenhauer's pessimism, contrary to appearances, is yet a measured pessimism, one that seeks to speak to the tornness of existence as well as to its fullness; one that delves deeply into the darkness to find therein the frailest openings for beauty and rapture, as well as for redemption, compassion, and consolation.

HOPE AND CONSOLATION

This brings us to the third and final problem besetting Schopenhauer's pessimism from that very pessimism's perspective. As I have suggested at several points, two key issues at stake in the clash between optimism and pessimism are *hope* and *consolation*. Both issues are connected with the deeper question of how to make sense of suffering, how to speak meaningfully and sensitively of suffering in such a way that unlocks opportunities for hope as well as consolation. What can we hope for? Wherein lies our consolation?—These are the recurrent questions filling out the moral background of any optimism or pessimism worth fighting for; and these, too, are questions central to Schopenhauer's philosophy.

As for consolation, we have seen that Schopenhauer believes his pessimism to be consoling, in stark contrast to the optimism it opposes. 'There is only one inborn error,' he writes, 'and that is the notion that we exist in order to be happy.' As long as we persist in this error, we suffer twice:

127. The specific term 'flute-playing pessimist' I draw from Gray, *Straw Dogs*, 47.

added to the actual pain is 'the theoretical perplexity as to why a world and a life that exist so that he may be happy in them, answer their purpose so badly' (*WWR*.II.634). Instead, Schopenhauer holds that we can be consoled only by the awareness of the necessity of our suffering, and of the fact of our suffering *together*.

And yet there are reasons to argue that one of the points on which Schopenhauer's philosophy fails most miserably is precisely that of consolation. This is an objection that could be formulated from different angles. The Leibnizian version would be that Schopenhauer, like Bayle, doubles suffering by placing such emphasis on it. The Baylean version would be that Schopenhauer, like Leibniz or King, doubles suffering by adding to it the knowledge of our responsibility—not only by our natural guilt, but by a failure of the will. There are moments when Schopenhauer echoes the uncomfortable suggestion made by Descartes and Leibniz that pain can be overcome by force of will; that the extent of our suffering is up to us. Since life is a phenomenon of the will, according to Schopenhauer, 'a man is always referred back to himself':

> It is and remains the will of man on which everything depends for him. Sannyasis, martyrs, saints of every faith and name, have voluntarily and gladly endured every torture, because the will-to-live had suppressed itself in them; and then even the slow destruction of the phenomenon of the will was welcome to them. (*WWR*.I.326)

In other passages, Schopenhauer seems to assume a kind of hierarchy of suffering, in which a heroic response or 'melancholy disposition' (that is, to bear a single great pain voluntarily while disdaining lesser joys and sorrows) is considered a worthier kind of suffering than that dependent on 'deceptive' forms of joys and evils (*WWR*.I.319). What is so problematic about such passages is that they suggest that our suffering, or at least the extent or form of our suffering, is voluntary; that it could be avoided by an effort of the will. Not only would this seem to take away the consolation offered by the inevitability of suffering—but it risks overburdening the will in much the same way as in the optimism or eudaemonism he so despises.

This, to my mind, is one of the main challenges to the moral integrity of Schopenhauer's pessimism: that in emphasising the voluntary negation of the will, he ends up overburdening the will. Schopenhauer seems unaware of this objection—which nevertheless has its antidote in the very emphasis on human fragility and incapacity that is central to his system. Even so, I am not convinced that Schopenhauer does enough to save the consolatory force of his philosophy. Be that as it may, the most important point to make, perhaps, is that, whether or not his consolation works, Schopenhauer certainly *believes* that it does: even if his philosophy does not drive to consolation, it is certainly driven by it.

But can we say the same of hope? I have suggested that it would be wrong to see Schopenhauer's pessimism as a philosophy of sheer denial and despair; that it is also oriented on positive horizons, such as consolation and compassion; that it even has redemptive force. But could we go so far as to speak of hope—a term which Schopenhauer himself tends to avoid? Hope remains a more problematic concept for pessimism than consolation, gilded as it is with intimations of an afterlife: earlier pessimists are not agreed on whether or not hope is a thing worth saving. In Schopenhauer's case, we might expect him to steer clear of hope as the last disaster in Pandora's jar—and yet we have seen glimpses and musings of an other-worldly salvation, and these glimpses are enough to know that hope still has force for him; that pessimism is to offer hope as well as consolation.

Thus, in the manuscript notebook entitled 'Senilia', Schopenhauer wrote this passage, to be added immediately after a paragraph in his essay on ethics, in which he has yet again emphasised the 'badness and baseness' reigning in the human world:

> Nevertheless, in [the human world] there occur, though quite sporadically but always surprising us anew, appearances of honesty, of goodness, even of nobility, and likewise of great understanding, of the thinking mind, even of genius. These never extinguish entirely; they glimmer out at us like individual gleaming points from the great mass of darkness. We must take them as a pledge that a good and redeeming principle lies in this *Samsara*, which can achieve a breakthrough and fulfil and liberate the whole. (*PP*.II.199)

What is this, if not a *hopeful* pessimism?

CHAPTER NINE

Dark Matters

PESSIMISM AS A MORAL SOURCE

But where danger threatens
That which saves from it also grows.

FRIEDRICH HÖLDERLIN[1]

There is a crack in everything
That's how the light gets in.

LEONARD COHEN[2]

IT BEGINS WITH AN observation—but where does it end?

Having travelled through 'the worlds of death and darkness', 'these great abysses of grief', 'this storm of life';[3] having passed through the wastelands of evil and suffering; having scaled the heights of optimism, and burrowed down into the depths of pessimism; having measured out our lives, not with coffee spoons,[4] but in Bayle's balances—what are we left with? With the terrible silence of Job or of Wordsworth's Michael, who, smitten by his grief, 'never lifted up a single stone'?[5] Is it true what the optimists say, that pessimism only fosters despair? That turning our eyes

1. 'Wo aber Gefahr ist, wächst / Das Rettende auch' (Hölderlin, 'Patmos', in *Poems and Fragments*, 462–3).

2. Leonard Cohen, from his song 'Anthem'.

3. De Quincey, *Suspiria de Profundis*, 92, 119, 87.

4. 'I have measured out my life with coffee spoons': T.S. Eliot, 'The Love Song of J. Alfred Prufrock', in *Poems*, vol. I, 6.

5. Wordsworth, 'Michael', in *Selected Poems*, 130; see Trilling, *Sincerity and Authenticity*, 92.

to the 'terrible side of life' blinds us to the good; that it leaves us defeated and 'sorrowing the sorrow for which there is no consolation'?[6] Do we run up against the limits of language in the face of such dark matters, as some have suggested? 'One profound sigh ascended from my heart,' writes De Quincey of the ultimate catastrophe, 'and I was silent for days'.[7] Can we hope for answers where we hardly dare to speak the question? If philosophy begins with a minor chord—*must it end there?*

This book has taken us deep into some of philosophy's darkest pages, and we have come a long way on this strange odyssey of theodicy, passing some familiar faces, such as Kant and Rousseau, as well as some possibly less familiar ones, such as Bayle and Maupertuis. We have heard some authors raise themselves up as God's defence counsel, where others played the devil's advocate. We have witnessed some sing of the goodness of creation, while others lamented its terrors. We have watched from the shadows as they weighed the goods and ills of life, the brighter and darker sides of our existence, until we too would ask that 'pillar of fire', that 'pillar of darkness': '*in what scales should I weigh thee?*'[8] Among so many presences, the absences of this book may stand out all the more. Where, outside the margins, are Pascal, Leopardi, Cioran, Hartmann, Kierkegaard, or Nietzsche? Where is Calvin; where are the Greeks? But the aim of this book was never to be exhaustive, and this should serve as enough of a justification: if it does not suffice, neither will any other.[9]

Instead, the aim of this book has been to connect the early modern debate on the problem of evil with the rise of philosophical pessimism, and to show how both debates have influenced each other. I have argued that the problem of evil emerges as a way of tracing deeper changes in the moral and cultural background of the early modern era as well as our current age. I have argued that the problem of evil can be better understood as a cluster of related questions (as *problems* of evil), having to do sometimes with creation or annihilation, sometimes with mental and physical suffering, sometimes with the possibility of this-worldly happiness, sometimes with hope and consolation. I have argued that our philosophical

6. Schopenhauer, *WWR*.I.252; De Quincey, *Suspiria*, 102.

7. De Quincey, *Suspiria*, 91.

8. Ibid., 100; my emphasis.

9. But here is one, regardless. The focus on this book has been the early modern period: the development I am tracing begins with Bayle (the emergence of pessimism out of the problem of evil) and ends with Kant and Schopenhauer (the failure of theodicy; the emancipation of pessimism as a philosophy in its own right). Discussing these other authors (especially Nietzsche, whose absence I too regret) would have required a book double this size; I leave these, then, as questions for another day.

senses should be attuned to a multitude of shifting assumptions in the background, on the conceptual and metaphysical as well as on the moral and methodological plane. What constitutes an evil? Which evils, if any, are most problematic for any justification of existence? How should we weigh them? Does any creature have a legitimate complaint against its creator? Could it be better never to have been at all? I have argued that these questions change significantly in the course of Bayle's reworking of the problem of evil, and that it is precisely through such questions that the problem of evil becomes, first and foremost, a problem of suffering.[10]

Parallel to this, I have tried to show how the debate on the problem of evil has given rise to the philosophical traditions of (value-oriented) optimism and pessimism, which by the nature of their subject matter have been shadowed by many misunderstandings. Not only has this will to misunderstand been profoundly unhelpful, it has also led to many undeserved criticisms *on both sides of the debate*, and it is for this reason that I have tried to do justice to the optimists as well as the pessimists and to read both sides with as much generosity as I could muster, while also critiquing them on their own terms. The result of this approach has been eye-opening, at least for this scholar, who has found that pessimism, so little taken seriously, has less to do with calculating evils or with moral complacency than with trying to find a way of speaking about suffering that does justice to experience while also being sensitive or even consoling. And that optimism, surprisingly or unsurprisingly, wants much of the same thing. The debate is about the value of existence, yes, but more than this, it is about the moral background of our being in the world, about how to give sure footing to grounding goods: such as compassion, consolation, and sometimes even hope. The disagreement lies mainly in the path they plot towards that common and forgiving goal.

But there are also differences, and the gap widens over time. The key intuition shared by the pessimists is the sense that there is something particularly jarring about being offered *the wrong kind of consolation*—whether by philosophers or by anyone, but philosophers (so say the pessimists) seem to be particularly good at getting consolation wrong. The pessimists commonly recognise this at the particular level, and they point to cases in which philosophers have tried to reason away our grief by putting it into perspective: approaches that, to borrow Julian Barnes's words,

10. It is, furthermore, through such questions that the debate on suffering finds its continuation or even its culmination in the modern anti-natalism debate, where the problem of evil is again linked to the ethics of creation. I hope to return to this in future work.

'try to handle grief by minimising it'.[11] But the history of the debate on suffering shows the pessimists recognising this at a more general level too, and this, for them, is the deepest problem with theodicy, its original sin. *Theodicy goes wrong when it tries to handle our grief, our suffering, by minimising it.* This may gain us something in coping benefits, but according to these thinkers the costs are too high, for if we shallow out our grief, we shallow out everything.

This is not the whole story of pessimism and the problem of evil, but it is a key part of its plot. And so, if we are to conclude anything from this exercise, it is that, despite misgivings to the contrary, the historical traditions of both philosophies have more in common than either of them have acknowledged; that optimism cannot be understood without pessimism, just as pessimism cannot be understood without optimism; and that neither can be understood without also understanding the questions posed by the problem of evil.

Why the Dark Matters

Now I will say a few things about why all of this matters: to me, and perhaps to all of us. This may seem a strange move: after all, throughout this book I have resisted and cautioned against the temptation to reduce ideas to experience, let alone to biography. It may also be controversial, since these days philosophy (i.e. 'real', 'serious' philosophy) is not supposed to want to be 'important'; that is, philosophers are not supposed to care too much about their subject matter. Throughout history, there have been many competing visions of the proper place of philosophy, and the one that seems to have won out is a vision of philosophy as parallel to the vision of science: a mainly left-brain activity characterised by the dispassionate search for truth.[12] As one of my first anonymous reviewers commented: 'isn't it true that most philosophers today shy away from becoming too "personal", too "intimate" perhaps to the liking of their peers?' The intuition is a pervasive one, to such an extent that it would disqualify those who turn to philosophy in order to find hope or

11. Barnes, *Levels of Life*, 78.

12. See Stump, *Wandering in Darkness*, 23–5, commenting on certain tendencies in the analytic tradition; and Van Fraassen, *The Empirical Stance*, who offers an alternative to the common view of philosophical positions as consisting purely or primarily in beliefs about the world: 'A philosophical position can consist in a stance', such as an 'attitude, commitment, approach', which may well include beliefs 'but cannot be simply equated with having beliefs or making assertions about what there is' (47–8).

consolation: such persons, in view of philosophy's self-proclaimed gatekeepers, have no business there, and should look to theology instead. 'I'm not entirely sure why contemporary philosophers are so keen to appear hardheaded,' writes Alex Douglas in an article on the issue: 'They might be afraid that scientists will make fun of them.'[13]

The concern behind this 'hardheadedness' is only understandable, if perhaps a little superfluous: of course, we shouldn't be doing philosophy if we're only looking for ways to twist reality into a version we find palatable—but was there ever a committed philosopher who did *that*? Even the least sophisticated of the optimists believed their visions of reality to be deeply truthful. And so, caricatures aside, why not look to philosophy for answers to some of the bigger questions of life? If 'a philosopher's motivation in striving to glimpse an ultimate reality beyond appearance . . . is to find comfort in the vision'—is anything so wrong in that?[14] I am reminded of one of my first classes in philosophy, where our teacher cautioned against the overvaluation of philosophy as an answer to everything, then cautioned equally against its undervaluation—and I now suspect that it's the latter lesson that contemporary philosophy should take most to heart, lest we compartmentalise it away. If philosophy is to be restricted solely to the conceptual analysis of things we're not supposed to care about anyway, then this may still be a worthwhile exercise, but it also means we will have lost something, and I think this *something* is worth saving. 'It has been a long time since philosophers have read men's souls,' writes E.M. Cioran: 'It is not their task, we are told. Perhaps. But we must not be surprised if they no longer matter much to us.'[15] Or, more boldly, in the words of Charles Renouvier: 'Life can be of no interest to a thinker unless he or she seeks to solve the problem of evil. Philosophy, the true philosophy, is that which teaches us to live and to die.'[16]

I'm not sure I would want to go so far, but perhaps there is something to the notion that we lose something if we force ourselves not to care

13. Douglas, 'Philosophy and Hope', 27.

14. Ibid., 28.

15. Cioran, *The Trouble with Being Born*, 39. See Van Fraassen, *The Empirical Stance*, 17: 'Philosophy itself is a value- and attitude-driven enterprise; philosophy is in false consciousness when it sees itself otherwise. . . . it is the enterprise in which we, in every century, interpret ourselves anew. But unless it so understands itself, it degenerates into an arid play of mere forms.' Van Fraassen notes that this danger also lurks in some contemporary philosophers' treatment of the problem of theodicy as a 'lovely logical problem of . . . consistency' but not something of real importance (29–30).

16. Renouvier, *Les Derniers Entretiens*, 61 (my translation); see Krusé, 'The Inadequacy', 399.

where *care* or *concern* is precisely what is due. I hope that if one thing has become clear through the pages of this book, it is that the philosophers represented here *care* about their subject matter—and that it is *right* that they do so. The caring part (I have argued throughout) is crucial to their enterprise, and this is true for both sides of the debate, those arguing for theodicy and against it, the varieties of optimism as well as those classified loosely as pessimists. While I have tried throughout this book to do justice to both sides, it may nevertheless seem that my sympathies lie ultimately with the pessimists, just as Neiman's lie with the optimists.[17] To some extent this is correct, but it is so only because of the particular historical context in which this book was written; in a different time or situation my sympathies might have fallen elsewhere. This again seems to be a tendency due the topic: throughout this history, optimists and pessimists have articulated their philosophies in order to take position *against something*, and they have done so on strongly moral grounds. Both philosophical currents spring pivotally from a position of care or concern.

This book, however, is *not* an articulation of pessimism, and it did *not* emerge out of a sentiment of either moral or societal concern. Instead, it sprang from a typical series of scholarly coincidences: learning about Bayle in my undergraduate years, writing my doctoral thesis on him, becoming interested in the problem of evil, starting a project on this, and then changing it halfway through in order to connect the debate on theodicy with the philosophy of pessimism. But it is perhaps inevitable for any scholar of pessimism *or* optimism that studying this topic opens their eyes or unlocks new fields of vision or even changes their way of seeing things. 'Occasionally,' writes Robert Macfarlane, 'once or twice in a lifetime if you are lucky . . . you encounter an idea so powerful in its implications that it unsettles the ground you walk on.'[18] At its best and deepest, the philosophy of pessimism has this potential: it changes everything, from the way we think and speak about suffering and happiness to the way in which we decide whether or not to have children. More than a philosophy, it is also a style, a mode of thought, a sensitivity that travels with you into the margins of the books you read, the things you hear and see around you, the way you console people and the way you wish to be consoled yourself. The result for me, personally, has been that the writing of this book has

17. Or more specifically: with authors such as Rousseau who hold 'that morality demands that we make evil intelligible'. Neiman, *Evil in Modern Thought*, 8.

18. Macfarlane, *Underland*, 87, writing there of the ecological phenomenon known as the 'wood wide web': underground mycorrhizal fungi networks connecting trees and plants.

given rise to deep concern over some cultural perspectives closely linked to the questions of optimism and pessimism—and it is this concern that, while not triggering the beginning of this book, nevertheless will form its conclusion.

The concern in question has much to do with certain misperceptions of both optimism and pessimism, with the result that the former is widely overvalued by our culture, just as the latter is strongly undervalued. Dienstag has made this point in general for future-oriented pessimism, and I think much of his argument can be extended to the value-oriented kind as well, and especially to some specific issues haunting the current (and future) generations. To explore this fully would require a book in itself: here, I will just say a few things about the ways in which optimism has become more 'danger' than a thing that 'saves', and where pessimism may serve us better as a moral source.

Happiness and the New Suffering

This takes us back to chapter 4, and the long debate on happiness. There, we witnessed the clashing cultural narratives of optimism and pessimism, represented *in this aspect* by Maupertuis and La Mettrie, respectively, who offered different answers to the question of the extent to which we are in charge of our own happiness. The question at stake in this part of the debate on (value-oriented) pessimism is not so much whether the goods of life outweigh the evils, but to what extent the balance is controlled by us. How much responsibility do we carry for our own happiness? Should we stress the role of will and agency in our lives, or tone it down? The contrasting intuitions that motivate such questions could be a different way of dividing the optimists from the pessimists, even though it cuts across the usual categories.[19] For while the one view is motivated by the instinct that we must emphasise human agency at all costs, the other believes that compassion and consolation are best served by resisting any view of reality that would make us responsible for our own suffering. In our current culture, one narrative has prevailed, and it is repeated like a mantra across wellness manuals, yoga videos, self-help books, and commercial advertisements alike: *you are responsible for your own happiness*. It is presented as a message of hope and encouragement, and many find as much comfort and inspiration from this narrative as Rousseau did from the

19. Thus Maupertuis can be called an optimist in this sense, but a pessimist in others; and La Mettrie vice versa; see chapter 4.

art of suffering: For is it not indeed a hopeful thing that we can improve ourselves?

It is, and at the same time, it is not. For all its merits and benefits, there is also a danger in this line of thinking, and it is one of which the historical pessimists were deeply aware, having to do with what I have called *the overburdening of the will*. The flipside of making individuals responsible for their own happiness is that they must be individually responsible for their suffering as well. If happiness is radically in our power, then so too is unhappiness. So how does this speak to our suffering? The message overwhelmingly brought out by the modern mindfulness industry, positive psychology, self-styled spiritual movements, commercials, and Western consumer culture as a whole is that if we suffer misfortunes, then either we have attracted them, or we have not worked hard enough at controlling our reactions: *if we're not happy, we are doing something wrong*. This mindset has been called *responsabilism* by the late Mark Fisher and *magical voluntarism* by David Smail: 'the belief that it is within every individual's power to make themselves whatever they want to be'.[20] It has shaky roots in ancient philosophy, strongly diluted, as well as in Eastern spirituality, though in both cases it has been stripped of any deeper reflection on what *the good* entails, let alone our responsibility to other creatures.[21] Its message may seem innocuous, or too superficial to merit philosophical scrutiny, but its consequences can be deeply damaging.

A few years ago, all the flats in a London high-rise were being sold off to foreign investors, causing much anxiety and stress among the occupants. But rather than taking responsibility for the problems created by this event, the council hired a company to offer mindfulness courses to the people affected: 'The council encouraged residents to look inwards, towards their brain chemistry, and in doing so cast itself as a solution, rather than a cause of the problem.'[22] According to this brazen mechanism, people were first deprived of their homes and emotional tranquillity, then made cunningly responsible for the very stress caused by this deprivation. The pervasive idea of magical voluntarism allows politicians

20. This is Mark Fisher's formulation in his article 'Good for Nothing'; see Smail, *Power, Interest and Psychology*.

21. Purser, *McMindfulness*, 8. For the most extreme version of this 'philosophy', see Rhonda Byrne's *The Secret*, according to which 'Everything that's coming into your life you are attracting into your life. And it's attracted to you by virtue of the images you're holding in your mind. It's what you're thinking'. Cited in Gunn and Cloud, 'Agentic Orientation as Magical Voluntarism', 62. But see also Kate Bowler's critique of the 'prosperity gospel' in her book *Everything Happens For A Reason*.

22. O'Brien, 'How Mindfulness Privatised a Social Problem'.

to 'deny links between depression and economic insecurity', writes Mark Fisher: 'Each individual member of the subordinate class is encouraged into feeling that their poverty, lack of opportunities, or unemployment, is their fault and their fault alone.'[23] Not only does this make things worse for those suffering depression and other mental health problems, but it offers a structural excuse to those agents implicated in social injustice. As Ronald Purser writes in his critique of the modern mindfulness industry: 'Societal problems rooted in inequality, racism, poverty, addiction and substance abuse and deteriorating mental health, can be reframed in terms of individual psychology, requiring therapeutic help. Vulnerable subjects can even be told to provide this themselves.'[24]

This, then, is the ugly side of the modern quest for happiness, where it has been carried too far: where the hopeful view that we can change our lives has been twisted into the uncompassionate view that we are each the cause of our (un)happiness, and that no one need concern themselves with anyone else's suffering. This was surely never the intention of the concerned optimists of the past, who would have been horrified at the shallowing down of principles that were supposed to *deepen* human solidarity with creation and with each other, not weaken it. Nevertheless, the tendency to explain suffering away and to emphasise human self-mastery has clung to optimism from the start—and it is here that pessimism again reveals its value, by warning us that to overburden the will is to make us all the more miserable; it is to overwhelm us with a sense of failure for things that are ultimately out of our control. Again in Fisher's words: 'A particularly vicious double bind is imposed on the long-term unemployed in the UK now: a population that has all its life been sent the message that it is good for nothing is simultaneously told that it can do anything it wants to do.'[25] As the pessimists already knew, nothing adds to our despair as much as being told we have called it upon ourselves.

At the same time as the happiness hype, shadowing it like its darker twin, is another kind of desensitisation. In a recent article, Amelia Tait points to people reacting in online forums to the death and suffering of immigrant children with reactions such as 'bummer' or 'too bad', and asks: 'has the internet made evil our new normal?'[26] In their book *Evil Online*, Dean Cocking and Jeroen van den Hoven have investigated 'features of

23. Fisher, 'Why Mental Health is a Political Issue'.

24. Purser, *McMindfulness*, 35.

25. Fisher, 'Good for Nothing'.

26. Tait, 'As People Celebrate Migrant Children Dying in Custody, Has the Internet Made Evil Our New Normal?'

our online worlds that erode empathy and moral character' and create a 'moral fog' that makes ordinary people capable of things they might well consider bad or evil in offline circumstances.[27] In Tait's words, 'It is not really, then, that the internet allows us to say things we would never have dared say before—it also makes us want to say them in the first place.'[28] And it's not just saying: it's *doing*, too. The internet has become a weapon placed loosely in the hands of trolling users who encourage or manipulate others to inflict self-harm or even to kill themselves, until even suicide becomes a game in a world that affects reality all the more deeply for pretending not to belong to it.[29]

According to Susan Neiman, it is surely a sign of moral progress that we have abolished 'public execution by torture': not only have we ended the practice, but the very idea of seeing such horrors now makes our stomachs turn: 'This is a change not just of moral sense but of moral sensibility; it's deep, and it's visceral, and it's not three hundred years old.'[30] I wholeheartedly agree, and would ask in turn what it means that we are increasingly accepting of depictions of extreme violence for entertainment purposes. As Alan Bennett writes in his diary: 'if a naked woman being pressed to death and a priest disembowelled is not unusual, it seems to me to put a modern audience on the same footing as a 17th-century crowd watching the executions'.[31] It is true that most of such depictions are fictional, but I am beginning to wonder to what extent we can hide behind this justification, especially when it is paired with a conflicting one: that the depicted crimes actually do occur, or have done so in the past.[32] Unlike those seventeenth-century executions, which at least were not *intended* as entertainment, the new aesthetic of suffering is just that: it's entertainment.[33] What does it say about a culture aiming at ever

27. Cocking and Van den Hoven, *Evil Online*, 4, 16, where they also warn: 'A large part of socialization and moral education now takes place in digital environments not at all designed with the education of morally sensitive, prosocial future citizens in mind.'

28. Tait, 'As People Celebrate Migrant Children Dying'.

29. For a range of horrific examples, I refer to Cocking and Van der Hoven, *Evil Online*, 1–32. At least as disturbing as the actions themselves is the popularity it bestows the perpetrators in many cases, and the number of views and likes begotten by online evil.

30. Neiman, *Moral Clarity*, 290.

31. Alan Bennett, *Diary*, 4 January 2018.

32. Nor are the depictions always fictional, as is demonstrated by the rising phenomenon of real violence to humans and animals in online videos.

33. Note that I am in no way equating the two: I am questioning the innocence of the latter without denying the horribleness of the former.

bigger kicks and thrills that depicting violence (and, increasingly, sexual violence) in the most explicit and sensationalistic ways is considered an acceptable means of getting them? As I have argued in my unconventional critique of *Candide*, it *matters* how we speak of suffering, because speaking *of* suffering is always speaking *to* suffering as well.

So is there a connection between the narrative that places happiness entirely in our power and the desensitisation trend, whether by the distortions of the online world or by the gradual dulling down of our affective responses to representations of other people's suffering?[34] Surely it is at least *easier* to withhold sympathy if our fortunes are seen to belong to us in a non-contingent way. Surely it is not entirely a coincidence that platforms such as Facebook pressure us to share our successes and not our failures with people we are nevertheless supposed to call 'friends', to such an extent that happiness has become not just an aim or a privilege, but a duty, and failure to comply not just unfortunate, but shameful.[35] Now there is nothing new about humans concealing their misfortunes: Schopenhauer calls it one of our most common tendencies, and suggests that it is the fear that our sufferings will be met with contempt rather than with 'sympathy or compassion' that makes us conceal them (*WWR*.I.324). But we have never in history lived lives quite this public on quite this scale from quite this young an age, nor have we had to carry so entirely the burden of what has become a fully secular sin: *failing to thrive*. And so there is a special courage in those who dare to bare their wounds before a culture that tends to receive such revelations with distaste.

These, of course, are only my impressions, and I will not insist on them. My point is a modest one: we could do with more generosity, more compassion, and especially more sensitivity to other creatures' suffering in our culture, without that suffering becoming sensationalised as yet another kick or thrill. If pessimism can teach us anything, it can teach us this, and I think Schopenhauer was right when he argued that opening our eyes to others' suffering will open our hearts to them, and will foster a sense of sympathy and connectedness with other persons, and potentially with animals too, whose suffering the pessimists have always taken more deeply into account.[36]

34. See also Neiman, *Moral Clarity*, 371–4.

35. See Freitas, *The Happiness Effect*.

36. Though some recent pessimists, disturbingly, do not: e.g. Dienstag, *Pessimism*, 249; and Ligotti, *The Conspiracy against the Human Race*.

This is the ethics of pessimism: it unfolds immediately into a full and certain sympathy. While it blushes sometimes at doing so, it need not apologise, for its message is a sound one, aligned with what George Eliot said of the arts: 'The greatest benefit we owe to the artist, whether painter or poet or novelist, is the extension of our sympathies.'[37] It is this extension that the philosophy of pessimism, at its best and fullest, also offers us, not necessarily in replacement of optimism, but as its necessary counterpart. For where pessimism is not callous, it is kind.

The Point of Pessimism

Wherever did we get the idea that it is intellectually deficient or shallow or complacent or arrogant to want to do justice to the suffering of the world? For be not mistaken: that is the main drive behind any philosophical pessimism that deserves the name. As I have tried to show throughout this book and especially this conclusion, the point of pessimism has always been to resist the urge of minimising pain or grief or suffering, whether by turning our eyes to other things or by overburdening the will or by explaining suffering away as the optimists have so often done. This is why compassion and consolation are such major concerns for the pessimists—and why their project, ultimately, is a *moral* one. In this sense, it would seem mistaken to see pessimism as an *overall* philosophy, which it cannot be—and this is something that the more consistent pessimists fully recognise. With the exception of Schopenhauer, the pessimists in this history have another thing in common, and it is their profound discomfort with *systems*, whether philosophical or theological in nature. Pessimism, these philosophers acknowledge, cannot do its work as a system on its own accord, but only as a *complement* to any philosophy (even an optimistic one) that lays claim to describing and evaluating experience—the human as well as the animal kind. It has its role and value rather as a critical element, as a test for any philosophy or theory of life that paints an image of experience in which suffering is insufficiently weighted. The main point of pessimism, against such descriptions, is to pause theory where it goes too far, and remind us: *There is also this . . .*

Herein too lies the enduring value of the problem of evil, which perhaps always had less to do with the nature of God's attributes than with something more basic: that the ills or evils of existence should never be

37. George Eliot, 'The Natural History of German Life' (1856), 110.

met with the kind of dismissive acceptance that characterised at least some of the optimists; that evil should indeed be considered a *problem*, not just for God's goodness, but for existence itself. This is why something is lost if we consider evil a non-problem in a secular age: for there is something jarring, disruptive, unsettling about evil and suffering that requires a problem to do it justice. And this too is where Bayle and Benatar are so strangely and yet, it seems, so naturally aligned. If Benatar is right and the issue at stake is fundamentally one of *creation*, then the problem of evil is relevant to anyone who considers bringing another being into existence. More than this, it is relevant to anyone who has ever existed—that is, *to all of us*—since it has to do with other, less justificatory questions too, such as how to speak of suffering, how to relate to it, and how to ground our compassion as well as consolation, maybe even our hope.

It is as easy to ridicule the pessimists for their bleakness as it is to ridicule the optimists for their *naïveté*, but there is something profound being articulated in both philosophies, and in the case of the former, it is the attempt to bring everything down to this pinpoint: the experience of the truly miserable among us. Even one creature whose life is not worth living should be enough to halt us in our steps: even one grain of suffering constitutes a problem of evil. There are states worse than non-existence, argues Malebranche of those who are born into a fallen world; and it is in trying to express fully what such a state is like that pessimism finds its depth. This kind of description, which is itself an exercise in empathy, seems to be what Wittgenstein is aiming at in one of his notebooks of around 1944 where, against the background of world catastrophe, he writes about the suffering of a single person:

> No cry of torment can be greater than the cry of one man.
>
> Or again, *no* torment can be greater than what a single human being may suffer. . . .
>
> The whole planet can suffer no greater torment than a *single* soul. . . .
>
> No greater torment can be experienced than One human being can experience. For if a man feels lost, that is the ultimate torment.[38]

Circling around what he wants to say, he ends up saying the same thing four times, and it is at heart the very point that the pessimists were making: *This too is life*; *how shall we speak of it?*

38. Wittgenstein, *Culture and Value*, 45e–46e; his emphasis.

Does such a philosophy detract in any way from the value or colour of life; does it make life seem less worth living? This has been the main objection of the optimists from early on: that pessimism, with its emphatic focus on the 'terrible side of life', poisons it for us, cutting us off from either hope or happiness. And the concern is valid in some cases, for just as optimism has its shadow side, pessimism has also. At its best, it is a philosophy of fragility, sensitivity, compassion, and consolation; at its worst, it is callous in its own way and ruins us for joy by telling us that it is impossible.[39] At its worst, it can be just another strategy of desensitisation, a way of cutting us off from the suffering of others and of stifling participation in the wider moral and social realities that stretch out beyond our narrow selves. This is certainly not what 'my' pessimists were getting at, as they proved themselves capable of a sensitivity and sympathy for the suffering of other creatures that was exceptional in their age and may be so still. But, sirens of suffering, could they also be lovers of life?

As Cioran wrote of reading Schopenhauer: 'The more I read the pessimists, the more I love life.'[40] If this is true, if reading the pessimists could make us love life *more*, then the optimist objection would seem to fail—but all depends on the manner of this love. Surely Cioran did not mean that reading about others' misery makes his own pale in comparison, for we know enough of the importance of sympathy in the pessimist tradition (let alone of Schopenhauer's resistance to *schadenfreude*) that this could never be the point of pessimism. And surely he is not trying to mirror the aesthetic strategy traditionally wielded by the theodicean optimists, according to which light and dark shades are both needed to make a beautiful painting or tapestry, and discords have as much place in music as harmony does. This, however, was how De Quincey thought we should come to terms with suffering, since 'the rapture of life . . . does not arise, unless as perfect music arises—music of Mozart or Beethoven—by the confluence of the mighty and terrific discords with the subtle concords'.[41] The context, it should be noted, is not a theodicean one: De Quincey was not trying to justify life or even to say that happiness is within our reach. His was an attempt to travel deep into the heart of suffering and find some hidden meaning there, having to

39. See Stump, *Wandering in Darkness*, 479: 'there can be ideology in the promotion of despair as well as in the raising of hope. And moral scorn is a delicate matter, easily mishandled.'

40. Cioran, *On the Heights of Despair*; cited in Dienstag, *Pessimism*, 121.

41. De Quincey, *Suspiria*, 160.

do less with happiness than with awe, solemnity, depth, rapture—different kinds of goods that give a value to life beyond the search for earthly enjoyment:[42] 'Either the human being must suffer and struggle as the price of a more searching vision, or his gaze must be shallow, and without intellectual revelation.'[43]

Maybe it is this, then: maybe this is one way in which pessimism could make us love life more. Not by reminding us that things could always be worse, but by imbuing us with an appreciation of the fullness and fragility of existence, a sharpened sense of the darker and lighter materials of which our lives are made, a heightened receptivity for the *innocent* as well as the *terrible* or *serious* side of life (to use Schopenhauer's terms), and a deepened sensitivity to the suffering of others. Most of all, I suspect it is by that very sympathy that pessimism can make us love life more: by opening our hearts to other creatures, by extending our love or at least our kindness to them—for if the pessimists are right, it is by filling out the background of existence that we are reminded to take kindly to these people, these animals, with whom we share a world. Nor does this mean that we must stand idly by, helpless and hopeless in the face of the insurmountable reality of suffering. Marilynne Robinson writes of cultural pessimism that it 'has the negative consequence of depressing the level of aspiration, the sense of the possible'.[44] This may be true of cultural pessimism that has got out of hand, but the kind of compassionate, even *hopeful* pessimism argued for here is morally active precisely because it opens new horizons for us, wielding that terror that must always be the counterpart of vision where change is most urgently needed and most difficult to achieve. And I would go further still. If even that strand of pessimism most oriented towards resignation (Schopenhauer's version) retains a profound ethical orientation; if even here the recognition of suffering in the world is tightly linked to the commitment to lessening that suffering—what this tells us about pessimism is that this is a philosophy that sees itself as charged with the highest ethical potential. Far from dissuading us from ethical or political action, the point of pessimism is to motivate us.

42. This, roughly, is also the existentialist response to Schopenhauer's pessimism; see Young, *Willing and Unwilling*, 109.

43. De Quincey, *Suspiria*, 161.

44. Robinson, *Givenness*, 29.

Fragility

Throughout the ages, then, the tension between optimism and pessimism has had to do with the conflicting demands of their double orientation: towards hope and, at the same time, towards consolation. This means, on the one hand, to do justice to the reality of human suffering, without which, as pessimism in particular recognises, consolation is impossible. And, on the other, to offer a perspective that opens up new possibilities, new perspectives for the future, without which, as optimism in particular recognises, hope is impossible. This tension arises again and again in literature as well as the history of philosophy. I will just point out two more passages, one as subtle in its optimism as the other is in its pessimism.

The first passage occurs at the end of Tolstoy's *War and Peace*, where Pierre looks back at his past sufferings and draws from them a lesson that, without discounting or playing down these hardships, nevertheless manages to place them in a wider narrative of hope and meaning:

> 'They say: sufferings are misfortunes,' said Pierre. 'But if at once, this minute, I was asked, would I remain what I was before I was taken prisoner, or go through it all again, I should say, for God's sake let me rather be a prisoner and eat horseflesh again. We imagine that as soon as we are torn out of our habitual path all is over, but it is only the beginning of something new and good. As long as there is life, there is happiness. There is a great deal, a great deal before us.'[45]

I believe there is great wisdom in this. But I also think this is something we should handle with great caution; something we should not make into too general a point. It is a wonderful thing when out of deep tragedies or great suffering comes 'the new and the good'; when bad experiences teach us new things, help us to reach beyond ourselves, to grow as persons. Speaking of the value of life, this is surely one of those things that makes life and living valuable to us: this possibility of bad things giving entry to the good. But while we should be deeply grateful when this is the case for us, it is not something we can count on, nor is it something that is dependent on our will. Not all that doesn't kill us makes us stronger. Not all suffering gives way to the new and good; not all bad experiences help us to grow. Some diminish us; some tragedies make life stop short in its tracks. Some suffering cuts us off from the attainment of the 'new and good', and, in Hilary Mantel's words, makes us 'foreign to ourselves':

45. Tolstoy, *War and Peace*, 1053.

> All of us can change. All of us can change for the better, at any point. I believe this, but what is certainly true is that we can be made foreign to ourselves, suddenly, by illness, accident, misadventure, or hormonal caprice.[46]

These words are drawn from Mantel's memoir, *Giving up the Ghost*, and they comprise the second passage I want to mention, which seems to stand as a kind of counterpoint to Tolstoy's muted optimism: where Pierre counterposed light to darkness, Mantel counterposes darkness to light. My own pessimism, if it deserves the name, arises exactly at this point. I believe, with and perhaps beyond Mantel, that there are those to whom the path of happiness is closed—truly closed. That there are experiences that can cut us off from ourselves and from our very capacity for happiness: from the good and from the true. To recognise this is not to forfeit hope or to give up on such persons, let alone on ourselves: it is rather to acknowledge that this *too* is life; this *too* is what it means to be alive. As Julian Barnes writes of 'the lostness of the griefstruck' after the death of his wife: 'everything you do, or might achieve thereafter, is thinner, weaker, matters less. There is no echo coming back; no texture, no resonance, no depth of field.'[47] Or De Quincey of the death of his sister: 'the terrific grief which I passed through, drove a shaft for me into the worlds of death and darkness which never again closed'.[48] Or Kate Saunders of the death of her son: 'My world is dark and will always be dark. The death of a child is a wound that will never heal, and there's no getting used to hefting round that sack of everlasting sorrow.'[49] Or Hannah Gadsby of the damage that has been done to her: 'I will never flourish.'[50]

And this is the great risk, the original sin of any overly optimistic description of reality or of the human capacity to flourish: the suggestion that this flourishing is entirely up to us, that it resides firmly in our human hands; that we are radically responsible for our own happiness.[51] While many have drawn hope from this belief, it is not simply a message of hope

46. Mantel, *Giving Up the Ghost*, 54.

47. Barnes, *Levels of Life*, 100; see also John Gray, *Straw Dogs*, 101, on Varlam Shalamov's suffering in the gulag: 'At its worst human life is not tragic but unmeaning. The soul is broken, but life lingers on. As the will fails, the mask of tragedy falls aside. What remains is only suffering. The last sorrow cannot be told.'

48. De Quincey, *Suspiria*, 92.

49. Saunders, in C.S. Lewis, *A Grief Observed*, 93.

50. Gadsby, in her comic-tragic stand-up show *Nanette*.

51. Equally, that 'everything happens for a reason'; see again Bowler's book of the same title.

or inspiration: it can quickly become an imperative, and as soon as it does, it reveals its ugly side, in its overburdening of the will. If this gains us hope, it fails in consolation.

And yet it seems equally unconsoling to tell us, as some pessimists have done, that there is never a way back from that heart of darkness; that 'it is only in sermons or on the stage that human beings are ennobled by extremes of suffering';[52] that 'Suffering improves no one (except those who were already good), it is forgotten as all things are forgotten, . . . it wastes itself as everything is wasted.'[53] For in spite of everything, there are indeed those who have 'touched the true bottom of life'[54] and yet have resurfaced; who have been broken as few things are broken and yet have rebuilt themselves. Such as the tragic and yet not tragic Charlotte Salomon, who found her way back again from the zero point of existence, breaking away from a history of abuse and a family line of suicide to which she believed herself to be destined, travelling deeply into herself and somehow managing to create the world anew.[55] Such stories are meaningful to us not because they are exemplary, but *because they are authentic*: because these are lives that were really lived, because these were real people speaking to us of the possible without suggesting that it is possible for all of us. If there is such a thing as an authentic theodicy, then surely, this is it. And so, while it would be deeply mistaken to make an example out of the kind of transcendent suffering we see in Salomon or Etty Hillesum (thus turning the extraordinary into the ordinary), it seems equally mistaken to rule their experience out altogether (thus turning the extraordinary into the impossible).[56]

52. Gray, *Straw Dogs*, 99.

53. Cioran, *The Trouble*, 176.

54. Varlam Shalamov, cited in Gray, *Straw Dogs*, 100.

55. The result was the astonishing collection of autobiographical paintings combined with narrative and music titled *Life? Or Theatre?*, available online at https://charlotte.jck.nl. Salomon was murdered in Auschwitz in 1943. For an overview of her life and work in relation to her troubled family background, see Harding, 'A Young Woman Who Was Meant to Kill Herself'.

56. Etty Hillesum, upon the death of her friend and lover Julius Spier in September 1942, and awaiting deportation herself, nevertheless expressed a cosmic gratitude: 'I find life very beautiful and meaningful. Yes, even as I stand here by the body of my dead companion, one who died much too soon, and just when I may be deported to some unknown destination. And yet, God, I am grateful for everything' (*Etty*, 518). See Paul van Tongeren, *Dankbaarheid*, who connects Hillesum's 'gratitude for everything' with Nietzsche's *amor fati*, while warning that this is a 'possibility that can only be shown in practice' (99; my translation).

There is a fine balance to tread here, and when they are at their best, the pessimists tread it well. Hume's suggestion that there is something in grief and mourning that is profoundly valuable serves as a challenge to the optimists as well as the more callous kinds of Stoicism, and even to Schopenhauer's blunt dismissal of any kind of longing as purely negative. As Marilynne Robinson writes, in one of those passages that clings to the soul of any who have read it:

> To crave and to have are as like as a thing and its shadow. For when does a berry break upon the tongue as sweetly as when one longs to taste it, and when is the taste refracted into so many hues and savors of ripeness and earth, and when do our senses know any thing so utterly as when we lack it? And here again is a foreshadowing—the world will be made whole. For to wish for a hand on one's hair is all but to feel it. So whatever we may lose, very craving gives it back to us again. Though we dream and hardly know it, longing, like an angel, fosters us, smooths our hair, and brings us wild strawberries.[57]

This perhaps is the meaning of that hope which the pessimists hardly dare call by name: that it is through longing and grief and mourning that we may find some form of consolation. That there is something meaningful about speaking about suffering or craving or grieving, as long as we find the right way of bringing it to words: 'Grief can, after all, in some ways, turn out to be a moral space.'[58] This is the 'paradox of grief', in Julian Barnes's words, but it is also the hope most compatible with pessimism, the kind that always retains its openness for an influx of something else: the saving force that grows alongside Hölderlin's 'danger'; the single 'crack in everything' through which Cohen's 'light comes in'. 'If you don't feel despair, in times like these, you are not fully alive,' writes Paul Kingsnorth: 'But there has to be something beyond despair too; or rather, something that accompanies it, like a companion on the road.'[59]

Pessimism, then, need not stand in the way of joy or happiness or love of life,[60] but it requires a different attitude to it, as receptivity rather than entitlement: receptivity to something that it is either given or not given to us to enjoy, and always in the knowledge that 'Nothing is so delicate or so

57. Marilynne Robinson, *Housekeeping*, 152–3.

58. Barnes, *Levels of Life*, 103.

59. Kingsnorth, *Confessions*, 147; the context is that of the environmental crisis. There is much still to say on the value of pessimism in an age of climate change: too much to say it here. This, too, is a question to which I hope to return.

60. Cioran, *The Trouble*, 212: 'No one has loved this world more than I'.

fragile as a happy state.'[61] The binding concept is perhaps that of *fragility*, as the place where optimism and pessimism can meet; as the point of entry of that awareness of the terrible side of life, and at the same time of hope itself.[62] For it is precisely through the sense of the fragility of all things that pessimism, without insisting on hope, can nevertheless leave the door open to it, so that, on the day when 'mystic gladness' irrupts into our lives or happiness finds us, despite everything, as a thief in the night, we can greet it with a gratitude all the richer for having been deepened by compassion.[63]

Hopeful Pessimism

Halfway through the writing of this book I came across a bench by a beach in Scotland that had black balloons tied to it. The bench itself was dedicated to the memory of a boy who had died one year before that day. There were flowers on the bench, and beside the flowers, a bunch of papers, with hundreds of names of persons, followed by those persons' ages: fifteen, seventeen, twenty-one, thirty-two. On the first page was a handwritten note, telling us that this was a list of people lost to suicide, and suggesting to us these three things:

> Be kind to people.
> Look out for loved ones.
> Its ok to not be ok.[64]

And this is what the ethic of pessimism, in its strongest, clearest, cleanest form, most pivotally represents: that 'It's ok to not be ok.' That to make suffering a question primarily of our will is merely to increase suffering, by heaping guilt upon it. That it's a wonderful thing to live a life rich in

61. Fontenelle, *Du Bonheur*, 265. This is not to say that happiness is utterly out of our hands or that we should not strive for it, but that this striving should take on a different character, and go hand in hand with the 'extension of our sympathies' (Eliot) towards our own fragility as well as others'.

62. Hope, as a Christian virtue, may seem to stand in direct contradiction to the pessimism, and yet it need not be so: for where hope occurs in the pessimist tradition, it is a deeply fractured concept, often value-oriented in nature, having to do rather with openness or with resistance to the final closure of any system or explanation. If life and flourishing are ultimately uncontrollable, this can also be a hopeful thing; just as optimism, if carried too far, can be a creature of cruelty. On fragility or (in Dutch) *broosheid*, see Prins, 'Het wordt niet beter', and his forthcoming book on the topic; as well as Nussbaum, *Fragility*.

63. The term 'mystic gladness' comes from George Eliot's poem, 'Self and Life', 445.

64. It turns out that the note was put up by 'Project Tag', a 'campaign aimed at supporting people with mental health issues' (*Fife Today*, 13 August 2018).

wonder, and meaning, and happiness; and we should be deeply grateful if we are so blessed. But that our own happiness should not excuse us either from an awareness of the fragility of life, happiness, and good itself, or from a due consideration and concern for those less fortunate, less blessed, less beloved, or the truly miserable among us, who also walk this world.

The message of pessimism is that this, too, is a part of life, and that it deserves a place in our language, our shared experience; that we are not justified, that it is never justified, to close our eyes to that other, darker, 'terrible' side of life. This is also the meaning of compassion in the ethic of pessimism, which need not at all be in conflict with optimism, but should stand shoulder to shoulder beside it as its necessary complement and companion. As Schopenhauer wrote, this is how deep down we should greet each other, not as *Madame* or *Monsieur*, but as 'fellow sufferer, compagnon de misères'.[65]

In times of great crisis such as we are living through now—'the time of the great, strange plague',[66] and beneath it, the dim reality of an earth we are on the verge of breaking beyond repair—we could do worse than take on board some of pessimism's notions. As Thomas Berry wrote in the 1990s, two things are needed for real cultural or personal transformation, *terror and vision*. In order to transform our lives or our culture, we need to be attracted to a different vision of reality, but sometimes we also need to be 'so frightened that we are willing to undertake a drastic restructuring of our lives, a reordering of our personal life, our environment, our associations—a kind of rebuilding of life from the ground up'.[67] If this is right, then this is another way in which pessimism can serve us as a moral source: by unsettling us out of our comfort zones and imbuing us with some of the dauntlessness that the pessimists show us by their example, a willingness to sing even of the most terrible things, thereby to open our eyes, thereby to open our hearts. The 'evil facts' of life are, in William James's words, 'a genuine portion of reality; and they may after all be the best key to life's significance, and possibly the only openers of our eyes to the deepest levels of truth'.[68]

Noam Chomsky has argued for optimism over despair. We might equally, and perhaps more meaningfully, argue for hope over optimism. If optimism risks, on the one hand, an overburdening of the will, and on the other, an understatement of the reality of true and dire damage done

65. Schopenhauer, 'On the Suffering of the World', in *Essays and Aphorisms*, 50.

66. Kingsnorth, 'Finnegas'.

67. Berry, *Befriending the Earth*, 94.

68. James, *Varieties of Religious Experience*, 163.

to the world and to ourselves—could not pessimism serve us better as a moral source? And where pessimism risks stumbling into resignation—could not hope help us to mind the gap? If optimism and pessimism both have their faces turned towards a common goal, could we not find in both the materials by which to travel forwards?

Why, then, not a philosophy of hopeful pessimism to guide us into the future?

ACKNOWLEDGEMENTS

AS I HOPE WILL HAVE BECOME clear in the course of this book, pessimism need not stand in the way of gratitude, and my gratitude is all the greater for having travelled these dark matters, not alone. For their questions, suggestions, and comments on these pages, and for other kinds of conversation and correspondence, I thank Alex Douglas, Robin Douglass, James Harris, Anthony La Vopa, Vassilios Paipais, Awee Prins, John Robertson, Jens Timmermans, Wiep van Bunge, Richard Whatmore, and John Wright. For sending me draft versions of unpublished work and answering my queries, I thank Geertje Bol, Sam Duncan, Emilio Mazza, Gianluca Mori, Samuel Newlands, and Bernhard Ritter. For their insightful suggestions and corrections of the manuscript, I thank two anonymous reviewers; and for his support throughout the writing process, I thank editor Ben Tate of Princeton University Press. I also thank the Leverhulme Trust and the University of St Andrews, as well as the Lichtenberg Kolleg-Göttingen Institute of Advanced Study, for having made this journey possible.

Hardly any of this book has been previously published: the exceptions are a few sections in chapter 7, which were published in my article 'The Left Hand of the Enlightenment' in *History of European Ideas*, and parts of chapter 9, which were published in my essay 'Pessimism' in *The Philosopher*. I thank the editors of both journals for allowing me to reprint these sections here.

For their invaluable support and inspiration throughout the process of writing this book, I thank my friends in Scotland and beyond, who need not be named: they know who they are. But my deepest thanks go to my family, who have had their share of challenges over the years, and whose trials have sometimes informed the silent undercurrents of this book. Above all, I thank my mother Mañec, who is also my first and finest reader, and whose wisdom and kindness have no match upon this earth.

Finally, some words to the dead: for this book, aside from many things, is also a book about grief. In fact, it is a book lined with loss, as the philosophers I talk about talk about death themselves, about grief, about the possibility or impossibility of consolation. Sometimes they talk about particular people they or others have loved and lost, and so there are some ghosts as well that haunt these pages, such as Cicero's daughter, or La Mothe le Vayer's son, or Bayle's brother, or De Quincey's sister. Some of these long-departed souls have been introduced into the history of philosophy to prove a point—for which I would apologise, had the point not been such an important one, one that honours the dead as much as it may serve to console the living.

This is the word I barely dare to speak: that the loss of a loved one, whether by death or separation or the many vicissitudes of life, can devastate as few things can, but can also fill the heart with a deepening and heightening of sorts: a deepened sense of the fragility of life; a heightened sense of gratitude. As some of the voices in this book will suggest, an awareness of the dark stuff of life can achieve the same, so that pessimism, despite the assurance of the pessimists that philosophy cannot console us, nevertheless emerges as a philosophy of consolation. This intimation may not meet with everyone's agreement, but as Voltaire himself wrote after the loss of his lover and companion: 'they say that no two people grieve alike, and so there you have how my grief is'.

And so I dedicate this book to the memory of my father, Bart van der Lugt. Eeuwige dank.

Mara van der Lugt
St Andrews, 1 May 2020

BIBLIOGRAPHY

BIBLIOGRAPHICAL NOTE: with a few exceptions, spelling and punctuation have been modernised for all early modern sources cited in translation and most English texts; I have, however, left capitalisation mostly intact in sources cited directly or in my own translations. The bibliography is divided into 'Main Primary Sources', 'Other Primary Sources', and 'Secondary and Modern Sources'.

Main Primary Sources

A bibliography of authors named in chapter headings, with conventions and abbreviations, and notes on translations. For others not listed, see 'Other Primary Sources'.

BAYLE

DHC *Dictionnaire historique et critique* (first published 1696). All citations are from the English translation, ed. Pierre Des Maizeaux. 5 vols. London, 1734–1738 (though at times modernised or adjusted by me). Since Bayle prepared three editions of the *DHC* (1696, 1702, and 1720 [posthumously published]), I indicate the origin of any passage as follows: *Xenophanes*[1]*.E* (article *Xenophanes*, Remark E, passage present in the first edition).

Dialogues of Maximus and Themistius, trans. and ed. Michael W. Hickson. Boston, MA: Brill, 2016.

EMT *Entretiens de Maxime et de Thémiste*. 2 vols. Rotterdam: Reinier Leers, 1707. In *OD*.IV.

OD *Œuvres diverses*. 4 vols. The Hague [Trévoux], 1737.

Political Writings, trans. and ed. Sally L. Jenkinson. Cambridge, UK: Cambridge University Press, 1999.

RQP *Réponse aux questions d'un provincial*. 4 vols. Rotterdam: Reinier Leers, 1704–1707; also in *OD*.III; references are to both editions.

Selections *Historical and Critical Dictionary: Selections*, trans. and ed. Richard Popkin, with the assistance of Craig Brush. Indianapolis, IN: Hackett, 1991.

Various Thoughts on the Occasion of a Comet [*Pensées diverses sur la comète*], trans. Robert C. Bartlett. Albany, NY: State University of New York Press, 2000.

HUME

DNR *Dialogues concerning Natural Religion and other writings*, ed. Dorothy Coleman. Cambridge, UK: Cambridge University Press, 2007.

EHU *An Enquiry concerning Human Understanding: and Other Writings*, ed. Stephen Buckle. Cambridge, UK: Cambridge University Press, 2013.

EMPL *Essays, Moral, Political, and Literary*, ed. Eugene F. Miller. Indianapolis, IN: Liberty Fund, 1987.

FE 'Fragment on Evil'. In *DNR*, 109–12.

Letters *Letters of David Hume*, ed. J.Y.T. Greig. 2 vols. Oxford: Oxford University Press, 2011.

Mem. 'Memoranda'. In E.C. Mossner, 'Hume's Early Memoranda, 1729–1740: The Complete Text'. *Journal of the History of Ideas* 9(4) (October 1948): 492–518, at 499–518.

NHR *Dialogues and Natural History of Religion*, ed. J.C.A. Gaskin. Oxford: Oxford University Press, 1993.

THN *A Treatise of Human Nature*, ed. David Fate Norton and Mary J. Norton. Oxford: Oxford University Press, 2000.

KANT

I have used the common German abbreviations for Kant's *Critiques*, and English abbreviations and initialisms for other works. References are solely to the Prussian Academy edition (*AK*), even when cited in translation, with the exception of English editions that do not supply the *AK* pagination, in which case both are cited.

AK *Immanuel Kant: Gesammelte Schriften (Akademie-Ausgabe)*. 29 vols. Berlin: Georg Reimer, Walter de Gruyter, 1900–.

'Conjectures' 'Conjectures on the Beginning of Human History' [*Mutmaßlicher Anfang der Menschengeschichte*] (1786). In *AK* 8:107–23/*PW*, 221–36.

'Danzig' 'Danziger Rational theologie nach Baumbach' (1784). In *AK* 28:1227–1319.

'Dialectic' 'Dialectic of Pure Practical Reason'. In *KpV*, *AK* 5:107–48.

'Essay' 'On the Failure of All Philosophical Trials in Theodicy' [*Über das Misslingen aller philosophischen Versuche in der Theodizee*] (1791). In *AK* 8:255–75/*RRT*, 19–38.

Groundwork *Groundwork of the Metaphysics of Morals* [*Grundlegung zur Metaphysik der Sitten*] (1785), trans. and ed. Mary Gregor. Cambridge, UK: Cambridge University Press, 1998.

KpV *Critique of Practical Reason* [*Kritik der Urteilskraft*] (1788); trans. and ed. Mary Gregor. Cambridge, UK: Cambridge University Press, 2015.

KrV *Critique of Pure Reason* [*Kritik der reinen Vernunft*] (first version A, 1781; second version B, 1787); trans. and ed. Paul Guyer and Allen W. Wood. Cambridge, UK: Cambridge University Press, 1998.

KU *Critique of the Power of Judgment* [*Kritik der Urteilskraft*] (1790); trans. and ed. Paul Guyer and Allen W. Wood. Cambridge, UK: Cambridge University Press, 2007.

'Lecture' *Lectures on the Philosophical Doctrine of Religion* (especially part 2: *Moral Theology*). In *AK* 28:989–1126/*RRT*, 338–451.

MS *The Metaphysics of Morals* [*Die Metaphysik der Sitten*] (1797), trans. Mary Gregor, ed. Lara Denis. Cambridge, UK: Cambridge University Press, 2017.

PW *Political Writings*, trans. H.B. Nisbet, ed. Hans Reiss. Cambridge, UK: Cambridge University Press, 1991.

RBMR *Religion within the Boundaries of Mere Reason, and Other Writings*, trans. and ed. Allen W. Wood and George di Giovanni. Cambridge, UK: Cambridge University Press, 2018.

Religion *Religion within the Boundaries of Mere Reason* (1793), trans. George di Giovanni. In *RRT*, 39–216.

RRT *Religion and Rational Theology*, trans. and ed. Allen W. Wood and George di Giovanni. Cambridge, UK: Cambridge University Press, 2001.

TP *Theoretical Philosophy, 1755–1770*, trans. and ed. David Walford, in collaboration with Ralf Meerbote. Cambridge, UK: Cambridge University Press, 1992.

Other works cited

Correspondence, trans. and ed. Arnulf Zweig. Cambridge, UK: Cambridge University Press, 2007.

Observations on the Feeling of the Beautiful and Sublime and Other Writings, trans. and ed. Patrick Frierson and Paul Guyer. Cambridge, UK: Cambridge University Press, 2011.

KING

DOM *De origine mali* (first published 1702): I cite from the posthumous English translation by Edmund Law, *An Essay On the Origin of Evil*, ed. Law. 2 vols. London: J. Stephens, 1732.

Note: Law expanded his translation with (i) remarks drawn from King's manuscripts and (ii) lengthy footnotes added by Law himself. While it is sometimes unclear whether King's remarks are entirely by King or rather paraphrased/edited/enhanced by Law, I cite them as King's (adding '1732'), since Law generally distinguishes his own additions clearly by the footnotes.

LA METTRIE

AS *Anti-Senèque* (first published 1748). In *Œuvres philosophiques*, vol. 2. Berlin, 1764.

DB *Discours sur le bonheur* [i.e. *Anti-Senèque*], ed. John Falvey. Studies on Voltaire and the Eighteenth Century, vol. 134. Banbury: Voltaire Foundation, 1975. [Critical edition, based on the 1751 text but with alternative passages.]

DP 'Discours préliminaire' (1750), trans. Ann Thomson, in her book *Materialism and Society in the Mid-Eighteenth Century: La Mettrie's Discours preliminaire.* Geneva: Librairie Droz, 1981.

MM *Machine Man and Other Writings*, trans. and ed. Ann Thomson. Cambridge, UK: Cambridge University Press, 1996. [Contains half of *Anti-Senèque* in the 1751 version used by Falvey, 119–43; and includes the *System of Epicurus.*]

LEIBNIZ

A *Sämtliche Schriften und Briefe*, ed. Preussischen Akademie der Wissenschaften. Darmstadt: Otto Reichl, 1923–.

EdT *Essais de theodicée sur la bonté de dieu, la liberté de l'homme, et l'origine du mal* (1710) [*EdT*]. Citations are to the standard paragraph number and the page number of the English translation by E.M. Huggard: Leibniz, *Theodicy: Essays on the Goodness of God, the Freedom of Man, and the Origin of Evil.* Chicago: Open Court, 1998; followed by the page number in (G).

G *Die philosophischen Schriften von Gottfried Wilhelm Leibniz*, ed. C.I. Gerhardt. Berlin: Weidmann, 1875–1890.

Other works cited

Confessio philosophi, trans. Robert C. Sleigh. New Haven, CT: Yale University Press, 2005.

Discourse on Metaphysics, trans. Peter G. Lucas and Leslie Grint. Manchester: Manchester University Press, 1953.

Textes inédits, ed. Gaston Grua. 2 vols. Paris: Presses Universitaires de France, 1948.

Philosophical Essays, trans. Roger Ariew and Daniel Garber. Indianapolis, IN: Hackett, 1989.

Philosophical Papers and Letters, trans. Leroy E. Loemker. Dordrecht: Kluwer Academic Publishers, 1989.

Selections, trans. P. Wiener. New York: Scribners, 1951.

MALEBRANCHE

All references are to the *Œuvres complètes* [*OCM*], followed by reference to the translation used, except where the translation is my own (e.g. *OCM*.XI.82/*TE*, 91).

OCM *Œuvres complètes*, ed. André Robinet. 20 vols. Paris: Vrin, 1958–1967.

SAT *The Search after Truth*, trans. and ed. Thomas M. Lennon and Paul J. Olscamp. Cambridge, UK: Cambridge University Press, 1997 [1674–1675].

TE *Treatise on Ethics*, trans. Craig Walton. Dordrecht: Kluwer Academic Publishers, 1993 [1684].

Works cited from the OCM

Recherche de la vérité (1674–1675)

Traité de la nature et de la grâce (1680)

Méditations chrétiennes et métaphysiques (1683)

Traité de morale (1684)

Réponse au livre des vraies et des fausses idées (1684)

Réponse aux réflexions philosophiques de M. Arnauld (1686)

Entretiens sur la métaphysique et sur la religion (1688; with preface added 1696)

Entretiens sur la mort (1696)

Réponse . . . à la troisième lettre de M. Arnauld . . . touchant les idées & les plaisirs (1699/1704)

Abrégé du traité de la nature et de la grâce et du dessein de son auteur (1704)

Avis touchant l'entretien d'un philosophe chrétien avec un philosophe chinois (1708)

Other editions consulted

Dialogues on Metaphysics and on Religion, trans. David Scott, ed. Nicholas Jolley. Cambridge, UK: Cambridge University Press, 1997 [1688].

Œuvres, ed. Geneviève Rodis-Lewis. 2 vols. Paris: Gallimard, 1992.

MAUPERTUIS

EPM *Essai de philosophie morale.* Leiden, 1751; first published 1749 in pirated edition.

ROUSSEAU

Confessions *Confessions*, trans. J.M. Cohen. London: Penguin Books, 1953.

CWR *The Collected Writings of Rousseau*, ed. Roger D. Masters and Christopher Kelly. 13 vols. Hanover, NH: University Press of New England, 1990–2010. From this edition, I cite the following texts:

Emile and Sophie, Or, The Solitaries (XIII, 685–721).
Letter to Beaumont (IX, 19–101).

Discourses *The Discourses and Other Early Political Writings*, ed. Victor Gourevitch. Cambridge, UK: Cambridge University Press, 2016. From this edition, I cite the following texts, as well as *DOI* and *LV* below:

Letter to Philopolis (223–8).
'Preface to *Narcissus*' (92–106).

DOI 'Discourse on the Origin of Inequality'. In *Discourses*, 111–222.

Emile *Emile or On Education*, trans. Allan Bloom. London: Penguin Books, 1991.

LV Letter to Voltaire. In *Discourses*, 232–46.

OCR *Oeuvres complètes*, ed. Bernard Gagnebin and Marcel Raymond. Paris: Gallimard, 1959–1995.

Reveries *Reveries of the Solitary Walker*, trans. Peter France. London: Penguin Books, 2004.

SCHOPENHAUER

PP *Parerga and Paralipomena: Short Philosophical Essays* (1851) [*Parerga und Paralipomena*], trans. and ed. Sabine Roehr, Christopher Janaway, and Adrian Del Caro. 2 vols. Cambridge, UK: Cambridge University Press, 2014–2017.

WWR *The World as Will and Representation* (1819–1859) [*Die Welt als Wille und Vorstellung*], trans. E.F.J. Payne. 2 vols. New York: Dover Publications, 1966–1969.

WWR.Cam *The World as Will and Representation*, trans. and ed. Judith Norman, Alistair Welchman, and Christopher Janaway. 2 vols. Cambridge, UK: Cambridge University Press, 2014–2018.

Other editions consulted

Essays and Aphorisms, trans. and ed. R.J. Hollingdale. London: Penguin Books, 2004.

Hauptwerke, Intelex Past Masters electronic edition. 6 vols. Charlottesville, VA: InteLex Corporation, 2003.

On the Suffering of the World, trans. and ed. R.J. Hollingdale. London, Penguin Books, 1970.

The Two Fundamental Problems of Ethics, trans. and ed. Christopher Janaway. Cambridge, UK: Cambridge University Press, 2014 [1840].

VOLTAIRE

Candide/CRT *Candide and Related Texts*, trans. David Wootton. Indianapolis, IN: Hackett, 2000.

D *Correspondence*. In *OCV*, vols. 85–135 [the '*D*' refers to the number of a letter in this edition].

Dictionary *A Pocket Philosophical Dictionary* [*Dictionnaire philosophique portatif*], trans. John Fletcher. Oxford: Oxford University Press, 2011 [1764].

'Lisbon' 'Poem on the Lisbon Disaster'. In Voltaire, *A Treatise on Toleration and Other Essays*, trans. Joseph McCabe. Amherst, MA: Prometheus Books, 1994 [1756].

Letters *Letters on England* [*Lettres philosophiques*], trans. Leonard Tancock. London: Penguin Books, 2005.

Memnon 'Memnon the Philosopher' ['Memnon, ou La Sagesse humaine']. In *Voltaire's Romances*, trans. Peter Eckler. New York: Peter Eckler, 1889 [1749].

OCV *The Complete Works of Voltaire* [*Les Oeuvres complètes de Voltaire*], ed. Theodore Besterman et al. Oxford: Voltaire Foundation, 1968–.

Other editions consulted

Voltaire, *Letters concerning the English Nation*, ed. Nicholas Cronk. Oxford: Oxford University Press, 2009 [1733].

Other Primary Sources

A bibliography of primary sources by authors not mentioned in the chapter headings; with the exception of 'modern' (roughly twentieth-century) primary sources, which are included in 'Secondary and Modern Sources'.

CMM Shaftesbury, Anthony Ashley Cooper, third Earl of Shaftesbury. *Characteristics of Men, Manners, Opinions, Times*, ed. Lawrence E. Klein. Cambridge, UK: Cambridge University Press, 1999.

EM Pope, Alexander. *An Essay on Man*, ed. Tom Jones. Princeton, NJ: Princeton University Press, 2016; references are to book and verse, e.g. *EM*, I.81.

FIN Jenyns, Soame. *A Free Inquiry into the Nature and Origin of Evil. In Six Letters to —*. Third edition. London: R. and J. Dodsley, 1758 [1756].

FME Bolingbroke, Henry St John, Viscount Bolingbroke. *Fragments or Minutes of Essays*. In *Works*, vol. 5. London: David Mallet, 1754.

NRL *Nouvelles de la république des lettres*, ed. Jacques Bernard: May–June 1703 (Amsterdam: Henry Desbordes and Daniel Pain, 1713) and January 1706 (The Hague: Adriaan Moetjens, 1713).

RND Wollaston, William. *The Religion of Nature Delineated*. London: S. Palmer, 1725.

SJW Johnson, Samuel. *The Yale Edition of the Works of Samuel Johnson*, general editor Allen T. Hazen. 23 vols. New Haven, CT: Yale University Press, 1955–.

Solomon Prior, Matthew, *Solomon on the Vanity of the World*. In *The Literary Works of Matthew Prior*, ed. H. Bunker Wright and Monroe K. Spears. Oxford: Clarendon Press, 1959, vol. 2, 306–85.

Encyclopédie, ou dictionnaire raisonné des sciences, des arts et des métiers, etc., eds. Denis Diderot and Jean le Rond d'Alembert. University of Chicago: ARTFL Encyclopédie Project (Autumn 2017 edition), Robert Morrissey and Glenn Roe (eds), online at http://encyclopedie.uchicago.edu/.

Mémoires pour l'histoire des sciences & des beaux arts [*Mémoires de Trévoux*], vol. 37. Paris: Chaubert, 1737.

Alembert, Jean d'. 'Jugement sur *Emile*'. In *Œuvres*. Paris: Didier, 1853.

Alès de Corbet, Pierre Alexandre d'. *De l'Origine du mal, ou Examen des principales difficultés de Bayle, sur cette matière, etc . . .*, 2 vols. Paris: Duchesne, 1757–1758.

Aristotle. *Metaphysics*, trans. Hugh Lawson-Tancred. London: Penguin Books, 1998.

Arnauld, Antoine. *Réflexions philosophiques et théologiques* (1685–1686). In *Œuvres d'Arnauld*. 43 vols. Lausanne: Sigismond d'Arnay, 1775–1783, vol. 39, 155–856.

Augustine: all works consulted are available at http://www.augustinus.it.

Contra secundam iuliani responsionem imperfectum opus
De Genesi ad litteram imperfectus liber
De ordine
Enchiridion de fide, spe et charitate

Aurelius, Marcus. *Meditations, Books 1–6*, trans. Christopher Gill. Oxford: Oxford University Press, 2013.

Austen, Jane. *Pride and Prejudice*. Ware: Wordsworth Editions, 2017 [1813].

Bentham, Jeremy. *An Introduction to the Principles of Morals and Legislation*, ed. J.H. Burns and H.L.A. Hart. Oxford: Oxford University Press, 2005.

———. *Deontology or, The Science of Morality*, ed. John Bowring. 2 vols. London: Longman, Rees, Orme, Brown, Green, and Longman/Edinburgh: William Tait, 1834.

Borowski, Ludwig Ernst. *Darstellung des lebens und charakters Immanuel Kant's*. Königsberg: Friedrich Nicolovius, 1804, vol. 1.

Boswell, James. *Life of Johnson: An Edition of the Original Manuscript*, vol. 1, ed. Marshall Waingrow. Edinburgh: Edinburgh University Press/New Haven, CT: Yale University Press, 1994.

Buffon, Georges-Louis Leclerc, Comte de. *Œuvres complètes de Buffon*. 12 vols. Paris: Garnier, 1853–1855; vol. 2, 1853.

Byron, Lord. *The Major Works*, ed. Jerome J. McGann. Oxford: Oxford University Press, 2008.

Châtelet, Emilie Du. *Selected Philosophical and Scientific Writings*, trans. Isabelle Bour and Judith P. Zinsser, ed. Judith P. Zinsser. Chicago, IL: University of Chicago Press, 2009.

Cicero, Marcus Tullius. *Letters to Atticus*, trans. Evelyn Shuckburgh. Online at http://www.perseus.tufts.edu/hopper/text?doc=Perseus%3Atext%3A1999.02.0022%3Ayear%3D45&force=y (accessed 25 February 2021).

———. *On Old Age. On Friendship. On Divination* [*De senectute. De amicitia. De divinatione*], bilingual edition, trans. William Armistead Falconer. Cambridge, MA: Harvard University Press, 2014.

Clarke, Samuel. *A Demonstration of the Being and Attributes of God and Other Writings*, ed. Enzio Vailati. Cambridge, UK: Cambridge University Press, 1998 [1705].

Crousaz, Jean-Pierre de. *Commentaire sur la traduction en vers de Mr. l'Abbé du Resnel, de l'essai de M. Pope sur l'homme*. Geneva: Pellisari & Co., 1738.

——. *Examen de l'Essai de M. Pope sur l'homme*. Lausanne: Bousquet & Co., 1737.

Dante Alighieri. *Inferno*, trans. Henry Francis Cary. London: Folio Society, 1998.

Darwin, Charles. 'Letter no. 2814' (22 May 1860). *Darwin Correspondence Project*, online at https://www.darwinproject.ac.uk/letter/DCP-LETT-2814.xml

——. *The Autobiography of Charles Darwin, 1809–1882*, ed. Nora Barlow. London: Collins, 1958.

De Quincey, Thomas. *Suspiria de Profundis* [1845–1891]. In *Confessions of an English Opium-Eater and Other Writings*, ed. Grevel Lindop. Oxford: Oxford University Press, 1989, 87–181.

Descartes, René. *The Passions of the Soul*, trans. Stephen Voss. Indianapolis, IN: Hackett, 1989 [1649].

—— and Princess Elisabeth of Bohemia, *The Correspondence between Princess Elisabeth of Bohemia and René Descartes*, ed. Lisa Shapiro. Chicago, IL: University of Chicago Press, 2007.

Eliot, George. 'Self and Life'. In *The Spanish Gypsy, The Legend of Jubal, and Other Poems, Old and New*. Edinburgh: William Blackwood, 1870.

——. 'The Natural History of German Life' (July 1856). In *Selected Essays, Poems and Other Writings*, ed. A.S. Byatt. London: Penguin Books, 1990, 107–39.

Eliot, Thomas Stearns. 'The Love Song of J. Alfred Prufrock.' In *The Poems of T. S. Eliot Volume I: Collected and Uncollected Poems*, ed. Christopher Ricks and Jim McCue. London: Faber and Faber, 2015.

Epictetus. *How to Be Free: An Ancient Guide to the Stoic Life. Encheiridion and Selections from Discourses*, trans. A.A. Long. Princeton, NJ: Princeton University Press, 2018.

——. *Letters, Principal Doctrines, and Vatican Sayings*, trans. Russel M. Geer. Indianapolis, IN: Bobbs-Merrill, 1964.

Erasmus, Desiderius. *Collected Works of Erasmus. Vol. 39: Colloquies*, trans. Craig R. Thompson. Toronto: University of Toronto Press, 1997.

Fontenelle, Bernard Le Bouyer de. *Du Bonheur*. In *Œuvres*, vol. 3. Paris: Michel Brunet, 1742, 243–69.

Goethe, Johann Wolfgang von. *Faust: Part One*, trans. David Luke. Oxford: Oxford University Press, 2008 [1808].

Haller, Albrecht von. *Über den Ursprung des Übels*, ed. Eduard Stäuble. Zürich: Atlantis Verlag, 1953 [1734].

Hölderlin, Friedrich. *Poems and Fragments*, bilingual edition, trans. Michael Hamburger. London: Routledge and Kegan Paul, 1966.

Hutcheson, Francis. *An Essay on the Nature and Conduct of the Passions and Affections*. London: J. Darby and T. Browne, 1728.

James, William. *The Varieties of Religious Experience*. London: Penguin, 1985 [1902].

——. *The Will to Believe, and Other Essays in Popular Philosophy*. New York: Longmans Green and Co., 1897.

Jaquelot, Isaac. *Conformité de la foi avec la raison*. Amsterdam: Henry Desbordes, 1705.

Johnson, Samuel. *The Letters of Samuel Johnson*, ed. Bruce Redford. 5 vols. Princeton, NJ: Princeton University Press, 1992–1994.

Maimonides, Moses. *The Guide of the Perplexed*, trans. and ed. Shlomo Pines. 2 vols. Chicago: University of Chicago Press, 1963 [ca. 1190].

Milton, John. *Paradise Lost*, ed. John Leonard. London: Penguin, 2003 [1667–1674].

Nietzsche, Friedrich. *Beyond Good and Evil*, trans. Judith Norman, ed. Rolf-Peter Horstmann and Judith Norman. Cambridge, UK: Cambridge University Press, 2018 [1886].

———. *The Gay Science: With a Prelude in German Rhymes and an Appendix of Songs*, trans. Josefine Nauckhoff and Adrian Del Caro, ed. Bernard Williams. Cambridge, UK: Cambridge University Press, 2001 [1882–1887].

Pascal, Blaise. *Pensées*, trans. A.J. Krailsheimer. London: Penguin Books, 1995 [1670].

Plato, *Theaetetus*. In *The Dialogues of Plato*, trans. Benjamin Jowett. Oxford: Clarendon Press, 1871, vol. 3.

Petrarca, Francesco. *Petrarch: The Canzoniere, or, Rerum vulgarium fragmenta*, trans. Mark Musa. Indianapolis, IN: Indiana University Press, 1999.

Puisieux, Madeleine de. *Les Caractères*. London [Paris], 1750.

Sade, Donatien Alphonse François de. *La Nouvelle Justine, ou les malheurs de la vertu, suivie de l'histoire de Juliette, sa sœur*. 10 vols. Hollande, 1797.

Schlegel, Friedrich. *Philosophical Fragments from the Philosophical Apprenticeship*. In *The Early Political Writings of the German Romantics*, trans. and ed. Frederick C. Beiser. Cambridge, UK: Cambridge University Press, 1996, 159–68.

Schmid, Carl Christian Erhard. *Versuch einer Moralphilosophie*. Jena: Cröker, 1790.

Schultens, Albert. *Liber Jobi cum nova versione ad Hebraeum fontem et commentario perpetuo*. 2 vols. Leiden: Johannes Luzac, 1737.

Shakespeare, William. *Much Ado About Nothing*, ed. Jonathan Bate and Eric Rasmussen. London: Random House, 2009.

Sherlock, William. *A Discourse Concerning the Divine Providence*. London: D. Brown et al., 1715 [1694].

Simon, Richard. *Histoire critique du Vieux Testament*. Rotterdam: Reinier Leers, 1685 [1678].

Spinoza, Benedictus de. *Ethics: Proved in Geometrical Order*, trans. Michael Silverthorne, ed. Matthew J. Kisner. Cambridge, UK: Cambridge University Press, 2018.

Stewart, Dugal. *The Philosophy of the Active and Moral Powers of Man*. 2 vols. Edinburgh: Adam Black et al., 1828.

Suárez, Francisco. *The Metaphysics of Good and Evil According to Suárez: Metaphysical Disputations X and XI and Selected Passages from Disputation XXIII and Other Works*, trans. Jorge J.E. Gracia and Douglas Davis. München: Philosophia, 1989.

Toland, John. *A Collection of Several Pieces of John Toland*. 2 vols. London: J. Peele, 1726.

Tolstoy, Leo. *A Confession*, trans. Jane Kentish. London: Penguin Books, 2009 [1882].

Warburton, William. *Letters from a Late Eminent Prelate to One of His Friends*. London: T. Cadell and W. Davies, 1809.

Wharton, Edith. *The House of Mirth*, with an introduction by Danuta Reah. London: Macmillan Collector's Library, 2017 [1905].

Wordsworth, William. *Selected Poems*, ed. John O. Hayden. London: Penguin Books, 1994.

Secondary and Modern Sources

A bibliography of secondary and modern sources (roughly twentieth-century onwards); newspaper articles and other media are listed separately below ('Newspaper and Magazine Articles'; 'Other Media').

'optimism, n.'. *OED Online*. Oxford: Oxford University Press, September 2020. Online at https://www.oed.com/view/Entry/132073 (accessed 1 November 2020).

'pessimism, n.'. *OED Online*. Oxford: Oxford University Press, September 2020. Online at https://www.oed.com/view/Entry/141727 (accessed 1 November 2020).

Adams, Marilyn McCord and Robert Merrihew Adams (eds.). *The Problem of Evil*. Oxford: Oxford University Press, 1990.

Adams, Robert Merrihew. 'Justice, Happiness, and Perfection in Leibniz's City of God'. In Jorgensen and Newlands, *New Essays*, 197–217.

Alberg, Jeremiah L. 'Rousseau and the Original Sin'. *Revista Portuguesa de Filosofia* 57(4) (October–December 2001): 773–90.

Alvarez, Al. *The Savage God: A Study of Suicide*. London: Bloomsbury, 2002 [1971].

Antognazza, Maria Rosa. *Leibniz: An Intellectual Biography*. Cambridge, UK: Cambridge University Press, 2009.

——. 'Metaphysical Evil Revisited'. In Jorgensen and Newlands, *New Essays*, 112–34.

Atwell, John E. *Schopenhauer: The Human Character*. Philadelphia, PA: Temple University Press, 1990.

Aycock, Roy E. 'Lord Byron and Bayle's "Dictionary"'. *Yearbook of English Studies* 5 (1975): 142–52.

Baker, Gordon and Katherine J. Morris. *Descartes' Dualism*. London: Routledge, 1996.

Barber, W.H. *Leibniz in France, From Arnauld to Voltaire. A Study in French Reactions to Leibnizianism, 1670–1760*. Oxford: Clarendon Press, 1955.

Barnes, Julian. *Levels of Life*. London: Vintage Books, 2014.

Battersby, Christine. 'The *Dialogues* as Original Imitation: Cicero and the Nature of Hume's Scepticism'. In D.F. Norton, N. Capaldi, and W.L. Robison (eds.), *McGill Hume Studies*. San Diego, TX: Austin Hill Press, 1979, 239–52.

Baum, Wilhelm. *Weimar—Jena—Klagenfurt: Der Herbert-Kreis und das Geistesleben Kärntens im Zeitalter der Französischen Revolution*. Klagenfurt: Kärntner Druck- und Verlagsgesellschaft, 1989.

Baumgardt, David and Jeremy Bentham. *Bentham and the Ethics of Today: With Bentham Manuscripts Hitherto Unpublished*. New York: Octagon Books, 1952.

Beauchamp, Tom L. 'An Analysis of Hume's Essay "On Suicide"'. *The Review of Metaphysics* 30(1) (September 1976): 73–95.

Beeson, David. *Maupertuis: An Intellectual Biography*. Studies on Voltaire and the Eighteenth Century, vol. 299. Oxford: The Voltaire Foundation, 1992.

Benatar, David. 'Anti-Natalism'. In Benatar and Wasserman, *Debating Procreation*, 9–132.

——. *Better Never to Have Been: The Harm of Coming into Existence*. Oxford: Clarendon Press, 2006.

——. *The Human Predicament: A Candid Guide to Life's Biggest Questions*. Oxford: Oxford University Press, 2017.

—— and David Wasserman. *Debating Procreation: Is It Wrong To Reproduce?* New York: Oxford University Press, 2015.

Berry, Thomas, with Thomas Clarke. *Befriending the Earth: A Theology of Reconciliation Between Humans and the Earth*. Mystic, CT: Twenty-Third Publications, 1991.

Bishop, John. 'On Identifying the Problem of Evil and the Possibility of Its Theist Solution'. In Trakakis, *The Problem of Evil*, 42–54.

Boehm, Omri. *Kant's Critique of Spinoza*. Oxford: Oxford University Press, 2014.

Bol, Geertje. 'Themes in von Herbert's Letters to Kant: Deception, Happiness and Meaning'. MA thesis, University of St Andrews, 2019.

Bost, Hubert. *Pierre Bayle*. Paris: Fayard, 2006.

—— and Antony McKenna (eds.). *L'Affaire Bayle. La bataille entre Pierre Bayle et Pierre Jurieu devant le consistoire de l'Église wallonne de Rotterdam*. Saint-Etienne: Institut Claude Longeon, 2006.

Boudot, Anne-Marie. 'L'être et le néant selon Malebranche'. *Cahiers de philosophie de l'université de Caen*, no. 43: 275–96.

Bourke, Joanna. *The Story of Pain: from Prayer to Painkillers*. New York: Oxford University Press, 2014.

Bowler, Kate. *Everything Happens for a Reason. And Other Lies I've Loved*. London: SPCK, 2018.

Brachtendorf, Johannes. 'Kants Theodizee-Aufsatz—Die Bedingungen des Gelingens philosophischer Theodizee'. *Kant-Studien* 93(1) (2002): 57–83.

Braiterman, Zachary. *(God) After Auschwitz: Tradition and Change in Post-Holocaust Jewish Thought*. Princeton, NJ: Princeton University Press, 1998.

Braun, Theodore E.D. and John B. Radner (eds.). *The Lisbon Earthquake of 1755: Representations and Reactions*. Studies on Voltaire and the Eighteenth Century, vol. 2. Oxford: Voltaire Foundation, 2005.

Brooke, Christopher. 'Rousseau's Political Philosophy: Stoic and Augustinian Origins'. In Patrick Riley (ed.), *The Cambridge Companion to Rousseau*. Cambridge, UK: Cambridge University Press, 2001, 94–123.

Camus, Albert. *The Myth of Sisyphus*, trans. Justin O'Brien. London: Penguin Books, 2005 [1942].

Cartwright, David E. 'Schopenhauer on Suffering, Death, Guilt, and the Consolation of Metaphysics'. In E. von der Luft (ed.), *Schopenhauer: New Essays in Honor of His 200th Birthday*. Lewiston, NJ: Edwin Mellen Press, 1988, 51–66.

——. 'Schopenhauerian Optimism and an Alternative to Resignation? *Schopenhauer-Jahrbuch* 66 (1985): 153–64.

Cassirer, Ernst. *The Question of Jean-Jacques Rousseau*, trans. Peter Gay. New Haven, CT: Yale University Press, 1989.

Cavallar, Georg. 'Kants Weg von der Theodizee zur Anthropodizee und retour. Verspätete Kritik an Odo Marquard'. *Kant-Studien* 84(1) (1993): 90–102.

Chester, David K. 'The 1755 Lisbon Earthquake'. *Progress in Physical Geography* 25(3) (2001): 363–83.

Chignell, Andrew (ed.), *Evil: A History*. Oxford: Oxford University Press, 2019.

Cladis, Mark S. 'Tragedy and Theodicy: A Meditation on Rousseau and Moral Evil'. *The Journal of Religion* 75(2) (April 1995): 181–99.

Chomsky, Noam, interviewed by C.J. Polychroniou, *Optimism over Despair: On Capitalism, Empire and Social Change*. London: Penguin Books, 2017.

Cioran, E.M. *The Temptation to Exist*, trans. Richard Howard. New York: Arcade Publishing, 2012 [1956].

Cioran, E.M. *The Trouble with Being Born*, trans. Richard Howard. New York: Arcade Publishing, 2012 [1973].

Cocking, Dean and Jeroen van den Hoven. *Evil Online*. Hoboken, NJ: Wiley, 2018.

Cohen, Andrew Jason. *Toleration and Freedom from Harm: Liberalism Reconceived*. New York: Routledge, 2018.

Cohen, Joshua. 'The Natural Goodness of Humanity'. In A. Reath, B. Herman, and C.M. Korsgaard (eds.), *Reclaiming the History of Ethics: Essays for John Rawls*. Cambridge, UK: Cambridge University Press, 1997, 102–39.

Comte-Sponville, André. *Traité du désespoir et de la béatitude*. Paris: Presses Universitaires de France, 1984.

Condren, Conal, Stephen Gaukroger, and Ian Hunter (eds.). *The Philosopher in Early Modern Europe: The Nature of a Contested Identity*. Cambridge, UK: Cambridge University Press, 2006.

Dees, Richard. 'Morality above Metaphysics: Philo and the Duties of Friendship in Dialogues 12'. *Hume Studies* XXVIII(1) (April 2002): 131–48.

DeGrazia, David. 'Is it Wrong to Impose the Harms of Human Life? A Reply to Benatar'. *Theoretical Medicine and Bioethics* 31(4) (2010): 317–31.

Dews, Peter. *The Idea of Evil*. Oxford: Wiley-Blackwell, 2009.

Dienstag, Joshua Foa. *Pessimism: Philosophy, Ethic, Spirit*. Princeton, NJ: Princeton University Press, 2006.

D'Iorio, Paolo. 'Nietzsche et l'éternel retour. Genèse et interprétation'. In Marc Crépon (ed.), *Nietzsche. Cahiers de l'Herne*. Paris: l'Herne, 2005, 235–57.

Douglas, Alexander. 'Philosophy and Hope'. *The Philosopher* 107(1): 25–8.

Douglass, Robin. 'Free Will and the Problem of Evil: Reconciling Rousseau's Divided Thought'. *History of Political Thought* 31(4) (2010): 639–55.

——. *Rousseau and Hobbes: Nature, Free Will, and the Passions*. Oxford: Oxford University Press, 2015.

——. 'The Moral Psychology of The Social Contract: Rousseau's Republican Citizenship'. Forthcoming.

Duncan, Sam. 'Moral Evil, Freedom and the Goodness of God: Why Kant Abandoned Theodicy'. *British Journal for the History of Philosophy* 20(5) (2012): 973–91.

Dye, James. 'Demea's Departure'. *Hume Studies* XVIII(2) (November 1992): 467–82.

Dynes, Russell R. 'The Lisbon Earthquake of 1755: The First Modern Disaster'. In Braun and Radner, *The Lisbon Earthquake of 1755*, 34–49.

Eagleton, Terry. *Hope without Optimism*. New Haven, CT: Yale University Press, 2017.

Erskine-Hill, Howard. 'Pope on the Origins of Society'. In G.S. Rousseau and Pat Rogers (eds.), *The Enduring Legacy: Alexander Pope Tercentenary Essays*. Cambridge, UK: Cambridge University Press, 1988, 79–94.

Falvey, John. 'Introduction' to La Mettrie, *Discours sur le bonheur* [*DB*: see Main Primary Sources], 11–109.

Fernández, Jordi. 'Schopenhauer's Pessimism'. *Philosophy and Phenomenological Research* 73(3) (2006): 646–64.

Ferrari, Jean. *Les Sources françaises de la philosophie de Kant*. Paris: Librairie Klincksieck, 1979.

Fonnesu, Luca. 'The Problem of Theodicy'. In Knud Haakonssen (ed.), *The Cambridge History of Eighteenth-Century Philosophy*. Cambridge, UK: Cambridge University Press, 2000, 749–78.

Forman, David. 'Leibniz and the Stoics: Fate, Freedom, and Providence'. In John Sellars (ed.), *The Routledge Handbook of the Stoic Tradition*. London: Routledge, 2016, 226–42.

Fox, Michael. 'Schopenhauer on Death, Suicide and Self-Renunciation'. In Michael Fox (ed.), *Schopenhauer, His Philosophical Achievement*. Brighton: Harvester Press, 1980, 147–70.

Freddoso, Alfred J. 'Suarez on God's Causal Involvement in Sinful Acts'. In Latzer and Kremer, *The Problem of Evil*, 10–34.

Freitas, Donna. *The Happiness Effect: How Social Media is Driving a Generation to Appear Perfect at Any Cost*. New York: Oxford University Press, 2017.

Gisler, Monika. 'Optimism and Theodicy: Perceptions of the Lisbon Earthquake in Protestant Switzerland'. In Braun and Radner, *The Lisbon Earthquake*, 247–64.

Gleeson, Andrew. 'God and Evil without Theodicy'. In Trakakis, *The Problem of Evil*, 202–12.

Gouhier, Henri. *Cartésianisme et Augustinisme au XVIIe siècle*. Paris: Vrin, 1978.

Gourevitch, Victor. 'Rousseau on Providence'. *The Review of Metaphysics* 53(3) (March 2000): 565–611.

———. 'The Religious Thought'. In Patrick Riley (ed.), *The Cambridge Companion to Rousseau*. Cambridge, UK: Cambridge University Press, 2001, 193–246.

Grandjean, Antoine. *Voudriez-vous revivre?* Vallet: Éditions M-Editer, March 2011.

Gray, John. *Straw Dogs: Thoughts on Humans and Other Animals*. London: Granta, 2003.

Greenberg, Sean. 'Leibniz on King: Freedom and the Project of the "Theodicy"'. *Studia Leibnitiana* 40(2) (2008): 205–22.

Greene, Donald. '"Pictures to the Mind": Johnson and Imagery'. In Mary M. Lascelles et al. (eds.), *Johnson, Boswell, and Their Circle: Essays Presented to Lawrence Fitzroy Powell, in Honour of His Eighty-Fourth Birthday*. Oxford: Clarendon Press, 1965.

———. *Samuel Johnson's Library: An Annotated Guide*. Victoria, BC: English Literary Studies, University of Victoria, 1975.

Griffiths, A. Phillips. 'Wittgenstein and the Four-Fold Root of the Principle of Sufficient Reason'. *Proceedings of the Aristotelian Society, Supplementary Volumes* 50 (1976): 1–20.

Guéroult, Martial. *Malebranche*. 3 vols. Paris: Aubier-Montaigne, 1955–1959.

Guidi, Marco. 'Jeremy Bentham's Quantitative Analysis of Happiness and its Asymmetries'. In Luigino Bruni and Luigi Porta (eds.), *Handbook on the Economics of Happiness*. Cheltenham: Edward Elgar, 2007, 68–94.

———. 'Pain and Human Action: Locke to Bentham'. *Departmental Working Papers*, University of Brescia, Department of Social Studies, STO 1–95 (1995), 1–26.

Gunn, Joshua and Dana L. Cloud. 'Agentic Orientation as Magical Voluntarism'. *Communication Theory* 20(1) (February 2010): 50–78.

Hamlyn, D.W. 'Eternal Justice'. *Schopenhauer-Jahrbuch* 69 (1988): 281–8.

Hanley, Brian. *Samuel Johnson as Book Reviewer: A Duty to Examine the Labors of the Learned*. Newark, NJ: Associated University Presses, 2001.

Halévy, Elie. *La Jeunesse de Bentham*. Paris: F. Alcan, 1901.

Harris, James. *Hume: An Intellectual Biography*. Cambridge, UK: Cambridge University Press, 2015.

——. 'Hume's Four Essays on Happiness and their Place in the Move from Morals to Politics'. In Emilio Mazza and Emanuele Ronchetti (eds.), *New Essays on David Hume*. Milan: FrancoAngeli, 2007, 223–35.

Hart, David Bentley. *That All Shall Be Saved: Heaven, Hell, and Universal Salvation*. New Haven, CT: Yale University Press, 2019.

——. *The Doors of the Sea: Where Was God in the Tsunami?* Grand Rapids, MI: William B. Eerdmans, 2005.

Havens, George R. 'Voltaire, Rousseau, and the "Lettre sur la Providence"'. *PMLA* 59(1) (March 1944): 109–30.

——. 'Voltaire's Pessimistic Revision of the Conclusion of his *Poème sur le désastre de Lisbonne*'. *Modern Language Notes* 44(8) (December 1929): 489–92.

Haxo, Henry E. 'Pierre Bayle et Voltaire Avant Les Lettres Philosophiques'. *PMLA* 46(2) (June 1931): 461–97.

Hazard, Paul. *European Thought in the Eighteenth Century from Montesquien to Lessing*, trans. J.L. May. London: Hollis and Carter, 1954.

Healy, Róisín. 'Suicide in Early Modern and Modern Europe'. *The Historical Journal* 49(3) (September 2006): 903–19.

Hernandez, Jill Graper. *Early Modern Women and the Problem of Evil: Atrocity and Theodicy*. New York: Routledge, 2016.

Hickson, Michael. 'A Brief History of Problems of Evil'. In Justin P. McBrayer and Daniel Howard-Snyder (eds.), *The Blackwell Companion to the Problem of Evil*. Chichester: Wiley-Blackwell, 2013, 3–18.

——. '*Reductio ad malum*: Bayle's Early Skepticism about Theodicy'. *The Modern Schoolman* 88(3–4) (July–October 2011): 201–21.

——. 'The Message of Bayle's Last Title: Providence and Toleration in the *Entretiens de Maxime et de Thémiste*'. *Journal of the History of Ideas* 71(4) (October 2010): 547–67.

——. 'Theodicy and Toleration in Bayle's Dictionary'. *Journal of the History of Philosophy* 51(1) (January 2013): 49–73.

Hillesum, Etty. *Etty: The Letters and Diaries of Etty Hillesum, 1941–1943*, trans. Arnold J. Pomerans, ed. Klaas A.D. Smelik. Grand Rapids, MI: William B. Eerdmans, 2002.

Holden, Thomas. 'Religion and Moral Prohibition in Hume's "Of Suicide"'. *Hume Studies* 31(2) (2005): 189–210.

——. *Spectres of False Divinity: Hume's Moral Atheism*. Oxford: Oxford University Press, 2010.

Horkheimer, Max. 'Schopenhauer Today'. In Horkheimer, *Critique of Instrumental Reason: Lectures and Essays Since the End of WWII*, trans. Matthew J. O'Connell et al. New York: Seabury Press, 1974, 63–83.

Immerwahr, John. 'Hume's Essays on Happiness'. *Hume Studies* XV(2) (November 1989): 307–24.

Irwin, Kristen. 'Reason in Bayle and Leibniz'. In Leduc et al., *Leibniz et Bayle: Confrontation et dialogue*, 289–301.

——. 'Which 'Reason'? Bayle on the Intractability of Evil'. In Jorgensen and Newlands, *New Essays on Leibniz's Theodicy*, 43–54.

James, Susan. *Passion and Action: The Emotions in Seventeenth-Century Philosophy*. Oxford: Clarendon Press, 1997.

Janaway, Christopher. 'Schopenhauer's Pessimism'. In Christopher Janaway (ed.), *The Cambridge Companion to Schopenhauer*. Cambridge, UK: Cambridge University Press, 1999, 318–43.

Jolley, Nicholas. *Causality and Mind: Essays on Early Modern Philosophy*. Oxford: Oxford University Press, 2013.

——. 'Is Leibniz's Theodicy a Variation on a Theme by Malebranche?' In Jorgensen and Newlands, *New Essays*, 55–70.

Jorgensen, Larry M. and Samuel Newlands (eds.). *New Essays on Leibniz's Theodicy*. Oxford: Oxford University Press, 2014.

Jossua, Jean-Pierre. *Pierre Bayle ou l'obsession du mal*. Paris: Aubier Montaigne, 1977.

Kendrick, T.D. *The Lisbon Earthquake*. London: Methuen, 1956.

Kilby, Karen. 'Evil and the Limits of Theology'. *New Blackfriars* 84(983) (2003): 13–29.

Kingsnorth, Paul. *Confessions of a Recovering Environmentalist*. London: Faber and Faber, 2017.

——. *The Wake*. London: Unbound, 2015.

Kivy, Peter. 'Voltaire, Hume, and the Problem of Evil'. *Philosophy and Literature* 3(2) (Fall 1979): 211–24.

Kjørholt, Ingvild Hagen. 'Cosmopolitans, Slaves, and the Global Market in Voltaire's *Candide, ou l'optimisme*'. *Eighteenth-Century Fiction* 25(1) (Fall 2012): 61–84.

Kleingeld, Pauline. 'Kant's Second Thoughts on Race'. *The Philosophical Quarterly* 57 (2007): 573–92.

Kremer, Elmar J. 'Leibniz and the 'Disciples of Saint Augustine' on the Fate of Infants Who Die Unbaptized'. In Latzer and Kremer, *The Problem of Evil*, 119–37.

Krusé, Cornelius. 'The Inadequacy of the Hedonistic Interpretation of Pessimism'. *The Journal of Philosophy* 29(15) (21 July 1932): 393–400.

Kuehn, Manfred. *Kant: A Biography*. Cambridge, UK: Cambridge University Press, 2002.

La Vopa, Anthony J. *The Labor of the Mind: Intellect and Gender in Enlightenment Cultures*. Philadelphia, PA: University of Pennsylvania Press, 2017.

Labrousse, Élisabeth. *Pierre Bayle, Tome I: Du Pays de Foix à la cité d'Érasme*. The Hague: Martinus Nijhoff, 1963.

Lærke, Mogens. *Les Lumières de Leibniz. Controverses avec Huet, Bayle, Regis et More*. Les Anciens et Les Modernes—Études de Philosophie, vol. 20. Paris: Classiques Garnier, 2015.

——. 'The End of Melancholy. Deleuze and Benjamin on Leibniz and the Baroque'. In U. Beckmann et al. (eds.), *Für unser Glück oder Das Glück Anderer. Vorträge des X. Internationalen Leibniz-Kongress*, vol. I. Hildesheim: Georg Olms Verlag, 385–91.

Lam, Wing Kwan Anselm. 'Rethinking the Source of Evil in Rousseau's Confessions'. In Eve Grace and Christopher Kelly (eds.), *The Rousseauian Mind*. New York: Routledge, 2019, ch. 3.

Lamb, Jonathan. *The Rhetoric of Suffering: Reading the Book of Job in the Eighteenth Century*. Oxford: Clarendon Press, 1995.

Langdon, David. 'On the Meanings of the Conclusion of *Candide*'. In *Studies on Voltaire and the Eighteenth Century, vol. 238*. Oxford: The Voltaire Foundation, 1985, 397–432.

Langton, Rae. 'Duty and Desolation'. *Philosophy* 67(262) (1992): 481–505.

Latzer, Michael J. and Kremer, Elmar J. (eds.). *The Problem of Evil in Early Modern Philosophy*. Toronto: University of Toronto Press, 2001.

Lauer, Gerhard and Unger, Thorsten (eds.). *Das Erdbeben von Lissabon und der Katastrophendiskurs im 18. Jahrhundert*. Göttingen: Wallstein Verlag, 2008.

Lecaldano, Eugenio. 'Hume on Suicide'. In Paul Russell (ed.), *The Oxford Handbook of Hume*. New York: Oxford University Press, 2016, 660–8.

Leduc, Christian, Paul Rateau, and Jean-Luc Solère (eds.). *Leibniz et Bayle: Confrontation et dialogue. Studia Leibnitiana*, vol. 43. Stuttgart: Franz Steiner, 2015.

Lennon, Thomas. *Reading Bayle*. Toronto: University of Toronto Press, 1999.

Lewis, C.S. *A Grief Observed: Readers' Edition*, with contributions from H. Mantel, J. Martin, J. Bailey, R. Williams, K. Saunders, F. Spufford, and M. Freely. London: Faber and Faber, 2015 [1961].

——. *The Problem of Pain*. London: William Collins, 2015 [1940].

Ligotti, Thomas. *The Conspiracy against the Human Race*. New York: Penguin Books, 2018.

Litwin, Christophe. 'Amour de soi et pensée du néant: Rousseau héritier de Malebranche?' In Blaise Bachofen, Bruno Bernardi, André Charrak and Florent Guénard (eds.), *Philosophie de Rousseau*. Paris: Classiques Garnier, 2014, 275–88.

——. '"Le principe nécessaire de tous nos maux naturels": Jaucourt aux lumières de King, Leibniz et Rousseau'. In Gilles Barroux and François Pépin (éds.), *Le Chevalier de Jaucourt. L'Homme aux dix-sept mille articles*. Paris: Société Diderot, 2015, 195–212.

——. 'Rousseau and Leibniz: Genealogy vs. Theodicy'. In Eve Grace and Christopher Kelly (eds.), *The Rousseauian Mind*. Abingdon: Routledge, 2019, ch. 7.

Lobel, Diana. 'Being and the Good: Maimonides on Ontological Beauty'. *Journal of Jewish Thought & Philosophy* 19(1) (2011): 1–45.

Lovejoy, Arthur O. 'Rousseau's Pessimist'. *Modern Language Notes* 38(8) (December 1923): 449–52.

——. *The Great Chain of Being: A Study of the History of an Idea*. Cambridge, MA: Harvard University Press, 1936.

Lucci, Diego. 'William Wollaston's Religion of Nature'. In Wayne Hudson, Diego Lucci, and Jeffrey R. Wigelsworth (eds.), *Atheism and Deism Revalued: Heterodox Religious Identities in Britain, 1650–1800*. London: Routledge, 2016, 119–38.

Macfarlane, Robert. *The Wild Places*. London: Granta, 2017.

——. *Underland*. London: Hamish Hamilton, 2019.

Mack, Maynard. *Collected in Himself: Essays Critical, Biographical, and Bibliographical on Pope and Some of His Contemporaries*. Newark, NJ: University of Delaware Press, 1983.

Magee, Bryan. *The Philosophy of Schopenhauer*. Oxford: Clarendon Press, 1997.

Mahon, James E. 'Kant and Maria von Herbert: Reticence vs. Deception'. *Philosophy* 81(3) (2006): 417–44.

Mantel, Hilary. *Giving Up the Ghost: A Memoir*. London: Fourth Estate, 2013.

Malherbe, Michel. 'Hume and the Art of Dialogue'. In M.A. Stewart and John P. Wright (eds.), *Hume and Hume's Connexions*. Edinburgh: Edinburgh University Press, 1994.

Martínez Solares, J.M. and López Arroyo, A. 'The Great Historical 1755 Earthquake. Effects and Damage in Spain'. *Journal of Seismology* 8 (2004): 275–94.

Mason, Haydn. *Pierre Bayle and Voltaire*. Oxford: Oxford University Press, 1963.

———. 'Voltaire's "Sermon" against Optimism: The *Poème sur le désastre de Lisbonne*'. In Giles Barber and Cecil P. Courtney (eds.), *Enlightenment Essays in Memory of Robert Shackleton*. Oxford: Voltaire Foundation, 1988, 189–203.

Mauzi, Robert. *L'Idée du bonheur dans la littérature et la pensée françaises au XVIIIe siècle*. Paris: Armand Colin, 1967.

Mazza, Emilio and Gianluca Mori. 'Hume's Palimpsest: the Four Endings of the "Dialogues"'. In Kenneth W. Williford (ed.), *Hume's Dialogues concerning Natural Religion: A Philosophical Appraisal*. Routledge, forthcoming.

McBrayer, Justin P. and Daniel Howard-Snyder (eds.), *The Blackwell Companion to the Problem of Evil*. Chichester: Wiley-Blackwell, 2013.

McKenna, Antony. *Études sur Pierre Bayle*. Paris: Honoré Champion, 2015.

McMahon, Darren. *The Pursuit of Happiness: A History from the Greeks to the Present*. London: Penguin Books, 2007.

Meister, Chad and Paul K. Moser (eds.). *The Cambridge Companion to the Problem of Evil*. Cambridge, UK: Cambridge University Press, 2017.

Mendes-Victor, Luiz A., et al. *The 1755 Lisbon Earthquake: Revisited*. Dordrecht: Springer, 2009.

Moreau, Denis. *Deux Cartésiens: La polemique entre Antoine Arnauld et Nicolas Malebranche*. Paris: Vrin, 1999.

———. 'Malebranche on Disorder and Physical Evil: Manichaeism or Philosophical Courage?' In Kremer and Latzer, *The Problem of Evil*, 81–100.

Mori, Gianluca. 'Bayle et Hume devant l'athéisme'. *Archives de Philosophie* 81 (2018): 749–74.

———. *Bayle philosophe*. Paris: H. Champion, 1999.

Morris, Katherine. 'Bête-machines'. In Stephen Gaukroger, John Schuster, and John Sutton (eds.), *Descartes' Natural Philosophy*. London: Routledge, 2000, 401–19.

Mossner, Ernest Campbell. 'Hume's "Four Dissertations": An Essay in Biography and Bibliography'. *Modern Philology* 48(1) (August 1950): 37–57.

———. *The Life of David Hume*. Oxford: Clarendon Press, 2001.

Murray, Geoffrey. *Voltaire's Candide: The Protean Gardener, 1755–1762*. Studies on Voltaire and the Eighteenth Century, vol. 69. Oxford: Voltaire Foundation, 1970.

Nadler, Steven. 'Choosing a Theodicy: The Leibniz–Malebranche–Arnauld Connection'. *Journal of the History of Ideas* 55(4) (October 1994): 573–89.

———. *The Best of All Possible Worlds: A Story of Philosophers, God, and Evil in the Age of Reason*. Princeton, NJ: Princeton University Press, 2010.

Nagasawa, Yujin. 'The Problem of Evil for Atheists'. In Trakakis, *The Problem of Evil*, 151–62.

Neiman, Susan. *Evil in Modern Thought: An Alternative History of Philosophy*. Princeton, NJ: Princeton University Press, 2015.

———. 'Metaphysics, Philosophy: Rousseau on the Problem of Evil'. In A. Reath, B. Herman, and C.M. Korsgaard (eds.), *Reclaiming the History of Ethics: Essays for John Rawls*. Cambridge, UK: Cambridge University Press, 1997, 140–69.

———. *Moral Clarity: A Guide for Grown-Up Idealists*. London: Vintage, 2011.

———. 'What Happened to Evil?' In Andrew Chignell (ed.), *Evil: A History*. Oxford: Oxford University Press, 2019, 358–82.

Neuhouser, Frederick. *Rousseau's Critique of Inequality: Reconstructing the Second Discourse*. Cambridge, UK: Cambridge University Press, 2014.

———. *Rousseau's Theodicy of Self-Love: Evil, Rationality, and the Drive for Recognition*. Oxford: Oxford University Press, 2008.

Newlands, Samuel. 'Evils, Privations, and the Early Moderns'. In Andrew Chignell (ed.), *Evil: A History*. Oxford: Oxford University Press, 2019, 273–305.

———. 'Hume on Evil'. In Paul Russell (ed.), *The Oxford Handbook of Hume*. New York: Oxford University Press, 2016, 623–43.

———. 'Leibniz on Privations, Limitations, and the Metaphysics of Evil'. *Journal for the History of Philosophy* 52 (2014): 281–308.

———. 'Malebranche on the Metaphysics and Ethics of Evil'. In Sean Greenberg (ed.), *Oxford Handbook on Malebranche*. Oxford University Press, forthcoming.

———. 'The Problem of Evil'. In *The Routledge Companion to 17th Century Philosophy*, ed. Dan Kaufmann. London: Routledge, 2017, 536–62.

Norton, David Fate and Mary J. Norton. *The David Hume Library*. Edinburgh: Edinburgh Bibliographical Society, 1996.

Nussbaum, Martha C. *The Fragility of Goodness: Luck and Ethics in Greek Tragedy and Philosophy*. Cambridge, UK: Cambridge University Press, 2001.

Nys, Thomas and Stephen de Wijze (eds.), *The Routledge Handbook of the Philosophy of Evil*. Abingdon: Routledge, 2019.

O'Hagan, Timothy. 'Review of Neuhouser, *Rousseau's Theodicy*'. *Mind* 119 (2010): 219–25.

———. *Rousseau*. London: Routledge, 1999.

Oppy, Graham. 'Problems of Evil'. In Trakakis, *The Problem of Evil*, 68–80.

Paganini, Gianni. 'Job, Bayle et la Théodicée'. In Leduc et al., *Leibniz et Bayle*, 363–80.

Pearce, Kenneth L. 'William King on Free Will'. *Philosophers' Imprint* 19(21) (2019): 1–15.

Pearson, Roger. *The Fables of Reason: a Study of Voltaire's 'Contes philosophiques'*. Oxford: Clarendon Press, 1993.

———. *Voltaire Almighty: A Life in Pursuit of Freedom*. London: Bloomsbury, 2006.

Phemister, Pauline. *Leibniz and the Environment*. New York: Routledge, 2016.

Pihlström, Sami and Sari Kivistö. *Kantian Antitheodicy: Philosophical and Literary Varieties*. London: Palgrave Macmillan, 2016.

Pike, Nelson. 'Hume on Evil'. In Marilyn McCord Adams and Robert Merrihew Adams (eds.), *The Problem of Evil*. Oxford: Oxford University Press, 1996, 38–52.

Pinker, Steven. *Enlightenment Now: The Case for Reason, Science, Humanism, and Progress*. London: Penguin Books, 2019.

Pitassi, Maria Cristina. *De l'Orthodoxie aux lumières: Genève, 1670–1737*. Geneva: Labor et Fides, 1992.

Pittion, J.-P. 'Hume's Reading of Bayle: An Inquiry into the Source and Role of the Memoranda'. *Journal of the History of Philosophy* 15(4) (October 1977): 373–86.

Pitson, Tony. 'The Miseries of Life: Hume and the Problem of Evil'. *Hume Studies* 34(1) (2008): 89–114.

Pomeau, René. *La Religion de Voltaire*. Paris: Nizet, 1994.

Popkin, Richard. 'Bayle and Hume'. In R.A. Watson and J.E. Force (eds.), *The High Road to Pyrrhonism*. San Diego, CA: Austin Hill Press, 1980, 149–60.

Prins, Awee. 'Het wordt niet beter, het kan niet beter: over existentiële professionaliteit en de toekomst van de herstelbeweging'. In Dienke Boertien and Wouter Kusters (eds.), *Filosofie bij herstelondersteuning. Opnieuw denken over geestelijke gezondheid*. Utrecht: Kenniscentrum Phrenos, 2018, 142–53.

———. *Uit verveling*. Kampen: Klement, 2007.

Purdy, Jedidiah. *After Nature: A Politics for the Anthropocene*. Cambridge, MA: Harvard University Press, 2015.

Rateau, Paul. 'L'Univers progresse-t-il? Les modèles d'évolution du monde chez Leibniz'. In Rateau, *Leibniz et le meilleur des mondes possibles*, 143–74.

———. *Leibniz et le meilleur des mondes possibles*. Paris: Classiques Garnier, 2015.

———. *Leibniz on the Problem of Evil*. Oxford: Oxford University Press, 2019.

———. 'The Theoretical Foundations of the Leibnizian Theodicy and its Apologetic Aim'. In Jorgensen and Newlands, *New Essays on Leibniz's Theodicy*, 92–111.

Rees, D.A. 'Kant, Bayle, and Indifferentism'. *The Philosophical Review* 63(4) (October 1954): 592–95.

Renouvier, Charles. *Les Derniers entretiens*, ed. Louis Prat. Paris: Vrin, 1930.

Rétat, Pierre. *Le Dictionnaire de Bayle et la lutte philosophique au XVIII*[e] *siècle*. Paris: Les Belles Lettres, 1971.

Richardson, Joseph. 'William King—European Man of Letters'. In Christopher Fauske (ed.), *Archbishop William King and the Anglican Irish Context, 1688–1729*. Dublin: Four Courts, 2002, 106–22.

Ricoeur, Paul. *Freud and Philosophy: An Essay on Interpretation*, trans. Denis Savage. New Haven, CT: Yale University Press, 1970.

———. *The Symbolism of Evil*, trans. Emerson Buchanan. Boston, MA: Beacon Press, 1969.

Ritter, Bernhard. 'Solace or Counsel for Death: Kant and Maria von Herbert'. In Corey Dyck (ed.), *Women and Philosophy in 18th Century Germany*. Oxford University Press, forthcoming.

Robinson, Marilynne. *Housekeeping*. London: Faber and Faber, 2005 [1980].

———. *The Givenness of Things*. London: Virago, 2015.

Rorty, Amélie Oksenberg. 'Rousseau's Therapeutic Experiments'. *Philosophy* 66(258) (October 1991): 413–34.

———. 'The Two Faces of Stoicism in Rousseau and Freud'. *Journal of the History of Philosophy* 34 (1996): 335–56.

——— (ed.). *The Many Faces of Evil: Historical Perspectives*. London: Routledge, 2001.

Rosenblatt, Helena. *Rousseau and Geneva: from the First Discourse to the Social Contract, 1749–1762*. Cambridge, UK: Cambridge University Press, 1997.

Rutherford, Donald. *Leibniz and the Rational Order of Nature*. Cambridge, UK: Cambridge University Press, 1995.

——. 'Leibniz and the Stoics: The Consolations of Theodicy'. In Latzer and Kremer, *The Problem of Evil in Early Modern Philosophy*, 138–64.

——. '*Patience sans espérance*: Leibniz's Critique of Stoicism'. In Jon Miller and Brad Inwood (eds.), *Hellenistic and Early Modern Philosophy*. Cambridge, UK: Cambridge University Press, 2003, 62–89.

Ryan, Todd. 'Hume's Reply to Baylean Scepticism'. In Sébastien Charles and Plínio J. Smith (eds.), *Scepticism in the Eighteenth Century: Enlightenment, Lumières, Aufklärung*. Dordrecht: Springer, 2013, 125–38.

——. 'Pierre Bayle and the Regress Argument in Hume's *Dialogues concerning Natural Religion*'. In *Libertinage et philosophie à l'époque classique (XVIe–XVIIIe siècle)* 14 (2017): 161–87.

——. *Pierre Bayle's Cartesian Metaphysics: Rediscovering Early Modern Philosophy*. New York: Routledge, 2009.

Safranski, Rüdiger. *Das Böse oder Das Drama der Freiheit*. München: C. Hanser, 1997.

——. *Schopenhauer and the Wild Years of Philosophy*, trans. Ewald Osers. Cambridge, MA: Harvard University Press, 1991.

Savulescu, Julian. 'Rational Desires and the Limitation of Life-Sustaining Treatment'. In Helga Kuhse, Udo Schüklenk, and Peter Singer (eds.), *Bioethics: An Anthology*. Malden, MA: Wiley-Blackwell, 2016, 665–82.

Schrecker, Paul. 'Malebranche et le préformisme biologique'. *Revue Internationale de Philosophie* 1(1) (15 October 1938): 77–97.

Schulte, Christoph. 'Zweckwidriges in der Erfahrung. Zur Genese des Mißlingens aller philosophischen Versuche in der Theodizee bei Kant'. *Kant-Studien* 82(4) (1991): 371–96.

Schwarzbach, Bertram Eugene. 'The Eighteenth Century Confronts Job'. In Mordechai Feingold (ed.), *History of Universities, Volume XXII/1*. Oxford: Oxford University Press, 2007, 141–98.

Schwartz, Richard B. *Samuel Johnson and the Problem of Evil*. Madison, WI: University of Wisconsin Press, 1975.

Scott, John T. 'The Theodicy of the Second Discourse: The "Pure State of Nature" and Rousseau's Political Thought'. *American Political Science Review* 86(3) (1992): 696–711.

Senior, Nancy. 'Les Solitaires as a Test for Emile and Sophie'. *The French Review* 49(4) (March 1976): 528–35.

Sheehan, Jonathan. *The Enlightenment Bible: Translation, Scholarship, Culture*. Princeton, NJ: Princeton University Press, 2005.

——. 'The Poetics and Politics of Theodicy'. *Prooftexts* 27(2) (Spring 2007): 211–32.

Shell, Susan Meld. *Kant and the Limits of Autonomy*. Cambridge, MA: Harvard University Press, 2009.

——. 'Kant's Secular Religion: Philosophical Theodicy and The Book of Job'. In Oliver Thorndike (ed.), *Rethinking Kant: Volume 3*. Newcastle upon Tyne: Cambridge Scholars, 2011, 20–32.

Simmel, Georg. *Schopenhauer and Nietzsche*, trans. Helmut Loiskandl, Deena Weinstein, and Michael Weinstein. Amherst, MA: University of Massachusetts Press, 1986.

Sivado, Akos. 'The Ontology of Sir William Petty's Political Arithmetic'. *The European Journal of the History of Economic Thought* 26(5) (2019): 1003–26.

Smail, David. *Power, Interest and Psychology: Elements of a Social Materialist Understanding of Distress*. Ross-on-Wye: PCCS Books, 2005.

Smith, Norah. 'Hume's "Rejected" Essays'. *Forum for Modern Language Studies* 8(4) (October 1972): 354–71.

Smuts, Aaron. 'Five Tests for What Makes a Life Worth Living'. *Journal of Value Inquiry* 47 (2013): 439–59.

——. *Welfare, Meaning, and Worth*. New York: Routledge, 2018.

Spark, Muriel. *The Only Problem*. Edinburgh: Polygon, 2017 [1984].

Starobinski, Jean. *Blessings in Disguise, or the Morality of Evil*, trans. Arthur Goldhammer. Cambridge, UK: Polity Press, 1993.

——. *Jean-Jacques Rousseau, Transparency and Obstruction*, trans. Arthur Goldhammer. Chicago, IL: University of Chicago Press, 1988.

Sully, James. *Pessimism: A History and a Criticism*. London: Henry S. King & Co., 1877.

Stewart, M.A. 'An Early Fragment on Evil.' In M.A. Stewart and John P. Wright (eds.), *Hume and Hume's Connexions*. Edinburgh: Edinburgh University Press, 1994, 160–70.

——. 'The Stoic Legacy in the Early Scottish Enlightenment'. In Margaret J. Osler (ed.), *Atoms, Pneuma and Tranquility: Epicurean and Stoic Themes in European Thought*. Cambridge, UK: Cambridge University Press, 1991, 273–96.

Strickland, Lloyd. 'Leibniz on Eternal Punishment'. *British Journal for the History of Philosophy* 17(2) (2009): 307–31.

Stump, Eleonore. 'The Problem of Suffering: A Thomistic Approach'. In Trakakis, *The Problem of Evil*, 12–25.

——. *Wandering in Darkness: Narrative and the Problem of Suffering*. Oxford: Clarendon Press, 2010.

Tallis, Raymond. *Enemies of Hope: A Critique of Contemporary Pessimism*. New York: Palgrave, 1997.

Taylor, Charles. *A Secular Age*. Cambridge, MA: The Belknap Press of Harvard University Press, 2007.

——. *Sources of the Self: The Making of the Modern Identity*. Cambridge, UK: Cambridge University Press, 1989.

Thacker, Eugene, *Starry Speculative Corpse* [*Horror of Philosophy*, vol. 2]. Winchester: Zero Books, 2015.

Thomson, Ann. *Materialism and Society in the Mid-Eighteenth Century: La Mettrie's Discours preliminaire*. Geneva: Librairie Droz, 1981.

Tolstoy, Leo. *War and Peace*, trans. Constance Garnett. Mineola, NY: Dover Publications, 2017 [1869].

Tooley, Michael. 'The Problem of Evil'. In Edward N. Zalta (ed.), *The Stanford Encyclopedia of Philosophy* (Spring 2019 edition), online at https://plato.stanford.edu/archives/spr2019/entries/evil/ (accessed 1 April 2020).

Trakakis, N.N. 'Anti-theodicy' (1). In Chad Meister and Paul K. Moser (eds.), *The Cambridge Companion to the Problem of Evil*. Cambridge, UK: Cambridge University Press, 2017, 124–43.

——. 'Anti-theodicy' (2). In Trakakis, *The Problem of Evil*, 94–106.

——. (ed.) *The Problem of Evil: Eight Views in Dialogue*. Oxford: Oxford University Press, 2018.

Trilling, Lionel. *Sincerity and Authenticity*. Cambridge, MA: Harvard University Press, 1972.

Van der Lugt, Mara. *Bayle, Jurieu and the Dictionnaire Historique et Critique*. Oxford: Oxford University Press, 2016.

——. 'Pessimism'. *The Philosopher* 107(4) (Autumn 2019): 50–7.

——. 'The Left Hand of the Enlightenment: Truth, Error, and Integrity in Bayle and Kant'. *History of European Ideas* 44(3) (2018): 277–91.

Van Fraassen, Bas C. *The Empirical Stance*. New Haven, CT: Yale University Press, 2002.

Van Tongeren, Paul. *Dankbaarheid: Denken over danken na de dood van God*. Zoetermeer: Klement, 2015.

Vanden Auweele, Dennis. *Pessimism in Kant's Ethics and Rational Religion*. Lanham, MD: Lexington Books, 2018.

Vyverberg, Henry. *Historical Pessimism in the French Enlightenment*. Cambridge, MA: Harvard University Press, 1958.

Wade, Ira O. *The Intellectual Development of Voltaire*. Princeton, NJ: Princeton University Press, 1969.

Walker, D.P. *The Decline of Hell: Seventeenth-Century Discussions of Eternal Torment*. London: Routledge & Kegan Paul, 1964.

Wasserman, David. 'Pro-natalism'. In Benatar and Wasserman, *Debating Procreation*, 133–264.

Wellman, Kathleen. *La Mettrie: Medicine, Philosophy, and Enlightenment*. Durham, NC: Duke University Press, 1992.

Whelan, Ruth. 'Reason and Belief: The Bayle–Jacquelot Debate'. *Rivista di Storia della Filosofia* 48(1) (1993): 101–10.

Williams, Bernard. *Ethics and the Limits of Philosophy*. London: Routledge, 2011.

——. *Truth and Truthfulness: An Essay in Genealogy*. Princeton, NJ: Princeton University Press, 2002.

Wills, Garry. *Saint Augustine: A Life*. New York: Penguin Books, 2005.

Wilson, Catherine. 'Leibnizian Optimism'. *The Journal of Philosophy* 80(11) (November 1983): 765–83.

Wirz, Charles. 'Note sur *Émile et Sophie, ou les solitaires*'. *Annales de la Société Jean-Jacques Rousseau* 36 (1963–1965): 291–303.

Wittgenstein, Ludwig. *Culture and Value*, trans. Peter Winch, ed. G.H. von Wright and Heikki Nyman. Oxford: Blackwell, 1980 [1977].

——. *Tractatus Logico-Philosophicus*, trans. C.K. Ogden. London: Routledge, 2005 [1922].

Woods, David. 'Schopenhauer's Pessimism'. PhD thesis, University of Southampton, 2014.

——. 'Seriously Bored: Schopenhauer on Solitary Confinement'. *British Journal for the History of Philosophy* 27(5) (2019): 959–78.

Wootton, David. 'Pierre Bayle, Libertine?' In M.A. Stewart (ed.), *Studies in Seventeenth-Century Philosophy*. Oxford: Oxford University Press, 1997, 197–226.

——. *Power, Pleasure, and Profit: Insatiable Appetites from Machiavelli to Madison*. Cambridge, MA: The Belknap Press of Harvard University Press, 2018.

——. 'Unhappy Voltaire, or "I Shall Never Get Over it as Long as I Live"'. *History Workshop Journal* 50(1) (Autumn 2000): 137–55.

Wright, John P. 'Dr. George Cheyne, Chevalier Ramsay, and Hume's Letter to a Physician'. *Hume Studies* XXVIX(1) (April 2003): 125–41.

——. 'Skepticism and Incomprehensibility in Bayle and Hume'. In Jeffrey Burson and Anton Matytsin (eds.), *The Skeptical Enlightenment: Doubt and Certainty in the Age of Reason*. Oxford University Studies in the Enlightenment. Liverpool: Liverpool University Press, 2019, 129–60.

Wykstra, Stephen J. 'The Humean Obstacle to Evidential Arguments from Suffering: On Avoiding the Evils of "Appearance"'. In Adams and Adams, *The Problem of Evil*, 138–60.

Yandell, Keith E. *Hume's 'Inexplicable Mystery': His Views on Religion*. Philadelphia, PA: Temple University Press, 1990.

Young, Julian. *Schopenhauer*. London: Routledge, 2005.

——. *Willing and Unwilling: A Study in the Philosophy of Arthur Schopenhauer*. Dordrecht: Martinus Nijhoff, 1987.

Zwagerman, Joost. *Door eigen hand: Zelfmoord en de nabestaanden*. Amsterdam: De Arbeiderspers, 2015.

NEWSPAPER AND MAGAZINE ARTICLES (ALL ACCESSED 1 DECEMBER 2020)

Barnes, Julian. 'A Candid View of *Candide*'. *The Guardian*, 1 July 2011. Online at https://www.theguardian.com/books/2011/jul/01/candide-voltaire-rereading-julian-barnes

Bennett, Alan. 'Diary: Finding My Métier'. *London Review of Books* 40(1), 4 January 2018. Online at https://www.lrb.co.uk/the-paper/v40/n01/alan-bennett/diary

Fisher, Mark. 'Good for Nothing'. *The Occupied Times*, 19 March 2014. Online at http://theoccupiedtimes.org/?p=12841

——. 'Why Mental Health is a Political Issue'. *The Guardian*, 16 July 2012. Online at https://www.theguardian.com/commentisfree/2012/jul/16/mental-health-political-issue

Harding, Jeremy. 'A Young Woman Who Was Meant to Kill Herself'. *London Review of Books* 40(5), 8 March 2018. Online at https://www.lrb.co.uk/the-paper/v40/n05/jeremy-harding/a-young-woman-who-was-meant-to-kill-herself

Kingsnorth, Paul. 'Finnegas'. *Emergence magazine*, March 2020. Online at: https://emergencemagazine.org/story/finnegas

O'Brien, Hettie. 'How Mindfulness Privatised a Social Problem'. *The New Statesman*, 17 July 2019. Online at https://www.newstatesman.com/politics/health/2019/07/how-mindfulness-privatised-social-problem

'Project Tag brings positive messages to north east Fife'. *Fife Today*, 13 August 2018. Online at https://www.fifetoday.co.uk/health/project-tag-brings-positive-messages-to-north-east-fife-1-4782869

'Schrijver Joost Zwagerman maakt een einde aan zijn leven'. *De Volkskrant*, 8 September 2015. Online at https://www.volkskrant.nl/cs-bf09e5da

Srinivasan, Amia. 'He, She, One, They, Ho, Hus, Hum, Ita: How Should I Refer to You?' *London Review of Books* 42(13) (2 July 2020). Online at https://www.lrb.co.uk/the-paper/v42/n13/amia-srinivasan/he-she-one-they-ho-hus-hum-ita

Tait, Amelia. 'As People Celebrate Migrant Children Dying in Custody, Has the Internet Made Evil Our New Normal?' *The New Statesman*, 24 July 2019. Online at https://www.newstatesman.com/science-tech/internet/2019/07/people-celebrate-migrant-children-dying-custody-has-internet-made-evil

Townsend, Chris. 'Nietzsche's Horse'. *Los Angeles Review of Books*, 25 April 2017. Online at https://blog.lareviewofbooks.org/essays/nietzsches-horse/

OTHER MEDIA

Cohen, Leonard. 'Anthem', from *The Future* (music album, Columbia, 1992).

Gadsby, Hannah. *Nanette* (TV show, Netflix, 2018).

Salomon, Charlotte. *Life? or Theatre?: A Song-Play* (autobiographical artwork, available online at https://charlotte.jck.nl [1941–1943]).

REFERENCE IN ACKNOWLEDGEMENTS

Voltaire's quote on grief is from his letter to the comte d'Argental, 23 September 1749 (*D*4024); cited here in English translation by Roger Pearson (*Voltaire Almighty*, 208).

INDEX

A NOTE ON THE TYPE

THIS BOOK has been composed in Miller, a Scotch Roman typeface designed by Matthew Carter and first released by Font Bureau in 1997. It resembles Monticello, the typeface developed for The Papers of Thomas Jefferson in the 1940s by C. H. Griffith and P. J. Conkwright and reinterpreted in digital form by Carter in 2003.

Pleasant Jefferson ("P. J.") Conkwright (1905–1986) was Typographer at Princeton University Press from 1939 to 1970. He was an acclaimed book designer and AIGA Medalist.

The ornament used throughout this book was designed by Pierre Simon Fournier (1712–1768) and was a favorite of Conkwright's, used in his design of the *Princeton University Library Chronicle.*

Printed in the USA
CPSIA information can be obtained
at www.ICGtesting.com
JSHW080527030823
45746JS00002B/2